HEBREW WOMEN JOIN THE FORCES: JEWISH WOMEN FROM PALESTINE IN THE BRITISH FORCES DURING THE SECOND WORLD WAR

Hebrew Women Join the Forces:

Jewish Women from Palestine in the British Forces During the Second World War

ANAT GRANIT-HACOHEN

TRANSLATED BY

Ora Cummings

VALLENTINE MITCHELL
LONDON • PORTLAND, OR

First published in 2017 by Vallentine Mitchell

Catalyst House,
720 Centennial Court,
Centennial Park, Elstree WD6 3SY, UK

920 NE 58th Avenue, Suite 300
Portland, Oregon,
97213-3786 USA

www.vmbooks.com

New in paperback in 2017

British Library Cataloguing in Publication Data:
An entry can be found on request

ISBN 978 1 910383 10 0 (cloth)
ISBN 978 1 910383 31 5 (paper)
ISBN 978 1 910383 11 7 (Ebook)

Library of Congress Cataloging in Publication Data
An entry can be found on request

In fond memory of Jean Baker,
a soldier and a lady

'A [female] Hebrew soldier in uniform – a novel concept in Jewish History'

(Moshe Shertok in a speech to the Women Workers' Council Congress, Tel Aviv, 26 February 1942)

Contents

List of Figures

Forward and Acknowledgements

'I must go! If only they'll take me – I will go ... I am too ashamed to sit here doing nothing ... when I could be making myself useful ... these last few weeks I've been feeling so emotional, agitated and restless.' So wrote a young woman from the Yishuv (Jewish society in pre-state Israel) in a letter to her soldier father informing him of her decision to volunteer for the British army.[1]

She was one of the Yishuv women who volunteered for service in the British forces during the Second World War. Between 1942 and 1946, some 3,000 Jewish women aged between 18 and 45 served in the ATS (Auxiliary Territorial Services) and a further 600 joined the WAAF (Women's Auxiliary Air Force). The recruits came from all walks of Yishuv life and served mostly in Egypt, Palestine (Eretz Israel),[2] Syria and Lebanon, Italy and even in Austria (once the war was over). The women were among the 30,000 volunteers from Eretz Israel who served in various branches of the British army and air force in the Middle East Theatre of the Second World War, as well as in the Jewish Brigade. This is the story of the female Jewish volunteers from the Yishuv during the period between the beginning of negotiations over recruitment (March 1941) and July 1946 when the last of the soldiers were released from duty.

Female enlistment in any army, let alone a foreign one, was unheard of in Jewish history. As Moshe Sharett (Shertok) pointed out at the Women Workers' Council Congress, 'A female Hebrew soldier in uniform – a novel concept in Jewish History'[3] In the absence of political independence, Jewish men had traditionally served in the armies of the countries in which they lived, but Jewish women had never served within any organized military framework. This was the first time Jewish women had participated in an organized recruitment drive for service in a regular army, and in some cases they even had a numerical majority. Thousands of women donned uniform and left their homes and their homeland, most of them wishing to participate in the effort to defend the Yishuv, as well as to assist the Jewish nation in its time of greatest need.

This book compares female military service in the British Forces with that of their male counterparts from the Yishuv and touches on female service in other armies and countries during different periods in history. It also presents female military service as part of Yishuv women's struggle for the right to participate in renewing Jewish life in Eretz Israel, together with a gender oriented cultural and social study of woman's role in national struggles worldwide. New light will be shed on such issues as the Yishuv Council of Women's Organizations, the body that initiated the recruitment drive in the first place; the ethnic and social composition of the recruits, according to marital status, address, date of birth and date of immigration to Eretz Israel, with a focus on hereto un-researched documents. An analysis of the social composition and internal relations among the recruits will challenge the various myths that emerged from previous literature on the subject. A study is made of the way the women maintained their Jewish and national identities while serving in the foreign army, the positions they filled in Haganah and Lehi[4] on behalf of their organizations, as well as the contribution of the women's service in the British Forces to the development of the general gender discourse vis-à-vis the place of women in the Israeli armed forces.

In addition, the book describes the role of women in the Yishuv's national and wartime historiography, since this has been virtually ignored in previous historical accounts of the Yishuv. There was no glory attached to the issue of female wartime service and no myths have emerged, as they have, for example, for the Palmach and Israel's War of Independence. In recent years, students of gender and women's issues, together with the historiography of the Jewish Yishuv in Eretz Israel, have begun to study the relationships between the structuring of masculine or feminine identity and the structuring of a national identity by means of memory. Until now women have been excluded from the the Second World War narrative and historiography and this book aims to shed new light on their real contribution to the war, national and Yishuv effort

Formerly, the main narrative regarding the recruits referred to them as belonging to the 'organized' Yishuv or as having 'conformed' with it. The books of Bracha Habas, for example, express this narrative.[5] This book brings for the first time the voices of those women who were not part of this aspect of the Yishuv, and they enlighten and enrich the story from additional aspects. So far, no academic studies have been devoted to the service of Yishuv women in the British Forces. The monograph devoted to this issue will present both the British and the Yishuv viewpoints and will attempt to add new aspects of the British attitude to the women volunteers from the Yishuv.

The study of women and gender has changed the understanding of key processes and phenomena relating to gender and nationalism. The phenomenon of Yishuv women's service in the British forces is presented in this book as a test case in the study of gender and nationalism. The recruitment initiative set off a process that paved the way for women into what had previously been a male-only stronghold – the military. In addition to an obvious gender statement, female military recruitment was also a clear statement vis-à-vis women's wish to participate in the Yishuv's struggle for nationhood alongside their male counterparts and an expression of ideological independence and the realization of their long fight for their position in Yishuv society. The book attempts to understand the Yishuv experience, its social fibre, the power of female unity and, above all, the conflict of interests between feminism and nationalism.

In writing this I made use of primary sources in archives in Israel and in the UK: the British National Archives, the Imperial War Museum and the National Army Museum. Some of them had already been researched and I present them here from a different, hereto un-researched aspect; some are revealed for the first time, such as the war diary of Audrey Chitty, the supreme ATS commander in the Middle East. Chitty used her diary to record her meetings in Eretz Israel during negotiations for establishing the women's units. The diary is in her own handwriting, is classified 'Very Private' and contains, among other things, her personal impressions of the meetings and of various persons in the Yishuv.

In the course of my research, I conducted some sixty interviews, two of which took place in the UK with former British commanders who served with the Yishuv recruits and gave me their British perspective. For most of my interviewees this was the first time they were being asked about the service in the British forces. I also made use of interviews that had been archived in various research institutes. These are of supreme importance in hearing the female voice, albeit from a time distance. To verify, explain or comment on my findings, I cross-referenced interview information with primary sources at my disposal. Research leaned on relevant literature from Israel and the wider world, on press reports from the time as well as prose and poetry.

This book is based on my PhD dissertation, 'Hebrew Woman to the Flag! The Service of Yishuv Women in the British Forces During WWII – National and Gender Aspects', which was written in Bar-Ilan University's Department of Land of Israel Studies and Archeology in September 2007. The Hebrew book, an adaptation of the thesis, *Hebrew Woman to the Flag*, was published by Yad Itzhak Ben Zvi Publishing, Jerusalem and Galili Institute for Research of Defence Force, Ramat Efal, in 2011. I extend my gratitude for their generosity.

My thanks go to the Hadassah-Brandeis Institute and the Helen Gartner Hammer Translation Prize that helped make the translation of the book possible. Special thanks to Gabi Raviv and Naomi Yekutieli for their generous donations.

I would like to thank the people who helped me in this work: first and foremost, Professor Margalit Shilo, who was my teacher, mentor and guide in preparing this work, who had faith in the project from its onset and who stood by me throughout with wisdom and devotion. Every 'minor or major' comment of hers enlightened, illuminated and enriched the work.

In the course of my research, Orly Levy of the Haganah Archive and Michael Lachs of the IDF Archive pointed me in the direction of rare books and documents. Batya Leshem, of the Central Zionist Archives helped me locate documents. Maury Kantor of the Yad Tabenkin Archive revealed new documents to me. At Bet Ariela, the library team spared no effort to help me, especially Dagobert (David) Rubin, who had himself served in the RAF during the Second World War, a 'born historian', who led me to priceless 'hidden' treasures from that period.

Daphne Hill, a former ATS officer in the Middle East, who died before the research was complete, helped me find my way through labyrinthine archives in the UK and provided valuable information about the period and the people. Elizabeth Talbot-Rice, an ATS officer, showed me Audrey Chitty's private diary. The late Jean Baker, wartime commander of the WAAF in the Middle East, shared her private diary with me and was invaluable in shedding light on the period from a British perspective.

Special thanks to Ora Cummings, who dedicated this English translation to the memory of her late parents, Meira Beres from the Jewish Yishuv and John Cummings from Scotland, who met and married in RAF Ismailia in Egypt in 1945.

Thanks also to Jenni Tinson and Toby Harris of VM Publishing for their devoted treatment of me and the book. Also, to Heather

Marchant the editor of the book, for the meticulous editing.

Thanks to my own family, for being with me throughout the long and exhausting path – David, Ophir and Omer. To my late father, Arieh Granit, one of the first pilots in the Israel Air Force, who instilled in me my deep interest and curiosity in all aspects of the Second World War; to my mother, Zmira Granit and my father-in-law, Eliezer Cohen.

And last but not least, my heartfelt thanks go to the subjects of this study – the dozens of amazing women I met and interviewed and those I wasn't fortunate enough to meet, who stood up and took action, often flouting the social conventions of the time and even in defiance of their own families; women who taught me and other women of my generation the meaning of personal and public courage, loyalty and devotion to an ideal. Although they had never even heard the term, these women were genuine feminists, and they turned the work of historic research into an experience that was both personal and utterly fascinating.

Anat Granit-Hacohen

NOTES

1. 'Why did I join?' Conversation with Hanna Levin, ATS recruit and new immigrant, in *Olam Ha'isha* (20 February 1942), p.2 (Hebrew). Levin subsequently served as mayor of Rishon Le'Zion.
2. Eretz Israel was the Hebrew name of Palestine until 1948.
3. Moshe Sharett, 'Recruitment of Women', speech at the Women Workers' Council Congress, Tel Aviv, 26 February 1942; *Davar Hapo'elet*, 3–4 (23 April 1942), p.8 (Hebrew).
4. Haganah – an organization established in the early years of the British Mandate in order to provide security on a national level vis-à-vis the Arab population. Lehi (Stern Gang) – a right-wing nationalist military organization, active during the 1940s especially against British targets.
5. Bracha Habas (1900–68) was an educator, writer and journalist, editorial member of *Davar* and *Davar Layeladim* (*Davar* for children), in which she wrote a regular column. She wrote hundreds of newspaper articles and wrote and edited more than fifty books for adults and children.

Introduction

British Rule in Palestine

During the British Mandate (1920–48), Palestine transposed from a failing Eastern-Ottoman government into the Western-style government of one of the most advanced European powers of that period. Thus, after 400 years of Turkish rule, it changed from a small, insignificant corner of the Ottoman Empire, into a country with its own political status.[1] The new regime, under an industrial imperialist power, with a democratic parliamentary rule of law, defined Palestine's political and administrative boundaries, rehabilitated it from the physical destruction it had suffered during the First World War and determined its government and its administration. The regime also encouraged, directly and indirectly, the country's development and modernization in all walks of life.[2] The British regime arrived in the country equipped with advanced ideas and work methods with regard to all aspects of its development and design. Its activity here was a blend of British and local initiatives, especially those of the Jewish population. Britain's contribution to the country's development was expressed in several spheres: road and rail transport; promoting and developing Yishuv systems for public health and sanitation; providing significant resources for enforcing law and order; and establishing a framework of modern master plans and urban plans.

The British brought to their mandatory regime three unique concepts: for the first time, the words 'Palestine' and 'Palestinians' were used to describe the country and its inhabitants; the establishment of a civil service employing civil servants; and the appearance of a 'civil society' (a term used to describe the aggregate of non-governmental organizations and institutions that manifest the interests and will of citizens).[3] The Second World War broke out about twenty years after the beginning of the British Mandate for Palestine. During this period the relationships were formed between the Zionist Movement and the

British government as well as between the Jewish Yishuv and the British administration in Palestine. Some people see the British administration in Palestine as an independent body with its own viewpoint of events in the Middle East in general and in Palestine in particular, a view that differed from that of the government in London; and others view the administration in Palestine as a branch of the government in London.[4] It would seem that both characteristics worked alongside each other.

Relations Between the Yishuv and the British Administration

The Balfour Declaration of 2 November 1917 and the Mandate for Palestine that was approved in July 1922 by the League of Nations, led to Britian's commitment to 'establish a national home for the Jewish people'. The mandatory regime was generally characterized by cooperation between the British government and the Zionist movement, out of a desire to advance this objective, although the period saw changes in Britain's commitment toward the Zionist ideal and Zionist aspirations. The British Mandate for Palestine can be divided into three sub-periods in accordance with changes in British policy vis-à-vis the Zionist ideal: the first period (1917–1925/6) was characterized by British support and sympathy for the 'national homeland' (Balfour Declaration); the second period (1926–1936) exhibited a double commitment to the Jews and the Arabs in equal proportion; the third period (1936–1948) saw a pro-Arab approach on the part of Britain, which intensified over time and became anti-Zionist.[5]

From a social aspect, British presence in the Yishuv was barely felt until the Arab uprising that took place between 1936 and 1939. They were few in number and were concentrated mainly in Jerusalem, belonging to a specific social stratum of senior administration and rank. The number of Jews who intermingled with them was relatively small and these too belonged to a specific social milieu. The Jewish population's interaction with the British authorities was restricted to the District Office or members of the British police and these too were infrequent.[6]

Palestine During the War

With the outbreak of the Second World War in September 1939, Britain headed the fighting forces against Nazi Germany and Fascist

Italy. Large numbers of British forces were concentrated in Palestine in order to defend the Middle East against Italian or German invasion of the region. The reinforced forces that arrived in the area in order to depress the Arab uprising were joined in early 1940 by two divisions, consisting of 40,000 soldiers from Great Britain and Australia/New Zealand. The British presence was felt more acutely during the war and its effect on social life in the Yishuv was considerable. Palestine had become the home front for the Middle Eastern theatre of war, a place for military exercises, training, vacations, rehabilitation and redeployment. Military bases and arsenals were built, together with workshops, a study centre, military academies and a medical centre that served the Allied Forces who were hindered in transporting troops from Britain by German submarines in the Mediterranean Sea. Altogether some 100,000 troops served in Palestine during the war years, manning the garrison and forming the logistic foundation for the British forces.

Recruiting Yishuv men into the British Forces

When war broke out, the Jewish Yishuv was ambivalent in its attitude to the British administration. The Yishuv leadership was faced with the question of whether to continue with the struggle against the British government and its anti-Zionist policies (following the publication of the White Paper of May 1939), or to concentrate efforts in the war against the Nazi enemy by cooperating with Britain. The solution provided a new political way for cooperating with Britain. In contrast with the pre-war years, this cooperation was now expressed mainly in the recruitment of a large number of Jews into the British army. With the worsening situation of the Jews in Europe, the Zionist movement believed that the establishment of a Jewish fighting force would turn Zionism into an international issue that other countries would be unable to ignore.[7] During the war some 25,000 Yishuv men were recruited and distributed among the land forces, the Air Force, the Royal Navy and various other divisions of the British Forces.[8] The British did not recruit men from the Arab countries.

During the first two years of the war and, especially since the fall of France in May 1940 and after Italy joined the war, Britain's standing in the Middle East was at its lowest ebb. In fact, Britain was the only country fighting against Nazi Germany. In addition, the French army's surrender in Syria at the beginning of July 1940 increased fears of a renewal of the Arab uprising. The appearance of General Irvin

Rommel on the Egyptian border, as well as the occupation of Cyprus and Crete, the uprising in Iraq and Germany's invasion of Syria, looked like the collapse of Britain's status in the Middle East. The atmosphere of fear and concern for the Jewish settlements in the north reached a peak in June 1941 and led the Yishuv leadership to prepare plans for a general recruitment drive, with names such as 'Northern Plan', 'Massada', and 'Guarding the Homeland'. The British prepared their own plans.[9] But the British were able to stabilize the north African front and from the Palestine point of view, the war was already over in the autumn of 1942. From then on, the direct effects of the war on day-to-day life in the country were reduced until they disappeared altogether.

At the beginning of the war, Chaim Weizmann, president of the World Zionist Organization, informed the British government of the movement's intention to join the war effort alongside the allied forces and to make its own contribution. The intention was to establish a Jewish division-sized force as part of the British army. The force's commanding officers would be Jews and it would be embellished with national symbols such as a flag and a badge. The establishment of this force was accompanied by furious debate within the Zionist movement, over its objectives, character and the place in which its soldiers would serve. The fiercest polemic took place between Weizmann and David Ben-Gurion, Chairman of the Jewish Agency Executive. According to Weizmann, the main objective in establishing the force would be the political rewards it would bring at the end of the war, whereas the question of where it would serve was of secondary importance as far as he was concerned. Ben-Gurion, who lived in the Yishuv and was aware of the potential danger it was under, pressed for the force to be based on Jewish volunteers from the Yishuv serving solely in Palestine.

Moshe Sharett (Shertok), head of the Jewish Agency Political Department, supported the Jewish recruitment drive (women as well as men), and throughout the war years he invested most of his time and energy in it. He promoted including people from the Yishuv in the war effort on Britain's side and conducted stubborn negotiations to establish an independent Jewish force, which eventually happened in September 1944. For Sharett, the first objective of the recruitment was its actual participation in the war and not in defending the Jewish Yishuv. He said that the Yishuv recruits would act 'wherever there is war and wherever our participation is needed'.[10]

From the very beginning of the war, British Prime Minister, Winston Churchill, supported the establishment of a Jewish force, which was intended to free British forces stations in Palestine to go and defend Britain. However, as soon as his support of Zionist interests became harmful to Britain's interests in the Middle East, especially when Britain was in need of the support of the Arab states, Churchill didn't hesitate to drop the idea. He was unable to face the firm opposition of his cabinet ministers and military commanders and, notwithstanding the Zionist struggle to establish a military force within the framework of the British army, in October 1941 he rejected the idea.[11] It was only after he became aware of the extent the annihilation of Europe's Jews that Churchill took a stand and the idea of a Jewish force was approved.[12]

Even before the war hundreds of men from the Jewish Yishuv took part in various ways in the activity of the British forces in Palestine, initially individually, as drivers, translators and guides; and later, in an auxiliary framework – Orde Wingate's 'Special Night Squads' and the police force annexed to the army. With the outbreak of war, thousands of people, mainly new immigrants, were recruited spontaneously in the military bases, police stations and other government offices. September 1939 also saw the recruitment of individuals into the British army's Palestine Buffs Regiment. From this period and until the end of 1942, recruitment was among the main issues on the Yishuv's agenda. In September 1940, recruitment began of Jewish companies into the Palestine Buffs alongside Arab companies.[13]

At first, the drive to recruit volunteers was not conceived as a national calling. The Jewish Yishuv's institutions did not support the recruitment of its men, mainly because of the differences of opinion with the British authorities over the establishment of a Jewish force; it was even considered as 'crossing the line' of Yishuv discipline. In July 1940, following the decision to establish infantry brigades that would precede the Jewish force, the Yishuv institutions changed their minds about military service. They called on the Yishuv population to consider volunteering for service in the British forces as being the 'order of the day', even though the induction regime did not alter the voluntary nature of the mobilization. The public's attitude to the call was mixed. Some parts of the Yishuv rejected it out of hand; for example, people who had come from Eastern Europe saw the army as an alien and hostile body, a tool for conducting pogroms. The communal agricultural settlements refused to release working hands and the Revisionist movement had its own political motives for opposing cooperation with the British. But against all these, there were many who felt a duty to join up and considered the act of volunteering to be a contribution to the defence of the country.

News of the Annihilation in Europe

From early 1942, the year in which the recruitment of Yishuv women into the British forces began, the American Jewish press began publishing information about the mass murder of Jews in the territories of the Soviet Union. In March 1942, first news reached Palestine of the activity of Nazi murder squads in the Balkan states and in White Russia. Two months later, *Hamashkif* published information on the fate of the Jews of Lithuania, and at the end of May the first news started to flow in and be published about the slaughter of Jews in occupied Poland.

At the end of July 1942, the first news reached Palestine of deportations from Warsaw and later of the destruction, but the local newspapers continued to be reserved as to the reliability of the Jewish agencies that had provided the information. By late October, reliable information was already received about the 'final solution'. This was followed one month later by the testimony of a group of sixty-nine Yishuv Jews, who had arrived in Palestine as part of an exchange for German citizens held by the Allied Forces.[14] The Yishuv began to absorb the incoming information and to respond to it. Thus, for example, in late 1942, women of the Labor Movement issued a desperate cry to the women of the world to act against the slaughter of Jews. In early 1943, news reached the Yishuv of the Valley of Death in Poland and of the heroism of the fighters in the Warsaw Ghetto. This information sent a shock wave throughout the Yishuv and motivated men and women to join the army in order to help Britain in its efforts to defeat Nazi Germany.

Attempts at Forced Recruitment

In September 1939 the Jewish institutions in Palestine conducted a population census, of which one of the objectives was to gauge the number of potential military recruits the Jewish Yishuv could draw on, when the time came.[15] The results of the census were impressive, although the extent of actual recruitment was not compatible with the hopes pinned on it. As a result, starting in May 1941, the institutions attempted to organize volunteering by issuing 'mobilization orders'. A year later, in June 1942 an extensive recruitment regime defined potential conscripts according to age and marital status. According to the order, 'All men aged between 20–30, single and married who have no children', were liable to be conscripted into the army. Nonetheless, the recruitment regime did not change the voluntary character of the recruitment and, in fact, there was no legal way to force it on people. The strained relations with the British since spring 1943 symbolized the beginning of the end of voluntary recruitment, whose extent had never been significantly reinstated. After November 1942, when the Allied victory turned the tide in the North Africa Campaign and ended the Axis threat to the Middle East, the British command, under which most of the Yishuv volunteers served, began to lose its military importance and focus in the region and its military bases turned gradually into large centres for logistics and training.

Three waves of recruitment to the British forces took place up until 1942: the first consisted of the onset of male recruitment that lasted until the 'large rally' in October 1941; the second continued until June 1942 (during which 'mobilization orders' were issued to the Yishuv), and the third wave lasted from June to October 1942. Female recruitment commenced at a time when male recruitment was in decline and there was hope among the Yishuv leadership that this drive would encourage men to step forward.[16] With the developments in the war in North Africa and Britain's increasing need to transfer as many troops (who had hereto fulfilled administrative positions) as possible to the front, the army decided to recruit Yishuv women as well.

Female recruitment was an additional link in the already complex relationship between women and emerging Jewish nationalism. In order to understand the unique situation of female military recruitment in the context of gender and security, it is necessary to first familiarize oneself with the background struggles the women of the Yishuv conducted for their status in Yishuv society, as well the history of Jewish women's military service.

Women in the Jewish Yishuv in Palestine

'Here he comes and he goes – from within us, the Hebrew man',[17] thus he was welcomed by the poet Ya'akov Cohen. And what about the new Hebrew woman?

Whether on purpose or inadvertently, within the reality prevailing in the Yishuv at the time and contrary to the utopian narrative, some change was already taking place in the traditional representation of women and they were striving to participate in Zionist activity and in the national discourse. The image of the 'new Hebrew woman' was created in order to challenge the traditional Jewish idea of femininity, while embracing her and understanding her in a new light. Thus the process of recreating the new woman called upon traditional as well as new forces to produce a many-faceted figure. Nonetheless, a certain image still adhered to the New Hebrew Woman; one that had no grasp on reality, of a woman whose status is equal to that of the Hebrew male. Thus evolved the 'ethos of equality' that Yishuv women supposedly enjoyed.

Female equality in the new Yishuv society was an important factor in the pioneering, Zionist-Socialist ideology. Thinkers and theorists of that ideology were convinced that the removal of capitalism and its replacement with socialism would bring a cure for the 'woman problems'. It is no wonder therefore that this idea was included in the complexity of principles that shaped the new Zionist society that aspired to set an example of enlightenment, based on principles of justice and equality. Even before the 1920s the labour movement had issued a declaration committing itself to social equality, including equality between men and women. However, in truth things did not turn out as expected and the discrepancy between dream and reality was patently obvious throughout. The Yishuv's pioneering society had a male orientation, full of palpably, physically, emphatically male orientations and inequality between men and women was maintained.

Women in Education and in Instating the Hebrew Language

Although the women of the First Aliyah were engaged in farm labour in Palestine, their effect on the Yishuv's agriculture was marginal. Their effect on education, on the other hand, was significant. This particular wave of immigration was noteworthy in the special role played by its female members in instilling the Hebrew language. Also, the development of nationalist Hebrew education for girls as well as for boys was a unique feature of this group of immigrants. Their inclusion in education was the cherry in the icing of women's participation in the national renaissance enterprise, since it opened the door to their acceptance as equal members of the new society.[18] During the Second Aliyah, too, women played a pivotal role in education. The level of female teachers at this time improved and some of them were graduates of European high schools and universities.[19] Not only did the establishment of the high school in Tel Aviv during that period in time create the new Yishuv intelligentsia, but it also actualized the 'new Hebrew female'. Among other things, the high school's teachers instilled in their pupils new ideals, including the idea of female emancipation.

Women's Organization in the Yishuv

The various waves of Jewish immigration to the Yishuv – from the Second Aliyah in the early twentieth century and up to the Fifth Aliyah in the 1930s, were marked by various kinds of organization – professional and social – whose objective was to promote the interests of their members. Women, too, knew that they had to establish various bodies in order to promote their own interests and improve their social and economic standing. These bodies were part of their efforts to participate in the nation building process. Working women in the Second Aliyah, for example, started to organize themselves, both individually and as part of the male organizations, in order to work together toward professional achievements.

Most of the 'female citizens' (women of the Second Aliyah who were not labourers) lived in towns and villages, but only a few of them worked for their living. They established various aid and welfare organizations and, unlike those of the philanthropic organizations that preceded them, their efforts had new features. They created a new framework that helped women to obtain vocational training, established workshops in various locations around the country and also acted as social workers.[20] The 'Working Women's Federation,' for example was established in Jerusalem in 1920, with the objective of helping pregnant women and new mothers to follow their babies' development and to provide material aid. This women's federation established a countrywide network of mother and baby stations under the name 'Tipat Halav' (Drop of Milk), which operate to this day.[21]

Notwithstanding the ethos of equality, with the beginning of the British Mandate of Palestine a struggle evolved over the rights of women to vote in the elections to the Elective Council. The 'Association of Hebrew Women for Equality in the Land of Israel' was established in 1919 and consisted of already existing women's associations. Sara Azriyahu established the association and a key figure in it was Dr Rosa Welt Straus, whose connections with international women's organizations paved the way in 1920 for their acceptance into the International Women's Alliance as members in the struggle for voting rights for women. The Association was a non-party body and consisted of women with a wide variety of political affiliations from all walks of Yishuv life: Labour-Socialist; the religious sector and the civil women's sector. Their struggle ended in January 1926 when woman's right to vote and to be elected to the Elective Council was included in the organization's rules.[22]

In 1927 the mandatory authorities approved an election constitution, which included equal rights for women in the political life of the Jewish Yishuv in Palestine.[23] However, notwithstanding their achievement, it would appear that their right to vote did not change women's low status, especially in the economic/employment structure, and it can safely be said that traditional values remained unchanged. Rachel Elboim-Dror is convinced that not only did the struggle for voting rights fail in equalizing the status of women in the Yishuv to that of men; indeed an opposite result was achieved. According to her, in creating an illusion of equality, the victory in this struggle was actually a stumbling block and, in fact, served as camouflage against criticism and demands for change. Inequality was also palpable in the kibbutz movement.[24]

The Movement of Working Women

An important step in organization of working women was the establishment of the Working Women's movement within the General Labour Federation of Hebrew Workers in Eretz Israel (henceforth Histadrut), which was born out of women's protest against their discrimination at the Histadrut's founding congress in late 1920. Following an uncompromising struggle, a special women's section was established in the Histadrut, headed by an elected representation known as the 'Working Women's Council'.[25] The Council worked hard on behalf of women in towns and in the agricultural settlements to improve their lives and working conditions. It acted on two levels: on the one hand, as a socially orientated movement representing salaried women and, on the other, as a movement representing housewives, seeking expression for bourgeoisie values such as establishing a home and raising a family. It acted as educator of the single woman and as representative of the working establishment.[26]

During the second half of the 1920s with the onset of the economic crisis in the Yishuv, the Women's Council embarked on a new initiative in an attempt to provide a solution for unemployed women workers. The 'Associations' established in 1926 by Hanna Chizik constituted an independent women's commune, based on temporary communal life together with employment outside the 'association'. Twelve such 'associations' were established.[27]

The achievements of the women were blocked when there was estrangement or lack of contact between the Working Women's Movement, whose influence was especially obvious in the agricultural settlements, and the salaried urban women. According to some researchers these and the mutual feedback between the two groups left women at the fringes of the major change processes during that time. Bat-Sheva Margalit-Stern, for example, claims that attempts to solve the special problems of working women within the Histadrut framework enjoyed only partial success. Wherever women's organization presented a real or imaginary threat to the Histadrut establishment, a deliberate process of dissolution and withdrawal took place. According to Dafna Izraeli, already at the beginning of their journey, the women's movement avoided defining itself as struggling against male dominance.[28]

Religious Women's Organizations

The organization of religious women in the Yishuv encompassed both the civil circles of this population and the settling socialist public. First of all, religious women established the Women's Mizrachi Federation in 1918, with independent branches throughout the Yishuv, unlike other women's groups belonging to the Hadassah and WIZO (Women's International Zionist Organization), which were first established abroad and subsequently set up branches in the Yishuv. The Mizrachi Working Women's organization was also established as a uniquely local enterprise. In 1940 a centre for Mizrachi women's organizations was established in Palestine, headed by Rebbetsen Sara Herzog, with the objective of educating women in the spirit of Mizrachi; participating social and welfare aid to the movement, especially to women; helping the party in general elections and forming ties with Mizrachi women worldwide. One of the organization's more important endeavours consisted of establishing religious women's farms, in order to solve the problems of the religious working woman.

Other Organizations

Other women's organizations were also active in the Yishuv during the early 1940s, such as the WIZO, which was established in 1921 as a

Federation of Hebrew Women, but changed its name in 1933 to the Federation of Zionist Women and, with Henrietta Szold at its head, joined the WIZO as the Israeli Federation;[29] the Hadassah Women's Federation in America, established in 1912 on the initiative of Henrietta Szold; the Mizrachi Women's Federation, established in America in 1915, and then in Canada; the Pioneer Women Federation which was established in 1925 in the USA and Canada and later also in Mexico; the Women's League for Eretz Israel New York was established in 1927. All the aforementioned organizations were members in the Council for Women's Organizations established in the Yishuv in 1936. The Women's Council established by the women of the Yishuv played a weighty role in initiating the drive for female service in the British armed forces and, with the help of factors in the Yishuv and in the military, led it to fruition.

Women in the Military During the First World War

From the birth of history, war and armies were conceived as essentially a male dominion, since the best masculine traits were given expression on the battlefield.[30] Women were always seen as creators of life and not belonging to a world in which life is taken, and were therefore placed in the hinterland, while men were posted in the battlefront.[31] A view of the army and military activity as central, and a view of military courage as major social value, are usually detrimental to women.[32] Women's presence in the army is conceived as contradicting this ideal and undermining the organization's male supremacy, since, with the introduction of women, it could have lost an important part of its characteristics.[33]

Women were left out of the battlefield in the First World War and anyone who wished to fight had to masquerade as a man. By adopting a male identity, many women assured themselves power and independence, such as an equal-rights social status, which had always been the province of men only.[34] Women's presence in the vicinity of fighters was seen during many periods in time – from the middle ages to the present day – as essential and helpful to maintaining the morale and abilities of the male soldiers. These women, commonly known as 'camp followers', stayed with the fighting forces close to the war front, in the role of wives, nurses and often even of prostitutes.[35]

The First World War brought about a drastic change in the image of the soldier and the definition of his tasks. The military recruitment of men and their definition as both skilled and as citizen provided them with a single identity: that of 'soldier', thus creating an analogy between civilian and soldier. Each of the countries fighting in the war underwent an outburst of fervent nationalism, characterized by militarism, which in turn was identified with the term 'nation'. For the first time in history the differences between the military references to front and rear were obscured, and the terms 'home' and 'domestic' turned into adjectives to describe the military idiom 'front'.[36] The very act of various countries' including women in their military brought about the change in women's status during the twentieth century.

As for the role of women in the various armies during the war, different forms of military service can be discerned in accordance with the selection of jobs open to women.

Administrative positions: United States of America. From the time the US entered the war in 1917, over 13,000 women had joined the US Navy, mostly in office jobs. At first the women were employed as hired civilians and not as regular soldiers, as telephone operators and, overseas, as nurses. All plans for establishing a women's auxiliary force and employing women as soldiers, especially in service and clerical positions were torpedoed by the American War Office. But about a year later, and for the first time in American history, women were awarded full ranks and status in the army.

Auxiliary regiments: Britain. Until the day that Britain announced that it was at war with Germany, on 14 August 1914, no civilian or governmental authority had given any thought to or made any plans for integrating women in the case of war breaking out.[37] Only in 1917 – and in accordance with a government decision – were the Women's Auxiliary Army Corps (WAAC) established in Britain, with the objective of releasing men for war service. Thousands of female volunteers served in these regiments in positions that included nursing, cooking, secretarial work, telephone operators, etc. The military authorities decided that women would not serve in command positions and the only status they were given was that of supervisors and administrators. Helen Gwynne-Vaughan was appointed the first WAAC commander. The Air Force's Women's Auxiliary Division (WAD) was established with some 32,000 women recruits under the command of Dame Jane Trefusis-Forbes.

In fighting positions: Russia. The most outstanding example of women's military participation was the establishment of the Russian army's Battalion of Death, which was founded by Maria Botchkareva, who was its first commanding officer.[38] The hundreds of volunteers who served in the regiment bore weapons, underwent extensive and demanding training, and fought in painful battles. The regiment was established by women with a distinct social and political agenda. According to Laurie Stoff, from the very establishment of the regiment there emerges a direct connection between female participation in battle and the women's movements that fought for female equality in the early decades of the twentieth century, both in Russia and the west.[39]

Women in the Army during the Second World War

According to Nazi doctrine, which was based heavily on Adolf Hitler's conservative worldview, women were supposed to stay at home, as full-time housewives and mothers. At the beginning of the war, even unmarried women were not recruited into the army. But a change took place in 1941, when the war made it necessary for women to fill various positions in the war industries and in administrative-clerical roles in the women's auxiliary units. About half a million women, excluding nurses who served in units of their own, served in the various auxiliary forces in Germany. In 1945 women filled around 85 per cent of all the available administrative and clerical posts in the German army. These women wore uniform and were subject to military discipline, but were not known officially as 'soldiers'. Unofficially they were known as 'Blitzmädchen' (bomb girls). Women were not allowed to use firearms and in November 1944, Hitler issued a detailed order on this issue.[40]

Toward the end of the war, when Allied planes were already dropping bombs on German towns and cities, the anti-aircraft batteries were becoming a crucial factor in Germany's air defences and women were included in this. Between 65,000 and 100,000 women served in these Luftwaffe (air force) units; in some of the units employed in detecting enemy aircraft, women constituted 90 per cent of the workforce. Still, women were not permitted to fire anti-aircraft cannons, since Hitler was convinced that German public opinion would object.

Women in the US Army

The USA joined the war alongside the Allied forces in December 1941 after the Japanese attacked the American naval base in Pearl Harbour, Hawaii. The first proposal to establish a Women's Army Auxiliary

Corps (WAAC) had already been presented to Congress in May 1941, but, as in the previous war, it included an employment plan for women, with none of the status and benefits that military service provides to its recruits. Only after it entered the war did the American War Office recognize the need for an urgent recruitment drive for women. The establishment of a women's auxiliary army was announced in May 1942, with the resources for the immediate recruitment of 150,000 women. In September 1943, the auxiliary force was dispersed and replaced by the Women's Army Corps (WAC) that became an integral part of the US army and its recruits enjoyed military status and full military benefits. The force, at its height, numbered 100,000 women, and all in all, some 150,000 served in it throughout its existence. The women in the auxiliary army filled mostly clerical and communications positions; some of them served overseas on the Pacific front.[41]

In addition to the positions filled in the land and sea forces, women also served as pilots in the Women Airforce Service Pilots (WASP). They were entrusted with transporting aircraft from base to base and were also test pilots. About 1,000 women served in this company.[42] Despite the great respect paid to these women by various military parties, public opinion was hostile as a result of a slur campaign waged against them, mostly in 1943. The subsequent willingness of women to join up suffered a severe blow.

Women in the British Armed Forces

Besides military service, another form of service was open to women – the Home Guard. Faced with the threat of German invasion, and as a result of massive bombing by the German Luftwaffe, Britain had turned into one big battlefront and the differences between the terms 'front' and 'rear' became blurred. Women and men, who were unable for whatever reason to serve in the army, sought a semi-military framework that could provide them with the civil legitimacy they wanted. The Home Guard, which was established in May 1941, filled the void. However, although the organization called for a merger of 'home' and 'national', as its name would suggest, and notwithstanding its generally democratic roots, women were excluded from joining it until 1943.[43]

The women's Auxiliary Territorial Services (ATS) in the Second World War was in fact a continuation of the women's auxiliary services established in the First World War. It was established in 1938 as a regiment of volunteers and did not belong to an official military framework. Women were required to fulfil non-combatant functions in order to release as many men as possible to join the forces. Thus the jobs available to them at first were cooking, driving, clerical, communications and so on. The WAAF – Women's Auxiliary Air Force – was established in 1939. The two women who commanded the auxiliary forces in the First World War were also given command of them in the Second World War. Trefusis-Forbes stayed on to the end of the war, but Gwynne-Vaughan was obliged to leave the service in 1941 and was replaced by Jean Nox. Toward the end of 1941, the scope of positions available to women was expanded and they were now able to participate in 'operational' positions too. The most prestigious of these consisted of service in anti-aircraft batteries, although they were forbidden to fire on and bring down enemy aircraft.

In April 1941, the ATS became an official part of the British Army. All in all, by the end of the war some 487,000 British women served the various sectors of the British armed forces: the ATS (222,000), WAAF (185,000) and the WRNS (Women's Royal Naval Service, 80,000). In December 1941 the second National Service Act was passed by Parliament, as a result of which 125,000 women were recruited, by law, into the armed forces. Thus, most of the 600,000 women in the British armed forces during the Second World War had volunteered to serve.[44]

Women in the Soviet Army

For the first two years of the Second World War, the Soviet Union was an ally of Germany (in accordance with the Ribbentrop-Molotov agreement). After Germany invaded the USSR on 22 June 1941 in Operation Barbarossa, the Soviets broke away and joined the Allied forces in the war against the Germans. Until then, women had been employed mainly in factories and in other auxiliary positions. As the war intensified and following the fierce battles waged by the Soviets against the Germans in which 50 per cent of the country's able-bodied men were killed in battle, the shortage of manpower became acute. The new circumstances and the mandatory military recruitment meant that women were recruited directly into the army, without having first served in 'auxiliary forces' as in other armies. Since public opinion on female recruitment required no consideration, women were recruited solely on the basis of the army's war needs.

Aside from filling 'feminine' jobs, such as storekeepers, telephone operators, nurses, etc., Soviet women were assigned to almost all the combative roles in the army, serving as pilots of light bombers, carrying out operational sorties; they served as team members in the armored corps; filled combat roles in the infantry and carried out sabotage operations and bridge building for the engineering corps. Soviet women also served in anti-aircraft batteries. But, unlike the British ATS, they were allowed to fire and bring down enemy planes. Regiments of women fought alongside those of men in the defence of the major cities, such as Leningrad, Odessa, Kiev, Minsk and others. According to various estimates, some 800,000 women served in the Red Army, of which around half a million fought in the front lines. In addition to these, some 200,000 women fought with the partisans. Altogether, women constituted around 8 per cent of the entire Soviet army.[45]

Women's military service in the Soviet army was a unique phenomenon that had no previous equal in any other army or in wartime. These women served as role models and inspiration to feminist movements round the world, including the Women's Labuor Movement in the Yishuv which was struggling for equality and the inclusion of women in the war, and to female members of the Palmach (Hebrew acronym for 'striking forces'), who were fighting to achieve their position in the organization. In a Palmach women's congress that took place in September 1943, Zvia Katznelson said, 'The same great Russia ... that raised the image of the fighting woman; [Russia] and not England'. And she added, 'Why don't they make do with the ATS for women? Why do women there, of all places, recoil from the ... status of auxiliary? Is it not firmly connected to civil liberty there? Is not the liberated woman in society and in the workplace also a party to the struggle for the values of the newly achieved precious life?'[46]

Women and Security in the Yishuv

Several organizations operated in the Yishuv in order to cope with issues of security and defence: 'Bar Giora' and 'Hashomer' were established before the First World War to defend Jewish settlements against Arab marauders; the Haganah organization was established in the early years of the British Mandate in order to provide security on a national level vis-à-vis the Arab population; the Palmach, the recruited fighting arm of Haganah, although established with the encouragement of the British in order to defend the Yishuv against the possibility of a German invasion in the Second World War, its main importance lay in the fact that it was part of the evolving Jewish force under the auspices of the Yishuv institutions. The two right-wing nationalist military organizations (IZL – Irgun Zvai Leumi, and Lehi – Lohamei Herut Israel [known by the British as the Stern Gang]) were active during the 1930s and 1940s and in these, too, women filled various and varied positions.[47]

The role of women in the defence and security of the Yishuv since the Second Aliyah and until the Second World War is worthy of research, in light of the reality in the field, on the one hand, and in light of Zionist ideology and rhetoric, on the other: how did men conceive the role of women in defence and how did women see themselves as partners to the effort. Women's struggle for equality in the various organizations should be measured against a background of their struggle for equality in the evolving Yishuv society.

As a national liberation movement, Zionism considered masculinity to be a supreme value and all the characteristics of the Jewish people in the Diaspora were seen as feminine traits. Everything pertaining to Diaspora life was tagged 'female', soft and weak, whereas everything connected to Hebrew nationalism was considered 'masculine', daring and strong and this symbolism seeped into every aspect of the Yishuv's culture. There was no room in the new nationalist 'masculinity' for women and femininity as cultural symbols, and women identified with the masculine definitions, which played a major role in the Zionist ethos. The ideal of the fighting male (especially by way of restoring the image of historical Jewish heroes) and on whom the Zionist revolution's 'new Jew' was modelled did not include a parallel female image.[48]

The first test of the Yishuv's female-equality ethos can be found in the 'Hashomer' organization, which was initially established as 'Bar Giora' in 1907 and became 'Hashomer' two years later. Between 1907 and 1920, the organization consisted of 105 members, including 35 women. The inclusion of women was more of a myth than reality, since apart from two – Mania Shohat and Rachel Yanait Ben-Zvi – women in Hashomer were considered unworthy of even participating in the organization's meetings.[49]

During the First World War a small underground movement called NILI (a Hebrew acronym that translates as: strength of Israel will never lie) was active in the Yishuv with Sara Ahronson filling a key role.[50] A women's initiative to join the army as soldiers developed toward the end of the war (October 1917) when voices in the Yishuv started calling for volunteers to join the British forces and take part in the liberation of the Galilee. The leaders of the volunteer committee included Rachel Yanait Ben-Zvi. An all-male Jewish regiment was eventually established (attached to the 40th Royal Fusiliers) and became known as the Jewish Brigade. However, all 400 women who also volunteered for service were rejected.[51] In contrast with Britain, female recruitment in the Yishuv in the First World War did not in the end materialize. Only two sisters were recruited, Nina and Bella Berlin, who also served as nursing sisters in a hospital.

Women in the Haganah

The Haganah organization was established in 1920 in order to solve the problem of Arab attacks on Jewish settlements. Subsequent years provided Haganah members with plenty of opportunities to test their fighting abilities, and for the organization's female members the scope of their involvement. Their activity developed in accordance with the shifting character of the organization in light of changing reality in the Yishuv, although their actual status remained obscure.[52] Hundreds of the Haganah's female members lived on kibbutzim and moshavim (cooperative settlements), where they were granted automatic membership in the organization. But most of them lived in the towns and cities, especially in the three larger ones, Tel Aviv, Haifa and Jerusalem. Together with dozens of female students, most members of Haganah were hired clerks, unskilled labourers and secretaries.

Female Haganah members filled mostly 'traditional' posts such as cooking and nursing. Although most of them were resigned to these tasks and saw their longed-for equality in the very fact of their participation in the military and their contribution to the overall effort, there were many others, especially kibbutz members, who refused to accept the situation. Individual women who managed to penetrate blatantly male provinces, such as filling bullets, signals and pigeon handling, were held in high esteem among the women. They saw themselves as full partners in the national effort, unlike rank and file women who filled tasks that were seen as 'feminine'.

During the Arab riots of 1936–39 the number of women in Haganah constituted around 20 per cent of the organization's members (of the 24,947 members, 5,487 were women). Notwithstanding their relatively large number, only a few were included in defence missions.[53] Still, following pressure on the part of Haganah's female members, especially those from the kibbutzim, the movement's leadership decided to establish a system to provide military training to women. And, indeed, between 1940 and 1941, an independent 'women's regiment' was formed in Tel Aviv, under the command of Neuta Halperin, which brought together women and officers. The regiment devised methods especially for women, who then underwent field and weaponry training. The women in Haganah struggled to be included in regional defence, in communications, medical services, in accompanying illegal immigrant ships, receiving immigrants, teaching skills, demonstrations, acquisitions and accompanying convoys, but not in participating in war. In July 1942, for the first time in the history of the organization, a woman – Shulamit Klibanov – was appointed national commander of Haganah and this subsequently led to changes in the organization's view of female occupation.[54] Apart from her, Rosa Cohen – mother of assassinated Israeli Prime Minister, Yitzhak Rabin – served as commander of the Haifa branch of Haganah, and Yanait Ben-Zvi was a member of the Jerusalem command of Haganah.[55]

Women in the Palmach

In May 1942, four months after the beginning of recruitment to the British army, the Palmach started its own recruitment drive in the course of which sixty women were drafted, a women's company to each platoon. During the War of Independence some 1,000 women served in the Palmach (out of a force of 6,000). Recruitment to the Palmach was voluntary; ten women took part in a Palmach platoon commander's course and twenty-nine completed a Company Commanders' course. These included women who accompanied convoys and fighters on active duty. But most of them filled mainly social tasks that involved support for the male fighters, or, as they were referred to in the Palmach, 'mothers'. Women fighters who served in male platoons, commanded men and were even wounded in battle, were an exception to the rule.[56]

Women in the IZL and Lehi

The IZL was an underground organization founded in Jerusalem in 1931. It was established by officers who had dropped out of the Haganah because they wished to take firmer action in the future against the Arab aggression of the time. Most IZL members had previously belonged to the Betar movement.[57] During the 1930s the

IZL focused its activity on the defence of Jewish settlements and in terrorist acts aimed at breaking the national institutions' policy of 'restraint' in face of Arab aggression. In this way the IZL differed from Haganah, which practiced a defensive line. When the White Paper was published in 1939, IZL went into action against the British. But, when the Second World War broke out, IZL members volunteered to join the ranks of the Allied forces. The Lehi organization, under the leadership of Avraham ('Yair') Stern, broke off from IZL in the summer of 1940 as a result of IZL commander David Raziel's announcement that there would be no more attacks on British targets.[58] According to Lehi concepts, the British occupation of the Land of Israel was not legal, so that the organization focused its attacks against British targets, unlike Haganah and the IZL, who involved themselves mainly in fighting the Arabs. There were about 800 women in Lehi (around 20 per cent of the entire membership). IZL and Lehi women filled various positions: communications, propaganda, recruitment and training, first aid, intelligence (especially smuggling documents, tailing and lookouts), cooking and storekeeping. They were usually excluded from fighting missions or in purchasing activity (aside from escorting men on these missions, as decoys and in hiding confiscated material). Many women trained and even instructed in the use of various kinds of arms, especially personal weapons, which were essential to underground activity. Only a few were trained in heavy weaponry such as mortars or mines. Most of the women in the underground organizations were included in various activities that concerned instruction and training and worked on an equal basis with their male counterparts. Nonetheless, women employed as escorts, communications officers and couriers had an advantage over men; because of their innocent appearance they suffered fewer body searches. Some of the women participated in platoon commander courses and a very few in company commander courses. But women in the underground continued to feel discriminated against because of their exclusion from operational activity.[59]

NOTES

1. Gideon Biger, *The Role of the British Administration in Changing the Geography of Palestine, 1918–1929* (London: University College, 1979), pp.420–30. On Britain's contribution to the development of the country, see for example, Nahum Gross, 'Hamediniut hacalcalit shel hamimshal habriti hamandatori be'eretz Israel' [Economic Policies of the British Mandatory Government in Eretz Israel], *Katedra*, 24 (August 1982), pp.153–80.

2. The League of Nations' mandatory system left the task of development to the power that undertook the mandate, although from a very early stage, the Jewish Yishuv in the country had already developed a form of alternative government, at least internally, with regard to essential services. Thus, a kind of distribution of tasks was created between the British regime and the Yishuv institutes. The regime dealt mainly with issues of law and public order, building system of roads and railways, mail, etc., whereas the Yishuv concerned itself with its independent political activity, immigration (in accordance with British restrictions), settlement, security, education and health services. Dan Horowitz and Moshe Lissak, *Miyishuv lemedina: yehudei Eretz Israel betkufat hamandat habriti kekehila politit* [From Yishuv to State: Eretz Israeli Jews during the British Mandate as a political community] (Tel Aviv: 1977), p.207.
3. This process resulted in the creation of a political entity under the name Palestine. Bernard Lewis, 'Hamandat Habriti bekontext hashva'ati' [The British mandate in comparative context'], in Yehoshua Ben-Arieh (ed.), *Yerushalaim betkufat Hamandat: ha'asiya vehamoreshet* [Jerusalem in Mandate period: the action and legacy] (Jerusalem 2003), pp.25–8. Tom Segev is convinced that unlike the cultural imperialism in France, Britain did not attempt to subject its colonies to its own basic values. Tom Segev, *One Palestine, Complete : Jews and Arabs under the Mandate* (New York 2000).
4. On relations between the British civil administration in Palestine (which replaced the military administration in 1920) and the government in London, and especially on the issue of Palestine, see Motti Golani, 'Britania ve harchra'at 'milchemet haezrahim' be Eretz Israel' [Britain and the defining 'civil war' in Eretz Israel], *Zion*, 54, no.4 (1989), pp.455–94; Gabriel Sheffer, 'Me'atzvei hamediniut hamandatorit, stereotypim obasar vadam?' [Mandatory policy makers, stereotypes or flesh and blood?], *Keshet* 4 (Summer 1970), pp.167–78.
5. Yehoshua Ben-Arieh, *Jerusalem and the British Mandate* (Jerusalem: Yad Izhak Ben Tsvi, 2003), pp.4–18.
6. The number of British people in the country increased significantly, as did their distribution in various locations. In 1936, 930 British police personnel served in Palestine, a number that had grown to some 4,000 in 1939. Gelber, Forming the Yishuv, pp. 410-411.
7. Yoav Gelber, 'Aspectim politiim lehakamat hakoah halohem beyishuv haeretzisraeli btkufat milhemet haolam hashnia' [Political aspects in establishing the fighting force in the Yishuv during the Second World War], *Yalkut Moreshet*, 22 (November 1976), pp.31–62. Notwithstanding Ben-Gurion's 12 September 1939 declaration that the White Paper must be fought as if Hitler did not exist, and that Hitler must be fought as if there was no White Paper (David Ben-Gurion, *Bama'aracha* [In the campaign] [Tel Aviv 1957], p.18), there was no way to combine these two polar trends and the declaration was disregarded in practice. The Zionist leaders continued with recruitment while simultaneously striving to achieve a Jewish state within a pro-British framework.
8. 'The Recruitment for Late August 1944' (undated); Central Zionist Archive (henceforth: CZA), S25/5097.
9. Yoav Gelber, *Toldot hahitnadvut: Hahitnadvut ve mekoma bemidiniut hazionit ve hayishuvit 1939–1942* [History of volunteering: volunteering and its place in Zionist and Yishuv Policies 1939–1942] (Jerusalem 1989), pp.42, 513–24.

The military failures were seen as a preview for the possible British withdrawal from the region, a withdrawal that could have left the Yishuv to face its fate vis-à-vis the hostile Arab countries and raised fears of an enemy invasion and life under German-Italian occupation on sufferance of the Arabs.

10. Moshe Sharett, *Policy Making; The Diaries of Moshe Sharett* (Tel Aviv 1979), p.168. Nonetheless, he was convinced that the recruitment would eventually also lead to defense of the Yishuv.
11. According to Michael Cohen, despite the well known myth of Churchill's special affinity for the Zionist interest, which included his attitude to the establishment of a Jewish force, he was first and foremost British and acted in defense of Britain's interests. Michael Cohen, *Churchill and the Jews* (London 2003), pp.203–27, 331–3. On Churchill's personal intentions, see, Winston Churchill, *The Second World War: Their Finest Hour*, Vol.2 (London 1950), pp.373–7. See also, Winston Churchill, *The Second World War: Triumph and Tragedy*, Vol.6 (London 1954), p.597.
12. The Jewish Fighting Force (JFF or Brigade) was established in September 1944 and consisted of some 5,000 soldiers, most of them recruited into various units of the British army. Its troops participated in several battles in Italy. They were particularly active at the end of the war and after it among the Holocaust survivors.
13. The original plan was for the squads to serve initially as garrison companies and they would later be reassigned as combat companies. Gelber, *Toldot hahitnadvut: Hahitnadvut ve mekoma bemidiniut hazionit ve hayishuvit 1939–1942*, pp.253–5. According to Mordechai Naor, the British tried to minimize the volunteering of thousands of Yishuv Jews into their army in order to avoid 'annoying' the Arabs: Mordechai Naor, 'Ha'itonut Hayehudit be'retz Israel betkufat milhemet ha'olam hashniya' [Jewish Press in Eretz Israel during WWII], in Dina Porat and Mordechai Naor (eds), Ha'itonut *Hayehudit be'Eretz Israel nochach hashoa 1939–1948* [Jewish Press in face of the Holocaust] (Tel Aviv 2002), p.16. Piere Van Paassen defined the participation of people from the Yishuv as 'the best kept secret in the war', a hint at the fact that the British wanted to minimize the part played by the Jewish Yishuv in the Second World War. Pierre Van Paassen, *The Forgotten Ally* (New York 1943), pp.175–236.
14. Yoav Gelber, 'Ha'itonut ha'ivrit be eretz Israel al hashmadat yehudei Europa (1941–1942)' [Hebrew press in Eretz Israel on the destruction of European Jewry (1941–1942), in Dina Porat and Mordechai Naor (eds), *Ha'itonut hayehudit beeretz Israel nochah hashoa 1939–1945* [Jewish press in face of the Holocaust 1939–1945] (Tel Aviv: 2002), pp.35–65; Dina Porat, *Hanhaga be'milkud: Ha'Yishuv nokhakh Ha'shoa 1942–1945* [Leadership in a trap: the Yishuv in face of the Holocaust 1942–1945] (Tel Aviv: Am Oved, 1987), pp.61–4.
15. The census took place on 11–13 September and one of its objectives was to serve as an 'internal program for the establishment of a Hebrew army, when conditions for this were ripe'. 134,043 people registered for the census, 85,781 men (70 per cent more than those who were obliged to register) and 50,262 women (42 per cent of the women of relevant age in the Yishuv). Yehuda Slutsky (ed.), *Sefer toldot ha'aganah* [History of the Haganah], B and C (Tel Aviv 1973), pp.295–6.

16. 'Voluntarily', 15 November 1942, Haganah History Archive (HHA), 33/4.
17. Ya'akov Cohen, 'Ha'ivri hahadash' [The new Hebrew], in Ya'akov Cohen (ed.), *Ha'ivri hahadash: musaf lesifrut, leumanut ulehaim* [The new Hebrew: supplement on literature, nationalism and life] (Warsaw 1912), p.11. The basis for the Zionist legend about the 'new Hebrew' appears to have been contributed by another young Zionist intellectual, Micha Yosef Berdeczewski, who borrowed the phrase from Friedrich Nietzsche's theory of 'the super man'.
18. Margalit Shilo, 'Ha-Ishah – "Ovedet" o "Haverah" be-Mifal ha-Tehiyyah? Al Mekomah shel ha-Ishah ba-Aliyah ha-Rishonah (1882–1903)' [The woman – 'laborer' or 'member' in the Revival Project? On the place of the woman in the First Aliyah (1882–1903)], *Yahadut Zemanenu*, 9 (1995), pp.129–31. Ahron Bar-Adon believed that it is difficult to exaggerate their contribution to the establishment of the Hebrew kindergartens (the first was opened in Rishon Le'Zion in 1898), to the revival of the Hebrew language, to the children, to their mothers and to the female members of the Yishuv in general. Nonetheless, the revival of Hebrew was a very heavy process, which actually lasted until the first decade of the twentieth century. Ahron Bar-Adon, 'Ha-Imahot ha-meyassedot u-menat helkan be-tehiyyat ha-ivrit ve-hithavvutah (1882—1914)' [The founding mothers and their role in the revival of Hebrew and its formation (1882–1914)], *Lashon ve-Ivrit*, 3 (May 1990), pp.18–19.
19. In particular, Fania Matmon Cohen (who, together with her husband, established the Herzliya High School, the first Hebrew high school in 1905), Sara Azriyahu and Yehudit Harari. Margalit Shilo, 'Ledmuta shel ha'isha ba'aliyah hashniya: ha'ezrahit' [To the Woman's Image in the Second Aliyah: the Woman Citizen], *Israel*, 6 (2004), pp.89–92. For more on the Hebrew language during the Second Aliyah, see for example, Michael Grunzweig, 'Ma'amada shel ha'ivrit b'yemei ha'aliya hashniya' [Status of Hebrew in the days of the Second Aliyah], in Mordechai Naor (ed.), *Ha'aliyah hashniya 1903–1914* [The Second Aliyah 1903–1914] (Jerusalem 1985), pp.198–212.
20. Most of the studies on the Second Aliyah focus on its labour-socialist element, even though these represented a minority. Thus, too, most of the studies on women of this wave of immigration focused on those among them who were employed, despite their low number (only 200 out of 2,000 people). Margalit Shilo's study sheds light on the organization and work of the urban female citizens, who constituted the majority in the Second Aliyah and were given little attention in the studies. The work of women such as Sara Thon, Ada Geller, Miriam Hofein and others laid the foundation for modern social work in the state of Israel. Shilo, 'Ledmuta shel ha'isha ba'aliyah hashniya: ha'ezrahit', pp.83–105. For further works that deal with the female citizens and their organization, see, Hanna Herzog, 'Irgunei nashim bahugim ha'ezrahi'im, perek nishkach behistoriographia shel haYishuv' [Women's organizations in civil circles – forgotten chapter in historiography of the Yishuv], *Katedra*, 70 (February 1994), pp.111–33; Gur Elroi, *Immigrantim: hahagira hayehudit le Eretz Israel bereshit hame'a haesrim* [Immigrants: Jewish immigration to Eretz Israel in the early twentieth century] (Jerusalem 2004).
21. The network operated until 1948 under the auspices of the General Labor Federation and, after the establishment of the state it was part of the services provided by the Health Ministry until 1995. Shifra Shvarts and Zipora Shory-

Rubin, 'On Behalf of Mothers and Children in Eretz Israel: The Activity of Hadassah, the Federation of Hebrew Women and WIZO to Establish Mother and Infant Welfare Centers—Tipat Halav, 1913–1948', in Ruth Kark, Margalit Shilo and Galit Hasan-Rokem (eds), *Jewish Women in pre-State Israel: Life History, Politics and Culture* (Waltham, MA: Brandeis University Press, 2008), pp.299–318, pp.248–69. See also, Herzog, 'Irgunei nashim bahugim ha'ezrahi'im, perek nishkach behistoriographia shel haYishuv', p.132.

22. Hannah Safran, 'International Struggle, Local Victory: Rosa Welt Straus and the Achievement of Suffrage 1919–1926', in Ruth Kark, Margalit Shilo and Galit Hasan-Rokem (eds), *Jewish Women in pre-State Israel: Life History, Politics and Culture* (Waltham, MA: Brandeis University Press, 2008), p.327.
23. Sylvia Fogel-Bijaoui, 'Ha'omnam baderekh le'shivion? Ma'avakan shel hanashim lezkhut behira ba'Yishuv Ha'yehudi be'Eretz Israel: 1917–1926 [Really on the Way to Equality? Women's Struggle for Suffrage in the Yishuv in Eretz Israel: 1917–1926], *Megamot*, 34, no.2 (1992), p.263. The struggle of the women's movement paved the way to inclusion of women's right to vote in the Knesset Constitution, a right that is a corner stone of Israeli democracy.
24. Rachel Elboim-Dror, 'Ha'isha hazionit ha'idialit' [The Ideal Zionist Woman], in Yael Atsmon (ed.), *Hatishma Koli: yitsugim shel nashim batarbut ha'israelit* [Will you hear my voice: representation of women in Israeli culture] (Jerusalem 2001), p.143. Nonetheless, it must be stressed that the Women's Federation continued to act on behalf of extensive legal and financial equality. The thing that troubled female kibbutz members in the early 1930s was the disparity between the ideal of an egalitarian society and the reality. Instances of inequality in employment and the political system in kibbutz society stood against its utopian aspirations and remained an inseparable part of kibbutz ideology. Henry Near, 'What Troubled Them? Women in Kibbutz and Moshav in the Mandatory Period', in Ruth Kark, Margalit Shilo and Galit Hasan-Rokem (eds), *Jewish Women in pre-State Israel: Life History, Politics and Culture* (Waltham, MA: Brandeis University Press, 2008), p.173.
25. The Working Women's Council was subjected directly to the Histadrut executive committee and responsible for liaising on behalf of the female Histadrut members between one committee and another. Bat-Sheva Margalit-Stern, 'Tenu'at ha-Po'a lot be-Eretz Yisra'el: Mo'etzet ha-Po'a lot 1921–1939' [The Women Workers Movement in Eretz Israel: Mo'etzet ha-Po'alot 1921–1939] (PhD thesis, Haifa University, 1997), p.295.
26. Bat-Sheva Stern, 'Hinuch nashim betnuat hapo'alot haeretz israelit: bein masoret lekidma' [Education of women in the Israeli Working Women's Movement: between tradition and progress], *Historia*, 3 (1999), pp.292–314 (p.402).
27. In fact this initiative would have far-reaching objectives: assistance in coping with problems for immigrant women, through vocational training and preparation for employment; entering new professions; communal living for women with the objective of providing them with mutual support and self education in order to enable each woman to discover her own inner strength to advance her. Deborah Bernstein, 'Ma'amadan ve'hitargenut shel nashim ovdot bayishuv ha'ironi beshnot haesrim vehashloshim' [Status and organization of working women in the urban Yishuv during the 1920s and 1930s], *Katedra*, 34 (Tevet 1985), pp.132–6.

28. Margalit-Stern, 'Tenu'at ha-Po'a lot be-Eretz Yisra'el', p.313; Daphna Izraeli, 'Tenu'at ha-Po'alot be-Eretz Yisra'el mi-Reishitah ve-Ad 1927' [The women's labour movement in Eretz Israel from its beginnings until 1927], *Katedra*, 56 (1984), pp.110–40.
29. Esther Zmora led the merger between the movements and served as the first Chairwoman of WZO until 1941. Esther Zmora, *Nashim Ivriyyot Tziyyoniyyot* [Zionist Hebrew Women] (Tel Aviv 2002), p.9.
30. By definition, an army is an 'organization whose objective is to ensure the nation's security by means of fighting expertise, so that those people in fighting situations enjoy a preferred status both in the organization and in society in general'. Yehezkel Dar and Shaul Kimchi, 'Nashim tse'irot be'irgun gavri' [Young women in a masculine organization], *Soziologia Israelit*, D,1 (2002), p.62.
31. Gerard Degroot and Corinna Peniston-Bird, 'Arms and Women', in Gerard Degroot and Corinna Peniston-Bird (eds), *A Soldier and a Woman: Sexual Integration in the Military* (Essex 2000), pp.3–18.
32. Judith Buber Agassi, 'Status of Women in Religion', in Dafna Yizraeli, *Women in a Trap: On the Status of Women in Israel* (Tel Aviv 1984), p.227. Elisabetta Addis et al., 'Introduction', in Elisabetta Addis, Valeria Russo and Lorenza Sebesta (eds), *Women Soldiers: Images and Realities* (New York: 1994), p.xi.
33. Miriam Cook describes the relationship between gender and war as two structures in need of each other: war is conceived as masculine activity, while masculinity is conceived as active participation in war. The two spheres are built on a dichotomy and on organizing reality through binary thinking. Miriam Cooke, 'WO-Man, Retelling the War Myth', in Miriam Cooke and Angela Woollacott (eds), *Gendering War Talk* (Princeton 1993), pp.177–204.
34. Susan Grayzel, *Women's Identities at War: Gender, Motherhood and Politics in Britain and France during the First World War* (London 1999), p.52: during the American War of Independence (1776), women dressed themselves as young soldiers and joined the American army in its war against the British occupier. When their identity was discovered, they were barred from service and banished from the army. The same happened in the American Civil War (1861–65). Joshua Goldstein, *War and Gender: How Gender Shapes the War System and Vice Versa* (Cambridge 2001), pp.107–11; DeAnne Blanton and Lauren Cook, *They Fought Like Demons: Women Soldiers in the Civil War* (New York 2002), pp.94–106.
35. Women accompanied the British army during the wars with France and India (1755–65), thus helping to raise the morale of the soldiers, with the authorities' approval. Scott Hendrix, 'In the Army: Women, Camp Followers and Gender Roles in the British Army in the French and Indian Wars 1755–1765', in Gerard Degroot and Corinna Peniston-Bird (eds), *A Soldier and a Woman* (Essex 2000), pp.33–48. During the American Civil War, most of the women serving at the front – both on the northern and southern armies – were nurses, but there were others who were known as 'Daughters of the Regiment', whose job, like that of women a hundred years before them, was mainly to support and encourage the soldiers, to launder and cook for them. These women usually remained behind the lines, but occasionally got caught up in battle. Blanton and Cook, *They Fought Like Demons*, pp.110–20.
36. Buber Agassi, 'Status of Women in Religion', p.227; Billie Melman, 'Lahafoch et hamilhama lehistoria: Hamilhama Hagdola, Historia ve historionim,

1914–1918' [Turning the war into history: the Great War, history and historians], *Zmanim*, 65 (Winter 1998–99), p.19. For more on the reversed terminology see Nira Yuval-Davis, 'Front and Rear: The Sexual Division of Labor in Israeli Army', *Feminist Studies*, 11, no.3 (1985), pp.649–75; and Ilana Beit El, 'Gvarim, gavriut umilhama: migdar bemilhemet haolam harishona' [Men, masculinity and war: gender in the First World War], *Zmanim*, 65 (Winter 1998–99), pp.112–20.

37. The army's attitude – if there was one – to the role of women in wartime, was that they were hospital nurses working in accordance with rules laid down by Florence Nightingale; as soldiers' wives or as carriers and spreaders of sexually transmitted diseases. As such they presented a threat to the army as an organization and the labour force it employed. It would appear that the regiments were ultimately established as a result of confusion, frictions, conflicting interests and lack of communication between the government offices and various military bodies, and not as the result of organized intention. Jane Gould, 'Women's Military Services in First World War Britain', in Margaret R. Higonnet, Jane Jenson, Sonya Michel and Margaret Collins Weitz (eds), *Behind the Lines: Gender and the Two World Wars* (New Haven 1992), pp.114–25.
38. Botchkareva started her military career as a soldier in the Russian army. Following the February 1917 Revolution she was given special authority to establish a women's regiment. Goldstein, *War and Gender*, pp.72–6.
39. Laurie Stoff, 'They Fought for Russia: Female Soldiers of the First World War', in Gerard Degroot and Corinna Peniston-Bird (eds), *A Soldier and a Woman* (Essex 2000), pp.66–83.
40. D'Ann Campbell, 'Women in Combat: The World War II Experience in the United States, Great Britain, Germany and the Soviet Union', in Gerald Martel (ed.), *The World War Two Reader* (New York 2004), pp.258–9.
41. In addition to this force, some 90,000 women served in the voluntary auxiliary arm, known as WAVES (Women Accepted for Volunteer Emergency Services) and employed mainly in air control and monitoring functions relating to the naval fleet, and in communications systems. Some 25,000 women served in the Marine Corps reserves (in the First World War women served in this force). Some 75,000 women served as officer/nurses. Michael Rustad, *Women in Khaki: The American Enlisted Woman* (New York 1982), pp.27–37.
42. Goldstein, *War and Gender*, pp.88–94. Ann B. Carl wrote her book, A Wasp Among the Eagles, on this squadron, describing her experiences as a fighter pilot. Ann B. Carl, *A Wasp Among Eagles: A Woman Military Test Pilot in World War II* (Washington DC: Smithsonian Institution Press, 2010).For more about American women in the Second World War, see, for example, Emily Yellin, *Our Mothers' War: American Women at Home and at the Front During World War II* (New York 2004).
43. Penny Summerfield, 'She Wants a Gun not a Dishcloth! Gender, Service and Citizenship in Britain in the Second World War', in Gerard Degroot and Corinna Peniston-Bird (eds), *A Soldier and a Woman* (Essex 2000), pp.120–1.
44. For more information on British ATS see Jeremy Crang, 'The Revival of the British Women's Auxiliary Services in the Late Nineteen-thirties', *Historical Research*, 83, no.220 (2010), pp.343–57.

45. Reina Pennington, '"Do Not Speak of the Services you Rendered": Women Veterans of Aviation in the Soviet Union', in David M. Glantz (ed.), *The Journal of Slavic Military Studies*, 9, no.1 (March 1996), p.120; Rustad, *Women in Khaki*, pp.36–7. Most of the women in the Red Army were in their 20s and childless. Joshua Goldstein points out that no data exists as to the exact number of women in military service, and information is based on assumption. Goldstein, *War and Gender*, p.65.
46. Alon Kadish, *Lameshek ve'laneshek: ha'hachsharot hameguyasot ba'Palmach* [To farm and to arms: The Palmach recruited groups] (Ramat Efal 1995), p.119.
47. On the IZL, see for example, David Niv, *Etzel: ha'irgun hatzavai hale'umi* [Etzel: national military organization] (Jerusalem 1978). On the Lehi, see for example, Ya'akov Banai, *Hayalim almonim: sefer mivtzaei Lehi* [Anonymous soldiers: book of Lehi operations], ed. Israel Eldad (Tel Aviv 1989); Joseph Heller, *Lehi, 1940–1949* (Jerusalem 1989). [Hebrew]. Women took part in these activities, including personal terrorist activity against British officers and soldiers.
48. On comparing 'Diaspora' with 'effeminacy' see Daniel Boyarin, 'Neshef ha-Masekhot ha-Koloni'ali: Zionut, Migdar, Hikkui' [The colonial masked ball: Zionism, gender, imitation], *Teoria ve'bikoret*, 11 (1997), pp.123–44; Rachel Elboim-Dror, 'Nashim ba'utopiot hazioniot' [Women in Zionist Utopias], *Katedra*, 66 (December 1992), pp.111–42; David Biale, *Eros and the Jews: from Biblical Israel to Contemporary America* (New York: Basic Books 1992), p.232.
49. Hashomer had a blatantly male gender orientation. Although its members were ostensibly in favour of women's rights, in reality they refused to include women as equal members in the association and prevented them from taking part in guard duty. It was only through a struggle that women were considered members, even if they were still forbidden from guard duty. Margalit Shilo, 'Ha'isha ha'ivriya hahadasha – panim rabot la, hashomeret kemikreh mivhan' [Many faces to the New Hebrew Woman, the woman member of Hashom as a test case], *Bikoret ve-parshanut*, 34 (Summer 2000), p.8. On gender relations within the organization, see, Smadar Sinai, 'Gender Relations in the 'Hashomer' Organization and in Kfar Giladi 1907–1939' (PhD thesis, Bar Ilan University, 2009).
50. On the legend of Sara Ahronson see, Billie Melman, 'Lahafoch et hamilhama lehistoria: Hamilhama Hagdola, Historia ve historionim, 1914–1918' [Turning the war into history: the Great War, history and historians], *Zmanim*, 65 (Winter 1998–99), pp.6–23; Billie Melman, 'The Legend of Sarah: Gender, Memory, and National Identities [Eretz Yisrael/Israel, 1917–90], in Ruth Kark, Margalit Shilo and Galit Hasan-Rokem (eds), *Jewish Women in pre-State Israel: Life History, Politics and Culture* (Waltham, MA: Brandeis University Press, 2008), pp.465–522.
51. Shilo points out that the women's requests sounded like a blatantly feminist declaration, but they were nonetheless aware of the traditional role of women in the army and all the positions they were offering to fulfil were purely feminine ones, such as nursing the wounded, administrative work, food supply, etc. Margalit Shilo, *Etgar hamigdar: nashim ba'aliyot harishonot* [Challenge of gender: women in the first waves of immigration] (Bnei Brak 2007), pp.273–4.
52. On women in Hagana see Tali Moav Halbani, 'Woman in the Yishuv's Defence from the 1920s until the Establishment of the Women Corps' (MA thesis, Haifa

University, 1998); Debora Almog, 'Women in the Israeli Defense Forces' (MA thesis, Hebrew University, Jerusalem, 1987); Dganit Boni-Davidi, 'Women and Gender in the Hagana Organization between 1920–1948' (MA thesis, Bar- Ilan University, 2004).

53. On the frustration of female Haganah members see, for example, Bracha Habas (ed.), *Me'ora'ot 1936* [1936 Arab Uprising] (Tel Aviv 1940), pp.521–3. When it came to including them in the defence of settlements, the women members became the 'weak party', the defended rather than the defenders. And they were obliged to see the men, who until then they had seen as their equals – in rights as well as in obligations – setting out armed from their homes in order to defend them.
54. Klibanov (1902–69) was a member in Haganah from 1930 and helped in training women instructors. In 1934 she was the commander of the Magen David Adom (Red Star of David, Jewish equivalent of the Red Cross organization) in Haifa. Between 1944 and 1949, she was a member of the Assembly of Representatives. Over the years she was active in women's labour councils and served as an emissary to the Displaced Persons (DP) camps in Europe in 1947. Lifschitz and Lerer, 'A Portrait'; http://www.aka.idf.il/yohalan/main/main.asp?catid-40768&docid-42546.
55. Boni-Davidi, 'Women and Gender in the Hagana Organization', p.151; Yonit Ephron, 'Ahayot, lohamot, imahot: ethos umeziot bemivhan bnot dor 1948' [Sisters, fighters, mothers: ethos and reality in the test of the 1948 generation of women], *I'yunim Be Tekumat Israel*, 10 (2000), p.357.
56. Ofra Elad, '"Kol bahur ve tov laneshek, bahura al hamismar!": Ha'havera ba'Palmach' [Every man is good for arms, a woman, on guard duty! Woman Member in the Palmach], in Yehiam Weitz (ed.), *Palmach: Shtei shibolim veherev* [Palmach, Two Sticks of Corn and a Sword] (Tel Aviv, 2001), p.216; Kadish, *Lameshek ve'laneshek*, p.118.
57. Betar was the youth movement of the Revisionist movement in Palestine.
58. The new organization was initially called 'IZL in Israel', and only at the end of 1942, following Stern's death, was it given the name Lehi.
59. Zipora Atzmon, 'Ma'amad haisha besherut haetzel ve'halehi' [Women's status in the ranks of Etzel and Lehi] (MA thesis, Toro College, 1993). Esther Raziel Naor was a member in the supreme command. Yehuda Lapidot, *Hayom Sara haktana: sipuran shel lohamot haEtzel* [Today little Sara: the story of the women fighters in the Etzel] (Tel Aviv 2003), pp.100–109. Conversations with senior members of Lehi reveal an egalitarian attitude to women. Ya'akov Eli'av and Mordecai Schreiber, *Wanted* (New York: Shengold Publishers, 1984), p.206. Because of the underground's revolutionary character its ideology leaned on socialist ideologies, which demanded of its members a harsh and Spartan lifestyle. However, Lehi had no ideological institutional backing to provide it with the philosophical guidance enjoyed by the IZL.

Part One

Recruitment Initiative

1

Council of Women's Organizations and Volunteering for the Army

On 24 December 1941 all the newspapers in the Yishuv published the announcement that the British army had decided to recruit women. Two items connected with this announcement were published alongside it: the first by the Council of Women's Organizations (CWO), under the headline 'Hebrew Woman in the Homeland!' and called on the Yishuv's women to 'carry out [the spirit of] our announcement on the willingness of women to volunteer'. It went on to say that recruitment gives women the 'right to participate at the front line of the war' and would complete the spirit of Jewish volunteering in Palestine. The second announcement was published on behalf of the national institutions – the National Committee (the shadow government of the Jewish community in British Mandate Palestine) and the Jewish Agency – and bore the heading 'To the Daughters of the Yishuv'. It reviewed the position of women beside men in every effort and sacrifice both in the Jewish Yishuv and among freedom fighters worldwide, presented the Second World War as a war of fate and called not to 'undercut the role of the Hebrew woman in the war of fate'.[1]

In honour of the event, Chaim Weizmann, President of the World Zionist Organization, sent a telegram to Mrs Hadassah Samuel, Chairwoman of the CWO, in which he expressed his confidence that 'women will promote the call with enthusiasm and that the CWO will take advantage of promoting the idea of liberty'.[2] The CWO fought to allow Jewish Yishuv women to participate in the war effort in the way women from Britain, the United States, Australia and South Africa were permitted to do and it was the CWO that initiated the recruitment drive.

This chapter will discuss the CWO and the role it played in recruiting women into the British forces from the establishment of the council, through the initiative to recruit and up to the actual recruitment enterprise and the connections it maintained with the recruits in the course of their military service.

Council of Women's Organizations

The CWO was established with the outbreak of the Arab uprising in 1936 and was active until 1946. Its objective was to 'act on behalf of the full participation of the Hebrew woman in special activities in the political and social arenas', and to represent the Hebrew women inwardly and outwardly in issues where it finds itself 'authorized to represent them or at a time when it is required [to do so] by the national institutions'.[3] The CWO accepted the authority of the national institutions, as various other women's councils in the world acted as a branch of their governments' institutions.

The initiative behind the establishment of the CWO appears to have actually come from abroad as early as 1935. A congress was convened in Prague in late May 1935 of the World Zionist Organization that dealt with organization and propaganda. About a month later, the WIZO Executive entrusted the Federation's Palestine executive with the establishment of a local Council of Women's Federations. The Council's objective was to represent all the local organizations belonging to international women's federations that were active in the country. However, it would appear that the riots in 1936 accelerated the establishment of the new body. And, indeed, following the call by WIZO to all the women's organizations in the country, representatives of the women's federations in Israel convened in July in order to establish an 'initial committee for the creation of a federation of Hebrew women in Israel'. Two committees were elected at that meeting, one for drafting regulations and one for publicity.[4]

This was not the first time that a national body had been established of women's organizations in the Yishuv with the objective of fighting on behalf of all-female issues. Women's organizations in the Yishuv were well versed in mutual struggles over issues that concerned all women, such as that for equal rights. As already mentioned, 1919 saw the establishment of the Hebrew Women's Union for Equal Rights in Eretz Israel, a body formed by women's organizations already existing in the country.

Notwithstanding their success in achieving voting rights for Yishuv women, the women's organizations felt that this was not enough and that they had to join forces in order to improve the status of women in the Yishuv. In August 1927, representatives of nine organizations convened in Tel Aviv in order to establish the Council of Hebrew Women's Organizations in Eretz Israel. This council had two declared objectives: 'a. To unite and improve the public work of women in Eretz Israel; b. To create a united force, inwardly and outwardly.' The Regulations also determined that 'any organization annexed to this council is autonomous in its activity, so far as this does contradict the objectives of the council'. Each local federation sent a single representative and every centre of women's federations sent two representatives. In the end the council did not function and, after establishing the council and investing means on its behalf, the Women's Federation, whose idea it was to convene it, failed for a long time to maintain it.[5]

In May 1929, World WIZO initiated the establishment of an alternative council. This initiative was joined by Israel WIZO Federation, the Workers' Council and the Council of Women in Eretz Israel. The objective of the Council was to provide official representatives of the female public in Israel vis-à-vis Jewish women overseas and, as such, to influence the decisions taken by the women's organizations regarding their activity in the country. In this case, too, the power of these women's organizations was not fully realized. They never succeeded in putting the joint framework into action because the disagreements and competition among the member organizations triumphed over the need for cooperation. Nonetheless, the cooperation between the Women's Federation, the Working Women's Council and the Movement for Working Women did achieve success in one sphere: the Jewish National Fund's (JNF) change of policy vis-à-vis granting women equal rights to property belonging to their families.[6]

Established in 1936 the CWO consisted of 'nationwide Hebrew women's federations in Eretz Israel and of agencies [representing] international federations [for the benefit of] Zionist women in Eretz Israel who had no national federation'.[7] There were two kinds of membership in the council: one was active membership, which was granted to organizations that existed and acted in the country. These organizations include International WIZO, Women Workers Council, Federation of Zionist Women and the local WIZO chapter, the Women's Organization belonging to the Po'el Mizrahi and 'Amen', the

Mizrahi Women's Federation. The second kind of membership was passive and was granted to those organizations that acted in the country, but whose centres were overseas or who were connected to organizations there. These were: Hadassah, the Women's Zionist Organization of America, the Women's Mizrahi Federation in America, Federation of Women Members in America and the Women's League for Israel in New York. Hadassah Samuel, who was also the chairperson of WIZO, headed the Council.

Each member federation in the Council sent two representatives. The Council's presidency consisted of one representative of each organization, elected once a year from the two who represented it in the Council. Two members were elected from among the presidency to serve on the Executive and all its member groups shared the Council's budget equally. According to the Council's Rules: 'On issues of principle, only those decisions accepted unanimously by all the federations will be made public in the Council's name.'[8]

Activity of the Women's Organizations prior to the Recruitment Drive

Until 1941, the year of the initiative to recruit Yishuv women to the British forces, the CWO served as 'a mouthpiece for the country's women during a period of rioting and unrest that the Yishuv is subject to when it appeals at various times ... in protest to the Mandatory authorities', especially in protest against attacks on women and children on the part of Arabs during the uprising of 1936–39. This protest activity included a memo to the British High Commissioner regarding the murder of the nurses in Jaffa; protest at the attempt to set fire to a babies home in Jerusalem's Baka quarter on 1 July 1936; a telegram to the British Colonial Minister and various other organizations in Britain in protest against a bomb being thrown into the courtyard of a Tora study house for Yemenites on the Tel Aviv-Jaffa border, which left several students injured. In November 1938 (following *Kristallnacht*) the secretariat published its first memo in which it declared the Council's willingness to take in thousands of Jewish children from Germany in families and institutions affiliated to the women's organizations.[9]

Protest on the part of women and mothers is a well-known phenomenon and in all cases in which they participated the mere fact of their being wives and mothers was sufficient justification for their activity in public. In adopting a new ideology that Elizabeth Thompson defines as 'patriotic mothers', women and mothers channelled their domestic chores and their work as charitable activists into service on behalf of the nation and the demand for equal social rights.[10]

With the outbreak of war in September 1939, the CWO convened in order to prepare the Yishuv's female population for future events. It elected emergency committees and focused its activity on organizing women to protest against the 'White Paper' and the land rules. It appears that thousands of women responded to the CWO and set out to protest in the country's towns and villages.[11] In the course of 1940, the CWO decided that it should 'step up in support of the current campaign and to act in all the towns.' Further decisions consisted of discussions with the National Council the demand for 'including the CWO in all activities regarding the special situation [the war]';[12] sending calls to the women's organizations in the three largest towns, to harness the Council to various activities in the Yishuv; and to renew female participation in first-aid and civil defence services in the Yishuv.[13]

Hadassah Samuel and the Recruitment Initiative

Following several years of activity alongside the Yishuv institutions, the CWO, under the leadership of Hadassah Samuel, embarked on a daring initiative of its own. It would appear that the struggle for the right of local women to join the military served as a turning point in the cooperation among the women's organizations in the Yishuv. It was the first time that the joint framework had been maintained for such a long time (until after the war), when a single issue bound all the organizations together. As head of WIZO since 1933 and head of the Council of Women's Organizations since its inception, there is no doubt that Hadassah Samuel was the 'king pin' in the recruitment enterprise.

Hadassah Samuel (1897–1983) was tall and impressive, cultured and elegant.[14] One of five children, she was born in Jaffa and raised in Ekron (today Mazkeret Batya). Her father, Yehuda Gur (Grazovsky) was an ordained rabbi, a teacher, linguist and, later, the author of the Gur Dictionary. He was the first teacher of Hebrew at the Mikve Israel School. Her mother, Rachel, who came from a wealthy family of merchants from Romania, was a graduate of the School for Girls in Jaffa and a former pupil of Yehuda Gur in Mazkeret Batya. She was involved in voluntary work, alongside raising her family. In the Gur household, which served as a meeting place for teachers and writers, only Hebrew was spoken (according to Hadassah, her family was the first 'Hebrew family', rather than that of Eliezer Ben-Yehuda, as commonly believed). Hadassah spent her youth in Switzerland, where she studied psychology and was trained as a pianist.[15]

When Yehuda Gur was appointed to represent the Anglo-Palestine Bank in Beirut, the family moved to Lebanon, where Hadassah took advantage of her time there to learn French. In late 1917, the family was exiled to Haifa and later moved to Tel Aviv. During the First World War, Hadassah and her mother volunteered to sew armbands for the uniforms of the Palestine volunteers of the Jewish Brigade in the British Army. One of these volunteers was Hadassah's brother, Amihud. Her oldest brother, Asaf, joined the Jewish Brigade in the United States. Her mother helped with the social integration of Russian immigrants, who arrived on the ship, Ruslan, in December 1919.

The Zionist Commission arrived in the Yishuv in 1918 and four British officers were appointed to liaise between the committee and the local authorities. The four were billeted in the top story of the Gur family home. One of them was Edwin Samuel, son of the future British High Commissioner, Sir Herbert Samuel, a Jew and member of the British aristocracy. Before her first meeting with Edwin, Hadassah spoke no English and the two conversed only in French.

In December 1920 Hadassah Gur and Edwin Samuel were married in a wedding ceremony that caused many waves in the Yishuv.[16] Congratulations from various people and organizations continued to be published in the press even after the wedding. It would appear that in her marriage to Edwin Samuel, Hadassah combined her inherently deep-rooted Israeli nationalism and patriotism, with her newly formed connections within British high society.[17] Nonetheless, Hadassah admitted many years later that she did not enjoy parties and hanging around in the company of British society in Palestine and that she 'did not altogether belong to this society'.[18] In spite of his origins and status, and notwithstanding the various jobs and positions he was offered in other countries, Edwin Samuel was a Zionist and chose to live in Palestine.[19]

Shortly after her marriage and encouraged by her mother, Hadassah embarked on a career of public activity on behalf of WIZO and thus began her involvement in the country's feminine sector. In 1933 she was appointed Chairperson of WIZO, a post she held until 1950. Her first enterprise consisted of the establishment of the Hadassim Youth Village that provided a home and education for girls from Aliyat Hano'ar (youth immigration). The school was established thanks to funds raised by Hadassah Samuel from the Hadassah Organization in Canada.

Throughout the 1930s she used to travel to the WIZO offices in Tel Aviv at the beginning of the week, stay in her parents' home during the week and return to her home in Jerusalem at the end of the week. She often travelled overseas on propaganda and fundraising missions on behalf of the organization. Although most of her work with WIZO focused on education and welfare, her pet subject was agriculture, a love she had inherited from her mother, who was involved in promoting agricultural education in Tel Aviv schools.

Apart from the female sector, Hadassah's activity also stretched to the general public: she was a member of the executive of the Po'el Hazioni, Aliance, the Executive Committee of Youth Aliyah and the Soldiers' Welfare Committee. She was connected to the Yishuv leadership as well as the British Mandatory Authorities and her status opened many doors to her. In her private life she realized her concept that women were capable of achieving a great deal in public life. It seems that her worldview on the place of women in society, combined with her connections among senior figures in the Yishuv and her ties with British society, culture and language, rendered her the most appropriate person to lead the recruitment process that she herself initiated and worked toward its fulfilment. In this difficult and challenging mission, Samuel had the help and support of Beba Idelson, Secretary of the Working Women's Council (the women's branch of the Histadrut, the General Labor Federation).[20]

The idea of recruiting Yishuv women into the British forces was presented by Hadassah Samuel as a personal initiative of her own and not of the CWO; she also presented the army's decision to accept the initiative as her own personal triumph. And indeed, from the way in which negotiations were conducted and her correspondence with the military authorities (whose letters were addressed to her), it is fair to assume that there was a measure of truth in what she said. In her memoires, Samuel recalled saying to Yehoshua Gordon:[21]

> 'Everything is alright, what about the girls?' and he said: 'Let me take care of it'. I said to him: 'this isn't a political matter, it is of us, as women, wanting to join our boys and I won't let you take care of it. For nine months we fought, in the end *I won*'. [Author's emphasis][22]

Hadassah Samuel and Audrey Chitty – Nationalist Struggle or Personal Rivalry

Samuel made the first written approach to British Military HQ in Palestine on behalf of the CWO in March 1941 and, in doing so, set in motion the initiative for involving Yishuv women in the war effort. Over nine months, negotiations with the army and with Audrey Chitty, ATS commander in the Middle East, reached a conclusion. Samuel travelled to Cairo on behalf of the CWO even before Chitty's arrival in Palestine in order to sort out the details.[23] Chitty met Samuel on several occasions during her visit to Palestine, which began in December 1941.[24]

As already mentioned, Samuel was an opinionated and ambitious woman, who aspired to eventually receive the chairmanship of World WIZO.[25] Audrey Chitty was short in stature and had an ascetic appearance; short-haired and always dressed in army uniform, she had arrived in the Middle East determined to succeed in the mission imposed on her – the establishment of a women's auxiliary force in the region. It appears from Chitty's diary that Hadassah Samuel was her fiercest rival. The two first met for tea in a Jerusalem hotel on 17 December 1941, two days after Chitty's arrival in the city; Major Shaples, deputy administrative head at British Military HQ in Palestine, joined them. The following day, Chitty wrote in her diary, 'I like Mrs Samuel, she's a very nice woman, however, and I wish I could believe what she says without having a troublesome feeling that behind it all there lurks political intrigue.'[26]

At some point, Chitty started to feel that Samuel was 'threatening' her position and made every effort, backed by British Staff Officers, to erase the impression that Samuel was in control of and directing female recruitment in the Yishuv.[27] Two incidents increased this feeling in her. In early January 1942, the *Palestine Post* published a piece that praised Samuel for her part in establishing the ATS in Palestine. The article infuriated Chitty. An additional 'show of force' between the two took place against the design of a poster to encourage recruitment. After learning that the army had decided to approve the recruitment, Samuel asked the Jewish Agency to design a recruitment poster based on one she had seen in one of the British newspapers (probably *The Times*). The Jewish designers added some Hebrew words to the original English poster calling on Yishuv women to join up, and a large Star of David in the background. This aroused the anger of Chitty as well as of other army officers in the country, who didn't want the recruitment to appear as a purely Jewish initiative and they demanded that the poster be removed. Chitty called Samuel on the phone and the latter made it quite clear that removal of the Star of David would cause the recruitment drive to stop, and the British preferred to give in on this point.[28]

Government officials and various other British personnel, including Lady McMichael, wife of the British High Commissioner and Edward Keith-Roach, Governor of Jerusalem, caused Chitty to suspect that Samuel was planning to become commander of the training camp in Sarafend. Chitty felt that Samuel, out of some political motives of her own, was trying to take control of the ATS. It appears that Samuel did not intend to join up.[29] However, after consultation with Gordon, she asked to be made a Field Officer, a rank equal to that of Major. Although she never officially joined the army, the British treated her (so she said) 'as if I really was one of the commanders. They used to come to meet me at the railway station in an army car and I was able to go to all the camps and talk to all the girls in Hebrew.'[30] It seems that Samuel received an honorary commission and a uniform, which she wore with great pride on some of her visits to the British Army's female Jewish recruits.[31]

Notwithstanding the personal animosity between them, Chitty and Samuel had the sense to join forces for the good of the recruitment drive, which they both saw as the high spot of their careers. On the day the press announced the army's decision to establish a women's auxiliary force in Palestine, the CWO held a reception in JNF House in Tel Aviv, and the guest of honour was Audrey Chitty. About seventy women were invited from women's organizations representing the entire political spectrum in the Yishuv. Samuel spoke about the role of the Jewish woman in the history of the Yishuv and emphasized the importance of the historic decision of female military recruitment. Chitty made a faux pas when she wished the audience a 'Happy Holyday' (it was Christmas Eve), but the incident passed and she promised to help make the project a success. The event received broad media coverage and was written up in all the women's magazines. In January 1942, a large public rally took place in Jerusalem to encourage the recruitment drive; Hadassah Samuel, Audrey Chitty, as well as Moshe Sharett and other well-known figures attended the rally.

Reinforcing Positions

The law for female recruitment in Britain had been presented to Parliament in December 1940 and passed about four months later. As already mentioned, on March 30, 1941, Hadassah Samuel, on behalf of the CWO made the first written approach to British Army HQ in Palestine with the proposal to include women from the Yishuv in Britain's war effort. In addition to this initiative, and perhaps even before it, individual women (unconnected to any official framework) had made overtures to Sharett, Head of the Jewish Agency Political Department, suggesting that women could be included in the war effort, but this suggestion did not mature into action. From this stage and until late 1941, Samuel, on behalf of the CWO, conducted her correspondence with the military authorities. The army recognized the CWO, probably as a result of Samuel's status, as the body responsible for the country's women's issues in the Yishuv and did not demand intervention on the part of the Yishuv's official institutions. Starting with the first approach to the British army and until the women were demobilized from military service, the recruitment issue was the only one on the agenda of the CWO.

Although the first approach had been made in March 1941, there had been no response from the British War Office until October that year. Various considerations caused this delay, including political ones, such as Britain's wartime needs, for example, objective obstacles in transferring British recruits needed in their own country, training women in other countries and concern for the women's security. Only during the final two months of 1941, with the war expanding into the Middle East, did the army's decision to recruit women from Palestine ripen and details of the negotiations between the Yishuv and the military coalesce, although some of the issues remained open even after recruitment commenced.

In various forums, as well as in her correspondence with the army, Samuel reported that the issues raised in her dealings with the military authorities had been discussed with the Jewish Agency and been approved by its representatives or Moshe Sharett. There is no doubt that already in mid-1941 Sharett had been updated as to these negotiations and the CWO had his full backing for the process. From December 1941, when the matter of female recruitment was raised before the National Council and discussed in the Jewish Agency Executive, the issue was 'requisitioned' from the CWO and correspondence with the army was conducted with the Jewish

Agency's Political Department and especially with Sharett who stood at its head. Nevertheless, Hadassah Samuel continued to correspond with various factors in British military headquarters in Jerusalem and Cairo, mainly on administrative matters, following meetings she had had with officers and in wake of visits she had made to the women recruits. Shortly after the recruitment commenced, Sharett determined that 'were it not for the fact that the Hebrew woman demanded her right in Eretz Israel to determine her place in the forefront of the war from the country and its surrounds – it would not have occurred to any regime to deal with the question of female recruitment in Eretz Israel or in the Middle East.' Sharett admitted that while the CWO was demanding of the Yishuv institutions to lead the campaign for female recruitment, 'there was much scepticism among the military authorities and the Yishuv institutions [and I was among them] as to whether the matter was even capable of materializing in this part of the world. Still, where brains failed, the passage of time [sic] and the necessities of war prevailed.'[32]

After the decision to recruit Yishuv women to the British army, the negotiations between the CWO and the military authorities focused on a number of crucial issues: where will the women serve, their number, the military jobs they could fill, etc.

Locations

In March 1941, when the recruitment initiative was beginning to take practical form, the army headquarters in Palestine had not yet 'moved' the process and the War Office in London was still avoiding local recruitment. Brigadier Beddington, Commanding Officer in Palestine, replied to Samuel's letter regarding the recruitment and pointed out that the lack of suitable accommodation for the female soldiers made it hard to proceed with the drive and that there 'are other plans for this part of the world'.[33] Beddington informed Samuel that at that stage HQ would commit only to transfer the debate to a higher level.

A month later Beddington asked if Samuel's proposition (to recruit women) referred only to service in Palestine. Following consultations with Sharett, Samuel responded that the proposal referred to service not only in Palestine, but also throughout the Middle East. The next round of correspondence focused on the locations in which the women would be stationed and Samuel confirmed that 'the CWO was prepared for women to serve all over the Middle East and not only in Eretz Israel, apart from cases in which it would be better to restrict the scope of military service to Eretz Israel'.[34] This was the result of Samuel's concept that Yishuv society had a sophisticated view of female military recruitment, unlike the more traditional societies in the Middle East, who were opposed to female recruitment.

The Battalions

The matter of what the character the women's battalions would take was discussed from the very beginning of the negotiations both among the military authorities and in the Yishuv institutions. The latter preferred, naturally enough, that the battalions consist only of Jewish soldiers. But the British decided that the Jewish units (the ATS companies) would be open to everyone – to Jewish as well as non-Jewish women. The significance of this decision was that the Yishuv's efforts on this matter proved fruitless.

Beba Idelson was convinced that it was imperative to insist on Hebrew companies, thus representing the position of the Working Women's Council. Eliyahu Golomb, one of the Haganah leaders, believed that only one condition should be insisted on and that was that the Yishuv women should be concentrated in Hebrew companies, which would have provided larger frameworks than platoons. All the rest, Golomb believed, could take the form of a demand for presenting to the British, but not as a condition that could be construed as a potential deal breaker, so as not to stump the recruitment. Sharett explained that he had received a promise from the military authorities that Jewish women would usually be placed in Jewish platoons, but this could not be guaranteed. According to Yitzhak Tabenkin, one of the United Kibbutz Movement leaders, there should be no recruitment of Jewish women to an army that was not Jewish: 'There is no need to arrange service units for a non-Jewish army for Jewish girls', and 'first of all a Jewish army; and after that, Jewish women for a Jewish army. Without a Jewish army – there is no organization of Hebrew women!' [35] It would appear that this claim combined his opinions on maintaining the honour of the Jewish woman in the army and his worldview vis-à-vis the necessity of establishing an independent Jewish military force in the Yishuv.

Mina Ben-Zvi (Rogoz'ik), a graduate of the army's first leadership cadre, was assigned – with the army's approval – to carry out various activities to encourage recruitment. She participated in the Labour Federation's (Histadrut) fifth Congress, where she said that first of all it was necessary to ensure a large enough number of recruits and only then would it be possible to demand of the army that the platoons have a nationalist-Hebrew character: 'How can we create the Jewish character if there is not a large enough number of us there', she said, contradicting the position of her counterparts.[36]

Even though the Yishuv leaders voiced their opinion that Yishuv women should be recruited only into companies that consisted purely of women from Palestine, the army recruited them into mixed companies.

Number of Recruits

Correspondence between the CWO and the military authorities also included the matter of the estimated number of recruits from among the Yishuv women. In a letter to Colonel Sale, Administration Officer in the Jerusalem HQ, Samuel estimated the number of recruits to be between four and five thousand. Her aim apparently was to present the army with as optimistic as possible a forecast in order to justify the recruitment drive, but it would appear that her colleagues in the CWO and the Women Workers Council did not share this assumption. At its October 1941 meeting, the CWO secretariat estimated that some 2,000 of the Yishuv's women would volunteer for the British army. At the Women Workers Council convention, Idelson pointed out that 'we shall certainly be required to [provide] quite large numbers: two, three or five thousand women', but in light of the difficult situation in the Yishuv, 'we'll have to achieve this ... gradually. In other words, it is not necessary to talk of 4,000–5,000 women; rather it would be especially desirable if after ... each one thousand recruits – we'll begin with [counting] the next thousand. And then, we might be able to arrive at larger number.'[37]

It is worth remembering that at that time, Yishuv women were also serving in other security frameworks: about 5,000 women were members in the Haganah and thousands of women and girls were employed in the war industry, or were recruited to work in agriculture, in defence of the civilian population, etc. Nor was the Kibbutz Movement eager to release its members to serve in the army and it appears that the potential number of women recruits to the army was lower than Samuel's estimation. In the end, some 3,000 women joined the ATS (the only body open to female recruitment at that time), a statistic that fell short of Samuel's expectations.

Recruits' Wages

One of the controversial issues in the matter of female recruitment was the salary to be paid to the recruits from Palestine. The salary was lower than the average wages in the Yishuv (about 75 per cent) and even lower than that paid to British recruits. This was already known at the beginning of the negotiations with the army, since the salary policy determined by the British War Office discriminated between men and women: in Britain, too, the salary of women recruits was about 65 per cent of that of their male counterparts. This annoyed the CWO as well as the ATS Command and even before recruitment commenced, Chitty wrote in her diary that she feared the salary issue might discourage many women from joining the army.

The salary issue also played an important role in the negotiations in the months to come. In September 1941, Samuel proposed in writing that the salary of the female recruit should be equal to that of the British female soldier or of the male soldier from Palestine. In November, John McCandlish of British Forces HQ in Cairo informed Samuel of the imminent arrival in Egypt of Audrey Chitty and updated her on the on-going issue of wages for the female recruits from the Yishuv. At a meeting of the management committee of the Jewish Agency's Recruitment Department in December 1941, Samuel reported on her talks with Chitty and Major Shaples of the local HQ and said that the female recruits' wages would be 75 per cent of that of their male counterparts and that 'there was no point insisting since it wouldn't help and, anyway, by English law, women earn less than men'.[38] In February 1942, a special meeting of the Women Workers Council was devoted entirely to the recruits' wages.

In August 1942 there still remained several unsolved issues on the matter of wages, such as matching family allowances for Yishuv soldiers to that of British soldiers (in Britain it was referred to as a dependency allowance) and the wage discrepancies between soldiers in the various military professions, according to their rank and profession. The army promised to gradually cancel the discrepancies among the recruits, but this issue was not solved until the end of their service.

Military Professions and Other Issues

In September 1941, Samuel wrote to Colonel Sale summing up the major issues that had arisen in the negotiations conducted up to then between the CWO and the British army and formulated in consultations with the Jewish Agency. These included the matter of military scope available to recruits from the Yishuv; those offered them did not differ from the ones filled by the British recruits: cooking, secretarial work, driving, storekeepers and nursing.[39]

'Recruitment' Channels

The Jewish Agency and the CWO preferred that the entire recruitment drive should be conducted via Jewish Agency recruitment bureaus, in order to maintain control over the composition of the recruits and their 'quality'. The army did not agree to this and it was determined that recruitment would take place via both the Jewish Agency and the military bureaus (for whoever chose this option). The Jewish Agency announced that in order to put the drive into effect it would appoint its own recruitment and selection team and the CWO and the Jewish Agency promised the army not to discriminate against any recruit on the basis of political affiliation. The November 1941 meeting of the CWO called for restricting female recruitment to the Jewish Agency recruitment bureaus (where, it was agreed, representatives of the CWO would be present).

ATS: Commanding the Troops

Wishing to maintain the Jewish identity of the Yishuv women, the CWO, Haganah and the Jewish Agency tried to ensure that their own recruits would be given command of ATS companies where the majority of recruits came from Palestine. It was agreed with the army that during the first stage, British officers and NCOs – who would drafted in specially – would be appointed to command all the companies in the Middle East. Moreover, it was agreed that at a later stage a framework would be established in order to train the Jewish recruits to fill command staff positions. Hadassah Samuel promised to make every effort to ensure that this plan was put in motion.

Even after the recruitment drive began Samuel continued to liaise with the military authorities. In a summary of a meeting with Douglas Brown, the officer in command in Palestine in early August 1942, Samuel reveals that further issues were being dealt with: recruitment of Yishuv women for nursing positions (an issue that continued to concern the CWO and the Jewish Agency); establishment of a lending library in the Sarafend training camp; translation of orders into

Hebrew in all the ATS companies; solutions for matters of education and welfare; employing Jewish soldiers to play music at parties and concerts; equipment for the rest room in Dir Suneid (near Gaza); and releasing soldiers before the completion of their training in order to enable them to participate in the recruitment drive.[40]

With negotiations between the CWO and the military authorities finalized completed, it was agreed to broadcast the results on the radio and in the daily newspapers. The army's announcement was broadcast by the Voice of Jerusalem on 23 December 1942 and published the next day on the front pages of all the country's dailies. Publication of the announcement as well as its content was coordinated between the army and the Jewish Agency. The military authorities accepted Sharett's proposal to publicize the fact that the first round of recruits would consist of around 500 women (who had already registered with the recruitment offices and were awaiting their turn to step forward) and that further groups would be recruited in the months to follow. Publication was important both to the Jewish Agency and to the army in order to prove the success of the drive.[41]

Agenda of the Council of Women's Organizations: Focus on Military Recruitment

Throughout the months of negotiations with the military authorities the only ones kept up to date on its details were Samuel and members of the CWO executive – Beba Idelson, Ethel Agronsky and Lea Wilensky. The CWO's member organizations were officially informed of the decision on 2 October 1941, seven months after Samuel's first letter was sent to Army HQ. At that stage the Mizrahi Women's Organization, the Mizrahi Organization of Working Women and the Federation of Women were not members of the CWO, having resigned in early 1941 because of disagreements surrounding its rules. A letter was sent to the Working Women's Council and WIZO announcing the recruitment: 'After much work on our part, we are able to inform you that the recruitment of women to the army is about to take place.'[42] In accordance with the decision of the CWO secretariat, the organizations were requested to form local committees immediately, consisting of three representatives from each member organization, in order to discuss a plan of action for their own region. The organizations that had left the Council also held recruitment events among youngsters in order to encourage them to volunteer.

Following the aforementioned meeting, a further meeting of the CWO secretariat was held in Tel Aviv, this time with the inclusion of a representative of the Jewish Agency's Recruitment Department. It was decided at this meeting that in order to encourage Yishuv women to volunteer, the CWO would publish an announcement reporting on its recent activity in the sphere. Similarly, it would hold public assemblies throughout the Yishuv with the aim of creating a suitable atmosphere for recruitment. This meeting dealt mainly with practical, rather than conceptual issues, since these had already been formulated earlier, in the course of negotiations with the army.

It was decided at the meeting to demand that the army station women doctors in places where women soldiers would be serving; to provide English lessons to candidates for the cadre; to check who would be the professional instructors to be recruited, etc. There were still some standing issues about which the army had decided but the CWO and the Yishuv institutions were adamant about reversing the decisions. These issues included the recruitment of women to the position of registered nurses and not merely practical nurses, and the nationalist decision to force soldiers to wear an armband indicating that they were from Palestine.[43] These issues were indeed raised and dealt with by the army in the course of the recruits' service, apart from the matter of the nurses. At the same meeting it was decided to establish a separate section in the Jewish Agency's Recruitment Department that would be responsible for female recruitment and the inclusion of representatives of the CWO in the management of the Recruitment Department. Thus, in fact, the path was laid for the CWO to the Yishuv's recruitment mechanism.[44]

Throughout the period of female recruitment, the focus of the CWO was devoted entirely to this issue. All council and secretariat meetings dealt with the function of the soldiers, solving personal and national problems, visits by CWO members to the army camps, allocation of funds for the benefit of the recruits, etc. At the same time, member organizations in the CWO continued to deal with issues on their agenda, although many activities also provided a platform for female recruitment.

The recruitment of Yishuv women to the army was the result of a unique feminine initiative on the part of a civilian body of women. In their demand for recruitment, women's organizations actually undermined all conventional gender concepts of army and war. The initiative taken by women in the Yishuv on the matter of their military recruitment can be seen as an independent ideological expression and as the fulfilment of a lengthy struggle for their position in Yishuv society.

The Women Workers Council, Idelson and the Recruitment Issue

Even before the army had decided on recruiting women, the Women Workers Council (WWC) aspired to involve Hebrew women in the war effort by recruiting them into the army and by conceiving recruitment as the realization of the values it wanted to instil in the population of working women in the Yishuv. It expected that if the recruitment idea would be realized, the first to volunteer would be the Yishuv's working women, because 'it is better for a female member to demand of itself, rather than of a male' and 'We are only demanding of it a realization of the values that for years we have been striving to instil in it – to contribute to society and in general'.[45]

As an apolitical body, the WWC was elected, managed by and represented the Working Women's movement in Palestine. The Histadrut (General Labor Federation) defined the Women Workers Council as 'a special department beside the Executive Committee', to which it was subjected directly. It provided an address to female Histadrut members between one congress of working women to another as well as for workers' institutions and various other bodies in the country and overseas. It was one of the two major partners in the CWO and participated in all its initiatives and activities during the war. With Hadassah Samuel, Beba Idelson, in her capacity of Council Secretary, led the issue of female recruitment in the Yishuv.

Beba (Trachtenberg) Idelson (1895–1975) was the secretary of the WWC between 1931 and 1947. She was born in the Ukraine and was a member of the Ze'irei Zion (young Zionists), which, in 1916 established a Jewish self-defence group. In 1926, she immigrated to Palestine with her husband, Israel Idelson. She was integrated into the Labour Federation and the Jewish Agency and established a labour exchange for women workers. In addition to her position as Secretary of the WWC, Idelson held various posts in the Executive Committee of the General Labour Federation. Like other female members of her party (Labour), she was convinced of the need to restrict the spheres of activity and autonomy of the WWC and to turn it into a regular part of the Histadrut, with no special authorities or different modi operandi.[46]

Idelson viewed the uniqueness of the Israeli Women Workers Movement, in contrast to other women's movements elsewhere, from various aspects: in the very historical uniqueness of the return of the Jewish nation to its homeland; in its commitment to bring Jewish women to the country and help in forming their lives within a system of new conditions and concepts; to plan for a life of work, to establish new social types and to build a family on a basis of partnership and equality.[47] Unlike many of her colleagues in the Working Women's Council who were afraid that the unique qualities of the Working Women's movement would become blurred, Idelson saw the positive aspect of mutual elections to the Working Women's Council, the Histadrut and the Workers' Councils. Due to the mutual elections, claimed Idelson, many female members participated in the general campaign and in explaining the movement's issues.

As a result of its membership in the CWO, the WWC, under Idelson's leadership, continued to maintain and promote its political agenda in various ways, and the recruitment of women to the army was only a part of the council's activity during the war. It also dealt with other 'burning' issues that the women of the Yishuv had to contend with at that time, such as finding employment for the wives of recruited men who had to go out to work, arranging care for the children of recruited parents, solving women's problems in a wartime economy, etc. Throughout the period the Yishuv women were serving in the British forces, a silent competition prevailed among the various women's organizations, especially between WIZO and the WWC. This competition became apparent in Idelson's speech at the WWC meeting that dealt with the 'ripening' recruitment. She tried to emphasize the part of the WWC in the negotiations with the army and presented it as an 'initiative of ours [with other women's organizations ... [and the recruitment] is conducted between the Jewish Agency Political Department, with the participation of representatives of the CWO'.[48]

Further Objectives of Female Recruitment

As already mentioned, the CWO, headed by Hadassah Samuel, saw the importance of their recruitment in the women's contribution to the war effort and in their participation in bearing the burden of national duty. The WWC saw additional objectives in the recruitment of women, one of which was the women's contribution to the Yishuv's political efforts to achieve independence once the war was over. Sharett was sure that in 'the way we build our political strength depends on the measure of our use of them [the possibilities inherent in female recruitment]'.[49] The WWC, too, wanted to see an interpretation of female recruitment in the political arena and declared, 'the willingness of women to undertake any effort and sacrifice will add strength to our national demands'.[50]

The WWC wanted to see in female recruitment a means to bringing about a change in Yishuv society's attitude to women, once the war was over, and hoped that after being released from service, the women soldiers will contribute to a change in the social agenda. The women's military service was often referred to as 'occupation', an expression prevalent among the Jewish pioneers in relation to the country and the land: 'This summary proves that the women soldiers *occupied* important positions in Labour and this occupation will no doubt influence even in normal times the future of the working woman in Eretz Israel' [my emphasis]. With these words, the Working Women's Movement attempted to present female recruitment to the army as an act of pioneering, perhaps as a breakthrough toward the establishment of a new society, as the women pioneers of the second Aliyah saw themselves as groundbreakers in the status of the Hebrew woman in Palestine.[51]

Military recruitment of women was conceived by the WWC as part of the struggle of the working women in the world. In other words, not only as a national campaign, but as a socialist struggle to build a just society, in which a special place would be reserved for the women of the Yishuv. Representatives of the movement, the recruits and the leaders attached great importance to achieving the movement's objectives. In their speeches, they expressed the conflict of their activity as a women's organization within the framework of a male-dominated trade union. They called on the Histadrut institutions to ensure that there was a nucleus of female Histadrut members in every army company: 'We came here as fighters on behalf of *Hebrew labor* ... in our own camps' [original emphasis].[52] Although concentrating the activists in several separate units did indeed serve the Histadrut's interests by maintaining contact with the recruits, it was detrimental to the aspirations of the Working Women's movement to create a nucleus of activists in each unit and thus provide the units with a Hebrew character. According to Ben-Zvi, an officer and graduate of the Cadre, '[we] must ensure our increased influence in this service. It is very important ... to have a nucleus of female Histadrut members who were raised on the traditions of the Histadrut. Only a nucleus such as this can ensure the desired social character in the female units.'[53]

Representatives of the WWC in the CWO provided their colleagues in the movement with the first update on the recruitment program in November 1941, about a month after the debate in the CWO. In February 1942 a special session of the WWC was devoted entirely to the recruitment issue. The session approved de facto the decisions of the CWO as formulated with the army and the Jewish Agency and decided to entrust the CWO secretariat with convening a committee to deal with all matters pertaining to the recruitment. The session's decisions were distributed by the CWO to all the Working Womens' departments in the towns and villages, working mothers' organizations, female members' committees in the settlement movement, and homes and households.

Implementing Positions

After negotiations with the army had come to fruition, the Jewish Agency Political Department entered the arena and, starting in December 1941, the recruitment was navigated by the national institutions (the Jewish Agency and the National Council). The Jewish Agency's Political Department asked the National Council to raise the recruitment issue for discussion at it next session and to invite Hadassah Samuel as representative of the CWO to lecture on the recruitment plan. The National Council subsequently discussed the subject and established a committee on female recruitment, headed by Yitzhak Ben-Zvi, president of the National Council. Senior representatives of CWO participated in the meetings of the recruitment committee, despite the difficulties that appeared in the bureaus.

Rift Between the CWO and the Recruitment Centre

As already mentioned, in October 1941 it was decided on cooperation between the CWO and the Jewish Agency's Recruitment Department and on the establishment of a special unit to deal with female recruitment within the department's framework. As senior representatives of the CWO, Samuel and Idelson began participating in the department's meetings in December 1941 and through the early months of 1942. The meeting on 18 December 1941, for example, was devoted entirely to the subject of female recruitment.[54]

Following the army's decision to recruit women from the Yishuv, the Jewish Agency and the CWO wanted to oversee the recruitment and be able to control the 'quality' of the recruits. Here, in fact, the national considerations of the CWO leadership overrode the feminist interest to recruit as large a number of women as possible. In accordance with the agreement between the Jewish Agency Recruitment Department and the CWO, each of the recruitment committees in the country were joined by CWO members; moreover, it was decided also to include a member of the Histadrut Recruitment Committee. The uniqueness of female recruitment – from its nationalist and gender aspects – was given expression throughout the process, right from the stage of choosing the candidates for service, in order to conform with national criteria.[55]

In order to maintain the necessary control over the quality of the recruits, an organized system was established and headed by four recruiters, each veteran members of Haganah – one each from Haifa, Tel Aviv and Jerusalem and another representing the rest of the country. Later, two additional recruiters were appointed to represent the settlement community. Sonya Idelberg,[56] a veteran Haganah member, was initially appointed as a recruiter for the Tel Aviv area and later as a nationwide recruiter, first for the ATS and subsequently also for the WAAF. The recruiters' job, as determined by the Jewish Agency and the Haganah, was to receive each volunteer who came to the recruitment offices, to check their 'quality' and to instruct and prepare them for military life. The recruiters met once a week and were required to present a weekly report on their activity. Aside from registration and sorting of the recruits, the recruiters considered their job to also include persuasion and training of the recruits to be propaganda agents for the Jewish Yishuv in their encounters with the non-Jewish world in the course of their military service. To this end, the recruitment bureau provided lectures on the Yishuv's achievements in the fields of economics, education, etc.

The campaign for female recruitment was part of the mechanism established by the Jewish Agency in 1940 in order to deal with male military recruitment in the Yishuv. It had been decided at that time for the Yishuv to cooperate with the British military authorities and to this end, the Jewish Agency established its Recruitment Department. Representatives of the department were present in the Jewish Agency's recruitment bureaus all over the country and dealt with sorting names of all the men of conscription age (according to the institutions' decision) and in pro-recruitment propaganda. Haim Barles, Head of the Jewish Agency's Recruitment Department as well as head of the immigration department until 1948, was appointed to represent the Recruitment Department management in the Committee for Female Recruitment Matters.

June 1942 saw an organizational change in the recruitment activity of the Jewish Agency when the Centre for Yishuv Recruitment was established. This centre operated as the executive arm of the Jewish Agency in implementing the recruitment drive and its establishment ended a lengthy process of public awakening, begun at the initiative of Ben-Zion Israeli and his colleagues. The mechanism aimed at controlling the Yishuv's recruitment activity to the British army, as well as for defending and organizing the civilian population. Dr Dov Yosef (Bernard Joseph) was appointed chairman of the Centre for Yishuv Recruitment, assisted by Berl Raptor as representative of the Histadrut, and Ahron Netanel as representative of the civilian circles.[57] In every town and settlement local committees were established to act as representatives of the Centre and were subject to it. It was concluded that the women recruiters would be a part of the recruitment mechanism, both national and local. Representatives in the recruitment bureaus presented the Centre for Yishuv Recruitment with a weekly report of their activity.

And indeed, after the change in organization and despite the decision, the Centre for Yishuv Recruitment refused to implement the agreement with the CWO. In June and July 1942, the Council's secretariat wrote to Jewish Agency Political Department to complain that 'although we were the first to raise the issue of Yishuv women recruitment, demanded it of the authorities ... made great efforts to make recruitment a success', their representatives were excluded from Centre meetings.[58] Eventually, CWO pressure succeeded in placing two representatives in debates on female recruitment. It was further agreed that no decisions would be reached without their concurrence. However, even if the problem had been solved on a national level, on a local level – the local recruitment committees – no representatives of the CWO were included for several months.

Encouraging Recruitment

During the first two years of the recruitment drive – from late 1941 until late 1943 – much was done to encourage women to join the army. Some activities were conducted on the initiative of the CWO or the Yishuv institutions (together with the Council) and others were held separately by member organizations in the CWO. In these events the Council's major messages were presented regarding the importance of female recruitment to the war effort and satisfaction at the ability to release male soldiers to the war front.

CWO activities took place parallel to those of the Jewish Agency Recruitment Department and included speeches in cafes and movie houses and visits to the homes of dodgers. In addition to CWO activity, the WWC also arranged many events in the course of 1942 with the aim of encouraging working women to enlist in the army. To this end they organized propaganda meetings in factories and gatherings of domestic workers and professional women. The WWC also held large rallies in Haifa (in the presence of 500 people) and in Tel Aviv's Herzliya High School (with 600 attendees). These gatherings hosted recruits who came to describe their experiences in the military camps. It is hard to evaluate the moral and propaganda effect these activities had on the recruitment drive (but it can be estimated as high), at least until mid 1943.

As part of the effort to encourage recruitment, the Jewish Agency Political Department, with the knowledge of the CWO, called on employers to ensure the recruits' place in their work place, the rights after being released from military service and also to match their army wages to those prior to their recruitment. At a management meeting of the Recruitment Department, Eliyahu Golomb called on the Jewish Agency to negotiate with the Association of Industrialists in order to protect the women's pre-recruitment labour rights. The WWC, too, called on the Histadrut employers to ensure the rights of their women workers in order to encourage them to enlist. And, indeed, large public and private concerns responded by protecting the recruited women's rights, unlike smaller private enterprises that refused to cooperate on this matter. The Histadrut Executive Committee decided that the same laws applied to female soldiers employed by the Histadrut as to male soldiers and all their rights would be reserved for them. Already in the first months of the recruitment drive the Yishuv's large factories, such as Shemen, Asis, Elite and others, announced that every female volunteer for military service would be able to return to her former job with the same conditions and wages and tenure as well as promotions and pension rights she'd enjoyed before recruitment. The Hadassah Medical Federation, too, joined the Jewish Agency's call and announced that the rights of female recruits would be equal to those of their male counterparts.[59]

The Yishuv institutions, in coordination with the military authorities, started to include recruits in their efforts to encourage enlistment, as they did with male recruits. Mina Ben-Zvi remained in the country as a central activist in the campaign and twelve recruits who served in the country were placed at her disposal in order to participate in the recruitment drive. The soldiers participated in dozens of events in work places, organizations, gatherings and farewell parties for recruits, etc. In addition, drive-by parades were arranged of female ATS drivers in the city streets as well as marches, speeches in movie houses and theatres, etc.[60] In these events the soldiers spoke about their experiences in the army, the hardships as compared with their civilian jobs, and about the necessity for female recruitment and its potential contribution to the war effort. The soldiers also spoke about the fair attitude they enjoyed at the hands of the British. Sometimes the mere sight of female recruits in uniform was sufficient to arouse enormous pride throughout the Yishuv.

The efforts to obtain the temporary release of female soldiers from their military jobs in order to participate in the recruitment drive continued throughout 1942, since in wake of the war in Africa and the desperate need for working hands, it was hard for the army to relinquish the female soldiers who were required in the recruitment drive. Only at the end of that year, when the number of female recruits rose, did the military authorities agree to release several soldiers to this end. The brunt of recruitment activity took place during 1942–43. The Recruitment Department's Propaganda Committee held many sessions in which an extensive plan of action was determined for the various sectors in the Yishuv. The committee included public persons and journalists.[61] During the first months of 1942, mass gatherings took place in factories in Tel Aviv and its surrounds, in which female conscripts spoke and responded to questions about their lives. This propaganda on the part of the female conscripts continued until 1944.

Accompanying the Recruits to the Army

In addition to the recruitment drive, several events were arranged from the beginning of the year with the objective of creating an atmosphere of consensus in the Yishuv for the recruitment, and in support of the female conscripts. These events took place in Tel Aviv and other large towns on the initiative of the CWO or the Jewish Agency's Recruitment Department. In January 1942 a large farewell party took place in Tel Aviv for the first of the recruits to participate in the first leadership cadre. Hadassah Samuel, who was given the title 'Party Chairman', emphasized the role of the CWO and the Political Department in the efforts to include women in the war effort. In March 1942, on the day the first 500 Yishuv women were recruited to the ATS, a farewell party was held for 100 of the recruits, attended by recruits and their families. Idelson and Idelberg, the head recruiter, delivered speeches. Yitzhak Greenbaum[62] from the Jewish Agency Executive congratulated the recruits and CWO representatives handed out flowers and sweets. Descriptions of the farewell parties that took place in the various towns were published in the daily press. The recruits were seen as contributing to the war effort and the Yishuv newspapers, or at least some of them, tried to create an atmosphere of encouragement.[63]

The CWO continued to hold festive gatherings and events for the women soldiers throughout their service. For example, on 10 February 1943 the CWO arranged a national congress at Tel Aviv's Ohel Shem, as part of the International Women's Day celebrations. The objective of this gathering was to emphasize the achievements of the Hebrew soldier on the first anniversary of the recruitment and to encourage the continuation of the enterprise among the female population of the Yishuv. For the first anniversary of the first wave of recruitment of Yishuv women to the ATS, the CWO planned a series of events and activities, such as parties for the soldiers in every town in the country; a parade and a ball at the end for driving course graduates (that was ending in late January 1943); greeting cards, to be sent from all the meetings of WIZO and the WWC; regular reports in the press on the soldiers' achievements and greetings from Yishuv leaders; reports to the roof organizations overseas on the success of the recruitment drive, etc.

WIZO, under Hadassah Samuel's leadership, held separate gatherings of its own. In these events, too, soldiers described their lives in the army and discussed additional means of spreading information to encourage recruitment. The study day held by the CWO in the female soldiers' hostel in Cairo, which was attended by many soldiers from all over Egypt, provided a brief lecture about UNRRA (United Nations Relief and Rehabilitation Administration). Many women soldiers who attended the event asked to register with the organization after the war in an attempt to locate their relatives in Europe.[64]

Women's Magazines and Women Recruits

The women's magazines in the Yishuv – *Davar Hapo'elet* and *Olam Ha'isha* – were an important tool in spreading the messages and concepts of the CWO and WWC among the Yishuv's female population and recruits. They also provided the soldiers with a platform for expressing their concerns, impressions, complaints and experiences of life in the army.

Davar Hapo'elet

The first edition of this magazine was published on 11 March 1934 as a supplement to the *Davar* daily newspaper and, due to its large-scale distribution, many people were exposed to its contents who were hitherto unaware of the importance of women's magazines. In 1940 the circulation of the magazine was 18,000 copies, whereas in 1944, only 8,000 copies were distributed, particularly because of the paper shortage and budgeting problems caused by the war. The magazine reached male and female soldiers and, although its distribution statistics are known, it is not clear how many women read it and were influenced by its messages. Aside from its subscribers in the Yishuv, copies were also sent to various institutions overseas, as well as to all the Jewish centres in the Diaspora, such as the American Volunteer League in New York, WIZO, training kibbutzim and the Hehalutz movement.[65]

Rachel Katznelson-Shazar was the editor of *Davar Hapo'elet*. It was she who 'conceived, brought about and maintained it from its inception and to her retirement from the editorial office in 1961'. The magazine was considered an informal, cultural sounding board for the Working Women's movement and its objectives were to bring Hebrew culture to the working woman; in other words, to help women become fluent in the language and able to express themselves in written as well as spoken Hebrew. Additional objectives were to impart knowledge, provide emotional support, captivate the female reading public and reveal the female voice. *Davar Hapo'elet* was a cultural and informative tool of expression with ideological-gender, nationalist and social qualities and was active in forming the collective memory. The magazine strove to create a new feminine identity.[66]

From the moment of publishing the announcements calling for women to enlist and, in fact, even beforehand,[67] and throughout the military service, almost every issue until the end of the war, carried references of various kinds to the soldiers. It was, for example, the only magazine that published Sharett's speech at the February 1942 congress of the WWC.[68] In addition to reviewing the recruitment and service, the magazine followed the army's preparations for demobilization (from late 1943) and for subsequent civilian life – especially with regard to accommodation and professional training, with much respect for the work of the recruits in the army and consideration of their needs.

Olam Ha'isha

Olam Ha'isha was a bi-weekly magazine that began publication in February 1940, with the objective of instructing the literate woman during the war period and to report on the activity of women's organizations in the Yishuv. It was in fact the sounding board of the Federation of Zionist Women – WIZO, although this was not specifically emphasized. Its first editor-in-chief was Rachel Lifschitz and it appeared regularly until the end of December 1942; its publication was resumed in July 1945.[69] The magazine was commercial and even printed in a colour format; it was concerned mainly with fashion, cooking, childcare and the glamorous world of Hollywood and was parallel to current-day women's magazines such as *La'isha*, or *At*. It contained large numbers of advertisements and announcements of feminine interest and it also provided a literary platform for women writers.

Voice of the Soldiers

During the war, the two magazines provided a sounding board for various written works by women soldiers. Some of the pieces published in *Davar Hapo'elet* were commissioned. In August 1942, about six months after recruitment commenced, the magazine announced that it was aware of the anti-recruitment atmosphere in the Yishuv and the contribution the recruits were making to the war effort. Nor did it hesitate to point an accusing finger at itself, in stating, 'only a tiny part of their [the recruits'] lives is now being given ... in *Davar Hapo'elet* and other publications'. The magazine concluded, 'We must develop the mutual ties and condition for this are the ... soldiers themselves.' In order to increase the involvement in newspaper coverage, the magazine called on the soldiers and their families to send letters to the editor: 'help us to preserve the impressions of this period in the lives of our soldiers!'[70]

Olam Ha'isha, from the September 1942 issue and to the end of that year, devoted its front page to the recruits and even underwent a change in its regular format to conform with the changed circumstances of its readers themselves. After presenting the changes and the reasons, the magazine proposed introducing a 'special section in our magazine [devoted to the female Hebrew soldier]', with the intention of 'bridging the gap between the woman in the Yishuv and the women "over-there"' [thus in the original]. This section, the magazine stressed, 'will host Hebrew soldiers, whose talent for literary writing is well known'. Of its readers, the magazine asked them to open their hearts to the wishes of their sisters in the camps of the ATS.[71]

And indeed, true to the mission they had set for themselves, these magazines made a point of publishing letters, stories and poems written by soldiers about their experiences of life in the army camps, about the sights of war and about the relations with their British counterparts; there were letters complaining about the need to reinforce their ties with the Yishuv and against rumours regarding their 'morality'. About eight months after the beginning of recruitment, *Davar Hapo'elet* reported with pleasure that, 'relations between WWC and the soldiers in the country and abroad had strengthened, via letters, meetings and food supplies'.[72]

The two magazines followed the recruits through every stage of their military service: encouraging them to volunteer; keeping tabs on their service conditions and their life in camp; reporting impressions of visits by women's organizations and Yishuv institutions to the soldiers; photographs of soldiers participating in the war effort; reporting on establishment of rest homes and recreation clubs for their welfare; publishing their letters and providing them with a platform for their feelings and complaints and, finally, reports on the preparations and plans to assist them after their release from duty. In addition to all these, the women's magazines devoted commentary and editorials to the question of female recruitment, an issue that was paid very little attention in the daily papers.

Disputing the Authority of the Council of Women's Organizations to Lead the Campaign for Recruitment

One of the claims raised in various forums in the Yishuv referred to the very authority of CWO to lead the campaign. Even before the military authorities approved the decision on recruitment, the Jewish Agency Executive held a debate on the subject. Dr David Santor, representative of the non-Zionists (the Brit Shalom group) in the Executive, wanted to know who had authorized Hadassah Samuel to act on behalf of female recruitment. According to him, if the recruitment did indeed become a reality, it would have to be carried out via the Jewish Agency and not through other channels. Eliezer Kaplan replied that Samuel was acting with the full knowledge of the Jewish Agency's Political Department and in consultation with the CWO. Greenbaum testified that Sharett had reported to the Jewish Agency Executive on the initiative to recruit women from the Yishuv to military service and his report had aroused no objection or argument.

At a meeting of the United Kibbutz Movement (UKM) Council, Yitzhak Tabenkin claimed that no debates or real clarification had been held on the subject of female recruitment; he then put forward a blatantly patronizing argument according to which women had no authority to decide on issues that are allegedly 'feminine': 'Are women's matters only women's matters?' Tabenkin also doubted the legitimacy of the CWO to conduct negotiations on the recruitment by asking sarcastically: 'Which women decided? I know that they have representatives ... there are Jewish Lydias [leaders] and half-Lydias ... and I know of the Esther-icas among the Jewish women.'[73] He also added that he was not prepared to accept the authority of the WWC and its call for recruitment and that, 'I won't have it, because the Working Women's Council called for it, it's already an obligation'.[74]

Tabenkin's words also illustrate the discrepancy between the ideology of the workers' movement and reality. Already in the 1920s the workers' movement had declared its commitment to social equality, including equality between men and women. But in reality, things did not happen according to declarations and there was a marked difference between rules and reality in every way. Pioneer Yishuv society was noticeably male-labour oriented, with defined and categorical male components and the inequality between men and women in society was jealously maintained.

The debate over the 'legitimacy' and the authority of the CWO to conduct the struggle within the Yishuv institutions on behalf of women was not specifically typical of the recruitment issue. It was only a representative example of the ambivalent attitude of the women's movements in the world and in the Yishuv between ideological commitment to labour and social interests, and the unique interests of women. The Working Women's movement, for example, was ambivalent from its inception, since it operated on behalf of feminine objectives and the Yishuv's female population, but not as a separate organization, rather as part of a male-dominated organization. An examination of the complex relations between gender and status in the trade union raises the question of why, despite their fighting spirit and their status awareness, did the line workers not achieve their appropriate status and recognition in the trade union. Bat-Sheva Margalit Stern, who studied the subject, credits the partial success of the women's organizations in the labour movements in Israel and the world to their failure to overcome prejudice and unsympathetic social or economic government conditions. According to Dafna Izraeli, in spite of its extensive activity, the workers' movement failed in promoting specifically feminine issues because it operated within general frameworks and not as a separate entity.[75]

In response to Tabenkin's claim that the CWO had acted on 'its own accord' over the matter of recruitment, Rachel Katznelson-Shazar declared that the Jewish Agency Political Department was involved all the way and 'the CWO and the WWC did not make a move without the Political Department'.[76] She added that the matter had been discussed in various frameworks and still 'no-one had stood up to ask: what are you doing, girls?', and for that reason, there was no place now to doubt the role of the women's organizations and there was no place for male opposition.[77] Hadassah Samuel, too, felt the need – albeit in retrospect – to explain that, 'of course I did everything through the [Jewish] Agency'.[78]

Maintaining Contact with the Recruits

The CWO maintained contact with the recruits throughout their service: representatives visited them in their camps, provided emotional and financial support, established clubs and rest rooms where they could spend their vacations and free time, and made every effort to give them a feeling that they had a home, both in the Yishuv and abroad.[79] As already mentioned, the women's organizations made use of the women's magazines for passing on messages, decisions and reports to the recruited women, on the one hand, and as a platform for their letters and requests, on the other.

Various bodies in the Yishuv helped the CWO in maintaining contact with the recruits. These included the Soldiers' Welfare Committee, which was headed by Yosef Baratz from Degania. The Committee had been established in 1940 in order to supply the cultural and welfare requirements of the Yishuv recruits, since the British had at first refused to recognize the special needs of these recruits. But the Committee's activity was noticed only in early 1942, and even then, only within the boundaries of Palestine. In early 1943, Ya'akov Tsur was appointed to represent the Committee in Egypt, where he worked on behalf of the recruits, arranging concerts and literary and theatrical evenings in army camps, mainly in Egypt. In 1943 it was decided to institutionalize the cooperation between the CWO and the Soldiers' Welfare Committee and a joint committee was established and headed by Rachel Adiv (Kissel). The Committee's task was to prepare a plan of action on behalf of the women soldiers, to consolidate it and to activate it.[80]

In order to assure access to the soldiers, the CWO, in coordination with the Jewish Agency's Political Department, was recognized by the British military authorities as the sole representative of the Yishuv women and as a relief and welfare organization. At a meeting of the CWO secretariat in August 1942, Samuel reported with satisfaction that the army had recognized the Council as 'the official representative ... of the Jewish women with the right to direct access to the military authorities ... it is the [CWO] that appears before the army on those matters concerning the ATS'. Samuel added that she had also asked 'Mr. Shertok [Sharett] to inform me as representative of the CWO, of his own dealings with the army on instances that are close to the authority of the CWO'.[81] About two years later, the CWO was accepted as a member of the Church Army Clubs for HM Forces, thus making it the only women's organization, as far as is known, to have obtained this position in the British Army or any other army.[82] The new status made it easier for CWO representatives to enter army camps and also to maintain contact with the recruits.

Even after recruitment began, Samuel continued to correspond with British officers in order to solve problems that arose among the recruits. In fact, she dictated the CWO's agenda, which was devoted entirely to women's military service. Samuel sought solutions for the recruits' personal and national problems, arranged visits by CWO representatives in the camps, allocated resources for establishing clubs and restrooms in military bases, etc. At the same time, the member organizations in the CWO continued to deal with other issues, but the recruitment enterprise was incorporated into and given a platform in many of their activities.

NOTES

1. Both notices were also published in *Davar Hapo'elet*, 30 January 1942, p.2.
2. Telegram from Weizmann to H. Samuel, 17 January 1942, Central Zionist Archive, Jerusalem (CZA), S25/6001. The British Censorship disqualified the telegram.
3. 'Rules of the Council of Women's Organization in Eretz Israel' (undated), CZA, F49/2106.

4. Letter from WIZO to World WIZO, 7 August 1936, ibid., F49/2104.
5. Sara Azriyahu, 'Councils of Hebrew Women in Eretz Israel', *Ha'aretz*, 24 August 1927, p.87.
6. Hanna Herzog, 'Irgunei nashim bahugim ha'ezrahi'im, perek nishkach behistoriographia shel haYishuv' [Women's organizations in civil circles – forgotten chapter in historiography of the Yishuv], *Katedra*, 70 (February 1994), pp.130–1.
7. 'Rules of Council of Women's Organization in Eretz Israel' (undated), CZA, F49/2106.
8. Ibid.
9. Memo of the 'United Representation of Yishuv Women' (undated, probably from November 1938), ibid., F49/2104.
10. On the matter of patriotic or nationalist mothers in Lebanon or Syria during and after the French Mandate see, for example, Elizabeth Thompson, *Colonial Citizens: Republican Rights, Paternal Privilege and Gender in French Syria and Lebanon* (New York 2000), pp.140–50. On the role of mothers in protest in Russia, see for example, Amy Caiazza, *Mothers and Soldiers: Gender, Citizenship and Civil Society in Contemporary Russia* (New York 2002).
11. Minutes of the CWO, 26 May 1939, p.1, CZA, F49/2104. The participants at the meetings were very satisfied with this.
12. Already in October 1936, world WIZO had approached Eliezer Kaplan with the request to include its representatives in all committees connected to women's issues. Kaplan was a member of the Mapam leadership. Between 1933 and 1948 he was a member of the Jewish Agency Executive in Jerusalem as well as its treasurer. Later he would become the State of Israel's first Finance Minister.
13. Minutes of CWO meeting, 22 May 1940, CZA, F49/2104.
14. Samuel was fond of classical music and theatre and an avid reader of French and English literature. She was always meticulously dressed and well groomed. Her clothes were imported from London and Paris, or sewn to order by a high-end Tel Aviv seamstress. Interview with Ruth Horam, Jerusalem, 9 August 2007, Hadassah Samuel's niece, daughter of her sister, Nehama, who lived in the Samuel home between 1939 and 1945,.
15. Interview with Hadassah Samuel, 12 February 1972. Interviewer: Margalit Shilo, film 200/K, the Institute for Modern Judaism, department of verbal documentation, Hebrew University, pp.1–3.
16. In his memoires, Samuel wrote that the wedding, which took place in Government House on Jerusalem's Mount of Olives, was attended by 800 guests – officials in the army and the civil authorities, religious leaders and representatives of all the ethnic groups in Palestine. The Jewish ceremony was conducted by the two Chief Rabbis, the Ashkenazi, Abraham Yitzhak Hacohen Kook and the Sephardi, Ben-Zion Meir Uziel. After the ceremony, the groom was led to a corner of the hall where he was crowned 'Sheikh of the Bedouin tribes of Beer-Sheva' (a famous wedding photograph shows the groom in his Sheikh outfit, surrounded by the Sheikhs). Edwin Samuel, *A Lifetime in Jerusalem* (Jerusalem 1970), pp.54–5.
17. Miriam Vardi (Gur), Samuel's niece, said of her that she was a beautiful and hard woman, a great snob in her relationships with regard to people outside of her family, but very warm and devoted to members of her extended family – her brothers, nephews and nieces. In the Samuel household, much attention was

paid to discipline and cleanliness and only English was spoken to the children. Interview with Miriam Vardi, Jerusalem, 15 July 2006.

18. Interview with Hadassah Samuel, p.17. Horam is convinced that Samuel never considered herself a part of British society, but took advantage of her connections with the British to promote the issues that she believed in. Interview with Ruth Horam. Audrey Chitty's diary, too, indicates that 'Samuel was out for WIZO [and Zionism] entirely' and there was even suspicion as to her motives vis-à-vis female recruitment. Entry in Chitty's diary, 16 December 1941, National Army Museum, London (NAM), 9802-55-2.
19. In his memoires Samuel recalled that he first arrived in the country together with the Zionist Commission in 1918 and was captivated by Zionism. Probably one of the reasons for his wish to remain in Israel was the need to distance himself from the giant shadow of his famous father. Samuel, *A Lifetime in Jerusalem*, pp.24–5.
20. Yael Rozman et al. (ed.), *Nashim be-Yisra'el: Leksikon* [Women in Israel: Lexicon] (Tel Aviv: 1991), p.150 (for details on the activity of Beba Idelson).
21. In 1929 Yehoshua Gordon was appointed by the Jewish Agency to liaise between it and the British Police, on all matters concerning the Police Rangers, of which he was also the commander. Gordon died at the end of 1941, when the decision had been taken on female recruitment. Gershon Rivlin (ed.), *La'esh ve'lamagen: toldot hanotrut ha'ivrit* [To the fire and defence: history of Hebrew guardians] (Tel Aviv 1963), p.19.
22. Interview with Hadassah Samuel, p.11
23. The decision on recruitment was delayed until the arrival in the country of Audrey Chitty. In the CWO the fears were raised that 'if there is another postponement in fulfilling the recruitment [drive] the enthusiasm [for it] will wane among the women'. Minutes of CWO meeting, 17 November 1941, CZA, F49/2106. During that visit, Catherine Morrison-Bell, Chitty's assistant, took Hadassah Samuel to visit to the 501 Company in Madi, some 10 kilometres away from Cairo. At that time the company, which consisted entirely of female British soldiers, was the only one of its kind in Egypt.
24. Before Chitty's arrival in the Middle East, Vera Weizmann – wife of Chaim Weizmann – met with Jean Knox, Director of the ATS (1941–43) and Leslie Whateley, who was appointed commander-in-chief three years later. At their meeting, Mrs Weizmann updated the officers about WIZO and the CWO and its position in the Yishuv. Minutes of CWO meeting, 17 November 1941, CZA, F49/2106.
25. Ruth Horam recalled that Samuel was frustrated by the fact that she hadn't been appointed Chairwoman of World WIZO and hinted at intrigues within the organization's local chapter involving women who could not cope with her status and strong personality. Interview with Ruth Horam.
26. Audrey Chitty Diary, 18 December 1941, NAM, 9802-55-2.
27. Audrey Chitty diary, 18–19 December 1941, ibid. In her diary, Chitty added that, 'one of Samuel's games is to cause friction among us and to incite us against one another'.
28. Interview with Hadassah Samuel, p.12.
29. Samuel recalled that when Chitty asked her 'what about you?' she had replied, 'I was already older than army age [although she was 43 at the time, within the

range for military recruitment] ... I came and informed her that I was not going into the army.' Interview with Hadassah Samuel, p.14. In any case, in order to dispel any doubts, Chitty informed Samuel that if she was to become an officer, she would have to join a Leadership Cadre (first commanders training course) at the end of which she would be given a rank, like all the other recruits. Chitty's diary, 17 December 1941, NAM, 9802-55-2.

30. Interview with Hadassah Samuel, pp.12–13.
31. Interview with Ruth Horam. Nonetheless, in most of the photographs recording Samuel's visits to the recruits, she is dressed in 'civies'. Other Yishuv representatives also received uniforms and honorary commissions from the British army. Thus, for example, Amnon Zair (Rudi), delegate of the Soldiers' Welfare Committee in Egypt. Amnon Zair, *Vienna–Gan Shmuel* (Gan Shmuel 1980), pp.86–7.
32. 'Recruiting the Woman', lecture by Moshe Sharett before the Working Women's Committee, *Davar Hapo'elet*, 4–3 (23 April 1942), p.6. Sharett reiterated these words in other forums over the next months.
33. Letter from Brigadier Beddington to Hadassah Samuel, 2 April 1941, CZA, F49/2104.
34. Letter from Samuel to Beddington, 2 May 1941, ibid.
35. United Kibbutz Movement Council in Yagur, 6–7 February 1942, pp.38, 32, CZA, 45/140/2002. In fact, in light of the conditions made by the British army and Sharett's clarifications, Tabenkin's proposal negated the recruitment of women. At the end of the meeting, the Kibbutz Council decided to 'adopt', de facto, Tabenkin's line and not to support recruitment under the current conditions.
36. Mina Rogoz'ik at the fifth Histadrut Congress, p.97, Labor Movement Archive, Lavon Institute, 19–23 February 1942.
37. Idelson at a meeting of the Women Workers Council, 3 November 1941, ibid, IV-230–6. Idelson explained how she arrived at the proposed number: on the assumption that the age of the recruits will be between 20–25 (as proposed by the CWO at this stage), she calculated that out of some 18,000 women aged between 20–30 (single and married women without children) in the Yishuv, apart from a quota that has to be determined for mothers and for members of the kibbutz and moshav populations, this was a realistic number to strive for. Minutes of CWO, 13 October 1941, CZA, F49/2105.
38. Meeting of the Recruitment Department, 18 December 1941, CZA, S25/5063. In the announcement on the decision to recruit women, it was stated that the salary of a female soldier from Palestine would be half a shilling a day, plus a further four pennies war allowance and another five pennies professional fee. Every rise in rank promotion will be accompanied by a rise in salary. 'Formation of Auxiliary Territorial Service (Palestine)', 24 December 1941, ibid, S25/5099. Wages were determined according to seniority in service as well as the military professions. 'Wages and Awards' (undated), ibid, S37/674. The military wages determined for the Yishuv volunteers was two thirds that of their British counterparts, and family allowances were at first half and later two thirds of that given to the British service men and women. Yoav Gelber, 'Hitgabshut hayishuv hayehudi beeretz Israel 1936–1947' [Forming the Jewish Yishuv in Eretz Israel 1936–1947], in Moshe Lissak (ed.), *Toldot hayishuv beeretz Israel*

meaz ha'aliyah harishona: tkufat hamandat habriti [History of the Yishuv in Eretz Israel since the First Aliyah: period of British Mandate], B (Jerusalem 1994), pp.427–8.
39. Letter from Samuel to Sale, 5 September 1941, CZA, S25/6001.
40. Letter from Brown to Samuel, 11 August 1942, ibid.
41. Letter from Dodds (military HQ in Eretz Israel) to Moshe Sharett, 23 December 1941, ibid.
42. Letter from CWO secretariat to WIZO and the Working Women's Council, 12 October 1941, 12 October 1941, CZA, F49/2104.
43. Chitty allowed the recruits to wear armbands with the legend 'Palestine' even though this did not conform with regulations. HQ meeting, 8 September 1942, National Archives (NA), WO 169/3834.
44. Minutes of CWO meeting with representatives of Jewish Agency Recruitment Department, 12 October 1941, CZA, F49/2104. It was determined in this meeting that this unit would consist of four representatives of the CWO and three of the Recruitment Department; the management of the Recruitment Department would include two members of the Women's Recruitment Unit; in all places where local recruitment bureaus already existed, separate units would be established for female recruitment, consisting of a recruiter and a secretary.
45. 'Society and Volunteering', *Davar Hapo'elet*, 9–10 (4 July 1941), p.130.
46. For eighteen years Idelson was also a Labour Member of Knesset and Deputy Knesset Chairman. Ada Fishman Maimon, member of Hapo'el Hatza'ir and a founder member of Working Women's Movement in the Histadrut, presented a different approach from Idelson's. According to her, the WWC had to be the defining element in the movement's activity. Fishman Maimon strove to extend its authority and enhance it as an autonomous body within the Histadrut and adhered to the non-party principle in accordance with her party's decentralized and autonomous worldview. Bat-Sheva Margalit Stern, *Geula bekvalim: tenuat ha'poalot ha'eretz israelit 1920–1939* [Salvation in Chains: Working Women's Movement in Eretz Israel 1920–1939] (Jerusalem 2006), pp.136–9.
47. Beba Idelson, 'Moetzet Ha'Poalot: Tosefet o Yesod' [Working Women's Council: addition or foundation], *Baderekh* (Tel Aviv: 1965), p.254.
48. Idelson at the 22nd session of the WWC, 3 November 1941, WWC File, p.12, Labor Movement Archive, IV-230-6.
49. 'Recruitment of the Woman', lecture by Moshe Sharett, *Davar Ha'po'elet*, 3–4 (23 April 1942), p.8.
50. 'To Female Recruitment', *Davar Ha'po'elet*, 1–2 (30 January 1942), front page. The headline hinted that already in the previous world war, with the establishment of the Jewish Brigades, a 'volunteer' movement had formed that called for the recruitment of women, but to no avail. Now, however, at a time when thousands of women from various countries were partners to the war effort, the turn of the Yishuv had come to recruit.
51. 'A Year After the Daughters of the Yishuv Volunteered to the Army', *Davar Ha'po'elet*, 1 (31 January 1943), p.2. On the broad scale use of the word 'occupation' among members of the Second Aliyah in everything connected to work and the land, see for example, 'Occupation and Work', 'With the Occupiers of Work' and 'Occupying the Land', Bracha Habas (ed.), *Sefer ha-Aliyah ha-Sheniyyah* [The Second Aliyah Book] (Tel Aviv 1947), pp.67–156, 163–295, 403–77, respectively.

52. Speech by a female sergeant (no name given) at the Histadrut Executive Committee, 12 and 13 October 1942, p.46 (47), Labor Movement Archive, IV-230-6. At that same session the female sergeant expressed her fear that the recruitment enterprise might 'collapse' as a result of the falling numbers.
53. According to Ben-Zvi 'only in two of three units was a large number of Histadrut members concentrated. The other units have almost no Histadrut nucleus. I blame the selfishness of Histadrut bodies, who wanted to concentrate their own women in the units.' Mina Rogoz'ik, secretariat of the Histadrut Council, 7 September 1942, p.124, CZA, 45/14012002.
54. 'Information on the activity of the Recruitment Committee', 1 January 1942, CZA, S37/676.
55. The Jewish Agency's recruitment bureaus set criteria for approving a candidate for military service: in addition to minimal physical demands recruits also had to have a firm commitment to the Yishuv. In the Palmach, on the other hand, the physical criterion was the major component in choosing candidates, and as a Palmach doctor put it, 'it is necessary to select and recruit only the healthiest and the strongest [of women] who can withstand the effort of training'. Elad, Ofra, '"Kol bahur ve tov laneshek, bahura al hamismar!": Ha'havera ba'Palmach' [Every man is good for arms, a woman, on guard duty! Woman Member in the Palmach], in Yehiam Weitz (ed.), *Palmach: Shtei shibolim veherev* [Palmach, Two Sticks of Corn and a Sword] (Tel Aviv, 2001), pp.225–6.
56. Russian born Idelberg (1906), high-school graduate from Odessa, member of the Histadrut Council and the WWC, was a commander in the Haganah members' battalion in Tel Aviv, member of Ahdut Ha'avoda, Mapam and the Socialist left. Moreover, she was included in delegations to women's congresses in Europe during the 1950s. David Tidhar, *Enziklopediyah le'Halutsei ha'Yishuv ve'Bonav* [Encyclopedia of pioneers of the Yishuv and personages], 17 (Tel Aviv 1947), p.5195. Idelberg was the chief recruiter between January 1942 and August 1944.
57. Canadian born, Dr Dov Yosef was a leading lawyer in the Yishuv. From 1936 he had served as consultant to the Jewish Agency's Political Department and Sharett's deputy in the department's management. Berl Raptor was among the leaders of the Histadrut and a member of Ahdut Ha'avoda-Po'alei Zion party.
58. Letters from CWO to Jewish Agency Political Department, 24 June and July 1942, CZA, J1/3057; also 'Convening the activists with regard to female recruitment', 28 July 1942, ibid, F49/2104.
59. 'To Encourage the Recruitment of the Hebrew Women', 10 March 1942, CZA, S37/670. In April Bank Hapo'alim and Solel Boneh announced their intention to protect the rights of the female recruits in the same way as those of the men. 'To Encourage the Recruitment of the Hebrew Women', 3 April 1942, ibid. In contrast, the textile manufacturer, Ata, informed the Jewish Agency's Political Department that 'we see no necessity in the matter, that women who are permanently employed in our factory, should enlist'. One of the biggest hardships in the factories is the departure of trained female workers for various reasons and it is for this reason that they 'are obliged to influence our workers not to enlist'. Letter from Ata to Jewish Agency Political Department, 22 March 1942, ibid, S25/5099. Ironically enough, the wife of the company's MD enlisted in the army and served as an ambulance driver in 502 Company in Egypt. Interview with Naomi Yekutieli (Torok), Tel Aviv, 8 December 2005.

60. 'A Parade to Escalate the Recruitment in Eretz Israel' (no date provided), Labor Party Archive, 33/4.
61. Journalist, Bracha Habas, for example, was invited to a meeting of the Propaganda Committee on 7 May 1942 in Tel Aviv. Letter from the Recruitment Department to Bracha Habas, 6 May 1942, CZA, S37/670.
62. Between 1933 and 1948, Yitzhak Greenbaum was a member of the Zionist Executive and the Jewish Agency Executive. A member of the Mapam party, he was also the first Secretary of State in the Provisional Government.
63. 'Tel Aviv Accompanies its Daughters to the Army Camp' (press release), March 1942, CZA, S37/674.
64. Rachel Adiv, 'Soldiers' Study Day', *Davar Hapo'elet*, 8–9 (26 September 1944), p.141.
65. Tamar Shechter, 'Rachel Katznelson Shazar: Biography of Cultural Revolutionary' (PhD thesis, Bar Ilan University, 2004), p.322. On *Davar Hapo'elet*, see also Margalit Stern, *Geula bekvalim*, pp.156–71.
66. Margalit Stern, *Ibid.*, p.157.
67. The first reference to the issue appeared in issue number 10–9, 4 July 1941 (about five and a half months before the official notice). An article titled 'Society and the [female] Volunteers' that summed up the members' meetings in Nahalal and Petah Tikva, raised for first time the matter of recruitment (among other things).
68. In her book Habas pointed out that the speech increased motivation to volunteer for service and recalled that women and girls who listened to it cut it out of the magazine and kept it as souvenir. Bracha Habas, *Bnot hayil: sefer ha'ATS* [Women of valor: book of the ATS] (Tel Aviv 1964), pp.26–32.
69. It is possible that the magazine was not published during most of the war period because of budget problems caused by its relatively extravagant format. *Davar Hapo'elet* received financial support from the Histadrut throughout the period.
70. *Davar Hapo'elet*, 7–8 (31 August 1942), p.95.
71. 'We are Paying our Debts', *Olam Ha'isha* (28 September 1942), p.2.
72. 'From the Diary of the WWC', *Davar Hapo'elet*, 10–9 (30 September 1942), p.28.
73. Tabenkin may have been hinting at Esther, the Jewish woman who according to legend married Kazimiz the Great, King of Poland, in the fifteenth century, and estranged herself from her people, or to the Biblical Esther, who was Hadassah (Samuel).
74. UKM Council in Yagur, 6–7 February 1942, p.30, Israel Defense Forces (IDF) Archive, Tel Hashomer, 45/140/2002. Tabenkin seems to have been expressing the sentiments of other men in the Yishuv, like the worker in the Statistics Department in a large town who thought 'the WWC "damages" family life and [urges] women to revolt against their husbands by teaching them to go out to work ... and is thus responsible for a high divorce rate in the Yishuv'. Ya'akov Margalit (ed.), *Bayit bamoshav: haverot mesaprot* [A home on the moshav: women members recall] (Tel Aviv 1962), p.140.
75. Daphna Izraeli, 'Tenu'at ha-Po'alot be-Eretz Yisra'el mi-Reishitah ve-Ad 1927' [The women's labour movement in Eretz Israel from its beginnings until 1927], *Katedra*, 56 (1984), p.110. The Working Women's movement's disregard for the issue of releasing women from work at this time resulted from the concept that equality with men was obvious, both from the fact that building the national

enterprise stood above all else and because they believed that when solutions were found for the problems of the new society in general, the issue of women would also be solved. Yonit Ephron, 'Ahayot, lohamot, imahot: ethos umeziot bemivhan bnot dor 1948' [Sisters, fighters, mothers: ethos and reality in the test of the 1948 generation of women], *I'yunim Be Tekumat Israel*, 10 (2000), p.355.

76. Katznelson-Shazar counted the WWC and the CWO as separate entities, even though the WWC had been a part of the CWO since 1936.
77. Rachel Katznelson-Shazar, UKM Council in Yagur, 6–7 February 1942, p.43, IDF Archive, 45/140/2002.
78. Interview with Hadassah Samuel, p.12. In her correspondence with the British army, Samuel pointed out that the Political Department was involved.
79. The CWO maintained contact with recruits who served in the ATS as well as those in the WAAF. The resources allocated to various activities devoted to their welfare during the war are testimony of the importance attached to these connections. The money was spent on staff salaries and equipment for soldiers' hostels (largest outlay), gifts to military units, driving courses, cultural activities, visits to camps, etc. In the period between April 1942 and April 1944, 3,818,496 Palestine Lira were spent on these activities. Minutes of CWO meeting, 27 June 1944, CZA, F49/2105.
80. The CWO paid Adiv's salary and the Soldier's Welfare Committee agreed to pay for activities in and out of the camps. Letter from the General Secretary of the Jewish Soldiers' Welfare Committee to the Secretary of the CWO (addressed to Idelson), 16 December 1943, Labour Movement Archive, IV-230-6.
81. Minutes of CWO secretariat, 12 August 1942, p.2, CZA, F49/2105.
82. The Soldiers' Welfare Committee, too, was recognized as a welfare organization by the British army. It was in fact the reason for establishing the Jewish Soldiers' Welfare Committee. The 'Liaison Office' was established in June 1941 and was a special department of the Histadrut Executive. The objective of the Office was to care for recruits who were also Histadrut members. Later, the Office, headed by Baratz, came to the conclusion that there should be no distinguishing between members or non-members of the Histadrut. Thus the Office joined in activities of the Soldiers' Welfare Committee that acted on behalf of all the recruits. Ze'ev Sheffer (ed.), *Sefer Hahitnadvut: Parashat Hahitnadvut hatzvait shel yehudei Eretz Israel Be'milhemet ha'olam hashniyat* [Book of volunteering: the case of military volunteering of Eretz Israel Jews in the Second World War] (Jerusalem 1949), pp.438–9.

2

Dissent in the Yishuv over the Conscription of Women

The military conscription of women undermined somewhat the conventional concepts of army and war. The determination of women to enlist challenged, whether deliberately or inadvertently, the accepted concepts of women's place in society. The opposition was directed mainly at what men designated to be their biological and sociological task in building the nation. Female conscription in the colonial British forces created a unique situation that forced the gender-nationality issue to face special challenges.[1]

Moshe Sharett, who sported female conscription as soon as negotiations had ripened with the British army, was aware of the new challenge. In a lecture to the WWC in April 1942, he said, 'The act [female conscription] is daring, there is a novelty to it ... we have never experienced women soldiers and this is frightening, and it is no wonder that many recoil at the thought of this jump into the unknown.' Nonetheless, he was sure that 'the decision has to come by way of the act'.[2]

The decision on female conscription opened a Pandora's Box of responses, fears and suspicions. Some of the claims were rational, some were emotional; there were those that were based on the prejudicial and patriarchal thoughts prevalent in the Yishuv. This chapter will discuss with a plethora of opinions, people and groups who expressed them and will try to examine their reasoning from aspects of gender, society and religion.

Numerous Hurdles

In any country the conscription of women into an army has to overcome social, psychological and 'moral' hurdles. Mania Shohat, one of the founders of the 'Hashomer' organization, spoke about an inherent psychological barrier in women, who have internalized the concept that a woman's place is at home. According to Shohat,

> One hurdle [to female conscription] is psychological-historical: deeply rooted in the habit that a woman has to stay at home. [We] need to fight against this psychology. It's true that women are afraid to undertake this new role of participating in the war. This fear is based on being unaccustomed to this role and ways must be sought in order to overcome it.[3]

Such opinions were common to many societies.

It would appear that where the conscription of Yishuv women was concerned, the obstacles were more numerous, both because of the unique character of their national struggle (Yishuv vis-à-vis the British) and because it was a case of Jewish women serving in a foreign army. Sharett was sure that 'in the case of women there was disbelief. There is disbelief first and foremost as to whether a woman can be a soldier. There is disbelief a second time as to whether the Jewish woman is the same as all women in this respect under her unique circumstances.'[4] Cartoons published in the Yishuv depicting images of the recruits were a 'means for attacking' those who shirked military service, but they also expressed traditional fears of the newly created situation: a gender revolution in women enlisted in the military, while some men remain at home.[5]

The fears voiced in various circles in the Yishuv were subsequently expressed in diverse forms in writing, including satirical. Even before female conscription in the Yishuv became operative, the matter received two public references: the first was in Lea Goldberg's ditty 'Stand to Attention!' which she wrote as part of the play For She Will go to War and performed by the Matateh Theatre in late 1939. Thus, according to Goldberg: 'Once there were male soldiers here, now there are also female soldiers', and: 'Heroism does not depend on beauty and gender, look right, then march forward, since the days of the prophet Deborah we are heroines, stand to attention! Forward march!'[6] An additional reference appeared in a notice published by the *Davar* daily in support of the conscription of the Hebrew woman in the war effort, even before its official publication.[7]

On the day the announcement was made of female conscription to the ATS, *Yediot Ahronot* published a personal column in which the author referred to the issue of military conscription for married women. The writer went so far as to point out that 'the impression is

that most of the recruits will be married, so as to prove who wears the trousers!'[8] On that same day, Natan Alterman published a satirical poem in *Davar* under the title, 'Territorial Auxiliary Service'. About three months later, the Matateh Theatre performed the satirical play, Woman of Valor, which ridiculed the exchange of roles created in the home as a result of the woman of the house deciding to enlist.[9]

Reservations regarding female conscription were not restricted solely to the Yishuv. As already mentioned, female conscription to the US military was accompanied by hostile public opinion. In Britain, too, there was a public outcry when in December 1940, National Service Law Number 2 was presented to Parliament. The law was passed in April 1941, but was not implemented until August. Moreover, a special committee was established in order to examine service and welfare conditions in the three military branches in which women were in service; as well as the rumours regarding the dubious 'morality' of female recruits in Britain, rumours spread mainly by British male soldiers. Violet Markham headed the committee and Dr Edith Summerskill was its main spokesperson. Only after an extensive review of the service conditions and the work of the recruits was the committee able to refute the rumours and significantly improve the public image of female conscription. Some 125,000 British women were conscripted into the army by law.[10]

After the decision had been taken, the debate for and against female conscription in the Yishuv commenced, but not in the daily newspapers or on the radio. The army had ordered the press to announce the decision on female conscription on the front pages and all the papers, apart from *Hamashkif,* also published announcements from the CWO and the national institutions calling for Yishuv women to come forward and enlist. However, the way they dealt with the issue later depended on their political affinity. Some newspapers and journals published the issue in the form of news reports, some added photographs, and there were others still who almost completely ignored it. For example, *Davar,* which represented the labour movement, followed the recruitment drive, gave it support and provided it with a platform until the war ended and the women were released from service.[11] In contrast, the Revisionist Movement's *Hamashkif* completely and consistently ignored the conscription of women issue and published nothing about it throughout its existence.[12] The women's press provided the issue an important platform and in the children's paper *Davar Leyeladim*, it was emphasized as being a significant contribution to the war effort, as the editors wished to prepare their young readers for the recruitment of their mothers and sisters and for the expected change in their lives, and explained the need to volunteer even though it was not mandatory, because this was a war against a terrible enemy who threatened to destroy all of mankind.[13]

Arguments and demands for and against conscription were voiced in closed forums: party circles, the kibbutz movements – in the United Kibbutz Movement and the Hakibbutz Ha'artzi – in the Mapai center and in the Jewish Agency Executive, in the Labour Federation and in the Histadtrut Council, which, during the period discussed in this book, were the centres of power in the decision making processes of the 'organized Yishuv'.[14] Decisions reached by the organizations were published in journals, movement magazines and in newspapers identified with political parties or the various youth movements. Debates over whether is was appropriate to approve female recruitment to the British forces were based on a variety of aspects: women's employment in the military; concern over the respect and 'morality' of the recruited women; the potential harm caused by the recruitment to the Yishuv's economy and military forces; potential damage or improvement to women's status in Yishuv society, etc. The questionable absence in the daily papers of editorials on the various aspects of female recruitment, even if only because male voluntary recruitment or conscription in the Yishuv generally, and the matter of draft dodging in particular, attracted broad media coverage in the form of announcements, articles and editorial opinions, may testify to the ideological and polemical struggle with the issue. It would appear that the absence of ideological reference on the part of the daily press to the recruitment of women shows that the matter was on the fringes of the Yishuv's social-ideological experience.

Beginning in May 1941, the Yishuv institutions made attempts to instil order into the voluntary recruitment regime by way of a military draft in the course of which they located a potential pool of some 20,000 men and women for whom the draft was relevant. In June 1942 an extensive draft policy was decided upon with the publication of the 'Yishuv Mobilization Order', issued by the Jewish Agency and the National Council, making it mandatory to enlist in the army based on recruits' age and marital status.[15] The call was sent out to all men and women between the ages of 20 and 40. The women recruiters and organizations demanded that all women in the Yishuv who filled the defined criteria should be obliged to enlist, as were their male counterparts. But the national institutions rejected this demand. The recruiters felt that there was insufficient respect for female recruitment and that on a 'mandatory' order could ensure the recruitment of all the thousands of women who had not contributed to the war effort.[16]

On 4 December 1942 another order was published clarifying the one issued six months earlier. However, the wording was not to the liking of the CWO and the recruiters, whose members had hoped for an unequivocal recruitment order for female recruitment. The order stated, among other things that 'among the women *required especially* to volunteer for the army are those aged between 20 and 30, either single, or married without children' [author's emphasis]. The significance of the wording of this draft is that, unlike that for male recruitment, the Yishuv institutions merely recommended female recruitment, but did not make it compulsory.

CWO Chairwoman Hadassah Samuel advocated issuing a compulsory recruitment order for women and was convinced that it should be expanded to also include childless married women, even though she was aware of the opposition in various Yishuv circles to recruitment of these women. She aspired for compulsory military recruitment to receive preference over the other two formations – industrial and agricultural. Beba Idelson felt the same way and the two met with Yosef Gurion from the Recruitment Centre and Dr Dov Yosef, Advisor to the Jewish Agency's Political Department as well as head of the Centre, prior to publication of the December 1942 draft order, in an attempt to change its wording. But their efforts were in vain and the order was published in its original format.

Hanna Levin, a recruitment officer in the British army and graduate of the cadre course, provided a different version. At the December 1942 meeting of the Histadrut Council, she said, 'until the [issue of] the order, we were able to go to women and appeal to their better judgment; from today we won't be able to do so, since shirkers now have an official seal of approval [because of the clause that grants exemption to any woman in essential employment]'. Levin expressed her personal disappointment at the necessity for a draft order for women, saying, 'I didn't imagine that [a woman] would come to this, that someone would have to come and tell her: fulfil your duty! ... For me this is a serious blow.'[17]

Even Sharett believed, in spite of his support for recruitment, that women should not be forced to enlist, since the status of women in Yishuv public life did not permit the imposition of draft orders, as was the case with men. In his letter to the UKM Council in Givat Brenner he explained that 'the pioneering essence and primary character of this recruitment require the personal responsibility [of women] ... this position has to serve as sufficient basis for every woman who wishes to volunteer [for military service] to come forward and do so'.[18]

Indeed, following publication of the draft order, there was a rise (albeit temporary) in female recruitment. However, alongside encouraging reports on recruitment numbers, the absence of compulsory recruitment and threats of punishment caused frustration among the recruiters and the activists and these did not stop demanding of the Yishuv institutions to introduce compulsory recruitment for women. By late 1942 it seemed to the activists that compulsory recruitment was about to become a fact, but three months later they were disappointed to learn that all the recruitment activity had brought none of the substantial results they had expected, since 'the draft order for women is too flexible and does nothing to help in female recruitment. Similarly, there is no possibility at this stage to resort to pressure.'[19]

The frustration caused by a lack of sanctions and non-compulsory recruitment for women continued throughout 1943 and resulted in a fear that female recruitment would not reach its target figure of 5,000, which Hadassah Samuel had presented to the British Army.[20] Another weighty cause for frustration among the corps was the lack of a clear message on the part of the institutions on everything concerning female recruitment and, during 1943, the recruiters continued to struggle to have this issue clarified.

Support for Recruitment

The women's organizations in the Yishuv wanted to see female military recruitment as another link in placing Yishuv women alongside the men and contributing to settlement and security. They also wished to create a feeling of equality in women with regard to their place in the Zionist enterprise, and military recruitment was conceived by them as a step on the way to that longed-for equality. Various persons in the Yishuv leadership emphasized the importance of female recruitment both to the women themselves and to the Yishuv.

Two of the more outspoken supporters of female recruitment were Moshe Sharett and Eliyahu Golomb.[21] The two were both graduates of the Herzliya High School, the first coeducational institute of its kind in the country and both appeared in various forums in the Yishuv in attempts to gain support for female recruitment. Sharett's support for female recruitment came from a perspective of women's potential contribution to the political effort involved in establishing a Zionist state. According to him, there should be no disdaining any additional expression of political and moral strength because 'the Yishuv has to have this for itself, women need this for themselves'.[22] Golomb recognized the contribution of the women recruits to the war effort and compared it to that of the men: 'the value of female recruitment and the value of male recruitment – is equal in every sense ... Women and men are full partners', he said.[23]

Others shared this approach. Yosef Baratz, for example, a founding member of Kibbutz Degania and Chairman of the Soldiers' Welfare Committee, expressed his confidence in the success of the recruitment drive and expected that 'as women have achieved success in their pioneering task in the work force, so, too, will they find their rightful place in military service'. Shlomo Lavie, who was also a member of the Second Aliyah and a founder member of Kibbutz Ein Harod, said in a conversation with recruits in Sarafend that female involvement in the war first and foremost reinforces her own self worth and 'the effectiveness of [women's] contribution is certainly no smaller than ours'.[24]

Dr David Santor, the representative of the non-Zionists in the Jewish Agency Executive, had a different take on the contribution of women to the war. His position reflected his gender-based concept of women in society, according to which 'the Jewish woman can play very important roles in those professions *most suitable to women*' [author's emphasis]. This conforms with Joan Nagel, who found that 'the presence of women in blatantly male institutions such as the military or government is not usually welcomed, unless they fill auxiliary positions [such as those of] secretary, lover, woman'.[25]

In Favour of Recruitment

As already mentioned, from the earliest stages of the enterprise, when it appeared that female recruitment was a fait accompli, it was presented by the Working Women's Council as a test of women's future status in the Yishuv. The Council wanted to see as many as possible Histadrut members and members of the women's labour movement serving as 'soldiers' in women's struggle that was destined to be renewed when the war was over.

At the February 1942 UKM Council in Yagur, Rachel Katznelson-Shazar emphasized the approach of the Working Women's Council vis-à-vis female recruitment, although she was opposed to including women in a military organization. She said 'this recruitment determines the issue of working women in the country, the issue of women in the Yishuv. I am very well aware of this. In this I haven't the shadow of a doubt.'[26] A few months later, Katznelson-Shazar published a call in *Davar Hapo'elet* for the movement's members to enlist, reasoning that, 'there is a need for those who can create from the battalion of Hebrew women something for the future, so that the recruitment of the Hebrew woman does not remain only an event that came and passed by, leaving nothing behind'.[27]

Sharett, too, believed that recruitment would affect the status of women in the Yishuv. According to him,

> the strengths that she [the recruit] would obtain through facing this test – she will turn them into the property of the female community, the property of the [women] in Eretz Israel, the property of the working woman, the property of the mother, the property of the sister. The significance of this recruitment is ... withstanding the test of pioneering ... and withstanding the test of the Zionist recognition and reinforcing our Zionist strength for the days to come.

He also believed that woman's involvement in the war would help women in achieving civil equality.[28]

Thus women and men alike wished to see in the act of recruitment a step on the way to the longed-for equality of the sexes, even though it was quite clear to them that women were required to go a considerable way further before it was achieved. In a speech before the Working Women's congress in February 1942, Sharett presented female recruitment in this light when he said, 'equality between men and women is in fact dependent on women's enlistment'. Nonetheless, he added that 'equality cannot remain a given, and even to the extent that it can be a given, it is still not a given fact ... there is still great scope here for a war to be overcome, not only for our [sic] woman, but for the woman in the world'.[29] Shoshana Finkelstein of the UKM, for example, was aware of this concept when she said, 'they [the female kibbutz members who enlisted in the army] are setting out to defend together with the men, out of a *sense of equality*. But I wish to warn you: for this "togetherness" they will have to fight. It will not be granted them "in any case".'[30] [author's emphasis]

One of the more interesting claims raised with regard to women's military service is that it is a gauge of the 'enlightenment' of the society that allows it. Whoever presented this approach compared the Yishuv with other, less enlightened, societies that had still not internalized the concept that women can serve in the military. Nonetheless, it is possible to see in this a patronizing, 'tap on the back' approach on the part of men, for 'allowing' women to volunteer to serve their country.

In the same speech to the Working Women's congress, Sharett addressed the issue at hand – woman's place in human society at war and among our fighting nation – 'is not the concern of women alone, but a test for all'. Samuel, chairwoman of the CWO, felt that the fact that Yishuv women were being enlisted as truck drivers testified to 'an openness on the part of Yishuv society to new ideas such as women-soldiers, whereas in neighbouring countries in the Middle East, women's military recruitment arouses disapproval, especially [when they are] drivers'.[31]

In the fifth Histadrut congress that took place in April 1942, Sharett stressed this approach with the intention of showing that Yishuv society was more 'enlightened' on the matter of female recruitment than other societies. In response to the opposition, he said, 'there are weaker positions, there are weaker nations, who do not permit women to don uniforms and usually say: a woman's place is in the home ... but we cannot say: no'.[32] At the UKM congress in Yagur, Golomb claimed that female recruitment testifies to the social level in the Yishuv, since 'if this war requires a different cultural level of the fighting man and of the fighting unit – here, the Jewish Yishuv is equipped with this cultural level' (sic), and 'in the recruitment of [female kibbutz members] there has been discovered a certain measure of the excessive strength of the Yishuv'.[33]

Against Recruitment

At a lecture to the female forum of the Kibbutz Ha'artzi, the speaker – it is safe to assume that this was Ya'akov Riftin – presented the issue of female recruitment and objections to it as an attempt to 'defend' women against further enslavement. In this, he appears to have been expressing a defensive-patriarchal approach that wishes ostensibly to help women, while actually perpetuating their inferiority. Riftin was saying that female recruitment does not indicate women's involvement or social progress; on the contrary, in socialist terms it testifies to enslavement and 'regression' in women's status, since military service in a possessive regime is an element in enslavement and working women are sufficiently enslaved even without the army. Thus, he claimed, the involvement of women in wars should not be interpreted as an expression of progress and 'every fighting woman should not automatically be seen as an achievement for the progressive women's movement'.[34] Bat-Sheva Haikin of the UKM, too, believed that not only would female recruitment fail to advance the cause of women's status in society, it would cause a regression due to the kind of positions women would be required to fill in the military: 'from the aspect of women's status in society, I don't see in [female recruitment] a rise for my society', and 'military service constitutes a social regression to a very large extent. I respect someone who takes good care of an invalid, or a good storekeeper. But I have never agreed that this should be woman's only task in society.'[35]

In Defense of the Jewish Woman's Honour

In his song 'Women on Guard', from the musical Woman of Valor, Alterman wrote: 'If the woman stands on guard/what's needed of course is a guard for the woman.' Theoreticians of nationalism had already discussed the tendency of nationalists to compare the nation to a family unit with a man at its head, and in which both man and woman have 'natural' tasks that they are required to fulfil. Thus, as the women in a family have to defend their honour and in doing so, also that of the entire family, so on a national level, the woman is supposed to protect her honour, or have a man to protect it, so that national honour comes to no harm.[36]

The claim to having to protect the honour of a woman as an excuse against female military recruitment was discussed in equal measure in religious and secular circles. The male-patriarchal outlook, according to which it is a man's duty to safeguard the honour of a woman, crossed boundaries and worldviews and united groups, although each such group had its own reasons. In early 1943 the Po'el Mizrahi announced its negative stance toward female military recruitment. Nonetheless, it demanded the recruitment of women to the religious farms and to any other service for the benefit of the war effort. Hatzofe, the Po'el Mizrahi newspaper, also provided a platform for the movement's position.

Most interesting was the rationale of the socialist leaders of labour organizations, who opposed female recruitment on behalf of protecting the honour of Jewish women. The idea of their serving in a foreign army released in Yitzhak Tabenkin, who was among the leaders of the United Kibbutz Movement and one of the movement's leading intellectuals, a deeply rooted fear, memories of the violation of Jewish women's honour in the pogroms of eastern Europe: 'I want to hear the voice of the Jewish woman's blood who knows what a gentile soldier means to a Zhidovochka [slanderous name for a Jewish woman...] the woman in the forests of the Ukraine and the forests of Poland knew what it was like when armies came and armies went ... and there was something fateful about Hebrew women'.[37] According to Tabenkin, even if the chances of his fears being realized were small, because of the ingrained fear in the hearts of Jewish men, there is still reason enough to negate female military recruitment, without having to be ashamed for being 'concerned': 'It is possible that if only one percent of my fear is realized', he said, 'but that one percent has roots that are so deep and so important as to allow it to appear *without need for me to feel shame*' [author's emphasis].[38]

Tabenkin was not the first to liken the female image to a symbol of victimhood. A familiar phenomenon in wars was that the longer the fighting continued, the more intense becomes the process of sexualizing in the national discourse – i.e. the physical/sexual danger to women. The woman symbolizes the nation and any threat to her – whether real or imagined – serves as an example of a threat to the nation in its entirety. Tabenkin probably was over reacting when he adopted the echoes of the pogroms in Eastern Europe to reinforce his claims, but he was not alone in doing so. Others in the Yishuv exploited the image of the Jewish woman as a sex victim. According to Billy Mellman, toward the end of the First World War the symbolism of the violent soldier/torturer and the Jewish woman as the tortured victim was copied from the pogrom-ridden Eastern European reality to the reality of the Middle East, and the familiar motifs of torture and affronts to female honour were translated into the language of the orient. The stereotype of the torturer – the Kazak – was copied on to the Eastern-Moslem male and the stereotype of the Jewish woman from the shtetl in the Pale of Settlement was copied on to the Modern Hebrew woman in the Yishuv. The resulting symbolism had enormous power, since it could be attached to the historic picture of a persecuted ethnic/religious minority in times of war, such as, for example, the Armenians. During the period discussed in this book, these images were copied on to the British male/soldier and the female recruit, daughter of the Yishuv.[39]

Tabenkin expected to draw criticism for voicing his thoughts in Yagur, when he said, 'I know what kind of a name I shall have for this in the Yishuv'. And it seems this is what happened, since only months later he saw fit to clarify the meaning behind his words: 'My lack of faith is not in the Hebrew woman, but in the gentile soldier in a camp in which unarmed Jewish [women] are serving him ... *I can't believe the situation* to which the female Jewish soldiers are subjected.' [original emphasis][40] Tabenkin seems to have feared that women were incapable of defending their honour and morality and, in fact, repeated his suggestion to recruit women only to non-integrated, Jewish units.

The Kibbutz Ha'artzi, too, had members who expressed concern as to the 'personal safety and national honour' of the female recruits. Like Tabenkin they were sure that 'there was no need or right to place the women in the difficult situation of recruits in small military units, in the midst of the sea of army in the Middle East'. Shlomo Lavie, too, used a patriarchal patronizing tone in expressing his wish to defend women's honour and in doing so, the national honour, as well. In an address to the soldiers in Sarafend, he said 'Many of the allies in this war, who are not of our nation, wish to see in these sisters of ours no more than candidates for a life of debauchery ... *If we are to know how to safeguard their honour*, if we are to know how to respect the ideas on whose wings they are borne – their honour and ours will be maintained in their entirety ... the refuse will be disposed of on its own.' [author's emphasis][41] He asked the men to defend the honour of the female soldiers and thus their own honour would be spared.

In relating to this 'concern', one of the female soldiers said: 'After all, with so much of this attitude, you are less concerned for women, than bringing upon them derision. You should know, all you undecided, that the daughter of Israel has self-respect. She knows why she is going to the army.' An older recruit, mother to a recruited daughter, said that if she had feared for her morality, she would 'not have been sending her only daughter to the army'.[42] Hayuta Bussel, member of the Second Aliyah, reacted to the men's 'concern' by saying, 'I was always suspicious of this supervision, this idea of [men] taking upon themselves the role of special protector of society. I have always believed that this role was best left in the hands of women.'[43]

The debate surrounding the 'concern' for the 'honour' of the female recruits brings to mind the debate on the exclusion of female members of the Palmach from the fighting in the War of Independence, even though some of them had participated in operational courses and filled operational functions. Slogans such as 'if a girl [sic] should be injured, we'll be obliged to invest efforts and resources to rescue her', and 'how will she behave', 'how will she cope', etc. served those who opposed female participation in the war effort.[44]

The Moral Aspect

The Yishuv's discourse against the recruitment of women included an obvious fear of the Yishuv having no control over recruits of 'dubious quality', or that some of the female recruits would be unable to withstand the daily contact with non-Jewish soldiers. There was also a suspicion as to unseemly behaviour of British soldiers toward the female recruits from Yishuv. Thus, for example, at a meeting between Dr Dov Yosef and General Macandlish, the two discussed the possibility of posting Hebrew soldiers at the relaxation camp in Netanya, and Yosef expressed reservations on 'moral grounds'.[45]

Like the debates over upholding women's honour, so also was the moral issue discussed by religious and secular men alike. Both groups expressed male patronage over women and a desire to control their morality. In religious Zionist circles claims were voiced to the tune of 'the movement cannot accept responsibility for its female members who [volunteer for] military service' and that women should not be recruited since '[all] women are frivolous of mind'. The religious Zionist movement rejected the military recruitment of religious women, especially the younger ones among them, in the belief that a military structure was 'too harsh a framework to cope with'.[46] Even Tova Sanhedrai, chairwoman of the Working Women's Council in Hapo'el Hamizrahi, adopted the proposal to oppose female recruitment on moral grounds. She was at one with the decision 'that was also reached by me. There are many other areas in which we can act.'[47] However, other voices were also heard in Hapo'el Hamizrahi and some people were sure of the ability of religious women to withstand the army, 'since it is the duty of our members not to assimilate and not to be ruined'.[48]

When he came to explain his objection to female military recruitment, Dr Yosef referred to the 'dubious' image of the ATS battalions. First he described their image in the First World War and said, 'I would not have allowed my [own] daughter to enlist'. He added that in the current war, too, before the recruitment law was passed in the British Parliament, 'tens of thousands of girls were recruited who until then had been unemployed' and preferred that from the Yishuv the female recruits would be 'frequenters of cafés and not girls who work the land ... [in order] to scrub hospital floors'.[49]

The Jewish Agency and the Haganah wished to have control over the 'quality' of the recruits in general and of the participants of the first cadre course in particular. The participants of the cadre course were entrusted with forming the 'moral' image of the ATS companies. But it seems that the women, too, especially members of the Haganah and leading activists in the women's organizations, 'internalized' the male fears with regard to the recruits' 'moral fibre'. When Idelson and Shulamit Klinbanov chose the Haganah members for the cadre, they were accompanied by 'many doubts and not with regard to the necessity of this, but how and in what way we could preserve our feminine and Jewish identity in the midst of a foreign army.' Claire Epstein, one of the participants in the cadre, wrote that 'the soldiers' ranks require not only good professional levels, but also choice human material that will know how to withstand the harsh existence of Jews in the British army and the special existence of Jewish women in the British army'.[50] At the UKM Council in Yagur, too, Kibbutz Ein Harod member Ruth Haktin, member of the Working Women's Council, asked that control be maintained over the quality of the recruits and said, 'we have to allow a woman to go who has to go, *a woman who suits* this recruitment ... not anyone can go join this recruitment, only people of the highest quality' [author's emphasis].[51]

Sharett was aware of all these doubts and tried to dismiss them at every forum he attended. On his opinions about the inability of the Jewish girl to protect her honour, he said that there are all kinds of women, as there are all kinds of men and that there are 'in our population iniquities, too'. He made it clear to his audiences that the recruitment could not be prevented because of these, as immigration to the Yishuv could not have been prevented because it also included negative elements.[52]

The Moral Aspect as Reflected in Research

The 'dubious' reputations women were given when in the vicinity of male soldiers appears to have developed largely during the eighteenth century, at a time when 'camp followers' became a prominent phenomenon, with women attaching themselves to the British army at times of war with France and India (1755–65). These women remained close to the battlefront and were with the fighting forces not as fighters but as wives, sisters and lady friends, and sometimes as prostitutes. They accompanied the soldiers, lived inside or near the camps and helped raise the morale of the soldiers. Military authorities encouraged these women, whose presence lightened the lives of the soldiers.[53]

Researchers on gender indicate that in the middle of a national struggle, women are required to defend higher moral standards than men. Nira Yuval-Davis points at several tasks imposed on women in national struggles that defined the nation's boundaries. Women are required, among other things, to protect the boundaries of their nation's honour in everything concerning culture and sexuality and to define them in a way that includes relationships with people outside of the national collective that threaten the nation's unity. According to Sheila Katz, the growth of a nation and international conflicts depend almost entirely on some kind of male dominance over women and the view of women as a symbol. Some researchers have compared the female situation to that of nations under colonial rule, through the use of the term 'rape'. Just as the conquering male exploits a woman's body in a war, so also are peoples' national resources exploited in order to benefit the conquering nation.[54]

In the Yishuv, too, women's morality was connected to the national struggle and their military recruitment did not constitute the first time in which Yishuv women were required to mark out the national boundaries by means of their bodies and sexuality.[55] The secular outlook was certainly able to distinguish between prostitutes who provide sexual services in return for money and women who dated British men and sometimes even developed relationships that led to marriage. But it appears that from the national perspective, the secular attitude was not very different from that of the religious one and the nationalist-secular viewpoint did not distinguish between prostitution and intimate relations with British men: women who dated men outside the national collective were referred to as 'whores', suffered from absolute exclusion and in certain cases even experienced violence.[56]

The defence of the boundaries of the national collective sets female sexuality not only as a definer of the 'moral' and 'immoral', but also of the actual boundaries of the collective. Identifying female sexuality with the collective, with its boundaries and with its purity, places women in the position of gatekeepers, as standing on guard, but no less than this – as threatening. They have the power to reinforce and they have the power to undermine. Their status as setting the boundaries enhances their power, but also requires of them to be under supervision and control.[57]

The Markham and Summerskill Committee was established, as already mentioned, in Britain in order to conduct an investigation of service women's moral conduct. Only after extensive examination was the committee able to disprove rumours of drunkenness and promiscuity and to significantly raise the service women's public image.[58] In the United States, too, the recruitment of women to the military was accompanied by hostile public opinion, and gender and sexual stereotyping hindered the rate of enlistment. There, the general public saw female recruits as 'lesbians' and 'whores', and even male recruits objected to women in the army, for fear of their liberal behaviour.

Chauffeurs to Officers

One of the issues that aroused considerable concern in the Yishuv was the moral aspect of the fact that female recruits from the Yishuv were going to serve as private drivers to British officers. Opposition to this was based on the fear of sexual exploitation and improper behaviour toward women.[59] The subject continued to be raised at different forums and discussed with the military authorities.

At a debate on this matter that took place in the Recruitment Department, Samuel reported that Chitty, ATS Commander in the Middle East, had agreed to arrange for women to be appointed to this position only on rare occasions (Chitty, too, was probably aware of the image of woman-driver prevalent among the Moslem community of the Middle East). At the same meeting, Moshe Sneh (Kleinbaum), National Haganah HQ Commander, proposed recruiting women through the Jewish Agency and not sending them to work as officers' drivers. Even the representatives of the Working Women rejected this possibility 'even when it only involves fulfilling military roles'. Samuel replied that it might harm the entire recruitment issue if the Jewish Agency were to issue such a declaration, since 'then the girls they'll take are not of ours [not from the organized Yishuv] but 'wayward' girls and this will be even worse'. She thought it was better to cooperate with the army over this matter, but also to 'be constantly aware [in order to ensure that the drivers do not get a bad name]'.[60]

Ya'akov Hazan, too, as well as other members of Hakibutz Ha'arzi were opposed to the army employing Jewish soldiers as drivers to British officers, because of their objection in principle to recruiting women to jobs that appeared to them to be of 'low rank' and meant for 'natives'. They saw in this an attempt to humiliate the soldiers from Palestine, 'humiliation that was both national and political'.[61] However it would appear that this approach had no foundation, since the majority of jobs offered to recruits from the Yishuv were the same as those filled by British servicewomen, both in the UK and abroad.

Dr Santor objected to women working as drivers in general and especially as personal drivers to officers and demanded that 'only men should go to the battlefront and [the army] should deal with the matter of female drivers in such places as there is no real danger', and that 'there is no such need for the Jewish woman'.[62] Sharett tried to refute the claims regarding the potential dangers of promiscuity and said that it depended on the woman herself, on the living and service conditions and anyway, 'the English army is quite conservative and quite strict on these matters ... on no account will [they] agree to any female soldier, in whatever job, sleeping separately'.[63]

Rumours of Immoral Conduct

During the first year of their service and even later, the female recruits from the Yishuv were obliged to fight against the lies spread about them by their male counterparts, especially those serving in Egypt.[64] Sharett excelled in his ironic 'analysis' of the source of these rumours: 'the antagonism toward female recruitment on the part of Jewish soldiers doesn't come from their having any special kind of expertise on the matter, but from their fears, as men, of women serving at all'. Even the editor of the Book of Haganah admitted, 'this slander is deeply rooted in ... the habit of being more forgiving toward male behaviour than that of women'.[65]

The rumours being spread by soldiers were not only characteristic toward recruits from Palestine. Throughout 1942, the ATS commanders in the Middle East, led by Audrey Chitty, were obliged to deal with rumours regarding the inferior 'morals' of the ATS soldiers in the region. A proposal was raised at a meeting of the ATS command to cooperate with the military authorities in order to change the attitude of male to female soldiers and focus on the women's hard work and valuable contribution to the war effort. Even two years later, Leslie Whateley, ATS Director in the UK, was required to deal with the issue. At meetings with army commanders in Cairo, she discussed the troublesome rumours regarding the dubious morals of ATS servicewomen in the Middle East.[66]

The rumours reached the ears of persons and groups in the Yishuv, and the Jewish Agency tried to fight against them.[67] One of the bodies dealing with these rumours was the 'Committee for the Defence of the Honour of the Daughter of Israel in Tel Aviv', which was established in 1942 in Tel Aviv under the auspices of, and on the initiative of, the Chief Rabbinate and consisted of public figures.[68] The committee devoted a number of meetings to the 'morality' of the servicewomen. Thus, for example, Rabbi Meir Uziel, Chairman of the Rabbis' Union in Tel Aviv, reported on 'rumours' of a 'Jewish servicewomen employed as a servant to officers; quarrels and fights between Jewish and non-Jewish servicemen over servicewomen out of jealousy; 200 servicewomen who are incapable of serving in the army for reasons of morality and of dozens of servicewomen who returned to their homes in a condition of pregnancy [sic]'. Rabbi Professor David Prato proposed appointing a female 'Commander of Morality' over the servicewomen, in the style of the Military Rabbis. The meeting concluded with a decision for representatives of the committee to meet with Hadassah Samuel to discuss the problem with her. Attorney Tehilla Matmon, daughter-in-law of Yehuda Leib and Fanya Matmon Cohen, reported on the 'improper behaviour of servicewomen as a result of their living conditions and on instances of servicewomen being released from duty because of promiscuity'.[69]

Army rabbis, too, were aware of the source of the rumours spread about the servicewomen. Chief Rabbi Isaac Levy wrote in his memoires that 'dreadful stories were spread by word of mouth' about servicewomen being exposed to horrors because of ties with British officers, or that they would have to fill posts that were unsuitable to 'decent Jewish girls'. 'The source of the rumours was of course proven to be unsubstantiated', wrote the rabbi, 'some of the Yishuv servicemen considered their countrywomen to be their private property and were unwilling to come to terms with ... being rejected by [them]'.[70]

The rumours angered the servicewomen and other women in the Yishuv and they reacted in various ways. In many cases, they resorted to a measure of apology when explaining that they really were working hard, preserving their dignity and the dignity of the nation and that the rumours were totally unjustified. Even in the years following, the rumours did not cease altogether. In late 1943 an anonymous soldier was asked to defend the honour of a Jewish servicewoman when he wrote,

> a poisonous atmosphere is forming around the servicewoman ... and most shameful [is the fact] that the accusations and complaints against the Jewish servicewomen and her behaviour are coming from ... the kind of servicemen who unashamedly frequent brothels and are awash with a lasciviousness that is not in the least 'nationalist'.[71]

Even as late at 1944, the Jewish servicewomen were required to field the rumours in the Yishuv about their dubious morals. One of the servicewomen wrote in *Davar Hapo'elet*, 'A lot of slander is being hurled at her. The great light in her volunteering is sometimes enfeebled by the appetite for gossip among those citizens, which is at times hard to explain, except as an attempt to justify themselves for having evaded fulfilling their duty.'[72]

It should be stressed that, like in other countries, the rumours that spread throughout the Yishuv were not always baseless. Notwithstanding efforts at 'sorting' the recruits at the Jewish Agency's recruitment bureaus, hundreds of women from the Yishuv were recruited through the military bureaus. Some of these were women from Yishuv society's fringes, or individuals who had worked in prostitution before enlisting and continued to do so in the army. This issue will be dealt with thoroughly later.

A Shortage of Working Hands

Opposition to female recruitment on the grounds of a workforce problem and the claim that women were needed for work in the country mainly reached from circles in the kibbutz movements, on who there had already been imposed quotas of members for the army and the Palmach. Meir Ya'ari, one of the leaders of Hashomer Hatza'ir, objected to the military recruitment of women from the Kibbutz Ha'artzi. His grounds included real concern for the fate of the kibbutzim, but no less, he harboured a fear that military service would cause a reduced birth-rate and problems in the family. In light of a shortage of some 400 workers in Hashomer Hatza'ir kibbutzim, Ya'ari said, 'We shall not be able to recruit women instead of men', and added that, 'in my opinion, the kibbutz economy requires 40% men and 60% women for the home economy and with it that huge branch that is known as children ... that's the situation, there is a shortage of women'.[73]

Mina Ben-Zvi (Rogoz'ik), who was asked to respond to this claim in the speech she delivered to the Histadrut Congress in April 1942, saw things differently. She thought that manpower problems did not have to prevent women from fulfilling their duty: 'Since when have we been relinquishing out rights? Where is the balance that we are talking about so much everywhere and at every stage? This is an historic opportunity for society.'[74]

Women's Participation in a Military Organization

One argument against the recruitment of Yishuv women was voiced, of all places, in the female camp and touched on the objection to women participating in a military organization of any kind. The argument was developed by Katznelson-Shazar, whose position on the issue of recruitment conformed with the feminist concept. She refused to impose on women the features of brutality inherent in the 'new Hebrew person' and wanted to create a unique image for the pioneer woman to accommodate feminine characteristics and tasks, which are different from those of males. Already in the course of the First World War, Katznelson-Shazar was opposed to the recruitment of women to the British army, and in the Second World War she remained faithful to her view of the place of women in a male and gender-oriented organization – in the army as in the nascent civil society. At the UKM Council in Yagur, she raised an extraordinary argument against recruitment that leant on a woman's ability and devotion:

> Here the issue of the woman has been placed in the centre ... this matter is fateful ... it is a phenomenon that crosses all nations ... and the woman receives arms and will receive arms and will participate in everything and will even excel in murder. She'll do it, too, sure, with the same loyalty and serious attitude, as with other things that she undertakes.[75]

She didn't believe that by joining the army women would achieve any kind of change in their status and that all their hopes of equality would be refuted. In her opinion, a woman has to excel in those qualities she was gifted with and not in masculine qualities.

Tabenkin summed up his negative attitude to the recruitment of the Yishuv's women by declaring: 'I consider this thing [female recruitment] to be a *mistake*. Something bad.' [author's emphasis] Other movement members, too, believed the recruitment to be a big mistake for the entire Yishuv, but were prepared to support it since 'the kibbutz does make a habit of staying alone with being right. And we are also responsible for mistakes of the country's large general public.'[76] The Revisionist Movement also objected to female military recruitment. This objection came mainly from the position of the movement's enlisted men in the army who proposed to 'come out against all the matter of the ATS, not from a moral viewpoint but from one of political futility'.[77]

The Recruit – A Proven Success

The struggle for female military recruitment, which involved many reservations and serious concerns, ultimately bore fruit: the reports on the recruits' functioning in the army, on their contribution to the fighting forces and on their attempts to maintain a Jewish culture within a military framework, changed attitudes in the Yishuv's institutions to female recruitment. Senior persons in the Yishuv gave lie to the dubious morality of the servicewomen and dispelled fears as to their chastity in the role of drivers to British officers.[78]

On the first anniversary of the ATS, Dr Yosef sent a greeting card to the servicewomen in which he wrote that 'there were many among the people of the Yishuv who doubted and were reserved as to the necessity [of female volunteering] ..., now is not the time to argue about it and ... the large majority of them completely changed their minds'.[79] Katznelson-Shazar, who had opposed the recruitment, joined its supporters after learning of its dimensions and even wondered if the servicewoman might be the 'new person' that the working women's movement had so wished for.[80]

Sharett was sure that the only gauge for the success of the female recruitment enterprise was the practical test. He seems to have been right, as the main cause for the changed attitude toward servicewomen and toward the recruitment itself was the number of recruits by the end of 1942. It was hard to ignore this statistic and the positive reports of the persons from the Yishuv who went to visit them in the army camps. Thus, female volunteering received the Yishuv's stamp of approval and this paved the way finally to making it acceptable in the eyes of different groups in Yishuv society.

NOTES

1. On the complex relationship between nationalism and national struggle and the role of women in them, see, for example, Antonio Gramsci, *On Hegemony: Selections from the Prison Notebooks* (London: Lawrence and Wishart, 1971); Nira Yuval-Davis, 'Nationalism, Feminism and Gender Relations', in Montserrat Guibernau and John Hutchinson (eds), *Understanding Nationalism* (Cambridge: Polity Press, 2001), pp.120–41; Joan Nagel, 'Masculinity and Nationalism: Gender and Sexuality in the Making of Nations', *Ethnic and Racial Studies*, 21, no.2 (1998), pp.242–70.
2. 'Recruiting the Woman', Moshe Sharett, *Davar Hapo'elet*, 3–4 (23 April 1942), p.6.
3. Shohat (1880–1961), was also active in the Haganah and represented Mapam in the Histadrut. At that meeting, she said that women had to overcome the prejudices of the soldiers themselves. As she said, one of the soldiers told his girlfriend, 'you'll have to choose between me and the mud of the ATS'. Histadrut Secretariat, 7 September 1942, p.130, Israel Defense Forces (IDF) Archive, Tel Hashomer, 45/140/2002.
4. 'Conscription of Women', Moshe Sharett, lecture, IDF Archive. Sharett repeated these thoughts in letters he sent to the UKM Council that took place in Yagur,

6–7 February 1942, which discussed female conscription, and also at the meeting of the Givat Brenner Council in April 1942. IDF Archive, 45/140/2002.

5. Yosef Bass produced most of the cartoons. Dov Shtok, 'Hakdama' [Introduction], in Yosef Bass, *Hayamim halalau...* [Those Days...] (Tel Aviv 1944), pp.3–5, p.1.
6. The ditty (words by Lea Goldberg, music by Moshe Wilensky) was written for the play, which was first performed on 7 November 1939, shortly after the start of male conscription from the Yishuv to the British army. For She Will Go To War, ICDPA (Hamileh – The Israeli Center for Documentation of Stage Arts, Tel Aviv University) 26.1.9.
7. 'Management Meeting of the Conscription Department', *Davar*, 11 February 1941, p.4.
8. 'The Notebook is Open', *Yediot Ahronot*, 24 December 1941, p.2. Two days later a humorous conversation was published between the writer, B (sic.) Amitai and his wife regarding female conscription and his agreement to her enlisting in the army. 'She Wants to Enlist', *Yediot Ahronot*, 26 December 1941, p.2.
9. The play was written by N. Yitzhak (pen name of Yitzhak Nozhik) and the ditties were written by Alterman. The play dealt with female conscription into the British forces in general and that of mothers in particular, and what happened to their husbands who stayed at home and had to fill the role of 'house husband'. The play premiered on 24 March 1942.
10. Lucy Noakes, *Women in the British Army: War and the Gentle Sex 1907–1948* (New York 2006), pp.127–8. Baroness Edith Summeskill was an MP (1938–61) active on behalf of women's rights and, as a physician and politician, pioneered the cause for combining motherhood with a career. During the Second World War she struggled to integrate women in the 'Civil Guard' and in combat roles in the military. Penny Summerfield, 'Our Amazonian Colleague: Edith Summerskill's Problematic Reputation', in Richard Toye and Julie Gottlieb (eds), *Making Reputations: Power, Persuasion and the Individual in Modern British Politics* (London 2005), pp.135–50.
11. *Davar*, the daily newspaper of the Labour Federation, whose editor was Berl Katznelson, was established in 1925. Its main focus was on labour and workers' issues from the perspective of the majority in the Histadrut. Getzel Kresel, 'Ha'itonut ha'ivrit' [Hebrew Press], *Hebrew Encyclopedia* (Tel Aviv 1957), p.1060.
12. *Hamashkif* was established in 1938 and Zeev Jabotinsky was a regular contributor to it until his death in 1940. The movement changed its attitude to conscription to one of support only in the latter part of 1942. Yoav Gelber, *Toldot hahitnadvut: Hahitnadvut ve mekoma bemidiniut hazionit ve hayishuvit 1939–1942* [History of volunteering: volunteering and its place in Zionist and Yishuv Policies 1939–1942] (Jerusalem 1989), p.243.
13. 'Hebrew Women in the Homeland', in the children's weekly publication, *Davar Layeladim*, 18 January 1942, front page. Books and newspapers for children during the 1940s took an ideological stand toward building the national dialogue and their writings conformed with the public discourse. Their commitment and direction indicate the expectations of adult members of the intermediate generation and the objectives they set themselves as teachers and formers of the future generation. Yael Dar, *Umisfsal halimudim lukahnu: hayishuv lenochach*

shoa velikrat medina besifrut hayeladim ha'eretz Israelit 1939–1948 [And from the school desks we were taken: the Yishuv in face of the Holocaust and in advance of a state in children's literature in Eretz Israel 1939–1948] (Jerusalem 2006), pp.4–5. Because of its political affiliation to the adult *Davar*, the weekly used to respond to current events and included journalistic writing (reports and announcements) and literary writing.

14. It often happened that the same people held positions in different organizations. In the course of establishing the national institutions that typified the Jewish Yishuv in general and the Labour Movement in particuluar, a complex structure of secondary centres was created, some of which overlapped or crossed each other. Dan Horowitz and Moshe Lissak, *Miyishuv lemedina: yehudei Eretz Israel betkufat hamandat habriti kekehila politit* [From Yishuv to State: Eretz Israeli Jews during the British Mandate as a political community] (Tel Aviv 1977), p.92. Most of the debates on draft orders for men and women, for example, were conducted in the Histadrut offices, mainly in its Executive Committee, where the important decisions were taken. On the decision taking process in the Yishuv during the 1940s, see for example, Uri Brenner, *Mediniut hagius bemilhemet haolam hashnia, tseva hamedina baderech: prakim betoldot koah hamagen ha'ivri* [Recruitment policies in the Second World War, the nation's army in making: chapters on the Hebrew defence force] (Tel Aviv and Ramat Efal 1988), pp.159–60.
15. This notwithstanding, the recruitment regime did not change the voluntary character of the enlistment and in fact there was no official way to impose it. The crisis in relations with the British surrounding the Spring 1943 recruitment affair (emergency regulations issued by the British that actually prevented the recruitment regime) signalled the beginning of the end of volunteer recruitment, which indeed was not subsequently reinstated to any significant extent. Draft had been a side effect of volunteering, especially after attempts to impose the recruitment regime. Social and moral pressure was placed on the shirkers, who were referred to in derogatory terms. Gelber, *Toldot hahitnadvut*, p.434.
16. Sonya Idelberg, 'The Hebrew Woman in World War Two' (undated), p.5, Haganah History Archive, Tel Aviv (HHA), 3.19. Representatives of the CWO met with the Jewish Agency's Security Committee at a meeting in which the women demanded that the Jewish Agency issue a compulsory draft for women. According to a report at a meeting of the CWO secretariat from 13 October 1942, only Dr Emil Shmorek and Ya'akov Riftin were against a compulsory draft (Riftin also demanded a compulsory draft for women to enlist in Haganah). Minutes of CWO, 13 October 1942, Central Zionist Archive, Jerusalem (CZA), F49/2105.
17. Hanna Levin at the Histadrut Council, 2–3 December 1942, pp.61–2, Labour Movement Archive, Lavon Institute.
18. From Moshe Sharett to the UKM Council in Yagur, 6 February 1942, p.5, IDF Archive, 45/140/2002.
19. Minutes of conversation of recruitment activists in Tel Aviv, 14 February 1943, p.1, HHA, 33/4. The Working Women's Council expressed disappointment at the additional order issued on 4 December 1942 and claimed that 'it is still not sufficient, that it's working has to be clearer, more committal. Nonetheless, it takes a further step toward recognizing the civil duty of the Yishuv woman ...

the CWO must devote itself from now on to realizing this demand.' *Davar Hapo'elet*, 11–12 (10 December 1942) p.143.

20. Shohat, for example, recalled speaking in front of 300 women who did not wish to enlist and summed up that the 'situation is bad. If it doesn't change we won't reach the number we set for ourselves – 5,000.' Shohat in the Histadrut Council, 7 September 1942, p.130, IDF Archive, 45/140/2002.
21. Sharett was a graduate of Herzliya High School in Tel Aviv, which, among other things, made real the vision of the 'New Hebrew Woman' (see Chapter 3). He also lived for several years in London after the First World War, became familiar with the British mentality and was exposed to the struggle of Britain's women for equal rights and social status. Interview with Ya'akov Sharett, Tel Aviv, 5 December 2006. On Sharett's stay in London see also Moshe Sharett, *Yemei London: michtavim mishnot halimudim belondon*, 1 and 2 [London days: letters from years of study in London, 1 and 2], ed. Tamar Gadron, Ya'akov Sharett and Rina Sharett (Tel Aviv 2005). Sharett also had a personal relationship with Nelly Moshinsohn, daughter of Rosa Welt Straus, who headed the Women's Union.
22. Letter from Moshe Sharett to UKM Council in Yagur, 6 February 1942, p.5, IDF Archive, 45/140/2002.
23. Eliyahu Golomb, UKM Council in Yagur, 6–7 February 1942, p.12, ibid.
24. Ze'ev Sheffer (ed.), *Sefer Hahitnadvut: Parashat Hahitnadvut hatzvait shel yehudei Eretz Israel Be'milhemet ha'olam hashniyat* [Book of volunteering: the case of military volunteering of Eretz Israel Jews in the Second World War] (Jerusalem 1949), pp.536–7.
25. Letter from David Santor to Moshe Sharett, 22 December 1941, CZA, S25/5099; Nagel, 'Masculinity and Nationalism', p.261.
26. Rachel Katznelson-Shazar, UKM Council in Yagur, 6–7 February 1942, p.45, IDF Archive, 45/140/2002.
27. R.K. (Rachel Katznelson), 'In the [female] Soldiers' Training Camp', *Davar Hapo'elet*, 6 (7 July 1942), p.78.
28. Speech by Moshe Sharett at the recruitment camp in Na'an, May 1942, p.10, United Kibbutz Movement (UKM) Archive, Yad Tabenkin, B 15.
29. 'Female Recruitment', a speech by Moshe Sharett before participants of the Working Women's Congress in Tel Aviv, *Davar Hapo'elet*, 3–4 (23 April 1942), pp.36–8.
30. 'When the Recruits Left' (parts of farewell conversation in Ein Harod), *a bundle of letters* (118) 119, 29 May 1942, p.1, UKM Archive, container 1a, file 11.
31. In a letter to Brigadier Beddington of the Military HQ in Jerusalem, Samuel confirmed that the CWO was prepared for women to serve throughout the Middle East and not only in Palestine, with the exception of those cases 'in which it would be preferable to restrict service to Eretz Israel'. She was referring to female drivers, 'whose appearance was liable to arouse offense in countries out of Eretz Israel'. Samuel to Beddington, 2 May 1941, CZA, S25/6001.
32. Moshe Sharett at the Histadrut congress, 19-23 April 1942, minutes, p.212, Labour Movement Archive.
33. Eliyahu Golomb, UKM Council in Yagur, 6–7 February 1942, p.10, IDF Archive, 45/140/2002.
34. Riftin was well known for his opinions on the Marxist attitude to women. 'On the issue of recruitment to the Auxiliary Territorial Service', meeting of the

Political Committee, undated (December 1941 or January 1942), Hashomer Hatza'ir Archive, Giv'at Haviva, F. 3. 52 20. Lydia Sargent, a Marxist-Feminist scholar, claims that Marxism is 'gender blind' as presented in Marx and Engels's 'Communist Manifest'. At best feminism is less important than the status struggle, and at worst it is derived from the working class. The Marxist ideology, she claims, doesn't differentiate enslaved men from women and they are all part of the enslaved class which needs to free itself from the yoke of capitalism. Lydia Sargent (ed.), *Women and Revolution, A Discussion of the Unhappy Marriage of Marxism and Feminism* (Cambridge 1981), p.2.

35. Bat-Sheva Haikin at a meeting of the Mapai Center, 'Female Recruitment' (segments from the archived minutes of the meeting), 8 February 1942, HHA, 16/6.

36. See, for example, Ann McClintock, 'No Longer in a Future Heaven: Women and Nationalism in South Africa', *Transition*, 51 [1991], pp.104–23. *Hahayal Ha'ivri* addressed the identification of the woman with the national honour: 'The woman is the centre of the family and thus – the centre of the nation. More than anyone else she must realize her duty to her nation and to its unity. She'll bear responsibility to educate the next generation of free people. It is worth stressing, therefore, that there's no place like the army to grant her with such experience.' N.N. [sic], 'Towards the second year of the ATS', CZA, PR 2540; *Hahayal Ha'ivri*, B ((January 29 1943), pp.6–7.

37. The extent of the emotions behind Tabenkin's approach toward the Russians is illustrated in the stories he told of his father's home: 'my hatred for the Russians received a deep and sharp emotional dimension when their gendarmes came at night and arrested my father'. Arieh Pialkov and Yosef Rabinovitz (eds), *Yitzhak Tabenkin: pirkei haim, ha'ish ve po'alo, haverim ve talmidim mesaprim, sugiot bemishnato* [Yitzhak Tabenkin: chapters from his life, the man and his activity, friends and students recall, issues in his teachings] (Ramat Efal 1982), p.18.

38. UKM Council in Yagur, 6–7 February 1942, p.30, IDF Archive, 45/140/2002. Katznelson-Shazar admitted in the course of the congress that she too had reservations with regard to female military recruitment and for the same reasons as Tabenkin, but she met many kibbutz members, including young ones, and was convinced that 'the woman does not accept that she has to defend her honour.' Ibid. Still, Tabenkin did not deny women's participation in the country's security. Tabenkin, 'Defending ourselves under our own authority', pamphlet for recruitment and for defense, May 1942, IDF Archive. According to Baruch Kinari, Tabenkin's attitude to military recruitment was 'Palastinecentrist', and that he wanted to classify the main part of service in the British army to units that would focus on defending the Yishuv and not for the sole purpose of defending its inhabitants, but also in order to establish bases in Palestine in which the refugees from Europe would be accommodated after the war. Baruch Kinari, *Tabenkin beretz Israel* [Tabenkin in Eretz Israel] (Ramat Efal 2003), pp.487–8.

39. Various national movements used femininity as a symbol of mythical, a-historic and at times passive nationalism. The presentation of women as a passive national symbol reached a peak in the First World War when women became symbols in motivating and recruiting public opinion in Western Europe. Woman as a victim was used often for propaganda purposes by all sides of the conflict. The most obvious example of this sexualizing the national discourse, according

to Melman, was in the presentation of Belgian women as a symbol of the defeated Belgian nation that served as a central motif in British propaganda on the matter of the horrors committed by the Germans in Belgium. Billie Melman, 'Min ha-shulayim el ha-historiyah shel ha-Yishuv: Migdar ve-eretz yisre'eliyut (1890–1920)' [From the periphery to the center of Yishuv history: gender and nationalism in Eretz Israel (1890–1920)], Zion 62, no.3 (1997), p.371.

40. Tabenkin, 'Defending Ourselves', To Enlisting and to Defense, May 1942, p.16, HHA, 304/80P/3.
41. Sheffer (ed.), *Sefer Hahitnadvut*, pp.536–7.
42. 'Proposal for a female volunteer to speak in cinemas, theaters, etc. on Tel-Hai Day', 27 February 1942, CZA, S37/676; Hayuta Bussel, at the Histadrut Council in Petah Tikva, 26 May 1942, p.50, IDF Archive, 45/140/2002; 'Industrial female workers actions for volunteering to the auxiliary services – mass rallies in factories in Tel Aviv and its surrounds', 29 April 1942, CZA, S37/670.
43. Hayuta Bussel at the Histadrut Council in Petah Tikva, 26 May 1942, p.50, IDF Archive, 45/140/2002.
44. Ofra Elad, '"Kol bahur ve tov laneshek, bahura al hamismar!": Ha'havera ba'Palmach' [Every man is good for arms, a woman, on guard duty! Woman Member in the Palmach], in Yehiam Weitz (ed.), Palmach: Shtei shibolim veherev [Palmach, Two Sticks of Corn and a Sword] (Tel Aviv, 2001), p.239.
45. 'Minutes of meeting of Recruitment Center', 22 February 1943, p.2, CZA, S25/4888. On the same day, Hadassah Samuel met Catherine Morrison-Bell, ATS Commander of the Palestine Region, and reported on the Jewish Agency's reservations to recruitment. After a debate at higher levels, it was decided not to post Israeli soldiers as waitresses in soldiers' dining rooms, but to keep them in office jobs. Palestine Region Diary, 23–24 February 1943, National Archives, London (NA), WO 169/13839.
46. David Anitrilagator and Yosef Bernstein at a meeting of the Hapo'el Hamizrahi Centre, 27 January 1943, p.5a, CZA, 001/1247b; 'On recruiting the [female] member to the ATS', the part of Hapo'el Hamizrahi on the voluntary military recruitment of women, in 1942–1943, ibid.
47. Tova Sanhedrai at a meeting of the Hapo'el Hamizrahi Centre, 27 January 1943, p.5a, ibid. Galicia-born Sanhedrai (1906–92) was a founder member of the Working Women's Organization of Hapo'el Hamizrahi and world deputy of Emunah. Served four terms as a Member of Knesset.
48. Such as, for example, Shalom Rodel Adler at a meeting of the Centre, 27 January 1943, p.7, CZA, 001/106.
49. Yosef at a meeting of the Jewish Agency Executive, 21 December 1941, pp.23–4, CZA, S100/34b. Nonetheless, Yosef understood that he couldn't stop the recruitment drive and asked for assurance that the Jewish Agency would have control over the recruits and that they would serve in groups and not as individuals.
50. Arieh Lipshitz and Rachel Lerer (eds), *Shulamit Klibanov: Le diokana* [In her image] (Jerusalem 1969), pp.36–76; Claire Epstein, 'On Women's Auxiliary Service', *Davar Hapo'elet*, 1-2 (30 January 1942), p.4.
51. Ruth Haktin, Kivrat Haderech Shelly [My own piece of way] (Tel Aviv 1990), p.51. Haktin later became a Member of Knesset for Ahdut Ha'avoda party. She did much work on behalf of women's status in the kibbutz and in Yishuv society

in general and did much to integrate women in public institutions and to include them in social and economic activity within the kibbutzim. According to her, she was helped in this matter by Tabenkin and Zisling, founders of the UKM, initiators of Youth Aliyah and Ahdut Ha'avoda.

52. Moshe Sharett, 'Woman's Right to Volunteer', lecture at a meeting of the Mapai Centre, 8 February 1942, Moshe Sharett, *Policy Making; The Diaries of Moshe Sharett* (Tel Aviv 1979), p.279.
53. Scott Hendrix, 'In the Army: Women, Camp Followers and Gender Roles in the British Army in the French and Indian Wars 1755–1765', in Gerard Degroot and Corinna Peniston-Bird (eds), *A Soldier and a Woman* (Essex 2000), pp.33–48.
54. Women are required to bear the brunt of national representation, since they are 'built' as bearers of the symbolism of national identity and honour. Women, in their 'pleasant manner and dress', symbolize the boundary that separates between the various nationalities. In this respect, the feminine construction contains signs of the 'other'. Male society develops clear cultural codes as to what 'is a moral woman', and thus perpetuates women as being in a position of power that is inferior to that of her male counterpart. Yuval-Davis, 'Nationalism, Feminism and Gender Relations', pp.4–22; Benedict Anderson, *Imagined Communities: Reflections on the Origin and Spread of Nationalism* (London 1991); Sheila Katz, *Women and Gender in Early Jewish and Palestinian Nationalism* (Florida 2003).
55. In the case of the abandoned girls of oriental origin during the 1930s and 1940s, their erotic and sexual attachment to Arab men was conceived as the most blatant and dangerous expression crossing the national and religious boundaries, as was the ethnic and cultural attachment of Jews of oriental origin to Arabs. This attachment endangered the essence of national, racial and spatial division between Jews and Arabs. Tamar Razi, 'Building the Fringes of the Nation: Homeless Youths in Tel Aviv in the 1930s and 1940s' (PhD thesis, Bar Ilan University, 2006), p.240.
56. Deborah Bernstein, 'Tel Aviv lavsha mahsof ... Pnina hameshuga'at vegvulot hakrach' [Tel Aviv donned a décolleté ... Crazy Pnina and the city boundaries], *Teoria veBikoret*, 25 (Autumn 2004), pp.154–5.
57. Ibid.
58. Things reached such a state as to arouse the concern of ATS Commander Whateley for the image and morale of her recruits and she set out in 1944 on tours of duty in the Middle East and Europe where British soldiers were serving in order to disprove the rumours. Noakes, *Women in the British Army*, pp.127–8.
59. A letter from the Committee for the Defense of the Daughter of Israel to the Jewish Agency Executive referred to 'Worrying and distressing rumours [that] spread in our city on the subject of the Hebrew soldiers ... the least of them being – albeit so disastrous it has to be taken into consideration – is that female soldiers will be employed in the personal service of officers, instead of male soldiers.' Sharett replied to the committee, 'I am quick to inform you that there is no truth in [this] rumour.' Letter from the Committee, dated June 1942, CZA, S25/5099; letter from Sharett to the Committee, 2 June 1942, Municipal Archives, Tel Aviv, 888-8, container 5266.

60. Meeting of the Recruitment Department, 18 December 1941, CZA, S25/5063.
61. Ya'akov Hazan at the Hashomer Hatza'ir General Council, 11 April 1942, Hashomer Hatza'ir Archive, 3.20-5 (2). Other members referred mainly to the refusal of the British to allow Yishuv recruits to serve as doctors and nurses and to approve their service only as practical nurses ('with an Englishwoman as nurse and a Jewish woman scrubbing the floor – this is humiliating work').
62. Letter from David Santor to Moshe Sharett, 22 December 1941, CZA. S25/5099.
63. 'Woman's Right to Volunteer', lecture at a meeting of the Mapai Centre, 8 January 1942, Sharett, *Policy Making*, p.280.
64. Even more than a year after the beginning of their service, one of the soldiers wrote to his wife, 'For two weeks there has been talk of the expected arrival of Jewish ATS [soldiers]. Unfortunately the psychology is such that the English [soldiers] are waiting for them more than we are ... the thought sometimes creeps that it might be better if they were not to come here.' Aharon Ben-Yosef to his wife, 4 April 1942, CZA, S25/5099.
65. Letter from Sharett to UKM Council in Yagur, 6 February 1942, p.48, IDF Archive 45/140/2002. Haktin was impressed by the letter and said, 'I wondered how this person felt what each of us felt at a time when the recruitment is already underway'; Yehuda Slutsky (ed.), *Sefer toldot ha'aganah* [History of the Haganah], B and C (Tel Aviv 1973), p.765.
66. Michael Rustad, *Women in Khaki: The American Enlisted Woman* (New York: Praeger, 1982), p.104. Dame Leslie suggested inviting MPs from England to see the situation with their own eyes, but the deputy commander of the British forces did not agree with her view and didn't even raise an alternative proposal to solve the problem. On the other hand, according to her, the chief commander of the British forces in the Middle East who appreciated the work and contribution of the female soldiers, had a more positive approach. Dame Leslie Whateley, *As Thoughts Survive* (London 1949), p.163.
67. Moshe Yovel, of the Jewish Agency Political Department wrote, on the direction of Sharett, to a person who was conducting a propaganda campaign against female recruitment to the ATS. According to him, the rumours were based on 'mishaps' that happened to a number of soldiers in Ismailia and that this should not lead to conclusions on all the other servicewomen, although 'various army units have accepted men and women whose behaviour is not always a source of pride'. In the letter, he reports that 1,100 women have already enlisted and the drive has been successful both internally and externally. Yovel to 'Rafa', 18 June 1942, CZA, S25/5099.
68. The committee was established in order to 'fight against promiscuity and to defend the purity of life in the Yishuv', through activating existing laws and a demand for legislation of further anti-promiscuity laws. Daniela Reich, 'Between National Mission and Social Ostracism: Contacts Between Jewish Women to British Servicemen 1940–1948' (MA thesis, Haifa University, 2003), p.86. The committee acted within the Tel Aviv-Jaffa Religious Council, and received the spiritual support, sympathy and respect of the Chief Rabbis and was funded by the Rabbinate.
69. H. Giladi, minutes of meeting of Committee for the Defence of the Honour of the Daughter of Israel, 28 Tevet 1942, p.1, Municipal Archives, Tel Aviv, file

8119. Tehilla Matmon established the League for Women's Rights in Israel and was a member of the International Alliance of Women. She also established and edited the newsletter 'The Woman in the State', David Tidhar, *Enziklopediyah le'Halutsei ha'Yishuv ve'Bonav* [Encyclopedia of pioneers of the Yishuv and personages], 17 (Tel Aviv 1947), p.3722.

70. Isaac Levy, *Now I Can Tell: Middle East Memories* (London 1978), p.48.
71. 'Jew: Let us not Defile the Name and Dignity of the Servicewoman!' *Halohem*, November 1943, pp.4–5.
72. Hadassah Goldgart, 'To the Future of the Hebrew Soldier', *Davar Hapo'elet*, 1–2 (21 February 1944).
73. Yair Spiegel, 'Hashomer Hatza'ir in Defense and Security of the Yishuv, 1920–1947' (PhD thesis, Bar Ilan University, 2006), p.185.
74. Mina Rogoz'ik, the fifth Histadrut Congress, 19–23 April 1942, pp.96–7, Labour Party Archive, Lavon Institute.
75. Rachel Katznelson, UKM Council in Yagur, 6–7 April 1942, p.43, UKM Archive, file 15 b. In raising this argument, Katznelson disregarded the fact that women were designated for auxiliary tasks only and would not be taking up arms.
76. Yitzhak Tabenkin, UKM Archive, file 15b, p.33; Liova Levite (member of Kibbutz Ein Harod and member of UKM leadership, later Political Secretary of Mapam) at Givat Brenner Council, 15–16 April 1942, p.53, IDF Archive, 45/40/2002.
77. Letter from Revisionist servicemen to Ya'akov Rubin, 18 February 1943, Jabotinsky Institute, Tel Aviv, C-1/17. As mentioned, the Revisionists saw the British as foreign occupiers and not as a liberating force and objected to make recruitment to the British forces. Only at a later stage, in the latter half of 1942, did the political movement change its attitude and begin to support male recruitment. Gelber, *Hahitnadvut ve Mekoma*, p.243. In movement debates on recruitment to the British forces during 1942–43, no mention is made of female recruitment. Ibid., 10-1/14g, 1/1/15 - 6g.
78. After a visit to Egypt, Sharett reported: 'I am honoured to report that throughout Egypt and throughout Eretz Israel there is not a single ATS soldier who serves as driver to an officer.' Moshe Sharett at a meeting of the Histadrut Council, 7 September 1942, p.70, IDF Archive, 45/140/2002.
79. Dr Dov Yosef in the name of the Jewish Agency, 'Greeting on the Anniversary of the ATS', 24 December 1943, Labour Party Archive, File 17, IV-230-6.
80. R.K., 'Fighting Women's Day', *Davar Hapo'elet*, 2 (28 February 1943), pp.36–7. At the sight of the servicewomen who participated in the gathering and described their lives and the work they did, Katznelson wondered if the Working Women's movement might have made a fundamental mistake in all its propaganda until then, since 'it might have been better to make less of the discrimination and burdens imposed upon women and to place more emphasis on woman's lasting beauty, which manifests itself especially in women of our generation. In this way it might have been easier, too, to overcome the discrimination.'

Part Two

On Military Service

3

The Recruits as a Reflection of Yishuv Society

The women who volunteered for service in the British forces were an integral part of Yishuv society and represented a colourful mosaic consisting of locally born women, new immigrants, different ethnic groups and different professions and occupations. The groups differed from each other in their affiliation to the Yishuv institutions, its leadership and their personal interests, their education and occupations. Often, there was no connection between the different ethnic groups, who typically held preconceived opinions about, and were alienated from, one another.

Did the community of recruits to the British forces provide a demographic picture of the Yishuv, or did it represent a unique group;[1] what was the percentage of locally born women and that of new immigrants among the recruits; what was their marital status and age, what were their reasons for volunteering and did the frictions and stereotypes in Yishuv society on this issue affect the social cohesion and relations among the women themselves? This chapter will address these questions.

The Recruits: Data and Statistics

Between 1941 and 1942, the Yishuv population in Palestine consisted of 505,000 Jews (an increase of 237 per cent from that of 1926). Some 370,000 of these were immigrants (legal and illegal) who arrived in the country after the British conquest in 1917. During the early years of the century, the number of men arriving in the country was greater than that of women.[2] From the early 1920s and throughout the 1930s and 1940s most of the immigration consisted of families, so that the ratio of men to women was balanced out. Most of the female immigrants had no choice, being dependent on decisions made by the head of the family. This situation reflects a patriarchal family structure typical of the majority of Jewish families at that time.[3]

During the period under discussion, around 187,000 women of recruitment age (18–45), according to British army criteria, lived in the Jewish Yishuv. From the start of female recruitment on 18 January 1942 and up to the demobilization of the last of them in mid 1946, around 3,000 women served in the ATS.[4] Some 600 Jewish women from the Yishuv served in the WAAF.[5] The recruits constituted about 2 per cent of the total female Jewish population of relevant age in the Yishuv.[6] From among the men in the Jewish Yishuv who were recruited into the British forces some 19,000 served in the land forces, some 1,106 were in the Royal Navy and a further 1,900 served in the RAF. The overall number of recruits (male and female) from the Jewish Yishuv constituted around 6 per cent of the entire population of the Yishuv.

A statistical analysis of the female recruits[7] shows that the majority consisted of unmarried women in their 20s or 30s. Among the recruits there were also married women, mostly without children. In the period under discussion, most of the women in the Jewish Yishuv were married; about 50 per cent were already married by the age of 25. According to Roberto Baki, head of Central Office of Statistics in Jerusalem's Hadassah Hospital in 1944, only a small percentage of women went through their fertile years without getting married and most of the women in the Yishuv did marry.[8] Thus the decision of married women to enlist in the army is testimony to their decision to postpone enlarging their families for an indefinite period, in contrast to the majority of married women in the Jewish Yishuv.

The segmentation of the recruits in accordance with the regions in which they resided conforms with the situation in the Yishuv and that of the recruits themselves: thus, around 80 per cent of all the recruits to the ATS lived in towns (with above 90 per cent of them in the three largest towns, Haifa, Tel Aviv and Jerusalem).[9] Some 82 per cent of the recruits were foreign born, most of them from Eastern Europe, a third from central European countries and 2 per cent from Western European countries and the Middle East. About 73 per cent of the foreign born recruits had lived in Israel for up to ten years before joining the army and about 91 per cent had lived there for up to twenty years before recruitment.[10] Above 80 per cent of the Yishuv's population during the war period lived there during the twenty years prior to the outbreak of war,[11] so that the Yishuv's Jewish population was a distinctly immigrant one.[12]

The number of older recruits was unusual.[13] The recruits included about 6 per cent who were over 40 at the time of enlisting and there were even a few who were in their 50s, after having misrepresented their age at the recruitment office. Many women in their 40s, who admitted to their real age and wished to join the army, were rejected by the military authorities.

The Working Women's Council saw the advantages of an older recruit and hoped to take advantage of the older women by placing them in positions it considered 'more responsible and appropriate'.[14] It would appear that in this there was an internalization of the fear for the 'morality' of the young recruits. Senior female kibbutz members also preferred to recruit older women rather than to send young and inexperienced women, or as the UKM's Ruth Haktin put it 'we won't send young girls – which is why I am prepared to go [myself] and won't send my daughter'. When rumours started to spread in the Yishuv about the dubious 'morals' of the young servicewomen, a proposal was put forward to appoint a 'supervisor of chastity', from among the 'older female recruits'.[15]

The only sphere in which no synchronization existed between Yishuv statistics and female recruitment statistics was that of employment. A study of the recruits' employment shows clearly that – in contrast to male recruitment (at least in the early stages of the war) – most of the women who decided to volunteer for military service did not do so for lack of paid employment. On the contrary: 95 per cent of the urban recruits left regular employment in order to enlist in the army;[16] 30 per cent of the Yishuv's women worked outside the home,[17] as compared to 95 per cent of the servicewomen who were employed by some kind of workplace prior to enlistment. Nor was the military pay determined for Yishuv women, which was lower than the average wages paid in the Yishuv, particularly tempting and, due to discriminatory policies of the British War Office, lower by 25 per cent than that of male servicemen from Palestine.[18] As already mentioned, the wage paid to a British ATS servicewoman was 25 per cent lower than that of a male British serviceman. Unlike the Jewish recruits, Arab women enlisted from purely economic considerations and received free food and clothing from the army and all their expenses were covered.[19]

Social Characteristic of the Yishuv Servicewomen

Following a visit to the training camp in July 1942, about five months after the commencement of recruitment, Rivka Katznelson wrote in

Davar Hapo'elet, 'How amazing is ... variety of human figures. We have not yet become accustomed to being in the midst of such complete representation of candidates, age-groups, ethnic groups, countries of origin of the women of the Yishuv.'[20] And indeed, the servicewomen came from all levels of society and from all the different ethnic groups that made up the Jewish Yishuv: from the towns and from the agricultural sector (kibbutzim and moshavim); from the various ideological streams; veterans and new immigrants; religious and secular, women who were affiliated to the various frameworks (professional, security and others) and those who did not belong to any organization.

By March 1943, 2,694 Jewish Yishuv women had joined the ATS. Of these, 1,898 enlisted via the Jewish Agency's Recruitment Offices and 769 went straight through the army's recruitment centres. During the remainder of 1943 and until March 1945, recruitment took place in the military offices only and it is reasonable to assume that additional women, who did not belong to the 'organized Yishuv', also enlisted in the army in the course of this time. Those women who enlisted through the Jewish Agency's recruitment offices came mostly from the 'organized' Yishuv, whereas those who enlisted directly with the army recruitment offices were generally from the 'non-organized' Yishuv.[21] The various recruitment 'channels' can serve as an indication of the numbers of recruits who enlisted through the Yishuv institutions and others.[22]

The 'Organized' and 'non-Organized' Yishuv

The 'organized' Yishuv consisted of kibbutz and moshav members, students, youth movement members, political party members and Histadrut activists, members of Haganah and employees of the Yishuv. This population obeyed the rulings of the Yishuv on civilian and security matters, notwithstanding the absence of official means of enforcement.[23] As for military recruitment, if at first the male recruitment was based on personal considerations, then two years after its commencement, the Yishuv institutions directed recruitment into specific military units and even placed quotas on recruitment, especially from the kibbutzim.

Most of the servicewomen from the 'organized' Yishuv came from the kibbutzim and, especially, the moshavim, as well as Haganah members from the towns. Typically these recruits were highly motivated, idealistic and with feelings of national mission, and it was they who determined to a great extent the cultural profile of Yishuv women in the ATS and the WAAF. Among these recruits were several hundred urban Histadtut members, daughters of senior public figures, or salaried women employees.

With ironic hindsight, Esther Tal (Iterani) sums up the difference between those who enlisted through the Jewish Agency and those who went through the military recruitment offices:

> Jewish Agency recruits considered themselves and were considered by some in the 'organized' Yishuv to be upper-class patriots, emissaries of the Yishuv and not mere adventurers. The private recruits [those who enlisted directly through the army recruitment offices] became easily 'Anglicised' and soon acclimatized themselves to the British army lifestyle. Their counterparts looked down on them.[24]

This would appear to reflect the feeling of many of the recruits from the 'organized' Yishuv, although the expression 'Anglicised' may have been over sharp. According to the writer Orah Shem-Ur, 'the "non-organized" Yishuv rejected those who were tempted to go out with English men ... A young Jewish woman seen in the company of English people was automatically finished with Jewish society ... in this there was an overall silent consensus.'[25]

Toward the end of the 1930s there existed a broad stratum in the Yishuv (above 20 per cent), whose worldview excluded it from the mainstream organized Yishuv, from Yishuv life and from additional parameters: origin, culture, education and employment. The group consisted of people from poor neighbourhoods and various ethnic groups, illegal immigrants released from the quarantine camps, new immigrants from the eastern states, deserters from the Anders Army (Free Polish Army), sons and daughters of the veteran settlements and others. At the end of a lengthy and gradual process, some of these people were incorporated into the new society.[26]

Although it did not identify with the values of the Labour movement, the political leadership and the Histadrut, the non-organized Yishuv tied itself through day-to-day collective experience with the emerging nationality. Nonetheless, many of the Jewish townswomen experienced – as did immigrant groups everywhere – a blurring of boundaries in many spheres: family boundaries, boundaries of intimacy (sexuality in general and female sexuality in particular) and permitted and normative behavioural boundaries. Many women found themselves having to cope on their own with day-to-day existence, with no support or defence. Although the recruits from these social strata were conceived as having come from the fringes of society, their behaviour was generally no different from that of women from the 'organized' Yishuv. Many of them were patriotic, nationalistic and decent and they maintained their national identity in no less measure than their counterparts who had undergone 'sifting' in the Jewish Agency recruitment offices.

Recruits, Graduates of Youth Aliyah

During the 1930s around 6,000 girls and boys aged 15 and above were brought to Israel within the framework of the Youth Aliyah enterprise[27] and placed on farms and in educational institutions and, once their education was completed, they were integrated into the community.[28] However, their integration into Israeli society was accompanied by educational and psychological difficulties resulting from differences in mentality, language and qualifications and from being severed from their families. Many of them left the kibbutz framework and some even left the country. Many of the girls went to live in the towns and cities, where rumours of their inferior morals began to flourish throughout the land, to the disconcertion of all those involved in the educational enterprise. Yosef Horowitz, author of the book on Youth Aliyah, reported in 1942 that 'the girls of Youth Aliyah are involved mostly in housework and child care, although some of them also go out to work [in the big towns] as waitresses in the cafes and restaurants that have recently been springing up in their masses'.[29] These girls knew several languages – Hebrew, German, and some of them English as well – and, since the hourly wage of a waitress was higher than that of a housecleaner, many young girls preferred this work.

Dozens of girls, who married British soldiers or policemen, saw in that situation a chance to improve their destiny and attempted to start a new life in a new place. Recruitment to the British army provided one solution to the loneliness, alienation and the problems of employment of the Youth Aliyah graduates – male as well as female. Still, many of them enlisted as part of the wave of volunteering that swept the Yishuv as it faced a German invasion, not to mention the dangers their families were facing back in Europe.[30]

A report on the part played by female Youth Aliyah graduates in the British forces, reveals a total of 176 recruits to the ATS and ten to the WAAF (of 1,320 graduates). Of these, 148 were aged between 18–22 when they enlisted. 125 enlisted already in 1942 and a further forty-two in 1943.[31] Although the graduates of Youth Aliyah had received a kibbutz education, they did not belong to the 'organized' Yishuv.

Former Prostitutes

Several interviewees mentioned servicewomen who led what they described as a 'promiscuous' lifestyle. In the eyes of many of the young servicewomen, especially those from kibbutzim and moshavim and town-dwelling members of Haganah, women who had sexual relations with men outside of a regular relationship were 'promiscuous' and even 'whores' (expressions they use to this day). Even servicewomen who only 'necked', as they put it, with servicemen (especially British), were seen as such. They were generally servicewomen who had experienced upheavals and hardships in their lives before enlistment and sexual relationships provided a kind of compensation for the loss of family and human warmth.

Nevertheless, there were also servicewomen who had been prostitutes prior to their military service, although these constituted a very small number of women. Thus, for example, one of the servicewomen in the drivers 513 Company told her friends that she had been a prostitute before enlisting in the ATS.[32]

Jewish society under the British Mandate was one of immigrants, characterized by foreignness, alienation and inconsistencies with regard to norms and behaviour. Concepts of gender in general, and of sexuality in particular, were foggy and far from being well defined and unequivocal. The number of girls employed in prostitution, or those who were at least prosecuted or kept under surveillance, was low throughout the 1930s and 1940s, although the war years saw a rise in the extent of prostitution among young girls. Among those who turned to prostitution in the Yishuv were women in their 20s and 30s, including single immigrants, single mothers and servicemen's wives. Prostitution was a sphere that cut through national boundaries, since many of the clients did not belong to the Jewish/Hebrew collective. This crossing of boarders was typified by prostitution and the crossings created a kind of twilight zone in which the evolving national boundaries were blurred, in complete contrast to the hegemony of establishing boundaries and making them permanent. There is no doubt that from a symbolic point of view, prostitution was tied to a world of hedonism and nightlife, and was inconsistent with the hegemonic project of nation building.[33]

Communist Recruits

Among the recruits there were also some women who believed in the Communist ideology. Throughout the 1930s and 1940s, Communism engendered fear in the Yishuv as well as in the British army. The British Mandatory authorities' Central Intelligence Department (CID) was active in thwarting and collection information on the Communist Party in the Yishuv. This activity was part of a general effort on the part of all the intelligence organizations against communist parties in general, and against communist activity in the British colonies in particular, since the Communists placed themselves as radical opposition to 'every existing order' – not only against governments but also vis-à-vis all existing political institutions. The Yishuv branch of the Communist Party was conceived as the representative of an organization geared toward illegal and subversive activity and whose positions and activities were based on concepts, interests and directives, all with the backing of a foreign power.[34] After the German invasion of the Soviet Union on 22 June 1941 (Operation Barbarossa), Communist Party activists the world over embarked on activity to open a 'second front' in order to help the Russian nation in its time of need.

The Palestinian Communist Party, known by the Yiddish acronym Pakap (Palastina Kommunistische Partei), supported a blatantly anti-Zionist ideology. It established joint activities for Jews and Arabs and was the only political party in the Yishuv whose leadership was composed of both Jews and Arabs.[35] At the end of 1941 and during the following year the party's anti-Zionist energies were released in opposing the military recruitment of women to the British forces. The Communists were opposed to the Yishuv institutions' demand to separate Jewish units in the army, which they considered to be improper and insulting to the Arabs. Most of the struggle was turned against the Haganah movement, which motivated its members to collect arms from military arsenals – since a strong Haganah force might place Zionsim at an advantage over the Arabs in the struggle for the future character of the Land of Israel.[36]

Communist recruits reported to their superior officers and to the military authorities on the 'dangerous behaviour' of Zionist servicemen and women and revealed their names. The propaganda conducted by communist soldiers in the army aroused suspicion and concern in the

Haganah especially because of the potential effect it could have on the non-Zionist recruits (new immigrants from Europe) who had not yet developed an affinity for the Yishuv and its objectives. One of the female drivers in Company 511 in Tel el Kabir, an active communist, spread propaganda in the army, including painting a hammer and sickle on the front of her truck, alongside the name 'Natasha'.[37]

The army and the Yishuv institutions kept each other updated when any suspicions arose of female recruits being communists or party affiliates. Pessia Schreier, a member of Moshav Ein Vered in the Samaria region, was recruited into the army at the regional military recruitment office. A letter to the recruitment office contained information from the Jewish Agency recruitment office that she was a communist. The significance of such information was that she was untrustworthy and that a keen eye should be kept on her activities, even in the army. Next to the name of Esther Vigler in the list published by the British recruitment office there was a note to say that she was a communist.[38] Women members of Hashomer Hatza'ir kibbutzim who enlisted before receiving movement permission were suspected of being undercover communists.[39] Further, the recruitment office reported to the Jewish Agency on recruits suspected of social ties with Communist Party activists.

Communist women who enlisted in the army had a worldview that was well formed and firm, according to which communism and the ideology attached to it is the most just and correct one. Nonetheless, because of the army's suspicions, these women did not always declare their loyalties out loud and sometimes it was discovered by chance by their fellow company members. Thus, for example, one of the recruits was surprised to discover that several of her fellow servicewomen were

> active communists, among the more extreme of their kind, alienating themselves from Jews and from their Jewishness, openly cursing and vilifying the Zionist movement, the Jewish Agency and the Yishuv institutions and proudly declaring that it was not for the sake of the Jewish people that they went on those campaigns, but on behalf of the Russians and the Arabs.[40]

Rachel Ziv (Barshavsky), who came from one of the oldest families in Rishon le Zion, lost her father when she was 14 and his death left a huge void in her soul and, according to her, she was 'drawn' – out of her great loss – to activity in the ranks of the Communist Party. She did not see in herself a victim, rather felt the need to fight for the ideal and the way. The Second World War period provided a crossroads of major upheavals throughout the world and Ziv wished to 'save the world', while relinquishing her private needs on behalf of the collective. Ziv enlisted in the WAAF in 1943 and served in 107 MU camp in Egypt.[41] A picture of Soviet leader Josef Stalin was placed on another recruit's bedside locker, and the nightly update on her activity that day, as well the kiss she planted on the picture, would indicate the level of her ideological 'orthodoxy' at the beginning of her military service. Another recruit who believed in communism who served with her on the same base was one Deborah Sahish.[42]

Religious Women in Military Service

Before recruitment, religious women in the Yishuv had taken part in activities of organizations such as the Notrim (guards), Haganah, the Palmach and the underground movements,[43] albeit in small numbers. Among the recruits to the British army there were several dozen women, such as Sara Kopler (Bar-Adon) and Esther Leon (Ben-Shabat) from Haifa and Elisheva Erez (Pearlman) from Tel Aviv, who came from observant families, although during their military service they did not maintain a religious lifestyle or keep kosher. Only a small number of religious servicewomen managed to adhere to a religious lifestyle in the military.[44] The religious establishment did not encourage women to enlist in the army, and often opposed it mainly for moral reasons and out of the need to protect the women's honour. Although in many cases, their families, too, objected to their enlistment, many religious women felt the need and the desire to enlist and they did so privately and on their own initiative. Often, this involved rejection on the part of their parents.

The servicewomen who led a religious lifestyle in the army were able to do so, as did their male counterparts, despite the absence of a supportive environment. Religious servicemen wrangled with various Halachic issues that arose in the course of the military service, such as kashrut, determining Torah times, conducting services, travel on Shabbat and holydays while on duty, etc. and they consulted with rabbis, both in the military and in the Yishuv (including the Chief Rabbi of Israel, Rabbi Yitzhak Halevi Herzog). At times this was conducted via the system of 'Question and Answers'.[45]

The relatively small number of religious servicewomen made it harder for them than for their male counterparts, who often served together as a group. But the women were the ones who emphasized their religious uniqueness. Haviva Kotler, for example, pointed out that 'if [you] want to hold on at the cost of relinquishing an easy lifestyle and personal pleasures, then it's not so difficult'. She added that 'if she [the woman] wants to be in order from a religious aspect, it does not come easily and requires many compromises'. According to her, she was the only observant Jew in the whole camp and, even though she was among 'many liberated girls, having no framework in which to uphold my religiousness, I never forget that on Shabat [I] must take care not to write, not to travel, etc.'[46]

Motives for Female Recruitment

About 80 per cent of all the Yishuv's volunteers (male as well as female) enlisted during the first half of the war and the rest during the second half. By the end of 1942, when the Yishuv was still in danger of invasion, recruitment was one of the central issues on the Yishuv's agenda. However, in mid 1943, when the war took a turn for the better and the Allied Forces became stronger, military recruitment ceased being a cardinal matter in Yishuv life and sometimes even turned into a bother for many people in it. Female recruitment, which began in January 1942, started at a time when male recruitment was in decline.[47]

National Considerations and Solidarity with the Jewish People

Most of the recruits to the ATS in 1942 volunteered out of a sense of personal and national mission. Hanna Levin, graduate of the Cadre, put it thus: 'We are now entrusted with the duty of fighting the mutual enemy, to defend our national honour, to defend the honour of [our] land.' Another girl wrote to her soldier father, 'I have to go! If they will only take me ... I shall go ... I am ashamed to sit by indifferently at a time when I can be of use, if only a little ... for several weeks my heart has been in such turmoil, restlessness, impatience.'[48]

Many volunteers wanted to see in their very recruitment an expression of their equal status with that of their male counterparts. There is no doubt that the women's patriotic feelings were no less strong than the men's. But women were usually excluded from active and equal participation in the army and the war and were therefore unable to express their citizenship in a way that was equal to men's. The right to defend the country allowed access only to those defined as 'first class citizens', those who held political power and financial advantages, in other words: men. The ultimate expression of the right to defend is death (sacrificing life) and because women were denied active participation in the defence of the country, they were denied, by definition, the right to equal citizenship.[49]

Toward the end of 1942 and early 1943, when news began to reach the Yishuv of the annihilation of the Jews of Europe, large numbers of women volunteered for military service out of a sense of solidarity with the Jewish nation, even if they did not have relatives in Europe. Some of them felt that they were part of the same sequence of tortured Jewish women throughout history. A recruit from Nahalal wrote to her parents that she was enlisting 'because I am a daughter of Israel ... because I am a sister to all my persecuted and humiliated and raped sisters from the days of the [1648–57 Cossack] riots. In all the pogroms and in all the persecutions.'[50] New immigrants who had left their families behind in Europe and were deeply concerned about their fate were quick to do something to help the British army in its war against the Germans. Some even hoped to take advantage of the army in order to get back to Europe, to uncover what had happened to their loved ones.

Recruitment posters published and distributed by the Jewish Agency and the British army reinforced the powerful desire of Yishuv women to enlist in the army and to help the Jewish nation. Many of the recruits pointed out the effect of the recruitment posters on their decision to enlist, or, as Bracha Habas put it 'Today the recruitment office calls her in letters of fire.'[51] Posters and notices were seen everywhere in the Yishuv: in newspapers, on billboards, in the streets and in many public places. In these publications people in the Yishuv were called upon to contribute to the war effort. This propaganda drive presented recruitment to the British army as a patriotic service on behalf of the nation and the homeland. People looking at these posters raised their eyes to the image depicted on them and were called to climb one step higher in order to join the defenders of the homeland.[52]

The biblical pathos used in the posters also found its place in such songs as 'Hymn to the ATS', composed by an anonymous poet. The song contains expressions that placed the ATS recruits on the historical sequence of women in the Bible, such as 'we shall bless the women in the tent' (an allusion to the song of Deborah), 'Again we rise from the Bible', etc. Similar sentiments can be found in 'Song to the Soldier' (composed by Amram Gilboa and Avraham Mindelin). Another verse from the song of Deborah was used on the front page of *Olam Ha'isha*

(Women's World) that was devoted to female recruitment. But, effective though these were, more than advertising slogans were needed in order to persuade women to enlist in their masses in the army.

Personal Motives

It would appear that the entire variety of motives that drew men to enlist in the army applied to women as well. Nonetheless, it should be stressed that during the first recruitment period, male recruitment was the result of a personal decision and based on personal motives. At that stage, the decision to volunteer was not conceived as a national duty and was actually considered a 'hole in the fence' of Yishuv discipline. As already mentioned, it was only two years after the beginning of recruitment that it came under the organized auspices of the Yishuv institutions. On the other hand, almost all the women were recruited on their own initiative and not through an organized recruitment drive, apart from those women who took part in the Haganah recruitment cadre and about 150 kibbutz members who enlisted after being granted movement approval.

Apart from patriotic consideration and solidarity with the Jewish people, the recruits were also motivated by 'thousands of personal considerations – from crises and problems, whether individual or family related, identical mostly outwardly and so different inwardly, like the differences between the lives of one person and another'.[53] Women's military recruitment for personal reasons has also been known in other periods in history,[54] and in the Yishuv, too, these considerations shifted the balance in favour of the army rather than other security frameworks – the Palmach or employment in the wartime economy.

In Britain, too, alongside the national and patriotic motives, there were personal ones that influenced women's decision to enlist. Many women enlisted in the various British forces and women employed in the various wartime industries felt the war had given them the chance to get 'out of the cage'; in other words – from the protective but stressful home environment, to the public domain.[55]

Male servicemen were influenced by a broad spectrum of motives for enlisting: some, especially refugees from the Nazi regime, wanted revenge; there were adventurers who saw the army as a continuation of the adventure that brought them to Palestine; without a doubt the employment situation in the Yishuv had an effect on recruitment, at least at first (although most of the unemployed did not enlist). The army also supplied many people with a refuge from their day-to-day problems (debts, alimony payments, etc.) and also an escape from loneliness, for those who had no home and family.[56] The Oriental Jews, too,[57] most of who had large families and were older than the required age, sought refuge from their financial hardships, and there were also the youngsters who managed to hide their age and were drawn into the army out of a sense of adventure and a lack of alternative in civilian life. Unlike male recruitment, at least during the early stages of the war, most of the women who decided to enlist in the army did not do so for lack of employment; indeed most of the urban recruits left regular jobs to volunteer for service, notwithstanding the low salaries.

The broad spectrum of motives that let women to enlist in the army is described by Habas thus: 'Add to the list of recruits those who went with the flow ... the social outsider ... – the one who wants to join the army to "see the world", the woman who is escaping the troubles at home, the family crisis, the one who seeks a quick solution to her life or a way out of a crisis in her life'.[58] These motives that Habas and the recruits attributed to women from the 'non-organized' Yishuv can also be applied to women from the 'organized' Yishuv, who experienced similar hardships in their homes.

Feelings of Alienation and Isolation

Around 75 per cent of the recruits who were not born in the country had lived there for up to ten years prior to enlisting in the army. On the new immigrants, people from the 'non-organized' Yishuv who enlisted in the army, Shem-Ur wrote: 'There was no one to advise them whether to enlist or not: their parents were in Poland, Hungary, Romania, it's been two or more years since they've had any sign of life from them.'[59]

Although many of the female immigrants to Palestine were able to settle in the towns, finding accommodation and employment, many others living in the country had no family and no friends. For these women enlistment in the army provided a substitute for home and family. An example is Dora Margalit, who had come from an assimilated family in Poland, with a background that was far from Judaism and Zionism and arrived in the country along with hundreds of Jewish refugees in September 1939, after the German occupation of Poland. She described the feeling of alienation and loneliness thus: 'The country, its language and the people living in it are foreign to her

... She enlists in the British army and moves to Egypt ... wanders along the various paths and seeks a way to herself.'[60] Others, whose families had remained in Europe and all ties with them had been severed in the course of the war, felt a fierce need to enlist and to try to reach them at some stage and to discover what had happened to them.

A Sense of Adventure

Many servicewomen testified that in addition to their patriotic feelings and national duty, there was also a sense of adventure, a wish to 'see the world', that drove them to enlist in the British army, rather than to join other frameworks in the Yishuv, such as the Palmach. These feelings crossed the boundaries of social belonging and can be detected equally among recruits from the organized and the non-organized Yishuv. It should be noted that for many recruits military service provided a window to the world outside, especially for those who came from small towns and villages in the Yishuv. They were especially enchanted with the possibility of serving in Egypt, in Cairo or Alexandria, two cosmopolitan cities famous for their vibrant cultural life. Possibilities were available to the recruits that did not exist for other Yishuv women: new locations, archaeological sites, vacations in far off places, etc. Lea Nelson-Bernstein provided a good description of this when she wrote: 'The call-up papers arrived. [My] heart was in a fizz. To defend the homeland ... to get away from the narrow moshav society. To see the world ... I admit, it fascinated us all, especially me.'[61]

On the motives of the Youth Aliyah graduates who chose to enlist in the army, Horowitz wrote:

> These youths were well aware of the seriousness of the times, of the dangers lurking in wait for the Jewish Yishuv in the country and for the Zionist enterprise. They developed a desire to fight against Hitler and his regime that destroyed the peace in their homes and their families. And these youthful motives combined with the urge for adventure and a desire for far off places.[62]

Elisheva Erez, who came from a religious home, was the only one in her class to enlist in the army. She admitted that apart from the desire to contribute to the war effort, she was motivated by an urge for adventure that drove her to enlist. Zipora Shahar (Eitan) from Tel Adashim and Zipa Gov from Tel Aviv, were also captivated by the challenge and adventure offered by the army, in addition to their ideological motives.[63]

The longing for adventure was not restricted to the younger female recruits. Older women, too, with families of their own, felt a desire to experience some excitement in the course of their military service. One of these was a cook on one of the military bases in the country, in a location near her home and was able to visit once a week. According to her, 'In my heart of hearts all this [service conditions] appears to me utter luxury. I just lack a little adventure. Wicked old vixen that I am, how I would still yearn for something to happen, to shake me up a little.'[64]

A Wish to Serve Near their Husband

Approximately 6 per cent of the recruited women were married, mostly with no children. What induced them to volunteer for military service? Some of the married women, especially the younger ones, enlisted in order to be close to their husbands, who were also serving. In an exclusive interview in the *Palestine Post*, Audrey Chitty, the supreme ATS commander in the Middle East, encouraged married women without children, whose husbands were already in the army, to enlist, explaining that as well as the additional income, they would thus enjoy the double pleasure of serving alongside their husbands.[65]

Recruitment with a Romantic Background

Quite a few women enlisted in order to be near their boyfriends, usually British men they had met in the Yishuv. When war conditions required that servicemen be posted to Egypt or elsewhere and the distance made it difficult to maintain relationships, couples would decide that it would be best for them both if the woman were to enlist in the army, in the hope that she would be given a posting near her boyfriend. It was so in the case of Varda Simpson (Kahanovitz), from Binyamina, whose father was an agronomist. She met Leonard, a handsome British serviceman wounded in the Battle of Al Alamein, when he was posted to a camp near her home. The two fell in love, but once he had recovered and relocated to Egypt, they were able to meet each other only once in 18 months. In the end they came to a decision that it would be best if she were to enlist in the army in order to enable them to meet more frequently. And so she enlisted in 1944 and received a posting to Egypt.[66]

Other women enlisted in order to get away from a relationship. Esther Zolotov, who served in the WAAF, for a brief while had been in a relationship with a British serviceman who worked in the Criminal Investigation Department (CID) of the police. She joined the WAAF in order to end the relationship.[67] Another recruit, who had arrived in the country as a refugee with no family, wrote in her book that her employer had treated her well and was a loyal friend, but 'as soon as she felt that the friendship might develop into something called love, she left her job and enlisted'.[68]

Wanting to Play a Role in the Public Sphere

There were some women, mainly married and from the agricultural sector, whose husbands held various security posts and were often absent from home for long periods of time, who felt themselves to be giving up their own life in order to allow their husband to fulfil his own mission for the general good. Military recruitment offered them the opportunity to prove that they, too, were able to make a contribution to society and to the nation, not only on the family farm, but in the public sphere.

When Haya Mor (Markovsky) from Kfar Yehoshua decided to enlist, she described to the village secretariat the

> sense of discrimination *I was feeling* with regard to myself. I, as the partner of a man who has been working for many years in a public post, a very important and responsible post, was not always reconciled to my condition ... and now that the girls have grown, I am taking upon myself the full right – and I stress that I am rightly entitled to it – to demand of my family and of my partner in particular, that they make it possible for me, too, to fulfil a valuable public post and to do so for a lengthy period ... I don't wish to call this reparation, but I do want to have some equal rights. [author's emphasis][69]

This can be summed up by saying that the ideological motive – the desire to participate in the defence of the Yishuv or the feeling of solidarity with the Jewish nation and the need to help in face of the tragedy in Europe – was the main motive that drove the women of the Yishuv to enlist in the army. Nonetheless, many women had personal reasons for choosing military service rather than other kinds of service.

Relations Among the Recruits

The Working Women's Council hoped the reality that developed in the army would apply a new kind of social solidarity. Rachel Adiv wrote in *Davar Hapo'elet*: 'A perfectly cohesive working society, a society in which all semblance of previous social origin has been obscured, becoming a united community that enjoys equality of experience, of obligations and of rights.'[70] Habas asked rhetorically 'How did they [the recruits] cohere into a single, united community ... how did they all stand together [to face] the test?'[71] Adiv summed up with admiration that 'while overcoming [all the hardships] there arose and grew from out of all the various tribes of the Diaspora a single group of Hebrew women, working ... the cultural act ... that positioned ... all these was a completely new vision'.

Yet, with all the grandiose descriptions, the reality was quite different.

The army brought together women from the Yishuv's economic, political and social elites with women who were impoverished and came from the fringes of society, and as such, served as a microcosm of Yishuv society. It was a meeting that gave free expression to deeply rooted stereotypes and ingrained prejudices. In many countries, especially those with obvious ethnic splits, the army undertakes a social responsibility and, in addition to its security tasks, it plays an integrative role, by serving as a social melting pot to an immigrant society.[72]

Stereotypes and Elites in Yishuv Society and in the Army

Most of the stories from the war period, as well as memoires written decades later, constitute the narratives prevalent in the discourse on recruitment into the British armed forces in general and female recruitment in particular. These writings make much use of expressions such as 'choice human material' and, in contrast, 'not like us' and 'those women'. The first kind refer to women who were born in the Yishuv or who had lived there for a long time, city-dwelling Haganah members or female members of the agricultural sector. The second class of expressions refer to recruits who did not belong to the first group.

Some of the recruits felt themselves to belong (and were also seen as such by the others) to the cultural elite, while others belonged to the social political elite. An elite is a 'minority group or a categorized minority of individuals in a society that has achieved social recognition of their superiority in some sense and they influence or control all, or some, of the other parts of society'. Another definition of an elite group is: 'a group that holds a monopoly over resources typical of a certain moral area on which the activity of the group focuses'. In Yishuv society there existed political elites, economic elites and cultural elites, whose profiles conformed to those of appropriate political-ideological sectors.[73] Eastern European Jews, for example, were a dominant component in the political and cultural elites and between the political elite and the economic elite there were certain similarities in the background variables. People of the Second Aliyah, especially those who belonged to the Labour Movement, had significant weight in the economic elite, whereas members of the Fifth Aliyah were prominent among the cultural elite.

Two companies of women drivers serving in Egypt represent two poles in a sequence of conflicts and stereotypes that took place among the women recruits from the Yishuv. At one end there was Company 511, the drivers from Tel el Kabir. This company was riddled with conflict between the servicewomen who belonged to the elites and those who, by definition, did not, against a background of social, political and cultural gaps. At the other end was Company 513, the drivers from Camp Mina, near Cairo, that presented an example of the army as a 'melting pot'. This company was outstanding in its social cohesion and the special atmosphere that reigned in it. It would appear that both companies were representative of the Yishuv's social spectrum of the period, although in each one a completely different system of interpersonal relations had developed.

Company 511: Social Alienation

Interviews and memoires reveal that the drivers of Company 511 reflected the social alienation that existed among the Yishuv servicewomen. Habas defined the relations between the various groups in the company as:

> A serious internal problem that split the community in two and opened an abyss between both parts. ... the established Yishuv-born girls provided the core and spinal cord, and these [kept to themselves] within their own restricted society, while the others, many of whom were new immigrants, were untouched by Israeliness, lacking in language and roots.[74]

Company 511, which was stationed in a huge army camp with thousands of servicemen and women, was among the first ATS companies established in 1942 and toward 1944 it was commanded by a female Palestine officer. Conditions in the camp, which was located at a distance from any city, were harsher than in other ATS camps, both because of the weather (frequent sand storms) and because of the living quarters, which often had no running water. In addition to this company, the camp housed two others, 504 and 520. The servicewomen in all three were mainly from Palestine.

Like most of the ATS companies in the Middle East, in this one, too, there was a 'core' of girls from the agricultural sector, as well as urban women who did not belong to the 'organized' Yishuv, and a group of new immigrants, mainly from Austria and Germany. It would appear that these groups did not approach each other for most of their period in the military. Esther Tal from Nahalal, one of the company's drivers, summed up her attitude to the other servicewomen by saying: 'I looked at them [while still in basic training] from aside or from above'.[75] Lilli Glatt, then a new immigrant from Germany, who had arrived shortly before enlisting in the army and had neither relatives, nor status or roots in the country, had bitter memories of the hostile attitude toward her and her fellow immigrants on the part of the kibbutz and moshav girls.[76]

The women from Nahalal stood out from among the servicewomen from the kibbutzim and moshavim. Nahalal was the first agricultural settlement established in Palestine (1921) and its members, as did the members of Kfar Vitkin (est. 1930) in Emek Hefer, considered themselves to be the elite of the country's agricultural settlement. Although only twenty-one women (fewer than 5 per cent of all the women from the agricultural sector to enlist in the army) had been born or lived in Nahalal prior to enlistment,[77] they still managed to stand out in their demonstrations of nationalism, their social cohesion, and in their intransigent attitude toward any servicewomen who did not belong to their group. Debora Dayan described it well: 'There is a huge psychological difference between us (the first generation of settlers) – who already knew in our youth that every detail is but a small point in the midst of a big life – and our children, who from childhood see themselves as *the centre of the universe.*' [author's emphasis] Dayan believed that the second generation's sense of lordliness was not to their benefit.[78]

These traits were obvious among the second generation in Nahalal even before military recruitment. Various descriptions depict a second generation growing up in the moshav in a stern and demanding atmosphere of idealism and absolute commitment to the land and its settlement and, as Dayan put it, 'We want a healthy generation, with connections to the soil of the motherland ... a generation that makes do with little, in accordance with the land's ability to provide.'[79] The moshav education required of one to relinquish one's private thinking and family warmth, as Tal defined it: 'There [in the Ben Shemen educational institution to which she was sent after the death of her mother] I felt the love and warmth [I] *was forbidden in Nahalal.*' [author's emphasis][80] Various reports show that the youth in Nahalal were dissatisfied with the situation in the moshav and established a kind of opposition to the routine of life there, in the hope of improving the tissue of the moshav's interpersonal relations.

Aviva Dayan, from Nahalal, enlisted in the army the day after her wedding.[81] Her son, Yonatan Gefen, insists that she did it in order to escape a depressive mother and a political activist of a father who made it quite clear to her that as far as he was concerned 'making the desert bloom and work on the farm were more important than the second world war'. In his book, *Dear Woman*, Yonatan Gefen wrote about the future that awaits a woman on the moshav and the motivation of the second generation moshavniks to enlist in the British army: 'Mother and many others of her generation knew that the only way out lay in finding an objective even more sacred than the Hebrew agricultural settlement of Eretz Israel ... she escaped from a narrow-minded and demanding community'.[82] Dayan served as a driver in the ATS, although in Company 513.

The arrogant attitude of the Nahalal women toward their fellow recruits even attracted the attention of Amnon Zair (Rudi), representative of the Soldiers' Welfare Committee in Cairo and liaison officer between Haganah and the male and female soldiers in Egypt. He often found himself having to mediate between the groups of recruits and later wrote in his book, 'The worst of them all were the women from Nahalal. There was one company in which most of the women were from Nahalal. *As far as they were concerned, all those who weren't from Nahalal but from Tel Aviv and not members in Haganah were whores.*' [author's emphasis][83] Habas thought that conditions in the camp affected the development of the recruits' hard-line attitude: 'A particular type of servicewoman was created in that camp, *who was immune to everything.* It was here that the best traditions of the ATS were nurtured.' [author's emphasis][84] It seems that the same ATS 'traditions' that the leaders of the 'organized' Yishuv so applauded, were the cause of so much injustice to many other servicewomen.

Company 513: A Melting Pot

Established in late 1942, Company 513 was a unit in a small isolated army camp in the vicinity of the pyramids of Giza and near the Mina House Hotel (which gave the company its name – Company Mina), about four kilometres west of Cairo on the Cairo-Alexandria road.[85] This company, too, represented the variety of women who enlisted in the army, but it appears that the atmosphere and social cohesion that developed among the women of this company was unequalled throughout the ATS. The company's team spirit that was nurtured by long sweaty hours on the road over thousands of kilometres in convoys,[86] strenuous physical labour, and a collection of personal experiences, grew into a unique sisterhood, a friendship that remains to this day, nearly seventy years later. It was a company made up of veteran recruits from the agricultural sector, the Yishuv's 'cultural and economic' elite, who served side by side with new immigrants,[87] some of who were impoverished and devoid of formal education.[88]

Judith Spitz, who came from Germany about four years before joining the ATS, felt no alienation on the part of her native born counterparts. On the contrary, they 'adopted' her into their company. Erica Sharon (Ino), who arrived from Germany shortly before enlisting, also remembers the atmosphere of solidarity in the company that encompassed the veterans as well as the newcomers. Sharon had no family in the Yishuv and Shoshana Israeli (of the Yelin family), a member of the Yishuv's Jerusalem aristocracy, 'adopted' her as a sister. On vacations from the army, Sharon was invited to the Yelin home in Jerusalem and soon became one of the family.[89] The recruits from the agricultural sector respected the new immigrants, most of whom were from Germany or Austria, who were intelligent and well educated and, as they said, taught them a lot. The immigrant group, many of whom were appointed non-commissioned officers (corporals or sergeants) had a positive influence on the entire company.[90]

The atmosphere that developed among the servicewomen of Company 513 is reminiscent of the fellowships formed among soldiers in fighting units. Relationships in these units are characterized by friendship, as well as mutual solidarity and commitment, to the extent of self-sacrifice.[91] British women serving in British forces during the Second World War also reported on the sisterhood that developed during their military service and the ties forged with other women. These ties were based on physical proximity, loyalty and powerful fondness, as well as shared experiences of dressing, sleeping, eating and working.[92]

In other ATS companies, too, drivers participated in transport convoys and hard physical work, but in none of these did there develop a sisterhood similar to that in Company 513. It seems that the reason Company 513 achieved such social and professional cohesion is connected to the conditions on the camp, which was small and isolated, and also because of the personality of its commanding officer, Mary Mackenzie. Drivers from 513 were the first in the ATS to arrive at remote and even dangerous locations. A study of Company 513's war diary, the war diaries of other drivers' companies and literature of the period, reveals that under the command of McKenzie Company 513 made a name for itself in the ATS, achieved great distinction and prestige and served as a role model to other companies of drivers.[93]

The Recruits' Cultural Elite

The July 1942 rotation, in which 309 women were recruited, was seen as one of quality, since 'it consisted of graduates of the Herzliya High School in Tel Aviv and Rehavia in Jerusalem as well as graduates of the Reali High School in Haifa'.[94] These three schools, for which the fees were expensive, were considered the 'stronghold' of the urban Yishuv's cultural elite.

The daughters of intellectuals who immigrated from Germany in the course of the 1930s constituted a third, albeit separate, group of the recruited cultural elite. Many girls who moved to the Yishuv with their parents during the 1930s graduated from schools that had been established by immigrant intellectuals in order to preserve the German culture.[95] Esther Herlitz, who was educated at such high schools in Jerusalem, admitted that she was a 'great snob' when she enlisted in the army.[96] Her military service, as an instructor of new recruits in Sarafend and later as an officer in Egypt, introduced her for the first time to 'women who couldn't read or write [especially young women], draggers-on [especially recruits from Cyprus], lesbians and others, a connection that would not have been made under other circumstances'.[97] Even those who graduated from public schools maintained their German culture at home,[98] and there is no doubt that there was a certain alienation between Yishuv society and the immigrants from Germany.

With the evolvement of the archetypal and stereotypical image of the young Sabra –the New Hebrew – students at the Hebrew high schools, sons and daughters of the kibbutzim, moshavim and the youth movements, 'began developing a consciousness about their cultural uniqueness. They also produced and honed native status symbols and a peculiarly native Israeli style in language, dress and collective leisure culture.'[99] The revolution's second generation was controlled by a trend to ingrain the new and to cast it in institutional moulds, in order to ensure the achievements of the revolution and its stability. The Yishuv leaders attached enormous importance to the education of the Sabras and their success in this was considered a guarantee of the success of the entire educational enterprise. According to Yonatan Shapira, the crystallization of the education system around the desire to create a unique national and cultural awareness solely by use of the Hebrew language resulted in the growth of a younger generation with a fixed and conformist concept of reality. This concept depended on the interpretation of the leaders.[100]

The Herzliya High School took in many new immigrants (including, for example, Eliyahu Golomb). Many of its graduates, who were socially harmonious, as well as being active in the Haganah alongside their studies, volunteered for the British army after completing their schooling – the boys to the various forces and later to the Jewish Brigade and the girls to the ATS.[101] Not only did the establishment of the High School in Tel Aviv create the new Palestinei intelligentsia, it also made real the vision of the 'New Hebrew Woman'. Among other novel ideas, the school's teachers instilled in their students the ideal of women's liberation. The mutual educational ideals provided to the students of the High School consisted of knowledge of the homeland and restoration of the language. Dr Baruch Ben-Yehuda, the school's principal, wrote: 'It [the school] was a focus of love and knowledge of the homeland and a nest of unlimited fanaticism for the restoration of the Hebrew language. Both these had a strong influence on many of the country's youngsters, who studied in the school and served as an example of the new youth, straight backed, proud and deeply rooted in the homeland and in Hebrew speech.'[102]

Even the Reali High School in Haifa emphasized the image of the students as people of values and prepared them for being the national vanguard for settlement and self-sacrifice. Dr Arthur Biram, the school's principal, wished to reinforce the centrality of the school in the lives of its students and developed a tradition of outings, physical education and extra curricular activities. During the 1930s, with the increase in immigration, mainly from Germany, the school accepted large numbers of immigrant children and rules were made that would facilitate the social and educational integration of the newcomers.[103] In light of all this, it is possible to understand the attitude of the school's graduates to the recruits who did not come from a similar background, especially those who were not fluent in Hebrew.

Even sixty years after her military service, Sonya Peres (Gelman), who served as a driver in Company 511 in Tel el Kabir, was unable to conceal the revulsion she and her fellow servicewomen felt toward those she defined as the 'privileged snobs' from the Reali High School, who constituted a separate group within the company. Peres had been educated in the Ben-Shemen Educational Institution, where her father, Ya'akov Gelman, was a teacher. But, unlike many of the servicewomen in her company, she actually befriended the new immigrants from Germany and Austria who were shunned by the Yishuv-born recruits. She and her friends felt that the more educated women looked down on them as a 'lower and inferior class'.[104]

Erez, who served in Company 508 in Cairo Castle, considered herself one of the 'common people' – lacking a high school education or a well-off family. The father of her roommate was a professor in the Technion and four other fellow servicewomen were the daughters of Yishuv leaders, what was thought of as 'local aristocracy'. They formed a united group, did not connect to the others and most of their time was spent in discussing *belles lettres* – Hebrew and translated. One of the 'common people' was Hedda Boshes (Shmueli).[105]

Miriam Vardi (a niece of Hadassah Samuel and granddaughter of Yehuda Gur) also served in that Company. Due to her fluency in English she was employed as an orders coordinating clerk to various units and, according to Erez's definition, she belonged to the cultural 'elite'. Vardi was raised in Jerusalem's Rehavia neighbourhood and attended the Hebrew High School. She remembered that among her classmates were the children of Dr Dov Yosef and Gershon Agron, editor of the *Palestine Post*. Other school friends of hers were the sons and daughters of engineers, university lecturers and others. This was their natural reference group and Vardi believed that they did not consider themselves 'elite' because there was no weaker or different group toward which they could feel superior. Once in the army, when she encountered recruits from a different social and cultural background from her own, was she able to recognize the differences.[106]

Attitudes to Oriental Jewish Recruits

One of the most obvious stereotypes in the Yishuv that were upheld even in the army was expressed in attitudes toward the Oriental Jews, who constituted the largest group in the 'non-organized' Yishuv.[107] Their lives were conducted on the fringes of society from every aspect: they lived in neighbourhoods on the edges of the towns and cities, their education was usually insufficient, and in the eyes of the organized core of the Yishuv they were closer to Arabs in mentality and lifestyle, since the language they spoke was different from that of the European Jews. Their social and economic contribution to the Zionist enterprise in the country was considered by the 'organized' Yishuv as marginal and non-productive, and there prevailed an almost complete rift between them and the new society with its values, symbols and institutions. The only reference to them came from the people employed in the social services, especially in Tel Aviv.[108]

Those who did find employment were on the lowest rungs of the ladder: blue-collar workers, apprentices and vendors; the majority of the women who worked outside their own home, were employed as cleaners. These were mostly girls in their teens or women in their 50s; in other words, before starting and raising a family or afterwards. Only about 50 per cent of the Oriental communities went to schools belonging to the 'organized' Yishuv, most of these attended elementary school and only 13 per cent continued to high school education. About 33 per cent of them received various kinds of religious education, but even here, only 10 per cent continued after bar-mitzvah age.[109]

It is hard not to discern a patronizing note in the reports of recruiters on their interaction with these recruits. One of them stressed that she

> enjoyed seeing these 'orientals' taking an active part in everything ... such things have never been heard within the wall of the Old City. Their *horizons are widening*. They never imagined to themselves that the world is so complex and complicated. I have connected with these girls. They are full of good intentions. In spite of being tired after a day's work they are willing to help me in my work in the office. [author's emphasis][110]

It seems that the stereotypical attitude on the part of women from the 'organized' Yishuv toward women from the Oriental communities was so deeply rooted in the Yishuv, as to be thoroughly assimilated in the recruits' group as well.

In his well-known book, *Orientalism*, Edward Said claimed that the definitions of backwardness and failure were supported by anthropologists who portrayed the [East] as primitive and uncivilized and labelled it as backward and failing, as part of the definition of the 'other'.[111] Stereotypes can be preserved when people tend to seek information to confirm their validity while avoiding information that will force them to introduce changes to their preconceived beliefs. Nonetheless, in general, people tend to avoid collecting material on someone who belongs to a stereotypical group, in the assumption that mere belonging to such a group makes it possible to make conclusions as to his/her traits. An incident that took place in Company 531 in Tura, Egypt, may serve to demonstrate the way stereotypes regarding these recruits were maintained in Yishuv society. The company's Hebrew officers, Esther Herlitz and Victoria Ben-Artzi (Tov), were asked to recommend – as part of their job – suitable candidates for an officer-training course. One of the servicewomen in their company was Yemenite-born Sergeant Malka Livni, who they considered had the personality and the talents for becoming an officer. But they rejected her application because they believed that if she were to be granted a commission, she would be unable, after the war, to return to the social framework of the Rehovot neighbourhood from which she came.[112]

Alienation and Distance Between the 'Natives' and the Others

Several hundred servicewomen felt they belonged to the political and social elites of the Yishuv, which was composed mainly of members of the Labour Movement. Sonya Halperin from Kfar Vitkin, a driver in Company 503 stationed in Abassya in Egypt, wrote to her family that she had felt lonely since her recruitment and only recently had it become easier for her: 'A reinforcement came – B.C. [Bronka Cohen] – *one of ours*, courageous, energetic, argues from morn 'til night with those harebrained ... simpletons who are constantly concerned with their dances and who sanctify every language except for Hebrew.' [author's emphasis][113]

What was the source of the patronizing attitude toward the new immigrants? One of the basic tenets of the Zionist concept expressed itself in the rejection of the 'Diaspora Jew' image, at times even to the extent of 'demonizing' it. Rejection of the Diaspora and its way of life and, especially the stereotyping of the Diaspora Jew, served as a secret mechanism for honing the boundaries of the Zionist 'national religion' principle and its superiority over traditional Jewish religion. The constant rejection of Diaspora culture came to a certain extent from the need to emphasize the superiority of Zionist-pioneering culture over the traditional Judaism from which it grew. The deeper the moral and spiritual roots of the 'Zionist religion' became in the country, the stronger the ethos of rejecting the Diaspora became, reaching a peak during the 1930s and 1940s.[114] The anti-Diaspora ethos in the 'Zionist religion' was nurtured during the 1930s in the Yishuv's schools and was integrated into the public awareness from an early age via local literature and schoolbooks. It is not surprising, therefore, that when the Yishuv-born recruits met recently arrived recruits from various countries in Europe, they reacted with patronizing disdain toward the Diaspora women.

At the time of enlisting many of the foreign-born recruits were still involved in the process of rebuilding their personal and national identities. Identity, according to Eric Erikson's, is a 'sense of independence and continuity created in the course of a dynamic process of personal and social experience and of interactions, during which symbols, concepts and values are obtained, whether consciously or subconsciously'.[115] According to gender researchers such as Alison Weir, Sheila Ben-Haviv, Judith Butler and others, the process of identity building involvs a constant search for ways to settle the internal contradictions and exercise the individual's sense of independence. They claim that the dynamic nature of the identity building process can be either harmonious and calm or conflicting and riddled with crises. The identity of the new-immigrant recruits was based on personal experiences accumulated both in their countries of origin and in Palestine. These experiences were integrated into the new army experience they were obliged to achieve in a short time and, together, they were added to the new national identity they had not yet managed to assimilate.[116]

Most of the research on emigrant women relates to 'double discrimination' or their 'triple oppression'; in other words, their femininity that is influenced by their status (emigrant labourer) and their nationality (foreign).[117] Most of the recruits who immigrated to the Yishuv were a part of the waves of 'forced migration' that were the result of economic and political pressures as well as anti-Semitism. It was not the 'free emigration' that was typical – for example - of the First and Second Aliyahs to Palestine. By nature, the immigration experience includes severance from the world of one's childhood, one's parents, one's siblings and one's extended family. Although many of the immigrant women arrived with their close families, their experiences of immigration and assimilation in their new country were as painful and traumatic as those of other immigrant women in the past – indeed, of immigrants in general.

In addition to the usual hardships involved in integrating into a new society, in the case of the recruits was the Yishuv's alienating attitude, and especially that of the youth, toward the newcomers. This was joined by the immigrants' concerns for the families left behind in Europe, with which all contact had ceased and there was no knowing what had happened to them. Their Yishuv-born counterparts had no way of understanding these hardships.[118]

Some of the recruits admitted their patronizing attitude to the immigrants. One of these wrote in her diary: 'I think that [such] nurturing of emotional nationalism ultimately leads to severe fanaticism in human relations.' However, she managed to justify such behaviour by explaining to herself, 'But for us it is a life necessity as well as an existential necessity.'[119] These recruits, most of which were Haganah members, saw themselves as emissaries of something big, that must not be tarnished by unsuitable behaviour.

Displacement, migration and integration usually involve an encounter with different social and cultural systems that need adjusting to. Moreover, assimilation into a new society often involves a change of employment and profession. Various studies indicate that women follow a pattern of action – social integration by way of 'networks' that make it easier for immigrant women to assimilate and create friendships. These social networks are mostly voluntary, with their members choosing whom to connect with and under what circumstances, although they also exist in bureaucratic or organized bodies such as an army.[120] Although in the ATS servicewomen were not able to choose who to connect with, there were other conditions available that enabled them to establish such a support network – daily contact, age and gender, employment, etc. Nonetheless, connections and ties did not always form among the groups.

It was not only from the battlefield and in war that women were excluded by men, but also from some of their narratives. This also applies to the pushing out of women who did not belong to the Yishuv's normative framework at that period, by other women who had access to the centres of influence in the Yishuv and, subsequently, in the State of Israel. In the historiography of Palestine during the Yishuv period there is a marked interest in the group memory, ways of perpetuating and preserving certain narratives from the past and denying others. This interest consists also of the national identity and its boundaries, of what it includes and what has been excluded from it. The debate on memory and perpetuation is a study of identity itself and touches on the question of to whom does history belong.

Psychological studies have determined that direct contact between groups can bring a reduction in stereotyping, prejudice and discrimination. Research literature has identified four main conditions that must exist in order for hostility to be reduced between two groups: social-institutional support; a high potential for inter-interpersonal familiarity (frequent and constant proximity); equal status; and cooperation among group members.[121] All these conditions existed in the British army, but still didn't bring about a reduction in the social friction among the servicewomen. These did, however, manage to achieve teamwork and shared lifestyle on behalf of the war effort, even though this fact did not obliterate or reduce the intensity of the alienation and stereotyping that existed in society. From this aspect, it appears that the British army was not a 'melting pot' (except for one instance in Company 513), but a reflection of Yishuv society on all its various levels.

One of the focuses of conflict in the army (which hadn't existed beforehand in the Yishuv) took place between the servicewomen in the ATS and those in the WAAF. It can be stated with a measure of generalization that there had been virtually no social interaction between the two groups, and even to this day some rivalry exists between them. This happened for several reasons: the different service conditions; from the prestige and 'higher status' image attached to the WAAF as compared to the ATS; from the organizational framework and its differing character and the different relationship it had with the Yishuv institutions. If any connection was made among these groups, it was usually in the clubs in Cairo or Ismailia.[122]

NOTES

1. For critical views of Yishuv society, see, for example, Uri Ram, 'Hahevra ve'mada hahevra: sociologia mimsadit vesociologia bikortit beisrael' [Society and social science: institutional sociology and critical sociology in Israel], in Uri Ram (ed.), *Hahevra haisraelit: hebetim bikorti'im* [Israeli society: critical aspects] (Tel Aviv 1994), pp.7–39; Shlomo Svirsky, 'He'arot la'sociologia hahistorit shel tekufat hayishuv' [Comments on the sociological history of the Yishuv period], in Uri Ram (ed.), *Hahevra haisraelit: hebetim bikorti'im* [Israeli society: critical aspects] (Tel Aviv 1993), pp.54–82.
2. The number of women fortunate enough to be issued an immigration permit (Certificate) under the category 'wealthy' was several times smaller than that of men. The main channel of immigration available to women during the British Mandate of Palestine was under the category 'dependent' (unemployed), which

testifies to the discrimination inherent in the very definition of this category. Aviva Halamish, 'Aflayat nashim be'aliyah betkufat hamandat- ha'uvdot, hasibot, hahashlachot' [Discrimation against women in the Mandadory period – facts, reasons and repercussions], *Proceedings of The 12th World Jewish Studies Congress,* August 1997, pp.50–1.

3. David Gurevitz and Ahron Gretz, *Haaliyah, haYishuv ve hatnua hativit shel haochlosiya in Eretz Israel* [Immigration, the Yishuv and the natural flow of the population of Eretz Israel] (Jerusalem 1945), p.91; Deborah Bernstein, 'Daughters of the Nation: Between the Public and Private Spheres in Pre-State Israel', in Judith Baskin (ed.), *Jewish Women in Historical Perspective* (Chicago, IL 1998), pp.288–9. According to Gur Elroi, between 1905 and 1914 some 23,000 people immigrated to Israel via Odessa, of whom 60 per cent were men and 40 per cent women. It was a family emigration, rather than that of young singles. Gur Elroi, *Immigrantim: hahagira hayehudit le Eretz Israel bereshit hame'a haesrim* [Immigrants: Jewish immigration to Eretz Israel in the early twentieth century] (Jerusalem 2004), p.119. The composition of the population was affected by the immigration policies of the Mandatory government and its wish to ensure that the immigrants were able to support themselves in the developing economy and took into consideration natural population growth.
4. According to a report prepared by the Colonial Office in May 1946, 3,155 women enlisted in the ATS between 18 January 1942 and 30 June 1943, National Archives (NA), London, CO 537/1819. This number includes some 200 women who enlisted in Palestine within various frameworks: local Arab women, about thirty Czech Jewish refugees, about thirty-six non-Jewish Polish and Czech women, sixty-three Greek citizens (including five Jewish women) and fifty-one British citizens (including three Jewish women). 'Numbers of the recruits who trained in the ATS central training camp in the Middle East', Central Zionist Archive, Jerusalem (CZA), S25/5097. In a document titled 'Recruitment to the Army', dated 17.10.1939–1.3.1945, the number of ATS recruits stands at 3,336 (in other words, about 200 more recruits than in army reports); 23 March 1945, ibid. In another document, titled 'Eretz Israel recruits to the British army by months', apparently from early 1946, it was reported that 3,166 women enlisted in the ATS. Ibid.
5. According to Gelber, throughout the war period, 789 women served in the WAAF. Yoav Gelber, *Toldot hahitnadvut: Bein Britim, Aravim veGermanim* [History of volunteering: Between British, Arabs and Germans] (Jerusalem 1984), pp.300–4. According to Yosef Shavit, who relies on RAF data, 615 Jewish women served in the WAAF. Yosef Shavit, *Mitnadvim Bekahol: eretzisraelim besherut heil hate'ufa hamalchuti* [Volunteers in blue: from Eretz Israel to service in the RAF] (Tel Aviv 1995), p.136. According to Jewish Agency statistics, 609 women served in the WAAF up to the end of 1945. 'Recruits in the Land of Israel to the Air Force', 29 November 1945, CZA, S25/5097. These numbers, too, include non-Jewish women.
6. In terms of 2016 population statistics in the State of Israel, this is equivalent to over 27,000 women of military recruitment age.
7. Statistics refer to some 2,000 ATS servicewomen (about 67 per cent of all the Jewish recruits), whose details are preserved in the IDF Archive and in the CZA. With regard to the WAAF, existing statistics relate to 100 servicewomen and do not provide clear-cut conclusions as to the remaining recruits. Statistics were

taken from the IDF Archive, release forms (Vets Deposition) and registry of released servicewomen in the Histadrut's Liaison Office, as from the CZA S37, files of candidates for recruitment in the municipal recruitment offices. Insufficient data was found with regard to the women's continued service and their levels of education.

8. According to Baki this data differentiates between the Yishuv and other nations, but feared that marriage at a later age could have a detrimental effect on the Yishuv's demographic situation, since late marriage results in a lower rate of childbirth. The average marriage age for Sephardic women in the late 1930s was 18.12; among Ashkenazi women the age was 22.76 in the Old Yishuv and 24.7in the New one. Roberto Baki, *H'anohag Benisuin ve'beyeluda bekerv hashchavot hashonot shel he'Yeshuv ve Hashpaato al Atiddenu* [The custom in marriage and birth in different layers of the Yishuv and its impact on our future] (Jerusalem 1945), pp.114–15.
9. Around 120 women were recruited from twenty-one Moshavim, of the sixty-five Moshavim existing in the country in 1944. Most of these (sixty-six) came from the veteran workers' Moshavim in the Jezreel Valley, as well as from the Hefer Valley and the Sharon region. Around 180 women were recruited from the Kibbutz Ha'artzi and United Kibbutz Movement. The others came from Judea and Samaria and the kibbutz union. The Histadrut Liaison Office, dated 1946, IDF Archive, Vets Deposition, as well as forms filled by recruits, CZA, S37.
10. IDF Archive; Vets Deposition; CZA, S37.
11. Roberto Baki, 'Ha'ochlusia: Demographia' [Population: demography], *Hebrew Encyclopedia*, 1 (Tel Aviv 1957), pp.673–83.
12. Sharett expressed it best as: 'a Yishuv of immigration and the war caught us in the process of immigration ... in fact, this is how we were caught in the midst of a process of establishing [ourselves] in the country'. Histadrut Executive meeting, 12 February 1942, p.7 (80), Labour Movement Archive, Lavon Institute.
13. In the course of 1943, the maximum age for recruitment was lowered from 45 to 40. The minimum age remained 18 and candidates below this age required parental permission in order to enlist. 'Results of a meeting between ATS doctors and doctors of the Jewish Agency Recruitment Department', 28 March 1943, CZA, S37/676.
14. Meeting of Working Women's Council, *Davar Hapo'elet*, 1–2 (30 January 1942), p.14.
15. UKM Congress in Yagur, *Davar Hapo'elet*, 6–7 February 1942, p.38, IDF Archive, 45/140/2002.
16. Although large factories – as already mentioned – had committed themselves to preserving the rights of the recruits, many women had reservations about leaving their jobs and losing their rights after the war. On the other hand, *Davar Hapo'elet*, 1–2 (30 January 1942, p.3) stressed that 'the element of unemployment or income had almost no influence on the decision to enlist. On the contrary, many [women] relinquished organized employment.'
17. The place of women during the 1920s and 1930s was on the fringes of the employment market. A significant proportion of them worked at jobs traditionally considered 'feminine', such as services, housework, food preparation and sales, and clerical work that kept them on low wage scales. The

1940s saw little change in this respect. Deborah Bernstein, 'Hahalutza bein hadvadim: ma'amdan shel nashim bekoah ha'avoda btkufat hayishuv' [Pioneer woman between the boilers: women's status in the Yishuv's work force], *Megamot*, 28, no.1 (June 1983), p.10. This notwithstanding, official statistics on female employment in the British Mandate period do not provide a complete picture, since much of women's economic activity created a hidden labour market that included sub-leasing rooms, laundry services, housework and cooking, and more. Bat-Sheva Margalit Stern, 'La'malka ein bayit, la'melech ain keter? Ma'amadan shel nashim yehudiot beshuk ha'avoda be'eretz Israel hamandatorit' [The queen has no home, the king has no crown? Status of Jewish women on the labour market in Mandatory Eretz Israel], in Avi Bareli and Nahum Karlinsky (eds), *Calcala ve'hevra beyemei hamandat 1918–1948* (Be'er Sheva 2003), pp.109–17.

18. The wages issue was one of the reasons for reduced recruitment. Wages were determined according to tenure and the kind of work in the service. The average wage per head in the Yishuv for February 1942 was 2.4 Lira Palestine in a family of 3.3; in Tel Aviv this was 2.6 Lira Palestine, and in Jerusalem 2.3 Lira Palestine. 'Provisional summaries of the investigation into standards of living in February 1942', CZA, S19/329. The military wages of Yishuv volunteers were calculated at two thirds those of the British soldiers. Yoav Gelber, 'Hitgabshut hayishuv hayehudi be'eretz Israel 1936–1947' [Forming the Jewish Yishuv in Eretz Israel 1936–1947], in Moshe Lissak (ed.), *Toldot hayishuv be'eretz Israel meaz ha'aliyah harishona: tkufat hamandat habriti* [History of the Yishuv in Eretz Israel since the First Aliyah: period of British Mandate], B (Jerusalem 1994), pp.427–8.
19. Leslie Whateley, chief ATS Commander who visited the area and learned of their motives, was disappointed that the war and the contribution to the war effort were not the reasons for which Arab women enlisted. Dame Leslie Whateley, *As Thoughts Survive* (London 1949), p.168.
20. R.K. 'In the Training Camp for Servicewomen', *Davar Hapo'elet*, 6 (7 July 1942), p.78.
21. The use of the terms 'organized' and 'non-organized' Yishuv can be misleading with regard to the complex reality of the time and they are used here only because they are so commonplace in the research and discourse of that period.
22. The fact that about 1,600 ATS servicewomen (half of the overall number) registered with the Histadrut liaison office at the end of the war, is a further indication. By the end of August 1943, from a total of 3,072 servicewomen, 1,393 were Histadrut members (45.3 per cent). Of these 466 lived in Tel Aviv, 276 in Haifa, 159 in Jerusalem, 22 in the other towns and the remainder lived on kibbutzim and moshavim. 'Numbers of Servicemen and Women According to the Jewish Agency's Soldiers' Books', Labour Movement Archive, 3237.
23. Gelber, 'Hitgabshut hayishuv hayehudi be'eretz Israel 1936–1947', p.428. Ben-Gurion testified to the ability of the 'organized' Yishuv to impose its authority on the 'non-organized' Yishuv as 'although there is a known, but not large, part of the Yishuv that does not obey our orders, still I am not familiar with any ... organization in the world that, without having a power of enforcement or a parliamentary framework, has so many listeners and followers and on such cardinal matters'. Minutes of Jewish Agency Executive meeting, 8 June 1941, p.6, CZA, S100/33b.

24. Esther Tal's Memoires.
25. Orah Shem-Ur, *Bli ha'kuku ve'hasarafan* [Without a ponytail and the sarafan] (Tel Aviv 1992), p.85.
26. Gelber, 'Hitgabshut hayishuv haychudi be'eretz Israel 1936 1947', p.342.
27. Youth Aliyah was a program initiated by Recha Freier when the Nazis came to power in 1933, with the objective of bringing boys and girls from Europe to Israel. Once the Jewish Agency had approved the programme, Henrietta Szold was appointed to head the enterprise and served in this capacity until her death in 1945.
28. On Youth Aliyah as an educational institution, it has been written, for example, 'The Youth Aliyah enterprise is not a social organization purely for the purposes of immigration ... it has to be a movement, that is to say an educational movement, with educational objectives that are geared to the needs of the integrating country – Eretz Israel. And not those whose countries of origin are obligating them.' Bracha Habas, *Sefer Aliyat Hanoar* [Book of Youth immigration] (Jerusalem 1941), p.15.
29. Horowitz also pointed out that 'lately, there have been many rumours as to the fate of the girls of Youth Aliyah who have apparently become involved in prostitution ... but after an investigation ... this slander has to be utterly denied. There are only a few isolated instances to justify this claim ... on the other hand, there is no denying the fact that the presence of young girls alone in the city, with no family and without a certain circle [of people] looking out for them, constitutes a suitable background for all kinds of undesirable phenomena.' Yosef Horowitz, *Bograi aliyat hano'ar* [Graduates of Youth Aliyah] (Jerusalem 1942), p.72.
30. Daniela Reich, 'Between National Mission and Social Ostracism: Contacts Between Jewish Women to British Servicemen 1940–1948' (MA thesis, Haifa University, 2003), p.69. Dozens of girls, mostly of Austrian origin, chose this option.
31. Of them 169 were privates, seven were first corporals, nine were corporals and one achieved the rank of sergeant. Most of them (128) enlisted after having spent between one and four years in Palestine before the start of the recruitment drive. 'Recruits on Active Service', report on graduates of the Youth Aliyah in the army, 15 October 1944, CZA, S25/5040.
32. Group interviews with former members of Company 513 (Mina Company) in Haifa on 27 April 2006, and in Even Yehuda on 2 November 2006. She apparently stopped after enlisting.
33. Tamar Razi, 'Building the Fringes of the Nation: Homeless Youths in Tel Aviv in the 1930s and 1940s' (PhD thesis, Bar Ilan University, 2006), p.228; Deborah Bernstein, 'Tel Aviv lavsha mahsof ... Pnina hameshuga'at vegvulot hakrach' [Tel Aviv donned a décolleté ... Crazy Pnina and the city boundaries], *Teoria veBikoret*, 25 (Autumn 2004), p.153. On the connection between the development of the phenomenon of prostitution in Palestine and the waves of immigration starting at the end of the nineteenth century, see, for example, Elroi, *Immigrantim*, pp.146–62.
34. Yair Spiegel, 'Hahitmodedut hamodi'init vehasiculit shel mishteret hamandat umahleket hahakirot haplilit ba (CID) im hmiflaga hacommunistit ha'eretzisraelit 1920–1948' [The intelligence and counterintelligence dilemma in the

Mandatory police and its CID with the Communist Party in the Yishuv 1920–1948] (MA thesis, Bar Ilan University, 1999), pp.11–12.

35. However, in this party, too, the majority was Jewish, although for reasons of ideology and pressure from the Comintern (the union of Communist states), it was determined in the early 1930s that the party would be headed by an Arab. The Arab riots of 1929 and 1936 forced the Communist to face a serious dilemma. Most of the Jewish members tended toward a position whereby the unique interests of the Jewish population should not be ignored, which led to their tendency toward a differential approach to both parts of the public. Dan Horowitz and Moshe Lissak, *Miyishuv lemedina: yehudei Eretz Israel betkufat hamandat habriti kekehila politit* [From Yishuv to State: Eretz Israeli Jews during the British Mandate as a political community] (Tel Aviv 1977), p.46. This formula absolved the Jewish members from having to actively identify with the rioting Arabs.
36. Shmuel Dotan, *Adumim: hamiflaga hacomunistit be'eretz Israel* [Reds: the Communist Party in Eretz Israel] (Tel Aviv 1991), pp.342–3.
37. Testimony of Rachel Michelson (Katz), 7 April 1942, IDF Archive, 8 297/03/. Male communist recruits behaved in the same way in the army's transport units.
38. Letter from Yuval to Binyamini, 23 April 1942, CZA, S25/11161; official recruitment forms according to months, 28 September 1942, ibid. These must have been among the combined efforts of the Yishuv institutions and the Mandatory police to uncover communists. For many years the British police had refrained from involving Jews in the intelligence system, but, for lack of sufficient manpower, they were obliged to include Jews in their 'inner sanctum' – their secret service. There was hostility between the Communist Party and the Yishuv institutions, so that in this case, mutual interests were formed and the Jewish Agency reported to the British military authorities on people, including suspected communists. Spiegel, 'Hahitmodedut hamodi'init vehasiculit', pp.81–2.
39. Since it was common knowledge that the Hashomer Hatza'ir movement objected to female recruitment, including that of its own members, these women recruits were suspected of being communists. There was some basis to this suspicion, as some members of the communist faction who joined the army and spread communist propaganda had previously belonged to Hashomer Hatza'ir. Yair Spiegel, 'Hashomer Hatza'ir in Defense and Security of the Yishuv, 1920–1947' (PhD thesis, Bar Ilan University, 2006), p.194, ref. 78.
40. 'And, by the way, in the meantime they were sexually active – and with English servicemen, of all people.' That same servicewoman connected communist activity to the behaviour of other servicewomen who alienated themselves from the Yishuv by the very act of having relations with Englishmen, even though the communist women did not seek the company of Englishmen'. Bracha Habas, *Bnot hayil: sefer ha'ATS* [Women of valour: book of the ATS] (Tel Aviv 1964), p.63.
41. Interview with Rachel Ziv (Barshavsky), Tel Aviv, 2 February 2006.
42. Interview with Aviva Gil (Flentzbaum), Tel Aviv, 24 January 2006.
43. Individual young religious women took part in nationwide instruction courses, training camps and professional courses; they also worked as cooks in Haganah kitchens. Exact numbers in the Haganah are not available, but it would appear

that thousands of religious women were active in the organization. During the 1940s sixty-nine young religious women served as a separate religious platoon in the 'Comrades' Platoon' in the Tel Aviv district. Lilach Rosenberg-Friedman, 'Women and Gender in Religious Zionism: Organization, Settlement and Defence 1918–1948' (PhD thesis, Bar Ilan University, 2002), pp.259–60.

44. Interview with Sara Kopler (Bar-Adon), Tel Aviv, 26 June 2006; interview with Elisheva Erez (Pearlman), Hertzliya Pituah, 14 January 2006; Lilach Rosenberg-Friedman, *Mahapehaniyot be'al korhan: nashim umigdar bazionut hadatit betkufat hayishuv* [Inadvertent revolutionaries: women and gender in religious Zionism in the Yishuv period] (Jerusalem 2005), pp.281–9.
45. Dov Knohel (ed.), *Behitnadev am: mitnadvim dati'im bemilhemet ha'olam hashniya* [When a nation volunteers: religious volunteers in the Second World War], A and B (Tel Aviv 1989, 1990), pp.94–103. For example, religious servicemen protested that no book of rules was available to show soldiers the way to follow the commands of their religion. Although they did have the book *Mahane Israel*, specially published in 1941 by the Hafetz Haim, on rules and conduct for soldiers in military service, this was intended for Jews serving in a foreign army, while in their case this was a war that they saw as the war of the Jewish people. Ibid. pp.98–9.
46. Haviva Kotler, 'In Answer to the Chief Rabbinate (a)', 'Newsletter to the Religious Serviceman' 20 Adar 1945, in Dov Knohel (ed.), *Behitnadev am: mitnadvim dati'im bemilhemet ha'olam hashniya* [When a nation volunteers: religious volunteers in the Second World War], A and B (Tel Aviv 1989, 1990) pp.162–3.
47. Mostly as a result of the quotas imposed on the kibbutzim, the draft and the searches for evaders. Yoav Gelber, *Toldot hahitnadvut: Hahitnadvut ve mekoma bemidiniut hazionit ve hayishuvit 1939–1942* [History of volunteering: volunteering and its place in Zionist and Yishuv Policies 1939–1942] (Jerusalem 1989), p.425. Up to July 1940, men volunteered for the army 'who sought war'. Yoav Gelber, 'Aspectim politiim lehakamat hakoah halohem beyishuv haeretzisraeli btkufat milhemet haolam hashnia' [Political aspects in establishing the fighting force in the Yishuv during WWII], *Yalkut Moreshet*, 22 (November 1976), p.47. During this month the Jewish Agency, together with the 'organized Yishuv', became de facto an active factor in the recruitment. At this stage, the Haganah organization undertook responsibility for recruitment, directing people to the various units, in accordance with the national criteria it determined – the Jewish units or the Buffs. After the reawakening of the summer/autumn of 1940, recruitment sunk into decline that lasted throughout 1941. The Haganah organization hoped to re-establish itself with the help of the recruitment drive, after its status in the Yishuv had been undermined by the riots of 1936–39, but when this did not happen, it stopped dealing with recruitment.
48. 'What Did I Enlist For?' conversation with ATS member Hanna Levin, *Olam Ha'isha*, 42–43 (20 February 1942), p.2; Habas, *Bnot hayil*, p.17.
49. Nira Yuval-Davis, 'Nationalism, Feminism and Gender Relations', in Montserrat Guibernau and John Hutchinson (eds), *Understanding Nationalism* (Cambridge: Polity Press, 2001), pp.129–31; Elisabetta Addis and Valeria Russo, 'The Constitution of a Gendered Enemy', in Elisabetta Addis, Valeria Russo and Lorenza Sebesta (eds), *Women Soldiers: Images and Realities* (New York 1994),

p.xiv; Sylvia Walby, 'Is Citizenship Gendered?', *Sociology*, 28, no.2 (May 1994), pp.379–95. According to researchers who studied the connection between citizenship and sectors of society, the myth of citizenship in democratic and liberal societies leads to the mistaken belief that every member of society has equal status. There are various levels of citizenship and entire sectors do not enjoy full citizenship. The term 'citizenship' represents a complexity of relations between the individual and society from which women – for example – have been excluded. James Burk, 'Citizenship, Status and Military Service: The Quest for the Inclusion by Minorities and Conscientious Objectors', *Armed Forces*, 21, no.4 (Summer 1995), p.503.

50. Habas, *Bnot hayil*, pp.17–18.
51. Ibid., p.17.
52. On messages and designs of propaganda posters in general, see Peter Paret, Beth Irwin Lewis and Paul Paret, *Persuasive Images: Posters of War and Revolution* (Princeton, NJ: Princeton University Press, 1992); on the design of and messages in the recruitment posters for the British army, see Batia Donner, *Shamir Grafika Ivrit: Studio Ha'achim Shamir* [Shamir Hebrew Graphics: Shamir Bros. Studio), Catalog 3/99 (Tel Aviv 1999), pp.6–12;, and also Rachel Arbel (ed.), *Kahol Lavan be tsvaim: dimuim hazutiim shel hazionut 1897–1947* [Blue and white in colors: frontal images of Zionism 1897–1947] (Tel Aviv 1996). See also, for example, Hava Bronfeld-Stein, 'Beautiful Group Portrait with a Gun: Visual Representations of Women Soldiers in Israel Defense Force Albums 1948–1958' (MA thesis, Bar Ilan University, 2002), where there is an analysis of the messages the IDF tried to pass on in the official photographs of pretty girl soldiers during the early days of the State of Israel. On recruitment posters, see Tali Shilo, *Kum ve'hitgayes'* [Step Up to Enlist], Recruitment Posters – British Army, WWII in Eretz Israel, Proposal for Exhibition in Museology Studies 2005, pp.18–19; and Donner, *Shamir Grafika Ivrit*, p.7.
53. Habas, *Bnot hayil*, p.19.
54. There were women during the American Civil War (1861–65) who even wished to join the army for economic reasons, as well as out of patriotism, since a soldier's salary was especially high in comparison to that of a factory worker. Goldstein, Joshua, *War and Gender: How Gender Shapes the War System and Vice Versa* (Cambridge 2001), pp.107–11; DeAnne Blanton, and Lauren Cook, *They Fought Like Demons: Women Soldiers in the Civil War* (New York 2002), pp.94–106.
55. Gail Brayborn and Penny Summerfield, *Out of the Cage: Women's Experiences in Two World Wars* (London 1987), p.34. Summerfield draws a more complex picture of women's motives for enlisting in the military and the various industries. Some of them took the decision independently; others reported a domineering father or a depressing mother as catalysts for their decision to enlist.
56. From among the people from the non-organized Yishuv who left their stamp on the composition and character of the Hebrew units throughout the war, the new immigrants were a significant component. Gelber, 'Hitgabshut hayishuv hayehudi be'eretz Israel 1936–1947', pp.425–7. On recruitment of the new immigrants from the non-organized Yishuv, Shem-Ur wrote 'They enlisted quietly, with no farewell parties, because the truth is that most of them did not

enlist for reasons of nationalism, but because they had no work and they were tired of seeking a day's work and worrying about where their next day's meal was coming from.' Shem-Ur, *Bli ha'kuku ve'hasarafan*, pp.145–6.

57. Although today it is customary to use other terms in describing Jews from Asia and North Africa, the term Oriental Jews will be used here because of its frequency in the research and discourse of the period discussed in this book.
58. Habas, *Bnot hayil*, pp.19–21. According to *Davar Hapo'elet* 'until the end of August 1942, a small number of Oriental Jewish women registered with the recruitment office: women of Yemenite, Sephardi, Bukhari, Kurd, Persian, Alleppo origin. The reasons for their recruitment are varied: some of them found recruitment to provide a solution to their unemployment; others found a release from the restrictions imposed by their parents, from a violent husband. And there are also those who "feel intuitively that this is their duty".' Further, there was a report of a girl who was forced into marriage at the age of 16 and suffered severe violence at the hands of her husband before going into domestic service, where her employer persuaded her to enlist. Rachel H. [sic.], 'From the Writings of a recruiter', *Davar Hapo'elet*, 7–8 (31 August 1942), p.96.
59. Shem-Ur, *Bli ha'kuku ve'hasarafan*, pp.145–6.
60. T. Damon, *Beshvilai hagoral: Roman mehayai ha'ATS* [In the paths of destiny: a novel on ATS life] (Tel Aviv 1953), Introduction (unpaginated). Dora Margalit wrote the book under the pseudonym T. Damon. The book is surprisingly candid and not only does the author refrain from hiding the less pleasant parts of her behaviour in the army, but she even provides her motives for them. So far as can be compared with literature and reportage of the period, the book is also true in its descriptions of life in the ATS.
61. Ya'akov Margalit (ed.), *Bayit bamoshav: haverot mesaprot* [A home on the moshav: women members recall] (Tel Aviv 1962), p.239. Haim Guri wrote that Berniki (Noah, the daughter of Levi Eshkol) was 'a driver in the ATS ... decided to see and experience everything' and also 'like an excellent alchemist, she turned times into pleasures'. Haim Guri, Hasefer hameshuga [The crazy book] (Tel Aviv 1971), p.22.
62. Horowitz, *Bograi aliyat hano'ar*, p.63.
63. Zipora Shahar was the daughter of Eliyahu Eitan and sister of the former IDF Chief of the General Staff, Rafael Eitan; Zipa Gov was a member the Katz family, one of the oldest in Tel Aviv, cousin of the artist Ziona Tager. Interview with Elisheva Erez; interview with Zipora Shahar (Eitan), Nahalal, 7 January 2006; interview with Zipa Gov (Katz), Tel Aviv, 22 October 2006.
64. L.A. (sic.), 'From Life on Camp', *Davar Hapo'elet*, 11–12 (10 December 1942), p.151.
65. *Palestine Post*, 4 January 1942, p.4.
66. Interview with Varda Simpson (Kahanovitz), Kibbutz Ma'agan Michael, 4 March 2006.
67. Interview with Ruth Gruzin (Grosbard), Tel Aviv, 22 November 2005.
68. Damon, *Beshvilai hagoral*, p.9.
69. Haya Mor, Ka'et Haya, *Sefer Zikaron le Haya Mor* [Memorial book for Haya Mor] (Kfar Yehoshua 1972), p.48.
70. Rachel Adiv, 'Toward Release', *Davar Hapo'elet*, 3 (2 April 1945), pp.59–60.
71. Habas, *Bnot hayil*, p.12.

72. 'A "melting pot" is an analogy for the way in which heterogeneous societies become more homogeneous and stronger', translated from *Even Shoshan Dictionary*, p.1036. On this role played by the military, see Victor Azarya and Baruch Kimmerling, 'New Immigrants in the Israeli Armed Forces', *Armed Forces and Society*, 6, no.3 (1980), pp.455–82; David Horowitz and Baruch Kimmerling, 'Some Social Implications of Military Service and the Reserve System in Israel', *European Journal of Sociology*, 15 (1974), pp.262–76.
73. Translated from Duncan G. Mitchell and Moshe Lissak (eds), *Lexicon Dvir le sociologia* [A new dictionary of sociology] (Tel Aviv 1984), p.15; Moshe Lissak, *Ha'elitot shel hayishuv hayehudi be'eretz Israel betkufat hamandat* [The Jewish elites in the Yishuv during the Mandate] (Tel Aviv 1981), p.113.
74. Habas, *Bnot hayil*, p.249.
75. Esther Tal's Memoires.
76. Interview with Lilli Glatt, Ramat Gan, 15 January 2006. To this day the ties remain that were forged among the servicewomen in the company who were then new immigrants, and they hold occasional reunions to which the kibbutz and moshav members are not invited. An exception was the late Sonya Peres (Gelman), graduate of the Ben Shemen educational institution, who befriended them and remained in contact with them for many years after being released from military service.
77. According to a list of names from the Nahalal Archive, compiled by Yizraela Bloch. Until March 1943, twelve women from Nahalal enlisted in the British army out of the eighty-three recruits from the moshav, of the moshav's 238 members of the second generation. Mordechai Amitai (ed.), *Nahalal – hazon behagshamato: rishon lemoshavei ovdim 1921–1971* [Nahalal – a vision in realization: first of the workers' settlements 1921–1971] (Tel Aviv 1971), pp.249, 295.
78. Debora Dayan, *Be-Osher uve'Yagon* [In Joy and Sorrow], ed. Bracha Habas (Tel Aviv 1957), pp.49–50. Dayan, mother of Moshe, Aviva and Zohar (Zorik, who fell in the War of Independence), was the wife of Shmuel Dayan and they were both founders of Nahalal. As for the worldview of the second generation, Dayan thought, 'there is no blessing in this feeling. And it is possible that even the satiety that characterizes our children, as well as the lack of monumental desire in our children and aspiration for something far off is, in no small measure, the result of this sense of lordliness.'
79. Ibid., pp.49–-50.
80. Esther Tal's memoires.
81. Yosef Shprinzak, who attended Aviva Dayan's wedding, heard the bride's grandmother exclaiming, 'This is the first time in my life that I am seeing [a kala saldat] a soldier bride.' Meeting of the Histadrut Executive Committee, 12–13 October 1942, p.47 (48), Labour Movement Archive.
82. Yonatan Gefen, *Isha Yekara* [Dear woman], ed. Yigael Schwartz (Tel Aviv 1999), p.129.
83. Amnon Zair, *Vienna–Gan Shmuel* (Gan Shmuel 1980), pp.86–7. Even if this description provides an exaggerated picture, at least from a numerical aspect (not all the recruits from Nahalal were in that company and in any case they did not have a numerical majority in it), it does illustrate their extremism and their attitude to recruits who came from a different background.

84. Habas, *Bnot hayil*, p.174.
85. It was at the Mina House that the epic meeting took place between Churchill, Roosevelt and Chiang Kai Shek prior to the launching of Operation Overlord, the code name for the Battle (Allied invasion) of Normandy.
86. The drivers made hundreds of journeys in convoys. In January 1944 alone, they drove in fifteen convoys to various destinations, both far and near. Company 513 war diary, January 1944, NA, WO169/18025.
87. Among the first to join the company were Erica Sharon, Varda Brin (Hoofien, daughter of the Anglo-Palestine Bank manager), and others.
88. Such as the 16-year-old from Tel Aviv, who lied about her age in order to enlist. The other servicewomen were fond of this girl, and the fact that her father was a janitor at the Tel Aviv Municipality did nothing to mar the attitude of the others toward her. Group interview with women from Company 513.
89. Erica Sharon's parents were imprisoned in a camp in England together with hundreds of German-Jewish refugees, and she used to send them food parcels from Egypt. Shoshana Israeli was the daughter of cellist Telma and architect Eliezer Yelin. The ties between the two women continued up to the death of Israeli during the 1990s. Interview with Judith Spitz, Tel Aviv, 13 December 2005; interview with Erica Sharon.
90. Interview with Zipora Shahar (Eitan), Esther Yanai (Ben-Zvi), Rachel Brenner (Koris), Nahalal, 7 January 2006. The three recalled the extraordinary story of a fellow company member, the daughter of a Jewish mother and German father, both of whose brothers were members of Hitler Youth movement. She was forced to immigrate with her mother to Eretz Israel, while the father and two brothers remained in Germany. Toward the end of the war, she learned that the British in Egypt had taken her brothers prisoner and she set out in search of them. With the help of the company's commanding officer, Mary Mackenzie, she managed to have them released and they immigrated to Israel.
91. Orna Sasson-Levy, *Zehuiot bemadim: gavriut ve'nashiut batzava haisraeli* [Identities in uniform: masculinity and femininity in the Israeli army] (Jerusalem 2006), pp.91–4. Active service provides unique and legitimate opportunities for close and intimate relations among men, and the soldiers internalized the concept that their camaraderie is unique among fighting men and stronger than any friendships forged in civilian life. The relationships forged among the female recruits in the British army are reminiscent of the friendships forged among male warriors in various wars as they are reflected in poems, stories and in all forms of narrative that described, for example, the generation of the Israeli War of Independence.
92. Penny Summerfield, *Reconstructing Women's Wartime Lives: Discourse and Subjectivity in Oral Histories of the Second World War* (Manchester 1998), p.177.
93. Thus, for example, in February 1944, the first ATS convoy set out for Syria under the command of McKenzie herself. To this day, servicewomen from the company remember the first convoy of drivers to Benghazi in May 1945. The company's drivers were the first ATS servicewomen to arrive in Tobruk and the only ones who arrived in a convoy of lorries at the Libyan capital of Tripoli after a month-long journey. Drivers from Company 511 from Tel el Kabir were sent to Camp Mina and joined the 513 drivers in order to learn from them how to

arrange long-distance convoys. Company 513 war diary, 28 February 1944; 3 July 1945; 27 August 1945; 24 November 1945, NA, WO169/18025.

94. Rina Zamir (Sadovsky) recalled that all the graduates of the Rehavia School (her own school) were recruited into the ATS, apart from three (included herself), who joined the Palmach. Zvia Cohen, 'The Story of Rina Zamir', *Na'amat*, February 1978, p.7; Habas, *Bnot hayil*, p.21. This description should be looked at through recognition of Habas's worldview. Graduates of these schools, who were mostly members of Haganah, together with women from the agricultural sector, constituted a preferred reference group for Habas, who saw herself as representative of Second Aliyah ideology. Yael Dar Klein, 'Agadat hale'om hamithaveh: hasipurim leyeladim ve-no'ar shecatva Bracha Habas beshanim 1933–1940' [The legend of the developing nation: stories for children and young people written by Bracha Habas in 1933–1940] (MA thesis, Tel Aviv University, 1997), p.32. It should be stressed that the Reali School, unlike the Herzliya High School that was established as a private institution for sons of the middle classes, was a public school that admitted an annual quota of poorer students. Sara Halperin, *Dr A. Biram ve beit hasefer hare'ali* [Dr A. Biram and the Reali High School] (Jerusalem 1970), p.89. According to a letter from the Jewish Agency Recruitment Office to parents who objected to their daughter's joining the army, 'The army recruits only girls [from good families]. In Jerusalem, only the best of women have been recruited, doctors, nurses, students and workers. Among them are the daughters of Dr Herman, Dr Rupin, of Mr Riza, and dozens of others, the cream of our city.' Letter, 5 October 1942, CZA, S37/58.
95. Many scientists, scholars and teachers from Germany were integrated into various academic and educational institutions in the country with the help of special funding for that purpose. Others were integrated into seminars and high school and especially the new schools established by immigrants for their own children. Thus, for example, Baruch Kurzweil taught at the Hugim High School in Haifa, Ernst Simon was integrated into a seminar, etc. Yoav Gelber, *Moledet Hadasha: Aliyat Yehudei Merkaz Eiropa veKlitatam 1933–1948* [New Homeland: Immigration of Central Europe Jews and their integration 1933–1948] (Jerusalem 1990), pp.222–333.
96. Herlitz, who was born in Germany and was the daughter of the archivist George Herlitz, subsequently became Israel's first Ambassador to Denmark and a Member of Knesset. She first studied at the Rehavia High School, but later moved to the school established by Dr Paula Natan in Talpiot. In 1936, the school taught 230 students, of which 75 per cent were immigrants from Germany. The school's object was to teach the Hebrew language in an atmosphere of Palestine. Ibid., p.249.
97. Interview with Esther Herlitz, Tel Aviv, 9 December 2005.
98. The veteran Yishuv found it hard to integrate the immigrants from Germany and for their part, they too found it hard to integrate. Yishuv society did not identify, neither culturally nor socially, with these immigrants and there was no openness in the social structure toward them. Miriam Getter, 'Ha'aliyah migermania bashanim 1933–1939, klita calcalit mul klita hevratit tarbutit' [Immigration from Germany: economic integration vis-à-vis social and cultural integration], *Katedra*, 12 (August 1978), p.132. Ruth Meier, friend of Bracha

Fold, was unable to attend youth movement activities because, 'I have to read Goethe now. Father is not prepared for me to skip my German reading.' Sari Gal, *Bracha Fold* (Tel Aviv 1999). [Hebrew], p.159.

99. The cultural phenomena known as 'Sabra', an authentic native youth culture, emerged before the First World War among the sons and daughters of First Aliyah immigrants (e.g. Ahron Ahronson and Avshalom Feinberg) as well as among the first graduates of the Herzliya High School. But these were only 'early birds', and only in the 1930s and 1940s did this culture become widespread among many native youngsters in the kibbutzim, moshavim and the more established parts of the larger cities. Thus, Israeli-born Moshe Shamir, and German-born Uri Avnery, were typical of the Sabra phenomenon. Oz Almog, *The Sabra: The Creation of the New Jew* (Berkeley, CA: University of California Press, 2000), pp.5–7.
100. Yonatan Shapira, *Elite le'lo mamshichim: dorot manhigim bahevra haisraelit* [Elite with no heirs: generations of leaders in Israeli society] (Tel Aviv 1984), pp.73–89.
101. Udi Michelsohn and Aharon Lapidot, *Me'ah shnot gymnasia* [A Hundred Years of Gymnasia] (Tel Aviv 2004), pp.80–7. Although the students were united, there was alienation between them and the workers of the Second Aliyah. The first to burst through this divide was Golomb. Ahuvia Malkin, *Ha'activist: sipur hayav shel Eliyahu Golomb* [The activist: life story of Eliyahu Golomb], A (Tel Aviv 2007), p.15.
102. During the early years of the school, there was still no Hebrew curriculum and the students were required to help their teachers find new words in order to continue with the studies. Thus, they became non-passive partners in designing the Hebrew school's curriculum. As those who were destined to become the new Hebrew intelligentsia, the students were displayed before the leaders and political activists. Malkin, *Ha'activist*, p.14; Baruch Ben-Yehuda, *Sipura shel hagimnasia 'Herzliya'* [Story of the Herzliya High School] (Tel Aviv 1970), pp.69–70.
103. Halperin, *Dr A. Biram ve beit hasefer hare'ali*, pp.90–100, 215–20.
104. Interview with Sonya Peres (Gelman), Tel Aviv, 9 January 2006. Peres and her friends used such expressions as 'that one from the [Herzliya] High School', or 'her from the Reali'.
105. Interview with Elisheva Erez.
106. Interview with Miriam Vardi.
107. In late 1943, of the 533,000 Jews in Palestine, 423,000 were Ashkenazi (79.4 per cent), 47,000 (8.8 per cent) were Sephardi, 25,000 were Yemenite (4.7 per cent) and the rest were members of the Oriental Communities (Middle East, Asia and Africa) – 38,000 (7.1 per cent). Most of the latter belonged to the 'non-organized' Yishuv. Gurevitz and Gretz, *Haaliyah*, p.104/d.
108. Recognition of the need to create a municipal system for mass integration of immigrant families, many with large numbers of children and low income, was interpreted into the establishment of a public system of voluntary social services. These were accompanied by a constantly judgmental attitude on the part of those who were located within the narrow boundaries of the normative, functional parts of society. Veteran and new immigrants from among the middle classes who had settled in Tel Aviv brought with them from Europe a bourgeoisie tradition of social responsibility and a developed social awareness. A central

aspect of this tradition was a fear of the social fringes as an element threatening the stability of the bourgeois order. The strong concentration of professionals in the fields of education and social work, as well as mental health experts, who had settled in Tel Aviv, also influenced the development of systems for diagnosing and treating abandoned children. Razi, 'Building the Fringes of the Nation', pp.292–5.

109. Bernstein, 'Daughters of the Nation', pp.294–300.
110. Rachel H., 'From the Notes of a Recruiter', *Davar Hapo'elet*, 7–8 (31 August 1942), p.97. Servicewomen from the agricultural sector testified that their world had been narrow and they didn't know the world outside their farms. But they were considered the elite and their worldview appeared naive, as opposed to the perceptions of the 'primitive' and unsuccessful Oriental girls. Interview with Zipora Shahar and Esther Yanai; Interview with Aviva Gil. The subject was raised at one of the recruitment meetings of women from the Oriental communities and emphasis was laid on the fact that 'in [this sector] the propaganda activity on behalf of military recruitment is also an important Zionist and educational act'. Minutes of recruiters meeting, 20 August 1942, p.2, CZA, S25/5099. At a recruitment rally in factories, it was said '[recruitment] gatherings were held in the Mespro factory, where the speech was delivered by a Yemenite servicewoman'. No comment on the ethnic origin of the recruits appears in any of the reports on recruitment rallies. 'Mass recruitment rallies in factories in Tel Aviv and its surrounds', 29 April 1942, Ibid, S37/670.
111. Edward Said, *Orientalism* (London: Vintage Books, 1979), pp.11–13. According to Henriette Dahan-Caleb, the melting pot policy in the state of Israel during the 1950s leant on the colonialism and on the measure of the immigrants' exposure to western culture before their arrival in Israel. Henriette Dahan-Kalev, 'Mizrahi Women: Identity and History', in Ruth Kark, Margalit Shilo and Galit Hasan-Rokem (eds), *Jewish Women in pre-State Israel: Life History, Politics and Culture* (Waltham, MA: Brandeis University Press, 2008), p.55. According to Moshe Lissak the stereotypes and prejudices that developed mainly toward the immigrants from arab states (in the 1950s) were formed as a result of fear that such waves of immigration were a threat to the Yishuv tradition. As well as the need to assimilate thousands of immigrants in order to increase Israel's demographical status, there were many uncertainties with regard to them. Moshe Lissak, *Ha'aliyah hagdola be'shnot hahamishim: kishlono shel cur hahituch* [The big immigration of the 1950s: the failure of the melting pot] (Jerusalem 1999), pp.63–74.
112. In retrospect, Herlitz is full of regret over the incident that caused this servicewoman such injustice. Interview with Esther Herlitz. Clearly, the well-defined hierarchy that existed in the British army also influenced the judgment of the Hebrew officers.
113. H.S. (Halperin Sonya), 'Letter of a Servicewoman', *Davar Hapo'elet*, 9–10 (30 September 1942), p.27.
114. Almog, *The Sabra*, pp.127–8. In the modern world, this concept of creating a human stereotype that mimics the system of rejected values and is subjected to constant condemnation is typical of traditional religions that base their superiority, among other things, on reproaching the 'other'.
115. Erik H. Erikson, *Identity: Youth and Crisis* (New York: W.W. Norton & Company 1968), pp.19–22.

116. Dahan-Kalev, 'Mizrahi Women: Identity and History', pp.52–3. One of the experiences that formed Hanna Senesh's emigration process, for example, was her sense of inconsistency between the Zionist ideology and the inability to fulfil it, between her high expectations and aspirations and her experienced reality. The personal discrepancy she felt was two-fold, both as someone who came from central Europe and as a woman. She was unable to crystallize a new identity as a pioneer, especially as the very transformation of a Diaspora Jews into a 'new person' was inherently masculine. Ruth Glick, 'Experience of Immigration and Reforming an Identity in the Private Writings of Hanna Senesh' (MA thesis, Bar Ilan University, 2006), pp.112–13. On the role of Diaspora culture in the identity of young women who immigrated during the 1930s, see for example, Judith Baumel, 'Gesharim ben Etmol ve Mahar: Mekoma shel tarbut Hagola besipur haye'en shel Giborot *Ha'aliyah* Hahamishit' [Bridges between yesterday and tomorrow: the role of Diaspora culture in the stories of Fifth Aliyah heroines,' *Katedra*, 114 (February 2003), pp.125–30.
117. Joseph B. Glass, *From New Zion to Old Zion, American Jewish Immigration and Settlement in Palestine* (Detroit, WI: Wayne State University Press, 2000), pp.84–5. On the immigration of Jewish women to America in the early twentieth century see, for example, Paula Hyman, *Ha-Ishah ha-Yehudiyyah bi-Sevakh ha-Kidmah: Mekoma ve Yitzuga ba'et hachadasha* [The Jewish woman in a tangle of progress: her place and representation in modern Jewish history] (Jerusalem 1997), pp.312–35.
118. Ruth Meier described the hardships suffered by the young immigrants from Germany, 'This is not a good place for someone who came from Germany. All the children here go to the [youth] movements. They don't like children from Germany because they are Hitler and Nazis [sic]. Even the counsellors in the movements don't like them.' Gal, *Bracha Fold*, p.159. Esther Herlitz, too, testified that she hated studying in the Hebrew High School in Jerusalem because of the alienating attitude of the Yishuv-born children toward her and toward those of her friends who came from Germany. Interview with Esther Herlitz.
119. Habas, *Bnot hayil*, p.78.
120. Penina Morag-Talmon, 'Women's Networks: A New Perspective on Women's Studies in Israel in the Early 1950s', in Margalit Shilo et al., *The New Hebrew Women* (Jerusalem 2001), pp.132–3. For more on women's networks see, for example, Elizabeth Bott, *Family and Social Network: Roles, Norms and External Relationships in Ordinary Urban Families* (London 1957).
121. Ruth Gonnet, 'Yahasim ben kevutsot' [Intergroup relations], *Sotziologia Hevratit*, 8 (2000), pp.197–8.
122. In the eyes of the ATS servicewomen, the others were conceived as being 'privileged' and enjoying improved service conditions, even though in various places in the WAAF (such as Camp 107MU in Egypt) the women lived in tents for a long time. On the rivalry, see also, Habas, *Bnot hayil*, pp.220–3.

4

Military Mothers

Due to its very uniqueness, the issue of Yishuv mothers' volunteering for service in the British Forces in the Second World War is worthy of a separate discussion. Until this war, women with children had been involved in underground military organizations (actually, unlike the women Palmach members and women in organizations such as Hashomer, many of the female members of Haganah were married and had children), but they carried out their duties in the organizations in addition to their regular civilian activities. In research literature and especially that relating to different kinds of female service in the various armies during the Second World War, no data has been found on mothers in military service. When women were called to service in the Allied Forces, the call was for unmarried women, or married women without children.[1] Even Julia Cowper's official book on the ATS makes no reference to married women with children.[2]

Of the approximately 3,600 Yishuv women in the British Forces, about 120 were mothers (almost 3 per cent). These knew in advance that they would not be required to fulfil field positions and that they would only be given auxiliary posts. Their service period was not determined in advance and they were all aware that they would serve for as long as necessary.

Who were the mothers who volunteered for military service; what was typical of them and did they have a common denominator? What motivated them to leave a home and a family, a husband and children and to join an unfamiliar arena; how did their relatives respond and what price were they required to pay; how did the other servicewomen react to these women and what was the attitude of the Yishuv? These questions and others will be dealt with in this chapter.

Statistics

When the recruitment of women began *Davar Hapo'elet* published preliminary statistics according to which some 1,000 women had registered. The paper's editorial pointed out, 'the recruits' age is higher than could have been anticipated ... of them, about 15 per cent (150 women) were aged between 40–45. 40 per cent of them are married women and of these, around 10 have children.'[3] Like the other recruits, the mothers were employed in a wide variety of jobs in the army: in the ATS they were storekeepers, clerks, drivers (of trucks and private cars), nurses, cooks, etc. In the WAAF they were employed as storekeepers, clerks and some were given jobs in intelligence, communications and special operations, etc.

Most of the recruited mothers served in the ATS, especially during the first year of recruitment, in other words, 1942. Most of the mothers who served in the WAAF were recruited in 1943 (the first year of recruitment to this arm). Most of the mothers were married; others were divorced or widowed. At the time of their recruitment, most of the mothers (70 per cent) had one child; 25 per cent of them had two children and the rest had three or four children. Two of the mothers were under 20 years old when they enlisted; about 50 per cent of all the enlisted mothers were in their 20s or 30s; about 25 per cent were in their 40s; three women were over 50 in age (as mentioned, recruitment age was 18-45 and there were women who lied about their age in order to enlist).

The vast majority of recruited mothers had been born abroad. The percentage of foreign-born recruits was 80 per cent of all the recruits, although among the recruited mothers their percentage was higher (92 per cent). In addition, 86 per cent of the mothers had lived in the country for over twenty years prior to their military service, whereas, among the general body of recruits the percentage of those who had lived in the country more than twenty years did not exceed 9 per cent. These statistics can indicate their ties to the country and their motivation to volunteer. The percentage of mothers from towns was similar to that of city dwellers among all recruits. About 63 per cent of urban mothers who enlisted were salaried workers in various kinds of employment: labourers, domestic workers, teachers, clerks, waitresses, etc., as compared with the 95 per cent of salaried workers among the general body of recruits. Fewer than 20 per cent of the mothers worked in their own homes at the time of their enlistment and a few were self-employed (doctors, lawyers, artists, etc.).[4] These data indicate that most of the mothers left a regular job and salary in order to volunteer for military service. In other words, like the other recruits, the mothers, too, did not enlist in order to escape unemployment. However, the quota of employed mothers was significantly lower than that of the employed women among the general body of recruits, and it appears that more women who worked at home (housewives) volunteered for military service in greater numbers than their percentage in the general body of recruits. As for their military service,[5] the assumption is that most of the mothers served three years, a few served a year and others served four years. Some of these served in Palestine and spent their weekends at home. Many of them served in Egypt and went home for week-long vacations every three months.

Institutional and Military Reservations over Recruit of Mothers

Did the British army or elements in the Yishuv encourage mothers to enlist? It appears that the military command in Palestine, as depicted by Audrey Chitty, ATS Commander in the Middle East, did not expect mothers to enlist in the army and did not encourage them, but nor could it prevent them from doing so. In an exclusive interview with the *Palestine Post* at the onset of female military recruitment in the Yishuv, Chitty exhibited a conservative approach to gender, in keeping with that of the British government and army at that time on all matters pertaining to the recruitment of women and mothers into the army. She made it known that the recruits from Palestine would receive no special family allowance (although married male recruits with children were given family support in accordance to the number of children), since as far as the army was concerned it was better for women with maternal (sic), family commitments not to enlist. The job of a woman with small children was more important than any job offered by the army and the children were not to be made to suffer. 'Nothing is more urgent than this', she said.[6]

Even before the British Army had accepted and made public the decision to recruit women from the Yishuv, a meeting of the Working Women's Council (WWC) was held in Tel Aviv in November 1941. The meeting, which was devoted to female recruitment, concluded (among other things) that, 'mothers of dependent children must be exempt from service'.[7] In other words, the first stage of recruitment did not call for mothers of small children to enlist and reservations were even voiced in this regard. After the call for recruitment was made public, the CWO – as already mentioned – called on the female community in the Yishuv to come forward and contribute its share to the war effort, although there was no mention of mothers. About three months later, Sonya Idelberg, the chief recruiter to the ATS, participated in a meeting of the Management Committee of the Jewish Agency's Recruitment Department. She pointed out, seemingly in response to criticism on the part of women's organizations, that although the recruiters are not encouraging mothers to enlist, care must be taken to ensure that those who do are allowed to serve in Palestine. In contrast, Beba Idelson was convinced of the necessity of defining the recruitment of mothers 'that we can call on to volunteer' in the towns and villages. It should be stressed that it appears from her speech that she was referring to women who were mothers of adult children.[8]

Later, on International Working Women's Day, the WWC published a call in *Davar Hapo'elet* with an announcement for May to be recognized as 'The month for recruitment of the working woman and the *housewife*: to military service, to security and defence, to the agricultural economy and all the other fields of industry in need of reinforcement. Any woman who has more strength and ability – of her we shall demand more. And every recruitment will satisfy.' [author's emphasis][9] It appears that at this stage, about four months after the start of recruitment, and with impressive recruitment statistics (including mothers), the WWC was still trying to recruit every woman capable or willing to volunteer. The reasoning behind this was that women had struggled for so long for the right for an equal share in the burden, and were now being asked to implement this important objective. Thus, in its call to the Yishuv's women, the WWC actually implemented its ideological worldview, according to which the Hebrew woman or the Hebrew mother is an independent person, aware of herself, aware of her nationality and her status, enjoys equal rights and obligations and socially and economically active in the public arena.

In June 1942, the national institutions in the Yishuv involved themselves in encouraging military recruitment by advertising a command on the duty to enlist. In this command women between the age of 20 and 30, single or married and childless were 'especially required' (sic) to enlist in the army, whereas women between the ages of 20 and 45, who were not enlisting were given the choice of joining the country's defence services or to work for the economy. The call to duty did not apply to women of small children, possibly because of the complaints of husbands who objected to their wives being recruited without their approval.

On his return from Egypt in September 1942, after visiting the Yishuv recruits, Sharett reported to the CWO and announced that 'under no circumstances must mothers be encouraged to enlist, and they must be made aware of the fact that there is no chance of their raising their children at the expense of others'.[10] At the September meeting of the Histadrut Council, and five months after her speech at the Recruitment Department meeting, Idelson said: 'We haven't yet encouraged mothers to go to the army – a mother can stay at home and fulfil other tasks.'[11] Idelson may said these things in this forum because of the public pressure on the issue of recruiting mothers, although a month later, she still believed in the possibility of recruiting mothers, at least from kibbutzim and according to a predetermined quota.[12] Even Mania Shohat, who was frequently absent from home for long periods, leaving her children in the care of others, whether from the kibbutz or her husband, Israel, spoke at that meeting. She believed that 'a woman-mother does not need to enlist', but explained that mothers who had already enlisted 'did it out of a sense of responsibility, because others had not done so'.[13] In other words, mothers enlisted because of the 'order of the day' without being called. At this meeting the Histadrut Council approved the terms of the mobilization order, according to which: 'Women aged between 20–30 are required to enlist, whether to the army or in defence of the homeland, *with the exception of mothers*.' [author's emphasis]

Therefore, both the army and the women's organizations in the Yishuv did not encourage the recruitment of women-mothers. They themselves took the initiative and enlisted.

The Uniqueness of the Group of Enlisted Mothers

In his eulogy for his wife, Sonya, Yosef Halperin admitted that she had not capitulated to social conventions of her times (including that a woman's place is in the home), and did not make do with the four walls of her home, but aspired to burst through the existing framework: 'You didn't want – and your nature did not allow you – to be like "everyone else", because you were a fighting daughter of Israel, bearing the tall yearnings of your generation.' And he added that 'a roof, a family [home] – these did not fill your heart ... and you, for whom the space between the walls was so cramped, within the farm and the village, so wished to move, to stray from the framework.' Halperin also testified that his wife had been ahead of her time: 'Not only did you aspire to keep abreast of the times, you wanted to overtake them.'[14]

Is it possible to extend this definition to the other mothers who went and enlisted in the army? In any society, female military recruitment has to overcome social, psychological and 'moral' obstacles. Mania Shohat, one of the founders of 'Hashomer' and herself an example of heroism, pointed to a psychological block inherent in women who internalized the concept according to which a woman's place is in the home: 'one obstacle [facing the recruitment of women] is psychological-historical: a deeply rooted habit that women have to stay at home. This psychology has to be fought against.'[15]

In attempting to study the phenomenon of mothers who willingly left their homes and their children, without being obliged to do so by law, and in attempting to find reasons for their decision, it is worth bearing in mind that the concept of motherhood is composed of various spheres: biology, psychology, culture and society. To this day the theoretic deliberation continues on the question of whether maternity is something natural, biological, congenital or the sociological fruit of generations that, among other things, were also the cause of discrimination against women, or if it was a combination of both of these concepts.[16]

In her book, *From Non-essence to Motherhood*, Anat Palgi-Hecker tried to conceptualize the mother as a 'subject' and the essence of the motherhood experience out of a psychological overview of the concept of motherhood. She wonders whether it is possible to create an idea of maternal subjectivity that can represent motherhood in a way that is true without imposing on them a uniform concept of how motherhood is supposed to be.[17] Donald Winnicott, for example, wished to distance himself from definitions of the utopian or ideal mother that is hard to realize. He coined the phrases, 'common devoted mother' and 'good enough mother', in order to enable a large number of women to feel that they are fulfilling their maternal requirements, even if they have doubts as to their function and if there are other things in their lives.[18]

Carol Gilligan showed that the identity of women and mothers does not depend only on their relation to others and denial of their own independence, and there is no dissonance between the various functions they fulfil. The multiple identities of a woman means that she is not forced to choose between achieving her personal objectives and selfish passions and giving to her environment. She also refers to the growth of the emotional abilities of the mother, who is a single unit with her baby and also simultaneously at one with herself. There is also a legitimization, both outward and inward, of additional elements in the mother's adult soul and awareness that allow her to be free of the blame involved in her very existence.[19]

It would appear that the recruited mothers wanted to show that at a certain time in her life a woman can devote herself to her children and, during different periods in her life, like men, to realizing social and national ideals, without feeling any dissonance.

From the dawn of history and, especially, at the height of struggles for civil liberation, women have been given the role of 'biological reproducers', in other words, raising children as a reservoir for national evolution. According to Yuval-Davis there is often a conflict between the national interest and the interest of the individual with regard to the number of children they should bring into the world. Whereas the collective is in need of every additional member for the evolving nation, couples are also motivated by other considerations when deciding to expand their families, especially when times are hard. Bracha Habas hinted at this when she wrote that, 'with the woman's entry into a life of uniforms, reproduction statistics will drop, but what is preferable: liberation, with fewer people, or a larger, enslaved, population?'[20] And indeed, statistics showed that the birth-rate in the Yishuv dropped at the beginning of the 1940s. In 1945, the demographer Baki indicated the low birth-rate among newly arrived Jewish families, a lower birth-rate 'than was necessary to ensure the demographic future of the Jewish nation'.[21]

The Jewish Yishuv in Palestine wanted to establish a new society, built on the model of 'the new Hebrew', as opposed to the Jew of the Diaspora, and his partner in building the nation was to be the 'new Hebrew woman'. According to Zionist Utopia, in the future Jewish state there would be no room for a change in the status of women, or for change in the traditional Jewish family. These utopias laid the existence of a single model for all women – that of wife and mother. According to Rachel Elboim-Dror the ideal Zionist woman in those utopias was destined to fulfil the position of mother of the family and of the nation, although, in fact, she was divested of her children's education, which was handed over to society. Margalit Shilo believes that family building was given national significance and the Palestinei motherhood was conceived as an essential Zionist contribution to building the land and the nation. Deborah Bernstein indicated that women were expected to continue to fulfil traditional gender positions in everything concerning childbirth and raising children, which, once they were married, removed most of them from public activity.[22]

Many of the women of the Yishuv period faced, at the time and under the unique circumstances created in the course of her life, an insolvable conflict: the aspiration to participate in the process of realizing the Zionist vision versus her own desire not to relinquish motherhood. According to Yael Atzmon, women were actually caught in the contradiction between their personal identity and their experience and the dominant concepts. The separation between the public and the private, that was taken for granted, together with the unwavering primacy of the public domain, resulted in denial of the status and significance of the private domain and its repression.[23]

The mothers who chose to volunteer for military service are no longer alive. A study of the writings left behind by a few of them reveals that although the maternal element in these women's identity was central, it was not exclusive. In this respect, they were preceded by courageous and opinionated women in the Yishuv who, while attaching great importance to their motherhood, refused to internalize that it was the sole component in their identity. Such women were, for example, Rachel Katznelson-Shazar, as well as Hayuta Bussel and Miriam Baratz, initiators of the system of communal childcare in Kevutzat Degania at the end of the first decade of the twentieth century. According to Bussel, if a woman is to be a good mother to her children, she cannot be tied to her home. She must be open-minded, understanding, a modern thinker and socially involved. Shilo shows that even the new citizen (woman of the Second Aliyah who did not belong to the workers' movement) implemented the concept that even someone who works outside her home is beneficial both to herself and to the nation. Femininity was identified not only with the private sphere, while nationalism and Zionism were not indentified solely with masculinity (which was identified with the public sphere).[24]

These women appear to have preceded the feminist theories of the late twentieth century. Feminism, especially American, struggled against the restricted definition of femininity, and wanted to prove that motherhood was neither the exclusive, nor the central, definition of female identity and that there was a large variety of identities of the individual and the freedom to choose among them was legitimate.[25]

Military recruitment of mothers was not something that 'swept away' the women of the Yishuv, but it was still an exceptional group (for its period) whose members showed that a woman can devote herself to her children at a certain time in her life and, at other periods, to fulfil social and national ideals, like men, without feeling any contradiction between the two worlds. In her speech to the 1942 Working Women's Congress, Rivka Guber defined it thus: 'This is a complete blend of [female] citizen and mother.'[26] Borrowing from the sphere of psychoanalysis, we can say that these women saw themselves as a complete subject in its own right and not as a subject defined only by right of its connection to the other.

Motives and Dilemmas of Recruited Mothers

The group of mothers who enlisted in the British forces can be divided into two sub-groups: mothers of older children and mothers of young children, since both faced different dilemmas, especially in everything concerning the need to leave children at home. Only a few of the mothers had both older and younger children.

Mothers of Older Children

Some of the mothers enlisted together with their sons or daughters and served in parallel with them in the various military units. Although it is not possible to determine their exact numbers, a review of age-related data shows that this group numbered more than thirty (women in their 40s and 50s). Some examples are: Roza Meierzak and her daughter Hanna (Maron); Elza Yosef (a sergeant in the 513 Company) and her daughter Shoshana (a driver in the same company); Zahava Zimbel (who enlisted at the age of 52) and her daughter Ruth; Hanna Prizer and her daughter Ahuva; Yona Reiser and her daughter Ruth; Tuti Levy (who owned a guesthouse in Nahariya) and her daughter Ruth; Dvora Levinson and her daughter Shimona; Tzafrira Shoham (Yaffe) and her mother, and others. In certain cases the daughter preceded her mother and in others, it was the mother who enlisted first and was followed by her son or daughter when they reached recruitment age. In these cases, although the mother was absent from home for long periods, the children were old enough to care for themselves and did not require constant supervision.

Some of the recruited mothers had children of recruitment age who chose not to enlist, rather to stay in the country, either in their own homes or in various other frameworks. For example, Sara Mahram, an immigrant from Canada who lived in Rishon Le'Zion, left a married daughter who had recently given birth, to drive trucks with Company 513.[27] Zipora Kesse, from Kvutzat Schiller, a mother of an adult son, was among the first to enlist in order to serve as a moral guide to the younger recruits. Lipsha Segal-Jamson assisted recruits from the Lehi and IZL in Egypt. Her sister was 45 and the mother of a 19-year-old daughter, when she enlisted and served with the ATS in Egypt.[28]

Hanna Maron, who enlisted with her mother and underwent basic training with her in Sarafend, admitted that, in addition to her inner conviction of the need to do something to help the Jewish nation in its war, her enlistment was something of an act of defiance against her mother – who, in return, registered and was also recruited. Maron is convinced that her mother's motive for enlisting was her shaky relationship with her husband. She herself refers to her mother's service as 'quite a catastrophe'. In the course of their basic training, her mother refused to carry out various duties and Hanna was obliged to replace her. Eventually the mother realized that she was not cut out for army life and was released without even completing her basic training.[29] Shoham, on the other hand, who served at the same time as her mother and father, recalls the idealism and determination of her mother to enlist and to contribute her share to the national effort. According to her, her mother did not hesitate for long before enlisting, thus serving as a model to her daughter who followed in her footsteps.[30]

Older mothers, like other older recruits and like the Working Women's Council that supported recruitment, considered themselves as moral guides to the younger recruits. Tze'ira Weiner (Lerman),[31] for example, did not provide her motive for enlisting, but described in her diary why she chose to serve in Egypt and did not take advantage of the fact of being a mother to stay close to home. When she saw the young servicewomen being sent to foreign parts, with no prior life-experience, many of them with no roots in the homeland, she asked herself: 'Am I allowed to leave our daughters, those young servicewomen, to fend for themselves, and to evade being with them ... in the deserts and in all kinds of foreign places? Is it right? Is it moral, comradely, nationalist?'[32]

But beyond the idealism and the desire to leave home, it appears that a psychoanalytical explanation can also be found for women in their 40s and 50s to serve in the military, when they are still at the height of their physical and mental strength. Psychoanalysts such as Karen Horny and others point to the fears of women of that age of losing their attraction, which could influence mother-daughter relations and cause the mother to envy her young daughter. Society 'allows' women only a limited period in which to blossom, so that a woman is denied the ability to evaluate for herself those qualities that are not erotic, such as maturity, stability, wisdom, independence and independent judgment. According to this explanation, mothers of sons or daughters of recruitment age wished to take the same step as their offspring and thus to prove to themselves and to their environment that they were still worthy of attention and still had something to contribute to society as well to themselves.[33]

Mothers of Young Children

When they decided to enlist in the army, the some seventy women that constituted the second group were mothers of young children or teens. Some examples are: Sonya Halperin from Kfar Vitkin, who left her 12-year-old son Zika; Zimbel from Tel Adashim, who, in addition to the daughter who enlisted in the army, left at home three others in their early teen years; the artist Ziona Tager from Tel Aviv, who enlisted in the army and left an 8-year-old son at home (later, the former MK, Avraham Katz-Oz) in Kibbutz Einat; Haya Mor (Markovsky) from Kfar Yehoshua, mother of three daughters (two teenagers and one aged 9), enlisted in the army; Rivka Guber, and others. Haya Stein-Botovitzky, who enlisted in the ATS and served as a driver in Company 511, left behind a 14-year-old son at boarding school in Ben-Shemen. In March 1943 she was killed in the line of duty.[34]

It seems that a few of the recruits who were mothers of small children enlisted with the knowledge that after completing their basic training they would be serving near their children, but there were other mothers who were sent to serve in Egypt. These appealed to the Political Department of the Jewish Agency claiming that they had been promised by the Recruitment Offices when they enlisted that they would stationed in Palestine. And indeed, in August 1942 a letter was issued by the Political Department that it was intending to appeal to the military authorities in order to set a rule that mothers of young children were not to be sent to serve abroad when it was possible to post them inside the country. Up until now, according to the letter, there was no such ruling so that there had been no basis for the promises made to the recruits. The Recruitment Centre was asked to issue an order to all the recruitment offices and to the chief recruiter to refrain from giving out such promises. Not only was it forbidden to promise mothers that they would be able to stay close to their children, the letter said, but they had to be warned that they were liable to be sent to serve abroad.[35]

Mothers from this group found childcare solutions for their offspring: some children stayed at home with their father, others were sent to kibbutzim or moved in with relatives. Even the Jewish Agency's

Recruitment Office tried to solve the problem of childcare for children of recruited mothers.[36] At that time the revolutionary method of communal childrearing was already being practiced in the kibbutzim, but in other parts of Yishuv society children were raised individually in a family environment.[37] The need to find childrearing solutions for working mothers arose mainly in the towns, and to this purpose day centres and baby houses were established. In Kfar Yehezkel and Haifa, two educational institutes were opened to accommodate the children of male and female recruits, in order to help families with the burden of childcare.

The willingness of mothers to hand over their children to be cared for by strangers indicates the natural result of a lengthy process of de-legitimization of the nuclear family as a framework capable of supplying a child's physical, emotional and educational needs. The German school of thought in the Yishuv emphasized this process during the 1930s and 1940s. It appears that the conflict between family and the Zionist ideal that had remained unsolved in Yishuv society lead to the desire to reduce to a minimum all contact between parents and their children. According to this process, as many areas of responsibility as possible were transferred from the family into the hands of the educational institutions, youth movements, training courses and youth societies.[38]

Studies on the effects of Freudian psychoanalysis on Yishuv society discuss the various types of attitude to the family as expressed in constructivist commentary to psychoanalytic theory. According to this commentary the family was meant to serve as a tool for creating the 'new person' and a new uncomplicated society. According to these theorists the biological family in kibbutz society was divested of all its educational tasks by the very fact of transferring children to frameworks of communal sleeping arrangements and the creation of youth society, reducing contact between parents and their children to two hours a day and handing over the sole responsibility for their education to the kibbutz educational institution. All this aimed at reducing the harmful emotional effects accredited to the family, to undermine the family's bourgeois, anti-revolutionary foundations and to subject it to a collective.[39]

The socio-biological school of thought that dealt with women's status in the kibbutz and is represented by the researchers Yosef Teiger and Lionel Sheffer presents a different outlook on communal education. The contention of these researchers is that until the establishment of the State, there was a situation of equality between the sexes. The harsh economic and security conditions forced parents to exchange their own parental investment for a collective parental investment. Thus: the explanation for communal education for pre-school children and collective sleeping arrangements from earliest childhood.[40]

In January 1942, under the heading 'With Female Recruitment', *Davar* published a piece by a mother who had volunteered for military service, but was undecided as to how she would organize her private life vis-à-vis her national obligation: 'the "voice that distinguishes" was always accompanied by the gentle sub-voice of mundane worries ... the little one can be placed in an institution and the older brother can stay with his grandmother. Obviously this will involve expense but [the grandparents] will certainly help.' She added that she had barely given a thought to her husband and how he would manage, but 'I am the man who stands – or should be able to stand – in his own right, and of course it is not feasible that at a time like this, I should be having to do all the accounting. After all, we demanded and implored, so surely now you can't expect it to have come out of nowhere!'[41]

Writings left behind by women, speeches before various forums, in letters or articles published in *Davar Hapo'elet*, whether in real time or from a distance of years, all lend expression to the hesitations and misgivings of the mothers who found it hard to leave their children at home, alongside the desire to make their contribution to the war effort. As already mentioned, military recruitment was a voluntary act and the result of decisions made by the women themselves. In her 1955 memoires, Mor from Kfar Yehoshua admitted 'it was not easy to sever yourself from your dear ones and to set out to do the job. But the desire was so powerful and intense that I was unable to resist it ... how could anyone resist? And on the other hand, how does one leave one's children and home? The hesitations did not last long. We had to go, no matter what!'[42]

In June 1942, when the kibbutzim were still objecting to female recruitment, kibbutz member Shoshana P. wrote in *Davar Hapo'elet*, calling on another kibbutz member who was also a mother to a soldier and had herself enlisted to share her deliberations: 'It is no simple matter. I have a 6-year-old daughter. And it is here that there is the big struggle between the personal duty as a person and as a Jew, and my feelings as a mother. Is it permissible to leave a child at such a young age? And especially when her father is not at home?' Her husband had worked away from home for many years and shared her decision to enlist in the ATS. She testified that when the media announced imminent female military recruitment and she learned of the kibbutz's objection to this, 'for me this came as a harsh blow'. But she did not give in: 'Is it possible that I, who was raised and educated in this country with the ideology of the kibbutz, will now be obliged to rebel and not to give in? ... Of course I was not convinced by the words of the [kibbutz] Yagur Council and the day after the meeting, I travelled to Haifa and signed on.'[43]

Mor enlisted in the army in June 1942, as a married mother of three daughters. When she decided to enlist, she appeared before the moshav council and spoke about women's rights and her duty to fulfil tasks at a time such as this. She listed 'women whose daughters had already graduated from school and others whose daughters were about to complete their schooling', and stressed that 'with a little supervision in running a household, they will be able to replace the enlisted women. Unless? First of all, there has to be a willingness on the part of the male [husband], the rest of the family and the moshav.'[44]

Mor made use of various explanations, such as her desire to serve in the public domain and to fulfil her potential: 'Now, especially, a woman has the chance to emphasize her independence even in the field of military recruitment ... usually women stand on the sidelines, both through her own fault and because the tradition that is always with us ... now, women have a rare opportunity to fill such an important role.' Mor also referred to the length of time in the army as compared to the time it took to establish the farm: 'After all, a year or two, what are they compared to the long period we have already been through, establishing a large moshav, raising children, etc.'[45] It is worth remembering that the entire burden of the farm was on Mor's shoulders, as with all the other moshav women, although there were some who tried to present women's work in the moshavim as an 'ideal' solution when claiming that 'on a moshav the woman has found her salvation'.[46] It appears from Mor that the war provided her with an opportunity to prove herself and that she expected her family to receive the necessary support and assistance from the moshav.

In discussing the husband's role in childcare in the Yishuv, it should be remembered that the entire burden of childcare usually fell on the women, both in towns and in the agricultural settlements. This was probably due to the contemporary concept according to which, unlike the mother, the father does not develop emotional ties with his children, at least at first. According to Shilo, most of the women who immigrated to Palestine during the early twentieth century and who caused a huge revolution in their private lives and in that of their new homeland, did not demand of their men full equality and responsibility in raising the next generation, in their upbringing and in their education. They did not demand that their men share with them the shaping of the new person they had wished for as a result of the revolution they had created. In contrast, those mothers who volunteered to enlist in the army demanded that their partners bear the brunt of raising and educating their children.[47]

Rivka Guber

As part of the discussion on the mothers who left their young children at home, it is worth focusing on the case of Rivka Guber (1902–81), who was coined 'Mother of the Sons' after losing two of her boys, Ephraim and Zvi, in the War of Independence. Guber, a founder member of Kfar Bilu and a much admired figure in the agricultural sector, enlisted in the army as a mother of three – two teenaged sons and a younger daughter. She served as a cook in Sarafend (today's Zerifin). Although the camp was in the country, she went home only on weekends and every three months for a whole week, so that she was denied a day-to-day connection with her family.

Other mothers, as already mentioned, also named personal reasons, alongside their desire to contribute to the war effort, for enlisting, but it seems that Guber was the first to include the term 'sacrifice', in the discourse on female recruitment, which, until then, was solely in the male domain. About two years prior to the recruitment drive, Guber wrote to Shomo Lavie from Ein Harod: 'Who'll believe me that I am willing to sacrifice that which is dearest of all to me, that *I want* to give my dearest, because at a cheap price we won't buy our liberty.' [original emphasis][48]

Guber expressed herself in her published books and in articles she wrote for *Davar Hapo'elet*, often alluding to her military service and referring to the ideological motive for enlisting; if there were personal motives for this step, they were not mentioned. Moreover, Guber was a representative of a certain sector among the recruited women – women from the agricultural settlement in the Yishuv with much experience in working the land and establishing farms. As mentioned, most of the recruited women, including the mothers among them, were town dwellers and their background was different from hers. Thus, in this respect, too, Guber does not represent the majority of recruited mothers.

In her books, Guber described how she and her family were shunned when she decided to enlist, in defiance of the movement's stance on the matter. According to her: 'It was as if I was amazed by the power that pushed me toward the unknown, the army; when the heavy silence of my environment that had always been friendly until then, became so expressive of their condemnation of me as a mother; in those harsh days, when in the depths of my soul I was already close to collapsing ....' Only one friend, she stressed, dared to come to her home and to tell her to her face that she considered her recruitment to be a negative phenomenon and irresponsible toward her family. That woman friend was offered the post of emissary in America, but she was unable to overcome her maternal feeling and refused to leave her children in the hands of strangers for a lengthy period.[49] Bracha Habas, who included the story of Guber's recruitment (anonymously) in her book, *Bnot hayil* [Women of Valour], described it thus: 'The village accompanied her departure with a shocked silence, whereas her family – both the children and their father, who, for medical reasons, was himself unable to enlist – understood and encouraged her.'[50] She wrote of her suffering and guilt vis-à-vis her children who stayed at home:

> I remembered the nights ... when just soon after my departure, my little daughter contracted a painful ear infection and lost her balance for a few days. My partner [husband] had to be in the Bet She'an Valley, where he works as an instructor in outlying settlements and 14-year-old Ephraim cared for the girl on his own. Where did the words come from to describe my nights there in the barracks?[51]

In her book, *Rak Shvil* [Only a path], Rivka Guber wrote that Shlomo Lavie[52] helped her with her decision to enlist when he visited her at home after learning of her wish to do so. According to her, he had said,

> I've been told that you have three children and that you own a farm. Of course it's hard for you to go. I have come to tell you that there is not a single Jew in the world today who is allowed to think of himself that he is not obliged to take part in this war. But not everyone has the strength to go. If you feel that you have this strength – then you must go and not look to the right or to the left.

Guber wrote, after hearing these words, 'And with this strength I went'.[53]

Guber was reconciled with her decision and with her enlistment and admitted that she was 'happy to have withstood the test'. She did not see her departure from her home and family as desertion, as she was accused of at the time, but a mission: 'I had no intention of abandoning my family – I am not a person that fits that definition! I had hoped to leave them in a sympathetic environment, one that understands the size of the sacrifice my children made and also able to respect it.' She left behind 'a man who was my teacher and my guide, who gave me 22 years of endless love and devotion ... I am leaving sons that I nurtured with loyalty and in who I began to see signs of fruition ... all this I am leaving without pity – for what? ... The best proof is the happiness and willingness that are filling my soul as I take my leave.'[54]

Rivka Guber defended her ability to leave her children by comparing it to the importance of the ability to renounce the individual's needs on behalf of the society in which he lives: 'I taught my children to be good Jews ... I taught them not to follow the path of least resistance, I taught them to accept suffering with love and to fight for what was sacred to them to their last breath, because one has to fight for that which is dearest to him in life.' She added, 'I could point to no other person who could have gone before me. How can one [I] say to my peers, even if they are younger and uncommitted – Go! And possibly die? But *everyone must go and I am the first*, because no one is closer than me and dearer than my home [family].' [author's emphasis][55]

Guber served two years in the army and, according to her, she received the support and empowerment of her children who never complained: 'my dear children did not place so much as one stone on my heart, they always empowered me and encouraged me'. Nonetheless, she was aware of the price they had to pay during that period:

> Once, in those days, Zvi accompanied me to the car, I couldn't speak, there was a choking feeling in my throat. He began by saying: 'Don't worry, mother, after the war all this will seem good to us. And the main thing, if we meet someone who's lost an arm or a leg, it won't be hard for us to look him in the eye and he won't ask us: where were you, when I was suffering? *We, too, suffered.*' [author's emphasis][56]

Her son, Ephraim Guber's ambivalence toward his mother's military service is obvious in two letters he wrote. In December 1941 he wrote:

'To give Mother? The objective is without a doubt a noble cause, but the price is very high.' On the attitude of their fellow farmers he wrote, 'No doubt they are all thinking that Mother doesn't love us and is trying to escape from home. But it is we who know how much our mother loves us.' Although in a letter to his mother in the army, he wrote, 'it seems a long time since you left. Each day feels to me like a year.' Still, he appears to have internalized the concept: 'It is worth sacrificing everything on behalf of victory ... we promise you that we shall accept all the suffering with love, as you do.'[57]

Such a model in which one's private life is sacrificed and turned into a social/national issue brings to mind the revolutionary Soviet model on which women such as Mania Shohat were raised. Among the components that contributed to the formation of the pioneer discourse, that of the radical revolutionary movement in Russia in the nineteenth and early twentieth century is most outstanding. Revolutionary ideology, absorbed by the immigrants of the Second Aliyah, subjugated the needs of the individual to those of the community and, as they said, 'the professional revolutionary ... has to be completely loyal to the party and to the objectives of the workers – his private life and his public life are one and the same'.[58] Especially influential were the personalities of the revolutionary Russian women whose activity was outstanding in these movements. It should be noted that a significant number of Jewish women joined the revolutionary movements.[59]

In her speech at the fifth Working Women's Congress in February 1942, Guber recalled that she had announced her decision to enlist to her family and said, 'at this moment it is the big account that pushes aside all private considerations'. And with a note of profound self-persuasion, she added that she had heard her 14-year-old son say proudly: 'I knew that if female recruitment were announced, my mother will be the first to go. How could I have disappointed him? If there is one thing in the world that I am afraid of – *it is being tried by my sons*.' [author's emphasis][60] At the same time, Guber compared the education system that teaches people to prefer the needs of society to the religious attitude to life: 'That same specificity – the divine: before anything else – the divine, the religious and after that – my life ....It is a perfect blend of civilian and mother.'[61]

According to Nurit Guvrin the same happened to Guber as did to other female activists. In her opinion, not only was Guber's activity not valued as worthwhile in that sphere, as was her activity in immigration integration during the 1950s, she actually became a target for wicked attacks. Instead of praising her work, Guber became a victim of political backbiting. This, in Guvrin's opinion, is one of many examples of the ungratefulness of Israeli society vis-à-vis those who volunteered on its behalf for the most difficult of missions.[62]

The Recruits through the Eyes of their Children

The mothers who enlisted in the British army are no longer alive, but a few of them left behind written testimony from which there emerges a picture of strong, articulate, highly motivated women, fired by pioneer idealism, who decided to take action and contribute to the war effort, even at the cost of leaving their home and family. But the picture that emerges from the memories of their children, or from women who knew them, is rather different, especially with regard to their motive for enlisting.

Zipora Shahar recalls the mothers from the agricultural sector in the Jezreel Valley, whose husbands were busy with various security positions with Haganah or missions on behalf of their movements and were therefore absent from home for days on end. The entire burden of farm and family fell on the shoulders of their wives, who did hard physical work from dawn till dusk. When the opportunity arose for women to enlist in the army, they preferred this option and decided that the time had come for them do things for themselves. They connected public activity with self-fulfilment. In the women drivers' company in Egypt, Shahar served alongside a mother who had 'distributed her children among the local kibbutzim [sic] and spent all day weeping with yearning for them'.[63]

The length of time Mor from Kfar Yehoshua spent in the army was two and a half years, most of which was spent in Camp Genifa, near Suez in Egypt. Mor went home to her family only for a week once every three moths. Her ties with her family were maintained mainly through correspondence, as with most of the servicemen and servicewomen at that time. In a letter home about a month after recruitment she wrote that she had filed a request to serve in the Yishuv in order to be near her family: 'I had a meeting today with one of our officers and asked her to send me back home.' Also, 'Yesterday we were visited by Moshe Shertok ... we asked him questions and I raised the question of our [mothers'] situation. He promised to deal with it.'[64]

Rina Porat (Mor), Mor's daughter, recalls her father Emanuel being fiercely opposed to her mother's military service, and that there were many tensions between her parents. Her father was involved in security issues outside the moshav, and their farm, which consisted of various agricultural areas, was unable to continue to function without the presence of one of its owners. Porat testifies that when her mother enlisted, she herself was already wondering about the fact that both her parents were leaving the farm and the message this was giving the children: 'Could this mean that they don't want the farm? And if that's the case, shouldn't some firm conclusions be reached?' However, according to Porat, the decision had been made and her mother was going to enlist. During her mother's absence from home, her younger sister contracted a bad case of tonsillitis that had complications. Several years after Mor's military service, her relationship with her husband ended and the couple divorced.[65]

Zika, only son of Sonya Halperin from Kfar Vitkin, stayed with his father on the farm when his mother enlisted in the army. His mother had been active in Haganah and was employed as a cook. During the Arab riots (1936–39) she'd walk from the moshav to the Haganah hut, a distance of several kilometres, for a morning or evening shift, thus risking her life in order to cook for her comrades who were going on a mission or returning from one. Halperin served as a driver in Egypt and came home for a week every three months. Her service lasted three years. Zika recalls that he used to boast about his mother, who sometimes arrived as a driver in a convoy of trucks and passed through the village. Nonetheless, he also recalled the tensions and his parent's loveless marriage. Alongside his pride, he remembers that his schoolwork suffered during the years of his mother's absence and he worked off his anger with acts of mischief in the village.[66]

Ziona Tager, a Tel Aviv artist, enlisted in 1942, fired with a desire to participate in the war of the Jewish nation. Tager had been an independent, unconventional character from an early age and, as the daughter of a conservative, Sephardi family, she was the first woman in Palestine to study art in Paris in the 1920s. She served for about a year in an army camp in Haifa. Her only son, Avraham Katz-Oz, spent that period in Kibbutz Einat with a group of twenty other youngsters evacuated from Tel Aviv following an air raid by the Italian air force. Katz-Oz remembers his mother visiting him on the kibbutz, dressed in ATS uniform and loaded with sweets from the NAAFI, of a kind unknown at that time in the kibbutz. He remembers that period as very pleasant, especially because of the free atmosphere in the kibbutz, far from the horrors of war. Still, he was able to recall the tense relations between his parents and the lack of 'chemistry' between them. A few years later, the couple separated.[67]

Zahava Zimbel from Tel Adashim served together with her daughter, Ruth, leaving her remaining three children at home. She was too old to enlist and neglected to mention her real age in order to be accepted. She served as a cook in Camp Shneller in Jerusalem and on an army base in Haifa. In the course of her service in Jerusalem, she visited her home only at the weekends and once every three months she had a week's vacation, in accordance with British military custom. After transferring to the Haifa base, she came home every evening. Her daughter, Michal, recalls with pride her mother's determination to enlist and to this day, she continues to be proud of her mother for the step she took. Nonetheless, from what she wrote in an Internet site in memory of her mother, it emerges that Zahava Zimbel was released after a year of service due to her children's health issues.[68]The experiences of the children of the servicewomen resemble those of the second generation of parents who established the kibbutzim. These compared their generation to the 'Isaac generation', who defied their parents' generation, known as the 'Abraham generation', which sacrificed the needs of its family, especially that of its children, on the divine, ideological, kibbutz-socialist-Zionist altar of building the country and a new society.[69] They all, each according to his/her concepts, paid a harsh price, at times terrible, for the commitment and absoluteness of their parent's perception of life.

The Yishuv's Reaction

At first the daily press emphasized debates on the recruitment to the armed forces of married women with children. Thus, for example, under the headline, 'The Volunteer Movement is Making Waves', *Ha'aretz* published an article in December 1941 that dealt with the strong motivation of the women volunteers. The sub-headline was 'Mothers in Israel Wish to Enlist'. A few days later, *Davar* produced an article with the title, 'I Shall be Like a Mother to the Soldiers', about an 'old lady [sic] who comes with her 19-year-old only son to register him for military service. And the two – mother and son – are seriously deliberating over the military unit they would serve in.' The article went on to describe 'another mother, whose oldest son is already in military service', who is ten years above recruitment age (she is 55). To the question, 'What will you do in the army?' she replies simply and confidently: "I shall be like a mother. I shall take care of them, polish their shoes, write a letter on behalf of a wounded soldier.

I shall care for them as if they were my own children, I am a mother, after all!"'[70]

Later, the daily press stopped the publication of articles of this kind almost entirely. Quite possibly this was in response to orders from the army or from the Yishuv institutions as a result of problems among the families of recruits, as well as complaints from husbands who arrived at the recruitment offices demanding not to recruit their wives without their approval. The same seemed to have happened with regard to the women's magazines. *Davar Hapo'elet*, for example, pointed out about six months after recruitment began 'some of the women did not mention their marital status and there's a small percentage of mothers'.[71]

Several Yishuv circles, including a significant number of servicewomen, did not approve of the recruitment of mothers. A little of these emotions can be found in Habas's book, *Bnot hayil*. In describing the prevailing atmosphere in the basic training camp, Habas wrote: 'The mother-soldier was a special personality.' And she added, 'Many of the ATS girls [the recruits themselves] saw a certain exaggeration in the recruitment of mothers – since there is still some pretty important work to be done inside the country, in Haganah, and the Palmach, and it is not necessary for mothers to enlist and spend the nights weeping.' At the same time, she adds: 'Nonetheless, the general attitude to this unique test was respect and courtesy, especially to the test of the mothers, who had taken a definitive step in their lives without *breaking up or causing a crisis in their families*.' [author's emphasis] According to Habas, the very presence of the mothers, imparted 'more weight to the entire camp. And during those difficult hours of crisis and yearnings, all eyes turned inadvertently to the mothers, as to a moral authority, even when there was no military rank.'[72]

NOTES

1. Lucy Noakes, *Women in the British Army: War and the Gentle Sex 1907–1948* (New York 2006); Emily Yellin, *Our Mothers' War: American Women at Home and at the Front During World War II* (New York 2004); Mattie Treadwell, *The Women's Army Corps*: United States Army in World War II: Special Studies (Washington 1991); Michael Rustad, *Women in Khaki: The American Enlisted Woman* (New York: Praeger, 1982); etc.
2. Julia Cowper, *The Auxiliary Territorial Service* (London 1949). War Office, *Regulations for the Auxiliary Territorial Service* (London 1941) was distributed in Britain during the war and encompassed all aspects of women's service.
3. *Davar Hapo'elet*, 1–2 (30 January 1940), p.14. By the end of the war around 400 married women had enlisted, consisting of about 10 per cent of all the female recruits.

4. The data is according to lists of the Histadrut Liaison Bureau, Israel Defense Forces (IDF) Archive, Tel Hashomer, and Central Zionist Archive (CZA), Jerusalem, Section S37.
5. Statistics on the length of service related only to about one third of the mothers, which makes it difficult to reach firm conclusions. According to available statistics, seven women served up to one year, seven served about two years, seventeen women served about three years, and a further four women served almost four years in the army.
6. *Palestine Post*, 4 January 1942, p.4.
7. *Davar Hapo'elet*, 1–2 (1 January 1942), p.14.
8. Management Committee of the Jewish Agency's Recruitment Department, 14 April 1942, CZA, S25/5063.
9. *Davar Hapo'elet*, 3–4 (23 April 1942), p.1.
10. Moshe Sharett, minutes of CWO meeting, 15 September 1942, CZA, F49/2105.
11. Beba Idelson, Meeting of Histadrut Council, 7 September 1942, pp.128, 131, Labour Movement Archive, Lavon Institute.
12. Beba Idelson, minutes of CWO meeting, 13 October 1942, CZA, F49/2105.
13. Mania Shohat, meeting of Histadrut Council, 7 September 1942, pp.128, 131, Labour Movement Archive. Shohat was absent from home in order to realize an ideology, to fulfil personal aspirations, on behalf of a national mission, etc. The maternal aspect of her personality was actually expressed in her attitude to the members of the cooperative in Sedgera, toward whom she felt responsibility, concern and devotion, like a mother would to her children. Motti Golani 'Manya: aliata hakzara ve nefilata ha'aruka' [Manya: her short rise and long fall], *Israel*, 3 (2003), pp.9–11.
14. Yosef Halperin, 'In Memory of Sonya Halperin', *Davar Hapo'elet*, 9 (14 October 1947), p.214.
15. Mania Shohat at a meeting of Histadrut Council, 7 September 1942, p.130, IDF Archive 45/140/2002.
16. Simone de Beauvoir, *The Second Sex: Facts and Myths* (New York: Random House 1997).
17. Anat Palgi-Hecker, *Me'imahut le'imahut: hipus psichoanalyti feministy ahar ha'em cesubyect* [From non-essence to motherhood: a psychoanalytical feminist search for the mother as a subject] (Tel Aviv 2005), p.333.
18. Donald Winnicott coined these definitions and in doing so, rescued mothers from the discrepancy imposed on them by psychoanalytical theory. Ibid., pp.201–23.
19. Carol Gilligan, *In a Different Voice: Psychological Theory and Women's Development* (Cambridge, MA: Harvard University Press, 1982), p.32.
20. Nira Yuval-Davis,, 'Nationalism, Feminism and Gender Relations', in Montserrat Guibernau and John Hutchinson (eds), *Understanding Nationalism* (Cambridge: Polity Press, 2001), p.125; Bracha Habas, *Bnot hayil: sefer ha'ATS* [Women of valour: book of the ATS] (Tel Aviv 1964), p.10.
21. Roberto Baki, *H'anohag Benisuin ve'beyeluda bekerv hashchavot hashonot shel he'Yeshuv ve Hashpaato al Atiddenu* [The custom in marriage and birth in different layers of the Yishuv and its impact on our future] (Jerusalem 1945), pp.114–15.
22. Rachel Elboim-Dror, 'Ha'isha hazionit ha'idialit' [The Ideal Zionist Woman], in Yael Atzmon (ed.), *Hatishma Koli: yitsugim shel nashim batarbut ha'israelit* [Will

you hear my voice: representation of women in Israeli culture] (Jerusalem 2001), pp.114–15; Margalit Shilo, *Etgar hamigdar: nashim ba'aliyot harishonot* [Challenge of gender: women in the first waves of immigration] (Bnei Brak 2007), p.14; Deborah Bernstein, 'Po'alot ve-Halutzot ba-Aliyah ha-Sheniyyah – Tikvot ve-Akhzavot' [Female workers and pioneers in the Second Aliyah – hopes and disappointments], in Mordekhai Naor (ed.), *Ha'aliya Hasheniya 1903–1914* [The Second Aliyah 1903–1914] (Jerusalem 1985), pp.145–63.

23. Women of the Second Aliyah tried to bridge the impossible in frameworks offered to them by Zionist Movement. In some cases, the contradictions caused the physical and emotional breakdown of women. However, the women's movement tried to establish support institutions for women and civil circles established 'Hadassah' and the 'Federation of Hebrew Women', but these institutions fought only against the problematic aspects of identifying women with the private domain and proposed only technical solutions for the problem. Yael Atzmon, 'Historia shel kabalat ahrayut' [History of taking responsibility], in Yael Atzmon (ed.), *Hatishma koli: yutsugim shel nashim be tarbut israelit* [Will you hear my voice: representation of women in Israeli culture] (Jerusalem 2001), pp.134–35.
24. Margalit Shilo, 'Ledmuta shel ha'isha ba'aliyah hashniya: ha'ezrahit' [To the woman's image in the Second Aliyah: the woman citizen] *Israel*, 6 (2004), p.105.
25. Adrienne Rich, *Of Woman Born: Motherhood as Experience and Institution* (New York 1976), p.323. According to her, motherhood is but one aspect of the feminine entity, and women have been trying to overcome society's attempts to establish the concept that motherhood is the only thing that expresses their personality.
26. *Bundle of Letters*, 116 (181), 29 March 1942, p.10, United Kibbutz Movement (UKM) Archive, Yad Tabenkin.
27. Interview with Zipora Shahar. According to Shahar, Mahram used to ridicule her daughter for choosing to have a family instead of contributing to the war effort, as she did herself. One of the recruits who served in Beirut told Idelson, 'I enlisted, my daughter will stay at work. And I, a mother, older, went.' Report by Beba Idelson to secretariat of CWO, 30 May 1943, Labor Movement Archive, IV-23-6, WWC File, p.11.
28. Testimony of Raphael Sadovsky, an Egytian Jew who gave away the Lehi members who were involved in the murder of Lord Moyn in Cairo. Protocol of Sadovsky Confession, part 2, 4 April 1945, p.6, Haganah History Archive, Tel Aviv (HHA), 112/1029.
29. Interview with Hanna Maron (Meierzak), Tel Aviv, 28 February 2006.
30. Interview with Tzafrira Shoham (Yaffe), Kibbutz Ramat Yohanan, 11 March 2007.
31. In her case it is impossible to know if her children were of recruitment age or younger, but it can be assumed that they were young, because of the privilege that was apparently granted to mothers to choose to serve closer to home.
32. Slutsky, Yehuda (ed.), *Sefer toldot ha'aganah* [History of the Haganah], B and C (Tel Aviv 1973), p.765.
33. Palgi-Hecker, *Me'imahut le'imahut*, p.148.
34. Ya'akov Margalit (ed.), *Hineni shalcheni: mitnadvim batzava habriti kotvim* [Here I am, send me: writings of volunteers to the British Army] (Tel Aviv 1984), p.148.

35. Letter from Political Department to Recruitment Centre, 16 August 1942, CZA, S25/5099. One of the mothers who served as a cook in one of the military hospitals in Egypt wrote that most of the mothers had been sent to military bases abroad, whereas the single women were left to serve in Palestine. According to her, there were even instances of mothers asking to remain in Palestine and, after showing the recruitment officers pictures of their children, they received permission to do so. Z.S. [sic], 'My Work in the Army', *Davar Hapo'elet*, 9 (27 September 1943), p.133.
36. See, for example: a request to the management of the Ben Shemen Youth Village to accept the son of the servicewoman H.L: 'it depends entirely on you whether or not this [recruit] is not removed from the army, since this would be a complete tragedy for her and since she has already let her apartment and resigned from her job'. Letter from the Recruitment Office to the management of Ben Shemen Youth Village, 11 August 1942, CZA, S37/58.
37. Bat-Sheva Margalit Stern, *Geula bekvalim: tenuat ha'poalot ha'eretz israelit 1920–1939* [Salvation in Chains: Working Women's Movement in Eretz Israel 1920–1939] (Jerusalem 2006), pp.354–5. On communal childrearing, see Sylvia Fogel-Bijaoui, 'From Revolution to Motherhood: The Case of Women in the Kibbutz, 1910–1948', in Deborah Bernstein (ed.), *Pioneers and Homemakers: Jewish Women in Pre-State Israel* (New York 1992), pp.211–30. On the beginnings of this model, see Smadar Sinai, *Miryam Baratz: Dyokana shel Halutza* [Miriam Baratz: Portrait of a Halutzah] (Yad Tabenkin Ramat Efal 2002), and others.
38. According to Tamar Razi, kibbutz-style communal education, like the removal of abandoned children from their homes during the 1930s and 1940s, was an exaggerated expression of the concept that ruled the roost in the Yishuv: the family is the factor that holds back the realization of the Zionist revolution so that it is necessary to reduce to the minimum all contact between parents and their children, and to hand over to the authorities the responsibility for their education. Anti-family trends are typical of all societies based on revolutionary-collectivist ideology, but the Zionist and Palestine connection is unique because it did not take place in a nationalist framework and because it was not totalitarian in character. Tamar Razi, 'Building the Fringes of the Nation: Homeless Youths in Tel Aviv in the 1930s and 1940s' (PhD thesis, Bar Ilan University, 2006), p.221.
39. Ibid., pp.131–3, 207–11. This instance is similar to that of mothers who went out on a mission to the displaced persons camps in Europe to care for children of Jewish refugees and left their own children in the care of others. Lilach Rosenberg-Friedman indicates that it is possible to connect the phenomenon of the 'national mothers' to the lifestyle of some of the mothers. Many of the women emissaries were kibbutz members. The concept of national motherhood and that of children as a national asset was implemented in kibbutz society where children are part of the 'kibbutz ideal', in other words, essential to the continuation of the kibbutz way of life. The kibbutz's position at the spearhead of Zionist fulfilment encouraged – ideologically – the harnessing of parents to national missions. The institutionalized arrangements in the kibbutz – the communal education system and the children's houses in which children were de facto raised and educated – made it simple for mothers to go on lengthy

missions. This, indeed, was the reason that urban mothers, who undertook missions abroad, would often entrust the kibbutz with their children for the duration. To the mothers, the mission was of the utmost importance and for the national goal they were prepared to bear the pain of leaving their child. Lilach Rosenberg-Friedman, 'Zehuyot be'conflict ben shoah letekuma: shlichot hayishuv be'rikuzei she'erit hapleita be'Europa [Identities in conflict between the Holocaust and independence: Yishuv emissaries in concentrations of Holocaust survivors in Europe], *Israel*, 11 (2007), pp.117–20.

40. Under these conditions there was a need to concentrate the children in the centre of the kibbutz in order to ensure their survival and in order for the workforce thus released by their mothers could be turned to production and defence. Collective education for the children, that often included communal sleeping arrangements, made it possible for women to, among other things, have freedom from the burdens of homemaking and devote themselves to public activity. This was also an attempt at practical expression of the ideological value of equality between the sexes that was supposed to be typical of kibbutz life. In practice, however, there was no change in women's traditional role on the kibbutz, which even intensified because of communal education. Women acted as mothers to all the children. But, as a national symbol, motherhood became a reality with this method of education. Fogel-Bijaoui, 'From Revolution to Motherhood', pp.596–612.
41. *Davar*, 1 January 1942, p.2.
42. Haya Mor, Ka'et Haya, *Sefer Zikaron le Haya Mor* [Memorial book for Haya Mor] (Kfar Yehoshua 1972), p.55.
43. *Davar Hapo'let*, 5 (5 June 1942), pp.70–1.
44. Haya Mor, *Ibid.*, p.47.
45. Mor ignored the fact that women enlisted for indefinite periods (for as long as necessary) and they did not know what the length of their service would be when they signed on. Ibid.
46. According to Shmuel Dayan, one of the founders of Moshav Nahalal and Deganya, 'The women arranges her own life, her work is not beyond her ability. All her focus is on cooking, gardening or working in the cowshed and caring for a baby, housework, sewing, etc. Free of the need to organize her chores and of responsibility for herself, she has developed inner powers.' Shmuel Dayan, *Mosheve ovdim be eretz Israel* [Workers' moshavim in Eretz Israel] (Jerusalem 1945), p.117. According to Rachel Shar'abi, even if in the unique reality of moshav society women were considered equal partners to their husbands, the leading male ideologists were still bound by stereotypical concepts and believed a woman's place to be in the private sphere of her traditional format. Rachel Shar'abi, 'Pratit sh'ehi tziburit: mekoma shel ha'isha bemoshavei ha'ovdim harishonim' [Private and public: women's place in the first workers' moshavim], *Megamot*, 45, no.1 (June 2007), p.96.
47. Margalit Shilo, 'Ha'isha ha'ivriya hahadasha – panim rabot la, hashomeret kemikreh mivhan' [Many faces to the New Hebrew Woman, the woman member of Hashom as a test case], *Bikoret ve-parshanut*, 34 (Summer 2000), p.7. For more on the family structure during the Yishuv period and on the functions of the family and distribution of work in the family, see, for example, Deborah Bernstein, 'Bein ha'isha ha-adam ubein eshet habayit' [Between the woman as person and the woman in the home], in Uri Ram (ed.) *Habevra Ha'israelit:*

hebetim bikortiim [Israeli society: critical aspects] (Tel Aviv 1993), pp.89–95.

48. Letter to Shlomo Lavie, 1940, Rivka Guber, *Im habanim* [With the Sons] (Tel Aviv 1953), p.32. Guber recalled that after his enlistment, Lavie delivered an inspired speech in Sarafend, praising the servicewomen and the mothers who had enlisted in the army. To reinforce her words she turns to the book written by Haim Shorer, *Soldier Number Nine One Seven Two* (Tel Aviv 1946). Shorer mentioned that SL (Shlomo Lavie) did indeed write 'in his pleasant and simple language', about 'the servicewoman within us', but he does not mention the enlisted mothers. Ibid., p.23.
49. Guber, *Im habanim*, p.33; Rivka Guber, *Rak Shvil* [Only a path] (Tel Aviv 1970), p.61.
50. Habas, *Bnot hayil*, p.20.
51. Rivka Guber, 'Sooty Servicewomen', *Davar Hapo'elet*, 4 (1952), pp.60–4.
52. At that time Shlomo Lavie was 60 and of course well beyond the recruitment age for men. But later, sometime in 1942, he managed to lie about his age and join the army.
53. Guber, *Rak Shvil*, p.61.
54. Guber, *Im habanim*, p.35.
55. Ibid., pp.33–4.
56. Rivka Guber, *Morasha lehanhil* [Legacy to instil] (Jerusalem 1979), p.140.
57. Ibid. Her period in military service was not the only time her children were forced to stay home alone and take care of each other. When they were small and she worked as a teacher in Rehovot, Guber was often absent from home, leaving her 3-year-old son, Zvi, in nursery school, and his older brother, who was then in first grade, was entrusted with bringing the little boy home and caring for him, with the help of good neighbours, until she returned. Her husband worked away for a long time and was home only on the weekends. Rivka Guber, *Sefer Ha'ahim* [Book of the brothers] (Tel Aviv 1950), pp.48–9.
58. Tamar Hess, 'Autobiographical Writings by Women of the Second Aliyah' (PhD thesis, Hebrew University, Jerusalem, 2003), p.61.
59. Robert Stites, *The Women's Liberation Movement in Russia: Feminism, Nihilism and Bolshevism 1860–1930* (Princeton, NJ, 1978), pp.270–6; Guber, *Im habanim*, p.34.
60. Guber, *Im habanim*, p.34.
61. *A bundle of letters,* 116 (181), 29 March 1942, p.10, UKM Archive.
62. Nurit Guvrin, 'Nos'ot hakeylim, nashim be ma'arachot Israel be'reai Hasifrut ha'ivrit' [Bearing the banner, women in the wars of Israel as reflected in Hebrew literature], *Iton 77*, 264 (February 2002), p.23.
63. Interview with Zipora Shahar, Nahalal, 7 January 2006; Negev, 'Squad Sonya', *Yediot Ahronot*, 7 Days Supplement, 18 January 2007, p.56. *Davar Hapo'elet* pointed out that, 'Among the volunteers there are mothers of children, even of small children. Can there be any comparison between the mother who leaves her children and the feeling of the father who enlists? [...] Even when the [women] know that they could do no other, they are still subjected to yearnings, certainly more than once.' *Davar Hapo'elet*, 7–8 (31 August 1942), p.95.
64. Haya Mor, *Sefer Zikaron le Haya Mor*, pp.20–1.
65. Interview with Rina Porat (Mor), Tel Aviv, December 2006.
66. Interview with Zika Halperin, Petah Tikva, 23 October 2006.
67. Interview with Avraham Katz-Oz, Tel Aviv, 6 December 2006.

68. See Zahava Zimbel: www.aka.idf.il/yohalan/main/main.asp?catid+40768& docid-42546. Interview with Michal Ben-Arieh (Zimbel), Even Yehuda, 2 November 2006.
69. Nurit Leshem, *Shirat ha'deshe* [Song of the Grass] (Tel Aviv 1997), pp.6–7.
70. *Davar*, 2 January 1942, p.3.
71. *Davar Hapo'elet*, 7–8 (31 August 1942), p.107.
72. Habas, *Bnot hayil*, p.59. Habas's impression of the effect the recruitment had on the families is best credited to her ideological outlook, since she did not meet with the families, nor did she interview any of them in preparing her book. On women and 'writing committed' to Zionist ideology, see, for example, Yaffa Berlowitz, *Sheani adama ve adam: sipurei nashim ad kum hamedina* [I am Land and Man: stories of women up to the establishment of the State] (Tel Aviv 2003).

1. Clerks in a military office. Photographer: Zoltan Kluger. IDF Archive.

2. Esther Herlitz, Sarafend training camp, 1942. Courtesy of Esther Herlitz.

3. Hadassah Samuel with British officers, Jerusalem, 1942. Courtesy of David Samuel.

4. Miriam Makov (first left), No.27 Hospital, Suez, Egypt. Courtesy of Miriam Makov.

5. Wedding ceremony of Meira Beres and John Cummings, Egypt Courtesy of Ora Cummings.

6. Recruits from Company 513 in convoy, Egypt. Courtesy of Zipora Shahar.

7. Funeral of Uhma Levavi, 25 November 1944 Heliopolis, Egypt. Courtesy of Idit Levavi-Gabay.

8. At the officer's office. Illustration: Ziona Tager. Courtesy of Avraham Katz-Oz.

9. Ziona Tager with son Avraham. Courtesy of Avraham Katz-Oz.

10. Yaffa Tevua (Grinberg, first right), Lehi member, by the ambulance. Courtesy of Yaffa Tevua.

11. Tikvah Elhadef with British husband Bill Barry, Jerusalem. Courtesy of Ofra Gelbart-Avni.

12. Penelope Otto, commander of ambulance Company 502, Alexandria, Egypt. Courtesy of Naomi Yekutieli.

13. Haya Mor (Markovsky) with her family. Courtesy of Rina Porat.

14. Mary Mackenzie (centre), commander of Company 513. Courtesy of Zipora Shahar.

15. Lea Seideman with Jewish American husband Ben Segal, Jerusalem, 1946. Courtesy of Naomi Segal.

16. Hadassah Samuel (right) with Helen Pine, commander of Sarafend training camp. Courtesy of David Samuel.

17. Cooks in the military kitchen. Photographer: Zoltan Kluger. IDF Archive.

18. Jean Baker, commander in the WAAF, Egypt 1943. Courtesy of Jean Baker.

19. Erica Sharon (Ino), Company 513. Courtesy of Erica Sharon.

0. Hadassah Samuel with
TS commander Audrey
:hitty, Tel Aviv, 24 December
941. Photographer: Shimon
Rudi) Wissenstein, JNF
hoto Archive.

21. Naomi Yekutieli (Torok, right), ambulance driver Company 502. Courtesy of Naomi Yekutieli.

22. Hanna Maron (Meierzak), Alexandria, Egypt 1944. Courtesy of Hanna Maron.

23. Hagana members, Alexandria, Egypt, 1945. Courtesy of Orit Bar-Shira.

24. Recruitment poster, 1942. IDF Archive

25. Rivka Guber with husband Zvi and children, 1945. Kfar Bilu Archive

.6. In the military tent. Illustration: 'iona Tager. Courtesy of Avraham 'atz-Oz.

27. Prayer in Cairo Synagogue, 1945. Photographer: Lazar Dinar. JNF photo Archive.

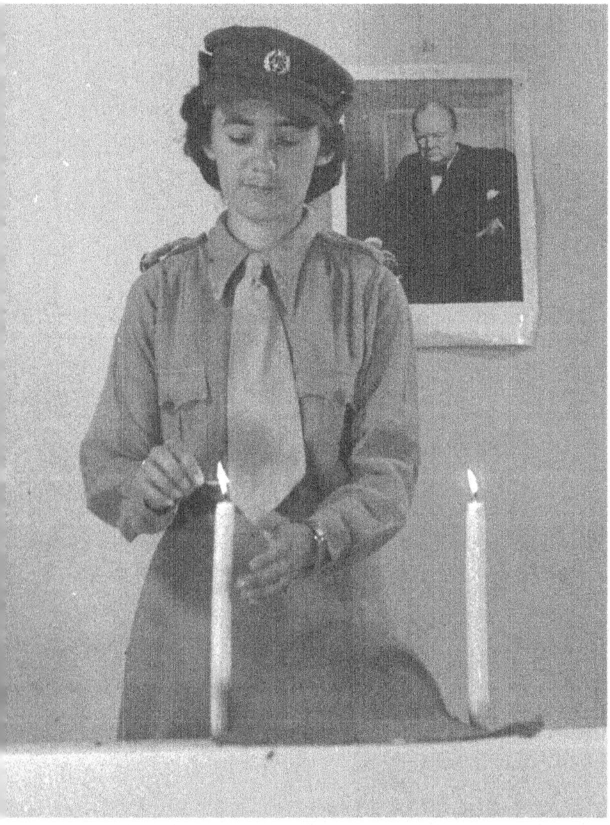

28. Woman recruit lights Shabbat candles, Egypt. Photographer: Lazar Dinar, JNF photo Archive.

5

Gender Aspects of Military Service

'It is an unrepeatable opportunity for the Jewish Woman, who has waited all these years of the discovery of the springs of her powers – that she'll seize this segment of the war needs which waits for the Yishuv to act upon, and will conquer it with her work and her personality.'[1] In this speech, Moshe Sharett, head of the Jewish Agency's Political Department, reflects his confidence in women's ability to contribute to the war effort under all circumstances and in every task required of them in their military service. The recruits, like the women's organizations who initiated their recruitment, wanted to prove that the Jewish woman is equal to her male counterpart in her willingness and ability to contribute to the war effort. Equality, from their point of view, was expressed in the ability to enlist in the army and to play a role in the war that threatened the Jewish Yishuv as well as the rest of the world. The women's organizations saw in the drive to recruit women into the army another chapter in women's aspirations to face, together with men, the challenges of settlement and security.

This chapter will examine the process of female recruitment in the Yishuv, the positions women filled in the army as part of the female alignment in the Middle East, the gender classification of these positions and the way the recruits conceived them. The question will also be examined as to whether the Yishuv recruits' service in auxiliary services contributed to the British war effort in the Middle East.

Service in the ATS

Yishuv women served in two British military forces: the ATS and the WAAF.[2] So long as the Middle East constituted the main Theatre of War, the women recruits served mostly in Egypt (over 2,000 in the ATS and most of the WAAF recruits), in Palestine (several hundred) and between 200–300 in Syria and Lebanon. In mid 1944, after the theatre of war moved to Italy, around 400 Yishuv servicewomen were transferred to that area. At the end of the war, several dozen recruits were also sent to serve in Austria.

The British army's first experience of establishing a Women's Auxiliary units took place as far back as August 1940 when Audrey Chitty, who later established the ATS, arrived in Cairo. She wanted to examine the possibility of recruiting British women residing in Egypt, to ATS companies, in accordance with the format accepted in Britain. At that stage there was still no thought in the British Forces High Command in the Middle East of recruiting women from the region. On the visit, Chitty was disappointed to learn that the British women working in the High Command, mostly daughters or wives of soldiers, were not interested in enlisting. She found a similar attitude among the British women in Jerusalem. Moreover, in wake of the battles in North Africa, most of the British women and children were evacuated from Egypt and sent back home to Britain. At that time, it was not possible to send ATS recruits from Britain, because of transport problems and the war needs in Britain, and the plan to do so was dropped. When Chitty returned home in September 1940, she arrived empty handed.

The next stage consisted of Hadassah Samuel's communication on behalf of the Council of Women's Organizations to the British army in Palestine regarding the recruitment of Yishuv women to the British forces. After lengthy negotiations a favourable decision was taken and made public on 23 December 1941 on the 'Voice of Jerusalem' and, the following day, in all the daily papers in the country.

The ATS Alignment in the Middle East

At first the Auxiliary Territorial Services in the Middle East were known as PATS (Palestine ATS) or ATS Palestine, but from February 1942 the army ceased to use this name, both for political reasons – in order to hide all hint of a connection between the recruitment of local women with the Jewish Yishuv in Palestine – and because the sexist connotations of the term 'pat'. The change to 'Auxiliary Services in the Middle East' aroused the anger of the Jewish Agency and Sharett wrote to Chitty with the demand to make use of the official term. As a result of his protest, the army returned to using the name ATS Palestine.[3]

The ATS alignment in the Middle East consisted of twenty-nine companies, which were a part of Britain's Middle East Forces (MEF). The ATS Command was located in the General Headquarters (GHQ) in Cairo. Chief Commander Audrey Chitty established the ATS alignment in the Middle East in January 1942; she was subsequently replaced by Controller Peggy Wagstaff. Her rank was higher than that of Chitty's because the ATS alignment had expanded in the course of the Second World War. The last commander of the ATS in the region was Mary Dixon, who served from late 1945 until the last of the servicewomen was released in mid 1946.

In addition to the senior command, from 1943–44 the organizational framework of the Middle East ATS included the distribution of regional or group commands, whose numbers were 16, 17, 18 and 21, in accordance with a similar distribution of the British forces in general. A senior ATS officer was given command of and made responsible for supervising, organizing and disciplining the ATS group in her region.[4] Within the Regional Groups there was a local distribution in accordance with the concentrations of ATS companies and the numbers of servicewomen in certain locations. Thus, for example, there was an HQ Palestine-Syria Group, under the command of Catherine Morrison-Bell; the Canal Group, whose HQ was in Tel el Kabir was commanded by Florence Fletcher; Tel el Kabir Group was commanded by Cranston, who was later transferred to command the Delta Group in 1945; Alexandria Group, under the command of Penelope Otto, and Egypt Group was under the command of Boyle. All the Group commanders held the rank of Senior Commander.

Table 1. Apparatus of ATS Companies in the Middle East*

Times of Activity	Location	Company
October 1942–July 1944	Ma'adi, Egypt	501 Communication unit (British recruits only)
End 1941–1946	Alexandria, Italy and Austria	502 Ambulance drivers
April 1942–December 1945	Abassya, Egypt	503 Drivers and clerks
April 1942–December 1945	Tel El Kabir, Egypt	504 Storekeepers
October 1942–December 1945	Haifa, Eretz Israel	505 Clerks
April 1942–December 1945	Suez, Egypt	506 Hospital workers
October 1942–December 1945	Dir Suneid, Eretz Isreal	507 Clerks, drivers
July 1942–December 1945	Cairo Citadel, Egypt	508 Clerks

August 1942–December 1945	Jennifa, Egypt	**509** Storekeepers, Clerks
November 1942–December 1945	Kasr El Nil, Cairo	**510** Clerks, bus drivers
October 1942–December 1945	Tel El Kabir	**511** Drivers
October 1942–December 1945	Jerusalem	**512** Clerks
December 1942–December 1945	Mina camp, Egypt	**513** Drivers
November 1942–April 1944	Tel El Kabir	**514** Clerks
February 1943–August 1945	Sarafend, Eretz Israel	**515** Clerks, ambulance drivers
March 1943–December 1944	Beirut, Lebanon	**516** Clerks
February 1943–July 1944	Alexandria, Egypt	**517** Drivers
April 1943–September 1944	Beirut	**518** Clerks, nurses
April 1943–December 1945	Beirut; Haifa	**519** clerks
April 1943–December 1945	Tel El Kabir	**520** Storekeepers
June 1943–October 1945	Sidi Bisher, Egypt: Sarafend	**521**
May 1943–December 1945	Alexandria	**522** Clerks
May 1943–December 1944	Egypt	**523** Clerks
June 1943–October 1944	Egypt	**524** Clerks
July 1943–December 1945	Kasr El Nil	**525** Clerks
November 1943–December 1945	Suez, Egypt	**526** Clerks
September 1943–	Sarafend	**528** Clerks
October 1943-December 1945 December 1945	Cairo	**529** Clerks
June 1944–December 1945	Tura, Egypt	**531** Computer workers, clerks
May 1942–December 1945	Sarafend	Eretz Israel and Syria Group, HQ Palestine-Syria
January–December 1945	Cairo	Delta Group HQ
January 1944–December 1945	Tel El Kabir	Canal Group HQ
April–December 1943	Tel El Kabir	Tel El Kabir Group
August 1943–September 1944	Alexandria	16 Area Group

January 1943–December 1944	Cairo	17 Area Group
December 1942–September 1944	Moaskar	18 Area Group
January–July 1944	Eretz Israel	21 Area Group
June–December 1942	Egypt	Egypt Group

*Based on War Diaries of ATS companies. NA, WO 169/6831-21590, WO 169/6831-21590.

The Cadre Course

The first twenty female recruits arrived at the Cadre Squad course in Sarafend on 18 January 1942. During the week that followed, a further forty women joined them and training began in earnest. The course, which was known as the 'Cadre', aimed at training commanders for ATS companies in the Middle East. The course was started with fifty-four Jewish and six Christian women (four Arab) from Palestine.[6] Chitty was determined to include Arab women in the Cadre as part of British policy vis-à-vis Arabs in the Middle East. Their participation in the course was made possible after Chitty met and persuaded the local female Arab leadership.[7]

In early December 1941, when it was known that Chitty was about to arrive in the country in order to finalize the negotiations over female recruitment, the Jewish Agency decided to prepare a group of several hundred volunteers to enlist as soon as the decision became official and to organize a group of female activists on behalf of recruitment to conduct some quiet propaganda. As already mentioned, the Haganah and the Jewish Agency both wanted to take control of the constituency of the candidates for the Cadre, since they wanted the Jewish commanders, graduates of the course, to be representative of the Yishuv in the army and serve as a 'moral' and cultural example to the other recruits. A special process was used for picking the candidates to the Cadre course, within the British army's general recruitment process, since it was the only time in which an effort was made to determine the constituency of recruits among women. With male recruits, on the other hand, entire groups were recruited in an orderly manner from the kibbutzim and Haganah, in accordance with organized draft procedures and quotas imposed by the Yishuv institutions. In all the subsequent batches of recruits, from 15 March 1942 and later, women were recruited on a personal basis through the Jewish Agency's recruitment office or directly through the army recruitment centres.

In order to implement the decision and monitor the constituency of the candidates, the Haganah established a special mechanism – a kind of 'Acceptance Committee' – that aimed at choosing those women that the Yishuv institutions considered the best of the bunch.

According to the decision of Ya'akov Dori – who was already called Chief of Staff – Rachel Shalon (Friedlander) was appointed recruiting officer responsible for sorting candidates to the Cadre course. Over three months the committee held interviews with the candidates in the Jewish Agency offices on Lilienblum Street in Tel Aviv, interviews that were attended by, in addition to Shalon, the Haganah representative Moshe Sneh (Kleinbaum) and representatives of the CWO, Hadassah Samuel and Beba Idelson.[8] Shalon received directions from Sneh and communication between them was conducted via go-betweens. One of the major problems in categorizing the candidates for recruitment was the fact that some women, who had been rejected by the Haganah, applied directly to the military recruitment office. The Haganah was unable to prevent this although attempts were made to determine the quality of each candidate and include her in the ranks of the Haganah.

The Jewish Agency's recruitment office was asked to provide its own candidates for the Cadre course by 5 January 1942, in order to enable them to be called for an interview with a military selection committee headed by Chitty herself.[9] The choice of candidates for the Cadre course caused considerable friction with the British high command in the country, especially with Audrey Chitty. The Jewish Agency had hoped at first to fill all the places in the course, but in accordance with military orders, a list of only forty-eight candidates was ultimately submitted. Chitty was determined to conduct the course purely in accordance with military considerations, which is why she insisted on choosing those candidates she found most suitable; in this she had the full support of the military high command in Palestine.[10] According to a decision of the military committee, out of the fifty-four Jewish recruits who participated in the course, thirty-two were recommended on behalf of the Jewish Agency and the Haganah, and a further twenty-two were recruited directly in the recruitment offices, without the 'supervision' of the Yishuv institutions. In total, the Haganah candidates constituted about 50 per cent of the sixty participants in the course, fewer than was hoped for by the Jewish Agency and the Haganah.[11]

The command course for women resembled the male version that preceded it. In early August 1940 the British decided to establish mixed Jewish/Arab infantry companies known as the 'Buffs' within the framework of the Palestine Regiment. In order to train a command team from these companies, the British army opened a Cadre course in Sarafend, where officers were trained, as well as sergeants and force commanders. A total of twenty-eight Jews and two Arabs took part. The Haganah and Jewish Agency wanted to have control of the constituency of the recruits but in the end the Yishuv institutions recommended only fifteen of the Jews. When the first course was completed, subsequent courses were opened for training local servicemen.[12]

One week before the women's course commenced, a Yishuv's male recruit officer (who had been released for the purpose of encouraging recruitment) still expressed male control over the constituency of the female candidates for the Cadre and hesitations as to their ability to influence the servicewomen: 'We all had reservations. The officers' course will begin soon and the face of the companies depends largely on the material [sic] participating in it. It must be stressed that those who were determined and sent by us are of the very best material.'[13]

The Cadre course aimed to train its participants as officers and Non Commissioned Officers (NCOs) in the ATS companies in the Middle East and in training future batches of recruits. The course was conducted in accordance with the experience accumulated in Britain with the formation of the ATS there, and its format in Palestine was proposed to the Jewish Agency by Claire Epstein.[14] According to her proposal, 'From the commencement of recruitment, we shall have a group of servicewomen prepared to help in determining the independent image of the units to which we must aspire.'[15] The course taught the same subjects as were dealt with by women commanders in the British army: drill, military discipline, administrative matters, punishment laws and others, but there was no weapons practice. Veteran Haganah members, who had undergone drill and weaponry practice prior to enlistment, were obliged to conceal their military expertise so as not to arouse their commanders' suspicions. The Haganah command even issued a clear directive that (organization) members were to march like new recruits, not like experienced soldiers.

Ten recruits dropped out of the course (nine Jews and one Arab), which was completed by forty-five Jewish recruits, three Arabs and two Christian women. Reasons for dropping out were mainly an inability to adapt to a military framework. At the end of the course, four Jewish recruits were given the rank of Junior Commander, eleven (including one Arab) recruits were made sergeant, eleven (including one Arab) recruits were given the rank of Lance Corporal, one recruit was made first corporal and twenty-three recruits (including one Arab) were made corporal. Most of the graduates of the course were sent to serve in Egypt, apart from Sergeant (later officer) Mina Ben-Zvi, who remained to assist in recruitment activity, and five of the corporals who stayed behind in Sarafend as part of the training camp's administrative staff.

Recruitment Process to the ATS

The recruits from the Yishuv volunteered for military service and were not forced to do so by law, as was the case in Britain. Thus the military term used by the authorities to describe their recruitment was Locally Enlisted (as opposed to Enrolled, which referred to people recruited by force of law).

The recruitment process was conducted along two 'channels' – some of the recruits had registered initially in the Jewish Agency's recruitment offices. Each volunteer underwent an initial selection, which included an interview with the local recruiter, who registered her personal details and had a medical examination.[16] The second stage took place in the recruitment office in Sarafend, and it, too, included an interview with a British officer and an additional medical examination. At the end of the process, the volunteer was either approved or rejected for service. The Jewish Agency's recruitment offices sent detailed lists of names to the military recruitment office of all the recruits who had successfully passed their own process. The women who enlisted directly with the military recruitment offices were interviewed by a British officer and underwent a medical examination. At the end of the process (in both types of selection) each recruit received a personal number with the prefix W/PAL, indicating that she was from Palestine.

The only places outside of Britain that the British army opened recruitment centres and training camps were Palestine and the Caribbean Islands. In Palestine these centres were located in the large cities, Tel Aviv, Haifa and Jerusalem – and the training camp in Sarafend, where basic training took place. From the onset, basic training was conducted according to the ATS format in Britain, except for a few changes in the hours, which had to accommodate the weather conditions and the need to devote several hours a day to the study of English. Until the end of 1943, each group of recruits underwent four weeks of basic training; this was later cut to two weeks.[17]

In the course of 1942, the year in which recruitment took place only to the ATS, a total of 2,264 women enlisted. In other words, almost 70 per cent of the recruits did so during the first year. Statistics show that the March 1942 group, which was the first extended batch after the Cadre course, was the largest (519 recruits) during all the years of service. This would illustrate the enthusiasm engendered among the women of the Yishuv by the prospect of enlisting.[18] After this high, the number of recruits dropped.[19] Sonya Idelberg, the Chief Recruiter, called on the national and public institutions to refrain from employing women of recruitment age and to remove women of recruitment age from the security services.[20] In wake of the criticism against the drop in recruitment numbers, the Council of Women's Organizations announced that all their members were unhesitatingly at the disposal of the recruitment drive. The next months during which higher numbers were registered were July 1942 (309 women), August 1942 (285 women) and March 1943 (267 women).

Most of the recruits who completed the first training course in April 1942 were sent to serve in Egypt, and sixty remained to serve in the Yishuv (most of these were destined to work in hospitals in Sarafend, Kantara or Kasasin). At the same time, there were only four ATS companies available to integrate them. Nine further companies were established in the course of the same year, seven in Egypt and two in Palestine, and thirteen additional companies were established in the course of 1943, eleven in Egypt and two in Palestine. Moreover, there were three companies in Lebanon.[21] In total, there were twenty-nine ATS companies in the Middle East.

About 80 per cent of all the Yishuv volunteers enlisted during the first half of the war, and the remainder during the second half. Female recruitment began during a low point in male recruitment, and the Yishuv institutions hoped that, by enlisting, the women would encourage men to do the same. By the end of 1942, there were three waves of recruitment to the British army: the first was from the beginning of male recruitment until the 'Recruitment Rally' that took place in the Yishuv in October 1941, as a result of which 9,947 men enlisted; the second wave lasted until June 1942 (when the draft was announced in the Yishuv) and during which a total of 3,136 men and women enlisted (1,100 women); the third wave lasted from June to October, 1942 and 4,615 men and women enlisted.[22] The Yishuv institutions hoped to see in the onset of the fourth wave the start of the idea of the Jewish Brigades. All in all some 25,000 men from the Yishuv enlisted in the British army and, together with the women who volunteered for service, recruits from the Yishuv reached a number of almost 30,000.

It should be pointed out that women registered with the military and the Jewish Agency offices in much greater numbers than the ultimate number of recruits. Dozens of volunteers who registered with the recruitment offices changed their minds for various reasons (family, financial and others), and many dozens were rejected on medical grounds. There were even those who had passed the medical examinations at the Jewish Agency's recruitment offices but were failed by the doctor at the military offices. According to different elements in the Yishuv 'the number of rejected applicants was too high, which makes it impossible to ignore the impression that rejection is too wholesale [sic]; and that it was not necessarily a medical consideration that affected their choice'.[23] Most probably it was the result of Britain's desire to control the number of female Jewish recruits and to reject those who seemed to be identified with the Jewish Agency or with the Yishuv's political objectives.

Service in the WAAF

The way the Royal Air Force (RAF) was deployed in the Middle East was different from that of the land army, of which the ATS was a part. It is for this reason that efforts on the part of the Jewish Agency and Haganah to persuade the authorities that recruits from Palestine should serve together in specific companies, as was possible in the ATS, failed. Yishuv women who served in the WAAF, therefore, were integrated into mixed companies of servicemen and women from the Yishuv, alongside those who came from the length and breadth of the British Empire. When it became clear to the Yishuv institutions that they were to have no influence over the lives of the WAAF recruits, as had become their custom with the ATS recruits, they did not maintain contact with them at first.

The chief national recruiter, Sonya Idelberg warned, 'the human fabric (in WAAF) is mostly assimilated, the camp is not united on the inside and lacks shape from a nationalist aspect'.[24] But this appears unjust to the WAAF recruits, most of who were loyal to the Yishuv and made a point of leading a Jewish lifestyle. Even in later stages of the war the servicewomen continued to feel neglected by the Yishuv authorities, the ties with them being loose. In spite of complaints, the CWO did continue to maintain ties with the servicewomen from the time they were still in basic training camp; they sent representatives to visit them, invited WAAF servicewomen to meet with the Organization's leadership and appointed liaison women in the WAAF camps.[25] The ties between the recruits and the Yishuv institutions tightened toward the end of the war and attitudes to them underwent a change.

The demand to send WAAF servicewomen from Britain to the

Middle East in order to operate communications and signals systems had been raised already in late 1941, but rejected mainly due to a shortage of manpower in Britain itself and because of transportation problems. In August 1942, the RAF Command in the Middle East reissued its demand that the Director of the WAAF, Air Chief Commandant Dame Katherine Jane Trefusis Forbes, send out an urgent dispatch of 3,000 communications operators from Britain. An alternative proposal was to recruit local women into the WAAF and to send them to train in Britain, or to send a team from Britain to train local women. At this stage there were still reservations as to sending servicewomen so far away from home, especially for reasons of security, and no steps were taken toward local recruitment.[26]

In early February 1943 Air Field Marshall Douglas appealed once again to the regional RAF Command to recruit local women to the WAAF and to be sent staff officers from Britain. This time the WAAF Committee approved the request for British women to be posted to the Middle East, on the condition that suitable accommodation be provided for them and military discipline be imposed. At this stage, too, the ban on posting British officers outside of Britain was lifted. In mid February a manpower shortage and problems of logistics involved in transferring women to the Middle East resulted in the WAAF HQ in England preferring local recruitment.[27]

The decision on recruitment of Yishuv women to the WAAF was made public on 26 April 1943 following correspondence between the Colonial Office and the Air Ministry in London and, at the height of the crisis between the Yishuv institutions and the British authorities that resulted in the closing of the Jewish Agency's Recruitment Offices. It is for this reason that most of the recruitment to the WAAF, from its very beginning, was conducted by way of the RAF recruitment offices in the Yishuv. Nevertheless, when the Jewish Agency's Recruitment Offices were reopened, several dozen WAAF recruits chose this channel through which to register. Each WAAF recruit was given a number that was preceded by ACW (Air Crew Woman), to signify that she was a soldier in the RAF, without indicating that she was from Palestine, unlike the ATS. The recruiters who worked at recruiting volunteers to the ATS were also employed in registering volunteers for the WAAF. In late 1944 the military recruitment offices in Haifa and Jerusalem were closed and only the one in Tel Aviv remained.

No course was held in the WAAF on the lines of the ATS Cadre course. The first basic training course was opened in the Lydda RAF camp on 26 May 1943. Since the twelve-strong team of WAAF instructors had not yet arrived from Britain,[28] male RAF personnel instructed the new recruits. Thirty-six Jewish recruits, six of who stayed behind to instruct the next batch of recruits, attended the ten-day course; the six were not given a rank. The remaining thirty were sent to Egypt. Most of the recruits to the WAAF (433) enlisted in the course of 1943 and the largest batch of recruits (ninety) joined in June. A further 176 women joined in the course of 1944. The last batch of recruits joined in August 1944 and included forty-six Christian Arab women.

Most of the WAAF recruits served in Egypt. A large number of them (more than 100) were posted to Maintenance Unit 107 (MU 107), near the Great Bitter Lake in Genifa. A further 100 served in the RAF's HQ in Cairo; twenty-five served at the Al-Jadida airport near Cairo; about seventy-five served at another airport near Cairo, Heliopolis; in Helwan, at the RAF's school of communications, thirteen recruits participated at various periods in courses in communications, radio, wireless, etc. Courses lasted for about six months. 110 servicewomen were posted at an airport near the school. Other recruits served in various maintenance units as well as in Ismailia. When rioting broke out in Egypt at the end of 1945, all the Jewish recruits serving in the urban camps were evacuated and concentrated in MU 107.[29]

Women's Occupations in the Army

'[Equality of Women] is not yet a thing in practice, with regard to equality in military positions filled by men and women. There is still a large field here to fight for and conquer, not only for our woman but for the woman in the world.' These are the words used by Sharett, head of the Jewish Agency's Political Department, to define the difference between women's tasks and men's tasks in the army. According to him, the women were prepared for this when they told him that 'every task in the war is important and every sacrifice will be welcome'. Sharett added, 'the tasks will be auxiliary tasks but the appearance of the woman [sic] in this lifestyle will be an independent appearance on the part of the woman. This is the entire idea behind female recruitment. This is all the justification for women's participation in the war.'[30] According to gender researchers such as Dafna Izraeli and Cynthia Enloe, the term 'auxiliary tasks' testifies to the lack of symmetry between the status of men and that of women and the difference between assimilating men and women in the army, since it leaves the impression that men are there to serve the nation, whereas women are there to serve the men and that 'men constitute the army, while women are in the army'.[31]

Most of the women serving in the army were located a long way from the battlefront. However, even when they reached it, or came close to it, the tasks they filled were still differentiated and defined. Yuval-Davis, for example, talks in terms of 'front' and 'rear' as being flexible and changing their significance in accordance with the character of the fighting, but maintaining their gender-related definition, because women remain, de facto, at the rear of the fighting forces.[32]

In the British army women served in an all-woman organization that aimed to support the male system and to assist it from the 'back seat' and behind the lines. They enlisted in the army in order to fill auxiliary tasks, in other words, all those tasks – mostly blatantly 'women's' (apart from drivers) – aimed at 'releasing as many men as possible to the front'.[33]

'Female' Tasks in the ATS

The document announcing the establishment of the ATS in the Middle East provided details of the military duties open to recruits from Palestine, most of them women: hospital workers (in February 1942 the army was planning to recruit assistant nurses and other hospital workers via the Red Cross, including women ambulance drivers who would be attached to hospitals),[34] clerks, cooks (including dieticians), storekeepers, assistant nurses, radiologists, masseurs and laboratory workers. At a later stage, various technical positions were made available to the recruits, but it would appear that the only trade that really symbolized a gender breakthrough was that of a driver. The variety of professional possibilities made available to recruits in Britain was also opened to their counterparts from the Yishuv, apart from operating communications equipment and service in anti-aircraft batteries.[35] In the Haganah, in addition to blatantly 'feminine' trades such as paramedics, cooks, etc., many women were also trained in communications, Morse and wireless, especially in order to ensure emergency communications between the settlements; indeed, communications was considered a 'female' domain.

Before 1941, only five 'non-operational' trades were open to ATS recruits in Britain: clerks, cooks, storekeepers, drivers and assistant nurses. Thus, according to Lucy Noakes, the ATS was considered a service where 'cleaners are called assistant nurses and some of them are servants to the officers'. The image of ATS service was influenced by a gender concepts and status, and was not flattering to women. Noakes is convinced that Dame Helen Gwynne-Vaughan, ATS

Commander during the First World War, who held that 'women were most suited to these tasks', contributed to this attitude.[36]

In comparison with the limited number of positions open to the female Yishuv recruits, male recruits from the Yishuv served in a variety of trades in the different sectors of the British army: the pioneer corps, infantry, engineering corps, the equipment corps, the Air Force, the transport corps (as drivers and water carriers). For most of their service the majority of them did not bear arms or fight at the front. An exception to this was the male soldiers of the Jewish Brigade which was established in September 1944 and fought on the Italian front, and several dozen men who served in commando units in the Western Desert. Nevertheless, many of these servicemen were posted near the front and frequently risked their lives.

Most of the servicewomen were placed in trades according to the compliance tests they took at the military recruitment offices. In addition to the aforementioned trades, there were several of the Yishuv recruits who filled special tasks. In the course of 1943, additional trades – with a technical nature – were made available to the Yishuv recruits, such as car and engine assembly, electricity and radio mechanics, testing machines and working in the arms industry.

Nonetheless, most of the trades offered to the recruits from Palestine were 'feminine' in character and reflected the traditional women's chores: nursing the sick, education, cooking and administration. In the army, these trades were turned into professions: practical nurses (working in hospitals), clerks, storekeepers and cooks. Many of the recruits, like their peers in the Haganah and the Palmach, came to terms with the tasks they were allocated and considered their participation in the military forces and the contribution they made to the overall war effort the equality they yearned for.

Practical Nurses

Nursing was the most widespread female trade in the army and indeed, several hundred of the Palestine recruits served in military hospitals in the Middle East. In Egypt they served in three companies – Kasasin, Suez and Cairo; and in Palestine, in two companies – in Sarafend, Be'er Ya'akov and in a convalescence hospital in Jerusalem.

In spite of the many complaints from Palestine recruits, they were accepted for service only as practical nurses. Even professionally trained, registered nurses were obliged, with the exception of extraordinary cases, to work as practical nurses. They were not allowed to treat patients and had to do all the hard physical work in the hospital. British army policy was that only British women could serve as registered nurses and staff nurses. This was probably due to the British army's suspicious attitude towards the women recruits from Palestine that stood in contrast to the claims of unity and equality the British tried to demonstrate in their propaganda to the countries of the Empire.[37] Possibly the famous British sense of honour had additional weight.

In order to specialize and rise in rank, practical nurses were required to spend an eighteen month period in three courses that would promise them professional stages C to A. Before completing this course, the recruit was referred to as an 'assistant nurse', but after completing the high professional stage, the recruits received greater professional respect from the British staff. Sometimes course lessons were given in Hebrew, when recruits, who had been nurses before enlisting, taught the material and exams were taken in both languages.

Work in the hospitals provided an endless source of resentment and tension between the recruits and the British staff, with the matron at their head. One of the reasons for the tension was the British nurses' struggle for their position and status in the eyes of the male members of the hospital staff. Under these circumstances, it is easy enough to understand the attitude of the Jewish recruits, who occupied, on the one hand, the lowest position on the hospital hierarchy and under subject to their command and authority and, on the other hand, they were mostly young women, full of energy and vitality and as such, they posed a threat to their British counterparts both among the patients and the male staff.[38]

One instance that testifies to the murky relationship prevailing in the hospitals took place in Hospital 13 in Suez. One night Sonya Peres was helping a British nurse treat newly arrived soldiers, wounded in the Battle of El Alamein. Throughout the night they worked with dedication, but as soon as the matron arrived in the morning, she reprimanded Peres with, 'Go clean the lockers and don't touch the patients, bloody native!' Sonya Peres was so offended by the nurse's words that expressed her attitude to the local recruits ('natives') that she gave the woman a ringing slap on the face, to the loud cheers of all the Palestine recruits in the vicinity.[39]

Another source of friction between British hospital staff and the Palestine recruits concerned the treatment of German POWs brought from the battlefront to the British field hospitals. Some of the Jewish recruits provided the same kind of treatment as they gave to the wounded of the Allied Forces, albeit with a heavy heart and mixed feelings; others, however, refused to provide this service. Zilla Babayouf, for example, who served in an Egyptian hospital, wrote to the Jewish Agency that the British nurses, headed by the hospital matron, were demonstrating insensitivity toward the Jewish recruits in forcing them to treat German patients. According to her, British military law exempted Jewish workers from treating Germans.[40] In the Yishuv the attitude of British hospital staff vis-à-vis the Jewish recruits was known, although some of the recruits showed empathy toward those nurses. One of these, for example, who had been a refugee before enlisting in the British forces and had no living family, actually tried to understand the British nurses, because they, too 'were separated from their parents' nest and left to nightmarish wandering; they, too were going through the storms of the spreading and intensifying war'. Nonetheless, she admitted 'the attitude of the [British] nurses was unbearable'.[41]

Yishuv recruits also served in Italy. Several months after the warfront moved from North Africa to Italy, starting in May 1944, 200 hospital workers were sent there. They served in several military hospitals in Italy (in Rome, Trani, Naples and Beri), most of them under the command of Jewish officers. Their service there continued in fact until the end of the war and even after it, throughout 1946.

Storekeepers and Clerks

Recruits who knew basic English were given placements as storekeepers and clerks, since these trades included the filing of forms and orders and required a minimal knowledge of the language. The Haganah and Lehi organizations, aware of the potential accessibility of the recruits to the forms and spare parts they needed for their activity in Palestine, took advantage of these postings for the benefit of these organizations.

Many hundreds of recruits served in various forms of administrative positions throughout the Middle East: in Lebanon and Syria (two companies); in Egypt: Tel el Kabir, in the Cairo Citadel, in Qasr al-Nil Bridge, in Qantara and in Alexandria; in Palestine: in Jerusalem (two companies), in Dir Suneid near Gaza (which was the main professional training camp in the Middle East) and Sarafend. Apart from companies made up specifically of clerks that consisted mainly of recruits from Palestine, dozens of recruits served as clerks in the administrative staff of ATS companies throughout the Middle East.

Administrative and clerical trades were traditionally reserved for women, but the recruits who filled them saw their work as a national mission that considerably empowered them as women.[42]

Among the hundreds of clerks there was a unique group of about thirty who served in Company 525 in Qasr al-Nil Bridge in Egypt. They were included in one of the British army's most secret projects – producing computer punch cards for data processing supplies destined for the planned invasion of Sicily in July 1943. They carried out their work, which at first had been done only by British recruits, in a secret cellar under harsh physical conditions. Among the Jewish women employed in this work were Ruth Breda (Hass) and Hanna Maron. Esther Herlitz was their sergeant in charge.

During the period under discussion, work in the storeroom was considered by the public 'un-feminine', as was factory work.[43] Egypt served as the British army's large supply and logistics base, and hundreds of Jewish recruits who served in the large camps established by the British were employed in the enormous stores that housed spare parts for cars and tanks, clothing, various kinds of instruments and other equipment. In Egypt the storekeepers served mainly in Tel el Kabir in three companies, in Genifa and in Tura; in Palestine they served mainly in Tira (near Haifa). The recruits who worked in the stores were employed mainly in disassembly, categorizing, storing and registering each item and piece of equipment that arrived mostly from India; they also filled order forms from the various units. Many of the storekeepers were kibbutz members with prior experience in their kibbutz warehouses, which made their training easier.

In an attempt to intensify their contribution to the war effort, the women wished to impart importance to the geographical location of their service; in other words, to its proximity to the battlefront. The physical dangers to which some of the recruits were exposed testified, in their eyes, to the value of their work. According to the concepts of the war period, the women distinguished between combat soldiers and those who served far from the battlefield, while still being considered soldiers, although not conceived as heroes – a title that was reserved for combat soldiers. Thus, women who served near the battlefront felt that their work was more heroic than that of their counterparts who served in the homeland.[44]

And indeed, the female recruits, especially those employed in non-glamorous trades such as storekeeping or office work, needed a sense of importance because of the nature of their trades, and they did their best to emphasize their proximity to the battlefront. During the first months following their enlistment, at the time of the Battles of Al Alemein, the recruits felt themselves close to the battlefront even if they didn't actually serve in its midst. One of the Jewish officers reported that 'We are not at the front, but not so far away from the front as to not feel what is happening there. Actually, our camp supplies the front, so that we were in the thick of things throughout: we felt what was happening, we saw what was being sent to the front and what was returned from there.' As for their feelings, she added: 'For over a month we were in a state of constant tension ... We worked day and night, without a break, packing tools, and sending cars and tanks to the front.'[45]

Like the hospital workers, recruits who worked as clerks were also sent to serve in Italy during the second half of 1944. Twelve servicewomen served in various capacities in Benvereta, the location of the Headquarters of the British Forces in the Mediterranean, as the Italian battlefront was known. A posting in Italy was the heart's desire of ATS servicewomen serving in Egypt as well as in Palestine. Their hope was to be fortunate enough to meet Holocaust survivors and to extend them help, but there was also the desire 'to serve in the vicinity of the Jewish Brigade, in total equality with the servicemen from Palestine'.[46] In other words, the servicewomen aspired to reach as close as possible to the front, out of a wish to emulate their male counterparts and adopt their combat identity.

Cooks

Generations of women were consigned to the private domain and cooking was a major component in their household chores. Army cooking, which was considered a 'feminine' trade, was open to the Jewish recruits, although from the first batch of recruits, none was placed in a kitchen trade and the army preferred to employ local civilians for this work. Only from the July 1942 batch of recruits were thirty-five cooks placed in the large kitchens on the army's camps in Palestine – Sarafend and Dir Suneid. At a later stage some of the cooks (some of them mothers) were transferred to serve in ATS companies near the military hospital in Qantara. Since the younger recruits were not enthusiastic about kitchen work, the veteran kibbutz members, who had gained expertise in cooking for large groups, volunteered to do the trade.

Rivka Guber, mother of three children, also served as an army cook. According to her, 'Many people wondered, even disappointed, over the fact that married women would "leave" their homes and children and choose so prosaic a stance as setting out to fight Hitler with a cooking spoon in their hands.'[47] She went on to write that there were not sufficient volunteers to prepare food for the early batches of recruits and when she and her friends heard that the British officers were denigrating the Jewish recruits for being too fussy to do the 'dirty work', and that there would be no choice but to hire Arabs to cook for the Jewish servicewomen, they volunteered to fill the void.

One of the cooks who stayed behind in Palestine after completing her basic training, was sent with several others to study cookery at a British school on a nearby military base. According to her, 'after cooking for years on the kibbutz, it was interesting to learn cookery methods that were new and belonged to another nation. We were happy to accept the ruling.'[48] After their training that cook was sent, together with five others, to work in a kitchen in Qantara. The matter of kashrut did not occupy the Jewish cooks, most of which had cooked in settlements belonging to the agricultural sector where kosher kitchens were not mandatory. In some places, the cooks were also active in the company's cultural activities and the tent they lived in was used by the choir for rehearsals, as a meeting place, for party planning and for welcoming the Sabbath.

It would appear that despite the harsh conditions involved in kitchen work (such as early wakeup calls and long hours beside huge cauldrons), the cooks were quite fulfilled by their labours and even gained the respect of their peers and commanders. When one of the cooks was asked how she managed to keep everyone satisfied, she replied, 'I always see in front of my eyes my son and his friends, who are serving in some remote place and their souls no doubt yearn for mother's cooking and the warmth of home.'[49]

Many women in the Haganah were given responsibility for kitchens, which were much smaller than those in the British army. There were even some who were recruited to the organization and sent to settlements in order to operate kitchens there. Women also helped in food distribution and during the Arab riots of 1936–39 they even established the 'Hospitality Company', an autonomous unit that provided food to the men guarding the posts. On the initiative of the Haganah, courses were opened where women were taught cooking and nutrition. Some women served as cooks in the Haganah and the Palmach and reported on a sense of satisfaction from their work, especially in light of the compliments they received from their fighting male counterparts. But there were also those who resented having to cook. Despite all the talk about women's role in the Palmach, many of the female members were frustrated by being placed in the kitchen, rather than being allowed to take part in operational activity.[50]

'Masculine' Trades in the ATS

In the course of 1943, further trades were made available to the Jewish recruits that had previously been carried out only by men: car and engine assembly, electricity and radio mechanics, machines testing and work in the weapons industry. Several dozen servicewomen were employed in various workshops for repairing machinery at Tel el Kabir. At first they were employed as apprentices to servicemen while learning their trade and a few were even promoted to the rank of sergeant responsible for entire departments in the workshops. Their job was to repair machinery and broken instruments, as well as to conduct final checks on them and to determine their usability. In order to be promoted to a higher rank or to receive a more responsible task in these skills, servicewomen were required to undergo theoretical and practical exams. The exams consisted of formulas in mathematics, electricity and radio, physics and mechanics. In the Haganah and Palmach, too, female members filled various technical posts, such as communications operators, for example; the 'girl Gideons' who operated the wireless equipment on the illegal immigrant ships,[51] weapons maintainance, etc., but the reference is to a only a small number of women members.

Women in the Police

In the first years of the war, only men served in the military police, but with the recruitment of women and the extended duties imposed on the men, the need developed for women to be included in this sphere, too. By doing this, recruits who worked as military policewomen, at first only in Britain and later in the Middle East, too, had thus penetrated an area that had hereto been considered 'male'.

Only about thirty recruits served in the military police, most of them in Palestine and some in Egypt. The proposal to establish a company of military policewomen according to the format of similar units in Britain was received in ATS HQ in Cairo during the second half of 1942. It was decided that the service would be on a voluntary basis, in other words, servicewomen would not be forced to serve in this capacity and recruitment to the police force would take place in the companies in Palestine and Egypt. The first training course took place Cairo in early 1943 and was attended by nine servicewomen, one from Greece, two from Britain and six from Palestine. The course lasted for six weeks and at its end five servicewomen were posted to Cairo and four returned to Palestine (two of them were from the Yishuv). A British officer was given command of the company in Palestine. The policewomen who were stationed in Palestine were billeted in Tel Aviv's Balfour Street, and not in an ATS camp, from there they would set out on patrol.

At first the trade's image was problematic due to the nature of the tasks assigned to the military police, as Habas wrote, 'According to the scale of values, it was unfit, at first, this service in the military police. The military policewoman was not seen by the [others] as being entrusted with order and discipline for the general good, but as an informer, who hands Jewish girls over to the law.'[52] The recruits from Palestine refused to comply and only a few months later did their assignments commence. A military policewoman's trade consisted of locating absentees and searching the personal property of servicewomen for subversive underground material, or smuggled goods (e.g. cigarettes). In Cairo, the policewomen were sent to locate servicewomen who were working as prostitutes. They were also employed in train duty, in the course of which they travelled on the night train from Cairo to Palestine and returned to Egypt the following day. Major Daphne Hill was the British officer in charge of the company in Cairo's military police. When there was a need to arrest a Jewish servicewoman (as in suspected involvement in the assassination of Lord Moyne), a military policewoman was present at the arrest. The work of military policemen was similar to that of their female counterparts.[53]

Drivers

Although most of the recruits were given 'feminine' trades in the army, and only a few of them started their service in trades that had been previously filled solely by men, there is no doubt that the one trade that most acutely expressed the gender reversal of women's work was that of drivers.

As a result of its widespread deployment and the need for logistic improvements, the British army required large numbers of drivers. Since many military drivers had been sent to the battlefront, there arose a need to train hundreds of servicewomen for driving missions throughout the military home front. It would seem that the image of women drivers in the Yishuv was tantamount almost to 'mythical'.[54]

This can be learned from Sharett when he asked, 'Is anyone willing to give up, in the name of women Jewish volunteers, the profession of driving?'[55] In the course of female recruitment various private and institutionalized bodies made use of photographs and drawings of servicewomen in propaganda announcements, commercial advertisements, political cartoons and press photographs. Even the Yishuv institutions singled out the women drivers of the ATS as a successful example of women's ability to replace men in various trades. Songs[56] and advertisements for cigarettes, coffee and soap, showed the driver as a liberated woman, swallowing up long distances in her vehicle, unafraid of the damages of the climate or the sights of war and appearing as a heroin, capable of bringing victory.

Several recruits testified that 'driving was, at that time, a symbol of feminism and all in all, a means of transport that turned into an objective that was difficult to achieve', and 'At that time there were no women drivers and the profession was most attractive, as if, today, someone suggested you become a space pilot.'[57] Driving, therefore, was considered the most 'combative' and 'operational' of all the professions open to them in the ATS (in the WAAF the recruits did not serve as drivers). In the Haganah, for example, only a few women were able to penetrate blatantly 'male' provinces, such as ammunition fillers, signalling and pigeon handling. In the Palmach the command positions – such as company commander – were considered the most prestigious. After command positions, scouting and sappers held considerable prestige. Five women passed a scouting course and two a sapper course.[58] There were no women drivers in the Haganah. Two women reported that they had completed driving courses in the Palmach. But the needs of the Palmach were not the same as those of the British army, from the point of view of trucking and travel.

Hundreds of women served as drivers in the ATS in Britain and their contribution to the war was considered much more significant than that of women who served as cooks, clerks and assistant nurses.[59] Service in anti-aircraft defence (colloquially known as ack-ack) was considered the most prestigious and most operational of all for British women.[60]

According to theories concerning women and geography (their place in space), the qualities traditionally connected to control of machines – strength, prestige and independence – led to the social concept that considers driving to be a masculine profession. The gradual admission of women to this profession caused a gender reversal. To women, who for years had been restricted to the private space, driving was conceived as liberating and breaking into the male public space and as 'conquering' new territories.[61]

Hundreds of servicemen from the Yishuv served in eight companies of truck drivers and containers in Egypt and transported supplies, water and ammunition to the fighting forces. Throughout the Middle East there were three companies of women drivers who specialized in driving trucks and most of these were from Palestine: in Egypt they were lodged in Camp Mina near Cairo (513), in Tel el Kabir (511) and in Abassya near Cairo (503). Each company consisted of about 120 women drivers. In the village of Kila, near Alexandria, a few dozen women drivers from Palestine served as part of number 517 Drivers Company. In addition to truck drivers, a further few dozen recruits drove various kinds of military vehicles in different companies and also as personal drivers to officers. Also about twenty servicewomen from Palestine served as drivers in the 502 Ambulance Company near Alexandria and some fifteen ambulance drivers served in Sarafend. Thus throughout the Middle East there were approximately 500 women drivers in the course of the Second World War. It appears that Company 513 in Camp Mina, under the command of Mary Mackenzie, became a byword in the ATS and achieved greater fame and prestige than other companies.

Training Women Drivers

An appendix to the decision on establishing the ATS in the Middle East, which detailed the occupations of the servicewomen, determined that the drivers 'drive new cars from the camps or the stations at which they arrive, to the army camps, will deliver repaired cars from workshops to the camps and will be employed as drivers to officers'.[62] Following several instances in which servicewomen from Palestine with no prior training were sent to serve as drivers, the military authorities demanded that recruits who were to serve as drivers receive suitable training before being sent to join their units. And indeed, in December 1942, the first driving course took place, funded by the CWO and attended by ten potential drivers.[63] In the months following, dozens of women were trained in these courses. Untill the end of 1942, servicewomen, who had declared prior experience in driving, learned from British instructors how to handle driving over sand (in Holon), in the course of their basic training.[64] Only in late 1943 was it decided to establish a driving school on Camp Mina and Mackenzie, who commanded Company 513, was appointed to command the school, too.

The drivers' course in Camp Mina was made up of two parts:

theory and practical. The theory part took place in a building that served as a workshop and contained dismantled cars. The drivers had to learn the name of each part, its location and its objective. They dismantled the motors and every other part of the car and then reconstructed them. The practical stage consisted of four weeks of practice in the desert. At first the recruits learned how to operate the car and then how to drive it. At a later stage in the course the servicewomen were taken on a drive over intercity roads and finally – in the streets of Cairo itself. The school also housed workshops in which trucks were prepared for operation and where they underwent mechanical testing, painting in camouflage colours and arming.

Truck Drivers

Due to the burden of work and the lack of women drivers during the first months of their military service, the drivers had to work long hours, sometimes into the night, and they barely had any spare time. The Mina drivers Company filled several tasks: transferring trucks from one workshop to another and placing them in order inside the workshop; driving trucks to a gigantic parking lot in the desert, where another group of drivers arranged the trucks according to type and size. Sometimes they were obliged to bring new cars to the camp that had been dismantled in Port Said, and back – to take the trucks (that were now ready for use) in long convoys as close as possible to the battlefront. The company's drivers were also responsible for the on-going transportation of supplies to the camp, such as food, spare parts, mail, etc. Some of them even drove heavy trucks that weighed over three tons – the kind of vehicles that British women drivers were not allowed to drive.[65] At the Tel el Kabir camp, too, drivers from Company 511 worked in the workshops, preparing trucks for their military use. The cherry on the icing of their work consisted of the long drives in convoys, during which the company's unique atmosphere evolved. Each convoy was made up of between thirty and fifty trucks, and the convoys to the seaports travelled along a regular route.

Dozens of servicewomen from Palestine were drivers for the company commanders in the ATS; a very few were employed as drivers of male officers. The drivers of Company 507 who drove the British officers in the Dir-Suneid base near Gaza, the largest British army training base in the Middle East, also drove many groups of officers and soldiers who came to the camp to participate in various training courses.

Ambulance Drivers

In the British army there was only one company of women ambulance drivers, Company 502, commanded by Penelope Otto. There was also a department of ambulance drivers in Sarafend, which was a part of Company 515,[66] and there were also several drivers in various other companies (e.g. Company 511 in Tel el Kabir), who did this trade in addition to driving in convoys or other routine driving work. Before the driving school was established in Camp Mina, the ambulance drivers received their training in this company and were subsequently sent to different locations such as Ismailia, Cairo, Palestine, etc.[67]

Most of the women drivers in Company 502, which was also coined 'the posh company', were women from upper class families in Britain. Some of them were even minor royalty and had joined the army with their own private ambulances as part of the nursing service.[68] The drivers in this company had more privileges and better conditions than other ATS servicewomen (e.g. the right to wear silk stockings, later stay-out times, better living conditions, etc.). Toward the end of their service in Egypt, in late 1944, and the transfer to Italy, the servicewomen from Palestine constituted about half of the company, and most of them were former students of the veteran drivers.[69]

During the battles at El-Alamain, in the second half of 1942, the drivers of Company 502 were the closest of all the ATS servicewomen to the battlefront and were able to experience the sights of battle. Day and night they transferred wounded men from the collection point at Mersa Matruh, near to the front, to the hospitals, mainly in Alexandria, and from the hospitals to ships, trains or aircraft that conveyed them to the home front.[70] They drove over mine fields, alongside skeletons of military vehicles and tanks, scattered by the roadside. Through long nights of bombing, they slept in their ambulances, alert, waiting for a call. When the need arose to evacuate women soldiers from Egypt, the drivers were given a certificate to say that they belonged to the Red Cross, in case they were taken captive by the Germans. Sometimes the drivers transported shell-shocked soldiers to the military mental hospital in Ismailia.[71]

In the second half of 1944, the company was transferred to Italy after the front had been removed to there, as part of the British forces. In Italy, the ambulance drivers collected the wounded, newly arrived from the battlefront, from railway stations or airports and drove them to various hospitals. They received no first aid training and did not treat the patients, only drove them. There were no medical teams in the ambulances and the wounded were therefore under the sole responsibility of the drivers. Apart from transporting the wounded, the drivers carried out all the hard physical work involved in maintaining the ambulances, including changing grease and oil, and changing wheels, etc. Each of the drivers passed a course in motor mechanics and was well-versed in dealing with technical problems that arose in their vehicles.

The Drivers' 'Masculine' Image

Women who served as drivers in the army wanted to adopt a 'masculine' and 'combative' gender image for themselves in order to feel that they were making an active contribution to the war effort, especially in comparison with women employed in other military trades and also in comparison with men who held clerical trades in the army.[72] In the Yishuv, too, there were women who didn't give in to patriarchal concepts and even succeeded in conquering for themselves a place in 'masculine' trades, in face of male objection,[73] although there were women who refused to 'adopt' the masculine elements of the 'new Hebrew male'. At the beginning of the century women from the social elite devised an alternative feminine discourse to the nationalist maternal one, by developing new patterns of female behaviour that expressed itself in acts, dress, creating a physical feminine culture and also in describing and representing women.[74]

Women in the military are a minority group in a male-controlled organization.[75] From a social, cultural and historic point of view, the army is conceived as a male organization that leans on clear definitions of femininity and masculinity in order for it to exist and continue to be motivated. In the army gender is an inherent, crucial, noticeable and formal principle. Delegation of work along lines of gender, and delegation of power in accordance with gender, lead to manpower policies that restrict women to certain military trades and this policy participates in a circular way in concepts of femininity and masculinity. In restricting combat tasks to men, the army and the state create and perpetuate the image of the man as strong, brave and morally superior, since he is prepared to sacrifice himself in defence of the state and its citizens.[76] In parallel, blocking their ability to participate in battle creates an image of women as being weak and in need of defence, together with children and the aged.[77]

The incidence of women soldiers in male trades clearly constitutes their gender identity in accordance with a model of dominant masculinity, by means of three central practices: emulating the physical and behavioural concepts of the combat soldier; diminishing the significance of sexual harassment; separating themselves from other women and from traditional 'femininity'.[78] In the British army the women drivers adopted some of the masculine practices, although other practices were dictated by the army and its conditions, for example, wearing long trousers (when carrying out routine maintenance work and while driving in convoys) or long khaki dungarees (worn by ambulance drivers), when the women's official uniform consisted only of a skirt and blouse; work in a dirty environment, in a garage, or in work places; strict hair standards, etc.[79] So as to prove to the military command that women were capable of carrying out the work as well as men, Company 513 commander Mary Mackenzie insisted that the women under her command themselves carry out all the routine maintenance work on the trucks and vehicles they drove. This heavy physical work gave the servicewomen the feeling that they were similar to their male counterparts, sometimes to the extent of minimizing their feminine identity and emphasizing the masculine identity, which gave them a sense of satisfaction and belonging.

Nonetheless, it was very important to the women drivers in the British army to appear 'feminine' after working hours. The drivers of Company 513, for example, recall how once a week they would drive to Cairo after working hours, dressed in clean, shining uniform. On occasion they would go for a swim in the pools belonging to one of the hotels in Cairo, or to dance in one of the hotels' ballrooms. Some of the servicewomen even defied the military rule that forbad the wearing of silk stockings – their uniform stockings were heavy and khaki in colour – even risking being tried by their commander.[80]

Special Tasks in the ATS

The army had special tasks in which only individual servicewomen were employed, usually in a blatantly 'masculine' environment. Miriam Shor (Mattersdorf) served in the army's recreation centre near Netanya that hosted groups of vacationing soldiers from all over the Middle East. As part of her job, Shorr organized trips around Palestine and Syria, to the holy places and the famous tourist sites. In this capacity, she was in contact with tourist agencies in the region and provided information on the sites.[81]

Friedl Stern, graduate of the Bezalel Art Academy and later a well-known cartoonist, was a single servicewoman in a team of camouflage professionals at the central training school near Gaza. She held this position as a result of her art degree. Groups of senior British officers used to arrive at the camp from all over the Middle East and it was Stern's task to teach them camouflage techniques for vehicles and personnel. For this work, described as excellent and impressive, Stern was awarded a citation in May 1946.[82]

There were additional special tasks servicewomen from Palestine were called upon to fill, which they saw as a gender breakthrough. Some of them were responsible for cleaning and maintaining weapons, a skill particularly sought after by the Haganah members in the ATS, and the Haganah movement went to great lengths to ensure that these women received places on weaponry courses. The servicewomen subsequently received the highest salaries of all the ATS recruits, according to military occupations rating. At first, military authorities refrained from allowing Palestine recruits access to weapons and they were employed in watch repairs only. Only after substantiating their expertise were the Jewish women 'promoted' to the position of being allowed to repair various kinds of weaponry.[83]

One of the singular skills required in the army consisted of repairing tanks in special workshops. The use of state of the art systems in British army tanks was highly clandestine and repairs were carried out under a heavy cloak of secrecy in remote desert locations. When tanks went out of service, the need arose to find spare parts with which to repair them. Aliya Kravi (Rachlevsky), a driver with Company 517, was entrusted with transporting the appropriate parts for the tanks from the workshops in the Alexandria region. After receiving the suitable authorizations she used to drive a pick-up truck into the desert to the military training areas, where she dropped off the parts for re-commissioning and use in subsequent battles.[84]

One of the recruits was given a posting as the single female soldier in an otherwise all-male team in the Railway Traffic Office (RTO) at the railway station in Alexandria. She was employed in directing train convoys travelling to and from the front in accordance with the traffic orders issued to the team. With the British forces' retreat from El Alamein the workload increased and the team worked around the clock. Since it was forbidden to register the name of the units for fear of them falling into enemy hands, the servicewoman was obliged to remember by heart the names, serial numbers and locations and their connection to the vehicles. She also knew by heart numerous telephone numbers of the units with which she stood in contact. For this work the servicewoman was awarded a citation.[85]

Haganah member Stella Levy served in the ATS at first as a clerk and later as a Teleprinter Operator – the only one of the Palestine recruits in the ATS to hold such a position – because she possessed a French passport. Levy served in British Forces HQ in Jerusalem.[86]

Another special role filled by a small number of Palestine recruits was that of Training and Education NCO, as part of the British Army's Department for Education or within the framework of the companies to which they belonged. In the Department for Education the position included arranging lectures by Jewish and non-Jewish lecturers on various subjects in the army's units. The lecturers were usually recruits with an academic background and they were required to lecture on their field of expertise. In addition to them, civilian lecturers from the Hebrew University of Jerusalem and British lecturers in the University of Cairo were also commissioned to give lectures. The NCOs also worked on establishing a framework of vocational/re-acclimatization courses to prepare recruits for their discharge, supplying books and records for musical evenings, concerts, etc. According to records, four Palestine recruits filled this particular task: Tsilli Brendstater (Avraham), who had initially served in the regional offices of the Department for Education in Jerusalem (Camp Schneller) and was removed from her job after being accused of Zionist activity in the army; she was later posted in Cairo and continued to be involved in educational activity; Tamar Eshel (Shoham) first served with the British Forces in England (where she was studying for a university degree), after which she was transferred to the Middle East and posted to the British Forces Headquarters in Cairo as a Training and Education NCO and librarian; Tamar Grizim (Schtamm) from Jerusalem, who immigrated with her mother from Germany in the 1930s, served in this position with Company 509 in Genifa, Egypt; Yehudit Bar-Rav-Hai, who served with Company 522 in Alexandria, headed the department that organized vocational courses for soon-to-be-discharged servicewomen.

Trades in the WAAF

Distribution of recruits in accordance to their trades in the WAAF was as follows: around 300 of the women filled administrative positions; sixty-two were logistics and storekeepers; about ninety served as nurses in various clinics; fifty of the recruits were wireless operators, telephone or teleprinter operators; thirty-two served in meteorological stations; about fifty were placed in maintenance units as electricians and electronics technicians; about twenty recruits worked in operations rooms.

Most of the WAAF recruits served in Egypt. About 100 servicewomen served in Camp 107 MU in Genifa near the Bitter Lake; a further 100 were stationed in RAF HQ in Cairo; twenty-five servicewomen were stationed in Al Jadida airport near Cairo; about seventy-five recruits served in another airport near Cairo, Heliopolis; in Heluan, the RAF's communications school, thirteen recruits underwent training at various times in communications, radio, wireless and so on. The courses lasted about six months. 110 servicewomen served in the airport close to the school. Individual recruits also served in various maintenance units and in Ismailia. The recruits had believed that they would be able to choose their military trade, but in fact it was the Air Force that determined and posted them in accordance with its needs. This caused considerable discontent among the recruits.[87]

Just as the drivers in the ATS enjoyed a 'combat' and operational aura, so too in the WAAF those fortunate enough to enjoy prestige were the ones who worked on the RAF bases in Egypt in the special order rooms, or as they were known, the filter rooms. To these rooms the data that flowed from the radar stations in the area regarding the movements of enemy aircraft was transferred via wireless or telephone.

The servicewomen in the filter rooms used long sticks to move model aircraft along a large sand-covered table in the middle of the room, in accordance with instructions they received through their earpieces. The officers on the balcony above reported on aircraft movement to the RAF HQ in the region, which in turn sent out aircraft to intercept the enemy planes. In the filter rooms, servicewomen worked around the clock in three consecutive shifts. It was work that required maximum concentration and responsibility for human life.[88]

Parachute folding was another prestigious job. In the WAAF, too, some of the recruits were employed in work that was physical and 'masculine', albeit different from that in the ATS. Rachel Ziv, for example, who served in Camp 107 MU as an aircraft mechanic, wrote to her mother: 'I would like to describe to you the place I am working in: machines, pumps and pipes. The worktable is high and I have to stand on a crate in order to reach it. My hands are covered in grease; in fact the entire place is completely smeared with grease. These are engine parts that have been repaired, and here are also planes.'[89]

The Jewish Officers

The female Jewish officers formed a unique group in the WAAF and the ATS. They, like their British counterparts, dealt mainly with administrative and disciplinary matters – food, accommodation, military tribunals, etc. – while in their actual work, the servicewomen were subject to the authority of the professional commanding officer. In addition to all their routine tasks, the Jewish officers were also expected to form the spearhead of the national struggle and, as Habas defined it, 'All the time [she] lives with the feeling that everything – the nation's honour and the fate of Zionism and the future of Palestine – lay heavily on her shoulders and are dependent on the things she does, be they large or small.'[90] They were burdened with the struggle over the use of the Hebrew language and flag, to prevent marriage with non-Jewish servicemen and to turn a blind eye to illegal activity on the part of fellow Haganah members. The officers were also required to adapt themselves to the mentality and customs that had been deeply rooted in the British army and were alien to the spirit of the Yishuv, such as personal servants, a private driver, and an unyielding social hierarchy.

Appointment of the Jewish officers, especially those who would command ATS companies, was a source of pride among the Yishuv institutions and the Council of Women's Organizations. Even before the beginning of recruitment, the Jewish Agency had recommended its candidates for commissions to the Cadre course, even though the final decision was in the hands of the British Command. Later, too, the Jewish Agency, especially Sharett, tried to advance recruits to officer status, although the recommendation and the decision on granting such status to recruits from Palestine lay solely in the hands of the British Command.

Throughout the war, seventeen Yishuv recruits serving in the ATS were commissioned.[91] Four of them received their commission immediately on completing the Cadre course: Ruth Berman,[92] Shoshana Gershonovitz,[93] Dvora Horef and Rachel Maklef-Hivner.[94] Four others (Mina Ben-Zvi, Miriam Levy-Kornfeld, Lea Spector and Poria Rafael, all graduates of the course) received their commissions in the course of the following three months, although all eight were only platoon commanders and not company commanders. Other officers were Shoshana Werner,[95] Victoria Ben-Artzi (Tov), Esther Herlitz, Varda Brin (Hoofien), Rivka Yaffe, Yocheved Dostrovsky, Hanna Finkelstein, Yehudit Herman and Ilsa Orgler.[96]

In the course of their military service three of the Yishuv recruits were promoted to the rank of Company Sergeant Major, a powerful rank in the British Armed Forces (especially with regard to discipline), and dozens of others became sergeants and corporals. In the WAAF, six of the recruits reached officer rank by the end of the war. Four of them – Ellen Alroi, Rachel Caspi, Nora Miller and Mussia Salzovsky – were made Assistant Section Officer (equivalent of lieutenant) in December 1943 and the other two, Shoshana Katz (Kalmanovitz) and Dvora Aroch completed officer training at a later stage.

For over two years only British officers were allowed to serve as Company Commander, with the exception of two Jewish officers.[97] In late 1944, only after a lengthy campaign by the Jewish Agency, led by Sharett, were four more Jewish officers given command of companies in which most of the servicewomen were recruits from Palestine: Werner received command of Company 507 in Tel el Kabir, Ben-Zvi received command of Company 522 in Alexandria, Berman received command of Company 520 in Tel El Kabir, and Ben-Artzi assumed command of Company 531 in Tura, near Cairo. Thus these companies became 'Hebrew'. Most of the officers served until 1945 and in that year only ten officers remained in active service – a fact that concerned the Yishuv institutions.

The first officers' course took place in Sarafend at the end of 1942, and lasted only one month. In July 1944 the course was extended to two months and its training programme was adapted to match its equivalent in Britain. The first officers, who had undergone training in the Middle East, completed a brief course before being posted to the various units, because the previous training standards had not been appropriate. The division for training NCOs was opened in Sarafend in August 1943 and continued to function until February 1945. Thirty recruits participated in the course and the selection of candidates, and components of the course were conducted in accordance with the British format. The main problem in adapting the programme was one of language.

Throughout the service, there were also frictions and misunderstandings between the officers and their soldiers, often because of various differences in mentality and culture. Possibly the main consideration facing the Yishuv institutions in recommending candidates for officer training was the measure of their loyalty to the institutions, their connections and status in the Haganah, rather than good human relations or leadership qualities. The British, on the other hand, realized that the potential officers had to have 'a sense of humour and a sense of proportion' and even some human weaknesses, since 'someone with weaknesses will be able to understand the weaknesses of those under her command'.[98] On the frictions with the officers, Habas wrote, 'There was one earnest officer who invested her entire being into her job, dutifully filled all the nationalist principles and demands of the Haganah, insisted on the rights of those under her command, defended them and cleared all the paths in they way', yet despite it all, 'the foreign walls and the tensions between ranks did not fall and it so happened that resentments developed against her that haven't faded even from a distance of years'.[99]

Service Conditions

Service conditions were not always easy: 'Convoys in the desert, huts and tents and hospitals dipped in blood and sand, stores and workshops in furnace-like heat, remote clusters of camps, surrounded by bamboo fences scorching in the wind and sun and uncomfortable khaki uniform, year after year.'[100] The ATS camp was separated from the main camp surrounded by straw mats with pieces of broken glass scattered on top to keep out undesirable elements. The living conditions of the ATS and WAAF servicewomen alike differed from one camp to another and depended on location of the camp and its characteristics.

In Ismailia the conditions were comfortable, with the servicewomen living in stone houses previously used to house British families from the Suez Canal Administration (before the war). The drivers of Company 502 and the clerks in Company 522 also lived in nice houses in Alexandria. In Cairo's Qasr al-Nil clerks lived in stone houses (military barracks). Servicewomen from Company 503 in Abassya (a suburb of Cairo) lived in an elegant villa. A few WAAF servicewomen lived in private homes in the prestigious Heliopolis neighbourhood in Cairo and several dozen WAAFs, such as Ruth Ziv Rartakov, daughter of founders of Kibbutz Geva, who served in the filter room, lived in fancy boats parked on the Nile and enjoyed the personal service of Sudanese servants.[101] The servicewomen in the drivers' company on Camp Mina, lived in large wooden huts, each housing forty women (a platoon), while the company sergeant had a small changer of her own.

However, for many of the servicewomen the conditions were harsh, far from comfortable. Tel el Kabir, for example, was a distance from the city, and servicewomen there lived in tin huts, which were scorching hot in summer and freezing cold in winter. In Genifa, between Suez and Ismailia, servicewomen spent their entire service period living in tents. In many camps, especially during the first months of the women's military service, there was often a lack of running water or electricity. Hundreds of WAAFs spent the first year of their military service in tents on RAF MU 107, the largest of the RAF camps, until huts were built to house them.

The servicewomen were allowed a few hours off a week and every second weekend they could leave camp. Once every three months they received a week's vacation which they could spend off camp, visiting their families or touring the Middle East. Often the servicewomen would spend their free time in the clubs and hostels specially built for them in the large Egyptian cities or in the rest and recreation rooms established for them on some of the camps. In this the Council for Women's Organizations played a significant part. Although the matter of servicewomen's welfare was officially the responsibility of the Soldiers' Welfare Committee, the CWO made a point of also seeing to the needs of the women when they were on leave in Palestine and had no sleeping arrangements.

Most of the ATS companies in Egypt were located far from the cities of Cairo and Ismailia. The servicewomen took advantage of their free time, except when the battles were raging at El Alamain, visiting the cities for shopping and recreation. Since the companies did not provide regular transport for this, many of the servicewomen would hitch rides in military cars. Most of these journeys were uneventful, although some ended in serious accidents. There were also instances of sexual assault against the servicewomen on the part of male drivers or other passengers. This is what happened to Sara Kopler, an occupational therapist in a hospital near Ismailia. She and a woman friend spent the day together in town after which they hitched a ride back to their base. On their way back, her friend in the back seat called out that the soldier next to her was 'touching her up', and trying to undress her. The driver, too, started to pester Kopler, and the two women had to fight the men off. As soon as a chance presented itself, Kopler opened the door and they both jumped out of the speeding command car. Kopler was badly wounded and her right arm remained permanently paralyzed.[102]

Not all the serious road traffic accidents that took place in the military were reported in the Yishuv and if they were heard about, they were seen as a necessary evil and as part of military service. News of traffic accidents apparently didn't put the women of the Yishuv off enlisting in the army, probably because most of them took place during 1943–44, after the majority of recruits were already in the middle of their military service.

Expressions of Appreciation for the Work of the Yishuv Recruits

Most of the servicewomen worked hard during their military service and their contribution to the war effort was significant. Like the British women who received praise for their part in the war effort and military service,[103] so also were the women recruits from Palestine similarly praised, although formal British sources have dismally few references to their service.[104] According to a rare report written at the height of the war, 'Despite the fact that only half of them speak English ... the Eretz Israeli ATS is an undoubted success.'[105] According to Mary Mackenzie, commander of Company 513, for example, 'the servicewomen [most of who are from Palestine] work very hard, but they are always in high spirits, even though their living conditions are extremely difficult'.[106] The work of the WAAFs was summed up by a British officer, 'I didn't have it easy with you. You always demanded your rights, insisted on communicating with each other in your strange language. In short, you were "strange birds". But I knew I could rely on you. Before, I have had no ties with Jewish people. If such are the Jews in Palestine – you will go far.'[107]

In the Yishuv, too, there was much praise for the recruits' hard work and their contribution to the war effort. Yosef Baratz, Chairman of the Soldiers' Welfare Committee, who visited the servicewomen in Egypt, reported on his return to the CWO that 'the male and female commanders are aware of the value of the servicewomen's work'.[108] One of the Council's members reported that servicemen and representatives of the institutions who visited the camps recalled the 'praise being dished out "in high places" to the Hebrew woman in the army – her agility, her ability to understand, her devotion and her courage'.[109] One gauge of appreciation was reflected in citations. And, indeed, six Palestine recruits received official awards for excellence in recognition of their military service on behalf of the war effort.[110]

Most of the skills obtained by the servicewomen in the course of their military service did not prepare them for civilian life. The jobs they filled in the army were not available to them after the war, because of the different character of civilian work, because of gender concepts and also because the jobs were taken by male ex-soldiers. Thus, for example, most of the servicewomen who had served as drivers in the army did not continue with this work after their discharge.[111] The Haganah organization that tried hard to place servicewomen in military trades courses according to its needs, did not take advantage of their professional potential once they were discharged, which is the way the IDF acted in the years that followed.

NOTES

1. Sharett saw in female military service a twofold task: as an answer to internal Yishuv needs (social responsibility) and outwardly (the political aspect of the Yishuv's struggle to establish a state). 'Recruiting the Woman', Moshe Sharett's lecture to the Working Women's Council, *Davar Hapo'elet*, 3–4 (23 April 1942), p.6.
2. Unlike British servicewomen, women from the Yishuv were not recruited into the Navy's auxiliary service, the Women's Royal Naval Service (WRNS – popularly and officially known as the Wrens). On the other hand, 1,106 Jewish men from the Yishuv served in the Royal Navy's various departments in the Middle East. Yoav Gelber, *Toldot hahitnadvut: Bein Britim, Aravim veGermanim* [History of volunteering: Between British, Arabs and Germans] (Jerusalem 1984), p.300. According to Hadassah Samuel, it was she who refused to recruit Yishuv women to the WRNS, 'For the Navy, I told them, we have no way of moving forward and that is how it remained.' Interview with Hadassah Samuel, 12 February 1972. Interviewer: Margalit Shilo, film 200/K, the Institute for Modern Judaism, department of verbal documentation, Hebrew University, pp.12–13; according to the British version, from the beginning, Naval rules did not allow the recruitment of women from the Middle East. William Hough, 'Palestine's Part in the War', *Forum* (August 1945), pp.10–15.
3. Sharett to Chitty, 2 February, 1942, Central Zionist Archive, Jerusalem (CZA), S25/6001. The letter was sent in response to a pamphlet the army published, stipulating the new name.
4. Companies 502, 517, 522, 523 and 524 belonged to Area Group 16 and located in Alexandria; Companies 503, 508, 510, 513 and Number 63 Hospital in Halmia belonged to Area Group in Cairo 17; Companies 504, 506, 509, 511 and 514 belonged to Area Group 18 and were located in Moaskar; Area Group 21, which was located in Palestine, included Companies 507, 512 and 515 as well as the training base in Sarafend, which was reduced on 28 January 1944 – with the drop in recruitment numbers – to Platoon status. Area Groups War Diaries, National Archives, London (NA), WO 169/13841-13843 and WO 169/18009-18012.
5. Based on War Diaries of ATS companies. NA, WO 169/6831-21590, WO 169/6831-21590.
6. One of the Christian servicewomen on the course was a Russian married to a British serviceman, and the other participants who spoke Russian befriended her. Another Christian woman, an older woman from Vienna, was married to a Jew and had worked, apparently, in the kitchens in Sarafend before joining the course. Letter from Claire Epstein in Sarafend, 19 January 1942, p.1, Haganah History Archive, Tel Aviv (HHA), 33/10.
7. Chitty met with Mrs Speirs, probably an Englishwoman who worked with Arab women, and asked her to recommend Christian women for military recruitment. Speirs was sceptical as to the chances of finding suitable candidates because of the conservative nature of Arab society. Audrey Chitty's diary, 19 December 1941, National Army Museum, London (NAM), 9802-55-2. Ultimately, four

Arab women enlisted. About a month after the start of the course, Chitty met with four Arab women leaders, one of who, Mrs Mogannam, expressed her ambition that Arab women would contribute to the war effort, since 'your (British) objective is also our objective'. Chitty's diary, 24 February 1942, ibid. Despite the support of their leaders, only about 100 Arab women enlisted in the ATS throughout the war. Hadassah Samuel described a conversation with Chitty on her first visit to Jerusalem in December 1941 to sum up the issue of female military recruitment. According to her, Chitty 'wanted Arab women, I said it's your business. What were the Arab women who would go, a handful of Christians rolling about in the streets. I told her I wouldn't allow our girls to be with those girls.' Interview with Hadassah Samuel, p.12.

8. Sneh, who was a physician by profession, was Head of the National Command of Haganah in 1941–46 and later served as a member of the Jewish Agency Executive. Yoav Gelber, *Toldot hahitnadvut: Hahitnadvut ve mekoma bemidiniut hazionit ve hayishuvit 1939–1942* [History of volunteering: volunteering and its place in Zionist and Yishuv Policies 1939–1942] (Jerusalem 1989), p.737; Mina Rogoz'ik , 'The Female Haganah Member', Haganah History Archive (HHA), 16/2, p.6.
9. Letter from Chitty to the Jewish Agency recruitment department, 31 December 1941, CZA, S25/6001. The British selection committee had received lists prepared by the CID of checks made on the reliability of the candidates. According to Mina Ben-Zvi's testimony, they were asked about their participation in illegal organizations and the level of their loyalty to the Mandatory Government. Ben-Zvi recalled candidates who had been proposed by the Jewish Agency and the Haganah, such as Gershonowitz, Berman and others, who had been given permission to participate in the course, only after pressure from Sharatt. Female Haganah Members, HHA, 16/2, p.6.
10. The committee headed by Chitty approved only thirty-two of the forty-eight names submitted to it. Chitty saw this as a victory over the Jewish Agency. Chitty's Diary, 9 January 1942, NAM, 9802-55-2. The Jewish Agency also recommended twenty-five women for a commission after completing the course. List of names of Jewish Recruits, 4 February 1942, CZA, S25/6001.
11. In wake of information received by her, according to which anyone who had not been accepted for the Cadre course would not enlist in the army, Chitty made it clear to Samuel and the Jewish Agency that she expected those candidates who were not accepted for the command course to enlist in the first cycle of recruitment and would be marked as candidates for promotion. Letter from Chitty to Samuel, 10 January 1942, CZA, S25/6001.
12. Gelber, *Toldot hahitnadvut: Hahitnadvut ve mekoma bemidiniut hazionit ve hayishuvit 1939–1942*, pp.272–7; Hanoch Patishi, *Mahteret be'madim: 'Haganah' ve'hayalim ha'eretz Israelim betzava habriti* [Underground in uniform: Haganah and the Eretz Israel servicemen in the British army, 1939–1946] (Tel Aviv 2006), p.28.
13. Sentiments of the officer, Baruch Yitzhar at 'A meeting of soldiers released for recruitment activity', 8 January 1942, HHA, 33/4.
14. English-born Claire Epstein worked, until her enlistment, in the liaison department established in the Histadrut Executive for dealing with the interests of men enlisting in the British army. Dov Hoz headed the department until his death in a road traffic accident in 1940.

15. Undated memorandum from Claire Epstein (probably from mid November 1941), CZA, S25/5099.
16. The army agreed for the volunteers to fill a military registration form in the Jewish Agency's recruitment offices and provided relevant forms in English and Hebrew. The volunteer was then to bring the completed form when she came to the military recruitment centre. Letter from Dodds in the military HQ in Palestine to Moshe Sharett, 8 January 1942, ibid. S25/6001.
17. Julia Cowper, *The Auxiliary Territorial Service* (London 1949), p.77.
18. Up to 8 February 1942, some 1,100 volunteers had registered in the recruitment offices, with about 850 of them registering with the Jewish Agency. The main wave of volunteers took place during the first few days after the decision was published and before the commencement of recruitment, after which it slowed down, partly as a result of polemic in the Yishuv. Already at a meeting of the Recruitment Management on 17 February 1942, Haim Barless reported a 'phenomenon of registered women dropping out', in other words, non-appearance for actual recruitment. Later Schneifer and Idelberg expressed their concern that the Jewish Agency's 'reserves' were dwindling, with insufficient candidates for the second batch of recruitment and calls were made for immediate action to encourage recruitment. Meeting of Recruitment Department, 18 March 1942, CZA, S25/5063.
19. The recruits and the recruiters credited the women's organizations indifference for this, claiming that it 'is difficult for the non-enlisted to solicit others to enlist'; also for the fact that no well-known activists enlisted, to set a personal example for the recruits. In wake of the criticism, the women's press reported the recruitment of 'famous names' in the women's organizations, such as Hanna Levy-Salz, former WIZO President in Rheine District in Germany, as well as the daughters of senior members of the organization, such as the daughter of Ms Hanna Steiner, former WIZO President in Czechoslovakia. 'New Links in the ATS Israeli Chain', *Olam Ha'isha*, 52–3 (22 July 1942), p.3; *Davar Hapo'elet* reported on the recruitment of four members who filled a position in the working women's movement in town and country. 'Activity on Behalf of Recruitment of Women Members', *Davar Hapo'elet*, 6 (7 July 1942), p.80.
20. Minutes of the Congress of Recruiters, 23 September 1942, p.4, HHA, 33/4. These things were said despite reports on Labour movement members who had enlisted in May 1942. 'Increasing Female Recruitment in Tel Aviv', 4 May 1942, CZA, S37/670. Ida Priber, for example, who was a recruiter, felt uncomfortable with the fact that she herself was not enlisting and had indeed applied to the recruitment office, but was rejected on medical grounds. Ida Priber, *Ma'aglei hayim: roman autobiography* [Circles of life: an autobiographical novel] (Tel Aviv 1982), pp.147–8.
21. In Beirut (sixteen Jewish servicewomen), in a hospital out of town (twenty-four) and in Sydon (thirty). A report by Idelson to the secretariat of the CWO on a visit in Syria (as Lebanon was then known), 30 May 1943, WWC file, Labour Movement Archive, IV-230-6.
22. 'Volunteering', 15 November 1942, HHA, 33/4.
23. 'Report on Recruitment Rejects' (undated), CZA, S37/376. It is hard to assess the number of these recruits, or to verify those assessments.
24. In order to improve the situation, Idelberg suggested holding parties where national issues would be discussed, while demanding that the Jewish Agency's

Political Department arrange more frequent visits to the training camp. Letter from National Recruiter to the Yishuv's Recruitment Center, 29 June 1943, CZA, S25/5097. The Organization of Yishuv Recruits in the RAF conducted a lengthy struggle to concentrate the women recruits in Jewish companies, or at least to arrange separate accommodation for them, and demanded that they speak Hebrew, in order to solve the problem of misunderstanding the British officers. By the end of the war, the demands had not been addressed. Document from the Organization of Yishuv RAF Servicemen to the Jewish Agency's Political Department, 5 June 1944, p.8, ibid., S25/4795.

25. Minutes of CWO meeting, 14 December 1943, ibid. F49/2105. At that meeting, it was reported that Sharett's visit to the RAF training camp in Lydda (later the town of Lod) left a deep impression on the recruits.
26. Minutes of WAAF Command, 11 August 1942, NA, Air 49/294.
27. Minutes of WAAF Command, 11 February 1943, ibid.
28. For reasons of security, the ship bringing the British officers sailed around the Cape of Good Hope on a journey that lasted several weeks. Interview with Jean Baker, Tackley (near Oxford, UK), 17 May 2006.
29. Interview with Brucha Ben-Haim (Eisenberg), Nahalal, 7 January 2006.
30. 'Recruiting the Woman', Moshe Sharett addressing participants of the Working Women's Council, *Davar Hapo'elet*, 3–4 (23 April 1942), pp.36–8.
31. Daphna Izraeli, 'Migdur basherut hatzavai be Zahal' [Gendering in military service in the IDF], *Teoria vebikoret*, 14 (Summer 1999), p.98; Cynthia Enloe, *Does Khaki Become You? The Militarization of Women's Lives* (London 1983), p.10.
32. Nira Yuval-Davis, 'Front and Rear: The Sexual Division of Labor in Israeli Army', *Feminist Studies*, 11, no.3 (1985), pp.649–57.
33. The expression 'back seat' was coined by Penny Summerfield and Corinna Peniston-Bird, 'Women in the Firing Line: The Home Guard and the Defence of Gender Boundaries in Britain in the Second World War', *Women's History Review*, 9, no.2 (2000), pp.231–55. Another aspect of service in an auxiliary capacity was expressed in the matter of their weapons training. Female commanders in Haganah demanded to train the recruits, especially the drivers, in weaponry, in order to secure their personal safety, but the military authorities refused to allow this, with the excuse that they were serving in auxiliary services. Sonya Idelberg, 'The Jewish Woman in WWII' (undated), p.4, HHA, 3/19.
34. In the Jewish Agency's recruitment offices, women registered in accordance with their medical occupation in which they wanted to be employed in the army. Even before recruitment commenced to the ATS, several dozen Yishuv women enlisted via the Red Cross for hospital service (PANV – Palestine Aid Nursing Volunteers). At the head of this service in Palestine stood Lady MacMichael, the wife of the British High Commissioner. The artist Friedl Stern, for example, was one of these and worked at the hospital in Be'er Ya'akov before enlisting in the ATS.
35. Only British servicewomen in Company 501 in Cairo were employed in the ATS Communications Branch in the Middle East. This probably indicates the lack of trust and suspicion vis-à-vis the recruits, since communications was considered a classified area. Anti-aircraft batteries around towns, as had been installed in Britain, were not in use in the Middle East, which is why women were not integrated into their operation.

36. Lucy Noakes, *Women in the British Army: War and the Gentle Sex 1907–1948* (New York 2006), p.107.
37. According to Enloe, in a country with ethnic divides, the governing elite categorizes its ethnic minorities according to the measure of trust it engenders. It differentiates between the controlling community and communities whose loyalty is dubious or even defined as hostile and potentially harmful to the existing political order. The ethnic groups are defined according to their loyalty to the state, and are prejudged in policies of military recruitment, promotion, dispensing trades in the army, combat levels, etc. Cynthia Enloe, *Ethnic Soldiers: State Security in Divided Society* (Georgia 1980), pp.15–23. In indeed, in Egypt it was virtually impossible for Palestine recruits who were employed in hospitals to actually treat the sick and wounded. In Italy, when there was a manpower shortage and many wounded men were brought in from the battlefield (especially from the fierce Battle of Monte Casino in May 1944), Italian prisoners of war were employed in the kind of physical labour previously reserved for the Palestine recruits, who, under these circumstances, were allowed direct access to the patients, with the encouragement of the hospital director. Bracha Habas, *Bnot hayil: sefer ha'ATS* [Women of valour: book of the ATS] (Tel Aviv 1964), p.98.
38. Enloe, *Does Khaki Become You?*, p.100.
39. As a result of this, the matron issued a complaint against Sonya Peres, who, for her part, demanded that the nurse, too, be tried for insulting her. She even demanded to be allowed to be present at the trial. Although in her heart of hearts the officer who judged her was on her side, she was unable to overlook such behaviour and Peres was forced to leave, with a heavy heart, the hospital she loved so much. Interview with Sonya Peres (Gelman), Tel Aviv, 9 January 2006.
40. Letter from Zilla Babayouf to the Jewish Agency, 19 April 1945, CZA, S25/9885.
41. T. Damon, *Beshvilai hagoral: Roman mehayai ha'ATS* [In the paths of destiny: a novel on ATS life] (Tel Aviv 1953), pp.20–1.
42. At that time clerks in the Yishuv saw their professional advancement as a national enterprise, in other words, as a contribution to service, as increased national loyalty and as an effort to educate the public. David De Friss, 'Pekidim Ivr'im be Eretz Israel' [Hebrew Beaurocrats in Eretz Israel], *Teoria ve'Bikoret*, 9 (Winter 1996), pp.41–56. Moreover, many emissaries who were sent to the DP camps in Europe after the war and were employed in administrative trades, saw in their work a national mission, as well as empowering women. Lilach Rosenberg-Friedman, 'Zehuyot be'conflict ben shoah letekuma: shlichot hayishuv be'rikuzei she'erit hapleita be'Europa [Identities in conflict between the Holocaust and independence: Yishuv emissaries in concentrations of Holocaust survivors in Europe], *Israel*, 11 (2007), pp.129–30.
43. Hadassah Samuel suggested that for propaganda reasons, storekeeping and driving should be stressed, since they were 'more attractive than feminine, housekeeping trades.' Letter from Samuel to Sale, 5 September 1941, CZA S25/6001. Women from Britain who had worked in factories in the Second World War as part of the war effort, saw their work as 'getting out of the cage' – getting out of the private domain and into the public domain. Gail Brayborn and Penny Summerfield, *Out of the Cage: Women's Experiences in Two World Wars* (London 1987), p.34.

44. Penny Summerfield, *Reconstructing Women's Wartime Lives: Discourse and Subjectivity in Oral Histories of the Second World War* (Manchester 1998), pp.122–3. Soldiers in non-combat positions developed practices of identity that, on the one side, emphasized the similarity between themselves and fighters, for example, describing their trades as dangerous or stressful, or, on the other hand, intensified the differences between themselves and women soldiers in the same trades. Orna Sasson-Levy, 'Hatranut be'toch dikui: kinun zehuiot migdariot shel hayalot betafkidim "gavri'im"' [Subversion and Suppression: establishing gender identities of women in 'masculine' roles], in Yael Atzmon (ed.), *Hatishma Koli: yitsugim shel nashim batarbut ha'israelit* [Will you hear my voice: representation of women in Israeli culture] (Jerusalem 2001), pp.277–302.
45. 'From the sentiments of a Hebrew officer on the situation in the ATS' (undated, probably in 1943), p.1-2, CZA, S37/676. Esther Bacharach, who served as a clerk to the commander of Company 504 in Tel el Kabir, wrote that the local storekeepers worked very hard from 07:00 to 19:00. She stressed that their work was hard and more continuous than that of clerks. 'From the Words of Esther Bacharach' (undated, probably late 1942), ibid.
46. Habas, *Bnot hayil*, p.93.
47. Guber, 'Sooty Soldiers', *Davar Hapo'elet*, 4 (April 1952), pp.60–4.
48. Ts. Sh. [sic] 'My Work in the Army', *Davar Hapo'elet*, 9 (27 September 1943), p.133.
49. Habas, *Bnot hayil*, pp.213–21.
50. Talila Kosh-Zohar, 'Hee lo halcha basadot: ha'yitsug hanashi betextim shel dor tashach' [She didn't walk in the fields: women's representation in texts from the 1948 generation], in Hana Naveh and Oded Manda Levy (eds), *Sadan Mehkarim be safrut Ivrit Yom Krav ve'arbo ve'haboker shelemaharat: yitsugei milhement ha'aztmaut basifrut* [Research in Hebrew literature, day of battle and the following morning: representations of the war of independence in literature], 5 (Tel Aviv 2002), pp.307–8.
51. For example, in London, Tamar Eshel (Shoham) operated a secret communications station on behalf of the Haganah.
52. Habas, *Bnot hayil*, p.57.
53. Interview with Major (ret.) Daphne Hill, Richmond (London), 10 May 2006.
54. 'A myth is the permanent basis for culture, society and nation, created by the culture and at the same time its creator.' David Ohana and Robert Wistrich (eds), 'Mavo: Nohehut hamytosim' [Introduction: Presense of Myths], in *Mytos ve Zikaron: gilgula shel hatoda'a ha'israelit* [Myth and memory: incarnation of Israeli awareness] (Jerusalem 1996), pp. 11-37. There are some who see myth as being a presentation of the worldview in a certain culture and an expression of the social ethos. Clifford Geertz, *The Interpretation of Cultures: Selected Essays* (New York: Basic Books, 1973), p.5.
55. These sentiments were voiced in response to the demands of certain elements in the Yishuv to recruit women only into the Jewish units where men served. Thus, according to Sharett, the range of professions open to women would be greatly reduced. 'Recruiting the Woman', Lecture by Moshe Sharett, *Davar Hapo'elet*, 3–4 (23 April 1942), p.5.
56. Of the nine songs written during the war years and devoted to the women recruits, four referred to the drivers: 'Soldier Driver' by Zelig Posek and Avraham Mindlin; 'Song to the Woman Soldier' by Amram Gilboa and Mindlin;

'There Beside the Pyramids', words and music by Mordechai Zeira; 'Oh the Road' by Izakson and Mindlin.

57. Memoir of Esther Tal (Itrani); Negev, 'Sonya Squad', *Yediot Ahronot*, 7-Days Supplement, 18 January 2007, p.50.
58. Altogether ten women participated in a platoon commander's course and twenty-nine completed a squad leader's course. Netiva Ben-Yehuda, for example, served as a sapper officer in the battles for the Galilee in Israel's War of Independence. Ofra Elad, '"Kol bahur ve tov laneshek, bahura al hamismar!": Ha'havera ba'Palmach' [Every man is good for arms, a woman, on guard duty! Woman Member in the Palmach], in Yehiam Weitz (ed.), *Palmach: Shtei shibolim veherev* [Palmach, Two Sticks of Corn and a Sword] (Tel Aviv, 2001), pp.232–3.
59. Eileen Bigland, *Britain's Other Army* (London 1946), pp.144–8.
60. Although Britain was far from the actual battlefront, in mid 1941 in the battle that became known as the Battle of Britain, the country became one big battlefront. The proposal to include women in mixed male-female anti-aircraft batteries was raised by General Pile in August 1941. It was considered 'breathtaking and revolutionary'. By the end of 1943, some 56,000 women served in this system, some in mixed male and female teams. D'Ann Campbell, 'Women in Combat: The World War II Experience in the United States, Great Britain, Germany and the Soviet Union', in Gerald Martel (ed.), *The World War Two Reader* (New York 2004), pp.253–62. Nonetheless, the British government gave in to public opinion in refraining from referring to the women's role as 'combatant' and in an unequivocal order from Churchill forbidding them to fire from the batteries placed in these units. However, there is no doubt that these defence units were operational in every way.
61. In the course of the Second World War many hundreds of women served as drivers of different kinds of motor vehicles, mainly because of a shortage of manpower and not because of changed gender perceptions. This phenomenon accelerated the worldwide increase in women drivers. Jean Veevers, 'Women in the Driver's Seat: Trends in Sex Differences in Driving and Death', *Population Policy and Policy Review*, 1, no.2 (May 1982), pp.171–82. According to Hadassah Samuel, 'The appearance of women drivers might cause unpleasantness in countries outside Eretz Israel.' (She was referring, of course, to the Moslem countries). Letter from Samuel to Brigadier Beddington, 2 May 1941, CZA, S25/6001.
62. Appendix to document on decision to establish the ATS in the Middle East, 24 December 1941, ibid. S25/5099.
63. Due to the attractiveness of this profession in the eyes of the Yishuv women, and in order to encourage recruitment, the CWO agreed to fund the driving courses. It is not known whether the CWO or other Yishuv organizations funded additional training courses in other skills.
64. Sharett reported to the Recruitment Department (23 February 1942) that the first round of recruitment would not include driving practice, but that 'only those who already know how to drive will be accepted to this service'. CZA, S25/5063.
65. With the help of Penelope Otto, Commander of Company 502, Mary Mackenzie managed to persuade Audrey Chitty, ATS Commander in the Middle East, to permit the drivers in her company to drive trucks weighing above three tons.

This required special dispensation since according to ATS rules women drivers in the army were not allowed to drive such heavy trucks. After driving such a truck herself, Chitty promised to arrange the matter with army HQ. Mackenzie noted with satisfaction in the company's war diary that this ruling, which was implemented in Britain, was never implemented in the Middle East. 1 December 1942, NA, WO 169/6843.

66. In April 1943, WIZO donated twelve ambulances to the British army on the condition that only women drivers from Palestine would drive them. And indeed, the ambulances were attached to Company 515 in Sarafend. The drivers all took the ambulance driving course in Camp Mina.
67. Adelyn Bonin, *Allegiances* (Santa Barbara 1993), p.167.
68. FANY – First Aid Nursing Yeomanry, a nursing service that supplied medical aid and volunteered to serve in the British army in a separate, but affiliated capacity. At first they served in France until the evacuation from Dunkirk and eighty of them arrived in the Middle East. At the time of their merger with the ATS (due to pressure from Audrey Chitty) in November 1941, some of the drivers left the company and were transferred to Britain. Several were commissioned and took command of other companies.
69. The beginnings of the Palestine recruits in the 'posh' company were not easy. Pat Hall, a staff sergeant and one of the veterans, recalled in her memoires that twelve graduates of the cadre course were sent to Company 502 as reinforcements, due to a severe manpower shortage. This addition was of no use to the company since only two of the servicewomen could drive and only one of these actually wanted to do so. The British staff saw no use in teaching women to drive who did not wish for it. Thus, three of them were placed in the traffic office of the ambulance station, where their language skills proved most useful. Three of them were given administrative trades in the company's offices, two experienced laboratory workers were sent to help in the number 64 Unit's HQ, and one (Geula), stayed behind as clerk to one of the officers. Only at a later stage, did the company receive more drivers from Palestine. These were the friends of the first twelve servicewomen. Pat Hall, *Fearfully 502: A Lighthearted History of 11 M.T.C. / 502 M.A.C, A.T.S* (London 1946), pp.84–5.
70. Over six months of battle, the company's drivers transferred 22,339 wounded men, despite the harsh conditions that prevailed at the time and without so much as a single accident. In July 1942 alone, Otto noted in the company diary that they had transferred 2,883 wounded and the ambulances covered a distance of 23,629 miles. 502 Company Diary July 1942, NA, WO 169/6832.
71. Interview with Tirtza Raviv (Torok) and Yael Arieli (Kornberg), Jerusalem, 27 December 2006.
72. Often servicewomen in 'masculine' trades internalize the concept that femininity and military do not go hand in hand. 'Traditional' femininity symbolized the 'other' that has to be excluded and depressed in order to establish a positive personal identity. Sasson-Levy, 'Hatranut be'toch dikui', p.220.
73. Deborah Bernstein is convinced that women who felt total confidence in their right and ability to work alongside men and insisted on doing so, eventually managed to obtain the trades they wanted. Deborah Bernstein, *Ishah be-Eretz Yisra'el: Hashe'ifa Leshivion Betkufat Heyishuv* [A Woman in Eretz Israel: The aspiration for equality during the Yishuv period] (Tel Aviv 1987), pp.30–3. Still,

women were pushed out of every 'field' that was considered masculine. Sara Malkin, for example, wrote about the workers, 'They will be unable to come to terms with our conditions for equality and independence ... you are too earnest ... want to look like men, we'll be ridiculed.' Deborah Bernstein, 'Kolot min hagarin hakashe – misipuraihen shel tse'irot ha'aliyah hashniah' [Voices from the hard core – stories of young women from the Second Aliyah], in Yael Atzmon (ed.), *Hatishma koli: yitzugim shel nashim behevra ha'israelit* [Will you hear my voice: women's representation in Israeli society] (Jerusalem 2001), pp.123–4.

74. Billie Melman, 'Min ha-shulayim el ha-historiyah shel ha-Yishuv: Migdar ve-eretz yisre'eliyut (1890–1920)' [From the periphery to the center of Yishuv history: gender and nationalism in Eretz Israel (1890–1920)], *Zion* 62, (1997), pp.343–78. According to Melman these women did not dress like men in order to fulfil employment or defence needs, rather for the purpose of defining gender boundaries.
75. Yehezkel Dar and Shaul Kimchi, 'Nashim tse'irot be'irgun gavri' [Young women in a masculine organization], *Soziologia Israelit*, D, 1 (2002), pp.62–83; Iris Gerbi, *Hamehir hakaful: ma'amad ha'isha bahevra ha'israelit ve sherut hanashim be'Zahal* [Double price: women's status in Israeli society and women's military service in the IDF] (Tel Aviv 1996); and others.
76. Orna Sasson-Levy, *Zehuiot bemadim: gavriut ve'nashiut batzava haisraeli* [Identities in uniform: masculinity and femininity in the Israeli army] (Jerusalem 2006), p.3. According to Eyal Ben-Ari and Edna Schreiber, by delegating jobs to women the army wants to justify the missions entrusted to it. Thus, for example, it is natural to place them in care work or education – jobs that do not require physical strength. Eyal Ben-Ari and Edna Levy Schreiber, 'Binui guf, binui ofi ubinui uma: hamigdar ve hashirut hatzvai be Israel' [Building a body, building a character and building a nation: gender and military service in Israel], *Tarbut Democratit*, 4–5 (2001), p.115.
77. Cynthia Enloe, *Maneuvers: The International Politics of Militarizing Women's Lives* (California 2000), p.13.
78. According to Raewyn Connell, the term 'gender identity' assumes a single identity that has to be acquired, sympathized with and internalized. Raewyn Connell, *Masculinities* (California Press 1995), p.25. In keeping with this approach, masculinity is a social-cultural-historical structure that is built into the history of power relations of men between themselves. Judith Butler reckons that gender identity is a changing and fluid social structure and not a biological entity. She rejects the possibility of gender identity, or any other identity, as an 'authentic', self-existing identity, rather as one that exists only within the creation of the identity. Judith Butler, *Gender Trouble* (New York 1990), pp.25, 136.
79. Melissa Herbert, *Camouflage Isn't Only for Combat* (New York 1998), pp.96–107.
80. Interview with Zipora Shahar (Eitan), Esther Yanai (Ben-Zvi), Rachel Brenner (Koris), Nahalal, 7 January 2006.
81. Interview with Miriam Shor (Mattersdorf), Tel Aviv, 15 April 2007.
82. Interview with Friedl Stern, Tel Aviv, 16 April 2006.
83. Habas, *Bnot hayil*, p.57.
84. Interview with Aliya Kravi (Rachlevsky), Tiv'on, 24 May 2007; Habas, *Bnot hayil*, pp.130–1.

85. Habas, *Bnot hayil*, pp.126–7. The servicewoman is mentioned in this book under an assumed name.
86. Stella Levy, later the Chief Commander of the IDF Women's Corps (1964–70). Cohen, 'Six Women in Uniform Respond to Six Questions', *Lamerhav*, 5 May 1966, p.6. The British did not permit Yishuv servicewomen to serve as communications or teleprinter operators (classified work), probably because of their suspicions toward the Yishuv. Only British servicewomen from Company 501 were permitted to do this work.
87. Unlike the ATS, the RAF left the profession of communications open to recruits from Palestine and many of them served as operators of communication and teleprinter instruments. Data according to Yosef Shavit, *Mitnadvim bekahol: eretzisraelim besherut heil hate'ufa hamalchuti* [Volunteers in blue: from Eretz Israel to service in the RAF] (Tel Aviv 1995), p.136.
88. Interview with Brucha Ben-Haim.
89. Interview with Rachel Ziv (Barshavsky), Tel Aviv, 2 February 2006.
90. Habas, *Bnot hayil*, p.140. Ya'akov Tsur, Jewish Agency Emissary in Cairo, recalled that one of the officers exclaimed to him, '[I wish] this was over! I want to be a free person, to go to the cinema or to sleep with a man without having to ask Moshe Sharett for permission!' Ya'akov Tsur, *Karev Yom: dapei avar* [A Day is coming: pages from the past] (Jerusalem 1979), p.143.
91. Letter from Dov Yosef to the Hebrew Officers, 14 October 1945, CZA, S25/9885.
92. Berman was among the veteran recruits. After the war she served in Europe on behalf of the Haganah and still later, during the War of Independence, she commanded the 205 Battalion Women's Forces in Jerusalem. 'Women's Force Congress, Battalion 205 (undated), HHA, 16/25.
93. Gershonovitz was born in Russia and was a laboratory worker by profession, member of Haganah and graduate of the Cadre Course. In late 1947, she established the Women's Unit in Jerusalem and was later transferred to Tel Aviv where she started recruiting for the National Women's Forces with Shurika Braverman from Kibbutz Shamir. Gershonovitz was Ben-Zvi's deputy, the first commander of the Women's Force and between 1950 and 1952, she commanded the women in the Nahal. Her last position in the IDF was Chief Commander of the Women's Forces, from 1952–59.
94. Maklef-Hibner was the most senior Jewish commander in the ATS, with the rank of Senior Commander, equivalent of major. Her last position was that of HQ officer in Company 508 in Cairo and responsible for about 800 servicemen overseeing the distribution of equipment in the Middle East. She had immigrated to Palestine in 1938 and was active in the Haganah, participated in the Cadre Course and stayed on to instruct new recruits from the extended batch of recruits. She was the first commander of a Jewish company. After the war she became spokesperson for the Haganah and, with the establishment of the Women's Force, she served as human resources officer for about eighteen months.
95. Werner was a graduate of the Hebrew University of Jerusalem, a veteran member of Haganah and later, Commander in Chief of the Women's Force from 1949–52.
96. 'List of commissioned servicewomen in the ATS up to 1.8.1942' (undated), CZA, S37/674; 'ATS Companies in Late August 1945', 10 September 1945, ibid., S25/5097. The latter document includes additional names of officers: Hava

Angel, Malka Sand, Shoshana Klein. These might not have served as officers, but were commanders.

97. In early 1943, Maklef-Hibner was appointed Commander of Company 515 in Sarafend. In the summer of 1943, she was transferred to Egypt and to command Company 526. Horef replaced her as commander of Company 515.
98. Habas, *Bnot hayil*, p.148.
99. A servicewoman from Company 512 in Jerusalem wrote that 'we don't always agree with the means they [the officers] see to be correct, but their intentions are good'. Habas, Ibid., pp.139, 148. Thus, for example, it was reported that the officer Orgler was transferred to Company 505 'after a contretemps with the girls in Genifa'. 'ATS Companies in late August 1945', 10 September 1945, CZA, S25/5097.
100. Habas, *Bnot hayil*, p.10.
101. Interview with Ruth Ziv (Tartakov), Kvutzat Geva, 11 April 2006.
102. Interview with Sara Kopler (Bar-Adon), Tel Aviv, 26 June 2006. Kopler's story appears under the heading 'The Story of One Ride' in Habas' book, *Bnot hayil*, pp.204–12, and also in Tamar Ze'evi, 'Women's Heroism in the Light of the Maccabis', *Ha'aretz*, 7 December 1966, p.3.
103. The British nation appreciated the contribution the women of Britain made to the war effort. According to Prime Minister Winston Churchill the war effort would not have been achieved were it not for the women who stepped forward in their millions and undertook such a plethora of jobs. Noakes, *Women in the British Army*, p.120.
104. One of the reasons for this is that companies' war diaries are an administrative and technical source whose task it is to deliver a serious and 'dry' report on everything that has taken place in the company and thus they do not contain moral reports on the way tasks were carried out. An additional reason could be credited to the tension and suspicions that prevailed between the military authorities and the recruits from Palestine.
105. 'Report by the Finance Secretary to the Military Council on his tours of the Middle East to examine the utilization of manpower in this area', 17 November 1943, p.22, NA, WO 32/10153.
106. Company 513 War Diary, 1 December 1942, ibid., WO 169/6843.
107. Shavit, *Mitnadvim bekahol*, p.142.
108. Yosef Baratz, 'From my Visit to Egypt', *Davar Hapo'elet*, 11–12 (10 December 1942), p.149.
109. R.K. [probably Rivka Katznelson], 'Fighting Woman's Day', *Davar Hapo'elet*, 2 (28 February 1943), pp.36–7. Even Lea Goldberg's song 'Aunt Ela Woman Soldier' stressed the servicewoman as a heroin, as part of the educational ethos of the younger generation. *Davar La-yeladim*, 12, no.28–29 (1 April 1942), p.225. The song was dedicated to her friend Ella Wilensky, who enlisted in the ATS.
110. Sergeant Mariana Dan was awarded a BEM (British Empire Medal) and five others were mentioned in dispatches: Yehudit Herman, Bertie Lehman, Hanna Sardi, Nehama Marcus and Stern. National Army Museum, London, 78-247-9401. Kopler was awarded an MBE after the war, for her work on behalf of the war veterans. Greer Fay Cashman, 'From ATS to IDF', *Jerusalem Post*, 8 May 1995, p.12.

111. Toward the discharge of the servicewomen, representatives of the CWO (and servicewomen connected to it) distributed questionnaires among the servicewomen in order to learn what profession they would like to work in after discharge from military service. Rachel Adiv reported that of ninety-eight women in one of the companies, twenty-seven wanted to continue in agriculture, ten in office work, nine in social work, eleven (of the younger ones) to continue with their studies, five in cooking and the rest in dressmaking and childcare. Of forty drivers only two wanted to continue in the job. From a questionnaire handed out by Epstein in Company 511, it transpires that out of 130 women drivers only six wished to remain drivers after discharge from the army, twenty-five wanted to be nurses and twenty hoped to be mechanics in motor workshops. Minutes of CWO Secretariat, 21 March 1945, p.1, CZA, F49/2106.

6

Twice Recruited: Women Members of Haganah and Lehi in the British Armed Forces

Among the female recruits from Palestine to the British forces were several hundred who were also members of the Yishuv paramilitary groups, Haganah and Lehi (Stern Gang). There is no knowledge of IZL (Irgun Zvai Leumi; known as The Irgun) members enlisting in the British army. In the course of the military service, some of the Haganah and Lehi members were involved in illegal activity on behalf of their organization and the activity they carried out provides a far-reaching example of national allegiance. Thus there developed a unique phenomenon that has no parallel in other societies: women members of underground national liberation movements who also serve as soldiers in an army they are fighting against. Examples exist of female members of underground movements and organizations fighting for their countries via a foreign occupier, or members of revolutionary underground groups struggling for a change of regime, but this was done within the framework of the state or community in which they live and not as part of the regular army of another country.[1] The complex image of the British army, which was conceived in the Yishuv as a foreign and hostile occupier, but also as an element that fought Nazi Germany, the enemy of the Jews, enabled this situation of 'dual loyalty' both to the British army, to which the servicewomen swore allegiance, and to the underground movements of which they were members. However, this duality also provided the servicewomen who belonged to the underground movements with challenges relating to gender as well as nationality.

Military service in the British army also offered Haganah members new possibilities for self-fulfilment. In their organization they were obliged to fight for the right to fill various roles in observation posts, regional defence, communications, accompanying illegal immigrant ships, welcoming immigrants and instructing in vocational courses, etc. Service in the British army, especially when it took place outside the boundaries of Palestine – in Egypt, Lebanon and Austria – opened to them a whole list of complex, secret and responsible jobs that would not have been available to them had they stayed in the Yishuv.

In order to carry out the different chores imposed on them by their organizations, the servicewomen were often obliged to violate various military and civilian laws – from making unauthorised use of military property, via criminal activity (assisting people on the police wanted lists), to involvement in murder. They carried out these acts knowing that they were liable to heavy punishment, such as imprisonment and dismissal from the army. The servicewomen hoped that their organizations would be wise enough to take advantage of the knowledge and experience they had garnered from this activity in the future struggle for the establishment of the State of Israel.

Haganah Members in the British Army

The decision to recruit women to the British army was announced on 24 December 1941, about two years after the outbreak of the Second World War, and after thousands of Yishuv men were already serving in the British forces, whether in all-Jewish or mixed units. In July 1940, the Haganah started to order its male members to enlist in the British army, directing them to the Jewish units or infantry divisions in accordance with the organization's national criteria. It imposed recruitment quotas on organizations within it, such as field forces and the police, and even set dates for enlistment, so as to slot in the recruits and distribute them in the various units. A special recruitment drive took place in October 1941 among male Haganah, kibbutzim and moshavim members and over 15,000 movement members enlisted.[2]

It appears that at a certain stage the Haganah started to openly encourage its male members to enlist in the army, but it remained ambivalent on the matter of female recruitment. On the one hand, its 'official' stance on recruitment of its female members was positive, and some of its leaders even called out for women to enlist. Zilla Dobrin, a Haganah member, testified that the movement's HQ called in late 1941 for recruitment to the Cadre Course. Sara Kopler testified that several men, including Sharett, encouraged female Haganah members in Haifa to enlist in the army.[3] Nonetheless, among members of the organization, as with the other movements in the Yishuv, opinions were divided between supporters and opponents of female recruitment. Within the prevailing hesitant atmosphere in the Yishuv over the issue of female recruitment, especially on the matter of their 'morality', and because of the dilemma in the organization as to the necessity of women's involvement in the Yishuv struggle in the region, the Haganah's leadership did not invest too much effort, in the beginning at least, in persuading its members of the importance of female recruitment.

It would appear that the Haganah's lack of clarity on this issue caused considerable frustration among the recruiters, who asked for clear-cut instructions as to the organization's policies. Already in the early stages the recruitment chief recruiters claimed that the '[organization], on the whole, held a positive position, however [it] did nothing toward instilling in its members the recognition of the need for female recruitment ... this position must be re-examined. In principle [the organization], has to impose via a command on its members its attitude to the matter.'[4] Complaints were also raised against Eliyahu Golomb, of the Haganah's leadership, who had initially been supportive of female military recruitment, for his contradictory messages in recruitment drives – on the need for female military recruitment vis-à-vis the need for reinforcing Jewish self-defence inside the country.[5] Not only men, but there were also female Haganah members who opposed recruitment to the British army. The female members' regiment in Tel Aviv under the command of Neuta Halperin, for example, was the focus of female power in the Haganah. Throughout the period of female military service no effort was made by the regiment to encourage their recruitment and only individual members actually enlisted. Haya Ironi-Abrahami and her colleagues in the regiment's command staff believed that the place of women (Haganah members) was in Haganah and the Palmach, and not in the British army, and therefore did not encourage their fellow members to enlist. Ironi-Abrahami was impressed that most of the active female Haganah members who did enlist in the Cadre and others who enlisted in regular recruitment batches did not come from Tel Aviv, but from Haganah centres in other towns such as Haifa and Jerusalem, as well as from kibbutzim and moshavim in the agricultural sector.[6]

Other female commanders in different Haganah HQs also opposed military recruitment. Rachel Tsabari, for example, testified that a meeting of all the Haganah female commanders in the Jerusalem region held a meeting following the call for recruitment. Tsabari was particularly averse to the recruitment of Haganah commanders to the Cadre course and held that it was unseemly for underground activists to wear uniform. Moreover, she claimed that recruitment of the commanders would harm the organizational system of Haganah women. Most of the women in her region did, however, enlist in the army and, when Tsabari was asked to serve as an example for recruitment, she refused to do so and 'went on leave' until the outbreak of the War of Independence.[7]

Although the Haganah's policies during the early stages of recruitment were typically indecisive, once a consensus was reached in the Yishuv and its scope expanded, the organization recognized the potential contribution of its female members as servicewomen in the British armed forces. As a result it supported and even encouraged its members to enlist. Nonetheless, fewer than 10 per cent of the organization's female members ultimately enlisted in the army.

At the United Kibbutz Movement (UKM) Council in February 1942, Yitzhak Tabenkin related to the claim that female Haganah members were enlisting in the army out of a strong sense of discrimination and in protest against their non-participation in Haganah activity. He asked to sever the connection between the issues and said, 'There are things that we are paying for. For some kind of discrimination against the female member [sic] of Haganah and other things, we are paying for in a kind of tense sensitivity, in a kind of psychological tension that preceded the ripening of the matter.' On the other hand, Ruth Haktin from Ein Harod claimed that in discussing recruitment, it was necessary to deal with the status of women in the Haganah and in the Yishuv in general: 'I have some additional conditions, not only in [joining] the army, but also in all our positions in the country. In the ranks of the Haganah, in [the] workplace, too.'[8]

In May, three months later, Tabenkin was required once again to relate to the matter and claimed that, 'Female recruitment should not be seen merely as a women's issue but also of men's'. He admitted openly that, 'In discussing this question – we are discussing it out of male psychology. We shall give the woman [sic] her rightful place in the Haganah in accordance with her talents and her capabilities. This will be determined by the physiology and psychology of the woman, and not of the man.'[9]

Female Haganah Members in the Cadre

Preparations for the women's recruitment and their selection for the Cadre, the first command course, were entrusted to the Haganah as the main security organization in the Yishuv (in 1941 it became the military arm of the Jewish Agency), which also had the necessary organizational capability. The first to be called for the Cadre were Haganah members and women from the towns and agricultural settlements.[10] The attitude of the Haganah leaders and the Jewish Agency to the composition of the candidates for the Cadre was based on their aspiration to train them in shaping the image of the ATS companies.

Even before the beginning of the course, the Haganah sent its candidates on a preparatory course whose objective was the 'mental steadfastness [sic] of the candidates for officer and NCO training, their unity and ... communal life'. The program of this 'course' included four lectures: Sharett lectured on the Hebrew army and the Hebrew officer; Golda (Meir) Meirson lectured on the woman in war; Moshe Sneh lectured on security problems in the Yishuv; and Ya'akov Dori (Dostrovsky) lectured on the tasks of the commander.[11]

The outlines of the tasks and the objectives that the Haganah destined for its female members would appear to have been drafted by one of its leaders at a meeting with female Haganah members in the Cadre about a week into the course.[12] The very fact of a meeting of this kind – there is no knowledge of anything similar with male recruits from the Yishuv – indicates the fears, even among the Haganah commanders, as to the potential conduct of the recruits and the need to supervise their behaviour. Some of the women present at the meeting were veteran Haganah members and others were relatively new. Expectations of the new members were that their behaviour in the army would not differ from that of the veteran members. The 'senior member' used a patronizing tone toward the women, probably in order to emphasize that the recruits were not allowed to behave as they pleased in the army. The recruitment was presented not as a personal decision on the part of the recruits but a mission on behalf of the organization: '*You have not enlisted* in the army. *You were recruited* into the army ... and you have entered into service in the British military only thanks to the fact that the Hebrew Authority has ordered you to enter this service.' [original emphasis]

At this meeting, the Haganah presented the agenda it was imposing on its recruits, and from it there arises the need of men to clarify to women the measure of national recognition they were expected to exhibit:

> *Hebrew authority supersedes* and whoever doesn't understand this, *always and under all circumstances, even this contravenes other discipline is not a hebrew soldier....* at this time ... you are obliged to exhibit excellent obedience toward the British command ... but with this in mind, with Zionism in mind, bearing in mind the Hebrew organization within the Hebrew companies, [you] need to be equipped beforehand. [author's emphasis]

According to that 'senior' member, the Haganah members in the Cadre were supposed to set a moral and cultural example to the rest of the recruits. And indeed, these recruits seem to have internalized the message, since several of them (we know of at least five, including Ahuva Zilberstein) were even suspected of conducting activity on behalf of the Haganah and suspended from military service in the course of 1944. They were returned to service thanks to connections Haganah and Jewish Agency leaders had with the British army.

Activity Patterns of Female Haganah Members in the British Army

The Haganah organization was voluntary in character and succeeded in enforcing its discipline, its control and command over its members in the British army in several fields of operation. Eliyahu Golomb was the major influence in organizing the internal system of the Haganah and provided the source of internal discipline that everyone obeyed. Nevertheless, the Haganah's behavioural concepts in the British army were not clear and recognized in advance, but developed in the course of the war and after the significant increase in the number of Haganah members serving in it. Until the end of the war, the organization never had absolute control over the soldiers, mainly because of the social composition of the recruits, their distribution among the various camps and the refusal of many of them to accept the organization's authority. At the end of 1942, the number of company commanders from Palestine in the British army who were loyal to the Haganah was reduced.[13] The Haganah's power in the army was expressed, for example, in organizing 'protest rallies' and even hunger strikes that took place simultaneously in women's and men's companies. Following the search for weapons in the kibbutzim Hulda and Ramat Hakovesh, the Hebrew servicewomen in the ATS companies expressed their protest by refusing to enter the dining room and their male counterparts behaved in a similar manner in their companies.

The behaviour of the female Haganah members/graduates of the Cadre was already determined at that meeting (during the course) with the senior member of the organization and resembled that of their male counterparts serving in Egypt. It was determined at that meeting that every future unit of Yishuv recruits will include 'Jewish' Haganah members 'with a national and Zionist awareness'.[14] In other words, the organization would ensure that each company had its own representative and the representatives would form an inner core, whose mission it was to activate the periphery of each unit. An additional requirement imposed on that core of Haganah members was not to isolate themselves and to avoid being introverted, and not to distance themselves from other recruits who did not have a national awareness (passive, as the senior put it), but rather to befriend and try to influence them. Despite this directive, there was tension between the Haganah members and the recruits who were far from the 'Organized Yishuv'.

In order to help place recruits in the courses that were beneficial to the Haganah, and in order to identify new recruits who could be brought into the organization, Esther Herlitz was ordered by Shulamit Klibanov to remain in Sarafend as boot camp instructor for a year. According to Herlitz, in order to identify a potential Haganah member from among the new recruits, all that was needed (according to Klibanov's instructions) was to say the code, 'Greetings from Shulamit'. When the need arose to place a particular servicewoman in an armoury course, for example, or to another job that the Haganah required, the code was changed to 'Warm greetings from Shulamit'. Occasionally Haganah members were called to attend an instruction evening and, in order to conceal the real objective of this activity, the recruits would ask the course commander for a Pass to attend a wedding or some other family event.[15]

Contact Between the Recruits and the Haganah Command

In July 1942, about six months after the beginning of recruitment, Klibanov was given membership of the National Command of the Haganah and was the first woman to hold so senior a position in the organization.[16] In accordance with orders from the Haganah high command, two objectives were defined for her when she took up the post: to include women members in defence positions in the fighting forces, and to plan a training system for women, within the framework of homeland security that was established to counter the danger of a German invasion of Palestine. According to Klibanov the decision had already been reached by the Haganah HQ and the Histadrut Security Committee during the Arab riots as a result of pressure by Bat-Sheva Haikin and the Working Women's Movement. Israel Galilee and Rachel Katznelson-Shazar negotiated with Klibanov until Dori granted her the post.[17] Yoav Gelber is convinced that the first round of recruitment of female Haganah members to the ATS, which took place in protest at their inferior status in the organization, is what led to Klibanov's appointment.[18] It would appear that military recruitment prompted the appointment that had been decided upon earlier. In any case, the directives that Klibanov put into operation caused an about-turn in the work of female members of the Haganah.

One of Klibanov's recommendations was to appoint a key member who would be responsible for female Haganah members serving in the ATS. This woman would study their problems and liaise between them and the Haganah HQ. And indeed, Klibanov herself was appointed also to the post of chief recruitment coordinator on behalf of the organization and set Wednesday as the day of the week on which to meet with them. She tried to respond to issues that troubled the women and sought materials for parties, propaganda and social activity, and she also tried to visit them in the camps. Also, a team of Haganah recruiters was established which met once a week to discuss on-going problems, consultations, and defining and preparing educational-propaganda material for distribution among the recruits.[19] During the Cadre course in Sarafend, constant contact was already being maintained with the Haganah and the recruits received instructions and information.

Ruth Birak, a senior commander in the Haganah, was responsible for maintaining contact with the Haganah cells in the army, for ties with Soldiers Welfare Committee, for servicewomen's gatherings, etc.[20] Haganah members who served in the training camp in Sarafend were 'marked' as being the first to come in contact with the new recruits, and for this reason the Haganah wished to invest in their welfare. Their instruction and education were conceived as 'an urgency of the first order'.[21]

Illicit Activity of Haganah Members

In all cultures, war delegates to women a role that is bearable or secondary and, during long periods in history, the privilege of defending the homeland was given only to 'civilians of the highest order', in other words, men. War has been defined as the 'supreme test of masculinity'[22] and nationalism, which is identified with masculinity demands that men make their ultimate sacrifice: giving their lives for a new political entity – the nation. This sacrifice was not available to women. Although the recruits to the British army did not serve as fighters, in the course of their service they did have the chance to participate in illegal activity that was denied to their counterparts in Palestine, like smuggling arms and people, anti-British propaganda, transferring intelligence from army offices, forging documents, etc.

Female Haganah members in the British army were obliged to carry out conflicting missions that created a difficult situation: on the one hand they were required to develop the Jewish companies as excellent and obedient military companies and, on the other hand, they had to exploit the military framework for their organization's illegal activities, in particular, acquisition and illegal immigration.[23]

From the second half of 1943 further chores were imposed on the female Haganah members in the British army, in addition to their 'vocation' as guardians of the national authority and 'morality'. The British forces under Field Marshal Bernard Montgomery beat the German Panzer Army under Field Marshall Rommel at El Alamein and the threat of a German invasion of Palestine was finally lifted. Large weapon reserves were found in the Egyptian Western Desert and the Haganah wished to transfer them to Palestine as part of its preparations for the future struggle against the Arabs. At a later stage, when Jewish refugees started to escape from Europe, the Haganah members in the British army were required to deal with the refugees. The Haganah took advantage of the different military tasks filled by the Jewish servicewomen in the various companies and ordered them to participate in clandestine and illegal activity.

At the end of 1942, some 15,000 Jewish soldiers from the Yishuv were serving in Egypt, including some 2,000 women. The volume of activity that expanded alongside the advance of the British forces in North Africa required that the Haganah send representatives to Egypt, in order to organize local activity and to coordinate between the forces and Haganah command in Palestine. The male recruits from the Yishuv served in about seventy-five different units in the British army and the female recruits in some twenty-five units (out of the twenty-nine ATS companies in the Middle East).

In early 1943, a Haganah HQ was established in Cairo headed by Amnon Zair and Levy Abrahami.[24] Ya'akov Tsur and Ruth Klieger-Aliav, representatives of the Jewish Agency, joined them. This HQ set operated the Haganah members who remained in Egypt and in the Western Desert in acquiring weapons and transferring Jewish refugees through Egypt and North Africa to Palestine and coordinated their activity. Klieger-Aliav was involved mainly in the transfer of refugees who passed through Egypt, including the famous convoy of 'Tehran Children', and in transferring emissaries to the liberated territories in North Africa. A Haganah branch was also opened in Alexandria. The branch commander, albeit not officially appointed, but in accordance with orders from Golomb, was Gershon Ritov, who was serving in the Royal Navy. His wife was with the ATS and serving in Alexandria.

Since this refers to underground activity that is not grounded in any written documents, we can only make an educated guess as to the numbers of male and female Haganah members who participated in illegal activity while serving in the British forces. Almost 500 men, out of the approximately 5,000 Haganah members serving in the army, were involved in this activity. The estimate is that 400 female Haganah members served in the ATS, out of some 3,000 servicewomen, in other words, 15 per cent,[25] although most of these did not maintain active contact with the organization in the course of their military service. Of these, there appear to have been a several dozen who were 'in on the secret' and involved in illegal activity. Graduates of the Cadre and other recruits who filled various command positions in the Haganah in Israel constituted the organization's active core and were referred to as 'active material' or 'our aktiva'.[26]

Several dozen female Haganah members served in the WAAF, but only a few were involved in illegal activity. Among the first batch of recruits most were active Haganah members. Like their counterparts in the ATS who had taken part in the Cadre, they too had enlisted in accordance with unequivocal orders from their Haganah commanders. However, once in the WAAF, their ties with the organization loosened, at least during the first year of their service.[27] In late 1945, following a visit by a senior member of the Yishuv leadership to one of the larger RAF bases in Egypt, the institutions changed their attitude to the WAAF recruits and included them in various activities, most of them illegal, on behalf of the Jewish Agency and the Haganah.

Involvement in this activity also demanded utter secrecy. Often the servicewomen found themselves involved in some activity or other without even knowing about another servicewoman in their company, who was also a Haganah member. In the Haganah, the hierarchy often stood in contrast to that of the British army. On more than one occasion it happened that a senior ranking servicewomen was given an order by another servicewoman whose military rank was lower than hers, but whose status in the Haganah was higher than hers. The code name for the illegal activity carried out by Haganah members in the army was the initials: TTG, tilhas tizi gescheften.[28] The expression turned into a concept, at times a term to describe a Hebrew unit that acted in Egypt, and even to the transfer of information over the phone.

From late 1944, Egypt provided an important transit route for movement between Palestine and Europe and especially to Italy. With the help of the Jewish recruits it was possible both to take advantage of military movement to transport emissaries to Europe and to smuggle illegal immigrants from Italy to Palestine. ATS Jewish servicewomen in various units throughout Egypt were involved in these operations. Later, the operations also included ATS servicewomen stationed on the Italian warfront.[29] The smuggling activity required a system of forging documents, stealing uniforms and transporting refugees in military vehicles or trains.

In Ismailia an elegant villa housed a soldiers' hostel. Via the hostel, communications took place with the Yishuv soldiers who were camped in the Sinai Desert, and Haganah emissaries were smuggled through to Jewish communities in North Africa, from Libya to Morocco. Recha Shtessel managed the hostel and Lilli Steinberg helped her; both women were veteran Haganah members. They took advantage of their work in order to help in smuggling Jewish refugees as well as weapons destined for the Haganah arsenals in the Yishuv.[30] Shmuel Osia, who served in the Canal Region HQ, was responsible for smuggling out the 'cargo'. Jewish servicewomen in the hostel would report to him on which of the military police was on guard duty and then go to the roadblock to flirt with the guards, to distract them and ease the way out for the weapons-bearing trucks.

Two of the servicewomen helped smuggle a female member of Kibbutz Beit Oren into Egypt, who had been sent by the illegal immigration operation (Hamossad le Aliyah Bet) to carry out activity in North Africa.[31] The two waited for her beside Kibbutz Yad Mordechai, provided her with an ATS uniform, equipped her with forged military papers and accompanied her to Egypt, where she was delivered to the Haganah representative. Tamar Eshel (Shoham),[32] too, helped smuggle Haganah emissaries, who had arrived from the Yishuv masquerading as British soldiers, into Egypt. In this way she helped to transfer Haganah emissaries Rafael Racanati and Shlomo Havilio, as well as Asher (Arthur) Ben-Natan, who had been sent to Vienna to take responsibility for the Bricha operation (bringing Holocaust survivors to the Yishuv). Jewish ATS servicewomen in Italy also helped the female emissaries from Palestine to penetrate the refugee camps illegally.[33]

The Yehuda Arazi Affair

The best known instance of servicewomen's involvement in smuggling wanted people was the one of Yehuda Arazi, who was wanted by the British police in Palestine.[34] Arazi was smuggled into Egypt in May 1945. At first he was taken to Cairo and from there to Alexandria and billeted in a safe house – the apartment belonging to Gershon Ritov, commander of the Haganah branch in the town. The two female Haganah members who served in company 522 in Alexandria, Yehudit Bar-Rav-Hai and Rina Barkai (Nick), were entrusted with his safekeeping. The mission involved great personal risk, since, as servicewomen in the British army, they were collaborating with a fugitive from the law.

Bar-Rav-Hai was the first of the two to be called to the task. Ritov told her about it in the midst of a party in one of the units. On Ritov's orders, the company commander, Mina Ben-Zvi released her for a week on the pretext that she had some translating to do. When she arrived at Ritov's apartment she was horrified to see the man most wanted by the British Police in Palestine and Egypt. She moved into the cellar apartment in which Arazi was hidden, saw to his food supply and stayed with him until arrangements were made for him to depart from Egypt. During her stay in the apartment, they were forbidden from going out in the daytime, since Alexandria was teeming with detectives and secret police.

Barkai replaced Bar-Rav-Hai in guarding Arazi. Sometimes, when he couldn't bear to stay in the apartment, she would sneak out with him on a Saturday for a walk on the promenade. When she was on leave in the Yishuv, she visited his family at his request. And when she returned she brought with her the sum of £500 that the Haganah HQ sent him to use for arms purchases in Italy. When it was time for him to leave, Barkai equipped him with a soldier's IDs and a traffic order in the name of Ya'akov (Kova) Filler, a soldier in the 1039 battalion, and Arazi was driven to Cairo.

Prior to Arazi's arrival in Cairo, Hanna Yosselevitz, a Haganah member serving in Cairo, was occupied in forging documents for use in smuggling him out of Egypt. When Arazi returned from Alexandria to Cairo, Yosselevitz and Eshel stayed with him and even went out in the evenings – Eshel on a Nile cruise and Yosselevitz to the cinema; Arazi was in disguise. In July 1945, on his last day in Cairo, Eshel accompanied him, dressed in the uniform of a Polish airman, to an RAF base in Heliopolis. She handed him over to Harry Fredericks, a Jewish pilot who had volunteered to help the Haganah, who flew him in a British aircraft to Italy. Thus, the 'Arazi affair in Egypt' came to an end.[35]

Theft and Forgery

Toward the end of 1944, the smuggling began of Jewish refugees through the Suez Canal into Palestine and it was necessary to dress them in British army uniforms and equip them with military documents in order to avoid suspicion. Jewish servicewomen working in the quartermaster stores in Egypt provided the uniforms. Servicewomen in the company offices, who were responsible for pay books, supplied these documents. This was achieved in two ways: the servicewomen would report a so-called loss or theft of a soldier's document and issue a new one in the soldier's name. The old documents were then handed over to Haganah contacts, who gave them to the refugees. Another method consisted of stealing military documents from the company safe, reporting a theft and passing the stolen documents to the Haganah HQ in Cairo.[36] Servicewomen serving in company 520 in Tel el Kabir, for example, transferred military documents to the Haganah HQ in Cairo, rolled up in their corsets or stockings. Many servicewomen were involved in smuggling documents, including some who were not Haganah members.[37] Similar activity took place in Italy at the end of 1944 and during 1945.

Jewish refugees arriving from Europe were provided with military documents issued for the CMF – Central Mediterranean Forces. In order to enter Palestine as British servicemen they had to have documents issued to the Middle East Forces (MEF). Here, too, some of the Jewish servicewomen were able to help. Shoshana Geller (Rogel) and Hanna Peretz, who both served in Company 507 in Dir Suneid near Gaza, received the European documents, exchanged them to documents suitable to the camp and travelled by jeep to the railway station in Gaza. As one of them was 'having fun' in the station's bar with some military policemen in order to sidetrack them, the other boarded a train and handed over the documents to the Haganah activist for distribution among the new 'soldiers'. The documents from Europe were burned at a safe distance from the station.[38]

WAAF servicewomen also participated in this kind of activity. Rachel Kaspi, who was an officer in the WAAF, described their modus operandi: the servicewoman reported to the authorities that her service certificate had been lost or stolen, was tried for negligence and received a new document. She gave the 'stolen' document to the Jewish officer/Haganah member, who handed it over to the Haganah members who met the refugees. These were then dressed in WAAF uniform and equipped with the relevant documents.[39]

Smuggling Refugees

Jewish refugees were usually smuggled into Palestine from Egypt on troop trains. Several servicewomen accompanied the refugees in person to the railway station in Cairo and saw them safely into the carriages. One of the servicewomen, who had previously secured a pass for a vacation in Israel, accompanied each group on its way out of Egypt. In this way, the Haganah was able to smuggle, 'under the noses' of the British, hundreds of Jewish refugees without the need for official Immigration 'Certificates'.

Servicewomen in Company 507 in the training camp in Dir Suneid were systematically employed in smuggling refugees: a sergeant and Haganah member, who was responsible for arranging transportation for soldiers, shipped out two trucks that were on standby, instead of the one ordered. The 'empty' truck transported refugees. The traffic certificates were duly signed by the Sergeant Zfira Ogen (Katinsky), who was also a Haganah member. The sergeant travelled to Kantara or Rafah and returned with immigrants dressed in British army uniform. She then drove them to the railway station near the camp, where they boarded a train to Palestine.[40]

Ahuva Zilberstein (Strikovsky) of Company 509 in Genifa, the daughter of founders of Kfar Vitkin in the Hefer Valley and a veteran member of Haganah, was involved in an unusual operation to transfer refugees. On orders from Lea Spector, the company's Hebrew officer, Zilberstein travelled to Ismailia, where her mission, which was given the code name 'plaits', was defined. She was to escort a group of Jewish refugee children aged between 2 and 6 years who had come from Libya, to Palestine. The children were put on the train in Alexandria and another servicewoman had escorted them to Ismailia and from there Zilberstein and another serviceman would escort them to Palestine. The younger children were frightened and weeping and many had wet their trousers. The two Haganah escorts moved from carriage to carriage, collecting from the servicemen and women on the train vests and underwear to use as makeshift diapers for the children. In Palestine, the children were met by Jewish Agency emissaries, who placed them in various institutions in the country.[41]

The 502 ambulance drivers' company was transferred in late 1945 to Austria. Among other tasks, the servicewomen helped in the refugee camps. Some of the drivers made use of the ambulances in order to smuggle Jewish refugees, while the company commander, Penelope Otto turned a blind eye.[42] Ziva Talbar (Chizik) and Alice Hazor (Hirsch), for example, transported a group of Czechoslovakian Jews who had been smuggled from Poland by a group from the Jewish Brigade's Third Regiment. The group arrived in Vienna, but had trouble getting from the Russian region to the American and the women drivers carried out the transfer in several batches in their ambulances.[43] Ehud Avriel and Ben-Natan, of the Aliyah Bet leadership who acted in Austria, made contact with driver Naomi Yekutieli (Torok), in order to receive her help. When Yekutieli arrived in Palestine on vacation, the Haganah activists gave her money and jewellery, which she took back to Austria, in order to fund activities on behalf of the refugees. Yekutieli, Yael Arieli (Kornberg) and other Haganah members in the company, also supplied petrol from the army's petrol tanks to people from Aliyah Bet.[44]

The entertainment troupe, 'Me'ain Zeh', whose members came from the Jewish Brigade and the ATS, also helped to smuggle Jewish refugees. The troupe performed to servicemen and women from Palestine throughout the Middle East and Europe between mid-1944 and December 1945.[45] When it appeared in Italy, groups of refugees were in the audience. At the end of the performance, the entertainers hid the refugees in their equipment truck, hiding them behind the props. From there they were taken to a central location pre-determined by emissaries of the illegal immigration operation.[46]

Were the British and the Egyptian authorities aware that refugees were being smuggled into Palestine? Apparently they were. From a report by the British Mandate's Criminal Investigation Department dated August 1945, it appears that they were aware that 'many men, equipped with uniforms and military documents, who were smuggled from Europe via the Mediterranean Sea, were accommodated in transit camps in Egypt and from there were infiltrated into Palestine'.[47] The British army and Secret Police also operated a system of intelligence among the Jewish soldiers. They knew that Jewish servicemen and women were smuggling refugees in military vehicles and trains, but did not conduct any serious searches. They did not ignore the attempts at smuggling but seem to have understood that investing too much effort in eradicating them would not have been financially worthwhile. The Egyptian press occasionally published news on the illegal immigration of Jews, but the authorities made no special efforts to prevent it.

Propaganda Leaflets

An important part of the underground's work was the effect of its propaganda, which consisted of the distribution of publicity leaflets in Palestine and abroad. The Haganah organization attached a great deal of importance to explaining its position and struggle against the British and hoped to include in its ranks soldiers who were not already members. Servicewomen/Haganah members also participated in propaganda activity. When on leave in Palestine they received copies of *Eshnav*, the Haganah sounding board, which they smuggled back to their military bases. They laid the propaganda material on the train luggage rack, to be able to deny all knowledge of it in case the train was searched. WAAF servicewomen, too, distributed Haganah propaganda leaflets against British policies in the Middle East in their bases. In early 1946 a WAAF servicewoman was arrested by the military police on the suspicion of distributing Zionist propaganda among members of the Jewish community in Egypt.[48]

Arms Smuggling

Starting in summer 1942, after the British victory at El Alamein, there accumulated large quantities of weapons left behind by the German army in the Western Desert. Many Haganah activists serving with the British army in Egypt approached the Haganah HQ for instructions on arms acquisition in Egypt. As more and more Hebrew units joined the British forces in Egypt, so did the focus of acquisition and smuggling activity move from Palestine to Egypt.[49] Servicemen and women, members of Haganah, tried to find ways to transfer the weapons to the Yishuv, as part of the organization's preparations for the upcoming struggle against the Arabs that would come after the Second World War. Israel Carmi was the first to successfully smuggle a carful of arms from Egypt to Palestine.[50] Servicewomen, too, mainly from the ATS, participated in weapons smuggling, but there were also some cases of WAAFs helping in the operation, including one instance in which a WAAF smuggled a revolver out of Egypt in her bra.[51]

Abrahami coordinated the weapons smuggling activity from Egypt to Palestine, helped by Eshel and Yosselevitz, who were involved in many underground affairs. The two, assisted by other servicemen, prepared the cover for smuggling activity – forging bills of lading, transport and leave permits, work authorizations for vehicles, etc.[52] At times, when it was impossible to pass on information by telephone, servicemen would travel to remote units to transmit messages, especially regarding acquisition, such as where to transport it to. After passing on the information, they would be back in Cairo at dawn. Female Haganah members also helped in arms smuggling operations in ATS camps throughout Egypt.[53] Thus, for example, a servicewoman who was responsible for organizing the transports in Dir Suneid helped smuggle arms collected in the Western Desert and transported by car to locations in the south of the Yishuv – the kibbutzim Kfar Maneham and Nir Am. At a certain stage, a large quantity of ammunition had accumulated inside the camp. Haganah members were asked to bury the ammunition in a deep pit on the outskirts of the camp. Servicewoman Geller and Officer Werner participated in this activity.[54]

Some servicewomen transferred weapons for self-defence to Jews living in the Jewish neighbourhood of Cairo (Harat el Yahud). In early November 1945 anti-British riots broke out in Cairo and Alexandria. In Cairo a synagogue was burned down, a community school was robbed and several shops were damaged.[55] In Alexandria the riots were more severe, although there were few Jewish casualties. At the same time, the activity to train Jewish youth in self-defence was increased and Haganah emissaries, helped by soldiers-instructors, expanded the training to include weapons. The soldiers held on to the weapons themselves, since a system of stores and slicks had not yet been established.

During this period, Esther Herlitz was made responsible for transferring arms to the Jewish neighbourhood in Cairo. Herlitz, an officer in Company 531 in Tura near the pyramids, instructed the company's driver to transfer to the Jewish neighbourhood a crate of weapons that she had received from the Haganah contact. There, the weapons were transferred to Rakanati, the Haganah emissary in Cairo, who worked with Jewish youth. Herlitz updated the driver about the cargo she was carrying in her car and told her what to say if she was caught, since as a servicewoman she was liable to severe punishment for making use of a military vehicle for carrying out such activity. The mission went according to plan and the servicewomen returned safely to base.[56]

Several servicewomen were suspected of involvement in the theft and smuggling of weapons and they were arrested and searches were made of their property. On 20 December 1944 there took place, for example, a search of the offices of ATS Company 505 in Haifa. Female Military Police arrived on the site before the end of the working day, loaded with servicewomen into military cars and drove them to their living quarters, where a thorough search was made of their personal property. The policewomen were particularly interested in the contents of the servicewomen's correspondence and confiscated some of their letters, but there were no suspicious findings. Even the personal property and room of an officer from Haifa, who, prior to enlistment had been the secretary of Moshe Sharett, and was away from Egypt on leave at the time, was meticulously searched, obviously on suspicion of illegal activity.[57]

In addition to arms the servicewomen also smuggled various instruments needed by Haganah. Zilberstein, for example, worked in a store that contained ship compasses and radar equipment for aircraft. Her job consisted of responsibility for cataloguing the items, ordering equipment and its dispatch to the warfront in Egypt and subsequently in Italy. When a demand arrived from the Haganah for instruments of this kind, Zilberstein would hide them in a bundle of clothes or blankets and send them to the Hebrew companies or Haganah emissaries, as necessary. On such occasions, she reported that the goods were stolen. Tamar Eshel, too, smuggled a wireless set from the UK to Palestine that was made use of by the Haganah.[58]

Transferring Information

The Haganah organization was assisted by the servicewomen who worked in various military offices and enjoyed access to information essential to Haganah activity, especially during periods of curfew in the Yishuv and arrests of activists. In some cases military police, acting on information received, searched the property of servicewomen, but there is no knowledge of any servicewoman being caught smuggling documents.

Bar-Rav-Hai was an office clerk in the Stella Maris camp in Haifa between September 1945 and June 1946. She habitually transferred various important looking documents to two Haganah contacts in Haifa. When she found such a document, she would call the contacts and suggest 'going to the cinema'. Thus, one day Bar-Rav-Hai passed on the information to a member of the Haganah information service that British army had issued an order according to which all military vehicles were to be equipped with a certificate indicating that it was on duty. She handed over the certificate and, after they had copied it, she returned it.[59]

Liah Ronai (Ernst), who served in an engineering corps office in the British HQ in Beirut, was instructed to supply information to the Haganah. Her job required that she know about all the dispatches that arrived by sea at the port of Beirut. She also collected information on movements of British units destined to arrive in Palestine, such as, for example, an infantry company from Italy, or a paratrooper company planned to arrive in Hadera. Her Haganah contacts were Tuvia Arazi (Yehuda's brother) and Abraham Ernst (her own cousin). She brought the information with her when she went on leave to the Yishuv. Ronai had late night meetings with Bracha Habas in the Solel Boneh offices in downtown Haifa and the latter would pass on the information to Haganah HQ.[60]

Recruiting New Members

During the first months of their military service, the Haganah members were given instructions to co-opt additional servicewomen to the organization. The servicewomen established a kind of 'acceptance committee' to recommend people who appeared appropriate. When a suitable recruit was identified, the others held an initiation ceremony that included swearing on the Bible, as in the recruitment of new members to the Haganah in Palestine.[61] The veteran members delivered the list of new recruits to the Haganah HQ in Cairo and from there to the Yishuv. In this way several new members joined the Haganah.

Lehi Members in the British Army

The Lehi organization was established in the summer of 1940 after the IZL ceased its offensive action against the British army. Nonetheless, the female Lehi members/servicewomen in the British army felt no conflict of interests between their service in an army, which they saw as a repressive occupier, and their membership in the underground that had carved on its flag the use of terror against British individuals. They decided to volunteer for the army in order to help an element that fought against Nazi Germany and on behalf of the Jewish nation. They were prepared to play their part in the British war effort, simultaneously carrying out activities against it and for the benefit of the Yishuv, according to their worldview.

From the low number of Lehi members in the British army, a few dozen, out of the hundreds of members in Palestine,[62] and from interviews with Lehi women recruits, it can be concluded that, unlike Haganah the Lehi did not encourage its members to enlist in the army. Whoever did enlist did so in accordance with his/her own conscience and not on behalf of the organization. Initially, the Lehi activity in Egypt was coordinated by Binyamin Gefner, a former IZL member who had left after the split in the movement and went to join the British army. He enlisted despite the lack of encouragement and after others followed suite, the Lehi took advantage of the military jobs available to the male and female recruits for its own needs in Palestine – purchase and smuggling of arms, ammunition and explosives and also in conducting propaganda for the organization among Yishuv recruits and the Egyptian Jewish community.

Servicewomen in the Service of Lehi

All except one[63] of the female Lehi members were recruited into the organization in the course of their military service and had no direct connection to the underground in Palestine. They were recruited mainly due to the opinions they voiced on various occasions regarding events that were taking place in the Yishuv at that time. It is hard to estimate the exact number of the Lehi servicewomen in the British army, but the estimate is that eight servicewomen became active members of the underground, or at least expressed their support for its work in the course of their service. Seven of these women are known by name:[64] Yaffa Tevua (Greenberg), Ruth Gruzin (Grossbard), Ada Leibowitz (Ariel), Hassia Lurie, Malka Chachik, Yehudit Peri[65] and Lilly Tarif. Unlike Haganah members, only a few of who were actively involved in illegal activity, all the Lehi members in the British army, except Peri, were involved in illegal activity.

The recruitment method of these servicewomen into the underground movement was similar to that used in the Yishuv. The organization was very cautious in its recruitment of new members. At first information was collected (opinions voiced, personality) on a potential candidate, his/her reliability and ability to withstand harsh underground conditions. The subsequent interrogation was lengthy and thorough and only people who filled the criteria were accepted to face an acceptance committee. The same applied to the recruitment of servicewomen.[66]

Servicewomen who were also members of Lehi were subjected to the rules of secrecy typical of underground activity. They usually worked in small cells, one knowing nothing about the other and were barely familiar with other members, except for their personal contact person, who connected between her, as well as with all the other Lehi members in the army, and Yosef Galilee (Sitner), who replaced Gefner after he'd gone with his regiment to Europe. Galilee was enlisted in the RAF in 1940 and in the course of his service he was involved in acquiring explosives and arms for the underground organization in Palestine. He also conducted propaganda activity among the local Jewish community, as well as among fellow Jewish soldiers in the British forces, in order to co-opt them to the ideals of the Jewish underground in Palestine. From 1943, Galilee headed the Lehi cell in Egypt under the code name 'Nehemia'. It was he who organized in Egypt, in accordance with instructions from the Lehi centre in Palestine – in fact in accordance with instructions from Yitzhak Shamir (Yazranski) – the murder of Lord Moyne, Britain's Resident Minister in the Middle East.

Illegal Activity of Jewish Servicewomen/Lehi Members

Strangely enough, Yaffa Tevua, who served as a driver in Company 511 in Tel el Kabir, was inspired by Yosef Almogi of the Mapai party to enlist in the ATS. Like many of the servicewomen in the ATS, she spent her spare time in the camp Jewish Club and also in soldiers' clubs in Cairo and Ismailia, where she met servicemen and women from the Yishuv. On different occasions she used to insist openly on the Lehi's right to carry out attacks on the British. On one such occasion she was overheard by a Lehi member serving in the army, who introduced her to Galilee in Cairo. After the meeting, Galilee co-opted her to the organization, although she was never sworn in or underwent an official initiation ceremony. Her underground code name was 'Ilana'.

In the army Tevua was employed mainly in driving trucks in convoys. Her first mission in the service of the underground was to smuggle leaflets containing Lehi propaganda material. When she returned from one of her vacations, she brought with her copies of Lehi publications *Hama'as* (The Act) and *Hahazit* (The Front) that she'd received from Anchel Spielman, her contact in the Yishuv. She distributed the leaflets in the Jewish soldiers' clubs in Egypt. Tevua's job, which also consisted of parking trucks in the army base's car park, enabled her to smuggle grenades and bullets to the underground. Australian drivers brought in the trucks that arrived laden with weapons from the Western Desert, which the drivers made a habit of leaving in the trucks overnight. Tevua quickly set about collecting weapons and ammunition, stuffing them into her military kitbag and, on her next leave, she smuggled them into the Yishuv.

At a later stage, Tevua was given the post of camp ambulance driver. She moved into a separate tent from the other servicewomen and, after the death of her tent-mate (probably committed suicide), she had the tent to herself. This made her activity so much easier. Sometimes, she even smuggled weapons in the camp ambulance. Eliyahu Hakin and Eliyahu Beit-Tsuri, who carried out the murder of Lord Moyne, obtained weapons from various sources and transferred them to her. She took advantage of the fact that the British did not make a habit of checking the ambulance and transferred the weapons on to a Lehi member employed in Cairo as a civilian railway worker.[67]

Ruth Gruzin enlisted in the WAAF in 1943. While in the wireless course in Helwan, the RAF's school for communications in Egypt, she was overheard by a Lehi member/army serviceman, who introduced her to Galilee. Her code name was 'Dalia'. Together with Ada Leibowitz, she worked as a wireless operator at an Air Force base in Alexandria. On orders from the Lehi underground, Gruzin habitually removed from the camp's stores radio parts, especially crystals, and smuggled them into Palestine when she went on leave. The parts were used for the underground radio station in the Yishuv, from which Geula Cohen (right-wing, former Member of Knesset) used to broadcast. Gruzin also smuggled out pay books, provided to her by Leibowitz.[68]

Leibowitz, whose underground name was 'Ginger', was the only one of the servicewomen who had been a Lehi member prior to her recruitment to the British forces. She had joined Lehi after its split from the IZL, underwent a commanders training course and filled various positions in the underground, including secretary of the underground publishing house and bodyguard to senior Lehi member,

Ya'akov (Yashke) Eliav. Between 1941 and 1943 she was employed as a military secretary on a British army base in Palestine. At the end of 1943, she enlisted in the WAAF and served as a wireless operator in Alexandria. Leibowitz made a habit of stealing pay books from her base for the use of Lehi members and also supplied forged pay books to Hakim and Beit-Tsuri for use in their escape from Egypt following the murder of Lord Moyne.

There is little available information about other Lehi members in the British forces. Chachik was identified as an underground member by Rafael Sadovsky, an Egyptian Jew who helped the Lehi and IZL in their activity, but by the time of the murder of the British minister she had already dropped out of subversive activity.[69] Lilly Tarif, a Jewish servicewoman in ATS Company 525, was arrested on suspicion of involvement in the murder of Lord Moyne. The Military Police in Cairo suspected her of being a Lehi member or associate of it, after she had voiced her support for the September 1944 murder of police detective Thomas Wilkin in Jerusalem, by members of Lehi.[70] Hassia Lurie was a driver in the ATS and helped Galilee in coordinating Lehi activity in Egypt. When she met a Jewish pilot in the RAF, she asked to cease her work with the underground and was transferred to serve as a driver in one of ATS companies in the Yishuv.

Involvement in the Murder of Lord Moyne

The involvement of female Lehi members in the murder of Lord Moyne on 6 November 1944 received more publicity than all their other underground activity. Yaffa Tevua and Ruth Gruzin were partners to the preparations for the assault, but did not actually participate in it. Their job was to act as girlfriends to Hakim and Beit-Tsuri in reconnoitring potentially suitable locations for the murder. According to their testimony, they were both aware that there was going to be a murder and they were ready to participate in preparations for it, notwithstanding the heavy consequences, interrogations and imprisonment if they were caught. They were persuaded by Galilee of the necessity of employing personal terror tactics against Lord Moyne, who blocked the gates to Palestine to Jewish Holocaust survivors, and that it was necessary to shock the world out of its indifference to Britain's intransigence.

When preparations began in the Yishuv's Lehi HQ for the assassination, Gruzin was informed that she was to travel to Ismailia and collect forged pay books for Hakim and Beit-Tsuri. The two were supposed to arrive in Egypt disguised as British soldiers. Gruzin flew from Cairo to Ismailia and, in the lavatories of the YMCA club, which served as a meeting place for British army recruits, she received the pay books from a soldier/Lehi member. These she transferred to Palestine shortly after. When Hakim and Beit-Tsuri arrived in Egypt, she was given the task of escorting Beit-Tsuri in observing the home of Lord Moyne. Gruzin, who served in Alexandria, took part in observing the building when she was on leave from her base.

Tevua, who served in Tel el Kabir, was closer to Cairo and was therefore more accessible and mobile. She escorted Hakim several times in observing the Minister's residence in a Cairo suburb. They used to walk together arm in arm like a courting couple, a technique employed often by the Lehi in Palestine in planning its activities. In September 1944, Tevua arrived at the Jewish club in Cairo, where she met Galilee and, for the first time, Eliyahu Hakim. Tevua and Hakim went together to the home of Rafael Sadovsky, where Gruzin was waiting for them. The four went to the Astoria Café in Cairo and joined Beit-Tsuri who had also come from Palestine. Together they planned the observation process on Lord Moyne's residence in Cairo, with the objective of learning his habits and to decide on the best way to murder him.[71]

That same day, Gruzin accompanied Hakim on a walk to Lord Moyne's Cairo residence, while Tevua went with Galilee to reconnoitre the minister's office. From that day on, Tevua escorted Hakim twice a week and together they observed Moyne's home, which was ultimately chosen as the murder scene. On one occasion the two travelled to the site of the pyramids in order to try out the gun that was to be used in the assassination. From time to time they would dine in Cairo's oriental restaurants, trying to avoid meeting their fellow servicemen and women from the Yishuv, who could recognize Tevua. At one point, it was suggested that Tevua should wait with her military ambulance beside Lord Moyne's residence, so as to escape with the assassins immediately after the act. But this plan did not go into operation, probably because of the order from the Lehi HQ not to openly involve servicemen or women in an act that could cause harm to all the Yishuv's recruits.

A little while before the designated time for the murder, Tevua was ordered to drive to Alexandria and to bring back pay books and various documents for Hakim and Beit-Tsuri, with which the two were meant to make their escape from Egypt after the murder, dressed in British army uniform. She arrived in Alexandria, where she was informed that Galilee had been arrested on suspicion of placing a bomb at the pan-Arab Congress taking place there (with no connection to the planned murder). Tevua used her initiative, managed to locate Ada Leibowitz at her RAF base and obtained the forged documents.

Tevua returned to Cairo with the documents and updated Sadovsky on the events. He prepared a letter to the Lehi HQ and ordered her to take it immediately to the Yishuv. Since she was not in a position to take any leave of absence, she gave the letter to another servicewoman who was about to leave and asked her to hand it over to a contact. Tevua, who knew she was endangering the other woman, warned her that in the event of a search by the British army, she was to destroy the letter. Tevua's cover story to the other woman was that the envelope contained a letter to her lover in Tel Aviv. About a week before the date of the murder, Tevua herself went back to the Yishuv for a vacation. When the time came for her return to Egypt, her underground contact gave her a letter, two guns and a bag of explosives to deliver to Hakim and Beit-Tsuri for use in the attack on Lord Moyne. In order to avoid being searched, Tevua joined a convoy of women drivers that made its way from Palestine to Egypt. She placed the objects she'd received from the underground in a kitbag in an open command car and when she arrived at the camp it turned out that the bag had been stolen on the way, that the attack had already taken place and that Lord Moyne had been murdered.[72]

Several ATS servicewomen were arrested in wake of the murder on suspicion of involvement in the affair. Pictures of Beit-Tsuri and Hakim were published in all the newspapers in Egypt and two soldiers, apparently members of Haganah, testified that they had seen the two fugitives on various occasions in the company of ATS servicewomen. The Military Police scoured the ATS companies in Egypt for servicewomen who had been absent from their base on the day of the murder and even carried out a few arrests, but found that these women had nothing to do with the murder.[73] At this stage of the investigation the Military Police were not yet on the trail of Tevua and Gruzin, and they were not suspected of involvement in the murder.

Hakim and Beit-Tsuri were caught immediately after the murder and executed in Cairo after a trial that lasted several months. Sadovsky turned in Tevua, Gruzin and Leibowitz, together with the rest of the underground members involved in the murder, to the British authorities.[74] The women were arrested in May 1945, six months after the murder, released from the army and transferred to Palestine and sent to the women's prison in Bethlehem, where they spent two years.

Lurie was also arrested, for another matter (the weapons slick). The remaining underground members were not arrested.

Lehi members in the British forces, like their Haganah counterparts, carried out activity – arms smuggling and forging documents – that was enabled by the fact of their military service outside of the Yishuv. Other work, such as tracking or collecting information could have been done by underground members who stayed behind in the Yishuv, but the situation was completely different with regard to the enlisted women because they were serving in a regular army.

Effects of the Murder on Relations among Members of the Organizations

Following the Lord Moyne murder the British raised the level of surveillance and flash searches of Jewish servicewomen. One of the results of the new situation was a temporary hiatus in weapons acquisitions by the Haganah in Egypt. The Haganah HQ in Cairo redeployed and its members now included Shalom Levin, Gershon Ritov and Israel Levites, who were assisted – as before – by servicewomen Hanna Yosselevitz and Tamar Eshel. On occasion, Amnon Zair also took part in discussions.

Until the murder, there had been no interaction between the members of Haganah and Lehi in the army. Active Haganah members, who often had no idea of the existence of each other within the same company, were not familiar with the Lehi members working under complete secrecy for their own underground movement. But things changed after the murder. It took place at the height of the 'Hunting Season',[75] and it serves as an example of the way the struggle in the Yishuv leaked its way into the army. Indeed, the Haganah's objective during the Season was to keep track of the IZL members and hand them over to the British, but in wake of the murder, the Haganah HQ in Egypt was now required to follow the movements of Lehi members in the various army units, to report to the Yishuv of its findings and also to report on the trial of the murderers.[76]

Representatives of the Jewish Agency and Haganah – Teddy Kollek[77] and Reuven Shilo'ah (Zaslani) – arrived in Cairo and were asked by the British to reveal the plans of IZL and Lehi. Kollek received permission to 'recruit' servicemen and women from the Yishuv and serving in Cairo to help in locating 'dropouts' (the nickname given by Haganah members to members of the underground movements). Abrahami, too, received dispensation from the military authorities to release several soldiers for a few hours daily from their regular duty for this purpose. Eshel, who served in the Education Corps and worked in the library, was chosen for the mission together with Yosselevitz, Levin and Levites. However, in the end soldiers were hardly used in this mission and were employed instead in the field of acquisition, smuggling immigrants and illegal immigration.

Sonya Peres, who served as a truck driver in Company 511 in Tel el Kabir, was sometimes employed as substitute driver of the camp ambulance. Occasionally, and unknown to her, Peres was involved in smuggling weapons in the ambulance that Yaffa Tevua carried out on behalf of the Lehi. Ruth Kaplan (Melamed), too, sometimes replaced Tevua as the camp's ambulance driver but suspected her of underground activity. Peres and Melamed were Haganah members, but were not active.[78]

Tevua became ill shortly after the murder and was hospitalized near the camp. A few days later, a group of hebrew female officers accompanied by British Secret Police officers arrived to interrogate Tevua, but her condition did not allow this and the officers left the camp. Peres took Tevua's uniform and went immediately to the hospital. Although she was burning with fever, Tevua urged Peres to take her back to camp. Peres acquiesced and drove Tevua, lying on the ambulance floor so as to avoid being seen, back to camp. Back in Tevua's tent, Peres helped destroy and burn letters and documents that would indicate Tevua's ties with the underground and were hidden under the tent floor. By this time, Peres understood that her friend was involved in something much more serious but she did not betray her. Peres had no reservations over any moral dilemma, because she had no doubt that, under those circumstances, loyalty to a friend in trouble overrode any national considerations. After burning all the documents, Peres drove Tevua back to the hospital. Two days later, Tevua was arrested in hospital and taken for interrogation.[79]

The Recruits in the Narratives of their Organizations

Although women filled key positions in many and varied missions, often at the risk of endangering their lives, their part in history has been neglected. The service of recruits from the Yishuv in the British army in general has been excluded from the Yishuv's historiography (unlike that of the Palmach and Haganah, for example) and the part played by women recruits in the national narrative is smaller still.

Claims that not only were women excluded from the actual battlefronts, but from their part in the narratives,[80] has motivated gender researchers to study the issue.[81] The study began to emerge from the central national narrative and alienated its totality. In its wake, there emerged marginal accounts of social sectors that had disappeared, were pushed aside or silenced, to burst through the monolithic boundaries of narrative and to create a multi-voice discourse. The central narrative, therefore, has been given a new and critical light.[82] Thus also in the study of the role of women in Zionism and the Yishuv.[83]

In the memoires of male Haganah members who served in the British forces there is virtually no mention of their female counterparts. Testimonies of the activity carried out by female Haganah members were provided solely by the servicewomen themselves.[84] It would appear that women, too, contributed to the disregard of their part in the war and 'stood on the sidelines' as did generations of women before them. Halperin, commander of the Haganah's women's regiment in Tel Aviv, admitted, 'we didn't know how to make ourselves stand out. After all the work had nothing to do with significant events and we had been educated to modesty, to the fact that some things are best kept silent.'[85] Even Habas wrote that they were 'mere trifles, a few crumbs under the wheels of a huge history'.[86]

The study of the part played by the members of Lehi in the British forces underwent a process that was the opposite of that in the Haganah narrative. For many years, the activity of the Haganah remained obscure, whereas the role played by the Lehi women in the British forces is emphasized in books devoted to the Lehi operations and, in particular, the murder of Lord Moyne. Possibly in a small and compartmentalized organization such as Lehi, where the percentage of women members was larger, there was more scope for describing their activity. Lehi members who participated in preparations for the murder are the only ones who came out of it alive. The murder of Lord Moyne was an event that made international waves and its female participants were exposed and received considerable publicity.[87]

It would seem that the roles filled by female Haganah and Lehi members in the army and the missions they carried out were right for 'the hour' and the unique circumstances in which they lived. When these ended, so did their roles and they did not carry out similar activity in Palestine. Most of the Haganah members/servicewomen mentioned in this chapter were released from service at the end of the war, established families and returned to their 'regular' lives. The captured Lehi women spent two years in prison, until the British left the region in 1948. They took no further part in Lehi activity. Some of the Haganah and Lehi women who served in the British forces went on to join the Israel Defence Forces, where they served as regular soldiers

NOTES

1. Like men, women played roles in revolutionary movements worldwide. In the Second World War, too, women were members of various underground bodies, such as those in France, Holland and Belgium. On women in the French Underground, see, for example, Margaret Collins Weitz, 'Soldiers in the Shadows: Women of the French Sexual Integration', in Gerard Degroot and Corinna Peniston-Bird (eds), A Soldier and a Woman (Essex 2000), pp.135–51; on fighting Jewish women in underground movements in occupied Europe, who filled roles that Jewish men were unable to do (couriers, weapons smugglers, etc.), see for example, Ephraim Wichselfisch, *Nashim Yehudiot lohamot bemilhemet ha'olam hashniya* [Jewish women fighting in the Second World War] (Jerusalem 2000).
2. Hanoch Patishi, *Mahteret be'madim: 'Haganah' ve'hayalim ha'eretz Israelim betzava habriti* [Underground in uniform: Haganah and the Eretz Israel servicemen in the British army, 1939–1946] (Tel Aviv 2006), pp.47–8. The organization hoped to rebuild itself after its status in the Yishuv had been shaken by the 1936–39 Arab uprising, but stopped dealing with recruitment when this did not happen. Slutsky, Yehuda (ed.), *Sefer toldot ha'aganah* [History of the Haganah], B and C (Tel Aviv 1973), p.685.
3. Testimony of Zilla Dobrin, December 7, 1971, p.6, Haganah History Archive, Tel Aviv (HHA), 97.31. Interview with Sara Kopler (Bar-Adon), Tel Aviv, 26 June 2006. Kopler pointed out that the persuasion tactics of these men was the main reason for her decision to enlist in the army.
4. Minutes of recruiters' meeting, 8 March 1942, Central Zionist Archive, Jerusalem (CZA), S25/5099.
5. According to Israel Galilee of the Labour Movement leadership, leader of the UKM and member of the National Command of the Haganah, at a conference in Givat Haim, one of the participants reprimanded Golomb that she had decided to enlist, but after hearing his words, her decision seemed mistaken and she didn't understand why she should enlist. Galilee added that the impression from Golomb's words was 'that the Haganah was the enemy of female recruitment to the British army'. 'Conversation with Israel Galilee', 17 May 1942, p.2, HHA, Galilee Files, number 8.
6. Interview with Haya Ironi-Abrahami, Tel Aviv, 8 February 2006. According to her, no debate in the organization was devoted to the issue and even the 'Live Newspaper' (the Hagana's verbal sounding board for Sabbath eve debates that aimed at encouraging the female members) did not issue a call to enlist. This might have been due to the social composition of the regiment's members, who were mostly in their 20s, came from poor families, worked for their living and their activity in the regiment took place after work and on Saturdays.

7. According to her, the recruitment of women commanders who were of a high level lowered the quality of work in the Haganah. Testimony of Rachel Tsabari (undated), pp.3–4, HHA, 117/2. Mary Hayam, who had been a member of Haganah, recalled the debate on recruitment of Haganah commanders to the Cadre course. According to her, although this was considered prestigious and most of the women agreed to go of their own free will, 'there were still members who had to be pressured into going. At the time we used means against "evasion" – in other words, those who were supposed to enlist but were reluctant to do so. Later, there came the announcement on compulsory recruitment [following the June 1942 call] and any member who did not comply – was called for a hearing.' 'Female Haganah Members', p.6, HHA, 16/2.
8. UKM Council in Yagur, 6–7 February 1942, p.37, Israel Defense Forces (IDF) Archive, Tel Hashomer, 45/140/2002; Haktin's speech, ibid, p.21.
9. Arieh Pialkov and Yosef Rabinovitz (eds), *Yitzhak Tabenkin: pirkei haim, ha'ish ve po'alo, haverim ve talmidim mesaprim, sugiot bemishnato* [Yitzhak Tabenkin: chapters from his life, the man and his activity, friends and students recall, issues in his teachings] (Ramat Efal 1982), p.79.
10. In its early stages, the kibbutz movements opposed female recruitment, thus the first recruits, apart from a few from the agricultural sector in defiance of their movements' orders, came from the towns.
11. Letter from Rachel Friedlander to Moshe Sharett, 7 January 1942, CZA, S25/5099.
12. Lecture by a senior member of the organization, 4 February 1942, HHA, 117/16. The document indicates that the lecture was most likely given by Golomb. In his book, Gelber determines that it was indeed Golomb, but it could have been Sneh or Dori. Yoav Gelber, *Toldot hahitnadvut: Hahitnadvut ve mekoma bemidiniut hazionit ve hayishuvit 1939–1942* [History of volunteering: volunteering and its place in Zionist and Yishuv Policies 1939–1942] (Jerusalem 1989), p.487. However, the preparatory course was supposed to have taken place prior to the beginning of the Cadre, but a few days beforehand, it was still unclear when it would start and it is possible that the preparation was given in the middle of the course.
13. Yoav Gelber, 'Aspectim politiim lehakamat hakoah halohem beyishuv haeretzisraeli btkufat milhemet haolam hashnia' [Political aspects in establishing the fighting force in the Yishuv during WWII], *Yalkut Moreshet*, 22 (November 1976), pp.49–51; Patishi, *Mahteret be'madim*, pp.47–8. The officers who were loyal to the Haganah were appointed mainly in accordance with directions from the organization in Israel. Jewish Agency representative Yehoshua Gordon was a member of the committee that appointed officers, and he passed on, with the recommendation of the Haganah supreme command, the names of potential officers. The Agency, and in particular its political department, strived to strengthen the Hebrew units by integrating officers into them in the hope this would lay the foundation of a future Hebrew military force.
14. The Haganah History Archive houses a document containing the names of sixty-three female Haganah members, according to the companies in which they served. List of Haganah Representatives (undated, probably 1943–44), HHA, 33/10.

15. Esther Herlitz, *Esther: o Le'an kvar Isha Yechola Le'hagia* [Esther: or how far could a woman go?] (Tel Aviv 1995), p.23.
16. In the same month, she also replaced Judith Simhonit as a member of the Histadrut's Security Committee.
17. Testimony of Shulamit Klibanov (undated), p.4, HHA, 160.42.
18. Gelber relies on a letter by Galilee: 'Today, we decided in the Executive on a change in attitude to the issue of [training of the woman], to appoint a woman to the position and to issue an order to include women ...; to hold training camps in Glilot for many instructresses.' Letter from Galilee to his wife, 23 March 1942, HHA,. Galilee Files, no.8; Yoav Gelber, *Toldot hahitnadvut: Nos'ei hadegel* [History of volunteering: bearers of the flag] (Jerusalem 1983), p.492. Motti Golani is convinced that one of the repercussions of female volunteering for military service was a change in the status of female members in Haganah, and especially in the training of women recruits to the Palmach. Golani, 'Volunteering for the Army', 26 March 1989, p.1, HHA, 118/24.
19. Arieh Lipshitz and Rachel Lerer (eds), *Shulamit Klibanov: Le diokana* [In her image] (Jerusalem 1969), p.2. Thus, for example, there were recruits who participated in weapons practice (guns for self-defence) that was passed on to them by Haganah members who stayed in Israel. These lessons took place under absolute secrecy, over a period of time, by the light of an oil lamp in the Working Women's commune in Tel Aviv. In order to keep out uninvited guests a guard was posted outside the hut. Training ended when the recruits left the country and took up their work as ambulance drivers in Egypt. Haya Ironi-Abrahami, *Almoniot bekhaki: Sipuran shel havrot ha'Hagana be'Tel Aviv* [Anonymous women in khaki: the story of the female Members of the Haganah in Tel Aviv] (Tel Aviv 1989), p.128.
20. Birak, too, enlisted in the ATS at a later stage. According to Klibanov, in 1940 they were all focused on recruitment to the ATS. Shulamit Klibanov, 'Chapter Titles to the Matter of Membership in Haganah' (undated, probably the 1950s or 1960s), pp.1–2, HHA, 132.37. As the selection process for the Cadre began in December 1941, the reference is probably to that year.
21. 'Report on the Haganah Girls' (undated, probably from the late 1940s and early 1950s), HHA, 16/14. The document was probably written by Klibanov (there is a reference on the top of the document that was written by Shaul Avigur on 10 March 1953, in which he assumes that it was she who wrote the paper).
22. George L. Mosse, *Fallen Soldiers, Reshaping the Memory of the World Wars* (Oxford: Oxford University Press, 1991), pp.34–9. Masculinity was considered the epitome of ideals such as strength, morality, justice, faith and conscience, and as a means for personal and national renewal. On the connection between masculinity and nationalism, see also, Ilana Beit El, 'Gvarim, gavriut umilhama: migdar bemilhemet haolam harishona' [Men, masculinity and war: gender in the First World War], *Zmanim*, 65 (Winter 1998–99), pp.112–20.
23. Attempts to fulfil both these missions caused friction and misunderstanding within the organization, the repercussions of which were felt in the years to come after the soldiers were released from military service. Some 5,000 Haganah members served in the British forces. The British were aware of this. Slutsky, *Sefer toldot ha'aganah*, p.729.

24. Patishi, *Mahteret be'madim*, pp.127–41. In addition to dealing with Haganah matters in the army and maintaining on-going contact with soldiers who were also Haganah members, Zair (according to him) also dealt with problems of motivation among the servicemen and in bringing soldiers from Palestine closer to Zionsim and the national institutions. The servicewomen/Haganah members knew Zair and were in constant contact with him. Amnon Zair, *Vienna–Gan Shmuel* (Gan Shmuel 1980), pp.74–5; Slutsky, Sefer toldot ha'aganah, p.728.
25. At this stage, according to Klibanov's estimation, there were some 10,000 female Haganah members. Klibanov, 'Chapter Titles to the Matter of Membership in Haganah', p.2. In his book that deals with the IDF and the Haganah, Moshe Pearlman points out that 'thousands of women from the Yishuv served in the ATS ... almost all of who were Haganah members'. Moshe Pearlman, *The Army of Israel* (London 1950), p.36. He is inaccurate on this point.
26. Klibanov, 'Report on the Girls in the Haganah' (undated), p.5, HHA, 16/14.
27. In each ATS Company there was one Haganah activist who maintained ties with the HQ. This arrangement was not possible in the WAAF, which is why no ongoing contact took place between Haganah members in the WAAF and the HQ in Israel or in Cairo during the early stages of their service. Yosef Shavit, *Mitnadvim bekahol: eretzisraelim besherut heil hate'ufa hamalchuti [Volunteers in blue: from Eretz Israel to service in the RAF]* (Tel Aviv 1995), pp.134–5. Recruits who had been Haganah members prior to enlistment were sorry for this fact and, in retrospect, they believed this to have been a mistake on the part of the Haganah not to have taken advantage of their various jobs for its benefit at an earlier stage. Interview with Brucha Ben-Haim (Eisenberg), Nahalal, 7 January 2006; Interview with Ellen Elroi, Bat Yam, 4 February 2006.
28. Which stood for a combined Arabic and Yiddish derogatory phrase, 'Kiss my ass business.' Patishi, *Mahteret be'madim*, pp.224–6; Herlitz, *Esther*, pp.24–5.
29. On smuggling emissaries, see Yoav Gelber, *Toldot hahitnadvut: Nos'ei hadegel* [History of volunteering: bearers of the flag] (Jerusalem 1983), pp.84–95; Patishi, *Mahteret be'madim*, pp.181–6; During the war Meir (Monia) Mardor, a Haganah member and one of the leaders in the smuggling of arms into Israel, organized the Jews of Iraq and taught them self-defence. Among other things, a wireless instrument was arranged and its operator was Malka Rofe from Kibbutz Ma'oz Haim. Her operators were undecided as to whether to send her there dressed in ATS uniform. However, the sight of a female soldier would have aroused suspicion since women did not serve in this part of the Middle East, and the plan was dropped. In the end it was decided to smuggle her into Iraq in the uniform of a British male soldier, with the help of forged documents obtained by female Haganah members serving in the ATS. Meir Mardor, *Shlihut aluma: pirkei mivza'im me'iuhadim bema'archot hahaganah* [Silent mission: chapters on special operation in the service of defence] (Tel Aviv 1957), pp.96–7.
30. In Ismailia there were stone buildings that housed which British civil servants employed in the construction of the Suez Canal. When the British civilians were evacuated from Egypt in the middle of 1940 the houses were handed over to the recruits. The servicewomen's hostel was located in a neglected French villa

which was refurbished and adapted for its new purpose. Shtessel recalled that the villa provided cover for Haganah activity in the region and she often spent nights with guns under her pillow, not for her security, but in order to keep them hidden. The weapons, which the servicewomen had brought from the Western Desert in bundles of clothing aimed for the Tehran Children, were taken from the hostel. Often refugees were smuggled through the hostel in Ismailia, too. Zivia Cohen, 'From Ismailia to Beer Sheva', *Lamerhav*, 5 May 1966, p.6.

31. Possible reference to Klieger-Aliav, who conducted fundraising activity in Egypt on behalf of illegal immigration. According to her own testimony, she had travelled several times between Egypt and the Yishuv and twice had almost been captured by the British in Kantara. But she had always managed to save herself. Ruth Klieger Eliav and Peggy Mann, *Hamiflat ha'aharon* [The Last Resort] (Tel Aviv 1976), p.4.
32. Niece of Avshalom Feinberg of the Nili underground, Eshel had been a member of the Haganah from her youth. When war broke out she was studying in London where, as a British citizen, she first enlisted in the ATS in Britain and served in various positions. In 1944, she asked to be transferred to the Middle East, where she served in the ATS's Hebrew companies. Interview with Tamar Eshel (Shoham), Tel Aviv, 16 November 2005.
33. At the end of 1945, there was a growing need to reinforce the refugee camps in Italy with emissaries from Israel in order to help in educational activity in the camps. The only way to achieve this was to bring them in 'vacation groups' of ATS servicewomen. Yehuda Arazi, who oversaw the acquisitions activity in Italy, was asked to leave in Italy servicewomen who were supposed to go on leave in Israel and to send in their place, female refugees dressed in ATS uniform and equipped with military documents. In Israel, the documents were given to emissaries who could then leave for Europe.
34. Arazi was a key operative in the theft of weapons from the British army, transferring them to the Haganah. Following the Reichlin-Sirkin trial (two Haganah activists sentenced to many years in prison for their part in smuggling weapons to the organization), Arazi went underground in late 1943 and hid in various safe houses for over a year. He became the British police's most wanted fugitive and a large sum of money was offered to anyone who led to his arrest. The Haganah sought a way to smuggle him out of Israel and transfer him to Italy, where he could work on arms acquisitions. In a difficult and extremely dangerous operation, he was smuggled into Egypt dressed as a British soldier. Patishi, *Mahteret be'madim*, pp.297–300. On Arazi and his activity, see also Adir Cohen, *Beru'ah Se'ara: prakim mehayav upo'alo shel Yehuda Arazi* [In the eye of the storm: chapters from the life and activity of Yehuda Arazi] (Tel Aviv 1966); Adir Cohen, *Alon basa'ar: alilot rechesh upirkei ha'apala* [Oak in the storm: stories of purchasing and chapters in illegal immigration] (Tel Aviv 1973).
35. Tamar Eshel's Memoires, p.80. Testimony of Hana Yosselevitz, 12 January 1960, pp.2–3, HHA, 24.35.
36. Ironi-Abrahami, *Almoniot bekhaki*, p.174. The connection between female Haganah members serving in Dir Suneid and their handlers was conducted via Rachel Adiv, a civilian working on base on behalf of the Soldiers' Welfare Committee, who passed on their missions to the servicewomen. Fridel Stern, who served on this base as an instructor in a camouflage course, was not a

Haganah member, but collaborated with the organization. Interview with Tzfira Ogen (Katinsky), Tel Aviv, 20 December 2005.

37. Patishi, *Mahteret be'madim*, p.83.
38. Interview with Shoshana Geller (Rogel), Tel Aviv, 20 April 2007.
39. Shavit, *Mitnadvim Bekahol*, pp.134–5.
40. Bracha Habas , *Bnot hayil: sefer ha'ATS* [Women of valour: book of the ATS] (Tel Aviv 1964), p.135.
41. Interview with Ahuva Zilberstein (Strikovsky), Herzliya, 23 July 2006.
42. The illegal immigration activists in Italy may have already heard of Penelope Otto's Zionist sympathies. The connection between the ATS drivers and the Haganah emissaries who were involved in Aliyah Bet (illegal immigration) was formed via Ben-Natan (who was smuggled into Italy dressed as a soldier from the Jewish Brigade and from there to Austria). The ATS ambulance drivers arrived in the small town of Veldeu in Austria in order to remove wounded prisoners of war from the hospitals and take them to POW camps not far from Vienna.
43. Talbar, who came from Rehovot, was a member of the extended Chizik family and a member of Haganah. German-born Hazor, was a Haganah member from youth. She served at first as a driver with Company 511 in Tel el Kabir, and was transferred to the ambulance company in 1944, shortly before moving with the company to serve in Italy.
44. At first Arieli, born in Jerusalem to parents of German origin, had been a driver in Company 507 in Dir Suneid. In 1943 she was transferred to Company 502 as an ambulance driver. Yekutieli is one of three sisters (together with Aliza and Tirza) from Jerusalem's Torok family; all three served as drivers in the same company.
45. Eliyahu Goldenberg, who had been in the first military entertainment troupe from the Yishuv, established the troupe. Entertainment troupes in Palestine were based on the ENSA (Entertainment National Service Association) format. The troupe included Mordechai Zeira, Shlomo Duetscher (Drori), Hanna Maron, Yossi Yadin (Sukenik) and others. Shimon Lev-Ari, 'Hitpathut hate'atron hamishni 1928–1948' [Development of the alternative theater], in Moshe Lissak (ed.), *Toldot hayishuv hayehudi be'eretz Israel me'az ha'aliyah harishona: bniyata shel tarbut ivrit* [History of the Jewish Yishuv in Eretz Israel since the First Aliyah: building a Hebrew culture], A (Jerusalem 1993), pp.610–11.
46. Interview with Hanna Maron (Meierzak), Tel Aviv, 28 February 2006.
47. Ephraim Dekel, *Benitivei habricha* [On the roads of escape] (Tel Aviv 1959), p.359.
48. Shavit, *Mitnadvim bekahol*, p.140; Gelber, *Toldot hahitnadvut: Nos'ei hadegel*, p.88.
49. On the property theft from British army camps in Palestine and the court martials that followed (the most famous of which was the Reichlin-Sirkin trial), see Yoav Gelber, *Toldot hahitnadvut: Hama'avak letzava Ivri* [History of volunteering: The Struggle for a Hebrew Army] (Jerusalem 1991), pp.176–89, and Patishi, *Mahteret be'madim*, pp.109–13.
50. Carmi, who served in a commando unit in Egypt, wanted to prove to the Haganah HQ that it was possible to do so. He managed to smuggle rifles, machine guns

and appropriate ammunition. After crossing all the British army blocs and examinations he arrived in Palestine and displayed the goods at the Histadrut Executive building. Levi Abrahami testimony, 30 March 1950, HHA, 2.11.

51. Shavit, *Mitnadvim bekahol*, p.140.
52. Gelber, *Toldot hahitnadvut: Hama'avak letzava Ivri*, p.187. For more on the smuggling operations from Egypt to Palestine, see ibid., pp.178–81; Hanoch Patishi, 'The 'Hagana' Organization's Command of its Members Serving in the British army, 1939–1946' (MA thesis, Haifa University, 2003), pp.50–6.
53. On one occasion an Israeli serviceman with American citizenship smuggled arms in a suitcase on behalf of the Haganah. Yosselevitz went to the Red Cross office in Cairo and brought back the suitcase, which she then handed over to Za'ir, who removed it from Cairo. Testimony of Hanna Yosselevitz, 12 January 1960, p.2, HHA, 24.35. One of the servicewomen transferred suitcases full of weapons under the cargo trailer of a truck full of Polish soldiers, in which she had hitched a ride to Palestine. Habas, *Bnot hayil*, p.112.
54. Interview with Shoshana Geller.
55. According to a report by the Police Criminal Investigation Department (CID) dated 15 August 1945, the riots in Cairo were 'staged' by the Hebrew press as convincing proof for the purpose of transferring the Jewish minorities in the Arab countries to Palestine. Dekel, *Benitivei habricha*, p.359.
56. Interview with Esther Herlitz, Tel Aviv, 9 December 2005.
57. This was probably Ben-Zvi, who possessed a top-secret letter from the Haganah HQ in Cairo, which was destined to Sharett. She managed to hide the letter and handed it to David Hacohen, who passed it on. As for the reason of the search, speculation had it that her address was listed in the notebook of Sirkin (who was suspected of smuggling weapons out of the British military stores on the Carmel Mountain), or that the military police had discovered Haganah documents bearing her name. 'Female Members in the Haganah', p.9, HHA, 16/2.
58. Interview with Ahuva Zilberstein; Interview with Tamar Eshel.
59. Testimony of Yehudit Rav-Bar-Hai, 2 December 1952, pp.4–5, HHA, 11.34. On one occasion she delivered a sketch of a British radar unit that was parked in the vicinity of her camp, together with a description of the vicinity.
60. Liah Ronai, Haganah member, was born in Riga, Latvia, and graduated from the Hebrew High School there. She subsequently married the Habima Theatre actor Avraham Ronai. Interview with Liah Ronai.
61. Testimony of Yehudit Rav-Bar-Hai, 2 December 1952, pp.4–5, HHA, 11.34. Habas notes that the roof of a hotel in Alexandria served as a meeting point. On the roof they would exchange information, receive orders and at a certain point in time they even conducted initiation ceremonies to the Haganah, following a security check. Habas, *Bnot hayil*, p.113.
62. According to Gerald Frank, about twelve Lehi members served in the British army. Gerald Frank, *Hama'as* [The action] (Tel Aviv 1963), p.165. Nathan Yellin-Mor does not quote numbers, but describes how, 'Soon there was a web of Lehi people in the British army, especially of veterans who moved arms and ammunition to Eretz Israel ... here and there new members joined.' Nathan Yellin-Mor, *Lohamey herut Israel: Anashim, ra'aionot, alilot* [Fighters for the freedom of Israel: people, ideas, tales] (Tel Aviv 1989), pp.214–16.

63. Ada Leibowitz, a Lehi member in the Yishuv, who had been active before enlisting in WAAF. The British must have missed the fact that she was a Lehi member.
64. Interview with Yaffa Tevua (Greenberg), Haifa, 17 December 2005; Interview with Ruth Gruzin (Grosbard), Tel Aviv, 22 November 2005. Tevua, who was not at first a member of one of the organizations and was not experienced in the rules of secrecy, felt free enough to express her feeling and it is thus that her opinions became known. According to Frank, three female Lehi recruits served in the British army. Another recruit aroused Ogen's suspicions because of her ability to recite the poems of Uri Zvi Greenberg, despite being generally uneducated. Interview with Tzfira Ogen. At that time the only one to study the poems of Greenberg were members of the right-wing Betar youth movement or of the underground.
65. Peri enlisted in the ATS in 1942 at the age of 16 and was sent to Egypt. When the military authorities knew her real age, she was released and returned to the Yishuv. In 1944, she joined the Lehi officially. It is possible that in the course of her service she voiced opinions, which conformed to those of the underground, although there is no knowledge of her carrying out any activity on behalf of the Lehi. Nehemia Ben-Tor, *Lexikon Lehi* [Lehi Dictionary] (Tel Aviv 2007), p.694.
66. Leah Giladi, *Aleyhen lo katvu* [About them, nothing was written] (Tel Aviv 1997), p.23.
67. Ya'akov Banai, *Hayalim almonim: sefer mivtzaei Lehi* [Anonymous soldiers: book of Lehi operations], ed. Israel Eldad (Tel Aviv 1989), p.273.
68. Interview with Ruth Gruzin.
69. 'Protocol of Sadovsky's Admission', Part 2, 4 April 1945, p.4, HHA, 112/1029.
70. Special Investigations Department Top Secret Report by the Military Police in Cairo, 'Investigation of ATS suspects following the murder', 8 December 1944, National Archives, London (NA), FO 371/46109.
71. Banai, *Hayalim almonim*, pp.263–4. In an interview, Gruzin claimed that she had never met Tevua before their meeting in the Bethlehem Jail. Interview with Ruth Gruzin.
72. Interview with Yaffa Tevua.
73. For example, a driver in Company 513 was arrested and, following an interrogation, it was obvious that she had not been involved in the murder, but she did lead a promiscuous life in the army. She was released from service for improper behaviour and sent back to the Yishuv. Special Investigations Department Top Secret Report by the Military Police in Cairo, 'Investigation of ATS suspects following the murder', 8 December 1944, NA, FO 371/46109. In Company 531 in Tura, too, the military police had taken a servicewoman out of a morning parade on suspicion of being involved in the murder. Herlitz, *Esther*, p.25.
74. Sadovsky was arrested by the British when he arrived at the cemetery in which Hakim and Ben-Tsuri were buried and asked for their bodies to be exhumed. The British did not need to place much pressure on him until he broke down and provided them with all the information he had on the underground. He committed suicide later in an Egyptian jail. Sadovsky's Confession, Part 2, 4 April 1945, HHA, 112/1029.

75. On the 'Hunting Season' see, for example, Yehuda Lapidot, *Ha'saison: tzaid ahim* [The 'hunting season': hunting down brothers] (Tel Aviv 1994).
76. Memoirs of Tamar Eshel, pp.79–80. Because of her command of English, Ogen spent time (when on leave from the army) in the Haganah HQ in Cairo, translating information from the English press in Egypt during the course of the trial. These reports were transferred via Haganah channels to the Yishuv.
77. Kollek served from 1936 in the Jewish Agency's Political Department and during this time he headed the Agency's Intelligence Department; he was also active in the Haganah. In the Second World War, Kollek was involved in the 'secret cooperation' and dispatch of the parachutists behind enemy lines in Europe. After the establishment of the State, he worked for the Foreign Ministry and Mossad. Gelber, *Toldot hahitnadvut: Hahitnadvut ve mekoma bemidiniut hazionit ve hayishuvit 1939–1942*, p.726.
78. Interview with Sonya Peres (Gelman), Tel Aviv, 9 January 2006; Testimony of Ruth (Melamed) Kaplan, 10 March 2003, IDF Archive, 120/03/72.
79. Interview with Sonya Peres.
80. Miriam Cooke, 'WO-Man, Retelling the War Myth', in Miriam Cooke and Angela Woollacott (eds), *Gendering War Talk* (Princeton, NJ 1993), pp.177–204. It is true in viewing the woman's place in the 'War Myth' that a format of narratives has developed through which wars have been described throughout history. This includes the literary creation (prose and poetry) written about wars, but also their historiography (study of historical writings of wars). In Cook's opinion, it is not enough that women participate in war; they need also to recall and analyse the experiences of war, both of the fighting men and their own. Lynn Higgins, for example, is sure that women's attempts to tell the story is threatening to men, who see it as an invasion of their territory and breaking of taboos. Lynn Higgins, 'Sexual Fantasies and War Memories: Claude Simmon's Narratology', in Miriam Cooke and Angela Woollacott (eds), Ibid. (Princeton, NJ 1993), p.249. See also, Carol Cohn, 'Wars, Wimps and Women: Talking Gender and Thinking War', in Miriam Cooke and Angela Woollacott (eds), Ibid. pp. 232–46.
81. Joshua Goldstein, *War and Gender: How Gender Shapes the War System and Vice Versa* (Cambridge 2001), p.59. For further reading, see, for example, Cynthia Enloe, *Does Khaki Become You? The Militarization of Women's Lives* (London 1983); Joan Scott, 'Rewriting History', in Margaret R. Higonnet, Jane Jenson, Sonya Michel and Margaret Collins Weitz (eds), *Behind the Lines* (New Haven, CT 1992), pp.21–30.
82. Yaffa Berlowitz, 'Letivo shel hanarative hazioni hanashi – hathalat mea/sof mea' (To the essence of the female Zionist narrative – beginning/end of century), in Yehudit Bar El, Yigal Schwartz and Tamar Hess (eds), *Sifrut vehevra batarbut haivrit hahadasha: ma'amarim mugashim le Gerson Shaked* (Literature and society in the new Hebrew culture: essays dedicated to Gershon Shaked) (Tel Aviv 2000), p.421.
83. See, for example, the work of Margalit Shilo, *Etgar hamigdar: nashim ba'aliyot harishonot* [Challenge of gender: women in the first waves of immigration] (Bnei Brak 2007); Deborah S. Bernstein, 'Heker Nashim ba-Historiografyah ha-Yisre'elit: Nekudot Motza, Kavvanot Hadashot ve-Kavvanot she-ba-Derekh' [The study of women in Israeli historiography: starting points, new directions

and emerging insights], in Ruth Kark, Margalit Shilo and Galit Hasan-Rokem (eds), *Jewish Women in pre-State Israel: Life History, Politics and Culture* (Waltham, MA: Brandeis University Press, 2008), pp.7–25; Yossi Ben-Artzi, 'Have Gender Studies Changed Our Attitude Toward the Historiography of the Aliyah and Settlement Process?', in Ruth Kark, Margalit Shilo and Galit Hasan-Rokem (eds), Ibid., pp.26–44; Berlowitz, 'Letivo shel hanarative hazioni hanashi'.

84. The testimonies are kept in the Haganah Archive, in verbal interviews, in memoires that they themselves published and also in the book Bnot hayil, which is, according to the author's definition, a book 'about women and for women'. Habas, *Bnot hayil*, p.5. Tamar Hess indicates that women who write their memoires place themselves in the middle of things. In opening up the private story there is a unification of the personal and public narrative, and publishing it provides a potential to influence the male and female readers. Tamar Hess, 'Autobiographical Writings by Women of the Second Aliyah' (PhD thesis, Hebrew University, Jerusalem, 2003), p.20. See also, Martha Watson, *Lives of Their Own: Rhetorical Dimensions in Autobiographies of Women Activists* (South Carolina 1999), p.7.
85. Neuta Halperin, *Davar*, 20 December 1984.
86. Habas, *Bnot hayil*, p.114.
87. In contrast, research studies and books concerning the women in Lehi contain little mention of those who enlisted in the British forces. This could be because of the small number of Lehi women who enlisted. It could be that the writers, or Lehi women who did not enlist, took a dim view of military service, which was construed by them as open collaboration with the British, and only their involvement in the murder turned them into heroines in Lehi eyes.

7

Relations between Yishuv Servicewomen and British Servicemen

The recruitment of Yishuv women into the British forces was accompanied by considerable reservations, one of which was the fear of a personal encounter between Jewish women and British servicemen. Because of the unique nationalist circumstances of the time, there was also a fear of the women being unable to serve in this alien British army that the Jewish Yishuv was struggling against.

This unique situation created a complex relationship between the military authorities and the female Jewish recruits, which can be divided into several rounds: the attitude of the ATS High Command toward Zionism and the Yishuv; attitude of the local command in companies and camps toward the recruits; the religious pluralism and tolerance exhibited by the military authorities vis-à-vis the Jewish recruits; the trust and suspicions that characterized the relations between the two parties.

Attempts to Create a Sense of Unity within the British Empire

In recent decades, there is a tendency in research to refer to the Second World War as The People's War. This expression aims to indicate the democratic manner in which a national identity has been created, with emphasis on the role of the 'common person' and with disregard for the differences of class and gender and in contrast with the class distinctions that controlled the British army during the First World War. By using another expression – The People's Empire – Britain's propaganda machine wished to present the Empire at war as an entity in which unity reigned supreme among the various nations and races that comprise it. The joint national identity was achieved via movies and propaganda, motivational posters to encourage recruitment to the war effort, radio broadcasts and newspaper articles. All these stressed the British component shared by every member of the commonwealth and served as ammunition vis-à-vis that of Nazi Germany and even against the voices in the US that called out against British imperialism. The Films Unit was established in the Intelligence Office for the purpose of achieving these objectives and was incorporated in the efforts to recruit support for the war throughout the British Empire.[1]

Even within the scope of the British Mandate of Palestine (Eretz Israel) the British authorities and the Yishuv institutions wished to attach the Yishuv recruits to the fighting collective in the war against the Germans. However, the feeling that British propaganda tried to create – one of a single, united nation throughout the Empire – was not always realized with respect to the military. Command of the companies in the British army was entrusted solely to British officers and there were colonial companies scattered throughout all the theatres of war.[2] In many aspects, Palestine differed from the rest of the British colonies, such as India, South Africa or Australia. Being under British Mandate, its official legal status differed from that of the other colonies, from an international point of view, although the attitude of the British was in every way as to a colony.[3] To the overall complexity of Britain's attitude to the female recruits from the Yishuv, there should be added the nationalist-political element of the Zionist Movement, which was as yet inactive in other parts of the Empire.[4] Many British civil servants and army officers either found it hard to come to terms with the political aspirations of Zionism or opposed them from the start.[5]

Audrey Chitty and Zionism

A central component of the British High Command's relationship with the female Yishuv recruits was the attitude of Audrey Chitty, Commander of the ATS in the Middle East, to the Yishuv in general and the servicewomen in particular. This attitude should be understood within the framework of the overall attitude of the senior British Command in the Middle East to the Yishuv and its aspirations for a national homeland. One aspect of this attitude was the struggle to establish a Jewish force within the British army. The British were reserved as to the desire of the local Jewish population to enlist in their army and suspected that it was motivated by Zionist interests. Even before the enlistment of Jewish women from the Yishuv, there were some who feared that the establishment of a Jewish fighting force would help in preparing a military infrastructure in the country that would eventually rise against the British Mandate.[6]

Audrey Chitty was the highest-ranking woman officer in the British army sent to establish ATS companies in the Middle East.[7] Claire Epstein, one of the participants in the cadre, said of her that 'to this region they sent a female commander in chief from among the haters of Israel. So long as she was commander in chief of the ATS companies, I was in her sights.'[8] Esther Herlitz referred to her as an 'anti-Semite', and Hadassah Samuel called her a 'hater of Israel'.[9] A study of her diary sheds light on her personality and her motives.

From Chitty's diary, which she wrote in the course of her activity in the region and devoted to a description of her mission, there emerges the image of a professional army woman who arrived in Palestine in order to carry out her assignment – to establish ATS companies in the Middle East in accordance with the model set by the women's auxiliary forces in Britain. Chitty arrived in the country for a series of meetings from 15 December 1941 until 17 May 1942. It was a whistle-stop tour between Cairo and Jerusalem, in the course of which she was 'summoned' to India to examine the possibility of establishing an ATS force there, too. Chitty's objective was to give her mission a purely military character and was unwilling to accept political dictates or involvement that would disturb her in carrying out her objective, either from Samuel or from any other element in the Yishuv. In this, Chitty appears to have been an outstanding example of British officer training, whose graduates wanted only to prove that their decisions were based purely on military considerations.

It would appear that Chitty had no negative opinion, indeed no opinion at all, on Jews or Zionism before her arrival in Palestine. Her outlook on Jewish/Arab relations in the country can be condensed into the words of Raymond Kaparta, a police officer and commandant of the Police HQ in Hebron during the riots of 1929: 'I am neither anti-Semitic, nor anti-Arab. I am simply pro-British.'[10] Like many other Britons who were raised on the Bible, Chitty was happy to arrive in the Holy Land and some of her more emotional moments were experienced on a tour of the Old City of Jerusalem, by the Western Wall and in the Christian churches. More than anything she wanted to succeed in her military mission and felt that the ATS should reflect the various nations in the Middle East, and not be based only on the Jews and form a reason for political confrontation.

The decision on female recruitment was published in the press on 24 December 1941. A number of events that developed after the announcement polluted the atmosphere between Chitty and her Jewish interlocutors in the Yishuv. One of these was the Jewish Agency's refusal to hand over to the British Recruitment Office the names of the recruits who had registered with them. Another event occurred a few days after the announcement on recruitment[11] and Chitty wrote in her diary that she didn't understand why the Jewish Agency was opposed to Britain's efforts, 'since the entire existence of the Jewish race [nation] depends on a British victory in the war'.[12] But it seems that Edward Keith-Roach, the Governor of Jerusalem, voiced the most pungent opinions on the recruits and the Jews.[13] He warned her 'there is no point expecting any kind of loyalty from the Jewish recruits, since they have no loyalty or sense of commitment toward the Empire or the objective for which the British are fighting'. Keith-Roach added, according to Chitty, that a Jew would never do anything without bargaining over it and also that a Jew would never get straight to the point, but always in a roundabout way. Because of her disappointment at the negotiations with the Jewish Agency, Chitty felt that she had made a mistake in not going straight to recruiting Arab women, before the Jewish women.[14] It appears that her encounters with military leaders and British government officials on the one hand and with Yishuv representatives such as Sharett and Samuel on the other, gradually formed Chitty's opinions on Zionism and the Jews she met here. She internalized some of the images she had heard about,[15] although on a personal level she was quite fond of some of them and was impressed by their work. Thus, for example, after a dinner at the home of the Sharett's, she was particularly impressed by the broadmindedness and military career of Sharett in the Turkish army.

About two months after her first visit in the country, Chitty wrote in her diary:

> The more time I spend in Palestine and the more I am obliged to negotiate with these Jews, the more I find them surprising and hard to understand. They will never do with a 'no' when they want to hear 'yes'. They never get straight to the matter, they always go round and round, methods that for a straight thinking English woman like myself are hard to cope with.

Similar sentiments to those of Chitty's were written or voiced by other British military commandants of government officials who spent several years in Palestine.[16]

From a military aspect and in the best way possible, Chitty fulfilled the mission for which she came to the region. On 14 October 1943, she was awarded an Order of the British Empire for establishing the ATS in the Middle East. In explanation for the award, Julia Cowper wrote, 'Among other problems the officer had to overcome were political and religious issues ... in addition, there are considerable problems involved in operating a women's military service in an eastern country and in a region of mixed forces such as that in the Middle East theatre'.[17]

The British ATS Staff in the Middle East

According to the official ATS book, of the some 5,000 officers and women serving in the ATS in the Middle East – the British army's main theatre of war until 1944 – some 2,000 came from all over the British Empire. During the first few months of 1944, there were 300 female officers in the Middle East (280 British) and 4,834 servicewomen (about 1,500 of who were British and the others local recruits). This data indicates that most of the officers were British (more than 90 per cent), while among the regular servicewomen the British constituted only 33 per cent. The number of British female recruits in the Middle East constituted less than 1 per cent of the overall ATS deployment.[18]

It would appear that in Britain, the ATS suffered from an inferior image compared with the more glamorous one of the other women's auxiliary services, the WAAF and the WRNS, and were nicknamed the 'Cinderella Service'.[19] Like all the women serving out of Britain, they, too, were volunteers. Each candidate for service overseas was required to produce a letter from her family or husband authorizing her departure. According to ATS protocol, each candidate had to appear before a committee, headed by a senior officer. The objective of the interview was to sift out unsuitable candidates on personality or disciplinary grounds or those whose personal or family commitments would have prevented them from serving far from home.[20]

The first group of British staff officers arrived in the Middle East in January 1942 to serve as the training team for the Cadre Course and, from then on, further groups of recruits arrived in the region throughout the duration of the war.[21] The age of the British servicewomen in the Middle East ranged between 19 and 45, similar to that of their counterparts in Britain. Initially, the British ATS command in the Middle East included First World War veterans, or women who had served with the British Expeditionary Force in France and were experienced in cooperating with other armies. These servicewomen were also familiar with languages other than English. However, for most of the British servicewomen in the Middle East, this was the first time abroad. Their service overseas was conceived as one of the great adventures of their lives and one they were eager to experience, especially after their brothers, husbands or lovers had also been sent to serve across the sea.[22] Their service outside of Britain and 'out of sight', as well as in male company, raised considerable fears and there even developed rumours as to their dubious moral behaviour. It would appear that prior to their arrival in the Middle East the servicewomen had not received any political or propaganda instruction on events in the region, so that most of them had no preconceived ideas on Jews, Arabs or the conflict between them. Their preparation had focused mainly on service under conditions of war rather than on political instruction.

Concepts of command in the ATS companies appear to have been set even before their establishment. In all her talks in the country, Chitty made a point of stressing that all the company commandants would be British women, although each ATS recruit would be given an equal opportunity for promotion. And indeed, during the first couple of years all the company commandants, apart from two, were British and among the platoon commandants only a few were from Palestine or the British Empire. Only toward the end of 1944 were four Jewish women appointed company commandants.

The British Staff on the Cadre Course

On 18 January 1942 the first batch of Yishuv women were recruited to the Cadre course. Among several of the recruits an atmosphere of suspicion prevailed toward the staff, especially among the Haganah members who were chosen for the course. Mina Ben-Zvi, for example, felt that the British teaching staff 'looked at the new recruits as they would at the "native" women in the British colonies in India'. According to her, the British women received the Jewish recruits with typical British politeness; they were friendly and obviously willing to meet them halfway, but they were never able to dispel the sense of alienation and suspicion.[23] In contrast, Claire Epstein, who was born in England and was familiar with the British mentality, saw it differently. In her opinion, the welcome received by the recruits was 'warm and very pleasant ... there is a desire on the part of the British crew to learn Hebrew and they are still unspoiled by [the attitudes] of *the local English*' [author's emphasis]. Epstein also differentiated between the attitudes toward the cadre participants and the other male Yishuv recruits to the army (news of which had already been broadcast throughout the Yishuv): 'There is no comparison between this and the attitude encountered by the soldiers of BUFFS when recruitment began.'[24]

On her visit to the training camp, Dr Nadia Stein from WIZO was impressed by the mutual respect that reigned between the recruits and the British staff: 'the officers are full of praise for the enthusiasm and devotion of the [Jewish] recruits, whereas the recruits themselves revere these British women, for their spirit of devotion and self sacrifice ... who inspired them to prove the value of their activity under extremely dangerous circumstances'.[25] The impression of another recruit, for who this was the first encounter with British women, 'was very good. It seemed as if we had been sent the best and most choice kind of [people], and this made our integration much easier.'[26] And, indeed, it appears that the teaching staff in the cadre had been carefully chosen by Chitty and Helen Pine, who commanded the training camp in Sarafend. However, the team that trained the women who took part in the cadre course for command posts in the ATS was not typical of the British servicewomen or of the company commandant throughout the Middle East.

British Officers in ATS Companies

Most of the servicewomen subsequently forgot the names for the British officers who commanded their companies in the ATS and WAAF. It seems that in the Cadre course a good relationship developed between the Jewish recruits and the British officers, although in most of the ATS companies there was no direct contact between the Jewish servicewomen and their British company commandants.[27] This is due to the differences in mentality and culture as well as a clear hierarchy that separated the different ranks that the British army was very strict about.

Most of the day the servicewomen were employed in their work places and usually encountered their company commandant in the orderly room, when they were being tried for some misdemeanour or other,[28] or in the course of an official roll call, celebration, party or sports activity. Most of the contact with the servicewomen was conducted via their sergeant or platoon head and only on rare occasions did good relations develop between Jewish servicewomen and the British commanders in the ATS companies. In a letter to her family, Ella Wilensky, for example, wrote, 'Relations with the two English officers and the Jewish officer in the company are very good.'[29] The officer Rachel Schorr was on friendly terms with a British officer, the commandant of Company 503 in Abassya, a friendship that continued after the war when she visited her friend in England.[30] Some British officers even learned Hebrew from the Jewish servicewomen.

It would appear that only the servicewomen in companies 513 (the drivers' company in Camp Mina) and 502 (the ambulance drivers) took advantage of every opportunity to refer to their commanding officers by name. These officers, who left a lasting impression on their underlings, were Scotswomen Mary Mackenzie of Company 513, and Penelope Otto of Company 502.

Mary Mackenzie

Mary Mackenzie took up her post in ATS in the Middle East as commander of a platoon in Company 503 in Abassya near Cairo. The platoon consisted of some forty female drivers, mostly from Palestine. At the end of 1942, when large numbers of female Jewish drivers were recruited from the Yishuv, the platoon became an independent company (513) of women drivers under Mackenzie's command. The company was billeted in a camp near the Mina House Hotel close to the pyramids at Giza. In February 1944 the company was amalgamated with the camp's driving school and Mackenzie was given command of the school, in which (beginning with late 1943) all the ATS drivers in the Middle East had received their training. In early 1945, Mackenzie was promoted to the rank of Senior Commandant, a rank equal to that of Major.

Mary Mackenzie was in her late 20s, quite 'masculine' in appearance; she had adopted a 'somewhat stooped posture ... and tended to stand with both hands in her pockets'. She used to start drinking whiskey in the early morning and sometimes appeared drunk when she turned up for duty.[31] Her brother served in the Mandatory Police and she seemed – under his influence – to have developed mixed feelings vis-à-vis Zionism and the Yishuv recruits who served in her company. However, the more she came to know them and after witnessing their devotion to the hard work they were required to carry out, the more she learned to appreciate and respect them.

Mackenzie set a personal example to her soldiers and instilled in them a sense that women can carry out almost every job. She fought with the military authorities over the women's rights and obligations to drive in convoys and did not give in on the right to maintain the trucks they drove, including dangerous and complicated actions. She insisted on the women drivers' ability to carry out tasks as well as or even better than their male counterparts. As she was responsible for driving instruction in the school, Mackenzie established a teaching system that included training in motor mechanics, night driving, topography and military history. The study of military history was aimed at increasing the drivers' awareness of the weighty responsibility they were bearing. Mackenzie made a point of 'obtaining' complex missions and journeys for her drivers to carry out and they were the first drivers in the ATS to make their way to places that were both remote and dangerous.[32]

Mackenzie was first and foremost a professional officer. When necessary, she was a strict disciplinarian and insisted that in everything concerning order and military appearance, her soldiers conduct themselves to the letter. When the women would return from a vacation in Cairo, Mackenzie would be there at the camp gate checking them, even late at night, to ensure that they were not wearing silk stockings (forbidden in the army) instead of the regulation thick khaki ones supplied them. She was as strict, too, when it came to safety on the road.

Nevertheless, however strict she was, Mackenzie was always fair toward her soldiers and aware of their problems. On her special relationship with her soldiers, we can learn from Ruth Breda (Hass)'s story. Even when the war was over and the company's soldiers had been demobilized and sent to serve in Haifa, Mackenzie maintained contact with them. Breda was worried about the fate of her mother, who had remained in Czechoslovakia during the war. Mackenzie learned of her soldier's concern and informed her that the army was searching for her mother and that she would be able to go to Europe to continue with the search as soon as the situation improved.[33]

These testimonies present a picture of a highly respected commanding officer. However, like other British officers, Mary Mackenzie kept a distance between herself and her Palestine recruits and did not socialize with them. Nonetheless, by strength of her personality and behaviour, she was able to socially cohere the company, instilled in it an exceptional esprit de corps that was maintained for many years and contributed to the reputation it garnered, both in the ranks of the ATS and among the male command in the Middle East.

Penelope Otto

Otto, too, was in her late 20s, from a well-to-do family and a widow (her husband had been killed before she enlisted), when she was given command of Company 502 of ambulance drivers in Egypt. In August 1943 she was promoted to a rank equal to Major and appointed commandant of the Alexandria area.[34] Her recruits remember her as a beautiful woman with sparkling blue eyes, a very decent woman, determined as well as quiet and constrained, who gave the new recruits from Palestine a warm welcome.[35] Otto was given command of the Company when she was still with the nursing service in France at the beginning of the war. When France was occupied by the German army, the company was evacuated as part of the general evacuation of the British forces via Dunkirk in May 1940. In the course of the evacuation, Otto managed to heroically evade a German force that was chasing after her and, in doing so, rescue the company's ambulances. For this act of bravery Otto was awarded the Croix de Guerre. Her company was transferred with its ambulances first to east Africa and from there to Egypt where it was stationed permanently in Alexandria.

At first the company maintained its independence, but later, especially due to pressure from Audrey Chitty, it was incorporated into the ATS and Otto served as its commandant in Egypt. Later, she also served as commander of area group 16, which included the ATS companies in the vicinity of Alexandria. Due to her connections with the British military leaders, Otto obtained for her drivers the right (as they saw it) to serve as close as possible to the battlefront. She, like Mackenzie, insisted that the female drivers were capable of carrying out the most dangerous of missions in the best possible way.

Otto's soldiers maintained contact with her even when the war was over. Arieli, for example, visited her twice in the UK and Otto, for her part, responded to an invitation to visit her former soldiers in Israel in the early 1960s and even met Sharett, who knew of her exceptional personality and her kindness toward her soldiers.[36]

It would appear that despite the obvious differences in character and behaviour between the two commandants, they both knew how to combine in their personalities the right measure of stern discipline, professionalism and fairness. Both Mackenzie and Otto were awarded the MBE (Member of the British Empire) for their wartime work. Otto received hers on 18 February 1943 and Mackenzie received hers on 1 January 1945. The two were the only British officers to have carved a place in the hearts of their soldiers and they were repaid with the admiration and respect that were not granted to other British officers in the ATS. They both demonstrated special esteem for their Jewish soldiers, which naturally led to their unique attitude to them.

British Officers in the WAAF

Most of the officers in the WAAF were older than the recruits from Palestine, since the average age of the WAAF recruits as compared to those in the ATS was lower. In the WAAF, as in the ATS, the British soldiers and officers who served in the Middle East had volunteered to do so. According to researcher Penny Summerfield, the British recruits to the WAAF belonged to a higher social class and were more accustomed to mobility as well as being more open-minded than their ATS counterparts, most of which were working class.[37] The WAAF recruits from Palestine served in mixed bases alongside women from all over the British Empire, and in these bases it was rare for friendships to form between the two groups of recruits. This would appear to be due– as in the ATS – to the differences in mentality and the fact that most of the Jewish recruits were better educated and their spheres of interest differed from those of their British counterparts.[38]

Jean Baker

As in the ATS companies, most of the interviewees who had served in the WAAF were unable to name the officers and soldiers they served alongside. An exception to this was undoubtedly Sergeant Jean Baker, who served first in the basic training camp at Lydda and subsequently in Camp MU 107 near Genifa (the Bitter Lake) in Egypt. She was exceptional in her approach to her soldiers and always made sure to explore the person behind the uniform and to treat them with respect. Baker's job involved authority for all the administrational issues connected to the recruits' military service and she knew most of them personally. The thing that touched her heart was the fact that most of them had arrived in Palestine without their families as immigrants after much wandering. Baker was offered a commission but she declined promotion and chose to remain in her post on camp after deciding that her work as sergeant would be of more use to her soldiers than would a regular administrative post. She, too, like Mackenzie and Otto, held the Palestine recruits in special esteem.

After being demobilized in November 1945 following a two and a half year tour of duty in the Middle East, Jean Baker returned to England. Her soldiers continued to correspond with her, writing that they missed her both as a person and as a commander, stressing her sympathetic and democratic attitude to all her soldiers. For Baker, the service in this part of the world was an exceptional experience, due especially to her encounter with male and female soldiers from different nations and cultures.[39]

Gaps in Language and Communication

At the height of its strength in late 1943, the ATS alignment in the Middle East numbered some 5,000 soldiers and officers: 80 per cent of them were local recruits, the vast majority came from Palestine and many of them had emigrated from various countries throughout Europe. The others were Greek, Czech and Polish and Arab women (most of who had been released from service by the end of 1943); and there were also about 120 Cypriot women who had been recruited in Cyprus. Thus, in addition to inter-national issues, there was also the problem of language, which provided a source of misunderstanding between the recruits and their British commandants. Language difficulties caused objective problems to the management of a body composed of women from many different nations, since a very few of the recruits spoke English and none of the British officers knew Hebrew, Greek or Czech, the languages spoken by their soldiers. It became necessary, therefore, to employ the services of translators, who were not British, in order to maintain routine life in the army. In Company 502 ambulance drivers, for example, the language was initially Hebrew, with some recruits speaking German and two Cypriot recruits speaking only Greek.[40] Several driving instructors tried to overcome the problem and learned key terms in the language of the recruits, while others made do with gestures and demonstrations, which sometimes had amusing results.[41]

Many of the recruits from Palestine were new immigrants or had lived only a few years in the country before enlisting. Many were not fluent in Hebrew or in English. Although several companies provided

English lessons during the early stages of service, training and orders were given in English, all of which were translated into Hebrew by recruits who had various levels of fluency in English. In addition to Yishuv-born recruits who knew English, educated women who had emigrated from Central Europe and were fluent in English also helped in translating when necessary.[42]

The language barrier likely caused alienation and a sense of strangeness among the different groups. For example Pat Hall, a staff sergeant in Company 502, pointed out that one of the greatest hardships encountered by the British army in its struggle against Zionism was the lack of people capable of censoring correspondence. As far as she was concerned, any woman who spoke modern Hebrew was suspected of harbouring sympathy for the Zionist cause. Educated British recruits who had studied Biblical Hebrew in university or in theology classes in England were incapable of reading letters written in the modern version of the language and thereby couldn't help with military censorship. Even Dame Leslie Whateley, Director of the ATS, indicated that the language and cultural differences were among the problems she had encountered in the course of her travels in the Middle East. Yet despite the hardships, Dame Leslie was impressed that the British servicewomen and their Jewish counterparts worked well together.[43]

Frank Knight, an aircraft mechanic on Camp MU 107 in RAF Kaspareet in Egypt, held a different view of the language issue. He was the first to instruct the female aircraft mechanics at the camp in the winter of 1944. Most of the participants in the course were local recruits of various nationalities: Jewish refugees from Germany, Poland and Russia, French and Syrian recruits and also a few British women who had enlisted in Bermuda or the Bahamas. He would later write in the *Kaspareet Kronicle*, a journal published after the war and distributed among recruits serving in the camp, that communications – or language problems – made instruction difficult, but 'with perseverance, sign language and help from those who knew English, they all passed the course' and became qualified mechanics.[44]

It seems that notwithstanding the linguistic and cultural differences, in most of the ATS and WAAF companies, the Yishuv recruits and their commanding officers managed to develop a good and fair working relationship. This was probably the reason for the high level of motivation to overcome the difficulties of language and initial ill ease.

Pluralism and Tolerance

The British servicemen and women respected the freedom of worship of their counterparts who were members of other religions and allowed them to celebrate the religious holydays and other special dates. A study of the war diaries of the ATS companies reveals that Jewish religious and national holydays were celebrated in full. The British commandants cooperated out of respect for the servicewomen who respected their own heritage, whether out of sympathy for the importance of the holyday, or out of complete ignorance of its meaning and customs. The company staff cooperated in making it possible to observe the holydays and conduct the ceremonies, both by supplying manpower and allocating resources (a hall, vehicles, etc.).[45]

Margaret Broderick, who commanded Company 511 of women drivers, stood out from among the British officers in Tel el Kabir with her religious tolerance and the sensitivity she displayed toward her soldiers. Reports in the company diary reveal an intelligent woman, with an interest and knowledge of the significance of the Jewish holydays, who did her best to release most of her women from duty in order to spend the holydays with their families. Thus, for example, on the Jewish New Year and Day of Atonement, she authorized three days off for all the Jewish servicewomen under her command and they, in return, were expected to replace their British counterparts at Christmas, New Year's Day and another social occasion. Broderick was impressed by the Passover meal celebrated by the servicewomen of her company and exhibited an understanding of the holyday and its significance. She made a point of seeing that servicewomen who did not get to celebrate this traditional holyday with their families, received an unforgettable experience in the form of 'a Passover meal that we've arranged like one big family right here in Egypt'.[46] During the holydays, she entrusted the non-Jewish drivers, including the officers, with all the crucial driving missions and closed the company office, even in wartime. In this way she exhibited extraordinary consideration for the Jewish servicewomen.

Occasionally there would be an amusing moment, the result of the British staff's unfamiliarity with Jewish religious traditions,[47] and there were also instances where Jewish servicewomen tried to take advantage of the British officers' tolerance over religious holydays. But, in general, the officers were exceptionally accommodating of the recruits' needs during the important Jewish holydays, approving absences from work and being considerate of their need to go home for the holydays.

The Sabbath eve (Friday evening) also provided an opportunity for a meeting of hearts between the non-Jews in the ATS and WAAF and the world of the Jewish recruits: the British commandants participated in the meal and even reported on it in the company diary. Thus, for example, even when most of the servicewomen in Company 508 in the Cairo Citadel were given time off to go home for Passover, the remaining women continued to light Sabbath candles and even invited guests from other companies. In the absence of a Palestine sergeant who was responsible for organizing the service, the British area commandant, who was invited to participate, read a chapter from the Bible in English and, following the traditional part, they all enjoyed an evening of dancing.[48]

The British army made it possible for representatives of the Yishuv and army rabbis to make frequent visits (similar to visits of Christian army chaplains to their own congregants) to the Jewish servicewomen in the various companies. This is further evidence of the tolerance displayed toward the Yishuv servicewomen.

Sympathy for the Zionist Cause

The Zionist enterprise and the Jewish Yishuv were often on the receiving line of displays of solidarity on the part of British servicemen. Thus, for example, after a search for weapons at Kibbutz Ramat Hakhovesh, when the British high command in Cairo issued an order to the various companies to publish the event and to officially read it out to the servicewomen, Penelope Otto, ATS Commandant in Alexandria, wrote to Audrey Chitty, ATS Commandant in the Middle East, in response that this should be avoided because it would be a matter of 'rubbing salt in the servicewomen's wounds'. Indeed, the drivers of Company 511 in Tel El Kabir tore down the announcement from the notice board.[49] Margaret Broderick, commander of Company 511 near Tel el Kabir, began reading the announcement to the servicewomen by saying that she opposed the search, but she was obliged to follow orders. The servicewomen, two of who were from Ramat Hakhovesh and Yagur, protested and stood up to leave the hall. Broderick allowed all the servicewomen to leave and, at the door, told the two kibbutz members at the door to 'pass on my sympathies to your [kibbutz]'. To the servicewoman from Yagur, she went on to say, 'I'll try to visit Yagur soon'.[50]

Expressions of solidarity, albeit rare, also came from commanders and servicemen for Jews' illegal nationalist activity. Often, British servicemen were aware of the clandestine activity of the Jewish Haganah members and sometimes even helped in it, whether directly or in a circumspect way. Instructors at the driving school in Mina Camp, who felt solidarity with the Zionist enterprise and the Yishuv, forged reports on the use of arms and ammunition and provided them to the Jewish servicewomen, who then passed them on to the Haganah. Servicewomen from Company 507 in Dir Suneid near Gaza also received help from their friends in the camp. At a certain stage, at the height of the arms smuggling from Egypt to the Yishuv, soldiers from Palestine were arrested in the perimeter of the camp on suspicion of obtaining arms on behalf of the Haganah. Some of them were hidden for a while by Jewish servicewomen in the camp's garages. A British soldier employed in cleaning vehicles in the garage knew of the clandestine activity but did not betray the servicemen to the camp commandant.[51] Jewish servicewomen who recalled these events in their memoires were full of admiration for these British soldiers, who placed themselves at risk by defying military law because of their sympathy for the Zionist enterprise.

However, alongside the sympathy, there were also a few anti-Semitic clashes, such as the case of Rachel Caspi, an officer in RAF Ismailia, who described the way a British officer, the girlfriend of the camp commandant, greeted her each morning with the words, 'Here comes the bloody Jewess'.[52] Brucha Ben Haim (Eisenberg) encountered an anti-Semitic sentiment uttered by a British doctor in the course of a medical examination, but she insists that this was an isolated incident and that her relations with the British servicewomen and her commanding officers were completely fair.[53]

Conversion

A small number of Jewish servicewomen and men, converted to Christianity in the course of their military service, but these seem to have been extremely isolated cases. Although the British army did not encourage such things, it did supply the necessary services for the conversion. The military chaplains presided over the ceremonies at which ATS officers also were present. Thus, for example, a report in the diary of Company 522 that Private Stern converted to Christianity in 1944 in the camp's church and the company commandant was invited to the ceremony.[54] In Company 505, which was stationed in Haifa (Stella Maris), a sergeant converted to Christianity. According to Bar-Rav-Hai, the woman's roommate, the servicewoman made a habit of spying on the Haganah activists in the company and on one occasion she even reported to the military authorities on her share in the IZL attack near Hadera.[55]

Encounter with British Servicemen and Women

One of the female servicewomen wrote in *Davar Hapo'elet* in February 1944: 'A chapter in its own right is provided by the meeting of dozens of Hebrew women (full of Zionist motivation), with the wounded and their multi-national workmates. A correct illustration of the Jewish question, of Zionism, of our lives in Palestine, of our relations with our neighbours, brought us more friends.'[56] The women recruiters, too, believed that it was their duty not only to register them, but also to train the recruits as representatives of the Yishuv and to deliver the necessary propaganda: 'She was required to be able to describe our achievements in the country, the new settlements, the advances we have made in various fields – education, culture and economics. And in her (the recruit) meeting with people from abroad she has to be able to reply to questions, to impress on them the problems facing Zionism, to arouse their admiration for our enterprise.'[57] And so, the recruits were seen by the women's' organizations, the Yishuv instutions and also by themselves, as representatives of the Yishuv, on a mission to explain its issues vis-à-vis the non-Jewish recruits.

Some of the recruits, especially the Haganah activists among them, had confrontations with British soldiers and policemen during anti-White Paper demonstrations held in the Yishuv. In their eyes, the British police were oppressors of the Yishuv and its nationalist aspirations and represented a hostile regime. But for many other recruits, their first encounter with their British counterparts was when they began their military service.

The weight of the British element in Yishuv society rose to a noticable extent during the Arab uprisings of 1936–39. The arrival of a large British armed force in the summer of 1936 and its extensive reinforcements in the summer of 1938, first in the framework of preparations for the invasion of Syria and subsequently for training purposes, increased the friction between the British and the Jewish population in the Yishuv. At the beginning of this period the British were still seen as allies against the Arabs and as defenders of the Yishuv. Attitudes to them were generally positive and if there was any opposition to relationships between Jewish women and British soldiers or policemen, it was usually for family, moral or religious reasons.

Starting in 1940, after the invasion of Syria, Palestine became central for the British forces in the Middle East and various other free armies. It was then that connections expanded between the general Yishuv public and the many foreigners staying in the country.

Social interaction between Jewish women in the Yishuv and non-Jewish servicemen was created under different circumstances: starting with women working as clerks and translators in the various offices; and those who worked in various forms of the hospitality and services trades. Some of the encounters occurred spontaneously and others were formed in various functions organized by private bodies. Many of the meetings were organized by municipal-governmental bodies for 'purposes of state'. Tel Aviv cafes served as additional meeting places for soldiers and Yishuv girls. The elegant cafes were frequented by members of the well-off Yishuv bourgeoisie, public figures and British government officials, and the more common cafes were usually used by British soldiers and 'the daughters of distinguished Tel Aviv families'.[58]

Social Interaction in the Army

From an administrative aspect, the Yishuv recruits belonged to ATS companies. However, with everything connected to their work, they belonged to a professional army and were subject in their workplace to servicemen and officers. Thus day-to-day meetings between non-Jewish servicemen and the Jewish servicewomen were unavoidable in their shared workplaces. There were of course servicewomen who tried to refrain from friendships with the British servicemen they worked with, but in most case they were unable to maintain complete disassociation with their environment. Meetings with servicemen took place after work hours, too – at parties, balls and in joint trips to various locations. These meetings provided opportunities for both sides to get to know people from different cultures, far from home and in a tense wartime atmosphere. On many occasions the servicewomen took advantage of the holydays in their companies to invite their colleagues to spend some cultural and quality time with them.

In many companies there developed good relations between the servicewomen and their non-Jewish workmates. Ahuva Zilberstein, for example, who served in Company 509 in Genifa wrote home a few months after arriving in the camp, 'the attitude of the English [servicemen] is friendly and very nice, they are trying to behave fairly and humanely at work and even after work, and they are constantly repeating that it's been two years since they saw and spoke to a human girl'.[59] Good relations and social cohesion developed on RAF MU 107 (maintenance unit) between the Jewish recruits and their British counterparts. For example, Aviva Gil (Flentzbaum) from Kibbutz Ein Harod became friendly with her commanding officer in the aircraft spare parts store. The two kept up a correspondence for many years after the war and even visited each other's homes.[60] Rachel Ziv, an aircraft mechanic at the same camp, had a British friend who taught her to swim, supported her during hard times and even helped her prepare for her exams on the technical material connected to her work. During her vacations in Palestine, he used to visit her at her home in Rishon Le'Zion. They, too, continued to correspond after the war.[61]

The Jewish servicewomen stressed the friendly relations they developed with the non-Jewish servicemen and said they did not remember any cases of sexual harassment on the part of their work colleagues. Most of the relationships were platonic, which is why – so they explained – the soldiers respected them and stayed in contact even after the war.[62] It would be wise to be cautious in using the modern term 'sexual harassment' in connection to the Second World War period, since what is now considered harassment was at the time considered perfectly normal behaviour. There may have been sexual innuendo on the part of servicemen, but most of the servicewomen were naive and did not interpret the signs as harassment. Esther Herlitz, for example, recalled that this issue did not concern them in the least and that 'it was quite hard to think about sex at the time. ATS girls busied themselves with psychology, drills, lectures and more esoteric things ... who gave any thought to male soldiers? And from that specific point of view ...?'[63] Nonetheless, some interviews as well as servicewomen's memoirs mention lifts with non-Jewish servicemen, some of them drunk, in the course of which the soldiers tried to grope the women.[64] Other such journeys ended, as already mentioned, in injury and accidents.

Fraternizing with non-Jewish Servicewomen

After-work friendships between Jewish servicewomen and their non-Jewish counterparts were rare. Servicewomen from Company 507 in Dir Suneid, for example, have favourable memories of First Sergeant Eileen Chilvers, who was known as Chubby. Jerusalemite Yael Arieli already knew her from her training in Sarafend when Chilvers was a company sergeant. They became very close after they were both transferred to Company 507, Arieli as a driver and Chilvers as her commandant. Chilvers took an interest in the lives of the Palestine servicewomen, identified with their national struggle and even learned how to dance the *hora* on Shabbat eves and to read chapters from the Bible. She made a point of joining Arieli on visits to her parents in Jerusalem and the two maintained their friendship after the war.[65] Herlitz, too, befriended a British sergeant major she served with in Sarafend when the two were training camp instructors. The woman visited Herlitz and her family and they continued their friendship even after the war.[66]

An unusual relationship developed among the Company 513 drivers at Camp Mina. Corporal Grace Selassie, a 30-year-old from Ethiopia and a nurse by profession, as well as being a niece of Emperor Haile Selassie, was a member of the staff. Her father had been an ambassador in several countries, including Palestine. She had enlisted in the British army in Jerusalem in August 1942. Selassie spoke fluent Hebrew, apart from having a good command of Italian, French, Spanish and English. She had studied in England and asked to be allowed to serve as a registered nurse in the army, but was not allowed because she was black. Furious, she tore up her British passport and went on to be a driver. As a veteran in the company, she took the younger drivers under her wing and, in the evenings after work, she used to sit with them and tell them stories of her life all over the world. The servicewomen were fascinated by her and the cosmopolitan aura she exuded, which caused them to feel quite provincial in comparison.[67]

Social Events in the Army

Alongside the harsh discipline and hard work, the British army made a point also of holding social and sporting events for the soldiers, in recognition of their contribution and from the awareness of the importance of such activity in raising the morale of the soldiers.[68] And thus, despite the differences in culture and mentality, the Jewish recruits gradually were integrated into army life and even grew to enjoy it.

In Camp Tel el Kabir, for example, the parties and celebrations were a focus of attraction for Jewish servicemen from the vicinity. Hanna Rovina of the 'Habima' theatre troupe performed for the Jewish recruits and there was also a concert by the Palestine Symphony Orchestra. Many of the Jewish servicewomen recall with yearning the Friday night dance party the British made a point of holding each week. At first 'it was a military duty to attend those parties', probably due to some of the Jewish recruits' refusal to participate of their own free will.[69] However, it would appear that this approach, which aroused considerable debate among the recruits, was mainly a reflection of the attitude of the Haganah members and the older servicewomen. With the passing of time they, too, enjoyed the entertainment options available to them. The Cairo Citadel, had a swimming pool and cinema hall where a lively social lifestyle developed, which included parties and balls. Although the place was located inside the town, it was relatively remote and for security reasons all the recruits were often forbidden to go to town, both during the war itself and later when the civil uprising broke out in late 1945.

Toward the end of the war, when the battlefront had moved to Italy and there was an easing of work pressure on the companies remaining in Egypt, there was some extra time to spare, which was used for various activities. In Company 513, for example, a Bible quiz was held which attracted many of the servicewomen and for which prizes were awarded. The prize giving was held in the NAAFI in the presence of Company Commandant, Mary Mackenzie. A sports committee had been established in the company, which included servicewomen from the company and servicemen from other companies annexed to the camp.

For many servicewomen, the army and especially service beyond the boundaries of the Yishuv also provided an opportunity for adventure, and they took advantage of their vacations to take trips throughout the Middle East. In their trip to the Egyptian botanic gardens, to ancient sites such as the pyramids, Aswan and Luxor, Lebanon and Syria, as well locations in Italy, they were often accompanied by non-Jewish soldiers who had befriended them in the course of their military service. A look at the photograph albums of many of the servicewomen reveals the experiences and the good feelings that prevailed among the servicewomen and men on these trips. Often, when British servicemen went on vacation to Palestine to see the holy places, they made a point of visiting the families of the servicewomen who served with them in the same camp.

In every company in the British army, various events and holydays were celebrated and provided opportunities for diverse social activity, such as, for example, the King's Official Birthday, successes in battle and victory over Britain's enemies, the anniversary of the establishment of the ATS or the company itself, and parties were also arranged in celebration of the end of training different courses. Such occasions were invariably mixed, with Jewish servicewomen, their friends and their non-Jewish male colleagues. To mark the successful landing of British forces in Italy in September 1943, for example, a lavish party was held in the storage camp in Tel el Kabir, attended by all the servicemen and women together. VE (Victory in Europe) Day on 8 May 1945 was celebrated with parties and special activities. In Company 513 on Camp Mina, celebrations continued for two days. On the first day, all the servicewomen, together with their colleagues from the camp's driving school, went on a picnic and the following day they all took part in a dinner dance. VJ (Victory over Japan) Day was also celebrated in the company over two whole days.[70]

Sometimes these parties became a demonstration or an arena for a confrontation of nationalities, which enabled the Jewish recruits to show off their nationalism. One of the better-known confrontations took place in the Cadre and involved the course graduation party. The Jewish recruits had made extensive preparations and invited officers and a large number of guests to the party. On the same day, news came of the sinking of the illegal immigrant ship 'Struma', with the loss of all its cargo of passengers. The grieving recruits asked to be excused from attending the party but they were ordered to be there. A compromise was reached in which Claire Epstein delivered a speech in English before the show, expressing the feelings of the recruits from the Yishuv.[71]

In Company 513, an incident took place that involved a Purim party organized on behalf of poor Jewish children in Cairo. Hadassah Shafir from Kfar Yehezkel, who was active in organizing the company's parties and holyday ceremonies, insisted on reading parts from the Book of Esther in Hebrew. Mary Mackenzie, who had asked to see the programme before it was performed on stage, demanded that the pieces be first read in English and only afterwards in Hebrew. Shafir intentionally violated the order and even arranged for the choir to sing the 'Illegal Immigrants' Song'. The following day she was summoned to the office of the camp commandant, who informed her of her transfer to another camp in Dir Suneid near Gaza.[72]

'Forbidden Relations' in Uniform: Intimate Relations with non-Jewish Recruits

One of the reasons for the objections to female military recruitment was a fear of Jewish women marrying non-Jewish soldiers. As part of army life and the frequent encounters between the Jewish recruits and non-Jewish soldiers, the subsequent development of romantic relations was only natural. The Jewish recruits who fraternized or married non-Jews were considered to have overstepped the boundaries of the national collective.[73]

Almost all the interviewees (of the more than 50 women interviewed for this book) were able to recall four or five women who served with them in the same company and married non-Jews. It is thus possible to calculate that there were about 100 cases of 'mixed' marriages, in other words, about 4 per cent of all the unmarried female recruits from Palestine married non-Jews.[74] In the Yishuv itself, the phenomenon of such mixed marriage is calculated in the hundreds, or about 2 per cent of all the single women in the Yishuv and it seems that, at a cautious estimate, the number in the army was almost double that in the Yishuv.[75] Many of the Jewish recruits boycotted their friends who fell in love with British men and wanted to marry them. The boycott was especially typical of Haganah members – whether active or less so – who had enlisted in the army full of nationalist fervour.

Marriage to non-Jewish Servicemen

For many women from the Yishuv who married British soldiers, the marriage was seen as a means of escape from the painful routine of day-to-day life, although there were also many who married for love. Jewish servicewomen, too, married non-Jewish soldiers for these same reasons.[76]

The marriage of Jewish women to non-Jewish men in order to improve their social standing is well known in Jewish history. For example, in eighteenth-century Berlin, Jewish women married Prussian men in order to gain acceptance into German society.[77] In Eastern Europe, too, many Jewish girls were married to non-Jews. However, these phenomena, which until the establishment of the Yishuv had been seen as betrayal of the nation or the religion, were now considered as betrayal of Jewish nationalism and a breech of the national collective. The novelty in this was that the secular community, too, saw in this an unforgivable sin.

The female Jewish officers who dealt with all the applications for marriage did their utmost to prevent these unions. Their efforts were mainly expressed at times of political tension in the country, during periods of searches and arrests. Such marriages, in the eyes of the Yishuv and its representatives in the company, were conceived not only as a family union between a Jewish person and someone of a different religion, but worse – as crossing over to another side, a hostile one. The graduates of the Cadre course (and subsequently additional Haganah members) were entrusted with defending national honour. It seems that the male message did indeed seep down and become internalized throughout the period of female military service in the British army. It was 'interpreted' mainly into efforts invested by the commanders to prevent marriages of Jewish women to non-Jewish soldiers, sometimes even at the cost of hurting the women themselves and their personal happiness. Some of the commanding officers stressed that the message had been passed on to them unequivocally,[78] and others insisted that there was no need for the message to be blunt, but they understood themselves that this was one of their main objectives. It appears that women's organization leaders in the Yishuv also 'adopted' the task imposed on them by their male counterparts in defending the 'moral boundaries' of the women recruits. Thus, for example, Hadassah Samuel, who made frequent visits to the ATS camps, admitted that she saw her job, in part, as preventing marriage to non-Jewish soldiers.[79]

It would appear that the men did not 'rely' only on the officers to implement this order. Ya'akov Tsur, the Jewish Agency emissary to Cairo, recalled that one of the tasks imposed on him, in addition to being a 'confidante' to the servicewomen in Egypt, was to prevent marriage to British servicemen. He was aided by the powerful Yishuv discipline 'that controlled everything and erected a kind of iron wall between what was permitted and what was not'. This tight watch on the servicewomen was explained as 'not only in national loss', but also as 'a danger to the future of the *servicewomen themselves*' [author's emphasis].[80] In other words, the men wished to determine the servicewomen's future 'for their own good', and expected the Hebrew officers to set a personal example, which often proved too much for them.

In their efforts to defend the servicewomen's 'morality' the Jewish officers were also aided by the older servicewomen, who saw it as their job to guide the inexperienced younger women along the moral highroad. About 6 per cent of the recruits were over 40 years old when they enlisted and they were seen by the younger recruits as 'righteous moralists'. The older women often preached to the younger ones on 'decent behaviour' and told them to preserve their 'dignity'.

It appears that in attempts to prevent mixed marriage, a mutual interest developed between the Jewish officers, the British officers and the military authorities. These, too, did not encourage romantic ties between Jewish women and British soldiers, but for different reasons. When the British became aware of a serious relationship and intention to marry, they did their best to separate the couple, usually by posting the soldier or officer elsewhere and placing distance between him and his Jewish beloved. The effort to separate couples was the result of the army's experience with women in the underground movements, sent to extract information from British soldiers under the pretext of a romantic relationship. At a certain stage, British officers were even warned against intimate relations with Jewish women who were suspected of spying for the Haganah. Although instances of women forming ties with British soldiers and officers in order to get information from them were few and of little significance, they did harm to other relationships that were innocent and devoid of all devious intent. The suspicions on the part of the British soldiers and especially the officers disturbed the formation of new relationships and behind each genuine love affair there lurked a message of suspicion and fear.[81]

A case in point was that of a young beauty from Jerusalem, daughter of a senior police officer in the British Mandatory Police, well educated and fluent in several languages. She fell in love with a British officer when working in a hospital near Suez and became pregnant by him, but the officer refused to marry her. His commandant helped him obtain a transfer to somewhere outside Egypt and, when the woman learned of this, she managed to locate him, boarded the ship and threatened not to budge until he married her. The wedding was performed by a military chaplain on board ship.[82] There were also incidents in which couples were separated, but it was the servicewoman who was transferred elsewhere in an attempt to end the relationship.[83]

'Mixed' Marriage in Company 508

Elisheva Erez, who served in Company 508 in the Cairo Citadel, testified that in this company alone there were about ten cases of Jewish servicewomen falling in love with British soldiers and marrying them. Erez's roommate spoke fluent English and even before enlisting had had a relationship with a British policeman. In the Citadel she met a British officer from an aristocratic family, a chemist by profession. The two got married after the war and made their home in Britain.

Another servicewoman in the company married a colonel on the camp. The two went to England and several years later moved to

Washington, where the husband was appointed Britain's Military Attaché to the United States. A servicewoman from Jerusalem fell in love with a garage worker and went with him to England. A few years later, they returned to Israel and lived there together until the husband's death. Apart from one servicewoman who belonged to Jerusalem's 'cultural elite', the other servicewomen who fell in love with British soldiers – according to Erez – were uneducated. Most of them were new immigrants who had been in the Yishuv only a few years before enlisting and they lacked strong ties with Judaism or Yishuv culture. Contrary to stories from other companies, Erez could not recall boycotting those servicewomen in her company.[84]

British Military Command for the Middle East was situated in the Cairo Citadel. Servicemen and women serving in it were often forbidden to go out to Cairo at night, or required to return to camp before dark because of security problems in the town, so that a lively social life took place within the Citadel itself. Most of the Jewish company's servicewomen were employed as office clerks and, unlike the hospital workers or drivers, had regular working hours, so that they were better able to take advantage of their spare time. The Citadel provided a good space for the many parties, balls and entertainment evenings which were attended by the non-Jewish servicemen and servicewomen stationed there. Such a lively social life seems to have helped tighten the bonds between servicewomen from Palestine and non-Jewish soldiers and the mixed love affairs flourished in numbers greater than in other ATS companies, where the working and social conditions were different.

Haganah Members who Married British Servicemen

Haganah members, especially the older and more idealistic among them, who fell in love with non-Jewish servicemen were looked upon as a disappointment from the nationalist aspect. After visiting the training camp and after learning of such cases, Rivka Katznelson wrote: 'Among them [the recruits who married British men] are some who would have better remained in our ranks. Why did these leave their nation?'[85] It was a huge crisis, even among the Haganah members themselves, when their friends 'strayed' and fell in love with British men, despite and in contradiction to all the messages they had been exposed to. They were unable to reconcile themselves to their friends' 'betrayal'. Thus, for example, Zipora Shahar and her fellow servicewomen, veteran Haganah members before being recruited to the ATS, boycotted Aviva Cohen, their good friend from Tiberius and their roommate in Company 513, because she fell in love with and subsequently married a British soldier, a boycott that lasted almost forty years.

Lea Spector, a veteran Haganah member and a much-admired officer in one of the ATS companies in Egypt, fell in love with a British officer. When he received a posting to Italy, Lea was able to join him. However, when she learned that he was married, she returned, broken-hearted to the Yishuv.[86] Sara Lichtenstein, a veteran Haganah member from Haifa, was Haganah leader Ya'akov Dori's courier. She married a British sergeant and weapons expert and went with him to Australia. Some Haganah members had secret relationships (that did not culminate in marriage) with British soldiers,[87] and some recruits had their heart broken and committed suicide.

Mixed Marriage in the WAAF

Life on RAF camps in Egypt were different from that in the ATS companies particularly because the camps were mixed, in other words, men and women lived on the same camp, although in different living quarters. On RAF MU 107, about a hundred Jewish servicewomen were stationed, together with thousands of soldiers. The servicewomen worked mainly in aircraft spare parts stores or were aircraft mechanics under the command of men. Thus plenty of occasions arose for social interaction between Jewish servicewomen and non-Jewish soldiers that resulted in several love stories.

On other RAF bases, several dozen Jewish servicewomen worked as wireless operators or in the screening rooms for identifying aircraft movements. The British servicemen in these places were usually well educated and working in shifts under tense conditions which often paved the way to romantic liaisons between servicemen and women. Meira Beres from Tel Aviv served in Ismailia and married John Cummings, an air gunner from Scotland. After the war the couple went to live in Scotland. In 1949, they moved to Israel with their two small daughters and Cummings converted to Judaism. Five years later the family returned to the UK.[88]

In face of the fact that about 100 of the recruits married British men, it would appear that at least some of the fears that accompanied female recruitment did indeed materialize. In the Yishuv the messages passed on to the women were contradictory with regard to relations with the British forces (on the one hand they were encouraged to entertain them in order to extract information, and on the other, there was suspicion and alienation), but the army did not encourage these relations and even used means to prevent them. Indeed, the British ATS officers and their Jewish counterparts, together with their commandants, passed on frequent and unequivocal messages as to the personal and national danger lurking in such relationships. Nevertheless, it is possible that a mixture of elements that were absent in the Yishuv provide explanation for many of these cases: close proximity in the workplace and at social events between the recruits and the non-Jewish servicemen soldiers; the women's distance from home and family; the sense of loneliness and alienation that intensified in the army among some of the recruits, especially the new immigrants; the pressures of army life, threat of war, etc.

Several such marriages ended in disappointment and heartbreak and the servicewomen returned to the Yishuv, whether in wartime or shortly after, some pregnant, others who had no children yet. Still, many marriages were successful and lasted for decades.[89]

Loveless Sex

Some of the Jewish servicewomen had sexual relationships with non-Jewish officers and soldiers that involved no romantic ties. T. Damon (the pen name of Dora Margalit) whose 'life in the army was complex and full of adventure', openly and courageously recalled in her autobiography 'Along the Paths of Fate' about the less patriotic sides to her military service. As a refugee from Poland with no family and not a single relative in Palestine, she and her friends served in a hospital near Cairo and used to go out with British soldiers they had met at parties in the nearby base or at one of the clubs. Their dates invariably included sex.[90]

It is known that several of the servicewomen, both Jewish and non-Jewish, were employed in prostitution during their military service. In its fight against this phenomenon, the British army engaged units of the ATS Military Police in Cairo, such as the one under the command of Daphne Hill, who located the girls and brought them to face trial in their companies. One of them was a driver in Company 513, an immigrant from Germany who had been in the Yishuv for a short time before enlisting. She was classified a whore by the British, since she made a habit of staying in various hotels under assumed names to provide sexual services to non-Jewish soldiers in return for cash.[91] It should be stressed that the number of women involved was very small and it did not justify the image or rumours attached to the majority of recruited women.

Unwanted Pregnancy

The Palestine recruits were also hounded by the fear of unwanted pregnancy by foreign soldiers. And indeed some of them became pregnant by British soldiers, but the exact number of these is unknown. A few testimonies and documents reveal that the number of unwanted pregnancies were between twenty and thirty. Some of the married servicewomen became pregnant to their husbands in the course of the service and considered terminating their pregnancies.[92] However, this debate will focus on servicewomen who became pregnant to foreigners and were subsequently deserted. These servicewomen were denied the support of their families, whether because they had no relatives in the Yishuv or because they came from conservative families who took a dim view of their relationships with a foreigner.

In her book *Bnot hayil*, Bracha Habas describes several cases of Yishuv servicewomen who found themselves with unwanted pregnancies. One of these was a married woman whose soldier husband had been taken prisoner of war in Greece. After a vacation in the Yishuv, she learned that she was pregnant by her husband's friend. Another servicewoman insisted on continuing with the pregnancy even though she was no longer in contact with its father. Encouraged by its Jewish officer, the entire company joined forces to help the pregnant servicewoman, although she ultimately miscarried the foetus. A woman serving in Italy was in an advanced stage of pregnancy when she waited in vain for the arrival of documents from her American soldier lover who had promised to marry her. Since these never came, her officer took her under her wing, funded everything she needed for herself and her baby and the servicewoman decided to return to the Yishuv.[93]

Some of the pregnancies were terminated. For example, one of the servicewomen in Hanna Maron's company in Egypt found herself with an unwanted pregnancy. She felt unable to share her predicament with her commanding officer, or even return to her home, so she asked Maron for help. Maron had heard from other servicewomen about an old woman in Cairo who did abortions and took the servicewoman to her. However, when she saw the conditions under which the woman conducted her business, she changed her mind and took her friend to the Jewish hospital in Cairo, where, with complete discretion, the doctors carried out a termination.[94] Pregnant servicewomen who returned to the Yishuv with no means of support were aided by the Council for Women's Organizations.

Suspicion towards Recruits

Even though Audrey Chitty, ATS Commandant in the Middle East, did not particularly like the Zionist enterprise and the Yishuv leadership, her opinions did not influence the attitudes of the ATS field command staff toward the recruits from the Yishuv. Most of the time the local commandants were fair toward the recruits. There were even occasional expressions of admiration for the Zionist enterprise and the Yishuv. Nonetheless, the British High Command was open about its suspicions vis-à-vis nationalist activity or what could be construed as such, and also toward the Yishuv's Zionist and political aspirations and those of the Jewish recruits who represented it. These suspicions did not fade with time and accompanied the recruits throughout their service.

The British suspicions were not unfounded. Many servicewomen from the Yishuv involved themselves in illegal activity during the military service. The more intense the struggle of IZL and Lehi against the British, so the terrorist activity in the Yishuv increased, the searches among servicemen and women from the Yishuv grew more frequent and the more restricted their movement in the army became.[95] Even requests for a transfer to another company were often construed as involvement in Zionist activity. Daphne Hill, a Military Policewoman in Cairo, who had come to the Middle East in wake of the Lord Moyne assassination, testified that the feeling was one in which 'the Zionists are trying to impose themselves on the army, if we only let them'. She admitted that she had not promoted so much as a single Yishuv recruit above the rank of Corporal because 'I didn't trust them'.[96] The suspicions were mutual and there were numerous servicemen and women who did not trust the British until the end of the war.

NOTES

1. Several books and papers have been pubished on the expression 'The People's War' and especially on its visual implementation. See for example, John Ramsden, 'Refocusing "The People's War": British War Films of the 1950', *Journal of Contemporary History*, 33 (1998), pp.36–54; Geoff Eley, 'Finding the People's War: Film, British Collective Memory and World War II', *American Historical Review*, 106 (2001), pp.818–38. British women scholars claim that despite attempts to paint the war as one of the people, propaganda was

conducted on a clear gender-based distinction: with recruitment of the men, women became more identified with the home and as potential victims of air attacks. This gender policy, which was emphasized in films, pamphlets and weekly newspapers and in government policy that opposed recruitment of married women, focused on women's place in the home. Lucy Noakes, *Women in the British Army: War and the Gentle Sex 1907–1948* (New York 2006), pp.103–4; Wendy Webster, *Englishness and Empire 1939–1965* (Oxford 2005), pp.21–2.

2. Germina Moed, an ATS nurse in a Suez hospital, wrote to her family, 'They are coming to call me to watch over a difficult patient on ward 10, it's the ward of the Colonial army.' Ya'akov Margalit (ed.), *Hineni shalcheni: mitnadvim batzava habriti kotvim* [Here I am, send me: writings of volunteers to the British Army] (Tel Aviv 1984), p.123. Many army documents made a clear distinction with regard to the various colonial battalions in the army. 'Colonial Batallions' in 'Progressing Report [clause 11]', October 1944, p.4, National Archives, London (NA), WO 169/15659. This concept was also implemented in Palestine. The September 1939 decision on the establishment of mixed infantry battalions of Jews and Arabs, for example, was taken in accordance with British concepts concerning battalions consisting of various nationalities under British command. However, change took place in the course of the war and most of the Yishuv battalions contained only Jews and no Arabs, not because of a change in policy but because most of the recruits were Jewish. Sco Foundation for Palestine Inc., *Study of Jewish, Arab and British Policies*, 2 vols (New Haven 1947), p.1025.
3. According to Tom Segev 'the Mandatory system was designed to give colonialism a cleaner, more modern look. The Allied Powers refrained from dividing up the conqueror's spoils as in the past; rather they invited themselves to serve as "trustees" for backward people, with the ostensible purpose of preparing them for independence.' In reality it was merely a reworking of colonial rule. Tom Segev, *One Palestine, Complete : Jews and Arabs under the Mandate* (New York 2000), p.118. Edward Keith-Roach felt that Palestine's biggest tragedy occurred when it was placed under the supervision of the Colonial Ministry after being under the Foreign Ministry. Ultimately C system, which was adapted to undeveloped countries, was implemented (instead of A which was granted to Britain by the United Nations). Edward Keith-Roach, *Pasha of Jerusalem: Memoirs of a District Commissioner Under the British Mandate* (London 1994), p.90.
4. Probably apart from India, where the women's auxiliary force was not an integral part of the ATS. In 1944, female officers sent to train Indian recruits encountered problems. The Women's Army had a reputation in India, but some of the servicewomen did not like the British officers and were reluctant to cooperate with them. Julia Cowper, *The Auxiliary Territorial Service* (London 1949), p.116. According to Tom Segev, the British were impressed by 'spiritual Zionsim, the revival of the language, the establishment of the university. They did not like political Zionism, though, because it threatened the status of the Arabs.' Segev, *One Palestine, Complete*, p.154.
5. Keith-Roach wrote: 'Most of the British officers with whom they had come into contact were fed up with their political views and also their constant demands. Their policy had been aggressive from the start and by the time I arrived I found

that there was a general feeling among the soldiers of: "Better the Arabs we know than hordes of Jews from East-Europe".' Keith-Roach, *Pasha of Jerusalem*, p.81.

6. Yoav Gelber, 'Aspectim politiim lehakamat hakoah halohem beyishuv haeretzisraeli btkufat milhemet haolam hashnia' [Political aspects in establishing the fighting force in the Yishuv during WWII], *Yalkut Moreshet*, 22 (November 1976), pp.31–62; Michael Cohen, *Churchill and the Jews* (London 2003), pp.207–23.
7. Before arriving in Palestine, Chitty was in command of Girl Guides troops in England and held a position of command with the ATS in Surrey. Interview with Major (ret.) Daphne Hill, Richmond (London), 10 May 2006.
8. Interview with Claire Epstein, 20 September 1979. Interviewer: Yehudit (no surname available), Kibbutz Ginossar Archive. Two days before the end of the course the Struma ship sunk. Epstein, as English speaking, was chosen to report on the tragedy at the party. The British high command disapproved as it was seen by the British officers, including Chitty, as 'an attempt at rebellion', and was the reason she was not promoted to officer status but remained a sergeant. There is some truth to her claims, since a year later, when the matter of Epstein's commission was discussed, Chitty admitted to Sharett that Epstein had 'been a great disappointment'. Ultimately, Sharett was able to transfer Epstein to a Jewish company. Sharett's conversation with Chitty, 17 January 1943, Central Zionist Archive, Jerusalem (CZA), S25/6039.
9. Interview with Esther Herlitz, Tel Aviv, 9 December 2005; Interview with Hadassah Samuel, 12 February 1972. Interviewer: Margalit Shilo, film 200/K, the Institute for Modern Judaism, Department of Verbal Documentation, Hebrew University.
10. Segev, *One Palestine, Complete*, p.9. Sir Michael Hogan, a Crown Counsel who served in Palestine between 1936 and 1948, put it thus: 'There was a saying that anyone who came to Palestine was pro-Jewish to some extent, but after a while becomes mainly pro-Arab, and usually leaves [the area] pro-British.' Hadara Lazar, *Out of Palestine: the Making of Modern Israel* (New York: Atlas & Co., 2011), p.86. Dame Leslie Whateley, Director of the ATS who visited the Middle East in April 1945, wrote in her memoire that after consulting with many civil servants in the Mandatory government, she was still unsure as to who was in the right, the Jews or the Arabs. Dame Leslie Whateley, *As Thoughts Survive* (London 1949), p.168. Whateley had first visited Ramala, then Jerusalem, even though the number of Jewish recruits was vastly greater than that of Arab recruits.
11. About a week after the decision on female military recruitment was published, Chitty noticed a large Star of David in the background of the advertisement flyer. She was furious when she realized the significance of the symbol and demanded its removal. Samuel flatly refused. Chitty, who was excluded from discussions on the flyer, felt cheated and decided to have a new flyer printed in three languages. The incident is mentioned in Daphne Trevor, *Under the White Paper: Some Aspects of British Administration in Palestine from 1939 to 1947* (Jerusalem 1948), p.62.
12. Audrey Chitty Diary, 31 January 1942, National Army Museum, London (NAM), 9802-55-2.

13. Edward Keith-Roach wrote: 'High commissioners come and high commissioners go. To them Palestine is an incident in their official careers; to me and other officials here it is our lives.' Segev, *One Palestine, Complete*, p.513, ref. 90.
14. Chitty diary, 23 February 1942, NAM, 9802-55-2.
15. Scholars are divided as to the scope of anti-Semitism or hostility expressed by the British decision makers toward the Zionist issue. Eviatar Prizel, for example, insists that it is hard to find among them any recognition of Zionism as a movement with positive depth and vision. However, their attitude to Zionism and its aspirations was not unsympathetic, or contemptuous or indifferent, as was characteristic of British attitudes to other colonies of the Empire, and most of them took an interest in Zionism and its hopes. Still he felt this to be a negative and hostile attitude. Eviatar Prizel, 'Bere'i akum: hazionut ve hamatzav be'Eretz Israel al pi yomanim briti'im 1927–1931' [In a crooked mirror: Zionism and the situation in Eretz Israel according to British diaries 1927–1931], in Shmuel Almog et al. (eds) *Tmurot ba'historia hayehudit hahadasha: kovetz ma'arim keshai le Shmuel Etinger* [Changes in the new Jewish history: collection of papers as a gift to Shmuel Etinger] (Jerusalem 1987), pp.233-7. Gabriel Sheffer related to persons who held key policy making positions and were often described by Jews as 'Pro-Arab' or 'anti-Semitic.' He is convinced that their personality and motives are too complex to credit them with the hackneyed concepts of 'pro-Zionist' or 'pro-Arab' and common denominator seemed to have been their sense of responsibility to the post to which, so they believed, they were appointed, safekeeping the wholeness of the British Empire. Sheffer, Policy Makers, p.177. According to Segev, 'Many of the British brought with them imperialist arrogance and a powerful sense of cultural superiority. There were those who saw their dominion as a destiny and a mission.' Segev, *One Palestine Complete*, p.8.
16. Keith-Roach wrote: 'The Jews, inconsiderate toward Arabs, were morbidly hypersensitive with regard to themselves. This self-deception was almost pathological and they never admitted that the reason for Arab hostility might be because of faults in the Jews themselves. This lack of psychological honesty destroyed any chance of rapprochement', and, 'There were other men moving about poking their noses into every-thing that interested them ... They belonged to the Zionist Commission'. Keith-Roach, *Pasha of Jerusalem*, pp.221, 81. Lord Martin Charteris, head of Military Intelligence in Palestine 1945–46 believed that 'The Jews are incapable of seeing another's point of view, only their own.' Lazar, *Out of Palestine*, p.33.
17. Julia Cowper's Lists, NAM, 25-247-9401. Medals for Excellence were awarded to only twenty-six ATS soldiers in Britain and five from outside Britain.
18. Cowper, *The Auxiliary Territorial Service*, Appendix 6. At its height in 1943 the ATS in Britain and in other theatres of war numbered 212,500 soldiers. In that year, the number of ATS recruits formed 7.35 per cent of all the British land forces. Noakes, *Women in the British Army*, p.131.
19. This term refers to the unglamorous younger sister, who carried out all the household chores. The ugly khaki uniforms contributed to this image, in contrast to the blue or white uniforms of the other forces. It is probably the reason that Jean Nox, the second Commandant of the ATS, changed the cut of the uniform and its accessories when she took the post in March 1941, in the hope of

changing the image of the ATS in the eyes of Britain's women and the recruits themselves. Collett Wadge, *Women in Uniform* (London 1946), pp.120–3.

20. Cowper, *The Auxiliary Territorial Service*, p.102.
21. Wadge, *Women in Uniform*. pp.133–6. According to Samuel's reports, until April 1942, eighty female British officers and sergeants had arrived in the Middle East. Samuel emphasized that this damaged the chances of promotion of female Jewish soldiers. Executive meeting of Recruitment Office, 14 April 1942, CZA, S25/5063.
22. War Office, *Regulations for the Auxiliary Territorial Service* (London 1941), p.100.
23. Mina Ben-Zvi, 'The First ATS Cadre', *Niv Ahim*, 21 August 1991, p.8.
24. Letter from Claire Epstein to Jewish Agency Political Department, 19 January 1942, p.1, Haganah History Archive, Tel Aviv (HHA), 33/10. Reports on the special problems of the Jewish battalions in the army (that related to male service) say: 'The Higher Command is not infested with anti-Semitism, although there are political forces there that are opposed to us. Relations between the military command in Palestine and the Jewish Palestine government are excellent and the military command is influenced by the principles of the local authorities. The central military command in Cairo *is not so poisoned* and a more attentive ear can be found there.' [author's emphasis] Lecture by Amnon Zair (Rudi), apparently to the Haganah Command, 22 July 1943, HHA, 117/18.
25. Dr Nadia Stein, 'Dawn with our servicewomen', *Olam Ha'isha*, 40–1 18 (June 1942), p.10.
26. T.S. [sic], *Davar Hapo'elet*, 9 (27 September, 1943), p.133.
27. Samuel distinguished between two kinds of female British officers: 'there were those who had an extraordinary attitude toward the girls and remain friends to this day, and there were others who simply hated Israel'. Interview with Hadassah Samuel, 12 February 1972. Interviewer: Margalit Shilo, film 200/K, the Institute for Modern Judaism, Department of Verbal Documentation, Hebrew University, p.14.
28. This is the origin of the military term, 'orderly room' that existed on the company level. In more severe cases, servicewomen were judged by more senior officers, such as the regional commandant, in which case the military process was called a Court Martial.
29. Ze'ev Sheffer (ed.), *Sefer ha'hitnadvut: Parashat Ha'hitnadvut hatzvait shel yehudei Eretz Israel Be'milhemet ha'olam hashniyat* [Book of volunteering: the case of military volunteering of Eretz Israel Jews in the Second World War] (Jerusalem 1949), p.542.
30. Interview with Esther Herlitz, Tel Aviv, 9 December 2005.
31. Ruth Kolodny-Baki, *Tik Yozefina* [Josephine file], National government publication (Tel Aviv 1994), p.68. Also, Mary Mackenzie carried a pistol with her wherever she went. She died in the late 1950s, probably from alcohol abuse. Thus according to Varda Hoofien, who visited the UK in 1959, Gnazim Institute, Tel Aviv. notes for Bracha Habas, *Bnot hayil: sefer ha'ATS* [Women of valour: book of the ATS] (Tel Aviv 1964).
32. The first ATS convoy set off for Syria in February 1944, under the command of Mary Mackenzie. In May 1945, the first convoy of women drivers left for Benghazi in the Western Desert and Tobruk and were the first to arrive in Tripoli

in convoys after a month-long journey. This included an emotional encounter between the Jewish drivers and local Jews who had survived the atrocities committed by the Italian army.

33. Letter from Mary Mackenzie to Ruth Breda, 16 March 1946; group interview with former members of Company 513 (Mina Company) in Haifa on 27 April 2006. Days after the letter arrived, Breda was granted leave to search for her mother. The humane side of her personality, which was usually kept hidden, is also illustrated by the case of the pregnant servicewoman who wanted to have an abortion in a military hospital. Mackenzie persuaded her to keep the baby, 'in light of the tragedy that befell the Jewish nation, she had to see to the following generation and leave others to do the army's work'. Kolodny-Baki, *Tik Yozefina*, pp.81–5.
34. Adelyn Bonin, *Allegiances* (Santa Barbara 1993), p.194.
35. Interview with Naomi Yekutieli (Torok), Tel Aviv, 8 December 2005; Interview with Tirtza Raviv (Torok) and Yael Arieli (Kornberg), Jerusalem, 27 December 2006.
36. Habas, *Bnot hayil*, p.120; Interview with Yael Arieli.
37. Gail Brayborn and Penny Summerfield, *Out of the Cage: Women's Experiences in Two World Wars* (London 1987), 163. This reflects the feeling of many of the servicewomen who enlisted in the WAAF.
38. From partial data (the first 637 recruits to enlist at the Jewish Agency recruitment office in Tel Aviv) it transpires that 221 had basic education, 307 were high school graduates and 109 were university graduates. 'Division of female recruits according to age, education, civilian occupation and chosen military occupation', 13 February 1942, CZA, S37/674.
39. Interview with Jean Baker, Tackley (near Oxford, UK), 17 May 2006.
40. Pat Hall, *Fearfully 502: A Lighthearted History of 11 M.T.C. / 502 M.A.C, A.T.S* (London 1946), pp.18–19.
41. One of the incidents took place when a Jewish driver, who spoke only German and Hebrew, collided with a car belonging to a local civilian who spoke only Greek. A military policeman summoned to the site spoke only English and considerable commotion ensued. Ibid.
42. In some cases the ability to translate 'saved' the servicewomen; such as when they were tested on gas warfare and had not managed to study the material. The sergeant/translator, who was familiar with the material, answered the questions correctly in English and all the servicewomen passed the exam. Habas, *Bnot hayil*, p.120.
43. Hall, *Fearfully 502*, pp.18–19; Whateley, *As Thoughts Survive*, p.161.
44. Frank Knight, *Kaspareet Kronicle*, 50 (30 August 1998), p.3.
45. The deputy commandant of Company 509 in Genifa travelled to the army rabbi to fetch prayer books and bottles of wine for the Passover feast. Company 509 War Diaries, 28 March 1945, NA, WO 169/21581.
46. Company 511 War Diary, 19 April 1943, NA, WO 169/13858.
47. At Hospital 27 in Tel el Kabir, a British officer was instructed on a forthcoming fast and the special meal that preceded it. Full of goodwill, the officer drove with the Arab cook to the market in Ismailia and bought all the necessities for the festive meal. Several months later, the Jewish servicewomen, together with companies of Jewish soldiers and on orders from the Yishuv authorities,

announced a day of fasting in protest at British hostility in the Yishuv. The same British officer was sure that this was again a religious day of fasting and bought the necessary ingredients for another beginning of fast meal. Habas, *Bnot hayil*, p.123.

48. Company 508 War Diary, 24 April 1943, NA, WO 169/13855.
49. Company 517 War Diary, 23 November 1943, NA, WO 169/13864.
50. Report to Klinov, 18 January 1944, CZA, S23/91.
51. The soldier whose nickname was Lofty met Tzfira Ogen, who was the company sergeant major, after the war in London and told her that he had known about the secret activity being enacted on base. Habas, *Bnot hayil*, p.116.
52. Rachel Caspi, 'WAAF', *Niv Ahim*, 21 (August 1991), p.15.
53. Interview with Brucha Ben-Haim (Eisenberg), Nahalal, 7 January 2006.
54. Company 522 War Diary, 20 August 1944, NA, WO 169/18034.
55. Testimony of Yehudit Bar-Rav-Hai, 2 December 1952, p.5, HHA, 11.34; the report was incorrect.
56. S.A. [sic], 'Two Years to the ATS in Eretz Israel', *Davar Hapo'elet*, 1–2 (21 February 1944), p.2.
57. To this end, the recruits were given lectures and talks, provided by the **Office** and the recruiters equipped them with literature, facts and figures. Rachel H., 'From the Impressions of a Recruiter', *Davar Hapo'elet*, 6 (7 July 1942), p.80.
58. Daniela Reich, 'Between National Mission and Social Ostracism: Contacts Between Jewish Women to British Servicemen 1940–1948' (MA thesis, Haifa University, 2003), pp.110–11. The cafés were established in the1920s in Tel Aviv and their number grew considerably in comparison with the town's population growth in the early 1940s. On encounters between Jewish and British frequenters of Tel Aviv cafés during the period under discussion see Batya Carmiel, *Batei hacafe be Tel Aviv 1920–1980* [Coffee shops in Tel Aviv 1920–1980] (Tel Aviv 2007), pp.18–19, 42–3.
59. Sheffer, *Sefer hahitnadvut*, p.537. Friendships developed among the female drivers at Company Mina and the camp's British driving instructors. Before the lessons the instructors, who taught practical driving, allowed the drivers to practice on various weapons at their disposal, such as guns, rifles, submachine guns and mortars. The instructors were very patient toward them and did not mind repeating their directions dozens of times. Tzofia Hillel, 'Women in the Uniform of a Foreign Army', 1981, pp.55–7, Israel Defense Forces (IDF) Archive, Tel Hashomer, 1867/98/151.
60. Interview with Aviva Gil (Flentzbaum), Tel Aviv, 24 January 2006.
61. Interview with Rachel Ziv (Barshavsky), Tel Aviv, 2 February 2006.
62. Several interviewees stressed that the British servicewomen were much more sexually liberated than their Yishuv counterparts. Zipa Gov, who served in the WAAF in Ismailia, recalled how the British girls would book in to hotels every weekend with their boyfriends, while their conservative Jewish friends would go to the Jewish club. Interview with Zipa Gov (Katz), Tel Aviv, 22 October 2006.
63. 'ATS Roots and Treetop' (undated, probably from the 1980s), p.8, HHA, 16/36.
64. Interview with Sara Kopler (Bar-Adon), Tel Aviv, 26 June 2006.
65. Habas, *Bnot hayil*, p.180; Interview with Yael Arieli; Interview with Tzfira Ogen.
66. Interview with Esther Herlitz.

67. Tzofia Hillel, 'Women in the Uniform of a Foreign Army', 1981, pp.13–14, IDF Archive, 1867/98/151; 'Authorizations of Recruitment Office, by Month', August 1942, CZA, S25/11162.
68. In Company 506, a hockey game took place between the host team and servicewomen from Companies 504 and 511 from Tel el Kabir. RAF 107 MU held sports days that included water games and even a camp beauty queen contest. *Kaspareet Kronicle*, 50 (August 1998), p.1.
69. In a conversation, Sharett and a senior officer agreed it would no longer be an order to participate in parties. 'Report of Mr. M.S. [Sharett] on Egypt Visit, August 16–29, 1942', CZA, S25/6039. Further evidence of this approach can be found in a letter from a Hebrew officer in Tel el Kabir referring to the British officers who wondered how this could be, since they had arranged weekly parties and the Jewish girls did not attend. The officer explained that the Jewish servicewomen wanted 'parties, lectures and cultural activity' and the officers suggested they ask the Yishuv authorities to send lecturers and materials. 'We are serving the Yishuv; the Yishuv should defend our honor!' *Olam Ha'isha*, 56–7 (28 September 1942), p.3.
70. Company 504 War Diary, 13 September 1943, NA, WO 169/13851.
71. Several of the Cadre participants remember receiving on that day a message, apparently from Moshe Sneh, Head of the Haganah National HQ, approving their participation, so that they acquiesced and agreed to perform.
72. Interview with Zipora Shahar (Eitan), Nahalal, 7 January 2006.
73. Nira Yuval-Davis, 'Nationalism, Feminism and Gender Relations', in Montserrat Guibernau and John Hutchinson (eds), *Understanding Nationalism* (Cambridge: Polity Press, 2001), pp.127–8. Similarly, although ostensibly from a nationalist, secular point of view there was a distinction between prostitution and romantic ties with non-Jewish men; in fact the women and girls who forged ties with men outside the boundaries of the national collective were conceived as whores in every way. From a national perspective, secular and religious attitudes were quite similar. Deborah Bernstein, 'Tel Aviv lavsha mahsof ... Pnina hameshuga'at vegvulot hakrach' [Tel Aviv donned a décolleté ... Crazy Pnina and the city boundaries], *Teoria veBikoret*, 25 (Autumn 2004), pp.154-155.
74. There were twenty-nine ATS companies in the Middle East. Jewish recruits served in twenty-five of them, although they did not form the majority in all of them.
75. Estimate of the number of incidents in the Yishuv comes from Reich, 'Between National Mission and Social Ostracism', p.111. At that time there were some 23,000 single women in the Yishuv, aged between 20 and 45. Still it should be remembered that most of the mixed marriages took place in the larger towns, where most of the single women lived, so that the percentage of mixed marriages is closer to 3 per cent.
76. Ibid. Often women who wished to escape social or financial hardship by marrying non-Jewish men also found themselves in financial straights in their husbands' home countries. The husband's families were sometimes cold toward the foreign women and they found themselves rejected and excluded in alien and unfriendly places. Two servicewomen, sisters from a Sephardi family in Haifa, married British soldiers in the hope of improving their financial situation. On arrival in the UK, they discovered that their husbands were gravediggers.

The two packed their bags and returned to Palestine. Interview with Zipora Shahar. Nonetheless, dozens of other mixed marriages were happy and lasted for many decades.

77. A famous case in point was that of Rachel Varnhagen (1771–1833) from Berlin who held a literary salon between 1790 and 1806, frequented by aristocrats, politicians, scientists and authors. In 1814 Rachel married Varnhagen von Enze, a historian and diplomat, and was baptized a Christian. Deborah Hertz, 'Emancipation through Intermarriage? Wealthy Jewish Salon Women in Old Berlin', in Judith Baskin (ed.), *Jewish Women in Historical Perspective* (Chicago, IL 1998), pp.193–207.
78. Interview with Tzfira Ogen. In conversations with seniors in Haganah, Herlitz was impressed that this was her job even if she had not been told so specifically. Interview with Esther Herlitz. Ellen Elroi, an officer in the WAAF, does not remember receiving any orders to prevent marriage with non-Jewish servicemen. Interview with Ellen Elroi, Bat Yam, 4 February 2006. This could be because of the loose ties between Haganah and the WAAF recruits.
79. Interview with Hadassah Samuel, p.13.
80. Ya'akov Tsur, *Karev Yom: dapei avar* [A day is coming: pages from the past] (Jerusalem 1979), pp.142–3.
81. The officers all received a letter about information that had reached the British army according to which many Jewish women who were fraternizing with British servicemen, especially officers, were active spies on behalf of the 'dairy' (Haganah term for the IZL), and that many of the officers had already fallen prey to these Jewish women's charms. All officers were therefore warned to stay away from these Jewish women who were not carrying out their task as such, but as part of a certain task derogatory to the British army in general. Letter from Regional Security Officer on the matter of 'Espionage', probably 18 July 1946, Jabotinsky Institute, Tel Aviv, 31/3/10 C-4.
82. Interview with Sonya Peres (Gelman), Tel Aviv, 9 January 2006. The sevicewoman was released from the army after her wedding and went to the UK, where she had her son. Two years later she received false information that her husband had been killed in the war and she returned to Israel.
83. Amnon Zair described a similar case in his memoirs. An ATS servicewoman, Haganah member and schoolteacher, fell in love with an Australian RAF pilot who wanted to marry her. But the woman felt that the cultural differences between herself and the pilot's mother were insurmountable and that the older woman might be upset by the girl's Sabra forthrightness. Zair had her transferred to a company in Palestine, without revealing it to the pilot, whose heart was broken. Amnon Zair, , *Vienna–Gan Shmuel* (Gan Shmuel 1980), pp.87–8.
84. Interview with Elisheva Erez (Pearlman), Hertzliya Pituah, 14 January 2006.
85. Rivka Katznelson, 'In Basic Training Camp', *Davar Hapo'elet*, 6 (7 July 1942), p.78.
86. Interview with Esther Herlitz
87. Interview with Sonya Peres.
88. Interview with Aviva Gil; Interview with Ora Cummings, Tel Aviv, 6 January 2010.
89. Shoshana Little (Hasson), a survivor of the 1929 Arab riots in Hebron, met her husband, a British officer and engineer in the army. They married after the war

and lived together until his death in 2005, at first in the Gulf Emirates where he worked, and later in the UK. Interview with Shoshana Little (Hasson), Kibbutz Ma'agan Michael, 4 March 2006.

90. T. Damon, *Beshvilai hagoral: Roman mehayai ha'ATS* [In the paths of destiny: a novel on ATS life] (Tel Aviv 1953), pp.15–20.
91. Transcripts of her interrogation, 13 November 1944, NA, FO 371/46109.
92. Several of them considered terminating the pregnancy rather than compromise their military service, but were dissuaded from doing so. Others ended their service on becoming pregnant. For example, Naomi Epstein, whose husband was also recruited, realized she was pregnant and was sent to a military hospital to be tested. She was released from service and gave birth. Interview with Naomi Epstein, Tel Aviv, 7 March 2007.
93. Habas, *Bnot hayil*, pp.144–5.
94. Interview with Hanna Maron (Meierzak), Tel Aviv, 28 February 2006.
95. Yoav Gelber, *Toldot hahitnadvut: Nos'ei hadegel* [History of volunteering: bearers of the flag] (Jerusalem 1983), p.314.
96. Interview with Daphne Hill.

8

Bridge between Judaism and Nationalism

Paradoxically, the Yishuv's fears that leaving their country would distance the recruits from Judaism and Zionism proved unfounded, and their service actually reinforced their Jewish and Zionist identity. According to commonly held gender division, men symbolize patriotism – by being bearers of the new nationalism – while women fulfil their national vocation by being mothers.[1] The recruits presented a different concept. They wanted to demonstrate their patriotism and national identity within a military framework. Thus, for them, cultural activity was an important tier in the company life. In male companies, on the other hand, such activity was seen as an inferior pastime or secondary to their military activity.[2]

Throughout the generations, Jewish women filled a crucial role in upholding Jewish traditions and values. So it was in the case of the Marranos (Jews who converted to Christianity to avoid persecution) of Castilia and in Jewish society in Germany and Eastern Europe during the nineteenth century.[3] The Jewish women were the ones who defended the Jewish rituals and way of life and insisted on Jewish education for their children. Throughout the escalated integration processes undergone by Eastern Europe's Jewish population in the eighteenth and nineteenth centuries, the men handed over their traditional responsibility for their children's religious and general education to their wives. By doing so, they allowed themselves the liberty to conduct their lives in the non-Jewish world, to achieve positions of power and to continue with the assimilation process.[4]

The novelty in Jewish women's service in the British armed forces lay in the fact that they turned a blatantly gender-based issue – preserving the Jewish tradition and culture – into one of national significance and, in doing so, they saw themselves as partners in preserving and contributing to the Hebrew and Jewish culture within the nation building process. Almost every holyday or Sabbath became a focus not only of Jewish-religiousness, but also of nationalist activity, both in content and from the aspect of those taking part.

Building a national culture is neither an easy, nor a singular matter. The national culture designed by the elites, especially in a society composed of different cultural and ethnic groups, languages, social class, etc., tends to reflect and express only the culture of some of the groups. The other groups are pushed to the sidelines, even if they don't represent numerical minorities.[5] This constitutes the 'cultural hegemony',[6] in which the ideology of the controlling group is presented as universal, taken for granted and 'natural', and is internalized by the rest of the population. The control is expressed simultaneously in focal points of economic, political and ideological empowerment.[7]

The holydays and Sabbaths celebrated far from home provided the Jewish servicewomen with an opportunity not only to build and reinforce their national and Zionist identity, but also to seek and bolster their Jewish identity as well. As part of their efforts to maintain their national identity, the servicewomen, who were representatives of Yishuv society in the army, wished to transport the Hebrew culture[8] created in the Yishuv and, especially, the ceremonial motifs of the Kibbutz and Moshav sector, into army life. By using rituals in the army the Yishuv leaders hoped to bring the new immigrants closer to the dominant, integrating culture – the Yishuv's Hebrew culture.[9] Hebrew culture grew in the Yishuv in contrast to the Jewish culture of the Diaspora, but then by being in a foreign land the servicewomen actually reinforced the Jewish content, those same symbols of a culture the pioneers wanted to escape from.[10]

Sabbath in the Army

In the ATS companies in the Middle East the Sabbath became an important event in the lives of the servicewomen. Far from home, the servicewomen, including those who did not come from an observant family, felt a need to protect their Jewish identity, to practice rituals that are unique to Jewish women, such as the lighting of candles. The first Sabbath at the Cadre course in Sarafend was attended by the Chief Rabbi, Louis Isaac Rabinowitz, on 30 January 1942, at the camp movie theatre, which had been adapted to serve as a house of worship, in order to hold 600 participants. He wrote emotionally that, 'for the first time in history, the hall was filled by women in military uniform'.

The rabbi pointed out that this event turned into a tradition throughout their service: a white cloth spread over a coarse wooden surface that served as a table, blessing of the candles, the song, 'We have brought peace upon you', reading of a chapter from the Bible, followed by a party. The ATS servicewomen, he stressed, 'imparted a traditional Jewish feel to the occasion'.[11]

Lighting Sabbath candles in a tent became 'a tradition that must not be deviated from'. On the festive atmosphere that permeated the Sabbath, Ella Wilensky wrote: 'How good it is that we light candles between sacred and secular ... there is a "simple" lighting of candles: a blessing, reading chapters from the Bible [both in Hebrew and in English], some singing and sometimes there is even a concert.' Despite the religious connotations, the blessing and the candles were more of a nationalist symbol than a religious act. Sometimes, they even danced Israeli folk dances after the ceremony. When conditions were difficult, the servicewomen made a point of celebrating the Sabbath: 'the Hebrew corporal did not forget each Friday the Sabbath cake and even if pressure of work sometimes prevented them from preparing a real party, the women sat together, drank coffee and listened to recorded classical music on the record player.'[12]

Sometimes Sabbath services were shared by several companies. The first such service in the drivers' Company 513, which was newly established in Camp Mina, was celebrated in the NAAFI and a company of Jewish soldiers from the nearby camp in Almaza was invited to participate. All those present enjoyed the joint programme prepared by the two companies. On another occasion, thirty servicewomen from this company travelled to Cairo to participate in a Sabbath service and social evening with ATS Company 525. And once, the servicewomen of Company 509 in Genifa spent the evening in the company of 100 soldiers from the Jewish Brigade, who had also taken part in preparing the cultural entertainment.

It wasn't easy to hold a weekly Sabbath party, as ideas, programmes, songs and characters were, ultimately, limited. When a party was unsuccessful 'the prestige of Zionism dropped for a few weeks and the few hard-headed [servicewomen] who refused to give up on the holydays were despondent'. On the other hand, following a successful party, 'the status of the organizers [usually Haganah members] rose in the eyes of the company and the Hebrew soldiers in nearby companies'.[13]

Sabbath gatherings provided an opportunity to inform the servicewomen on events back home and around the world and to reinforce their involvement in activity in the Yishuv and the Jewish nation. This custom, too, began among the recruits from the Kibbutz and Moshav movements. Toward the end of 1942 and during 1943, information began reaching the Yishuv on events in Europe. This subsequently reached the army, too and servicewomen used various means to express their solidarity with their brethren in Europe. After candle lighting in one of the companies and the traditional singsong, two servicewomen took their place on either side of the piano, each holding newly arrived newspapers from home. One delivered the latest news on the Holocaust in Europe and the other described events in Palestine. According to Tzofia Hillel, 'Death and destruction on the one hand; building and creative activity on the other. We all sat and listened in profound silence, almost in reverence, each deep in her own thoughts.' On the effect of the news, 'Suddenly [there was] a sense of belonging to the country, things that until then were taken for granted, received a deeper significance and, with it a sense of powerful commitment toward the country.'[14]

When, in 1944, the war front moved to Europe, servicemen and women from Palestine, too, were transferred to Italy. The sea journey to Italy lasted a week and the servicewomen celebrated the Sabbath on board ship. One of them recalled how 'with the approach of the Sabbath all the servicewomen on the ship congregated in the large hall, sang quiet Sabbath songs and lit Sabbath candles. The following evening, when the Sabbath was out, they held a dance, with the women bursting into a fiery *hora* and other Israeli folk dances.'[15] Thus the English dancehall received a new, Israeli, connotation. Every week, throughout the course of their term in Italy, the servicewomen made a point of celebrating the onset of the Sabbath.

The Sabbath tradition provided a chance to bring together the servicewomen and the Jewish men serving in the Allied Forces. Sometimes these soldiers would also attend Sabbath eves in the ATS clubs and companies. For them, as for the male and female recruits from the Yishuv, Sabbath candles symbolized the Jewish home they had left far behind. As Bracha Habas wrote, 'The Sabbath candles ... were also as spotlights for the Jewish soldiers ... each and every Jewish soldier ... knew that on that evening, in an ATS company, however far away or near, he would find an open door and a group of his own people.'[16] Non-Jewish soldiers, too, were made to feel welcome. A particularly emotional Sabbath eve took place in No.65 Hospital in Italy. A non-Jewish soldier was brought there after being wounded in a dangerous commando operation, in which all his friends had been killed in action. The Jewish servicewomen working in the hospital, who knew that the soldier was unable to get out of bed, perhaps would never even walk again, decided to pay him special attention. When his pain was slightly alleviated, they held a Sabbath ceremony at his bedside, served a plate full of sweet things and fruit and lit Sabbath candles. For the first time after arriving in the hospital, the wounded soldier had tears in his eyes.[17]

As compared with the sense of solidarity and shared destiny that the Sabbath provided to its celebrants, its lack in other companies caused a feeling of loneliness and alienation. Zilla Babayouf, who served as a nurse in an Egyptian hospital, wrote to the Jewish Agency, 'The Jewish sergeant of German origin, who works in the company office speaks no Hebrew, lacks all national sensitivity ... and altogether does not try to do anything on behalf of the company; no Sabbath eve parties, lighting of candles or readings are conducted here.' And she added, 'We have no Jewish officer and our English officer is a big anti-Semite.'[18]

Spiritual and National Renewal

The Soldiers' Welfare Committee and the Working Women's Council provided the necessities for the parties and holydays. On each of her visits, Beba Idelson, Chair of the WWC, brought with her songbooks and notes, and in summing up one of these visits she determined that 'suitable material for parties, holydays and dances had to be supplied to the servicewomen'.[19] For the Jewish New Year in 1944, for example, the WWC sent gifts to all the ATS companies for use in their cultural activities. Like the other women's organizations, the WWC maintained contact with the Jewish recruits throughout their service, keeping them updated on its own educational activity in the Yishuv.

The holydays provided the servicewomen with a chance for 'spiritual and national renewal', in Rabbi Rabinowitz's view, and it appears that they spared no effort to make them as impressive as possible: 'In these days of blackout, this was made possible with the help of car headlights ... Chapters from the Bible and all kinds of decorations adorned the walls ... Bible readings, suitable songs, lectures, suitable literary pieces', satirical pieces (in which the servicewomen excelled) – all joined in making this an exciting event.[20] Tisha B'Av turned into a national day of mourning and the Passover Eve an exhibition of traditional ritual and modern interpretation. In addition to the Jewish holydays, the servicewomen also celebrated the

Hebrew and national days of memorial that had been reinstated in Eretz Iarael.

Jewish New Year and the Day of Atonement

Both these days are religious in essence and the Kibbutz and Moshav movements did not include in them any new nationalist components. These occasions provided an opportunity to demonstrate solidarity with the Jewish nation. In September 1942, servicewomen from one of the companies in Tel el Kabir decided, with their officer, to celebrate the New Year in public prayer, in solidarity with their brethren in Europe. A few of the servicewomen objected, on the grounds that it would be hypocritical to demonstrate a national characteristic by resorting to prayer. The servicewomen invited a Jewish soldier and a cantor from a neighbouring company. Religious books were donated by the Jewish community in Cairo. A make-shift stage was erected, together with an ark and curtain and the holyday was finally celebrated according to tradition when a prayer was raised in the camp's large NAAFI hall, in the presence of all the company's servicewomen. Haviva Kotler, an observant servicewoman, recalled standing beside a fellow servicewoman as the prayers were being said. It was her first time inside a synagogue and Haviva pointed out which prayer to follow.[21]

In Company 504 in Tel el Kabir, the New Year was celebrated at dusk, according to the Hebrew calendar. A festive meal was served beneath an open sky, attended by all the servicewomen, including the officers from the regional ATS HQ.[22] The regional commander gave her New Year blessings to the Jewish servicewomen and the meal was followed by prayers in the NAAFI hall. The following morning, which was the first day of the Holyday, more prayers were held in the NAAFI hall. Strictly speaking this was not traditional, since the meal came first and prayers were said after it, whereas according to Jewish tradition, the prayers should be said before the meal.

A joint party was held in the Tura area in Egypt, where the large caves served as bomb shelters, workshops and stores, for all the Hebrew companies present on Jewish New Year 1946. A special programme was produced which was embellished by portions from the Bible. The programme consisted of traditional Jewish components as well as pieces of modern Hebrew culture: portions were read from the New Year and Day of Atonement Prayer Book and a series of humorous pieces from military life; the songs, 'The First Regiment', by Yitzhak Yitzhak and Alterman's 'Song of Vengeance'. The participants read segments on the illegal immigration ships and the choir sang 'Our Father Our King'.[23]

The Day of Atonement provided non-observant Jewish servicewomen with an opportunity to turn the day of fasting into an act of national distinction and an exhibition of strength vis-à-vis the British staff. Zipora Shahar and Esther Yanai from Drivers' Company 513 recalled that on the Day of Atonement, out of respect for the sanctity of the day, they did not enter the camp dining room, even though they were both from secular socialist families and had never fasted in their lives. Like many other servicewomen, they did not eat in public, in solidarity with the Jewish nation and the Yishuv in Palestine.[24] Yael Arieli and Tirza Raviv from the 502 Ambulance Company remember that on the Day of Atonement, they too avoided the camp dining room in order to show the British staff that they were adhering to their own nationality.[25]

The Kol Nidre prayer, recited in one of the companies, is carved in the memory of one of the servicemen, who wrote in *Davar*, 'I don't recall a more powerful experience than the sight of servicewomen, sitting in rows and rubbing their eyes of tears as they took part in the Kol Nidre prayer – for a child, a father-mother, a friend ... each according to her personal emotions'.[26]

Hanukah – the Festival of Lights

To the Zionist Movement Hanukah was a holyday of supreme importance. Jewish tradition stressed its miraculous-religious significance, whereas the Zionist movement chose to celebrate the holyday's national content: a historical model for the national struggle against assimilation into non-Jewish cultures, a struggle for the political independence of the Jewish people in its own homeland, raising the standard for human heroism and self sacrifice, stressing activism and taking one's fate in one's hand, vis-à-vis national and personal passivity. The practical expressions of this holyday included, in addition to lighting candles, reciting Hebrew poems, a presentation of the story of Hanna and her seven sons, and singing Hebrew songs.

The holydays provided an opportunity to unite the servicewomen with Jewish history. The Hanukah party, which took place in one of the hospitals in Egypt, also welcomed Jewish servicemen from a nearby company. The servicemen prepared a show consisting of songs and poems based on eight Jewish characters from the days of the prophet Deborah and to their present day. The show was also translated into English and was highly praised by the hospital's matron and commander.[27]

Sometimes Jewish holydays were also used on behalf of Jewish refugees. For Hanukah 1944, the 503 Drivers' Company in Abassya near Cairo threw a huge party. The servicewomen printed an elaborate invitation that was distributed among all the male and female soldiers in the vicinity. The programme, which took place on the sixth night of Hanukah, included a candle lighting ceremony, singing the traditional Hanukah song and other songs, and presentation of a four-part comedy show, written by servicewomen Lily Feldman and Lea Meisel. Rivka Dromi built the scenery and the entire evening was accompanied by orchestral music. All the profits from the sale of programs and the buffet went toward Jewish refugee children.[28] Similar activity was conducted by servicemen from Palestine.

Purim

The Jewish Yishuv, including the pioneering community, was more attracted to the carnival-like character of Purim and its more folkloristic customs, than to its idealistic-religious aspect as presented by its traditional context.[29] The holyday gave the servicewomen and their non-Jewish counterparts an opportunity to unload some of the burden of military discipline and rejoice in grand parties, dress up in specially sewn costumes, play-act, dance and sing. In Company 508 in the Cairo Citadel, the servicewomen had managed to hold a successful Purim Ball, even though the company had been transferred to its new quarters only three weeks before. Several of the servicewomen produced an entertaining cabaret which was received with great enthusiasm by all.[30] Like other Jewish holydays, Purim, too, provided an opportunity to involve Jewish refugees in Egypt.

Even in Europe, Jewish servicewomen celebrated the festival of Purim, sometimes together with servicemen from the Yishuv. In Italy, servicewomen in the No. 15 hospital in Naples produced a musical together with servicemen from the Solel Boneh Engineering Corps Company. The show was composed and directed by one of the servicemen with lyrics by Mordechai Ze'ira, both of who served in the same company. One of the servicewomen, Hadassah Aharoni

(Melamed), played the part of King Ahashvarosh and Avremale Slutzky from Nahalal played the role of Queen Esther.[31]

Passover

The traditional Passover holyday stands on clearly determined religious foundations: two ceremonial days, the requirement to eat unleavened bread (matzo), reading the Hagadah and divesting the home of all non-Passover foods, and an overall spring-clean. In many homes attempts were made to turn the Passover meal (seder) into a warm, family-orientated event by making it especially festive. Nonetheless the conceptual differences between pioneers and the religious connotations of the Passover, as expressed in the Hagadah and the Seder ceremony, aroused ideological dissonances, and the kibbutz and moshav movements developed a new interpretation of the Hagadah that emphasized the significance of its being a celebration of liberty and the Feast of Spring and the beginning of the harvest season. To this end, various kibbutzim produced a special Passover Hagadah for reading at the Seder meal. The Hagadah contained Hebrew songs and texts praising the renaissance of the Jewish nation and the land, alongside chapters from the traditional, centuries-old Hagadah.[32] The Passover holyday turned from a religious one into a national one and was thus transferred from the home to the public domain.

Like most of the Yishuv recruits, many servicewomen celebrated the Jewish festival of freedom in Egypt, where the story began. Dressed in military uniform, they were fighting for the world's right to live in freedom. For many, this was more than vaguely symbolic. In the ATS companies, where most of the servicewomen were from Palestine, Passover services were held that combined traditional Jewish elements with agricultural and nationalistic elements, similar to those in the kibbutz and moshav movements. Claire Epstein, who was born into an observant Jewish family in London, was especially impressed by the service at Camp Tel el Kabir, which was attended by some 500 servicemen and women from the region. The servicewomen prepared a special kibbutz-inspired and decorated Hagadah, a women's choir sang Hebrew songs and servicemen recited the relevant texts in the Hagadah. The service took place in the NAAFI building, which had been especially prepared for the event with long rows of tables, white table cloths and traditional Passover decorations: flowers, green leaves and pictures. Appropriate texts lined the walls.[33] In No.1 Hospital

Company in Kantara, servicewomen introduced an entertaining review of army life into the Passover programme. Mazal Elazer, a graduate of the Cadre course, composed the 'Company 506 [department] B Charter', in which she likened Audrey Chitty to Pharaoh.[34]

Tu Bishvat

It would appear that in the Zionist Movement, special emphasis was given to Tu Bishvat. It was a Zionist holyday that took place in Palestine and fulfilled the cultural needs of the time. In many places, the holyday, which had been celebrated since the days of the First Aliyah, became the province of Zionist circles. The first to customize this holyday were the Hebrew teachers and its main motif consisted of planting trees – symbolizing the re-rooting of the Nation of Israel in its homeland.

In certain companies in Egypt servicewomen celebrated the holyday together with their commanding officers, even though they were serving in a foreign land and not in their homeland. The February 1943 issue of *Letter to the Hebrew Soldier* (published by the Soldiers' Welfare Committee) contained a report on the tree plating ceremony in an ATS company in Egypt, a ceremony that was an official event in the life of the company:

> Saplings had been laid along the length of all the huts and at the designated time, hundreds of servicewomen arrived for a festive roll call. The Order of the Day contained an official announcement on the planting and this commenced with the sound of the company choir singing in the background. The commanding officer gave her blessing to the Jewish servicewomen and wished them a happy holyday on behalf of the HQ.

The event was recorded in the War Diary of Company 509 in Genifa as 'a concert in honour of the Jewish holyday of trees'.[35]

Tu Bishvat also provided an opportunity for Yishuv servicemen, both at home and in Egypt, to express their love of the land and the country. A company of male soldiers serving in the Yishuv participated in a tree planting ceremony in Kibbutz Ma'ale Hahamisha. Hundreds of soldiers took part in the planting, together with representatives of the Yishuv's institutions and commanding officers, who delivered speeches at this important event. In Egypt, too, on the Libya border, servicemen marked the occasion, although they didn't plant trees, but there was a festive meal, bible reading and Hebrew songs were sung.[36]

Tel Hai Day

On this occasion there was an attempt on the part of the Kibbutz and Moshav movements to set this date in memory of the heroic death of Yosef Trumpeldor and the fall of Tel Hai in 1920. It was an event of national significance, one that stressed the value of heroism and fighting for national dignity, in work as well as in protecting the land. The Tel Hai celebrations that took place in the Yishuv consisted of a 'Yizkor' prayer, published articles, aphorisms and eulogies, blessing the time and the place and a rich repertoire of stories, poems and legends surrounding the Tel Hai myth, especially the death of Trumpeldor.[37] It would appear that, notwithstanding the blatantly nationalist character of the event, the British allowed it to be commemorated, possibly due to a lack of awareness of its true significance to the Jewish servicemen and women, or because of the religious elements woven into it. One of the Tel Hai Day celebrations was attended by servicewomen from companies 504, 506 and 511 in Tel el Kabir and about seventy Jewish servicemen from nearby transport companies. The event took place by moonlight on a Friday evening and was followed by a Sabbath ceremony, attended by all the celebrants.[38] Company 509 held a Tel Hai Day ceremony together with Jewish servicemen from Company 554, which was located nearby.[39]

Lag B'Omer

Lag B'Omer enjoyed a renaissance at the hands of the Zionist movement, which as a nationalist movement searched its history for events that could be harnessed for its nation-building aspirations. One of these was the Bar-Kochba uprising, which had traditionally been underemphasized in Jewish folklore for fear of being conceived as an uprising against their host countries. It stressed the foundations of national uprising against a foreign regime, the necessary courage and determination of those taking part, and their willingness to sacrifice their lives for their homeland. While still in the Diaspora, many folkloric foundations had already been thoroughly embedded into this holyday, such as the joy of nature, bow and arrow tournaments and bonfires. Its character as a holyday that worships national activism and Jewish heroism and the mix of traditional rituals with Zionist/ideological foundations made Lag B'Omer an important holyday.

One of the most memorable Lag B'Omers for the Jewish servicewomen was celebrated beside the pyramids in Giza. Rabbi Rabinowitz chanced upon the party when he drove women from Company 513 to their camp near the pyramids and was highly impressed by it. The servicewomen and their guests danced the *hora* and sang Hebrew songs around a huge bonfire they had lit. In response to a request by one of the servicewomen, the rabbi spoke about the special connection between this holyday and the history of the Jewish people and its struggle for liberty and freedom. His words and the special atmosphere in the area lent a unique significance to the event.[40]

Other Celebrations

A review of the holydays and the way in which the Jewish servicewomen celebrated them indicates the extent of their activity, commitment to tradition and the effort invested. However, it appears that the festive spirit was especially notable in companies in which Jewish servicewomen constituted the majority, since it should be noted that similar experiences were not reported everywhere. Thus, for example, Sharett reported that Company 503 in Abassya differed from other ATS companies in that 'there is no lighting of [Sabbath] candles in the women's quarters and this is explained as being compliant with the general aversion to religious practices'.[41] Tsilli Brendstater, a sergeant in the Education Corps, who began her service in Jerusalem and continued it in Cairo and Alexandria, recalled no special atmosphere or celebration of Jewish holydays, since she spent most of her service in the company of British servicewomen and her work was more individual in character.[42]

In the WAAF units, celebrations of Jewish holydays depended on location and the numbers of Jewish servicewomen on base. In RAF MU 107, near the Bitter Lake, where some 100 Hebrew women served, the atmosphere around the Jewish holydays was special. In Camp Al Jedida, for example, Rachel Caspi, the camp's Hebrew officer, was allocated a large tent in which to hold Jewish social activity, especially on the Sabbath, when candles were lit and the servicewomen provided the entertainment. In the RAF camp in Alexandria, on the other hand, where there were only eleven Jewish servicewomen among several hundred of other nationalities, no Jewish holydays or Sabbaths were celebrated. In order to feel something of the festive atmosphere, the Jewish servicewomen would visit the Jewish club in Alexandria.[43]

The Struggle for National Symbols

When Moshe Sharett, head of the Jewish Agency's Political Department, departed from the first Jewish servicewomen on the Cadre Course, he told them, 'So long as there is no Hebrew army, you must know that the language of command is English, but the language of your lives in a Jewish company will be Hebrew and it will be the obligation of the Jewish woman to remain faithful at the same time to the British army and to the Jewish nation.'[44]

The recruitment of Yishuv women aroused fears not only from a gender aspect, but also from cultural, national and linguistic aspects. Many servicemen feared that women would choose to use English as a means for achieving preferential treatment and promotions in rank. Day to day life in the army was conducted in English: orders, instructions and military tribunals were all in English. Most of the recruits were not fluent in English and were able to learn it in courses on camp. At first the English-speaking Jewish servicewomen helped their counterparts by translating orders, etc., but throughout the service, the Yishuv servicewomen strove to instil Hebrew as their language of choice in the army.[45] As with the Jewish holydays, the struggle for Hebrew and the right to fly the Hebrew flag took place mainly in companies with a majority of Yishuv servicewomen. It took place notwithstanding the restrictions and strict military rules and in spite of the suspicions of the British about all expression of Zionist nationalism.

Although the British permitted freedom of worship to servicemen and women of different religions, they considered the use of Hebrew to be nationalistic and undermining. They wished to instil the use of English as one that unites all the recruits and hoped to prevent the use of a 'local' language, which they saw as nationalist separatism.

Various researchers have shown that language plays a pivotal role in imparting a social identity. The cultural models used in cognitive activity and, in its wake, behavioural concepts, are enfolded and even preserved with language. According to cognitive anthropology, it is possible to nurture mutual constructions among groups with different cultural backgrounds if they can achieve fluency in the 'same' language and, thus, to achieve control of mutual social models.[46]

As part of the cultural concept and as a means for seminal political and national activity, there also emerged the concept of Hebrew language teaching: not merely the cultural practice of introducing the language to someone who is unfamiliar with it, but also as a fulfilment of a cultural, movement-affiliated and social-national mission.[47] Within the structure of images of the national renaissance, the phenomenon known as 'reincarnation of the Hebrew language' took a pivotal position, since it was considered a major component in Jewish identity. The reincarnation of spoken Hebrew symbolized the connection between the ancient Hebrew-Jewish nationalism and the new nationalist-Zionist culture that was being formed in Palestine. The moral status of Hebrew as a national language was also expressed in the noun 'Hebrew', as a title for everything relating to the new Jew in Palestine.[48]

The Struggle for Hebrew in the Army

At the end of the Cadre course, Rachel Katznelson-Shazar took her leave of the new officers and 'ordered' them to follow in the footsteps of the first male recruits: 'you must learn from those Hebrew companies that knew how to defend their language, their culture and the essence of their lives'.[49]

In their struggle to conduct their military lives in Hebrew, the Jewish servicewomen followed in the footsteps of Yishuv women from the First Aliyah. The Hebrew language and culture were conceived as part of the national struggle in which the recruited women were required to participate, with the model of recruited men setting them an example. From the start of their military service, especially those who enlisted in orderly groups, the men strove to emphasize their national uniqueness. Their struggle for the right to raise their flag and to turn Hebrew into an official language was directed both in order to fulfil external requirements – as part of the Zionist effort to achieve post-war British recognition for the establishment of a Jewish state, and internally – to emphasize their uniqueness as volunteers from the Jewish Yishuv in the British army. The female recruits were called upon to join this struggle. The efforts invested in instilling the Hebrew language in the male and female companies encountered considerable obstacles, since many of the servicemen and women were not fluent in Hebrew.[50]

According to Esther Herlitz,

> everything that was achieved in the companies was achieved through struggle and constant vigilance: [the servicewomen] fought for the ... Hebrew language; for orders to be translated into Hebrew; for the servicewomen's right to wear the badge

'Palestine' on their shoulders and for the right to celebrate the Sabbath and Jewish holydays.

As for the struggle over the Hebrew language, Herlitz added that it was hard to explain to clerks, all English speakers, the necessity to translate orders into Hebrew. Similarly, there was a 'need to find a servicewoman to undertake the job of translating, since the Jewish sergeant doesn't know enough English and because *it was necessary to stick to principles here.*' [author's emphasis][51]

Epstein, a sergeant major at Tel el Kabir, made a point of publishing orders in Hebrew as part of the struggle for national identity. Herlitz testified that the stubborn adherence of the minority in the various companies bestowed control of the language on those servicewomen who were not fluent in it.[52] In their last year of military service, time was allocated for the study of the Hebrew language as part of the army's educational programme and, in addition, lectures were given on the Yishuv and its culture.

The WAAF servicewomen, too, conducted a struggle over the use of the Hebrew language. Like their ATS counterparts, it was important to them, too, to emphasize their national identity. In various RAF camps in Egypt, British officers forbade Jewish servicewomen to speak Hebrew during work hours. In other camps attempts were made to prevent Hebrew conversation in the women's living quarters and canteens. This resulted in complaints, which the servicewomen directed at Sharett on his visit to Cairo. Eventually a compromise was reached: in the workplace and in public places, only English would be spoken.[53]

The Struggle for the Hebrew Flag

Another arena in which the servicewomen struggled for their national identity consisted of flying the Hebrew flag. This had already been recognized as the national flag of the Yishuv and thus as that of everyone who considered him/herself to be representatives of it. Already from the beginning of voluntary enlistment, an unofficial custom had evolved among the Zionist institutions to present each company with the Zionist flag prior to leaving the country. But once the Mandatory Government turned the army's attention to this matter, an order was issued in early February 1941 forbidding civilians to give flags to military units. Servicewomen were forbidden to fly flags, with the exception of the British flag and the flags of the Allied forces or friendly nations. The Hebrew flag was not included in this category. In late 1942, the ban was extended to outside the boundaries of Palestine. Nonetheless, the Jewish male and female companies continued with their efforts and attempts to fly the flag as a symbol representing the Jewish Yishuv in the Land of Israel and their national identity.

A well-known incident involving the raising of the Hebrew flag took place on United Nations' Day in Cairo on 14 June 1943. Jewish servicewomen from Company 513 were meant to march behind the British flag with other groups of servicewomen from various ATS companies. The Jewish women asked to fly the Hebrew flag, like the group of Czech servicewomen, who marched with their national flag (although it subsequently transpired that they had no permission to do so), but their request was denied. They refused to march without the Hebrew flag, but acquiesced only when their company commander, Mary Mackenzie promised to discuss the matter with the highest ranks. One of the servicewomen even compared the matter with the Nazi order for all Jews to wear a yellow Star of David to indicate their identity, with the ban on raising the blue and white Star of David flag. The repercussions of this incident were significant and even reached the Yishuv.[54]

A further incident, also concerning the flag, took place on the evening of the British Empire's soldiers' march to commemorate their victory of Nazi Germany in Europe in May 1945. Then, too, the military commanders claimed that the Hebrew servicewomen did not constitute an independent nationality, so that they are unable to raise the Hebrew flag. The servicewomen refused to march without the flag. In the end, notwithstanding their hurt feelings, they marched behind the Union Jack, but made sure to maintain a distance of one step behind the groups of women in front of them, their silver coloured 'Palestine' badges on their shoulders shining from afar, in an attempt to emphasize their nationality uniqueness.

For the Jewish servicewomen, the flag also symbolized their being representatives of the Yishuv. In her farewell speech to the servicewomen about to set sail for Italy in May 1944, the company's Hebrew officer clarified their dual undertaking – both as soldiers in the British army, but also as representatives of the Yishuv – in their encounter with the surviving Diaspora Jews. In January 1945, a twenty-six-strong group of Jewish servicewomen set out for Italy after serving in Egypt in administrative positions. According to Habas, the officer who wished to stress to the servicewomen that they were filling a double mission departed from them with the message, 'You are taking with you three valuable pledges: the Bible, our book of books from the dawn of our existence; the Zionist flag, that you must bear in your hearts forever; and Sabbath candles and candlesticks, our devoted friends that impress an atmosphere of holiness all around us.' The officer also called on them to speak Hebrew among themselves and to follow the ritual of the Sabbath and Jewish Holydays under all conditions without missing a single one.[55] And, indeed, the servicewomen, when they arrived in Europe, were aware of the 'dual mission' imposed upon them.[56]

Further Expressions of Demonstrating National Identity in the Army

Other expressions of the struggle to express their national identity consisted of wearing a badge on their shoulder with the word Palestine embroidered in English. Jewish Drivers in Company 513 had the audacity to don a shoulder badge with the word Palestine embroidered in Hebrew. In Company 511 in Tel El Kabir, the drivers adopted an original approach in order to distinguish them from the other servicewomen. After a meeting with Arab soldiers, members of the Trans-Jordanian Arab League, they decided to order shoulder badges embroidered with the words: Land of Israel. Although against army rules, the Jewish servicewomen wore it with pride and the company staff turned a blind eye to it.[57]

Jewish servicewomen working in hospitals, too, tried to distinguish themselves from their counterparts of other nationalities. They were determined to demonstrate their nationality by means of a symbol of their own, even if it wasn't recognized officially and wasn't permitted; and some of them pinned an embroidered Star of David to the lapel of their nurse's uniform. Servicewomen who were transferred to work in hospitals in Italy in 1944, embroidered white armbands with a red Star of David, which they wore openly in the hospitals, although this was forbidden when they were serving in Egypt. At the number 65 hospital in Italy, some of the nurses wore Star of David badges made of tin. This badge, which was fashioned for them by a Palestine soldier, replaced their shoulder badge.[58]

The WAAF recruits, too, struggled for their national symbols and wanted to wear the Palestine (in English) badge on their shoulders, like their counterparts in the ATS, but they were refused permission. Following Sharett's August 1942 visit to Egypt and conversations he held with the local commanders, the servicewomen continued to wear the badge, but the officers turned a blind eye and made no further reference to it, even though official policy was not changed.

Clubs and Hostels for Servicewomen

In addition to the cultural activity that was part of military service, the servicewomen also enjoyed several 'islands' of culture and a Hebrew atmosphere outside working hours. These consisted of clubs and hostels built for the servicewomen on and outside of camp in order to complement the Hebrew atmosphere that the women's organizations and Yishuv institutions wished to provide them. Hostels had already been established in 1942 in order to provide servicewomen with 'somewhere where they can sleep, eat and [enjoy] a Hebrew ... atmosphere' when they were on leave from their army base or in their spare time. And they were much appreciated. One of the women wrote, 'Next week I'll have a day and a half to rest and I want to rest in town, in an ATS hostel. To really rest. There are newspapers from the Yishuv there and a radio, which broadcasts from Jerusalem.'[59]

Although the main objective behind the hostels was to create an atmosphere of Hebrew culture, over time the women's organizations provided recreational activity and entertainment for servicewomen who wanted a break from army life, especially in those hostels in the larger towns where servicewomen spent their vacation time. Shortly after the hostels were established, Hadassah Samuel reported, 'We are disappointed by the hostels ... We have learned that [a Hebrew atmosphere] is not the objective of these houses. The girls go off camp and don't want to have further cultural demands made of them; they want only rest and recreation. [Otherwise], they will not visit the [hostels].'[60]

The CWO saw in the establishment of clubs, hostels and rest rooms for the servicewomen in Egypt and Palestine one of the most important aspects of its connection with the servicewomen. Several elements cooperated on this issue: the CWO initiated the hostels, the military authorities made them possible and shouldered their administration expenses and the Egyptian Jewish community helped provide all the necessary equipment.[61] The CWO invested significant sums of money on funding the salaries of the hostel manageresses, who also reported on their activity, on books and furniture, gramophones, etc. In order for servicewomen stationed far from home to enjoy the best possible conditions, the CWO also cooperated with the Soldiers' Welfare

Committee – in organization as well as funding. Three hostels were established in Egypt for Jewish servicewomen – in Cairo, Ismailia (where the hostel also served other objectives, such as weapons smuggling) and Alexandria – and their locations were chosen because of their proximity to ATS camps. In Palestine, clubs and restrooms were established for the servicewomen in Sarafend, in Company 507 in Dir Suneid in Gaza, in Company 505 in Haifa, and Company 512 in Jerusalem.

Although they operated under the auspices of the CWO, the veiled competition between WIZO and the CWW over the benefits each provided to the Jewish servicewomen during the war was clearly aimed at drawing them to these organizations after the war.[62] Thus, for example, each hostel was established by a different organization. The WIZO hostel in Cairo was managed by Malka Weinberg, one of WIZO's leaders in Egypt. The hostel consisted of 'about 50 beautifully furnished rooms, cool reading and writing halls, recreation, sport and shower rooms. Cultural life in these places is conducted exclusively in Hebrew.'[63] In these hostels, the servicewomen were able to entertain Jewish servicemen. Aside from their homely atmosphere the hostels also attracted the servicewomen for economic reasons, since the rooms and meals they offered were cheaper than elsewhere.[64]

Ties with the Yishuv

In their struggle to preserve their national and cultural identity, the servicewomen received support and encouragement through direct contact with representatives of the Yishuv and the CWO. In the course of their military service, the women and the men often expressed their need for ties with the Yishuv representatives who had sent them to the army. These ties took place in several ways: visits, whether in the companies or in the clubs and hostels; gifts from different organizations; letters from school children, as well as publishing stories and letters by servicemen and women in Yishuv newspapers. Life away from the Yishuv in a foreign and stressful wartime environment created in many of them a desire to receive official 'greetings from home', not only from their families but also from home in the broader sense of the word – the Yishuv.

The kibbutz movements retained their own communication channels. Each kibbutz established a special communications committee, with the objective of staying in touch with their enlisted members. The United Kibbutz Movement (UKM) sent its newsletter

'A Bundle of Letters' to each serviceman and woman. From February 1942, large numbers of letters of enlisted Yishuv men and women were published in many of the newsletters. The UKM Security Committee maintained an on-going correspondence with the servicemen and women.[65] The Soldiers' Welfare Committee distributed the 'Newsletter to the Hebrew Soldier', which reported on events in the Yishuv and was received by all the companies in which Yishuv servicemen and women served.

Visits to the Servicewomen

Yishuv representatives, such as Sharett and Yosef Baratz, chairman of the Soldiers' Welfare Committee, made frequent visits to the servicemen and women in Palestine and Egypt (Sharett also visited them in Italy). These visits had two main objectives: the first was to provide the servicemen and women with a sense of connection with the Yishuv and to raise their morale. Another objective was to obtain an impression of the working conditions, the lifestyle and the hardships they were obliged to deal with. On their return from the enlisted men and women, Sharett and Baratz met with the CWO to report on their impressions.

Senior representatives of the CWO made frequent visits to the servicewomen in their camps in order to encourage them. Sometimes visits took place in response to criticism voiced by the servicewomen in writing or verbally over the insufficient contact with the CWO. In most cases, visits were coordinated with the Jewish Agency's Political Department and sometimes they were even made on its behalf.[66] Usually, CWO representatives set out on visits individually and not in groups. In order to strengthen ties with the servicewomen in the WAAF, for example, it was decided 'to keep in contact with the officers, to summon all the servicewomen on training camp for a meeting over a cup of tea, once a fortnight, and to invite a lecturer to the camp once a fortnight'.[67]

After the onset of female recruitment, Hadassah Samuel often visited the servicewomen. Her first visit to a military base took place in February 1942, at the Cadre course in Sarafend. Between 1942 and 1943 she often journeyed to Egypt to meet the servicewomen and she also visited them in Palestine. In the wake of each visit, she provided the CWO with a report on her impressions, after which there was a debate on her conclusions. Thus, for example, shortly after the establishment of Company 504 in Tel el Kabir, one of the first ATS companies in Egypt, Samuel visited together with Audrey Chitty, Commander of the ATS in the Middle East, in order to view living quarters on camp.[68] Samuel also participated in a memorial service for servicewomen killed in a road traffic accident.[69]

In the course of 1942, Beba Idelson visited together with a group of artists 'somewhere in [Palestine], a remote location, where visitors are rare'. She arrived on a visit to the training camp at Sarafend and a company that was located 'in one of the towns' (probably Abassya in Cairo. Place names were not revealed for reasons of security).[70] In May 1943, Idelson also visited servicewomen serving in Syria (Lebanon). Her conclusion was unequivocal: 'Frequent visits! We are making a mistake if we wait for a permit from the Soldier's Welfare Committee or the Jewish Agency ... We shall go as merchants!'[71] Idelson brought the servicewomen the sum of 50 PL with which to purchase things for the recreation room on camp. Idelson's visit was also reported in *Davar Hapo'elet*.[72] At a meeting of the CWO she said, 'We must take advantage of ... people close to us visiting the servicewomen'.[73] Rachel Yanait Ben-Zvi, too, who had made two visits to Beirut and Sidon and visited the servicewomen, reported at the same meeting.

In addition to visits by representatives of the Yishuv, the army also permitted visits by army rabbis to companies of Jewish servicewomen.[74] The first rabbis arrived in the Middle East with the British forces in order to fulfil the religious needs of the Jewish recruits. The task of a military rabbi included, apart from dealing with religious issues, assistance in searches for relatives in Europe, help to servicemen's families, blessing and conducting marriage ceremonies (between servicemen and women from Palestine, or between Jewish servicemen and Jewish refugees), hospital visits, funerals, etc.

When the first Jewish recruits arrived in the British army, the rabbis made a point of contacting them, and this was repeated later with the female recruits. The first of these rabbis were from Britain – Rabbi Israel Brody, Rabbi Isaac Rabinowitz, who was the Chief Rabbi to the British Forces in the Middle East and senior rabbi with the Eighth Army, and Rabbi Isaac Levy. As the numbers of recruits from the Yishuv increased, local rabbis were also recruited.[75] The rabbis visited the servicewomen in their camps, helped in organizing Jewish holydays, prayed with them[76] and provided them with prayer books.[77] The rabbis also held conversations with the servicewoman on various, including personal, matters.

Gifts

Aside from visits to military camps, connections with the servicewomen also consisted of gifts – to the Jewish servicewomen on Jewish holydays and to the British staff on the Christian holydays – such as writing sets and boxes of chocolates for Christmas. Sometimes the CWO joined forces with other groups, such as the Soldiers' Welfare Committee or the Histadrut Executive, in sending gift parcels.

For Jewish New Year 1942, the CWO and Histadrut Executive sent each company of Jewish servicewomen in Palestine and abroad subscriptions to books published by Am Oved. For Hanukah 1943, the CWO sent each ATS company a copy of the book *Women Members in the Kibbutz*, edited by Lilia Besevitch. In the attached letter, the CWO secretariat explained the motive for their choice: 'We are sure you will be interested in the lives of the working women depicted in this book, the women who were among the pioneers in forging the way for the new Hebrew woman in Palestine.'[78] For Rosh Hashanah 1944, the gift consisted of copies of David Shimony's book of poems. On receiving the gift, a group of servicewomen in Heliopolis (Cairo) wrote to the CWO that 'your letter was doubly significant for us ... it symbolized the fact that you have not forgotten us ... and it also constituted a "living testimony" from home and from Eretz Israel ... the smell of the land and of nature emanates from it'.[79] On the significance of the gift she received, together with a letter from a girl in Kvutzat Degania, Rina Shoffman from Kfar Yehezkel wrote, 'Suddenly you get the feeling that behind you there stands the Yishuv, looking out for you ... the parcel itself has no value, the main thing is the letter that accompanies it.'[80]

Another kind of gift the CWO sent the servicewomen consisted of sets of candlesticks for Sabbath candles. It also provided the servicewomen with the necessary equipment for use in cultural activities on Sabbath Eves, as well as all the issues of *Davar Hapo'elet*. In one of the ATS companies, the servicewomen used the gifts to decorate their mess hall. The CWO helped the ATS servicewomen to organize various kinds of exhibitions, from which the proceeds were devoted to Jewish refugees in Egypt.

In addition to gifts and other objects, the CWO also sent sums of money to the servicewomen for use in funding cultural activity. The money was presented to the servicewomen during visits of CWO representatives in the various military bases. Thus for example, during her August 1942 visit, Hadassah Samuel brought 20 PL for each company outside of Palestine. In their many thank-you notes, the servicewomen made it clear that the gift symbolized an ongoing connection with them in the army, which they valued highly.[81]

Meeting with Diaspora Jews

Additional opportunities to test the national identity of the Jewish servicewomen emerged in their encounters with Diaspora Jews: the ties forged with the Jewish community in Egypt, the Zionist/educational activity with Jewish servicemen in other member armies in the Allied Forces, and their humanitarian and educational activity in the course of their encounters with Holocaust survivors, initially in Egypt and subsequently in Europe.

The Yishuv recruits constituted the advance guard in establishing relations with Jewish communities in the Diaspora and instrumental in dispelling the sense of alienation that prevailed between the Yishuv and the Jewish communities in nearby countries. The servicemen, and especially the servicewomen, were emissaries of the Zionist enterprise in these countries and it was they who attracted the attention of the Yishuv leaders to the troubled condition of the Jewish communities in the Middle East. According to *Davar Hapo'elet*, 'For the first time, the servicewomen were required to see themselves as representatives of the Yishuv in their encounters with [people] who are far from our lives and our aspirations. Together ... our soldiers will have the strength for this task'.[82] Most of the servicewomen, especially those serving outside the Yishuv, found themselves, inadvertently, in an unfamiliar arena. They filled a mission that the recruiters in the recruitment offices had spoken of – to be spokeswomen for the Zionist cause, not only before the non-Jewish world, but also before Jews who were far from it.

The Jewish Community in Egypt

'The Jews of Egypt signed a page that was all light in its relations with the ATS', wrote Habas and added,

> The families Weissman [in-laws of the pianist, Pnina Saltzman], Horowitz, Tsadikov, Vidon, de Menashe and Politi and many others, opened their hearts as well as their purses and homes to the volunteer recruits. House parties, festivals, balls and exhibitions, as well as fundraising drives and, especially, personal care of the servicewoman, when she was in trouble and when she was happy.[83]

And indeed it seems that the entire Jewish community in Egypt adopted the recruits from the Yishuv and provided them with a substitute home throughout their time in that country.

The Jews of Egypt were, apparently, the first Jews outside of the Yishuv that the servicewomen came in contact with. For the native Yishuv women, this was the first meeting with Diaspora Jews and for the new immigrants, most of who came from Europe, it was a particularly fascinating encounter with a different Jewish community. For the Jewish community in Egypt, the meeting with the Yishuv women was the first significant and lasting relationship with representatives of the evolving nationalism across the border, even though there had been connections between Egypt's Jews and the Yishuv beforehand.

During the First World War, over the course of several waves between December 1914 and December 1915, a total of 11,207 exiles arrived in Egypt from Palestine and Syria. These included Dr Haim Bograshov, principal of the Herzliya High School; David Levontin, Manager of the Anglo Palestine Bank; Yosef Aharonovitz, editor of Hapo'el Hatza'ir; the writer Deborah Baron and Yehuda Leib Riklis, as well as other well known figures. As a result, the local Jews, especially in Alexandria, were exposed to educational and cultural activity from Palestine, by people who joined the community in teaching Hebrew and Jewish nationalism.[84] During the 1930s, too, representatives were sent by the Yishuv to work with young people in Egypt, as part of the relationship that developed between the Yishuv and the local Jewish community. Hadassah Berlinsky, for example, was sent to Egypt in 1935 to take up a teaching position in the Jewish community. In the evenings and on Saturdays, she worked with groups of youngsters from the newly established Hehalutz movement and tried to instil in them 'the spirit of Haganah'.[85]

The Egyptian Jewish community's first contact with the Yishuv actually began during the early stages of ATS recruitment in the Yishuv. The community wanted to make its own contribution to the war effort, but the British had their reservations because of Egypt's neutral status. The Yishuv leaders were interested in involving Jews from various communities in joining the British forces, so that by early 1942, contacts were made between the Yishuv and the military authorities over the recruitment of women from the Egyptian Jewish community to the ATS in the Middle East. As the organizing recruitment body in the Yishuv, the Jewish Agency assisted the correspondence between the Jewish community in Egypt and the British military authorities. After some reservations, the British army permitted their recruitment and several dozen young Jewish women enlisted in Egypt and joined some of the companies of recruits from the Yishuv.[86]

The Jewish community in Egypt was considered the wealthiest of all those in the Islamic states, particularly the very wealthy elite Sephardi community. Egyptian Jewry consisted of a heterogenic society living within an external cosmopolitan community. Due to the swift growth of the community and the fact that it was based mainly on immigration, the Jewish community in Egypt became, in a relatively short time, a community consisting of various ethnic groups with different cultures, traditions and languages. Thus it differed from most of the Jewish Diaspora in the east. From a socio-economic aspect the Egyptian Jewish community during the period between the two world wars was composed of three definitive groups: the Sephardi elites, the educated bourgeoisie and the poor classes, who constituted some 25 per cent of the community. Thus the Jewish world that opened itself to the Jewish servicewomen in Cairo and Alexandria, a world of secure and wealthy Jewry, of warm welcomes and friendly ties forged with several community members, was only one aspect of Egyptian Jewry. The second aspect consisted of the Jews who lived in the outlying regions.

Up to the mid 1940s, the Jewish community, which was part of the eclectic foreign community in Egypt, enjoyed a relatively safe and respected status in Egyptian society as well as a higher socio-economic standing than most of the indigenous Egyptians. For the Jews, Egypt was home; they were patriotic and loyal to the king and were even represented in the Egyptian parliament and Senate.[87] The community's unique character was formed in the schools, since Jewish children in Egypt were usually given a European education as part of a multi-lingual culture. Nonetheless, Egyptian Jews avoided public expression of sympathy or support for the Jewish Yishuv in Palestine.

The Community's Relationship with Servicemen and Women from Palestine

Typically the Jewish community in Egypt did not involve itself in public or political activity, even on public-local issues, and especially not with regard to an organization that was 'foreign' to them, such as the Zionist movement.[88] Thus, Yishuv representatives were obliged to invest much effort in raising funds among the wealthy Jews of Egypt for use in the treatment and smuggling out of European Jewish refugees via Egypt.[89] However, in spite of the reservations of Egypt's Jews toward the Zionist movement, an attitude typical of other Jewish communities in the region, the relations that developed with the recruits from the Yishuv were unwaveringly warm. It seems that many in the community were filled with pride at the sight of uniformed Jewish soldiers and were happy to help them in any way possible. Nonetheless, there were others in the community who took a dim view of the relationship with the servicemen and women.[90]

In Cairo and Alexandria, the community's women operated clubs for the Jewish servicemen and women that also served as communication centres between them and Zionist functionaries, and the servicewomen also volunteered to work in them. Although the CWO established the clubs, the Jews of Egypt were the ones to furnish them and they also contributed the food and bedding for them, provided laundry services and commodities needed by the servicemen and women. The community's women also helped the servicewomen with Torah books and food for the holydays. According to memoires and various stories, it would appear that the women members of the Jewish community in Egypt 'adopted' the Yishuv servicemen and women (even the older ones among them), who spent long periods far from home. The generosity of these women has been deeply carved in the memories of the servicemen and women as well as those of the representatives of the Yishuv who spent time in Cairo during the war. Moreover, the CWO recognized their contribution and sent them gifts for the holydays in thanks for their devoted care of the Yishuv recruits.[91]

Several recruits had favourable recollections of the meetings in the homes of community members. Ruth Kaplan (Melamed) noted the Sabbath eves to which the Jewish servicewomen were invited in the homes of local Jews. Ora (Herzog) and Suzi (Eban) Ambash were among the organizers of these events.[92] Although not Zionists, the Polity family, who owned a newspaper chain and were among the wealthiest in Alexandria, treated the servicewomen warmly and even welcomed several of them in their home.[93] Jewish servicewomen were also invited to the sumptuous home of Baron de Maneshe, as well as that of the Russo family, both among the wealthiest in Alexandria. The wealthy Jews also hosted Yishuv leaders on visits to Egypt.

According to Herlitz, whereas the community hosted servicewomen as well as servicemen, the women also contributed to the community. Some of the younger among them taught Hebrew in the community school in Cairo and others were youth counsellors in the Zionist youth movements – but here, too, according to Herlitz, more could and should have been done.[94]

Encounters with the Jews of Libya

The connection between the Yishuv servicemen and the Jews of Libya began in early 1941, when Britain attacked the Western Desert, caused the collapse of the Italian army and conquered Cyrenaica, and soldiers from the Yishuv's 5MT Transport Company arrived in this part of Libya. The drivers made it to Benghazi, the capital of Cyrenaica, as well as to smaller communities in Libya – Derna and Barca. Their contribution mostly consisted of their presence. The meeting with Jewish soldiers in uniform raised the spirit of the local Jews, since there was little else at that time that the soldiers could do for them.[95]

In wake of the final battle in El Alamein (late October 1942) and the race after the retreating Axis armies, transport companies returned to Cyrenaica, followed by other Jewish companies. Since the retreat of the British army, the local Jews had been subjected to a cruel Italian regime that banished some 3,000 to concentration camps. The first encounter between the soldiers of Company 178 with the Jews of Tripoli took place in February 1943. The soldiers rehabilitated the education system with the help of education supplies from the Yishuv, established a school for some 500 students and set about arranging the immigration of Jews to Palestine. In addition, the soldiers set up a clinic where children received medical treatment.[96]

In early November 1945, as the activity of the Yishuv servicemen was drawing to a close, a pogrom took place against the local Jewish community. There was an outbreak of riots, which were apparently pre-meditated and erupted in response to the local Arabs' uncertainty as to the political outcome of the war. Around 120 Jews were murdered as well as five Arabs, several dozen others were injured and large quantities of Jewish property were looted and destroyed.

In May 1945, toward the end of the war, the female drivers of Company 513 set out in a convoy of trucks to the city of Benghazi in Libya. After carrying out their military mission, they met with members of the local Jewish community. Aviva Dayan from Nahalal described the emotional meeting:

> The Jewish community in Benghazi welcomed us with flowers and accolades. Hundreds of children, women and men came to greet us, watching proudly as we drove the trucks. The children

> did not leave us for the entire time we were in Benghazi [48 hours]. It was almost symbolic how, together with them, we heard for the first time the news of the Nazis' unconditional surrender.[97]

The women drivers of the same company set out in early November in an additional convoy. They transported trucks from Camp Mina to the port of Tripoli, where they were loaded on cargo ships destined for Sicily. The women drivers of this company were the first Jews to arrive in Tripoli after the riots and they met Jews from the local community. The convoy was stamped firmly in the memories of the women who participated in it, not least because of their encounter with the horrors and terror experienced by the Jews during the war. On their way to Tripoli, the drivers drove through Derna where they visited the local rabbi. The community members were very excited by the sight of Jewish women in military uniform.[98]

The Encounter with Jewish Soldiers in the Allied Armies

Sabbath eves and Jewish Holydays that provided social opportunities for Yishuv recruits to fraternize among themselves as well as with the British staff, also served as a meeting point with Jewish soldiers serving in the British forces in Egypt and Italy. The Jewish servicewomen wanted to attract those Jews to Zionism and Palestine.

ATS soldiers also met Jewish soldiers in parties on camp and in the Jewish clubs. Herlitz wrote on the contribution of the servicewomen to bringing these soldiers closer to the Yishuv: 'I don't know if these soldiers constituted an "external camp" or an internal camp, but we brought the idea of Eretz Israel and Zionism to these soldiers.' She adds that when Jewish members of the 6th Airborne Division were transferred elsewhere, or completed their service in Palestine, Yishuv servicewomen organized a reception for them in the ATS club in Cairo.[99]

There were two clubs active in Cairo: the Zionist club, which was maintained and managed by the Soldiers' Welfare Committee, and the Jewish club that was run by the local Jewish community. The Zionist club was usually a meeting place for servicemen and women from the Yishuv, who came to hear news from home and to read Hebrew newspapers. The Jewish club tended to attract Jewish servicemen from all the Allied armies. The Yishuv servicewomen visited both clubs, in order to meet Jewish men from other countries and thus to bring them closer to the Zionist ideal, to the Yishuv experience and its issues.[100]

The encounters in these clubs led to the marriages of dozens of couples from the Yishuv and the Diaspora. Most of Yishuv women moved to their husbands' country of origin after the war. Molly Nissim, for example, who served in the military police in Cairo, met her future husband, a Jewish soldier in the American army. After the war, the two married and went to live in the USA.[101]

Additional meeting places were provided by the hostels in the large Egyptian towns and cities. As part of the effort to create a Zionist, Yishuv-orientated atmosphere, a large segment of the activity in the hostels was devoted to events to which Jewish servicemen were also invited. In the Ismailia hostel, for example, 200 servicemen and women participated in a party, including Jewish soldiers from South Africa. Less than two weeks afterwards, there was another party, this time with the participation of American soldiers. The CWO encouraged these activities, but they were expensive and the Council decided 'to ask the hostel's staff not to hold more than two such parties a month, so as not to sabotage activity on behalf of the servicewomen'.[102]

Holocaust Survivors

Activity on behalf of the Holocaust Survivors began in late 1943, even before there was any real encounter with them. News of the Holocaust of the Jews of Europe started arriving in the Yishuv in late 1942 and during 1943 there gradually emerged a clear picture of its extent. The servicewomen drew their information from Hebrew newspapers, from reports provided by servicemen on vacation in the Yishuv and also from the British staff. Throughout 1944, Jewish refugees began to flow into Egypt after the liberation by the Allied Forces of various areas in Europe. The refugees arrived in Egypt with the help of the Haganah with the objective of making it to Palestine. In the camp in Suez, for example, several hundred women from Europe were concentrated.

Several operations on behalf of the refugees took place as a result of cooperation between the servicewomen and members of the Jewish community in Egypt, with the servicewomen being asked to prepare parcels for the refugees. Community members provided the clothes and commodities and the servicewomen provided the organizational framework, repaired, sewed and packed the parcels for sending to the refugees. The activity of the servicewomen was, in fact, the traditional work of philanthropic women, expressed in various kinds of handicrafts and fundraising.[103] They wished to alleviate, however slightly, the refugees' suffering, or, as Habas put it, 'naively and with endless love, officers worked together with servicewomen, in organizing parcels'.[104] British officers shared in these activities.

Activity on behalf of the Holocaust Survivors began in Palestine with a fundraising drive for financing the integration of the 'Tehran Children'. In 1942, an agreement had been signed between the Polish government in exile and the Soviet government, according to which Polish refugees caught in the latter's territories would be recruited into the Polish army (Anders Army). At the same time, an order was given for the evacuation of some 24,000 Polish soldiers and refugees and, between April and August 1942, they were transferred by sea to Tehran, which was then under British rule. Among them there were approximately 1,000 children and some 800 Jewish adults. Most of the children were orphans and only a few of them arrived with one parent or even two. Some of them had parents who handed them over, as their last chance for saving their lives, to Polish orphanages under the management of priests and nuns. The parents themselves stayed behind in the USSR and the children arrived in Tehran with members of the Christian clergy. In Tehran the Jewish adults established an orphanage, with the active help of the local Jewish community and emissaries from the Yishuv.[105]

As part of their activity on behalf the 'Tehran Children', the women recruits from Company 522 organized a craft exhibition with the help of Mina Ben-Zvi, which was held under the auspices of Baroness Rosette de Menashe, of the Rothschild family.[106] The city's Jews were invited to visit and purchase the donated objects, with all proceeds going to institutions in the Yishuv.

These campaigns were held with the knowledge and blessing of the British command, mainly out of humanitarian considerations. On another occasion, with the approach of winter, news arrived from Italy concerning destitute Jewish refugees. Amnon Zair, the Haganah representative in Cairo, received large quantities of South American wool from the local British high command. In a 'knitting campaign' yarn and knitting needles were distributed among the servicewomen who knitted sweaters for the refugees. The army announced a competition among the companies for the handsomest sweaters. Even the officers took part in the knitting competition.[107]

One of the attempts to meet with Jewish women in the refugee camp in Suez ended in frustration. A servicewoman from Number 27 Hospital was sent to the camp in early 1944 in order to help the Jewish women inmates. But she returned to her company disappointed, since most of her occupation had involved caring for British women who were being repatriated. The few Jewish women in the camp were visible only through a barbed wire fence that separated the two groups, and she was unable to make any real contact with them.[108] It would appear that one of the emotional encounters between Jewish servicewomen and Jewish refugees took place in Tel el Shati in Egypt. Servicewomen from Company 509 celebrated the Purim holyday in the refugee camp. The servicewomen prepared the evening's entertainment and thus the refugees were introduced to the Yishuv experience and received the taste for Jewish life that they had missed for so long.[109]

Activity in Italy

After the war Shaul Meirov (Avigur), one of the leaders of Aliyah bet, stated that 'It is impossible to describe the Aliyah bet rescue activities without the Jewish companies ... without the direct and indirect help we received in many different ways from our friends in uniform ... the rescue activity ... throughout the war period would have been reduced to the smallest dimensions.'[110] During the second half of 1943 the Jewish Agency started to relate to the Holocaust survivors not only as a cause for rescue (or 'rescue material' by Sharett's definition), but also as an issue that would influence the political fate of the Yishuv. For over a year the servicemen were at work in Italy, some as part of the British forces, others in the Jewish Brigade, mostly on their own initiative. Connections with the Yishuv were loose.

The increasing number of Jews being released from the camps and the growing number of Hebrew companies required the establishment of an extensive organizational infrastructure. At a meeting of representatives of the Jewish companies in Italy that took place on 8 January 1944, it was decided to establish a Committee for Refugee Affairs, or a Refugee Centre in Bari with the objective of setting up training and employment centres for refugees and to obtain licenses for instructors from the Yishuv. A year later, at a gathering of the Jewish companies in the British army and the Brigade in Fiuggi, it was decided to extend the framework and establish a Diaspora Centre, headed by Yehiel Duvdevani, founder of Kibbutz Giv'at Hashlosha and a leader of the UKM. The centre's activities began immediately with the victory of the Allied Forces over Nazi Germany in May 1945.[111]

Humanitarian Activity

Several dozen Jewish ATS servicewomen in Italy helped the soldiers with the refugee work. Most of the servicewomen's activity consisted of humanitarian as well as educational aid, which took place mainly after official work hours, although many of the servicewomen conducted their refugee activity as part of their military service.

According to reports received by the Jewish Agency, ATS servicewomen in Italy were involved in aid and education activity alongside their male counterparts. They helped in the Jewish youth club in Bari, taught in the school and kindergartens and were responsible for preparations of the summer camp for refugee children. Thus, for example, according to Yosef Bankover, an activist in Italy, in a letter to Kaplan in August 1944: '[You] see the girls in a Zionist Federation party, meet them to lead the gift ... and gradually the circle expands of girls who lend a hand to help the refugees.'[112]

Although the overall number of servicewomen in Italy increased between December 1943 and May 1944, during which 100 hospital workers were moved to Italy, the British army still required a further 400 Yishuv servicewomen for work in hospitals and stores in Italy. In response to pressure on the part of Jewish soldiers, Sharett asked for ATS servicewomen to be sent to work in the refugee camps. But the British commander of ATS in the Middle East rejected the request with the claim that the needs of war were more urgent. Ultimately, despite the need for working hands, the number of Jewish servicewomen in Italy did not grow.[113]

The meeting with Holocaust survivors presented an emotional experience for the servicewomen, both Yishuv-born and those who immigrated from Europe. A servicewoman in a military hospital in Italy used to fill her army kitbag with expensive medications, penicillin, vitamins and sterile bandages she had pilfered from the hospital stores. Although she did this with mixed feelings, knowing that it was theft, her moral commitment toward the Jewish refugees was greater. She was unable to refuse the soldiers and activists in the Diaspora Centre and consoled herself with the thought that it was for the refugees and this was no game, and that if she did not do this, after all they had been through, what was she worth? But it wasn't easy and certainly not pleasant.[114]

Hadassah Aharoni recalled the meeting with survivors of the concentration camps in Rome. Yishuv soldiers stationed in the vicinity of the servicewomen started to collect clothing and supplies for the refugees and included them in the effort. The servicewomen contributed items of their own, as well as cigarettes and chocolates they received from the army. Eventually the refugees arrived in the Rome region and were housed in villas on the outskirts of the city; the servicewomen joined them together with the equipment they had collected. Toward the end of the war, Aharoni volunteered to teach Hebrew in Rome's Great Synagogue. Her group of 'students' consisted of local Jews and Holocaust survivors.[115]

People from various companies congregated in Naples – female soldiers serving in Hospitals in Italy, soldiers from the Jewish Brigade, wounded soldiers from the Yishuv and even Jewish soldiers serving in other Allied armies whose military rabbis asked to help them – and helped in preparing food parcels for the Holocaust survivors.[116]

The Convoy of Children from Bergen Belsen

The most horrendous meeting of all was the one the Yishuv servicewomen had with a convoy of children from the Bergen Belsen concentration camp in the summer of 1945. One of the female Hebrew officers who commanded a company in one of the hospitals near Bari, received a request from the Diaspora Centre to prepare large quantities of clothes for boys and girls aged 8–14. The servicewomen donated their own clothes, spent their own money on sweets and toiletries from the NAAFI and even recruited military rabbis from America and South Africa who were serving in the vicinity. Two rabbis, two servicewomen and one officer from the Yishuv stood in wait in a forest outside of Bari. Two army trucks driven by drivers from one of the transport companies brought the children straight from the concentration camp.

The soldiers waiting for the convoy had their first encounter with the horrors perpetrated by the Nazis – children who had turned into walking skeletons, terrified and dressed in striped pyjamas. The children were taken immediately to the British transit camp nearby, where they were given hot soup. Some of them died of weakness several days after their arrival and the others received devoted medical treatment at the hands of the Jewish servicewomen, in addition to their regular hospital work. During the evenings they stood in their white nurses uniforms preparing parcels of clothes and sweets for each of the children. A few days later, the servicewomen threw a party for the children – who were on the way to recovery – in their apartment in town.[117]

Drivers form the 502 ambulance company helped soldiers from the Jewish Brigade get to each of the camps in Austria and were very helpful in treating babies and providing medical treatment. The Hefner sisters, two of who served in this company and the Torok sisters, three of who served in the company, served as the 'communication channel' between the emissaries in the camps in Austria and the companies in Italy. In return for their help the servicewomen received the respect of the soldiers who arranged the activity in Italy.[118]

Educational Activity

Several servicewomen who worked in the military hospitals in Italy taught in schools for refugee children established by Yishuv soldiers in Bari. Zvi Lamm,[119] one of the first Jewish soldiers to arrive in Italy, was among the founders of the school and also its principal. He was assisted in his work by three ATS servicewomen, Deborah Meir, who had managed the nursing school at Assaf Harofeh hospital, Rina Sholvis and Bella Mizrahi from Zichron Ya'akov. The servicewomen who taught at the school received teaching aids from the Yishuv and were thus able to convey to their students some of the experiences of Yishuv life. The school curriculum was Zionist. Thus, for example, the school marked the day of Binyamin Ze'ev Herzl's death. The children recited words in Hebrew and the servicewomen were overcome with excitement.[120]

One of the servicewomen took advantage of her vacation to accompany a convoy of refugee children on their way to convalesce in Santa Maria in southern Italy, a location that provided a place in which refugees could be housed and trained prior to their immigration (escape) illegally to Palestine. The villa in which the children were housed turned into a meeting place for all the Jewish soldiers in the region. Jewish soldiers in the American army brought the children food and sweets and one of the company's sergeants volunteered to drive the children to any destination they chose in his military vehicle. A Hebrew school was established for the refugee children and a connection was made between its first grade pupils and their counterparts in the Geula School in Haifa. The children from Haifa sent letters and pictures to the refugee children.[121]

NOTES

1. Joan Nagel, 'Masculinity and Nationalism: Gender and Sexuality in the Making of Nations', *Ethnic and Racial Studies*, 21, no.2 (1998), pp.242–70. Cynthia

Enloe, for example, claims that nationalism is based on male memory, submission and hope, whereas women are given a marginal and token place in nationalist movements and struggles. The position of Women in these cases is double: icons of the nation that are to be preserved and admired or spoils of war that must be disdained. In each case, according to Enloe, the lead players are men defending liberty, respect, homeland and their women. Cynthia Enloe, *Bananas, Beaches & Bases: Making Feminist Sense of International Politics* (California 1989), p.45.

2. Even at a relatively late stage of the war, the *Y.A.E.L Journal* (newspaper of Hebrew Transport Company 178) complained that 'there is still disdain within us for this branch of activity. It is seen as something special that is unconnected to organizing of daily life. The word "cultured" has become almost an insult.' 'On the Cultural Act Within Us', *Y.A.E.L Journal*, 68 (11 February 1945), p.5. Haganah History Archive (HHA), 0009/HHHA/086.
3. Renee Levine Melammed, *Heretics or Daughters of Israel*: *The Crypto-Jewish Women of Castile* (Oxford 2002); Paula Hyman, *Ha-Ishah ha-Yehudiyyah bi-Sevakh ha-Kidmah: Mekoma ve Yitzuga ba'et hachadasha* [The Jewish woman in a tangle of progress: her place and representation in modern Jewish history] (Jerusalem 1997); Marion Kaplan, 'Tradition and Transition: Jewish Women in Imperial Germany', in Judith Baskin (ed.), *Jewish Women in Historical Perspective* (Michigan 1998), pp.227–42; Shulamit Magnus, '"Out of the Ghetto": Integrating the Study of Jewish Women into the Study of "The Jews"', *Judaism*, 39, no.1 (1990), pp.28–36; and others.
4. Hyman, *Ibid.*, pp.17–47.
5. Motti Regev, 'Mavo le'tarbut isrealit' [Introduction to Israeli culture], in Ephraim Ya'ar and Ze'ev Shavit (eds], *Megamot bahevra haisraelit* [Directions in Israeli Society), 2 (Tel Aviv 2003), pp.824–6.
6. Antonio Gramsci, *On Hegemony: Selections from the Prison Notebooks* (London: Lawrence and Wishart, 1971), pp.88–133.
7. Yossi Yona and Yehuda Shenhav claim that the dominant culture in Israel is formed initially as an ethno-nationalist Zionist culture, and not as a civilian culture that enables a full and equal inclusion in a society of all the state's citizens and inhabitants. Despite all the various challenges facing it, the Jewish national culture maintained its hegemony firmly for a long time. Yossi Yona and Yehuda Shenhav, *Rav tarbutiut mahi? Al hapolitica shel hashonut beisrael* [What is multiculturalism? On the politics of diversity in Israel] (Tel Aviv 2005), pp.52–3.
8. Much use was made in the Yishuv of the term 'Hebrew culture', although in 1939 the feeling that prevailed among the shapers of Hebrew education was that 'culture we still don't have. Culture is not only a matter of language, but also [our] original literature is far away both in shape and content.' Haim Yehuda Roth, 'Al ba'ayot hahinuch hatichoni' [On problems of high school education], in Roth (ed.), *Al hahinuch hatichoni ha'ivri be'eretz Israel* [On high school education in Eretz Israel] (Jerusalem 1939), p.30.
9. In addition to all the routine military tasks, the servicewomen/Haganah members were also obliged to preserve Jewish national lifestyle on the military bases. The new system of celebrating traditional holydays was a Yishuv invention and became universally accepted. It was this that constituted the central level of New Hebrew Culture in Palestine. Ya'akov Shavit, 'Misimhat Beit Hasho'eva lemo'etzet hamorim lema'an hakakal: hamtza'at hagim ve'tekasim beyishuv

ha'eretz Israeli' [From Simhat Beit Hasho'eva to the Teachers' Council for the JNF: inventing holydays and ceremonies in the Yishuv], in Yossi Dahan and Henry Wasserman (eds), *Lehamtzi uma: anthologia* [Inventing a nation: an anthology] (Ra'anana 2006), p.350.

10. According to Shilo it was hard to determine if the women of the agricultural community were more connected to Jewish tradition than the men whose education in the Diaspora was more rounded. But among the women it could have been emotion that determined their attitude to Jewish tradition. Margalit Shilo, 'Hamtza'at masoret: girsa Eretz israelit' [Inventing tradition: an Eretz Israeli version], *Katedra* 110 (February 2004), p.165. On the growth and formation of local ethnic Hebrew culture in the Yishuv, see, for example, Itamar Even Zohar, 'Hatzmiha ve'hahitgabshut shel tarbut Ivrit mekomit ve'yelidit, 1882–1948' [The growth and development of local and indiginous Hebrew culture in the Land of Israel, 1882–1948], *Katedra*, 16 (1980), pp.165–89; Mordechai Zeira, *Kruim Anu: Zikata shel hahitiashvut haovedet beshnot haesrim el hatarbut hayeudit* [We are torn: Affiliation of the working settlements in the 1920 to the Jewish culture] (Jerusalem 2002); Zohar Shavit, 'Hitpathut kitvai ha'et ve'ha'itonot' [Development of journals and newspapers], in Moshe Lissak (ed.), *Toldot hayeshuv hayehudi beretz Israel me'az ha'aliyah harishona: bniyata shel tarbut ivrit* [History of the Jewish Yishuv in Eretz Israel since the First Aliyah: building a Hebrew culture], Part One (Jerusalem 1994), pp.190–4.
11. Louis Isaac Rabinowitz, *Soldiers from Judea: Palestinian Jewish Units in the Middle East 1941–1943* (London 1945), pp.54–5.
12. Ze'ev Sheffer (ed.), *Sefer Hahitnadvut: Parashat Hahitnadvut hatzvait shel yehudei Eretz Israel Be'milhemet ha'olam hashniyat* [Book of volunteering: the case of military volunteering of Eretz Israel Jews in the Second World War] (Jerusalem 1949), p.542; Bracha Habas, *Bnot hayil: sefer ha'ATS* [Women of valour: book of the ATS] (Tel Aviv 1964), p.65.
13. Esther Herlitz, *Esther: o Le'an kvar Isha Yechola Le'hagia* [Esther: or how far could a woman go?] (Tel Aviv 1995), p.22.
14. Ya'akov Margalit (ed.), *Hineni shalcheni: mitnadvim batzava habriti kotvim* [Here I am, send me: writings of volunteers to the British Army] (Tel Aviv 1984), p.149.
15. Habas, *Bnot hayil*, p.96.
16. Ibid., p.184.
17. Ibid., p.99.
18. From Zilla Babayouf to the Jewish Agency, 19 April 1945, Central Zionist Archive, Jerusalem (CZA), S25/5099.
19. *Davar Hapo'elet*, 6–7 (11 July 1943), p.94. The servicewomen, too, requested that the WWC send materials for their parties: K. (sic.) 'Our Sabbath parties are attended by [Jewish] soldiers ... and we have to plan. We really need literature, edited and prepared for Sabbath parties.' [Ibid.] Letters from Servicewomen, 7–8 (31 August 1942), p.95.
20. Rabinowitz, *Soldiers from Judea*, pp.57–60. On the Hebrew holydays and their similarity to a theatrical episode, see Naomi Yoeli, 'Massekhet: Zionist Ceremonies as Theatre' (PhD thesis, Tel Aviv University, 2002), pp.3–4.
21. Dov Knohel (ed.), *Behitnadev am: mitnadvim dati'im bemilhemet ha'olam hashniya* [When a nation volunteers: religious volunteers in the Second World War], A and B (Tel Aviv 1989, 1990), p.199.

22. The comment that all the servicewomen ate together is interesting. Notwithstanding the fact that hierarchy was strictly adhered to in the British army, this holyday cancelled the separation between the ranks and everyone sat around the same festive table.
23. Programme for Jewish New Year party in the Tura area, September 1945, IDF Archive, 36/1867/1998.
24. Interview with Zipora Shahar (Eitan), Esther Yanai Ben-Zvi, Nahalal, 7 January 2006.
25. Interview with Tirtza Raviv (Torok) and Yael Arieli (Kornberg), Jerusalem, 27 December 2006.
26. *Davar*, 15 February 1943, p.4.
27. Habas, *Bnot hayil*, p.77.
28. 'Program for Hanukah party in Company 503', IDF Archive, 36/1867/1998.
29. From the mid 1920s the Purim holyday became a central cultural activity in the kibbutz: a dramatic choir was established, rehearsals took place and scenery and costumes were produced. In the agricultural settlement movement, entertaining newsletters were published for Purim. Zeira, *Kruim Anu*, pp.233–7. The Purim parades in Tel Aviv were a veritable carnival of costume and dance that did not express traditional customs such as the Purim meal or gift parcels. Nili Arieh Sapir, 'Karnaval be tel aviv: Purim ba'ir ha'ivrit harishona' [Carnival in Tel Aviv: Purim in the first Hebrew town], *Jerusalem studies in Jewish folklore*, 22 (1983), p.120.
30. Company 508 War Diary, 22 March 1943, National Archives, London, WO 169/13851.
31. Testimony of Hadassa Aharoni (Melamed), Israel Defense Forces (IDF) Archive, Tel Hashomer, 120/03/72.
32. Zeira, *Kruim Anu*, pp.238–45. For more on Passover celebrations in the kibbutz and the kibbutz Hagadah, see: Arieh Ben-Gurion, 'Seder Pessach, hagadah ve tekes ha'omer b'Ein Harod' [Pessach Seder, Hagadah and the Omer ceremony in Ein Harod], *Mibifnim*, 46, no.3 (Spring 1984), pp.358–73; Muki Tsur and Yuval Danieli (eds), *Yots'im be hodesh he'aviv: Pessach eretz Israeli behagadot mehakibutz* [Going out in the month of spring: an Eretz Israeli Passover in the kibbutz hagadas] (Jerusalem 2004).
33. Interview with Claire Epstein; Company 511 War Diary, 19 April 1943, National Archives, London, WO 169/13858.
34. Passover Play by Mazal Elazar, IDF Archive, Demobbed Soldiers' Department.
35. Company 509 War Diary, 2 February 1945, NA, WO 169/21581.
36. Spitzer, 'Plantings in Soldiers' Camps', *The Hebrew Soldier*, G (25 February 1943) p.24; 'Echoes of Department A, Tu B'Shvat party', Haganah History Archive, Tel Aviv (HHA), 086/ HHHA /0009; *The Hebrew Soldier*, 11 (19 February 1943), p.15.
37. The battle for Tel Hai, where two women were killed, was a turning point for the servicewomen in the inclusion of the Hebrew woman in active defence of the Yishuv alongside their male counterparts. (Proposal for volunteer speech in cinemas, theatres, etc. on Tel Hai Day', 27 February 1942, CZA, S37/676. On the Tel Hai battle see Yael Zrubavel, 'Bein "historia" le "agada": gilgulei tel hai bazicaron ha'amami' [Between 'history' and 'legend': Tel Hai in the national memory], in Yossi Dahan and Henry Wasserman (eds), *Lehamtzi uma* [Inventing a nation] (Ra'anana 2006), pp.199–216; Yoeli, 'Massekhet: Zionist Ceremonies as Theatre', pp.332–42.

38. Company 511 War Diary, 19 March 1943, National Archives, London, WO 169/13858.
39. Company 509 War Diary, 24 February 1945, National Archives, London, WO 169/21581.
40. Rabinowitz, *Soldiers from Judea*, pp.57–70. This special Lag B'Omer is remembered by Hanna Golani, who previously served in Abassya in Company 503 and was invited to a bonfire together with fellow servicewomen and Jewish soldiers from the vicinity. Interview with Hanna Golani (Golanski), Natanya, 21 January 2006.
41. 'Report of Mr. M.S. [Moshe Sharett] on a journey to Egypt on August 16–29, 1942', CZA, S25/6039.
42. Interview with Tsilli Brendstater (Avraham), Tel Aviv, 5 February 2006.
43. Interview with Ruth Gruzin (Grosbard), Tel Aviv, 22 November 2005.
44. Moshe Sharett at a farewell party for the first recruits, 'Information on Recruitment Committee Activity, no. 13', 10 February 1942, CZA, S37/676.
45. Idelson reported that '80% of the second batch of recruits reported that they know English, which disrupted their work and attitude to Hebrew [sic.]'. Recruitment Department meeting, 14April 1942, CZA, S25/5063.
46. Although the use of the same language does not necessarily result in a mutual national biography. See, for example, Arabs and Jews in the State of Israel who use the Hebrew language without a mutual national and cultural identity being created among them. Debora Kalkin Fishman, 'Hasafa hemeshutefet: gorem melaked?' [The mutual language: a unifying element?], in Yitzhak Kashti and Rivka Izikovitz (eds), *Panim hamishtakfot bamar'ah: tarbuyot beisrael beshnot hatish'im* [Faces in the mirror: cultures in Israel in the 1900s] (Tel Aviv 1996), pp.69–94.
47. According to Zohar Shavit, for the people of the labour movement, the study of Hebrew aimed to achieve two objectives: use of the language, which is the basis of the Jewish culture, with the purpose of laying the foundations for the establishment of a new national culture; and to provide an opportunity for the establishment of a cultural life in which everyone will participate – veterans as well as newcomers. Zohar Shavit, 'Harachashta kvar at hamapte'ah l'otzrot tarbutainu? Hora'at ivrit ve'hamtza'ata shel tarbut leumit betnuat ha'avoda' [Have you already bought the key to our culture's treasures? Teaching Hebrew and inventing a national culture in the Labour movement], in Yossi Dahan and Henry Wasserman (eds), *Lehamzi uma: antologia* [Inventing a nation: an anthology] (Ra'anana 2007), pp.360–70.
48. Rafael Nir, 'Ma'amada shel halashon ha'ivrit betahalich hat'hia hale'umit' [Status of the Hebrew language in the process of national renaissance], in Moshe Lissak and Zohar Shavit (eds), *Toldot hayishuv hayehudi be'eretz Israel me'az ha'aliyah harishona: bniyata shel tarbut ivrit be'eretz Israel* [The history of the Jewish Yushuv in Eretz Israel since the First Aliyah: the building of Hebrew culture in Eretz Israel], A (Jerusalem 1999), p.37. For more on the development of the new Hebrew language, see Shlomo Morag, 'Ha'ivrit hahadasha behitgabshuta: lashon be' aspaklaria shel hevra' [Modern Hebrew in development: language as a reflection of society], *Katedra*, 56 (August 1990), pp.70–92.
49. Rachel Katznelson, 25 January 1942, Labour Movement Archive, 33/4, p.2.

50. Yoav Gelber, *Toldot habitnadvut: Hama'avak letzava Ivri* [History of volunteering: The Struggle for a Hebrew Army] (Jerusalem 1991), p.223.
51. Margalit, *Hineni shalcheni*, p.533.
52. Interview with Claire Epstein.
53. Yosef Shavit, *Mitnadvim bekahol: eretzisraelim besherut heil hate'ufa hamalchuti* [Volunteers in blue: from Eretz Israel to service in the RAF] (Tel Aviv 1995), pp.137–8.
54. In his memoires, Rabbi Levy wrote that the ATS servicewomen were actually those who were rebellious against the ban on marching with the Jewish flag. Isaac Levy, *Now I Can Tell: Middle East Memories* (London 1978), p.141. In contrast, Ben-Gurion did not hide his chagrin at what had happened on that occasion. According to him, 'they [the ATS servicewomen in Cairo] should have followed the order not to participate [in the parade]! I would like to have seen them shot for this ... The Englishman would respect a Jewish ATS company, especially when women who burst into hysterics and tears. I am not mocking this: I would have joined in these tears, in this shouting: we shall not go out ... no need to revolt, but this kind of demonstrative act, yes! We must now invest all our strength in this, how our male and female soldiers will behave.' Ben-Gurion at a meeting of the Mapai Central Committee, 23 June 1943, pp.7–8, Labour Movement Archive, 23/43.
55. Habas, *Bnot hayil*, pp.94–5.
56. Mira Hefner related to the mission imposed upon her as a Jewish servicewoman to help the refugees, but she was also familiar with the way the servicewomen were tested in light of the rumours spread about them in the Yishuv: 'We knew our work was serious, a double mission: as Jewish daughters of Eretz Israel it was our task to help the Jewish refugees as much as we could and as Jewish servicewomen we had to prove to everyone, especially those in the Yishuv, that they had been too hasty in judging the female soldiers of Israel.' Mira Hefner, 'Twenty Six' [the number of servicewomen to have arrived in Italy], *Bamahane* (newsletter of company 745, Solel Boneh), May 1944, pp.10–13.
57. Testimony of Rachel Michelson (Katz), 7 April 2003, IDF Archive, 297/03/8. The mission was given to Rivka Bogen. When she returned from her mission in Cairo, it transpired that a mistake had been made in the spelling of the word ISRAEL. She was sent again to Cairo and this time, she returned with the correct badges.
58. Habas, *Bnot hayil*, p.101.
59. N. [sic], 'In Khaki Uniform' (from a servicewoman's letters), 'Woman Member's Life in our Company', *Palmach Newsletter*, 15 (19 February 1943), p.2.
60. Hadassah Samuel, Minutes of Meeting of Council of Women's Organizations, 29 September 1942, CZA, F49/2105.
61. The commander of area group 16 met the Baroness de Menashe and Mrs Cohen of the Alexandria Jewish community to sum up issues concerning the hostel. At her meeting with the companies group in Tel el Kabir, Samuel proposed that WIZO would manage a rest room for servicewomen on camp. If the army were to provide a hut, WIZO would provide the furniture and a local woman to manage the place. Samuel presented the hostels as an issue which she nurtured and groomed: 'I travelled often to Egypt ... and thanks to the Jewish community

there I managed to do this ... and so I took care of those girls'. Interview with Hadassah Samuel, 12 February 1972. Interviewer: Margalit Shilo, film 200/K, the Institute for Modern Judaism, Department of Verbal Documentation, Hebrew University, p.13

62. On the competition between the organizations, see Herlitz, *Esther*, p.22. On 21 June 1942, for example, a hostel was opened by the WWC in Ismailia in the presence of Cranston, the British commander of the group of companies in Tel el Kabir.
63. The hostel in Cairo also contained 'service rooms, a concert hall, two libraries and an English and French library', and 'serious parties and dance evenings were held as well as a weekly chamber concert'. *Olam Ha'isha*, identified with WIZO, provided a detailed description of the Cairo hostel. *Olam Ha'isha*, 46–7 (28 September 1942), p.9. Report from Malka Weinberg, hostel manager, minutes of CWO meeting, 3 December 1942, CZA, F49/2105. As for the Ismailia hostel, established by WWC, there is no description in that publication, save a note of its existence. This is obviously another expression of the competition between the organizations.
64. The hostel in Ismailia was forced to compete with additional hostels in town such as the YMCA. Lillie Steinberg, deputy hostel manager, wrote to the CWO: 'Despite rising prices in Egypt, we have lately been running on the lowest prices and, among all the clubs in Ismailia, our hostel is the cheapest one.' Letter from Steinberg to CWO, 18 November 1943, Labour Movement Archive, IV-230-6, file 17.
65. David Cnaani from Ayelet Hashahar, member of the UKM Security Committee since June 1942, was in charge of all communications activity in the committee and devoted himself to correspondence with the servicemen overseas. Thus he was able to share with them the experience of the kibbutz and moshav. Uri Brenner, *Le Tsava yehudi azma'i: hakibutz hameuhad behaganah 1939–1945* [To an independent Jewish army: the United Kibbutz Movement in the Haganah 1939–1945] (Tel Aviv 1985), pp.403–4.
66. Thus for example, the CWO called on the Jewish Agency Political Department to reimburse Samuel's travel expenses for her March 1942 trip to Egypt, explaining that 'As you know, Mrs Samuel went to Egypt for a series of missions entrusted to her.' 22 March 1942, CZA, S25/5505.
67. CWO memorandum,12 December 1943, CZA, F49/2105. The relationship between the CWO and the WAAF servicewomen is particularly significant because no on-going ties were conducted between them and the Yishuv institutes – Jewish Agency and Haganah.
68. On this trip, Samuel managed to visit only this company (possibly because of the special circumstances), due to the army's new order forbidding civilian visits to the camps, following a crisis between the Yishuv institutions and the army, on suspicion of Zionist intervention in the recruitment offices.
69. Company 511 War Diary, 26 March–1 April 1943, National Archives, London, WO 169/13858.
70. Beba Idelson at WWC meeting, p.20, Labour Movement Archives, IV-230-1, file I.
71. Beba Idelson report to the CWO, 30 May 1943, p.1, Labour Movement Archives, IV-23-6, WWC file.

72. Beba Idelson, 'Visit to Yishuv Servicerwomen', *Davar Hapo'elet*, 6 (11 July 1943), p.94.
73. Beba Idelson at CWO meeting, 1 December 1943, p.2, CZA, F49/2104.
74. Although most of the servicewomen were secular, they saw the military rabbi as representing the Yishuv. As far as the working agricultural sector was concerned, the Rabbinical Establishment symbolized the corrupt side of Diaspora Jewry, an establishment expression whose authority and values it rejected and rose up against. However, since this institution was the creation of the British Mandatory Government, who saw in it the beginnings of Yishuv's cultural autonomy, the working settlement related to it as an additional expression of the developing nationalist settlement and respected it. Zeira, *Kruim Anu*, p.149. Simultenously, and from the same concept, the British established the Supreme Arab Council, headed by Haj Amin el Husseini, the Mufti of Jerusalem.
75. From 1942, young English-speaking rabbis were sent to serve in the British army, on permission of the Yishuv's Chief Rabbinate. Rabbi Ya'akov Lifshitz, for example, was appointed to the Fighting Jewish Division (the Jewish Brigade). In addition to their regular duties, the military rabbis organized activities and parties for the Jewish servicemen and women, established clubs and arranged hospitality for servicemen among the remote Jewish communities. They also assisted in distributing Hebrew newspapers and establishing libraries in various companies, and dealt with disciplinary matters. Yehuda Slutsky (ed.), *Sefer toldot ha'aganah* [History of the Haganah], B and C (Tel Aviv 1973), p.714.
76. One of the events that testified to cooperation between the recruits and the rabbis and remembered by the servicewomen was the 'prayer for the dead': for the dead children of the Diaspora. 15 servicewomen stood in a desert tent with the rabbi and said a prayer hereto unfamiliar to most of them.' Habas, *Bnot hayil*, p.63. Hadassah Samuel reported to the CWO secretariat praising the rabbis' assistance even though 'it wasn't their obligation to do so'. Hadassah Samuel, in minutes of the CWO, 29 September 1942, p.2, CZA F49/2105.
77. As well as the regular prayer books, the British army allowed the distribution of the *Book of Jewish Thought* by the UK Chief Rabbi Dr Joseph Herman Hertz. The book, which was first distributed among Jewish soldiers in the First World War, included the wise words of famous people.
77. From CWO Secretariat to ATS servicewomen, 17 December 1943, Labour Movement Archive, IV-230-6, file 17.
78. To the CWO, 20 September 1944, CZA, F49/2105.
79. *Bashelach vebamacheresha: Kovetz Hayalim Havrei Tenuat Hamoshavim* [In the sword and plough: Soldiers members of the Moshavim movement] (1948), p.92.
80. For example, summary of national WWC Secretariat, 24–25 August 1942, CZA, F49/2105.
81. Editorial, *Davar Hapo'elet*, 1, (31 January 1943), p.2.
82. Habas, *Bnot hayil*, p.244. On occasion Haganah oversaw relations with Egypt's Jews. Herlitz, for example, received directives from Haganah Command to befriend the Weissman family in order to influence their son-in-law Emil Najar, a communist, to embrace Zionism. According to Herlitz, following many Friday evening meals she shared with the family, together with other servicemen and women, Najar left Egypt, where he was head of the local Zionist Federation.

Years later, Najar was Israel's Ambassador to Turkey. Interview with Esther Herlitz, Tel Aviv, 9 December 2005.

83. Opionions differ on the development of the Zionist Movement in Egypt. According to some, the expatriates caused local Zionism to flourish and even raised Zionist awareness. See, for example, the meeting of Albert Moziri, founder of the *Israel* newspaper in Cairo with the expatriates and Zionist activists serving in the British forces. Hagar Hillel, *"Israel" be Kahir: Iton Zioni bemitzrayim haleumit 1920–1939* [*"Israel"* in Cairo: A Zionist newspaper in nationalist Egypt 1920–1939] (Tel Aviv 2004), p.36. Others doubted the value of this contribution. Ruth Kimhi, 'The Activity of the Zionist Movement in Egypt and its Relations with the Yishuv In Eretz Israel 1918–1948' (PhD thesis, Haifa University, 2005), pp.28–9.
84. Testimony of Hadassah Berlinsky (Rabinowitz), undated, p.5, HHA, 16/35. On the Yishuv and its connections with the Jewish community in Egypt, see, for example, Yoav Gelber, 'Peulot hamahlaka hamedinit shel hasochnut bemitzrayim' [Activity of the political department of the Jewish Agency in Egypt], *Katedra*, 67 (April 1993), pp.24–53; Yehuda Don, 'Yahasim calcali'im ben Israel ve Mitzrayim' [Economic relations between Israel and Egypt], *Katedra*, Ibid., pp.70–89, etc.
85. The British permitted only Jewish refugees or local Jews, non-Egyptian citizens, to enlist in the army. On relevant correspondence, see letter from Moshe Sharett to officer Morrison Bell, 19 February 1942, CZA, S25/6001; letter from Chitty to Sharett, 23 February 1942, ibid; letter from Sharett to Chitty, 9 March 1942, ibid. See also letter from Alfred Cohen, of the Commercial Office in Cairo, to Moshe Sharett, 20 July 1942, CZA, S25/5099.
86. The pinnacle of Jews in political life was the appointment of Joseph Aslan Qattaui Pacha to the post of Finance Minister in 1924 and to Transport Minister in 1925. Kimhi, 'The Activity of the Zionist Movement in Egypt', pp.2–9.
87. Ibid., p.96. According to Kimhi, the prevailing ethos among the community was that of the private individual, whereas the Zionist movement and the Yishuv existed in accordance with the collective ethos, which the Jews of Egypt found hard to identify with. The outspoken secularity of the Zionists and emissaries of the various movements in Egypt also disturbed the Egyptian Jews. More on the attitude of Egypt's Jews to the Yishuv can be found in the report presented by Eliezer Kaplan to the Jewish Agency Executive after a fundraising visit to Egypt. According to him, very large profits are made in Egypt and the Jews and Greeks have a large position in these profits, although 'these Jews are not interested ... in investing in Eretz Israel ... from a security aspect there is no discrepancy between Egypt and Eretz Israel, but they are willing to invest money if as a result they can get goods to Egypt.' Minutes of Jewish Agency Executive meeting, 24 August 1941, p.8, CZA, S100/33b. See also, Ya'akov Tsur, *Karev Yom: dapei avar* [A day is coming: pages from the past] (Jerusalem 1979).
88. In an interview, Ruth Klieger-Eliav recalls her ties with the Baron de Menashe who donated large sums of money, on her fundraising efforts among the community leaders, such as Chief Rabbi Nahum Efendi, and of her disappointment at Qattaui Pacha. More on fundraising efforts and relations in Egypt, see Ruth Klieger Eliav and Peggy Mann, *Hamiflat ha'aharon* [The Last Resort] (Tel Aviv 1976).

89. Moshe Mosenson, who served in Transport Company 178 in Egypt, wrote to his family that he entered a store in Cairo and the proprietor 'appears to be a Jew, but had no interest in meeting us'. On the other hand, 'Another, smaller shop. When it transpired that they were Jewish soldiers from [Palestine], the owners were overjoyed. Refused to accept payment from us.' Moshe Mosenson, *Letters from the Desert*, ed. Shlomo Grodzensky (New York: Sharon Books, Inc. 1945), p.94.
90. Cover letter to a New Year's gift box of fruit from the CWO to Mrs Vidon, 20 September 1943, Labour Movement Archive, IV-230-6, File 17.
91. Ora later married Haim Herzog, and Suzi married Aubrey Eban. The cultural entertainment included the weekly portion, followed by dancing until the small hours. Kaplan herself used to play piano and accompany the dancers. Ruth Kaplan (Melamed), IDF Archive, 120/03/72.
92. The Polity family, one of the Jewish community's many influential families, welcomed Haganah members in Cairo and whenever an important notice arrived it was at the Polity home that they congregated. Yizraela Be'eri (Grinker), *Rosh Hatsevet tahat etz hatomer* [Tribal chief under the date tree] (Nahalal 2005), p.68; Interview with Ruth Gruzin.
93. Sheffer, *Sefer Hahitnadvut*, p.533.
94. Yoav Gelber, *Toldot hahitnadvut: Nos'ei hadegel* [History of volunteering: bearers of the flag] (Jerusalem 1983), pp.8–15. On the meeting between Yishuv soldiers and refugees in Benghazi, the poet Amir Gilboa wrote 'I guard you, last night ...' on 31 January 1942, and 'Tonight, too, all throughout the years ...' the following New Year's Eve. Both poems were published in *LaHayal*, 31 December 1944, p.2. Gilboa enlisted in the British army in 1942 and served as a driver in the Hebrew Transport Company 178 until 1946, in Egypt and Italy. Hagit Halperin, 'Berl, ha'adama bo'eret' [Berl, the ground is burning], in Hagit Halperin (ed.), *Amir Gilboa, Hinai yamim ba'im* [Amir Gilboa, here days are coming] (Tel Aviv 2007), pp. 7–41.
95. Gelber, *Toldot hahitnadvut: Nos'ei hadegel*, pp.95–128. Yishuv servicemen and women described their meeting with the Jews of Libya in *Hahayal HaIvri*, Company 178 newspaper published between 10 January and 9 March 1943, which became a twice monthly newsletter, shared by several companies. 'At a meeting with the Jews of Tripoli', *Hayal Haivri*, 10 (7 February 1943), p.4, HHA, 086/HHHA/0006.
96. Ya'akov Margalit (ed.), *Bayit bamoshav: haverot mesaprot* [A home on the moshav: women members recall] (Tel Aviv 1962), pp.240–1.
97. Interview with Judith Spitz, Tel Aviv, 13 December 2005. In Tripoli Spitz and her driver friends met a young Jew who had undergone a fictitious tonsillectomy in order to be hospitalized and evacuated by soldiers. The young man subsequently emigrated to Israel.
98. Sheffer, *Sefer Hahitnadvut*, p.533.
99. Tzofia Hillel, 'Women in the Uniform of a Foreign Army', 1981, p.29, IDF Archive, 1867/98/151.
100. Interview with Major (ret.) Daphne Hill, Richmond (London), 10 May 2006, friend of Mollie Nissim.
101. Minutes of CWO meeting, 4 January 1944, p.1, CZA, F49/2105.
102. On the philanthropic activity of women in western and central Europe, see Michael Berkowitz, 'Transcending "Tzimmes and Sweetness": Recovering the

History of Zionist Women in Central and Western Europe 1897–1933', in Maurie Sacks (ed.), *Active Voices: Women in Jewish Culture* (Illinois 1995), pp.41–62.

103. Habas, *Bnot hayil*, p.143.
104. On the 'Tehran Children', see Ben Zion Tomer (ed.), *Adom ve'lavan vere'ah tapuhei zahav: yaldei Tehran* [Red and white and the scent of golden apples: the Tehran children] (Jerusalem 1972); Laurence Rosengart, 'Parashat Yaldei Teheran' [The Teheran Children Affair], *Beshvil Hazikaron*, 6 (1995), pp.15–20. On the children's integration in Israel, see Ada Shein, 'Hapulmus hayishuvi sviv klitat 'yaldai Teheran' [The polemic surrounding integration of the Tehran children], *Yalkut Moreshet*, 54 (1993), pp.133–61.
105. Tsadok Eshel, *Habahurot hahen: sefer bnot hahaganah b' Haifa* [Those girls: Book of Haganah girls in Haifa] (Tel Aviv 1997), p.86; Report by Ben-Zvi 'On an Exhibition and a Bazaar', to Delta Area Commander, ATS, 24 February 1945, CZA, S25/9885.
106. Amnon Zair, *Vienna–Gan Shmuel* (Gan Shmuel 1980), pp.82–3.
107. Habas, *Bnot hayil*, p.93.
108. Company 509 War Diary, 27 February, 1945, NA, WO 169/21581.
109. Slutsky, *Sefer toldot ha'aganah*, pp.737–8.
110. The Centre was established with the aim of organizing ties between Jews from all the European states beyond the front line and to organize the Jews in Italy in rehabilitating the Jewish community and national organizations, financially, in establishing schools, establishing the Zionist Federation and Hehalutz, legal and illegal immigration, removing Jewish orphans from monasteries and convents and establishing children's homes and a training farm. Hanoch Patishi, *Mahteret be'madim: 'Haganah' ve'hayalim ha'eretz Israelim betzava habriti* [Underground in uniform: Haganah and the Eretz Israel servicemen in the British army, 1939–1946] (Tel Aviv 2006), pp.70–80.
111. Letter from Baknover to Kaplan, 18 August 1944, CZA, S53/1600.
112. During his April 1944 visit to Italy, Sharett tried to obtain official recognition for the activity of Jewish servicemen and women among the refugees, but the British exhibited a suspicious attitude. Gelber, *Toldot hahitnadvut: Nos'ei hadegel*, p.240. In his talks in London, too, Sharett raised the issue of 'transferring ATS [women] for service in Europe, including nursing, [etc.]' (personal memo), January 1944, CZA, S25/6039.
113. Habas, *Bnot hayil*, p.230. Yishuv leaders considered the establishment of the Brigade, an army whose objective was not only to fight, like other armies, but also to assist the remains of the exiled nation and to bring them tidings of redemption, whether through simply being there, or through real action. Yaacov Lipshitz, *Sefer Habrigada Hayehudit: Korot hahativa hayehudit halohemet vehamatzila et hagola* (The history of the Jewish fighting brigade, saviour of the Diaspora) (Tel Aviv 1947), p.15.
114. Testimony of Hadassah Aharoni (Melamed), IDF Archive, 120/03/72.
115. Eshel, *Habahurot hahen*, p.87.
116. Habas, *Bnot hayil*, pp.103–4.
117. It is appropriate here to mention Rania Heffner, one of two sisters serving in an ambulance company (a third sister served as a clerk in another unit in Italy). After the war she scoured Europe, at great personal risk, and arrived in her

hometown near Warsaw, still dressed in her army uniform. With a great deal of effort, she managed to rescue her sister and son and another pregnant relative. Interview with Naomi Yekutieli (Torok), Tel Aviv, 8 December 2005; Habas, *Bnot hayil*, p.107.

118. Zvi Lamm volunteered for the British Army in 1943. After the War of Independence he became a teacher and pedagogue and later a professor at the Hebrew University's School of Education.
119. Habas, *Bnot hayil*, p.102.
120. Correspndence between schoolchildren in Haifa and children in the Hebrew school in Santa Maria, HHA, 086/HHHA/0013; *The Hebrew Soldier*, 76 (21 July 1944), p.11.

Part Three

Demobilization

9

The Ex-Servicewomen in Yishuv Society

Even while the war was raging (in early 1942), the future of the recruits was of concern to the Histadrut Executive Committee and it was obvious even then that real plans, involving all aspects of the Yishuv, would have to be made for when the women were released from duty. The CWO, too, started planning for the women's release, even in the course of the war. At a meeting of the CWO in August 1943, Beba Idelson said: 'There is no need for exaggerated fears regarding the future of the demobilized servicewoman, since the CWO is prepared to accept her, to train her in a profession where necessary and to arrange employment for her.'[1] This chapter deals mainly with the CWO's role in caring for the ex-servicewomen.

Professional Training toward Demobilization

Toward the end of the war, the British army instigated two programmes aimed at integrating ex-servicewomen in civilian society: the ABCA Plan (Army Bureau of Current Affairs) and the British Way and Purpose (BWP). According to Lucy Noakes, the two plans were conservative with regard to gender issues, with all the lectures focusing mainly on domestic tasks and the courses the women were offered prepared them for jobs that were only of a 'feminine' character.[2] Attendance of the lectures, which were given after working hours, was not compulsory. The lecture programme sometimes included current and relevant issues, in accordance with the servicewomen's national affinity. For the Yishuv women, the lectures included such subjects as local geography, the trades unions in the Yishuv and a view of the servicewomen's future in the country after release from military service.[3] The lecturers were professionals, or servicemen or women from adjacent units.

The situation was similar in Yishuv society. When military recruitment began, most of the working women were employed in traditionally female occupations, such as domestic service, clothing and textile, administrative, etc. (which was also expressed in wage discrepancies),[4] and the situation remained unchanged at the end of the war. Despite the debates prior to female recruitment on the need for change in women's professional status, the Yishuv's women's organizations adhered to the traditional gender concepts and offered the ex-servicewomen training in familiar 'feminine' occupations. Thus, it appears in a letter from Rachel Ziv, who served in the WAAF in Egypt, to her mother: 'There is a course on childcare, provided by a midwife from the Yishuv. She taught theory and also gave lessons in practical childcare.'[5] The significance of this 'professional training' actually consisted of paving the way for ex-servicewomen to settle into a domestic environment, including motherhood. The CWO prepared a programme for training the servicewomen in various spheres: cookery, social work, nursing, dressmaking, crafts such as spinning and weaving. The WWC wanted to show that female recruitment was a means for achieving change in social attitudes toward women in the post-war Yishuv and hoped that demobilized servicewomen would contribute to social change. According to the WWC, crafts were no more than extra curricular activity, a mere diversion of the mind, and demanded professional training courses (nursing, teaching, etc.) for the ex-servicewomen.[6]

Demobilization Problems

> For most of the ATS servicewomen, the demobilization period was a definitive test in their lives, no less than their period in service. Some of them set out and returned with no problems. Some set out as young girls and returned as mature women and brought with them, apart from life experiences and knowledge of people and the world, a profession and a path and a relationship to a woman friend or a male partner. But there were also those who returned uncertain and lacking in confidence after years of life in uniform within a military framework. Many had no home when they set out and had none when they returned, trailing behind them the thread of loneliness and alienation, with no roof to their heads, burdened with severe personal issues – illness, mental crises, broken families, a child with no father and without a source of income.[7]

Bracha Habas's words reflected the reality that many women, as well as men, encountered on their return to the Yishuv after a lengthy period of military service. It appears that Yishuv society did not know how to relate to them. Recruitment activists, who helped the servicemen and women with their demobilization, expressed their disappointment at the alienating attitude of the Yishuv toward its sons and daughters. Moshe Smilansky said, 'I have some things to say to the Yishuv with regard to the matter of the demobilized serviceman. The Yishuv has no positive or sympathetic attitude toward these sons [sic].' He tried to explain the reason for this: 'Perhaps this is because the Yishuv has so many issues to deal with', but the sad conclusion was that 'in reality, the attitude is flawed toward the soldier and also toward the demobilized soldier'.[8] It should be remembered the general atmosphere in the Yishuv at the end of the war, in the course of which there were revealed the horrors and the tragedy that befell the Jewish nation. In this reality, it would seem that the suffering of the demobilized soldiers, as well as those of other groups in the Yishuv, became dwarfed and they did not receive sufficient attention.

The demob dates for the servicewomen as well as the servicemen were determined according to various military considerations, such as tenure, family status and war needs (or the army's needs after the war). Although some were demobilized in 1943, most were released in 1945 after the war was over. Nonetheless, hundreds of recruits continued to serve until late July 1946.

Frameworks for Dealing with Demobilized Servicemen and Women

As the body that initiated the recruitment of Yishuv women into the British army and sent them to serve in it, the CWO felt duty bound to care for them once their service was over. Their activity in this respect was of considerable significance in light of the Yishuv's attitude to the ex-servicewomen and men. The sense of responsibility shared by the members of the women's organizations vis-à-vis the ex-servicewomen was best described by Beba Idelson, 'The CWO carried out the recruitment and it also undertook responsibility for putting the women back on track.'[9] Just as it had invested effort and resources in the welfare of the servicewomen during the war, so too did the CWO help the women to find accommodation, employment and even emotional support. Throughout the period of military service, the separate members of the CWO – especially WIZO and the WWC – were in competition with each other for the women's affection and affiliation, but as these were released from service, the organizations cooperated on their behalf. Many of the ex-servicewomen had been new immigrants, with no family or home in the Yishuv and they returned after their military service to their previous status. Although they received a regular salary throughout their service and a demobilization grant on their release, they were unable to provide for themselves for long. Military salaries were not high, even by Yishuv standards, and the CWO directed most of its efforts toward these specific women.

More than anything, the ex-servicewomen required employment and accommodation. But the Soldiers' Welfare Committee, which dealt with all the recruits during their military service, did nothing for them after their release. Concerned for their welfare the CWO called for the establishment of a 'central institute for the welfare of the ex-servicewoman that will unite and coordinate the various individual initiatives'. The CWO also called for the establishment of a Demobilization Office to provide ex-servicemen and women with all the necessary information, to 'imbue, from the beginning, a sense of friendly concern ... and a sense of security in the heart of the servicewoman, who was indeed returning home'.[10]

In late January 1944 the 'Yishuv Council for the Welfare of the ex-serviceman being released in the course of the war' was established. At the same time, the Jewish Agency formed a department to deal with ex-servicemen and women, headed by Yosef Gurion from Kibbutz Geva. The servicemen cared for themselves, too, and in late 1942 there began internal deployment that ultimately led in 1944 to the establishment of the 'ex-Servicemen's Association'.[11]

It would have been expected that at the end of the war, the CWO would be included in discussions on the future of the ex-servicewomen. But efforts to exclude the Council from the mainstream of decision making in the Yishuv continued even now. At a meeting of the CWO Secretariat in which he participated, Gurion was informed by Hadassah Samuel of the Council's commitment to the ex-servicewomen. She stressed that the CWO was 'established specifically for the purpose of female military recruitment and subsequent care for servicewomen and was a collective body consisting of representatives of women's organizations', and thus 'that body considers itself duty bound to continue its work and to return ex-servicewomen to civilian life'. Moreover, she said, that the lack of communication with Gurion's department made it difficult for the CWO to act. According to her, 'they [the women] were not seeking esteem', but they were concerned for the welfare of the ex-servicewomen. The women's organizations, she said, had accumulated many years of experience in guiding and advising women, and 'men cannot provide women with advice on career choice'. As far as she was concerned, she added, Gurion's department 'needs to be interested in cooperating with the CWO and should take advantage of us and not to see duality and fragmentation in the CWO's activity'.[12]

But Samuel's message to Gurion did not escalate the inclusion of CWO members in the ex-Servicemen's Welfare Department's meetings. At the beginning of recruitment, there was criticism as to the CWO's legitimacy to lead the move, and during the war there were efforts to exclude it from the Yishuv's recruitment centre. After the war, too, women representatives were excluded from debates on the future of the ex-servicewomen. Probably, it was still difficult for men to accept the role of the women's forum in initiating so daring a move and taking it to its successful conclusion.

Accommodation Problems

Even if the (temporary) issue of accommodation was shared by men and women, for the ex-servicewoman this problem was considered more urgent than for her male counterpart. According to a letter from the National Council to the WWC, 'Caring for the ex-servicewomen was more complicated than for ex-servicemen ... you can see for yourselves that it is not good to simply place a recently returned ex-servicewomen in a hotel. A servicewoman is even more in need of a special environment.'[13] Rachel Adiv wrote in *Davar Hapo'elet* that, 'It is easier to exist for a while without employment than without a roof over one's head. Under current circumstances in the Yishuv, the most complex issue is that of accommodation. Various activities are being invested in arranging accommodation in different locations.'[14] And indeed, the CWO rented houses in various towns in order to provide housing solutions, even temporary, for ex-servicewomen who had nowhere to live and even took advantage of various buildings belonging to WIZO and the WWC in which to house them. In Tel Aviv, for example, the Council commissioned the building of an additional storey on an existing house on Mikve Israel Street, in which to house twenty ex-servicewomen.

Other solutions were also presented for solving the housing shortage: in a building on Hayarkon Street, the army allocated eighteen rooms for housing fifty-five servicewomen; the building had been home to an ATS Company during the war. In Haifa, the government bought a residential building on Stanton Street in which to house fifteen ex-servicewomen. Three rooms, 'expropriated enemy property' (Templars in the German Colony), were allocated to ex-servicewomen; in Jerusalem, the Jewish Agency rented a building for ex-servicewomen. The WWC demanded of the British government, as well of local authorities, to build houses and to expropriate unused public buildings for housing ex-servicewomen and men.[15]

The WWC, also tried to prevent discrimination against unmarried ex-servicewomen and ensured them special rented apartments or houses within the public housing plan.[16]

The Agricultural Sector

Another channel for solving the issue of housing ex-servicemen and women was provided by the agricultural sector. At a meeting of servicemen in Italy, Haim Ben-Asher from Givat Brenner said,

> there is a greater and more burning issue – to what extent will we be able to establish and awaken a large settlement movement that will enclose thousands of servicemen and women ... probably with help from us, and with a willingness to go shoulder to shoulder together to conquer and settle new places ... a logical continuation of our pioneer voluntary work.[17]

By February 1944, the WWC had already called for the creation of women's farms and the establishment of cooperative working groups for those servicewomen, so it (the Working Women's Council) believed, 'that had learned to value the importance of working side by side'.[18] The WWC considered female military service to be a stage on the way to realizing the objectives of the working women's movement, which included agricultural settlement.

The WWC saw much importance in the integration of servicewomen, especially ones who were unmarried and had no family ties, in the kibbutzim and moshavim which were ready to take in hundreds of female members. In order to train the servicewomen for this kind of lifestyle, the CWO decided to prepare a proposal with regard to the number of servicewomen able to receive accommodation and training on the women's farms and at the schools in Nahahal and Nahalat Yitzhak. It is worth noting in this regard that the WWC saw the settlement of ex-servicewomen in agricultural farms from an ideological movement orientated view rather than from the viewpoint of the servicewomen. Most of these had come from towns and were unprepared for such a life, or as the WWC put it: 'Many of them will try to arrange for themselves some privacy, an individuality that has no intervention on the part of the collective and re-attachment within the framework.'[19]

Notwithstanding the efforts invested, the agricultural settlement sector did not provide the results expected by the initiators of the idea. Only 3,000 of some 30,000 servicemen registered into settlement cells and of these, only half actually settled. As for the women, few were found who were willing to join their destinies with the soldiers' settlements, and those that were, were wives of soldiers they had married before their recruitment.[20]

Employment and Vocational Training

It was clear to the CWO that on their return to the Yishuv many of the ex-servicewomen would require employment, such as nursing, social work and teaching. 'Among the servicewomen', Samuel located 'a large number [of women] with a tendency to social work' and decided to organize vocational training with this in mind. Toward the end of the military service period the CWO, with the help of civilian volunteers or relevant servicewomen, distributed questionnaires in order to determine the women's wishes vis-à-vis employment or vocational training.[21]

In July 1945, the CWO and the Committee for the Serviceman/woman's Future (which was established in conjunction with the National Council) organized a congress at the WIZO School in Tel Aviv. The agenda included: the Servicewoman's Future; Federation of (female) Members before Demobilization; Settling the Servicemen/women; and the Political Situation in the Yishuv. Chosen representatives of all the female companies in the Middle East attended the congress.[22]

In order to integrate the ex-servicewomen in the labour market the CWO needed to provide them with training. The WWC called on the government to establish a suitable fund to provide for vocational training and to allocate means for establishing constructive enterprises in which to employ ex-servicewomen. Further, there was a call to make professional training institutions available to them (nursing schools, teacher training schools, social services faculties), to provide them with intensive study courses and to adapt the agricultural economy to the needs of the ex-servicewomen. The WWC wished to encourage the ex-servicewomen to become familiar with a working rural lifestyle.[23]

In wake of cooperation between the CWO and other bodies, the country's nursing schools offered the ex-servicewomen training courses in nursing, and the Hebrew University's School of Social Studies proposed a project for training social workers. Taking into account the experience accumulated by the servicewomen in the army, these institutions gave them priority in enrolling for the courses. The CWO also provided student grants for the servicewomen who had studied in the Hebrew University and the Technion prior to their recruitment.[24]

In June 1945, the CWO drafted its proposals for training the demobilized women and specified its budget for each of the training channels. According to the proposal, 100 women were to be sent for agricultural training on women's farms, moshavim or kibbutzim. About eighty servicewomen who had worked in military hospitals expressed their interest in continuing with this work in Yishuv hospitals. Some of them lacked a high school education but their army work was taken into consideration and it was agreed that they would undergo a further course in order to compensate. Twelve ex-servicewomen were sent to be trained as social workers. Ten high school graduates with an aptitude for education and fluent Hebrew were accepted into youth training courses in a Jerusalem seminar provided by Youth Aliyah. Around twenty ex-servicewomen were sent for training in service positions (public kitchen management, housekeepers in institutions, storekeepers, housekeeping and cooking instructors). About twenty-five were sent for various administrative courses to become accounts clerks, shorthand typists and translators. Some were sent for training as elementary school cookery teachers. Also, several were offered courses in dressmaking, infant care and physical education.[25]

The CWO tried to find employment for the ex-servicewomen in the Yishuv institutions. One of the options was to place them in clerical work in the local inter-institutional committees. Also, some 1,700 of them registered in the Histadrut Liaison Bureau, which helped some find positions in Histadrut affiliated offices.[26]

In addition, ex-servicewomen and men were sent to work for UNRRA (the United Nations Relief and Rehabilitation Administration) with Jewish refugees in Europe even before the end of the war. These worked in Jewish refugee and displaced persons camps alongside women from the Yishuv sent on missions, and were employed in rehabilitation, Hebrew and Zionist education and organized immigration to the Yishuv. In May 1944, a meeting took place between the CWO and Jewish Agency representatives and a representative of UNRRA in which a proposal was raised to transfer ATS hospital workers to the organization. The registered nurses, who had not worked in their profession in the army, were dressed in army uniform so as to avoid the impression that they had left the army. The first UNRRA course opened in Petah Tikva on 18 July 1944 with sixty participants, including twenty-nine women. The curriculum included lectures on camp organization, warehouse and kitchen management, care for women and children, etc.[27]

Demobilization as a Result of Pregnancy or Illness

Already in 1943, the CWO turned to the matter of servicewomen seeking release from the army for reasons of health and according to its definition, 'They need recuperation, sometimes lengthy healing and, after all these, employment'.[28]

Several dozen servicewomen became pregnant in the course of their military service. Those who became pregnant unintentionally by British soldiers and decided to continue with the pregnancy were released from service. These recruits usually returned to the Yishuv and were denied the support of their families.

The CWO, as an institution that encouraged military recruitment, felt duty bound to care for these women in their time of need. It took care of their needs via its member organizations, such as baby houses or pioneer houses. The CWO undertook to pay the ex-servicewomen's private hospital fees and to house them in baby houses after their birth. Sometimes the CWO also paid for milk when breastfeeding was not an option. The Central Committee for Soldier's Family Welfare helped the CWO to bear the mothers' expenses. Sometimes the baby houses would employ the new mothers on the condition that alternative housing be found for them.

The member organizations in the CWO, especially WIZO and the WWC, were required to find solutions for ex-servicewomen who were wounded in the course of military service and were released from duty as a result. The council also undertook to find housing for servicewomen released on medical grounds and remained homeless in the Yishuv.

Shulamit Mariot (Hotori), for example, was released from duty after being hospitalized in a Yishuv hospital for dehydration.[29] Another case related to a Yishuv servicewoman who contracted tuberculosis in the course of her service and was hospitalized in an Egyptian hospital.

When she was released from hospital and from military service, the hospital contacted the CWO and requested help in finding her housing in the Yishuv.[30] The Council also asked the Central Committee, affiliated to the National Committee, to care for servicewomen who were released as a result of accidents or 'war tragedies' and not only on health grounds, the reason for most of the women's demobilization at that time.[31]

Victims of Military Service

Not all the recruits ended their service at the end of the war. Some (several dozen) were released after a brief period because of 'nervous ailments'. Some of these were sent to a special hospital (probably a mental health facility) in the Kantara region, before being transferred to the Yishuv.[32] Probably these were servicewomen who were unable to adapt to military life, or who had served in Egypt at the time of the battles in El Alamein in late 1942, who were prone to anxiety attacks due to the events around them and asked to be released on emotional grounds.

Twenty-four women lost their lives in the course of their military service: twelve were killed in traffic accidents (including one mother),[33] two in an aircraft accident or bombing, three died of an illness, five in various accidents and two names recorded no cause of death. One of the horrific accidents took place in Company 511 in Tel el Kabir after a group of servicewomen travelled to a Purim party in Engineering Corps Company 744. On their way back to camp their truck slipped into a ditch at the side of the road and overturned. An officer and twenty-three servicewomen were in the truck and Bat-Ami Yahalomi-Chizik of Metulla, Tamar Marek and Haya Stein-Botovitzky (mother to a 14-year-old son, a boarder at the Ben Shemen school) lost their lives. Many others were wounded and some were hospitalized nearby.[34] Several Yishuv servicewomen committed suicide in the course of their service, for various reasons – ranging from a sense of alienation and loneliness to failed relationships with British soldiers (these were mainly new immigrants with no family or friends in the Yishuv). One driver in ATS Company 513, who had come to the Yishuv from Germany, fell in love with a British officer who promised to marry her. When, at the end of the war, he was transferred to India, she went to say goodbye to him in the port of Suez and saw him on deck with his wife and children. She returned to Cairo, took a hotel room and committed suicide on 19 October 1945. On occasion servicewomen would threaten to commit suicide. One War Diary reported that Private Cohen was due to face a tribunal for some misdemeanour. She was clearly afraid of the outcome and threatened to take her own life.[35]

NOTES

1. 'Toward Increased Female Recruitment', *Davar Hapo'elet*, 8 (23 August 1943), p.116.
2. Lucy Noakes, *Women in the British Army: War and the Gentle Sex 1907–1948* (New York 2006), pp.130–1.
3. Company 504 War Diary, 3 August, 28 September 1944, National Archives, London (NA), WO 169/18016. The servicewoman's laconic report provides no indication to which future she was referring; probably she meant integration in the job market.
4. Deborah Bernstein, 'Hahalutza bein hadvadim: ma'amdan shel nashim bekoah ha'avoda btkufat hayishuv' [Pioneer woman between the boilers: women's status in the Yishuv's work force], *Megamot*, 28, no.1 (June 1983), p.10; Bat-Sheva Margalit Stern, 'La'malka ein bayit, la'melech ain keter? Ma'amadan shel nashim yehudiot beshuk ha'avoda be'eretz Israel hamandatorit' [The queen has no home, the king has no crown? Status of Jewish women on the labour market in Mandatory Eretz Israel], in Avi Bareli and Nahum Karlinsky (eds), *Calcala ve'hevra beyemei hamandat 1918–1948* (Be'er Sheva 2003), pp.115–17.
5. Interview with Rachel Ziv (Barshavsky), Tel Aviv, 2 February 2006.
6. Minutes of CWO meeting, 16 November, 1944, Central Zionist Archive, Jerusalem (CZA), F49/2105.
7. Bracha Habas, *Bnot hayil: sefer ha'ATS* [Women of valour: book of the ATS] (Tel Aviv 1964), p.15.
8. Moshe Smilansky, minutes of Yishuv Council for soldier demobilizing in the Course of the War, 15 June 1944, p.1, CZA, S25/4770.
9. Beba Idelson at a meeting of the CWO, 1 December 1943, p.2, CZA, F49/2104.
10. Rachel Adiv, 'Toward Demobilization', *Davar Hapo'elet*, 3 (2 April 1945), p.60.
11. Yoav Gelber, *Toldot hahitnadvut: Bein Britim, Aravim veGermanim* [History of volunteering: Between British, Arabs and Germans] (Jerusalem 1984), pp.212–22.
12. Minutes of CWO meeting, 30 May 1945, pp.1–2, CZA, F49/2106.
13. From National Council to WWC, 18 February 1945, ibid.
14. Rachel Adiv, 'Seminar for Servicewomen', *Davar Hapo'elet*, 8–9 (26 September 1944), p.141.
15. 'Resolutions of the 25th Meeting of the WWC', 5–7 June 1942, CZA, S25/9885. The WWC published a pamphlet to the servicewoman detailing its resolutions.
16. 'Toward Demobilization of Servicewomen', (Hebrew) from the Resolutions of the 25th Meeting of the WWC, ibid.
17. Haim Ben-Asher, meeting of UKM members in the Jewish Fighting Brigade in Fiuggi, 9 February 1945, pp.8–9, United Kibbutz Movement (UKM) Archive, Yad Tabenkin, a15.
18. *Davar Hapo'elet*, 10 (13 November 1944), pp.151–2.
19. Beba Idelson, 'On the Servicewoman's Future', ibid.

20. Meira Ya'akova, 'Hityashvut hayalim be'ertz Israel le'ahar milhement ha'olam hashnia' [Settlement of soldiers in Eretz Israel after the Second World War], *Katedra*, 102 (Tevet 2002), pp.125–35.
21. Minutes of CWO meeting, 18 June 1944, CZA, F49/2105.
22. Invitation to congress, 15 July 1945, CZA, S25/9885. A letter to female companies in advance of the congress included the message that although the servicewomen feel themselves an integral part of the entire population of servicemen/women and part of its activities and enterprises, there is still a need – especially on the part of the servicewomen themselves – to hold a congress of their own in order to discuss special issues. *Davar Hapo'elet*, 3 (2 April 1945), p.60.
23. 'Toward Demobilization of Servicewomen', from the resolutions of the 25th Meeting of the WWC, 5–7 June 1945, CZA, S25/9885.
24. Idelson, 'On the Servicewoman's Future', *Davar Hapo'elet*, 10 (13 November 1944), p.152.
25. 'Preliminary Proposals for Training Servicewomen Toward the Future', CWO from June 1945, CZA, F49/2106.
26. Minutes of CWO meeting, 18 April 1945, p.3, ibid. The Liaison Bureau served as the Histadrut's 'labour exchange' for its members. Lists of servicewomen in the Liaison Bureau from 1946, IDF Archives, submissions of the ex-Servicemen's Association; After her release from military service Ahuva Zilberstein was a clerk in the bureau and helped in referring ex-servicewomen to positions in the Histadrut offices. Interview with Ahuva Zilberstein (Strikovsky), Herzliya, 23 July 2006.
27. Report by Beba Idelson, minutes of meeting of CWO, 18 June 1944, CZA, F49/2105.
28. 'From the Journal of the Working Women's Council', *Davar Hapo'elet*, 9 (27 September 1943), p.135.
29. Mariot was the sister of Ahron Hotter-Yishai, the lawyer who represented Haganah members against the British. Interview with Mariot's sister, Yehudit Karasik, Ramat Gan, 15 March 2007.
30. Letter from Hospital No. 68 to Hadassah Samuel, 9 July 1943, Labour Movement Archive, Lavon Institute, IV-230-6, file 17.
31. Minutes of CWO, 28 September 1943, CZA, F49/2105.
32. Sonya Idelberg, minutes of CWO meeting on 27 april 1943, ibid.
33. Pnina Vilenchuk was killed in a road traffic accident in Syria on 17 September 1943; in Company 504 in Tel el Kabir, several servicewomen were killed, including Sara Ben-Shalom (29 May 1942); on 21 June 1942 Private Miriam Neuberg fell off a truck and was badly wounded and died the following day; according to reports, the funerals took place in Tel el Kabir and the servicewomen were buried in the military cemetery with full military honours. Private Berger of Company 504 in Tel el Kabir apparently drowned to death. She was taken unconscious to hospital, where her death was determined. She, too, was buried in the local military cemetery. Company 504 War Diary, 3 September 1944, NA, WO 169/18016.
34. Two days after the accident a funeral took place for the dead servicewomen. Many servicewomen from three companies serving in Tel el Kabir participated and the Purim party planned for the following day was cancelled. About a week

later, on 1 April 1943, a memorial service was held for the servicewomen, conducted by a military rabbi, and Hadassah Samuel arrived especially from the Yishuv to take part. The report on the accident in the Company War Diary did not mention the names of the dead servicewomen. An additional report and the only one on the accident was included in a letter from Zipora Kesse, who was sitting next to Tamar on the truck, to her friend's family in Kvutzat Schiller. Ya'akov Margalit (ed.), *Hineni shalcheni: mitnadvim batzava habriti kotvim* [Here I am, send me: writings of volunteers to the British Army] (Tel Aviv 1984), p.148.

35. Area Group 16 War Diary, 21 August 1943, NA, WO 169/13842.

Afterword

Missed Opportunity: A Historical View of Women's Military Service

In 1893, Malka Katz wrote from a township in Eastern Europe to the editor of *Hamagid* (a journal for educated East European Jews): 'Before knowing what my duties are, I would like to say, what does the honour of my nation demand of me? ... It is almost the only time in my life that I have actually heard one of the men saying specifically that we [women], too, *owe a debt to our nation*!' [author's emphasis]. And she added, 'Until now I have been instructed that a daughter's duty is to her parents, to her sons, etc. But duty to our nation ..., I dare not even mention!'[1]

There were women in the Jewish Yishuv who thought that volunteering for the military service in the British army and contributing to the war effort were a matter of national duty. They did it even though the Yishuv society expected them to stay behind, protected and caring for their families. Those women who enlisted undermined the regular gender order and defined their own duty toward their nation in wartime. They demanded to be allowed to enlist, succeeded in fulfilling their wish and motivated a process that ultimately achieved the broad support of the Yishuv. This struggle engulfed the concept that men and women were equal partners in building the country. Recruitment into the British army was therefore an important layer in the long lasting women's initiative to secure their status in the Yishuv.

In most of its aspects Yishuv women's service constituted a crossroads of gender and nationality. For example, the dissent aroused by the issue in the Yishuv reflected society's attitude to women. The deep fears that accompanied many of the Yishuv leaders testified to their ambivalence toward 'the new Hebrew woman': on the one hand, a declaration of her equality, on the other, deep suspicions as to her morality. Some of the suspicions emerged as justified; most of them were not.

Crossroads of nationalism and gender were also created in women's own concepts of military recruitment, in the underground activity of women members in the army, in the service of mothers, etc. The need to defend Jewish culture in the army, too, provided the recruits with a chance to construct their national and Zionist identities and thus to reinforce their Jewish identity, as part of their efforts to maintain a Jewish identity in a foreign army.

Concept of Women's Military Service in the War

The women who enlisted in the army in pre-State Israel, as well as in Britain and the US, aspired to penetrate new professions, to obtain a respectable position and to carry out their military tasks with devotion. To these were added national and pioneer-social ambitions. According to Ariela Friedman, the basis for women's self determination is their ability to express their wants and feelings. Moreover, real expression 'gives a sense of freedom – not freedom from others or freedom from responsibility for others, but the emotional freedom to be one's self and to take independent decisions'.[2] And indeed the Yishuv women's taking the initiative on military recruitment may be determined as an expression of ideological independence and the fulfilment of a lengthy struggle.

On the other hand, there are those who claim that the changes taking place in women and in their status in times of war are merely tenuous ones that have no influence on their status once the war is over. With demobilization, there is a gradual dissolution of gender concepts that empowered the women in the course of their service. This indicates both the limitations of women's power in the military system and the tenuousness, the localness and the flexibility in forming gender identities. The women, who formed their identities in accordance with combat identity, did not turn into men, they remained women but 'other', 'similar but different'. So long as the practice continues the servicewomen constitute a threat to the gender order. But when it ceases, the threat is removed and the social and gender order is restored.[3]

Women's military service, like other changes in traditional gender distribution of work power, contributed to the complex relationship that developed between the feminist movement and national groups, especially in countries under colonial rule. According to Yuval Davies, female emancipation symbolizes social change and the transition to modernity, although this did not actually happen in most of the countries that were granted independence and women remained in their old traditional positions.[4] According to researchers of gender and nationality, the politics of national liberation always preferred national liberation to women's liberation. Sheila Katz is convinced that western nationalism provided a 'Pandora's Box' in that it opened to women opportunities to shed the bonds of their old tasks, but, in doing so, they subordinated their personal and statuary needs on behalf of the homeland. Thus, she believes, their demands for liberation and equality were forever subordinated to the needs of the emerging nation as defined by the men.[5]

While women in the Yishuv hoped that the national struggle and the establishment of a new society would provide a window of opportunity to achieve a change in their social standing and equal rights, they did not neglect their personal and social interests, and in their discourse and activity they continued to talk and fight for equal rights (the result of equal obligations and shared burdens). Nonetheless, it would appear that the gender concepts that made possible the continuation of patriarchic control of Yishuv society, on the one hand, and the War of Independence, on the other, pushed all other discourse to the sideline, since 'there were always more burning issues' to deal with, due to 'lack of time and too much to do'.[6] Thus, for example, after being removed from combat positions in the War of Independence, many female Palmach wondered if this was indeed the right time to realize their dream of equality that had dissolved in the course of the war. Suddenly their struggle was conceived as 'so private and small' as compared with the big fight. Netiva Ben-Yehuda wrote in her book, 'A war as terrible as this … this isn't quite the time or place for trying to solve ideological issues of this kind; sexual equality. There are enough problems in war.'[7]

Effect of the Second World War on the Status of Women

Similar to studies on the effect of the First World War on women's status, studies of the effects of the Second World War contain two main narratives: according to one, the war created an image of a liberated woman, who discovered her value and importance due to her contribution to the war effort. According to the second narrative, no social change took place in woman's status. They may have felt a significant personal change in their lives, but the war was not presented as a period of women's liberation, rather as a period that was unstable and limited in time, the end of which signalled the safe return of women to their protected and protective homemaking.[8]

The entrance of women into the public sphere is examined in a similar manner. One of the oldest of feminist struggles is waged against the traditional distinction between the public and private spheres. Even during the Yishuv period and, later, after establishment of the State, the impression was that women would enter the public sphere only after realizing their obligations in the private arena, even though women were active in committees, political parties and voluntary organizations. According to another school of thought, this is due to the way in which reality is structured in dichotomist terms of private versus public and 'male' versus 'female'. According to a different school, men are the ones who particularly enjoy the genuine and full right to participate in public life, whereas women are not really invited to play a full, free and equal role in events in the public sphere.[9]

Marilyn Lake, who studied the effect of war on women in Australia, related to various studies that compared the place of women in the private sphere to that in the public sphere, i.e. their status in the work market. In this respect, she agreed with those researchers who detected a change and even regression in the status of women in various societies after the war, and even criticized them for failing to integrate into the work market. However, according to Lake, this observance disregards feminine concepts and a whole world of definitions for 'feminine' structure that had changed in the course of the war. These concepts are rooted in the discourse that awakened in the 1930s with regard to a new understanding of femininity that developed around sexuality and puberty. These concepts were reinforced in the wake of women's experiences in the Second World War.[10]

The Effect of Service in the British Army on Yishuv Society

According to Gelber, the main effect of military service in the British army was on the internal-Yishuv arena and especially with regard to women's place in Yishuv society and the underground resistance movements.[11] Ofra Elad is convinced that female recruitment into the British army caused significant change, albeit not immediate, in the decision to include women in the Palmach, initially as individuals (1942–43) and subsequently in large numbers with the addition of women from the recruited training programmes (Hachsharot).[12] This data must be considered with caution, since it would appear that a plethora of circumstances contributed to these changes, not only military service.

It appears that the effect of military service in the British army is especially noticeable in the establishment of the Women's Corps (Hen) in the Israeli Army, which was known at first as the Woman's Auxiliary Corps. Still, the decision to establish it was a strategic one on the part of Ben-Gurion, who was impressed by the organizational structure of the British army. The establishment of the Hen was not a result of a social process in the internal-Yishuv arena. Until its establishment, the status and jobs available to women were unclear. Some people believed that a certain number of women should be placed in combat positions, and, on the other hand, there were those who believed women should fill only auxiliary positions. In May 1948, with the publication of the Hen's first list of rules, the argument was determined and servicewomen were to be allowed to serve in static combat positions, in defending settlements, in administrative and professional positions and in auxiliary posts.[13]

On 5 May 1948, ten days before the declaration of the State, fifteen female officers and commanders who served in the ATS were summoned to participate in a course in the Borochov neighbourhood in Givatayim, together with fifteen additional female commanders in the Haganah. Thus was laid the foundation for the IDF's Women's Corps. Two military principles provided the foundations of the Women's Corps: that of the Haganah and Palmach members and that of the ex-ATS-servicewomen. The aforementioned members brought with them to the new corps the combat training guidelines and weapons experience, and the ex-servicewomen brought order, discipline and organization.[14] The first five Hen commanders were ex-ATS officers,[15] and additional officers, also ex-ATS, filled various positions of command and administration in the Corps.[16] The Hen was organizationally a part of the IDF personnel system, whose concepts conformed to a large extent with those of the British military.

Several dozens ex-servicewomen, especially those who had been Haganah members before their recruitment, participated in the War of Independence in various jobs as part of the women's battalions established alongside their male counterparts. Esther Lior, for example, a former driver in Company 513 in Camp Mina, drove an ambulance and transferred casualties under fire in the War of Independence. Brucha Ben-Haim, who served in a filter room for locating aircraft in the WAAF, served in Haganah as a wireless operator and in this capacity also participated in negotiations for an armistice agreement with Egypt in Rhodes (November 1948). Esther Rosenzweig enlisted in the IDF and was killed in the battle for the Etzion Bloc in the War of Independence. Several officers held positions of command in women's battalions in the War of Independence. Ruth Berman, a graduate of the ATS Cadre course and an officer, commanded Battalion 205 of the Women's Corps in Jerusalem.[17] But they were all exceptions that didn't prove the rule and most of the ex-servicewomen returned to their everyday routine after the war.

The army made use of the extensive administrative experience accumulated by the commanders in the British army in managing the new Women's Corps,[18] as it made use of the military experience of the male officers who joined the IDF after being released from service in the British army. But it appears that their effect on the Women's Corps, which was essentially an administrative rather than a combative force, was greater than the effect of the male officers on the IDF as a fighting force. Their contribution was expressed mainly on the organizational and administrative level and in equipping the army and formulating a military doctrine.[19] The appointment of five ex-ATS commanders as the first commanders in the IDF Women's Corps is testimony to the successful assimilation of the organizational heritage they brought with them. They formed the image of the corps that was an important feminine and national symbol for many years. Nonetheless, they perpetuated the concept that women in the army fill auxiliary positions and not combat positions, which conformed to male concepts with regard to the status of women in the military.

The experience accumulated by women as drivers in the British army helped the women of the Yishuv, even during the war, to become bus drivers in the public transport and drivers of jeeps in the Palmach. The IDF, too, provided driving courses for female drivers, which also included training in vehicle maintenance.[20]

Military Service as a Formative Personal Experience and as a Unique National Phenomenon

From a personal aspect most of the women saw military service as a personal, empowering and formative experience. Even the connections maintained among some of the servicewomen that lasted for many years after their release from service is testimony that the army was such an experience for them. After marriage, many of the women went out to work and some even nurtured distinguished careers: two became Members of Knesset, one an ambassador, others went into academe, etc. Yet, it seems that their work in the army had no effect on their subsequent professions.

When female military recruitment began in the Yishuv, Mania Shohat claimed that women have an inherent psychological block, which led them to internalize the fact that a woman's place is in the home. Apparently, during the war period the women who enlisted in the British army managed to rise above their own psychological blocks and those social-cultural blocks that society placed before them. But when their service came to an end, they returned to the same society that had not changed its fundamental, patriarchal concepts regarding women's place in it; and they had not changed their own concepts. Thus, as an experience, military service brought about no social change.

The uniqueness of women's military service was expressed mainly in its having been initiated by women – from a civilian women's organization (the CWO) and especially by Hadassah Samuel, who led the enterprise. In other countries in which women served in the military, it was inevitably the authorities that initiated the recruitment drive.[21] The feminine initiative provoked a process that, for the first time, broke through that male-dominated 'stronghold' – the military – and challenged men's ability to decide on female issues. This seems to have been the reason behind the repeated attempts on the part of persons and groups in the Yishuv to exclude women from the discourse – both by casting doubts on their legitimacy as women to lead the process and by their non-involvement in the centres of decision taking in the relevant institutions.

Also, female recruitment in the Yishuv was entirely voluntary, unlike in Britain (mostly), the USSR and even in Germany, where women were obliged by law to enlist in the army. The situation of female recruitment in the Yishuv was unique: more than 100 mothers left their homes and children and volunteered for service, a singular and unprecedented phenomenon in any other regular army and, in fact, does not exist to this day. The recruitment of women from the Yishuv was characterized by the relatively high personal level of many of the recruits, especially in comparison to the recruits from Britain, for example. The recruits displayed high personal and nationalist motivation, preserved their national and cultural identities and even carried out illegal and unprecedented missions on behalf of underground movements in the Yishuv.

The Yishuv women's service was unique even from the internal-Yishuv aspect. For the first time in the Yishuv's history, women from all walks of life came together in the army in a meeting that would not have taken place under other circumstances. Although the organizations that stood behind the recruitment of women – the CWO, Haganah and the Jewish Agency – tried to 'sift' the recruits in accordance with their own national requirements, it can be determined that the large majority of the recruits, even those who did not come from the 'organized' Yishuv, fulfilled the initiators' expectations, contributed to the war effort and preserved their national and personal identities.

And despite all this, the failure and missed opportunity were those of the women. The CWW that aspired to 'harvest the fruits' of its investment in the servicewomen throughout the war, expected to see them, on their release from service, integrating – in accordance with the movement's objectives – in 'building the nation anew and fitting into public positions and missions'. But this was not the case. The women merely returned to their traditional occupations.

The Exclusion of Women's Service in the British Army from Zionist Historiography

With the beginning of recruitment, Moshe Sharett determined that the fact and number of recruited women would establish the attitude toward them.[22] In 1943, Natan Alterman spoke on behalf of the entire Yishuv:

> and we remembered your exile
> and we remembered your walking in the desert
> and that you left at times of darkness and suffering
> to remote camps and a far off town
> and we shall tell it all in days to come
> and poems will be written, good as well as bad.[23]

In his book 'The Texture of Memory', James Young points out that 'memory is never shaped in a vacuum; the motives of memory are never pure'.[24] And, indeed, in the historiography of the Yishuv, the place of the servicewomen has become almost completely excluded. No aura has ever been created around the service of men and women from the Yishuv in the British army and no legends have developed, such as those of the Palmach and the War of Independence.

The recruits themselves wrote most of the books concerning the military service of men and women from the Yishuv.

Gelber, who wrote that to the 'organized' part of the Yishuv, military recruitment came to a certain extent as a surprise and especially the Jewish Agency's support for it, provides one explanation for this. According to him, after months during which the struggle against the 'White Paper' headed the Yishuv's agenda and its people had come to see Britain as its enemy, feared its persecutions, demonstrated against its regime and attacked its policemen and military – after all this, it was hard to make a sharp about-turn and enlist in its army.[25] Probably, Zionist historiography that tried to enhance the Yishuv's active struggle against what it saw as Britain's hostile regime, found it hard to explain a reality in which alongside active resistance there was an extensive system of cooperation – the service of thousands of people from the Yishuv in the British army. Possibly there were other reasons that contributed to this.[26]

And, indeed, within the general exclusion and the overall disregard for the army recruits, that of the female Yishuv recruits stands out sharply, even from the memoires of the men who served in the war. In Israel, both historiography and academic research almost completely ignored this particular chapter. Aside from Bracha Habas' book *Bnot hayil* (1964), which was based on the personal stories of the women recruits (under assumed names),[27] two others were published on the initiative of the ex-Servicemen's Association, Ruth Kolodny-Baki, *Tik Yozefina* [Josephine file] (1994) and Zivia Cohen (ed.), *Hitnadavnu letzava habriti* [We volunteered for the British Army], in 2003. Several memoires were also published, written by women who served in the British army, including Esther Herlitz's *Esther: o Le'an kvar Isha Yechola Le'hagia* [Esther: or how far could a woman go?] (1994) and Tsilli Brendstater, *Tsel misheli* [A shadow of my own] (2003). The only testimonies written were by groups and individuals who took part in the war. Exceptions to this were the servicemen employed in rescue operations and refugee aid in Italy and Austria, who mentioned the servicewomen who worked alongside them, whether in the form of reports to the Jewish Agency, or in later testimonies. This could be due to the fact that the servicewomen who worked with the Holocaust survivors were involved mainly in traditionally 'feminine' occupations, such as nursing and education. Other servicemen, those who were involved in illegal activity, avoided mentioning the women from the Yishuv who assisted them. Even in books on the meeting between Yishuv representatives and Holocaust survivors in Europe and in the Diaspora Centre no mention is made of the servicewomen.[28]

Contrary to Natan Alterman's promise, Yishuv society as well as, later, Israeli society did not remember the women who volunteered for service in the British army, not their exile, nor the time they spent in the desert. According to gender researchers, women were excluded de facto not only from the actual battlefields and the wars, but also from their share in their narratives.[29] The women themselves probably contributed to this exclusion from the narrative and their part in the war is largely forgotten. They stood on the sidelines, as women had done for generations before them, and did not know how to make themselves stand out.[30]

Service in the British Army: A Contribution to Female Equality or Meeting the "Need of the Moment"

Did female service in the British army have the potential to achieve a significant change in women's status in the Yishuv and to promote the desired equality? From the aspect of the number of women who enlisted, this service was a phenomenon that cannot be disregarded: about 2 per cent of the Yishuv's entire female 18–45 age group volunteered for service. Female military recruitment was a unique event in Jewish history, as Sharett said: 'A [female] Hebrew soldier in uniform – a novel concept in Jewish history.'[31] In the army, the recruits filled posts and missions that had been denied them in the Yishuv. Some of the professional posts were 'masculine' in essence and novel from a national aspect, both military/underground and cultural.

Miriam Bernstein Cohen anticipated the reality of demobilization and the return of the servicewomen to their former lives, when she wrote,

> and then [after the war] again they will regret and again the debate will begin
> on the weaker sex and their place
> on slave wages ... their spirit will take them
> on *the inequality between males and females*! [Author's emphasis][32]

In those days, the mere fact of female recruitment to the army was seen by women and men alike as an upgrade in woman's status, but this was not enough to translate into real social equality.

According to Orit Kamir, political Zionism forced Jewish women to make way for Jewish men to take centre stage and display their masculinity on a personal as well as a national level. According to her, Zionism 'invited' women to participate in the masculinization project of the Jewish collective, but 'to take a back seat'. Women had to maintain and support the hinterland, but in order to repair past damage from the Diaspora, they were required to emphasize Jewish femininity and not to stand out as masculine.[33] Women, for their part, according to Kamir, accepted this 'invitation' openheartedly.

From its very beginning, political Zionism carved on its flag the principle of sexual equality.[34] However thus, according to Kamir, the equality metered out to women within the conceptual system of fulfilling the Zionist vision meant that first and foremost equality had to exist in the fulfilment of the Zionist vision, as expressed in the masculinization of the Jewish collective and the Hebrew male in conquering and redeeming the land. This kind of equality does not conform with the equality of a liberal worldview, which calls for the equal right of each individual to realize him/herself in accordance with his/her concept of him/herself and an autonomous and understanding creature, rather as Zionist equality that is unable to grant equal opportunity to all of the nation's individuals. It promises each individual the right to participate in the Zionist enterprise in accordance with the gender-based positions designated for him/her.

The Zionist Movement's commitment was, therefore, to a woman's right to serve as a right-hand-person to the evolving Hebrew man, to be a devoted wife, to nurture the next generation of Zionist men and to participate in auxiliary positions in building the country. According to this explanation women's military service, as well as their involvement in the Yishuv's other national and security institutions, could never testify to genuine equality with men.

In 1964 a reception was held in the President's Residence in honour of Habas' book *Bnot hayil*. Rachel Katznelson-Shazar, the president's wife and herself a veteran women's rights advocate, rebuked the ex-servicewomen with, 'You went to the army and returned the same – [straight] to the kitchen and the babies ... why haven't you changed?'[35] Indeed, it would appear that the servicewomen contributed their share to this situation. The WWC had hoped that women would obtain a 'male' skill or profession in the army, such as driving, motor mechanics, mechanical engineering, telegraph and radio operators that they could continue working at after the war, but the recruits themselves didn't think so. Most of them internalized their wartime occupations as 'auxiliary' to those of their male counterparts, or as a 'mother and sister' to the servicemen. The recruits saw the war as a period in which social and gender orders were turned upside down, a period in which it was possible to do unacceptable things. They didn't think of adopting a pattern of masculinity or copying the 'male' occupations they filled in the army in their lives in the Yishuv, rather they aspired to fill 'feminine' jobs and expressed no desire to create a new feminine image.

It is possible that the Yishuv women's volunteer service in the British army could indicate a new and correct feminine awareness to breaking of conventions, or as Motti Golani put it (as paraphrased by Mania Shohat), 'It seems that their feminism was 'retroactive feminism and was certainly not well phrased'.[36] But their service did not change the gender discourse in Yishuv society, nor in that of society in the State of Israel. Their success in military service was good at the time and did not express any social change or change in status. The same applies to Britain and the US at the end of the war: when the men returned, the women were required to vacate the positions they had filled throughout the war and return to their homes. Society expects adult women, such as the ex-servicewomen on their return to the Yishuv, to first of all fulfil their ultimate female destiny – establish a family and raise children. And, indeed, the women who came back from the war resumed their private lives and didn't try to break through the 'glass ceiling' of the patriarchal approach to them.

Although military service was conceived as a chance to achieve equality between the sexes and as a definitive experience in the eyes of the servicewomen, it was created as a need of the moment and not as any cognitive-social revolution. Confirmation of this can be found in the extraordinary attitude of Hannah Senesh, who died carrying out a blatantly 'heroic' and 'un-feminine' mission.[37] Although she became a myth and a role model among the women of the Yishuv, she was unable to break through the 'glass ceiling'. The change in male attitude that was expressed in the willingness to recruit women into the military, to employ them in 'masculine' occupations and to break the accompanying social conventions, came from temporary practical and national considerations. Thus, after the state was established and conditions changed, women reverted to their traditional positions. Military service, therefore, did not improve their social standing, nor did it contribute directly to the struggle for full and real social equality for women in Yishuv society. Its influence was symbolic and it contributed to the myth of female equality, but since it was not accompanied by social and cultural change, its influence on the civil and political status of women in the Yishuv and, subsequently, in the State of Israel, was negligible.

NOTES

1. From Malka Katz, *Hamagid*, 32 (7 November 1893), pp.10–11, in Tova Cohen and Shmuel Feiner, *Kol alma ivriya: kitvei nashim maskilot bame'ah hatsha esreh* [Voice of the Hebrew woman: nineteenth century women's writings] (Tel Aviv 2006), p.127.
2. Ariela Friedman, *Ba'ah meahava: intimiut vekoah bazehut hanashit* [Coming from love: intimacy and strength in female identity] (Tel Aviv 1996), p.43.
3. Margaret Higonnet and Patrice Higonnet, 'The Double Helix', in Margaret R. Higonnet, Jane Jenson, Sonya Michel and Margaret Collins Weitz (eds), *Behind the Lines* (New Haven, CT 1987), pp.33–4.
4. Nira Yuval-Davis and Floya Anthias, *Woman, Nation, State* (New York 1989), pp.132–4.
5. Sheila Katz, *Women and Gender in Early Jewish and Palestinian Nationalism* (Florida 2003), p.164.
6. Dganit Boni-Davidi, 'Women and Gender in the Hagana Organization between 1920–1948' (MA thesis, Bar- Ilan University, 2004), p.151.
7. Netiva Ben-Yehuda, *Keshprartza hamedina* [When the State broke out] (Jerusalem 1991), pp.1–2. According to Yonit Ephron, ignoring the women workers' movement from the women's liberation at this time came from the concept of equality with men as a socialist given, and also due to the building of the national enterprise. The movement believed that once the issue of the new society was solved, it would be the turn of the new woman. Yonit Ephron, 'Ahayot, lohamot, imahot: ethos umeziot bemivhan bnot dor 1948' [Sisters, fighters, mothers: ethos and reality in the test of the 1948 generation of women], *I'yunim Be Tekumat Israel*, 10 (2000), p.355.
8. Penny Summerfield, *Reconstructing Women's Wartime Lives: Discourse and Subjectivity in Oral Histories of the Second World War* (Manchester 1998), p.255. For the first time in the First World War, millions of women participated in the war effort and many thousands served in the various auxiliary services. Nonetheless and despite the significant mobility – both spatial and gender – of women in the war, it seems that the traditional definitions of 'masculine' and 'feminine' remained, especially in wake of the emphasis on and perpetuation of 'motherhood' as the essence of womanhood and 'soldiers' as the essence of manhood. Susan Grayzel, *Women's Identities at War: Gender, Motherhood and Politics in Britain and France during the First World War* (London 1999), pp.190–206.
9. Orit Kamir, *Israel's Dignity Based Feminism in Law and Society* (Tel Aviv 2002), pp.73–4.
10. Lake lists several reasons for the reinforcement of these concepts: women had become accustomed to being independent when their husbands served far from home; women filled positions of responsibility both at home and in the war industry, etc. Marilyn Lake, 'Female Desires, The Meaning of World War II', in Gordon Martel (ed.), *The World War Two Reader* (New York 2004), pp.359–60.

11. Recruitment to the British army may have influenced the decision – or accelerated its implementation – to appoint a woman to the position of national command of Haganah. See for example, Yoav Gelber, *Toldot habitnadvut: Habitnadvut ve mekoma bemidiniut hazionit ve hayishuvit 1939–1942* [History of volunteering: volunteering and its place in Zionist and Yishuv Policies 1939–1942] (Jerusalem 1989), p.294.
12. Ofra Elad, '"Kol bahur ve tov laneshek, bahura al hamismar!": Ha'havera ba'-Palmach' [Every man is good for arms, a woman, on guard duty! Woman Member in the Palmach], in Yehiam Weitz (ed.), *Palmach: Shtei shibolim veherev* [Palmach, Two Sticks of Corn and a Sword] (Tel Aviv, 2001), p.216. According to Elad, women's recruitment to the ATS was a turning point in the attitudes of Jewish men in the Yishuv to the idea of women in the army, since, even if they didn't internalize the idea completely, it was inconceivable to disregard or fight it, especially in light of the extent of female volunteering.
13. The Hen was one of seven services in the Personnel Department (AKA) and the last corps in HQ, whose establishment had been decided on by the HQ Committee that determined the structure of the IDF. The commander of Hen was directly subordinate to the head of AKA. The developing women's status in the IDF (according to Ben-Gurion), was already discussed in the first months of the War of Independence, but only with the decision to establish the corps in accordance with the ATS model did preparations begin for it. Zahava Ostfeld, *Tsava nolad: shlavim ikariim bebniat tsava behanhagato shel David Ben-Gurion* [An army is born: main stages in building an army under the leadership of David Ben-Gurion], ed. Shoshana Stiftel (Tel Aviv 1994), pp.442–3.
14. Differences arose between the two groups over the organizational structure of the women's corps. Haganah members insisted that women had to serve in mixed male and female units, while ex-ATS servicewomen believed in complete separation (as in the British army). The compromise consisted of the first year being run according to the ATS model with training according to Haganah system. 'ATS, Roots and Heirarchy' (undated, probably from the 1980s), pp.6–8, Haganah History Archive, Tel Aviv (HHA), 16/36.
15. Lieutenant Colonel Mina Ben-Zvi (1948–49), Colonel Shoshana Werner (1949–52), Colonel Shoshana Gershonovitz (1952–59), Colonel Dina Wert (1959–64), Colonel Stella Levy (1964–70). Zivia Cohen (ed.), *Hitnadavnu letzava habriti* [We volunteered for the British Army] (Tel Aviv 2003), pp.203–8.
16. Thus, for example, in the first Hen HQ, Rachel Hibner was Administrative Officer; Victoria Ben-Artzi was Quartermaster Officer (she was followed by Hanna Levin and Ziva Talbar (Chizik)). Zivia Cohen, *Bat Hen: Sipuran shel hahayalot hamemalot tafkiding hiuni'im umeguvanim umosifot hen le Zahal* [Graceful: Stories of the servicewomen who fill varied and essential positions and add charm to the IDF] (Haifa 1972), p.15.
17. Alongside every battalion there was established a women's battalion under the leadership of a female commander. Haganah members saw in this a regression of the status they had previously achieved in the organization.
18. Veteran Haganah member, Tze'ira Lerman, admitted that the main consideration in the choice of ex-ATS servicewomen for senior command positions was the level and control of all organizational and disciplinary issues. Interview with Tze'ira Lerman (undated, probably from the early 1990s), HHA, 141.46. In the Hen, discipline, living accommodation, 'out of bounds' orders, etc., were

copied from the British army. Former British army officers in professional positions provided material from instruction courses or from their routine employment, all of which served the Hen. Nurit Gilat, 'Attitude of Israeli Society on Women's Military Service, 1948–1967' (PhD thesis, Haifa University, 2005), p.120.

19. Gelber believes that most of the initial contribution of ex-ATS servicemen consisted of their effect on the formation of the regular army's position in the State of Israel, since separation between the administrative and professional levels was unknown in Haganah. Yoav Gelber, *Gar'in Letsava Ivri sadir: Terumatam shel yozei Hatsava Habriti Lehakamat Tsahal* [Nucleus for Regular Hebrew Army: British Army Veterans' contribution to Establishment of IDF] (Jerusalem 1986), pp.527–30. It is worth remembering that most of the male Yishuv male recruits in the British army served in auxiliary positions and did not achieve combat posts (except for the Brigade, which was established in September 1944 and fought on the Italian front). A senior Haganah member said to participants of the women's Cadre course: 'Even in the army in general, in this war, even the male soldiers started in very, very [sic] non-military positions ... but they overcame their disappointment and fulfilled these menial jobs.' Lecture by Haganah senior, 4 February 1942, HHA, 117/16. Moreover, the recruits did not participate in forming military policies. Still, it should be mentioned that Sharett did not distinguish between combat and non-combat companies, since the main element for him was proximity to the front and not the recruits' jobs. Sharett, Moshe, *Policy Making; The Diaries of Moshe Sharett* (Tel Aviv 1979), 5, pp.168–9.
20. Beba Idelson in Histradrut Executive, 7 September 1942, p.128, Israel Defense Forces (IDF) Archive, Tel Hashomer, 45/140/2002; Cohen, *Bat Hen*, p.110. Women served as drivers in the IDF until 1960 and in the late 1970s the IDF again permitted the employment of women drivers.
21. In Britain, to some extent, it seems that the authorities' initiative was preceeded by lobbying of women organizations which existed since the First World War.
22. Sharett in a speech to WWC in February 1942, *Davar Hapo'elet*, 3–4 (23 April 1942), p.36.
23. Alterman, 'Two Sergeants', Seventh Column,' *Davar*, 5 Av 1943 p.39. The poem was devoted to Hanna Leibowitz and Miriam Langraf, the first Yishuv servicewomen to achieve the rank of Corporal in the WAAF and had their pictures in the local press.
24. James Young, *The Texture of Memory: Holocaust Memorials and Meaning* (New Haven, CT and London 1993), p.2.
25. Gelber, *Toldot hahitnadvut: Hahitnadvut ve mekoma bemidiniut hazionit ve hayishuvit 1939–1942*, pp.222–3. And 'we have to do some act of propaganda without stopping the political activity ... preliminary psychological training of the public'. Histadrut Executive meeting, 23 May 1940, p.14, Labour Movement Archive, Lavon Institute.
26. Additional possible reasons consisted of service outside the country's borders; the dissent aroused in the Yishuv by the recruitment, as well the political conflict between Sharett and Ben-Gurion, which caused Sharett to be excluded from the focus of influence and, as a result, the disregard for enterprises identified with Sharett.
27. Her choice to use assumed names might have allowed Habas to 'contribute' to the exclusion of the women recruits from the Yishuv's historical narrative.

28. See, for example, Idit Zartal, *Zahavam shel hayehudim: Ha'hagira hayehudit hamahtartit le eretz Israel, 1945–1948* [Jews' gold: illegal Jewish immigration to Eretz Israel, 1945–1948] (Tel Aviv 1996); Irit Keynan, *The Hunger Has Not Died Down – Holocaust Survivors and the Emissaries of the Land of Israel, Germany 1945–1948* (Tel Aviv 1997), etc. Possibly this is also a result of the relatively low number of servicewomen dealing with this.
29. Miriam Cooke, 'WO-Man, Retelling the War Myth', in Miriam Cooke and Angela Woollacott (eds), *Gendering War Talk* (Princeton, NJ 1993), pp.177–204.
30. Paraphrase of Neuta Halperin, Commander of a Haganah women's battalion, 'we didn't know how to make ourselves stand out.' Halperin added, 'In the end, the work was not connected to exciting events and we were trained to modesty, to the fact that some things are left unsaid.' *Davar*, December 20, 1984, Haganah Archive, 55/59.
31. Speech at the Workers' Council Congress, Tel Aviv, 26 February 1942 HHA, 55/59.
32. The song 'The ATS Marches' was performed by the Brigade's singing group 'Me'ain zeh'. Courtesy of Hanna Maron, a member of the group. Also, a cartoon published for International Women's Day, depicting a woman sweeping the floor and her husband saying: 'Doesn't it matter that you were an officer in the ATS – go out to work.' *Niv Ahim*, 21 (August 1991), p.12.
33. Zionism invested everything in emphasizing the new Jewish masculinity, whereas Jewish women symbolized Jewish feminism that brought about its destruction and discrimination. Orit Kamir, *Israel's Dignity Based Feminism in Law and Society* (Tel Aviv 2002), pp.74-5. Here, Kamir bases herself on Elboim-Dror, according to whom, the new Jewish Nationalism developed the symbols of 'the Judaism of Muscles' that presented masculinity, force and daring as the main images of the new culture. Women identified with definitions of masculinity, which were an integral part of the Zionist ethos, which rejected the feminine, spiritual and dependent symbols of Diaspora Judaism. This process contributed to women's denial of their femininity, to their efforts to appear masculine and to changes in their physical appearance. Thus reversal (inversion) was formed in the concept of sexuality: the man, who hereto had symbolized spirituality, unlike the woman who symbolized the material and the physical, exchanged his traditional characteristics. The Jew, Man of the Spirit, became a Man of Substance, Nature and Body. Rachel Elboim-Dror, 'Nashim ba'utopiot hazioniot' [Women in Zionist Utopias], *Katedra*, 66 (December 1992), pp.111–41.
34. The Israeli self-image of profound commitment to the value of equality remained so strong that only in the 1970s did gender researchers start to define it as a 'myth', and to reveal its damaging role in the smoke screen that hides the real inequality in the country. Kamir, *Israel's Dignity Based Feminism in Law and Society*, p.76.
35. Interview with Esther Herlitz, Tel Aviv, 9 December 2005.
36. Motti Golani, 'Manya: aliata hakzara ve nefilata ha'aruka' [Manya: her short rise and long fall], *Israel*, 3 (2003), p.7.
37. Senesh and her fellow parachutists were not included in this study. Although they were recruited into the WAAF, this was only in order for them to have the status of prisoners-of-war in the event of falling into enemy hands. In this respect their enlistment differed from that of the other servicewomen.

Bibliography

Archives

Central Zionist Archive, Jerusalem (CZA)
Gnazim Institute, Tel Aviv
Haganah History Archive, Tel Aviv (HHA)
Hamileh –The Israeli Center for Documentation of Stage Arts, Tel Aviv University
Hashomer Hatza'ir Archive, Giv'at Haviva
Israel Defense Forces (IDF) Archive, Tel Hashomer
Jabotinsky Institute, Tel Aviv
Labour Movement Archive, Lavon Institute
Municipal Archives, Tel Aviv
National Archives, London (NA)
National Army Museum, London (NAM)

United Kibbutz Movement (UKM) Archive, Yad Tabenkin

Interviews

Jean Baker, Tackley (near Oxford, UK), 17 May 2006
Michal Ben-Arieh (Zimbel), Even Yehuda, November 2, 2006
Brucha Ben-Haim (Eisenberg), Nahalal, 7 January 2006
Tsilli Brendstater (Avraham), Tel Aviv, 5 February 2006
Ora Cummings, Tel Aviv, 6 January 2010
Ellen Elroi, Bat Yam, 4 February 2006
Naomi Epstein, Tel Aviv, 7 March 2007
Elisheva Erez (Pearlman), Hertzliya Pituah, 14 January 2006
Tamar Eshel (Shoham), Tel Aviv, 16 November 2005
Shoshana Geller (Rogel), Tel Aviv, 20 April 2007
Aviva Gil (Flentzbaum), Tel Aviv, 24 January 2006
Lilli Glatt, Ramat Gan, 15 January 2006
Hanna Golani (Golanski), Natanya, 21 January 2006

Zipa Gov (Katz), Tel Aviv, 22 October 2006
Ruth Gruzin (Grosbard), Tel Aviv, 22 November 2005
Zika Halperin, Petah Tikva, 23 October 2006
Esther Herlitz, Tel Aviv, 9 December 2005
Major (ret.) Daphne Hill, Richmond (London), 10 May 2006
Ruth Horam, Jerusalem, 9 August 2007
Haya Ironi-Abrahami, Tel Aviv, 8 February 2006
Yehudit Karasik, Ramat Gan, 15 March 2007
Avraham Katz-Oz, Tel Aviv, 6 December 2006
Sara Kopler (Bar-Adon), Tel Aviv, 26 June 2006
Aliya Kravi (Rachlevsky), Tiv'on, 24 May 2007
Shoshana Little (Hasson), Kibbutz Ma'agan Michael, 4 March 2006
Hanna Maron (Meierzak), Tel Aviv, 28 February 2006
Tzfira Ogen (Katinsky), Tel Aviv, 20 December 2005
Sonya Peres (Gelman), Tel Aviv, 9 January 2006
Rina Porat (Mor), Tel Aviv, December 2006
Tirtza Raviv (Torok) and Yael Arieli (Kornberg), Jerusalem, 27 December 2006
Liah Ronai (Ernst), Tel Aviv, Janaury 12, 2006
Zipora Shahar (Eitan), Ester Yanai (Ben-Zvi), Rachel Brenner (Koris), Nahalal, 7 January 2006
Ya'akov and Rina Sharett, Tel Aviv, 5 December 2006
Tzafrira Shoham (Yaffe), Kibbutz Ramat Yohanan, 11 March 2007
Miriam Shor (Mattersdorf), Tel Aviv, 15 April 2007
Varda Simpson (Kahanovitz), Kibbutz Ma'agan Michael, 4 March 2006
Judith Spitz, Tel Aviv, 13 December 2005
Friedl Stern, Tel Aviv, 16 April 2006
Yaffa Tevua (Greenberg), Haifa, 17 December 2005
Miriam Vardi (Gur), Jerusalem, 15 July 2006
Naomi Yekutieli (Torok), Tel Aviv, 8 December 2005
Ahuva Zilberstein (Strikovsky), Herzliya, 23 July 2006
Rachel Ziv (Barshavsky), Tel Aviv, 2 February 2006
Ruth Ziv (Tartakov), Lea Itkin (Nahmias), Hana Weiss, Kvutzat Geva, 11 April 2006

Group interviews with former members of Company 513 (Mina Company) in Haifa on 27 April 2006, and in Even Yehuda on 2 November 2006.
Aviva Arbel (Kooperman), Ruth Nelkin (Telz), Esther Lior (Ben Shabat), Zipora Shahar (Eitan), Ruth Breda (Hass), Esther Yanai

(Ben-Zvi), Ruth Ofer (Fleischer), Hana Zilberg (Bielostotsky), Haya Levin (Alexandrovsky), Erica Sharon (Ino), Haifa

Transliterated Interviews

Interview with Claire Epstein, 20 September 1979. Interviewer: Yehudit (no surname available), Kibbutz Ginossar Archive

Interview with Hadassah Samuel, 12 February 1972. Interviewer: Margalit Shilo, film 200/K, the Institute for Modern Judaism, Department of Verbal Documentation, Hebrew University

Interview with Ruth Klieger-Eliav, March 23, 1964. Interviewer: Aharon Kedar, film 371, Haganah Archive

Miscellaneous

Donner, Batia, *Shamir Grafika Ivrit: Studio Ha'achim Shamir* [Shamir Hebrew Graphics: Shamir Bros. Studio), Catalog 3/99 (Tel Aviv 1999), pp.6–12.

Memoirs of Esther Tal (Itrani)

Memoirs of Tamar Eshel (Shoham)

Tali Shilo, Kum ve'hitgayes' [Step Up to Enlist], Recruitment Posters – British Army, WWII in Eretz Israel, Proposal for Exhibition in Museology Studies 2005

Publications

Addis, Elisabetta et al., 'Introduction', in Elisabetta Addis, Valeria Russo and Lorenza Sebesta (eds), *Women Soldiers: Images and Realities* (New York: 1994), pp.xi–xxii.

Addis, Elisabetta and Valeria Russo, 'The Constitution of a Gendered Enemy', in Elisabetta Addis, Valeria Russo and Lorenza Sebesta (eds), *Women Soldiers: Images and Realities* (New York: 1994), pp.49–58.

Almog, Debora, 'Women in the Israeli Defense Forces' (MA thesis, Hebrew University, Jerusalem, 1987).

Almog, Oz, *The Sabra: The Creation of the New Jew* (Berkeley, CA: University of California Press, 2000).

Alterman, Natan, *Ha'tur ha'shevii'* [Seventh Column] (Tel Aviv 1987).

Amitai, Mordechai (ed.), *Nahalal – hazon behagshamato: rishon lemoshavei ovdim 1921–1971* [Nahalal – a vision in realization: first of the workers' settlements 1921–1971] (Tel Aviv 1971).

Anderson, Benedict, *Imagined Communities: Reflections on the Origin and Spread of Nationalism* (London 1991).

Arbel, Rachel (ed.), *Kahol Lavan be tsvaim: dimuim hazutiim shel hazionut 1897–1947* [Blue and white in colours: frontal images of Zionism 1897–1947] (Tel Aviv 1996).

Arieh Sapir, Nili, 'Karnaval be tel aviv: Purim ba'ir ha'ivrit harishona' [Carnival in Tel Aviv: Purim in the first Hebrew town], *Jerusalem studies in Jewish folklore*, 22 (1983), pp.99–121.

Atzmon, Yael, 'Historia shel kabalat ahrayut' [History of taking responsibility], in Yael Atzmon (ed.), *Hatishma koli: yutsugim shel nashim be tarbut israelit* [Will you hear my voice: representation of women in Israeli culture] (Jerusalem 2001), pp.134–52.

Atzmon, Zipora, 'Ma'amad haisha besherut haetzel ve'halehi' [Women's status in the ranks of IZL and Lehi] (MA thesis, Toro College, 1993).

Azarya, Victor and Baruch Kimmerling, 'New Immigrants in the Israeli Armed Forces', *Armed Forces and Society*, 6, no.3 (1980), pp.455–82.

Baki, Roberto, *H'anohag Benisuin ve'beyeluda bekerv hashchavot hashonot shel he'Yeshuv ve Hashpaato al Atiddenu* [The custom in marriage and birth in different layers of the Yishuv and its impact on our future] (Jerusalem 1945).

Baki, Roberto, 'Ha'ochlusia: Demographia' [Population: Demography], *Hebrew Encyclopedia*, 1 (Tel Aviv 1957), pp.673–83.

Banai, Ya'akov, *Hayalim almonim: sefer mivtzaei Lehi* [Anonymous soldiers: book of Lehi operations], ed. Israel Eldad (Tel Aviv 1989).

Bar-Adon, Ahron, 'Ha-Imahot ha-meyassedot u-menat helkan be-tehiyyat ha-ivrit ve-hithavvutah (1882—1914)' [The founding mothers and their role in the revival of Hebrew and its formation (1882–1914)], *Lashon ve-Ivrit*, 3 (May 1990), pp.5–26.

Bashelach vebamacheresha: Kovetz Hayalim Havrei Tenuat Hamoshavim [In the sword and plough: Soldier members of the Moshavim movement] (1948).

Baumel, Judith, 'Gesharim ben Etmol ve Mahar: Mekoma shel tarbut Hagola besipur haye'en shel Giborot Ha'aliyah Hahamishit' [Bridges between yesterday and tomorrow: the role of Diaspora culture in the stories of Fifth Aliyah heroines], *Katedra*, 114 (February 2003), pp.121–48.

de Beauvoir, Simone, *The Second Sex: Facts and Myths* (New York: Random House 1997).

Be'eri (Grinker), Yizraela, *Rosh Hatsevet tahat etz hatomer* [Tribal chief under the date tree] (Nahalal 2005).

Beit El, Ilana, 'Gvarim, gavriut umilhama: migdar bemilhemet haolam harishona' [Men, masculinity and war: gender in the First World War], *Zmanim*, 65 (Winter 1998–99), pp.112–20.

Ben-Ari, Eyal and Edna Levy Schreiber, 'Binui guf, binui ofi ubinui uma: hamigdar ve hashirut hatzvai be Israel' [Building a body, building a character and building a nation: gender and military service in Israel], *Tarbut Democratit*, 4–5 (2001), pp.99–130.

Ben-Arieh, Yehoshua, *Jerusalem and the British Mandate* (Jerusalem: Yad Izhak Ben Tsvi, 2003).

Ben-Gurion, Arieh, 'Seder Pessach, hagadah ve tekes ha'omer b'Ein Harod' [Pessach Seder, Hagadah and the Omer ceremony in Ein Harod], *Mibifnim*, 46, no.3 (Spring 1984), pp.358–73.

Ben-Gurion, David, *Bama'aracha* [In the campaign] (Tel Aviv 1957).

Ben-Tor, Nehemia, *Lexikon Lehi* [Lehi Dictionary] (Tel Aviv 2007).

Ben-Yehuda, Baruch, *Sipura shel hagimnasia 'Herzliya'* [Story of the Herzliya High School] (Tel Aviv 1970).

Ben-Yehuda, Netiva, *Keshprartza hamedina* [When the State broke out] (Jerusalem 1991).

Berkowitz, Michael, 'Transcending "Tzimmes and Sweetness": Recovering the History of Zionist Women in Central and Western Europe 1897–1933', in Maurie Sacks (ed.), *Active Voices: Women in Jewish Culture* (Illinois 1995), pp.41–62.

Berlowitz, Yaffa, 'Letivo shel hanarative hazioni hanashi – hathalat mea/sof mea' (To the essence of the female Zionist narrative – beginning/end of century), in Yehudit Bar El, Yigal Schwartz and Tamar Hess (eds), *Sifrut vehevra batarbut haivrit hahadasha: ma'amarim mugashim le Gerson Shaked* (Literature and society in the new Hebrew culture: essays dedicated to Gershon Shaked) (Tel Aviv 2000).

Berlowitz, Yaffa, *Sheani adama ve adam: sipurei nashim ad kum hamedina* [I am Land and Man: stories of women up to the establishment of the State] (Tel Aviv 2003).

Bernstein, Deborah, 'Hahalutza bein hadvadim: ma'amdan shel nashim bekoah ha'avoda btkufat hayishuv' [Pioneer woman between the boilers: women's status in the Yishuv's work force], *Megamot*, 28, no.1 (June 1983), pp.7–19.

Bernstein, Deborah, 'Ma'amadan ve'hitargenut shel nashim ovdot bayishuv ha'ironi beshnot haesrim vehashloshim' [Status and organization of working women in the urban Yishuv during the 1920s and 1930s], *Katedra*, 34 (Tevet 1985), pp.115–44.

Bernstein, Deborah, 'Po'alot ve-Halutzot ba-Aliyah ha-Sheniyyah – Tikvot ve-Akhzavot' [Female workers and pioneers in the Second Aliyah – hopes and disappointments], in Mordekhai Naor (ed.), *Ha'aliyah Hasheniya 1903–1914* [The Second Aliyah 1903–1914] (Jerusalem 1985), pp.145–63.

Bernstein, Deborah, *Ishah be-Eretz Yisra'el: Hashe'ifa Leshivion Betkufat Heyishuv* [A Woman in Eretz Israel: The aspiration for equality during the Yishuv period] (Tel Aviv 1987).

Bernstein, Deborah, 'Bein ha'isha ha-adam ubein eshet habayit' [Between the woman as person and the woman in the home], in Uri Ram (ed.) *Hahevra Ha'israelit: hebetim bikortiim* [Israeli society: critical aspects] (Tel Aviv 1993), pp.83–103.

Bernstein, Deborah, 'Daughters of the Nation: Between the Public and Private Spheres in Pre-State Israel', in Judith Baskin (ed.), *Jewish Women in Historical Perspective* (Chicago, IL 1998), pp.287–309.

Bernstein, Deborah, 'Kolot min hagarin hakashe – misipuraihen shel tse'irot ha'aliyah hashniah' [Voices from the hard core – stories of young women from the Second Aliyah], in Yael Atzmon (ed.), *Hatishma koli: yitzugim shel nashim behevra ha'israelit* [Will you hear my voice: women's representation in Israeli society] (Jerusalem 2001), pp.116–33.

Bernstein, Deborah S., 'Heker Nashim ba-Historiografyah ha-Yisre'elit: Nekudot Motza, Kavvanot Hadashot ve-Kavvanot she-ba-Derekh' [The study of women in Israeli historiography: starting points, new directions and emerging insights], in Shilo Margalit et al. (eds), *Ha'ivriot hahadashot* [The New Hebrew Women] (Jerusalem 2001), pp.7–25.

Bernstein, Deborah, 'Tel Aviv lavsha mahsof ... Pnina hameshuga'at vegvulot hakrach' [Tel Aviv donned a décolleté ... Crazy Pnina and the city boundaries], *Teoria veBikoret*, 25 (Autumn 2004), pp.143–62.

Biale, David, *Eros and the Jews: from Biblical Israel to Contemporary America* (New York: Basic Books, 1992).

Biger, Gideon, *The Role of the British Administration in Changing the Geography of Palestine, 1918–1929* (London: University College, 1979).

Bigland, Eileen, *Britain's Other Army* (London 1946).

Blanton, DeAnne and Lauren Cook, *They Fought Like Demons: Women Soldiers in the Civil War* (New York 2002).

Boni-Davidi, Dganit, 'Women and Gender in the Hagana Organization between 1920–1948' (MA thesis, Bar- Ilan University, 2004).

Bonin, Adelyn, *Allegiances* (Santa Barbara 1993).

Bott, Elizabeth, *Family and Social Network: Roles, Norms and External Relationships in Ordinary Urban Families* (London 1957).

Boyarin, Daniel, 'Neshef ha-Masekhot ha-Koloni'ali: Zionut, Migdar, Hikkui' [The colonial masked ball: Zionism, gender, imitation], *Teoria ve'bikoret*, 11 (1997), pp.123–44.

Brayborn, Gail and Penny Summerfield, *Out of the Cage: Women's Experiences in Two World Wars* (London 1987).

Brendstater, Tsilli, Tsel misheli [A shadow of my own] (Tel Aviv 2003).

Brenner, Uri, *Le Tsava yehudi azma'i: hakibutz hameuhad behaganah 1939–1945* [To an independent Jewish army: the United Kibbutz Movement in the Haganah 1939–1945] (Tel Aviv 1985).

Brenner, Uri, *Mediniut hagius bemilhemet haolam hashnia, tseva hamedina baderech: prakim betoldot koah hamagen ha'ivri* [Recruitment policies in the Second World War, the nation's army in making: chapters on the Hebrew defence force] (Tel Aviv and Ramat Efal 1988), pp.159–72.

Bronfeld-Stein, Hava, 'Beautiful Group Portrait with a Gun: Visual Representations of Women Soldiers in Israel Defense Force Albums 1948–1958' (MA thesis, Bar Ilan University, 2002).

Buber Agassi, Judith, 'Status of Women in Religion', in Dafna Izraeli, *Women in a Trap: On the Status of Women in Israel* (Tel Aviv 1984), pp.210–27.

Burk, James, 'Citizenship, Status and Military Service: The Quest for the Inclusion by Minorities and Conscientious Objectors', *Armed Forces*, 21, no.4 (Summer 1995), pp.503–29.

Butler, Judith, *Gender Trouble* (New York 1990).

Caiazza, Amy, *Mothers and Soldiers: Gender, Citizenship and Civil Society in Contemporary Russia* (New York 2002).

Campbell, D'Ann, 'Women in Combat: The World War II Experience in the United States, Great Britain, Germany and the Soviet Union', in Gerald Martel (ed.), *The World War Two Reader* (New York 2004), pp.250–69.

Carmiel, Batya, *Batei hacafe be Tel Aviv 1920–1980* [Coffee shops in Tel Aviv 1920–1980] (Tel Aviv 2007).

Churchill, Winston, *The Second World War: Their Finest Hour*, Vol.2 (London 1950).

Churchill, Winston, *The Second World War: Triumph and Tragedy*, Vol.6 (London 1954).

Cohen, Adir, *Beru'ah Se'ara: prakim mehayav upo'alo shel Yehuda Arazi* [In the eye of the storm: chapters from the life and activity of Yehuda Arazi] (Tel Aviv 1966).

Cohen, Adir, *Alon basa'ar: alilot rechesh upirkei ha'apala* [Oak in the storm: stories of purchasing and chapters in illegal immigration] (Tel Aviv 1973).

Cohen, Michael, *Churchill and the Jews* (London 2003).

Cohen, Tova and Shmuel Feiner, *Kol alma ivriya: kitvei nashim maskilot bame'ah hatsha esreh* [Voice of the Hebrew woman: nineteenth century women's writings] (Tel Aviv 2006).

Cohen, Ya'akov, 'Ha'ivri hahadash' [The new Hebrew], in Ya'akov Cohen (ed.), *Ha'ivri hahadash: musaf lesifrut, leumanut ulehaim* [The new Hebrew: supplement on literature, nationalism and life] (Warsaw 1912), pp.7–11.

Cohen, Zivia, *Bat Hen: Sipuran shel hahayalot hamemalot tafkiding hiuni'im umeguvanim umosifot hen le Zahal* [Graceful: Stories of the servicewomen who fill varied and essential positions and add charm to the IDF] (Haifa 1972).

Cohen, Zivia (ed.), *Hitnadavnu letzava habriti* [We volunteered for the British Army] (Tel Aviv 2003).

Cohn, Carol, 'Wars, Wimps and Women: Talking Gender and Thinking War', in Miriam Cooke and Angela Woollacott (eds), *Gendering War Talk* (Princeton, NJ 1993), pp.227–46.

Collins Weitz, Margaret, 'Soldiers in the Shadows: Women of the French Sexual Integration', in Gerard Degroot and Corinna Peniston-Bird (eds), *A Soldier and a Woman* (Essex 2000), pp.135–51.

Connell, Raewyn, *Masculinities* (California Press 1995).

Cooke, Miriam, 'WO-Man, Retelling the War Myth', in Miriam Cooke and Angela Woollacott (eds), *Gendering War Talk* (Princeton, NJ 1993), pp.177–204.

Cowper, Julia, *The Auxiliary Territorial Service* (London 1949).

Dahan-Kalev, Henriette, 'Mizrahi Women: Identity and History', in Ruth Kark, Margalit Shilo and Galit Hasan-Rokem (eds), *Jewish Women in pre-State Israel: Life History, Politics and Culture* (Waltham, MA: Brandeis University Press, 2008), pp.45–60.

Damon, T., *Beshvilai hagoral: Roman mehayai ha'ATS* [In the paths of destiny: a novel on ATS life] (Tel Aviv 1953).

Dar, Yael, *Umisfsal halimudim lakhnu: hayishuv lenochach shoa velikrat medina besifrut hayeladim ha'eretz Israelit 1939–1948* [And from the school desks we were taken: the Yishuv in face of the Holocaust and in advance of a state in children's literature in Eretz Israel 1939–1948] (Jerusalem 2006).

Dar, Yehezkel and Shaul Kimchi, 'Nashim tse'irot be'irgun gavri' [Young women in a masculine organization], *Soziologia Israelit*, D, 1 (2002), pp.62–83.

Dar-Klein, Yael, 'Agadat hale'om hamithaveh: hasipurim leyeladim ve-no'ar shecatva Bracha Habas beshanim 1933–1940' [The legend of the developing nation: stories for children and young people written by Bracha Habas in 1933–1940] (MA thesis, Tel Aviv University, 1997).

Dayan, Debora, *Be-Osher uve'Yagon* [In Joy and Sorrow], ed. Bracha Habas (Tel Aviv 1957).

Dayan, Shmuel, *Mosheve ovdim be eretz Israel* [Workers' moshavim in Eretz Israel] (Jerusalem 1945).

De Friss, David, 'Pekidim Ivr'im be Eretz Israel' [Hebrew Beaurocrats in Eretz Israel], *Teoria ve'Bikoret*, 9 (Winter 1996), pp.41–56.

Degroot, Gerard and Corinna Peniston-Bird, 'Arms and Women', in Gerard Degroot and Corinna Peniston-Bird (eds), *A Soldier and a Woman: Sexual Integration in the Military* (Essex 2000), pp.3–18.

Dekel, Ephraim, *Benitivei habricha* [On the roads of escape] (Tel Aviv 1959).

Don, Yehuda, 'Yahasim calcali'im ben Israel ve Mitzrayim' [Economic relations between Israel and Egypt], *Katedra*, 67 (April 1993), pp.70–89.

Dotan, Shmuel, *Adumim: hamiflaga hacomunistit be eretz Israel* [Reds: the Communist Party in Eretz Israel] (Tel Aviv 1991).

Elad, Ofra, '"Kol bahur ve tov laneshek, bahura al hamismar!": Ha'havera ba'Palmach' [Every man is good for arms, a woman, on guard duty! Woman Member in the Palmach], in Yehiam Weitz (ed.), *Palmach: Shtei shibolim veherev* [Palmach, Two Sticks of Corn and a Sword] (Tel Aviv 2001), pp.211–51.

Elboim-Dror, Rachel, 'Nashim ba'utopiot hazioniot' [Women in Zionist Utopias], *Katedra*, 66 (December 1992), pp.111–43.

Elboim-Dror, Rachel, 'Ha'isha hazionit ha'idialit' [The Ideal Zionist Woman], in Yael Atzmon (ed.), *Hatishma Koli: yitsugim shel nashim batarbut ha'israelit* [Will you hear my voice: representation of women in Israeli culture] (Jerusalem 2001), pp.95–115.

Eley, Geoff, 'Finding the People's War: Film, British Collective Memory and World War II', *American Historical Review*, 106 (2001), pp.818–38.

Eli'av, Ya'akov and Mordecai Schreiber, *Wanted* (New York: Shengold Publishers, 1984).

Elroi, Gur, *Immigrantim: hahagira hayehudit le Eretz Israel bereshit hame'a haesrim* [Immigrants: Jewish immigration to Eretz Israel in the early twentieth century] (Jerusalem 2004).

Enloe, Cynthia, *Ethnic Soldiers: State Security in Divided Society* (Georgia 1980).

Enloe, Cynthia, *Does Khaki Become You? The Militarization of Women's Lives* (London 1983).

Enloe, Cynthia, *Bananas, Beaches & Bases: Making Feminist Sense of International Politics* (California 1989).

Enloe, Cynthia, *Maneuvers: The International Politics of Militarizing Women's Lives* (California 2000).

Ephron, Yonit, 'Ahayot, lohamot, imahot: ethos umeziot bemivhan bnot dor 1948' [Sisters, fighters, mothers: ethos and reality in the test of the 1948 generation of women], *I'yunim Be Tekumat Israel*, 10 (2000), pp.353–80.

Erikson, Erik H., *Identity: Youth and Crisis* (New York: W.W. Norton & Company, 1968).

Eshel, Tsadok, *Habahurot hahen: sefer bnot hahaganah b' Haifa* [Those girls: Book of Haganah girls in Haifa] (Tel Aviv 1997).

Even Zohar, Itamar, 'Hatzmiha ve'hahitgabshut shel tarbut Ivrit mekomit ve'yelidit, 1882–1948' [The growth and development of local and indiginous Hebrew culture in the Land of Israel, 1882–1948], *Katedra*, 16 (1980), pp.165–89.

Fogel-Bijaoui, Sylvia, 'Ha'omnam baderekh le'shivion? Ma'avakan shel hanashim lezkhut behira ba'Yishuv Ha'yehudi be'Eretz Israel: 1917–1926 [Really on the Way to Equality? Women's Struggle for Suffrage in the Yishuv in Eretz Israel: 1917–1926], *Megamot*, 34, no.2 (1992), pp.262–84.

Fogel-Bijaoui, Sylvia, 'From Revolution to Motherhood: The Case of Women in the Kibbutz, 1910–1948', in Deborah Bernstein (ed.), *Pioneers and Homemakers: Jewish Women in Pre-State Israel* (New York 1992), pp.211–30.

Frank, Gerald, *Hama'as* [The action] (Tel Aviv 1963).

Friedman, Ariela, *Ba'ah meahava: intimiut vekoah bazehut hanashit* [Coming from love: intimacy and strength in female identity] (Tel Aviv 1996).

Gal, Sari, *Bracha Fold* (Tel Aviv 1999).

Geertz, Clifford, *The Interpretation of Cultures: Selected Essays* (New York: Basic Books, 1973).

Gefen, Yonatan, *Isha Yekara* [Dear woman], ed. Yigael Schwartz (Tel Aviv 1999).

Gelber, Yoav, 'Aspectim politiim lehakamat hakoah halohem beyishuv haeretzisraeli btkufat milhemet haolam hashnia' [Political aspects in establishing the fighting force in the Yishuv during the Second World War], *Yalkut Moreshet*, 22 (November 1976), pp.31–62.

Gelber, Yoav, *Toldot hahitnadvut: Nos'ei hadegel* [History of volunteering: bearers of the flag] (Jerusalem 1983).

Gelber, Yoav, *Toldot hahitnadvut: Bein Britim, Aravim veGermanim* [History of volunteering: Between British, Arabs and Germans] (Jerusalem 1984).

Gelber, Yoav, *Gar'in Letsava Ivri sadir: Terumatam shel yozei Hatsava Habriti Lehakamat Tsahal* [Nucleus for Regular Hebrew Army: British Army Veterans' contribution to Establishment of IDF] (Jerusalem 1986).

Gelber, Yoav, *Toldot hahitnadvut: Hahitnadvut ve mekoma bemidiniut hazionit ve hayishuvit 1939–1942* [History of volunteering: volunteering and its place in Zionist and Yishuv Policies 1939–1942] (Jerusalem 1989).

Gelber, Yoav, *Moledet Hadasha: Aliyat Yehudei Merkaz Eiropa veKlitatam 1933–1948* [New Homeland: Immigration of Central Europe Jews and their integration 1933–1948] (Jerusalem 1990).

Gelber, Yoav, 'Peulot hamahlaka hamedinit shel hasochnut bemitzrayim' [Activity of the political department of the Jewish Agency in Egypt], *Katedra*, 67 (April 1993), pp.24–53.

Gelber, Yoav, *Toldot hahitnadvut: Hama'avak letzava Ivri* [History of volunteering: The Struggle for a Hebrew Army] (Jerusalem 1991).

Gelber, Yoav, 'Hitgabshut hayishuv hayehudi be'eretz Israel 1936–1947' [Forming the Jewish Yishuv in Eretz Israel 1936–1947], in Moshe Lissak (ed.), *Toldot hayishuv be'eretz Israel meaz ha'aliyah harishona: tkufat hamandat habriti* [History of the Yishuv in Eretz Israel since the First Aliyah: period of British Mandate], B (Jerusalem 1994), pp.303–461.

Gelber, Yoav, 'Ha'itonut ha'ivrit be eretz Israel al hashmadat yehudei Europa (1941–1942)' [Hebrew press in Eretz Israel on the destruction of European Jewry (1941–1942)], in Dina Porat and Mordechai Naor (eds), *Ha'itonut hayehudit be'eretz Israel nochah hashoa 1939–1945* [Jewish press in face of the Holocaust 1939–1945] (Tel Aviv: 2002), pp.35–65.

Gerbi, Iris, *Hamehir hakaful: ma'amad ha'isha bahevra ha'israelit ve sherut hanashim be'Zahal* [Double price: women's status in Israeli society and women's military service in the IDF] (Tel Aviv 1996).

Getter, Miriam, 'Ha'aliyah migermania bashanim 1933–1939, klita calcalit mul klita hevratit tarbutit' [Immigration from Germany: economic integration vis-à-vis social and cultural integration], *Katedra*, 12 (August 1978), pp.125–47.

Giladi, Leah, *Aleyhen lo katvu* [About them, nothing was written] (Tel Aviv 1997).

Gilat, Nurit, 'Attitude of Israeli Society on Women's Military Service, 1948–1967' (PhD thesis, Haifa University, 2005).

Gilligan, Carol, *In a Different Voice: Psychological Theory and Women's Development* (Cambridge, MA: Harvard University Press, 1982).

Glass, Joseph B., *From New Zion to Old Zion, American Jewish Immigration and Settlement in Palestine* (Detroit, WI: Wayne State University Press, 2000).

Glick, Ruth, 'Experience of Immigration and Reforming an Identity in the Private Writings of Hanna Senesh' (MA thesis, Bar Ilan University, 2006).

Golani, Motti, 'Britania ve harchra'at "milchemet haezrahim" be Eretz Israel' [Britain and the defining 'civil war' in Eretz Israel], *Zion*, 54, no.4 (1989), pp.455–94.

Golani, Motti, 'Manya: aliata hakzara ve nefilata ha'aruka' [Manya: her short rise and long fall], *Israel*, 3 (2003), pp.1–20.

Goldstein, Joshua, *War and Gender: How Gender Shapes the War System and Vice Versa* (Cambridge 2001).

Gonnet, Ruth, 'Yahasim ben kevutsot' [Intergroup relations], *Sotziologia Hevratit*, 8 (2000), pp.137–213.

Gould, Jane, 'Women's Military Services in First World War Britain', in Margaret R. Higonnet, Jane Jenson, Sonya Michel and Margaret Collins Weitz (eds), *Behind the Lines: Gender and the Two World Wars* (New Haven, CT 1992), pp.114–25.

Gozes-Savorai, Aya, *Sapperi Li Sapperi Li – Haverot ha-Palmah Mesapperot* [Tell me, tell me –female members of the Palmach tell their tale] (Efal: The Center for the History of the Defense Force, 1993).

Gramsci, Antonio, *On Hegemony: Selections from the Prison Notebooks* (London: Lawrence and Wishart, 1971).

Grayzel, Susan, *Women's Identities at War: Gender, Motherhood and Politics in Britain and France during the First World War* (London 1999).

Gross, Nahum, 'Hamediniut hacalcalit shel hamimshal habriti hamandatori be'eretz Israel' [Economic Policies of the British Mandatory Government in Eretz Israel], *Katedra*, 24 (August 1982), pp.153–80.

Grunzweig, Michael, 'Ma'amada shel ha'ivrit b'yemei ha'aliyah hashniya' [Status of Hebrew in the days of the Second Aliyah], in Mordechai Naor (ed.), *Ha'aliyah hashniya 1903–1914* [The Second Aliyah 1903–1914] (Jerusalem 1985), pp.198–212.

Guber, Rivka, *Sefer Ha'ahim* [Book of the brothers] (Tel Aviv 1950).

Guber, Rivka, *Im habanim* [With the sons] (Tel Aviv 1953).

Guber, Rivka, *Rak Shvil* [Only a path] (Tel Aviv 1970).

Guber, Rivka, *Morasha lehanhil* [Legacy to instil] (Jerusalem 1979).

Gurevitz, David and Ahron Gretz, *Ha'aliyah, haYishuv ve hatnua hativit shel haochlosiya in Eretz Israel* [Immigration, the Yishuv and the natural flow of the population of Eretz Israel] (Jerusalem 1945).

Guri, Haim, *Hasefer hameshuga* [The crazy book] (Tel Aviv 1971).

Guvrin, Nurit, 'Nos'ot hakeylim, nashim be ma'arachot Israel be'reai hasifrut ha'ivrit' [Bearing the banner, women in the wars of Israel as reflected in Hebrew literature], *Iton* 77, 264 (February 2002), pp.20–6.

Habas, Bracha (ed.), *Me'ora'ot 1936* [1936] Arab Uprising] (Tel Aviv 1940).

Habas, Bracha, *Sefer Aliyat Hanoar* [Book of youth immigration] (Jerusalem 1941).

Habas, Bracha (ed.), *Sefer ha-Aliyah ha-Sheniyyah* [The Second Aliyah Book] (Tel Aviv 1947).

Habas, Bracha, *Bnot hayil: sefer ha'ATS* [Women of valour: book of the ATS] (Tel Aviv 1964).

Haktin, Ruth, *Kivrat Haderech Shelly* [My own piece of way] (Tel Aviv 1990).

Halamish, Aviva, 'Aflayat nashim be'aliyah betkufat hamandat-ha'uvdot, hasibot, hahashlachot' [Discrimation against women in the Mandadory period – facts, reasons and repercussions], *The 12th World Jewish Studies Congress*, August 1997, pp.49–57.

Hall, Pat, *Fearfully 502: A Lighthearted History of 11 M.T.C. / 502 M.A.C, A.T.S* (London 1946).

Halperin, Hagit, 'Berl, ha'adama bo'eret' [Berl, the ground is burning], in Hagit Halperin (ed.), *Amir Gilboa, Hinai yamim ba'im* [Amir Gilboa, here days are coming] (Tel Aviv 2007), pp.7–41.

Halperin, Sara, *Dr A. Biram ve beit hasefer hare'ali* [Dr A. Biram and the Reali High School] (Jerusalem 1970).

Mor, Haya, Ka'et Haya, *Sefer Zikaron le Haya Mor* [Memorial book for Haya Mor] (Kfar Yehoshua 1972).

Heller, Joseph, *Lehi, 1940–1949* (Jerusalem 1989). [Hebrew].

Hendrix, Scott, 'In the Army: Women, Camp Followers and Gender Roles in the British Army in the French and Indian Wars 1755–1765', in Gerard Degroot and Corinna Peniston-Bird (eds), *A Soldier and a Woman* (Essex 2000), pp.33–48.

Herbert, Melissa, *Camouflage Isn't Only for Combat* (New York 1998).

Herlitz, Esther, *Esther: o Le'an kvar Isha Yechola Le'hagia* [Esther: or how far could a woman go?] (Tel Aviv 1995).

Hertz, Deborah, 'Emancipation through Intermarriage? Wealthy Jewish Salon Women in Old Berlin', in Judith Baskin (ed.), *Jewish Women in Historical Perspective* (Chicago, IL 1998), pp.193–207.

Herzog, Hanna, 'Irgunei nashim bahugim ha'ezrahi'im, perek nishkach behistoriographia shel haYishuv' [Women's organizations in civil circles – forgotten chapter in historiography of the Yishuv], *Katedra*, 70 (February 1994), pp.111–33.

Hess, Tamar, 'Autobiographical Writings by Women of the Second Aliyah' (PhD thesis, Hebrew University, Jerusalem, 2003).

Higgins, Lynn, 'Sexual Fantasies and War Memories: Claude Simmon's Narratology', in Miriam Cooke and Angela Woollacott (eds), *Gendering War Talk* (Princeton, NJ 1993), pp.249–59.

Higonnet, Margaret and Patrice Higonnet, 'The Double Helix', in Margaret R. Higonnet, Jane Jenson, Sonya Michel and Margaret Collins Weitz (eds), *Behind the Lines* (New Haven, CT 1987), pp.31–47.

Hillel, Hagar, "*Israel*" *be Kahir: Iton Zioni bemitzrayim haleumit 1920–1939* ["Israel" in Cairo: A Zionist newspaper in nationalist Egypt 1920–1939] (Tel Aviv 2004).

Horowitz, David and Baruch Kimmerling, 'Some Social Implications of Military Service and the Reserve System in Israel', *European Journal of Sociology*, 15 (1974), pp.262–76.

Horowitz, Dan and Moshe Lissak, *Miyishuv lemedina: yehudei Eretz Israel betkufat hamandat habriti kekehila politit* [From Yishuv to State: Eretz Israeli Jews during the British Mandate as a political community] (Tel Aviv: 1977).

Horowitz, Yosef, *Bograi aliyat hano'ar* [Graduates of Youth Aliyah] (Jerusalem 1942).

Hough, William, 'Palestine's Part in the War', *Forum* (August 1945), pp.10–15

Hyman, Paula, *Ha-Ishah ha-Yehudiyyah bi-Sevakh ha-Kidmah: Mekoma ve Yitzuga ba'et hachadasha* [The Jewish woman in a tangle of progress: her place and representation in modern Jewish history] (Jerusalem 1997).

Idelson, Beba, 'Moetzet Ha'Poalot: Tosefet o Yesod' [Working Women's Council: addition or foundation], *Baderekh*, Tel Aviv, pp.252–6.

Ironi-Abrahami, Haya, *Almoniot bekhaki: Sipuran shel havrot ha'Hagana be'Tel Aviv* [Anonymous women in khaki: the story of the female Members of the Haganah in Tel Aviv] (Tel Aviv 1989).

Izraeli, Daphna, 'Tenu'at ha-Po'alot be-Eretz Yisra'el mi-Reishitah ve-Ad 1927' [The women's labour movement in Eretz Israel from its beginnings until 1927], *Katedra*, 56 (1984), pp.110–40.

Izraeli, Daphna, 'Migdur basherut hatzavai be Zahal' [Gendering in military service in the IDF], *Teoria vebikoret*, 14 (Summer 1999), pp.85–107.

Kadish, Alon, *Lameshek ve'laneshek: ha'hachsharot hameguyasot ba'Palmach* [To farm and to arms: The Palmach recruited groups] (Ramat Efal 1995).

Kalkin Fishman, Debora, 'Hasafa hemeshutefet: gorem melaked?' [The mutual language: a unifying element?], in Yitzhak Kashti and Rivka Izikovitz (eds), *Panim hamishtakfot bamar'ah: tarbuyot beisrael beshnot hatish'im* [Faces in the mirror: cultures in Israel in the 1900s] (Tel Aviv 1996), pp.69–94.

Kamir, Orit, *Israel's Dignity Based Feminism in Law and Society* (Tel Aviv 2002).

Kaplan, Marion, 'Tradition and Transition: Jewish Women in Imperial Germany', in Judith Baskin (ed.), *Jewish Women in Historical Perspective* (Michigan 1998), pp.227–42.

Kark, Ruth, Margalit Shilo and Galit Hasan-Rokem (eds), *Jewish Women in pre-State Israel: Life History, Politics and Culture* (Waltham, MA: Brandeis University Press, 2008).

Katz, Sheila, *Women and Gender in Early Jewish and Palestinian Nationalism* (Florida 2003).

Keith-Roach, Edward, *Pasha of Jerusalem: Memoirs of a District Commissioner Under the British Mandate* (London 1994).

Keynan, Irit, *The Hunger Has Not Died Down – Holocaust Survivors and the Emissaries of the Land of Israel, Germany 1945–1948* (Tel Aviv 1997).

Kimhi, Ruth, 'The Activity of the Zionist Movement in Egypt and its Relations with the Yishuv In Eretz Israel 1918–1948' (PhD thesis, Haifa University, 2005).

Kinari, Baruch, *Tabenkin beretz Israel* [Tabenkin in Eretz Israel] (Ramat Efal 2003).

Klieger Eliav, Ruth and Peggy Mann, *Hamiflat ha'aharon* [The Last Resort] (Tel Aviv 1976).

Knohel, Dov (ed.), *Behitnadev am: mitnadvim dati'im bemilhemet ha'olam hashniya* [When a nation volunteers: religious volunteers in the Second World War], A and B (Tel Aviv 1989, 1990).

Kolodny-Baki, Ruth, *Tik Yozefina* [Josephine file], National government publication (Tel Aviv 1994).

Kosh-Zohar, Talila, 'Hee lo halcha basadot: ha'yitsug hanashi betextim shel dor tashach' [She didn't walk in the fields: women's representation in texts from the 1948 generation], in Hana Naveh and Oded Manda Levy (eds), *Sadan Mehkarim be safrut Ivrit Yom Krav ve'arbo ve'haboker shelemaharat: yitsugei milhement ha'aztmaut basifrut* [Research in Hebrew literature, day of battle and the following morning: representations of the war of independence in literature], 5 (Tel Aviv 2002), pp.304–46.

Kresel, Getzel, 'Ha'itonut ha'ivrit' [Hebrew Press], *Hebrew Encyclopedia* (Tel Aviv 1957), pp.1057–69.

Lake, Marilyn, 'Female Desires, The Meaning of World War II', in Gordon Martel (ed.), *The World War Two Reader* (New York 2004), pp.359–76.

Lapidot, Yehuda, *Ha'saison: tzaid ahim* [The 'hunting season': hunting down brothers] (Tel Aviv 1994).

Lapidot, Yehuda, *Hayom Sara haktana: sipuran shel lohamot haEtzel* [Today little Sara: the story of the women fighters in the IZL] (Tel Aviv 2003).

Lazar, Hadara, *Out of Palestine: the Making of Modern Israel* (New York: Atlas & Co., 2011).

Leshem, Nurit, *Shirat ha'deshe* [Song of the Grass] (Tel Aviv 1997).

Lev-Ari, Shimon, 'Hitpathut hate'atron hamishni 1928–1948' [Development of the alternative theater], in Moshe Lissak (ed.), *Toldot hayishuv hayehudi be'eretz Israel me'az ha'aliyah harishona: bniyata shel tarbut ivrit* [History of the Jewish Yishuv in Eretz Israel since the First Aliyah: building a Hebrew culture], A (Jerusalem 1993), pp.593–617.

Levine Melammed, Renee, *Heretics or Daughters of Israel: The Crypto-Jewish Women of Castile* (Oxford 2002).

Levy, Isaac, *Now I Can Tell: Middle East Memories* (London 1978).

Lewis, Bernard, 'Hamandat Habriti bekontext hashva'ati' [The British mandate in comparative context'], in Yehoshua Ben-Arieh (ed.), *Yerushalaim betkufat Hamandat: ha'asiya vehamoreshet* [Jerusalem in Mandate period: the action and legacy] (Jerusalem 2003), pp.25–8.

Lipshitz, Arieh and Rachel Lerer (eds), *Shulamit Klibanov: Le diokana* [In her image] (Jerusalem 1969).

Lipshitz, Yaacov, *Sefer Habrigada Hayehudit: Korot hahativa hayehudit halohemet vehamatzila et hagola* (The history of the Jewish fighting brigade, saviour of the Diaspora) (Tel Aviv 1947).

Lissak, Moshe, *Ha'elitot shel hayishuv hayehudi be'eretz Israel betkufat hamandat* [The Jewish elites in the Yishuv during the Mandate] (Tel Aviv 1981).

Lissak, Moshe, *Ha'aliyah hagdola be'shnot hahamishim: kishlono shel cur hahituch* [The big immigration of the 1950s: the failure of the melting pot] (Jerusalem 1999).

Magnus, Shulamit, '"Out of the Ghetto": Integrating the Study of Jewish Women into the Study of "The Jews"', *Judaism*, 39, no.1 (1990), pp.28–36.

Malkin, Ahuvia, *Ha'activist: sipur hayav shel Eliyahu Golomb* [The activist: life story of Eliyahu Golomb], A (Tel Aviv 2007).

Mardor, Meir, *Shlihut aluma: pirkei mivza'im me'iuhadim bema'archot hahaganah* [Silent mission: chapters on special operation in the service of defence] (Tel Aviv 1957).

Margalit-Stern, Bat-Sheva, 'Tenu'at ha-Po'a lot be-Eretz Yisra'el: Mo'etzet ha-Po'a lot 1921–1939' [The Women Workers Movement in Eretz Israel: Mo'etzet ha-Po'alot 1921–1939] (PhD thesis, Haifa University, 1997).

Margalit-Stern, Bat-Sheva, 'La'malka ein bayit, la'melech ain keter? Ma'amadan shel nashim yehudiot beshuk ha'avoda be'eretz Israel hamandatorit' [The queen has no home, the king has no crown? Status of Jewish women on the labour market in Mandatory Eretz Israel], in Avi Bareli and Nahum Karlinsky (eds), *Calcala ve'hevra beyemei hamandat 1918–1948* (Be'er Sheva 2003), pp.115–30.

Margalit-Stern, Bat-Sheva, *Geula bekvalim: tenuat ha'poalot ha'eretz israelit 1920–1939* [Salvation in Chains: Working Women's Movement in Eretz Israel 1920–1939] (Jerusalem 2006).

Margalit, Ya'akov (ed.), *Bayit bamoshav: haverot mesaprot* [A home on the moshav: women members recall] (Tel Aviv 1962).

Margalit, Ya'akov (ed.), *Hineni shalcheni: mitnadvim batzava habriti kotvim* [Here I am, send me: writings of volunteers to the British Army] (Tel Aviv 1984).

McClintock, Ann, 'No Longer in a Future Heaven: Women and Nationalism in South Africa', *Transition*, 51 [1991], pp.104–23.

Melman, Billie, 'Min ha-shulayim el ha-historiyah shel ha-Yishuv: Migdar ve-eretz yisre'eliyut (1890–1920)' [From the periphery to the center of Yishuv history: gender and nationalism in Eretz Israel (1890–1920)], *Zion* 62, no.3 (1997), pp.343–78.

Melman, Billie, 'Lahafoch et hamilhama lehistoria: Hamilhama Hagdola, Historia ve historionim, 1914–1918' [Turning the war into history: the Great War, history and historians], *Zmanim*, 65 (Winter 1998–99), pp.6–23.

Michelsohn, Udi and Aharon Lapidot, *Me'ah shnot gymnasia* [A Hundred Years of Gymnasia] (Tel Aviv 2004).

Mitchell, Duncan G. and Moshe Lissak (eds), *Lexicon Dvir le sociologia* [A new dictionary of sociology] (Tel Aviv 1984).

Moav Halbani, Tali, 'Woman in the Yishuv's Defence from the 1920s until the Establishment of the Women Corps' (MA thesis, Haifa University, 1998).

Morag, Shlomo, 'Ha'ivrit hahadasha behitgabshuta: lashon be' aspaklaria shel hevra' [Modern Hebrew in development: language as a reflection of society], *Katedra*, 56 (August 1990), pp.70–92.

Morag-Talmon, Penina, 'Women's Networks: A New Perspective on Women's Studies in Israel in the Early 1950s', in Margalit Shilo et al. (eds), *The New Hebrew Women* (Jerusalem 2001), pp.131–43.

Mosenson, Moshe, *Letters from the Desert*, ed. Shlomo Grodzensky (New York: Sharon Books, Inc. 1945).

Mosse, George L. *Fallen Soldiers, Reshaping the Memory of the World Wars* (Oxford: Oxford University Press, 1991).

Nagel, Joan, 'Masculinity and Nationalism: Gender and Sexuality in the Making of Nations', *Ethnic and Racial Studies*, 21, no.2 (1998), pp.242–70.

Naor, Mordechai, 'Ha'itonut Hayehudit be'retz Israel betkufat milhemet ha'olam hashniya' [Jewish Press in Eretz Israel during WWII], in Dina Porat and Mordechai Naor (eds), *Ha'itonut Hayehudit be'Eretz Israel nochach hashoa 1939–1948* [Jewish Press in face of the Holocaust] (Tel Aviv 2002), pp.11–23.

Near, Henry, 'What Troubled Them? Women in Kibbutz and Moshav in the Mandatory Period', in Ruth Kark, Margalit Shilo and Galit Hasan-Rokem (eds), *Jewish Women in pre-State Israel: Life*

History, Politics and Culture (Waltham, MA: Brandeis University Press, 2008), pp.193–206

Nir, Rafael, 'Ma'amada shel halashon ha'ivrit betahalich hat'hia hale'umit' [Status of the Hebrew language in the process of national renaissance], in Moshe Lissak and Zohar Shavit (eds), *Toldot hayishuv hayehudi be'eretz Israel me'az ha'aliyah harishona: bniyata shel tarbut ivrit be'eretz Israel* [The history of the Jewish Yushuv in Eretz Israel since the First Aliyah: the building of Hebrew culture in Eretz Israel], A (Jerusalem 1999), pp.31–9.

Niv, David, *Etzel: ha'irgun hatzavai hale'umi* [Etzel: national military organization] (Jerusalem 1978).

Noakes, Lucy, *Women in the British Army: War and the Gentle Sex 1907–1948* (New York 2006).

Ohana, David and Robert Wistrich (eds), 'Mavo: Nohehut hamytosim' [Introduction: Presense of Myths], in *Mytos ve Zikaron: gilgula shel hatoda'a ha'israelit* [Myth and memory: incarnation of Israeli awareness] (Jerusalem 1996), pp.7–18.

Ostfeld, Zahava, *Tsava nolad: shlavim ikariim bebniat tsava behanhagato shel David Ben-Gurion* [An army is born: main stages in building an army under the leadership of David Ben-Gurion], ed. Shoshana Stiftel (Tel Aviv 1994).

Paassen, Pierre Van, *The Forgotten Ally* (New York 1943).

Palgi-Hecker, Anat, *Me'imahut le'imahut: hipus psichoanalyti feministy ahar ha'em cesubyect* [From non-essence to motherhood: a psychoanalytical feminist search for the mother as a subject] (Tel Aviv 2005).

Paret, Peter, Beth Irwin Lewis and Paul Paret, *Persuasive Images: Posters of War and Revolution* (Princeton, NJ: Princeton University Press, 1992).

Patishi, Hanoch, 'The 'Hagana' Organization's Command of its Members Serving in the British army, 1939–1946' (MA thesis, Haifa University, 2003).

Patishi, Hanoch, *Mahteret be'madim: 'Haganah' ve'hayalim ha'eretz Israelim betzava habriti* [Underground in uniform: Haganah and the Eretz Israel servicemen in the British army, 1939–1946] (Tel Aviv 2006).

Pearlman, Moshe, *The Army of Israel* (London 1950).

Pennington, Reina, '"Do Not Speak of the Services you Rendered": Women Veterans of Aviation in the Soviet Union', in David M. Glantz (ed.), *The Journal of Slavic Military Studies*, 9, no.1 (March 1996), pp.120–40.

Pialkov, Arieh and Yosef Rabinovitz (eds), *Yitzhak Tabenkin: pirkei haim, ha'ish ve po'alo, haverim ve talmidim mesaprim, sugiot bemishnato* [Yitzhak Tabenkin: chapters from his life, the man and his activity, friends and students recall, issues in his teachings] (Ramat Efal 1982).

Porat, Dina, *Hanhaga be'milkud: Ha'Yishuv nokhakh Ha'shoa 1942–1945* [Leadership in a trap: the Yishuv in face of the Holocaust 1942–1945] (Tel Aviv: Am Oved, 1987).

Priber, Ida, *Ma'aglei hayim: roman autobiography* [Circles of life: an autobiographical novel] (Tel Aviv 1982).

Prizel, Eviatar, 'Bere'i akum: hazionut ve hamatzav be'Eretz Israel al pi yomanim briti'im 1927–1931' [In a crooked mirror: Zionism and the situation in Eretz Israel according to British diaries 1927–1931], in Shmuel Almog et al. (eds) *Tmurot ba'historia hayehudit hahadasha: kovetz ma'arim keshai le Shmuel Etinger* [Changes in the new Jewish history: collection of papers as a gift to Shmuel Etinger] (Jerusalem 1987), pp.225-46.

Rabinowitz, Louis Isaac, *Soldiers from Judea: Palestinian Jewish Units in the Middle East 1941–1943* (London 1945).

Ram, Uri, 'Hahevra ve'mada hahevra: sociologia mimsadit vesociologia bikortit beisrael' [Society and social science: institutional sociology and critical sociology in Israel], in Uri Ram (ed.), *Hahevra haisraelit: hebetim bikorti'im* [Israeli society: critical aspects] (Tel Aviv 1994), pp.7–39.

Ramsden, John, 'Refocusing "The People's War": British War Films of the 1950', *Journal of Contemporary History*, 33 (1998), pp.36–54.

Razi, Tamar, 'Building the Fringes of the Nation: Homeless Youths in Tel Aviv in the 1930s and 1940s' (PhD thesis, Bar Ilan University, 2006).

Regev, Motti, 'Mavo le'tarbut isrealit' [Introduction to Israeli culture], in Ephraim Ya'ar and Ze'ev Shavit (eds], *Megamot bahevra haisraelit* [Directions in Israeli Society), 2 (Tel Aviv 2003), pp.823–98.

Reich, Daniela, 'Between National Mission and Social Ostracism: Contacts Between Jewish Women to British Servicemen 1940–1948' (MA thesis, Haifa University, 2003).

Rich, Adrienne, *Of Woman Born: Motherhood as Experience and Institution* (New York 1976).

Rivlin, Gershon (ed.), *La'esh ve'lamagen: toldot hanotrut ha'ivrit* [To the fire and defence: history of Hebrew guardians] (Tel Aviv 1963).

Rosenberg-Friedman, Lilach, 'Women and Gender in Religious Zionism: Organization, Settlement and Defence 1918–1948' (PhD thesis, Bar Ilan University, 2002).

Rosenberg-Friedman, Lilach, *Mahapehaniyot be'al korhan: nashim umigdar bazionut hadatit betkufat hayishuv* [Inadvertent revolutionaries: women and gender in religious Zionism in the Yishuv period] (Jerusalem 2005).

Rosenberg-Friedman, Lilach, 'Zehuyot be'conflict ben shoah letekuma: shlichot hayishuv be'rikuzei she'erit hapleita be'Europa [Identities in conflict between the Holocaust and independence: Yishuv emissaries in concentrations of Holocaust survivors in Europe], *Israel*, 11 (2007), pp.117–52.

Rosengart, Laurence, 'Parashat Yaldei Teheran' [The Teheran Children Affair], *Beshvil Hazikaron*, 6 (1995), pp.15–20.

Roth, Haim Yehuda, 'Al ba'ayot hahinuch hatichoni' [On problems of high school education], in Roth (ed.), *Al hahinuch hatichoni ha'ivri be'eretz Israel* [On high school education in Eretz Israel] (Jerusalem 1939), pp.30–9.

Rozman, Yael et al. (ed.), *Nashim be-Yisra'el: Leksikon* [Women in Israel: Lexicon] (Tel Aviv: 1991).

Rustad, Michael, *Women in Khaki*: *The American Enlisted Woman* (New York: Praeger, 1982).

Safran, Hannah, 'International Struggle, Local Victory: Rosa Welt Straus and the Achievement of Suffrage 1919–1926', in Ruth Kark, Margalit Shilo and Galit Hasan-Rokem (eds), *Jewish Women in pre-State Israel: Life History, Politics and Culture* (Waltham, MA: Brandeis University Press, 2008), pp.361–80.

Said, Edward, *Orientalism* (London: Vintage Books, 1979)

Samuel, Edwin, *A Lifetime in Jerusalem* (Jerusalem 1970).

Sargent, Lydia (ed.), *Women and Revolution, A Discussion of the Unhappy Marriage of Marxism and Feminism* (Cambridge 1981).

Sasson-Levy, Orna, 'Hatranut be'toch dikui: kinun zehuiot migdariot shel hayalot betafkidim "gavri'im"' [Subversion and Suppression: establishing gender identities of women in 'masculine' roles], in Yael Atzmon (ed.), *Hatishma Koli: yitsugim shel nashim batarbut ha'israelit* [Will you hear my voice: representation of women in Israeli culture] (Jerusalem 2001), pp.277–302.

Sasson-Levy, Orna, *Zehuiot bemadim: gavriut ve'nashiut batzava haisraeli* [Identities in uniform: masculinity and femininity in the Israeli army] (Jerusalem 2006).

Sco Foundation for Palestine Inc., *Study of Jewish, Arab and British Policies*, 2 vols (New Haven 1947).

Scott, Joan, 'Rewriting History', in Margaret R. Higonnet, Jane Jenson, Sonya Michel and Margaret Collins Weitz (eds), *Behind the Lines* (New Haven, CT 1992), pp.21–30.

Segev, Tom, *One Palestine, Complete : Jews and Arabs under the Mandate* (New York 2000).

Shapira, Yonatan, *Elite le'lo mamshichim: dorot manhigim bahevra haisraelit* [Elite with no heirs: generations of leaders in Israeli society] (Tel Aviv 1984).

Shar'abi, Rachel, 'Pratit sh'ehi tziburit: mekoma shel ha'isha bemoshavei ha'ovdim harishonim' [Private and public: women's place in the first workers' moshavim], *Megamot*, 45, no.1 (June 2007), pp.75–102.

Sharett, Moshe, *Policy Making; The Diaries of Moshe Sharett* (Tel Aviv 1979).

Sharett, Moshe, *Yemei London: michtavim mishnot halimudim belondon*, 1 and 2 [London days: letters from years of study in London, 1 and 2], ed. Tamar Gadron, Ya'akov Sharett and Rina Sharett (Tel Aviv 2005).

Shavit, Yosef, *Mitnadvim bekahol: eretzisraelim besherut heil hate'ufa hamalchuti* [Volunteers in blue: from Eretz Israel to service in the RAF] (Tel Aviv 1995).

Shavit, Zohar, 'Hitpathut kitvai ha'et ve'ha'itonot' [Development of journals and newspapers], in Moshe Lissak (ed.), *Toldot hayeshuv hayehudi beretz Israel me'az ha'aliyah harishona: bniyata shel tarbut ivrit* [History of the Jewish Yishuv in Eretz Israel since the First Aliyah: building a Hebrew culture], Part One (Jerusalem 1994), pp.123–97.

Shavit, Ya'akov, 'Misimhat Beit Hasho'eva lemo'etzet hamorim lema'an hakakal: hamtza'at hagim ve'tekasim beyishuv ha'eretz Israeli' [From Simhat Beit Hasho'eva to the Teachers' Council for the JNF: inventing holydays and ceremonies in the Yishuv], in Yossi Dahan and Henry Wasserman (eds), *Lehamtzi uma: anthologia* [Inventing a nation: an anthology] (Ra'anana 2006), pp.331–50.

Shavit, Zohar, 'Harachashta kvar at hamapte'ah l'otzrot tarbutainu? Hora'at ivrit ve'hamtza'ata shel tarbut leumit betnuat ha'avoda' [Have you already bought the key to our culture's treasures? Teaching Hebrew and inventing a national culture in the Labour movement], in Yossi Dahan and Henry Wasserman (eds), *Lehamzi uma: antologia* [Inventing a nation: an anthology] (Ra'anana 2007), pp.360–70.

Shechter, Tamar, 'Rachel Katznelson Shazar: Biography of Cultural Revolutionary' (PhD thesis, Bar Ilan University, 2004).

Sheffer, Gabriel, *'Me'atzvei hamediniut hamandatorit, stereotypim obasar vadam?'* [Mandatory policy makers, stereotypes or flesh and blood?], *Keshet* 4 (Summer 1970), pp.167–87.

Sheffer, Ze'ev (ed.), *Sefer Hahitnadvut: Parashat Hahitnadvut hatzvait shel yehudei Eretz Israel Be'milhemet ha'olam hashniyat* [Book of volunteering: the case of military volunteering of Eretz Israel Jews in the Second World War] (Jerusalem 1949).

Shein, Ada, 'Hapulmus hayishuvi sviv klitat 'yaldai Teheran' [The polemic surrounding integration of the Tehran children], *Yalkut Moreshet*, 54 (1993), pp.133–61.

Shem-Ur, Orah, *Bli ha'kuku ve'hasarafan* [Without a ponytail and the sarafan] (Tel Aviv 1992).

Shilo, Margalit, 'Ha-Ishah – "Ovedet" o "Haverah" be-Mifal ha-Tehiyyah? Al Mekomah shel ha-Ishah ba-Aliyah ha-Rishonah (1882–1903)' [The woman – 'laborer' or 'member' in the Revival Project? On the place of the woman in the First Aliyah (1882–1903)], *Yahadut Zemanenu*, 9 (1995), pp.121–47.

Shilo, Margalit, 'Ha'isha ha'ivriya hahadasha – panim rabot la, hashomeret kemikreh mivhan' [Many faces to the New Hebrew Woman, the woman member of Hashom as a test case], *Bikoret ve-parshanut*, 34 (Summer 2000), pp.7–17.

Shilo, Margalit, 'Hamtza'at masoret: girsa eretz israelit' [Inventing tradition: an Eretz Israeli version], *Katedra* 110 (February 2004), pp.159–66.

Shilo, Margalit, 'Ledmuta shel ha'isha ba'aliyah hashniya: ha'ezrahit' [To the woman's image in the Second Aliyah: the woman citizen], *Israel*, 6 (2004), pp.83–105.

Shilo, Margalit, *Etgar hamigdar: nashim ba'aliyot harishonot* [Challenge of gender: women in the first waves of immigration] (Bnei Brak 2007).

Shilo, Tali, *Kum ve'hitgayes*' [Step Up to Enlist], Recruitment Posters – British Army, WWII in Eretz Israel, Proposal for Exhibition in Museology Studies 2005.

Shorer, Haim, *Soldier Number Nine One Seven Two* (Tel Aviv 1946).

Shtok, Dov, 'Hakdama' [Introduction], in Yosef Bass, *Hayamim halalau...* [Those Days...] (Tel Aviv 1944), pp.3–5.

Shvarts, Shifra and Zipora Shory-Rubin, 'On Behalf of Mothers and Children in Eretz Israel: The Activity of Hadassah, the Federation of Hebrew Women and WIZO to Establish Mother and Infant Welfare Centers—*Tipat Halav*, 1913–1948', in Margalit Shilo et al. (eds), *The New Hebrew Women* (Jerusalem 2001), pp.299–318.

Sinai, Smadar, 'Gender Relations in the 'Hashomer' Organization and in Kfar Giladi 1907–1939' (PhD thesis, Bar Ilan University, 2009).

Sinai, Smadar, *Miryam Baratz: Dyokana shel Halutza* [Miriam Baratz: Portrait of a Halutzah] (Yad Tabenkin Ramat Efal 2002).

Slutsky, Yehuda (ed.), *Sefer toldot ha'aganah* [History of the Haganah], B and C (Tel Aviv 1973).

Spiegel, Yair, 'Hahitmodedut hamodi'init vehasiculit shel mishteret hamandat umahleket hahakirot haplilit ba (CID) im hmiflaga hacommunistit ha'eretzisraelit 1920–1948' [The intelligence and counterintelligence dilemma in the Mandatory police and its CID with the Communist Party in the Yishuv 1920–1948] (MA thesis, Bar Ilan University, 1999).

Spiegel, Yair, 'Hashomer Hatza'ir in Defense and Security of the Yishuv, 1920–1947' (PhD thesis, Bar Ilan University, 2006).

Stern, Bat-Sheva, 'Hinuch nashim betnuat hapo'alot haeretz israelit: bein masoret lekidma' [Education of women in the Israeli Working Women's Movement: between tradition and progress], *Historia*, 3 (1999), pp.292–314.

Stites, Robert, *The Women's Liberation Movement in Russia: Feminism, Nihilism and Bolshevism 1860–1930* (Princeton, NJ, 1978).

Stoff, Laurie, 'They Fought for Russia: Female Soldiers of the First World War', in Gerard Degroot and Corinna Peniston-Bird (eds), *A Soldier and a Woman* (Essex 2000), pp.66–83.

Summerfield, Penny, *Reconstructing Women's Wartime Lives: Discourse and Subjectivity in Oral Histories of the Second World War* (Manchester 1998).

Summerfield, Penny, 'She Wants a Gun not a Dishcloth! Gender, Service and Citizenship in Britain in the Second World War', in Gerard Degroot and Corinna Peniston-Bird (eds), *A Soldier and a Woman* (Essex 2000), pp.119–35.

Summerfield, Penny, 'Our Amazonian Colleague: Edith Summerskill's Problematic Reputation', in Richard Toye and Julie Gottlieb (eds), *Making Reputations: Power, Persuasion and the Individual in Modern British Politics* (London 2005), pp.135–50.

Summerfield, Penny and Corinna Peniston-Bird, 'Women in the Firing Line: The Home Guard and the Defence of Gender Boundaries in Britain in the Second World War', *Women's History Review*, 9, no.2 (2000), pp.231–55.

Svirsky, Shlomo, 'He'arot la'sociologia hahistorit shel tekufat hayishuv' [Comments on the sociological history of the Yishuv period], in Uri Ram (ed.), *Hahevra haisraelit: hebetim bikorti'im* [Israeli society: critical aspects] (Tel Aviv 1993), pp.54–82.

Tidhar, David, *Enziklopediyah le'Halutsei ha'Yishuv ve'Bonav* [Encyclopedia of pioneers of the Yishuv and personages], 17 (Tel Aviv 1947).

Thompson, Elizabeth, *Colonial Citizens: Republican Rights, Paternal Privilege and Gender in French Syria and Leban*on (New York 2000).

Tomer, Ben Zion (ed.), *Adom ve'lavan vere'ah tapuhei zahav: yaldei Tehran* [Red and white and the scent of golden apples: the Tehran children] (Jerusalem 1972).

Treadwell, Mattie, *The Women's Army Corps*: United States Army in World War II: Special Studies (Washington 1991).

Trevor, Daphne, *Under the White Paper: Some Aspects of British Administration in Palestine from 1939 to 1947* (Jerusalem 1948).

Tsur, Muki and Yuval Danieli (eds), *Yots'im be hodesh he'aviv: Pessach eretz Israeli behagadot mehakibutz* [Going out in the month of spring: an Eretz Israeli Passover in the kibbutz hagadas] (Jerusalem 2004).

Tsur, Ya'akov, *Karev Yom: dapei avar* [A day is coming: pages from the past] (Jerusalem 1979).

Tsur, Ze'ev, Hakibutz hame'uhad beyushava shel Ha'aretz 1960–1980 [The United Kibbutz Movement in settling the country 1960–1980], B (Tel Aviv 1986).

Veevers, Jean, 'Women in the Driver's Seat: Trends in Sex Differences in Driving and Death', *Population Policy and Policy Review*, 1, no.2 (May 1982), pp.171–82

Wadge, Collett, *Women in Uniform* (London 1946).

Walby, Sylvia, 'Is Citizenship Gendered?', *Sociology*, 28, no.2 (May 1994), pp.379–95.

Watson, Martha, *Lives of Their Own: Rhetorical Dimensions in Autobiographies of Women Activists* (South Carolina 1999).

War Office, *Regulations for the Auxiliary Territorial Service* (London 1941).

Webster, Wendy, *Englishness and Empire 1939–1965* (Oxford 2005).

Whateley, Dame Leslie, *As Thoughts Survive* (London 1949).

Wichselfisch, Ephraim, *Nashim Yehudiot lohamot bemilhemet ha'olam hashniya* [Jewish women fighting in the Second World War] (Jerusalem 2000).

Ya'akova, Meira, 'Hityashvut hayalim be'ertz Israel le'ahar milhement ha'olam hashnia' [Settlement of soldiers in Eretz Israel after the Second World War], *Katedra*, 102 (Tevet 2002), pp.123–58.

Yellin, Emily, *Our Mothers' War: American Women at Home and at the Front during World War II* (New York 2004).

Yellin-Mor, Nathan, *Lohamey herut Israel: Anashim, ra'aionot, alilot* [Fighters for the freedom of Israel: people, ideas, tales] (Tel Aviv 1989).

Yoeli, Naomi, 'Massekhet: Zionist Ceremonies as Theatre' (PhD thesis, Tel Aviv University, 2002).

Yona, Yossi and Yehuda Shenhav, *Rav tarbutiut mahi? Al hapolitica shel hashonut beisrael* [What is multiculturalism? On the politics of diversity in Israel] (Tel Aviv 2005).

Young, James, *The Texture of Memory: Holocaust Memorials and Meaning* (New Haven, CT and London 1993).

Yuval-Davis, Nira, 'Front and Rear: The Sexual Division of Labor in Israeli Army', *Feminist Studies*, 11, no.3 (1985), pp.649–75.

Yuval-Davis, Nira, 'Nationalism, Feminism and Gender Relations', in Montserrat Guibernau and John Hutchinson (eds), *Understanding Nationalism* (Cambridge: Polity Press, 2001), pp.120–41.

Yuval-Davis, Nira and Floya Anthias, *Woman, Nation, State* (New York 1989).

Zair, Amnon, *Vienna–Gan Shmuel* (Gan Shmuel 1980).

Zartal, Idit, *Zahavam shel hayehudim: ha'hagira hayehudit hamahtartit le eretz Israel, 1945–1948* [Jews' gold: illegal Jewish immigration to Eretz Israel, 1945–1948] (Tel Aviv 1996).

Zeira, Mordechai, *Kruim Anu: Zikata shel hahitiashvut haovedet beshnot haesrim el hatarbut hayeudit* [We are torn: Affiliation of the working settlements in the 1920 to the Jewish culture] (Jerusalem 2002).

Zmora, Esther, *Nashim Ivriyyot Tziyyoniyyot* [Zionist Hebrew Women] (Tel Aviv 2002).

Zrubavel, Yael, 'Bein "historia" le "agada": gilgulei tel hai bazicaron ha'amami' [Between 'history' and 'legend': Tel Hai in the national memory], in Yossi Dahan and Henry Wasserman (eds), *Lehamtzi uma* [Inventing a nation] (Ra'anana 2006), pp.199–216.

Index